Dialogues

An Argument Rhetoric and Reader

GARY GOSHGARIAN

Northeastern University

KATHLEEN KRUEGER

JANET BARNETT MINC

University of Akron-Wayne College

Longman

New York   San Francisco   Boston
London   Toronto   Sydney   Tokyo   Singapore   Madrid
Mexico City   Munich   Paris   Cape Town   Hong Kong   Montreal

Senior Vice President and Publisher: Joseph Opiela
Acquisitions Editor: Susan Kunchandy
Development Director: Janet Lanphier
Development Editor: Karen Helfrich
Supplements Editor: Donna Campion/Teresa Ward
Media Supplements Editor: Nancy Garcia
Marketing Manager: Ann Stypuloski
Senior Production Manager: Bob Ginsberg
Project Coordination, Text Design, and Electronic Page Makeup: Nesbitt Graphics, Inc.
Cover Design Manager: Wendy Ann Fredericks
Cover Designer: Joan O'Connor
Publishing Services Manager: Al Dorsey
Printer and Binder: The Maple-Vail Book Manufacturing Group
Cover Printer: Lehigh Press, Inc.

For permission to use copyrighted material, grateful acknowledgment is made to the copyright holders on pp. 709–714, which are hereby made part of this copyright page.

Library of Congress Cataloging-in-Publication Data
Dialogues : an argument rhetoric and reader / [edited by] Gary Goshgarian, Kathleen Krueger, Janet Barnett Minc.—4th ed.
    p. cm.
  ISBN 0-321-10146-4
    1. English language—Rhetoric. 2. Persuasion (Rhetoric) 3. College readers. I. Goshgarian, Gary. II. Krueger, Kathleen. III. Minc, Janet Barnett.

  PE1431 .D53 2002
  808'.0427—dc21

                                                              2002073418

Please visit our website at http://www.ablongman.com/goshgarian

ISBN 0-321-10146-4

12345678910—MA—05040302

BRIEF CONTENTS

DETAILED CONTENTS

v

PART TWO   The Readings   261

CHAPTER 10   ADVERTISING AND CONSUMERISM   263

Hooking the Consumer   *264*

"With budgets that add up to hundreds of billions of dollars, the [advertising] industry exceeds the church and the school in its ability to promote images about our place in society—where we belong, why, and how we should act toward others."

"Although we like to think of advertising as unimportant, it is in fact the most important aspect of the mass media. It is the point."

"Ads have wandered away from their well-known hangouts in magazines and TV shows. Like alien-infected pod-people of early science fiction movies, they have stumbled out of these familiar media playgrounds and suddenly sprouted up everywhere."

PREFACE

*D*ialogues: *An Argument Rhetoric and Reader* focuses on promoting meaningful discourse, that is, the effective exchange of opinions and ideas. In this book, we seek to move away from more traditional models of confrontation and dispute and instead promote ways to create meaningful dialogue and understanding by presenting different points of view. The exploration of multiple perspectives on an issue or topic helps students to arrive at informed positions and develop their own compelling cases. While dialogue and consensus are encouraged, we realize that not all arguments can be resolved to everyone's satisfaction. However, understanding the principles of persuasive writing and the techniques of argument provides students with the foundation and tools with which to productively engage in negotiation. And while students may not always reach a consensus of opinion, they will be able to discuss diverse issues in a thoughtful and productive way.

Organization of the Book

As the title indicates, this book is divided into two parts. The rhetoric section consists of nine chapters explaining the strategies of reading and writing arguments. The reader section consists of eight thematic units containing over eighty essays—a challenging collection of thought-provoking contemporary and historical arguments.

Part 1: The Rhetoric

Part One of the book is designed to stimulate critical thinking, reading, writing, and research skills. It explores how issues are argued while emphasizing the actual process of persuasive writing, from brainstorming exercises to shaping the final product. Each of the nine chapters in Part One focuses on a particular facet or principle of persuasive writing, including a new visuals chapter that addresses how visuals can act as arguments in and of themselves, or as auxiliary support for arguments.

Chapter 1 offers an overview of argumentation, clarifies key terminology, and introduces the processes of debate, dialogue, and deliberation. Chapter 2 focuses on critical reading, presenting a series of activities designed to help students evaluate arguments and recognize their primary components. An extensive section on testing arguments for logical fallacies ends the chapter. Chapter 3 discusses how to begin writing arguments. It helps students find worthwhile and interesting topics to write about by demonstrating techniques for brainstorming, limiting topics, and formulating claims. Chapter 4 examines the presence of audience, encouraging students to think about the different kinds of readers they may have to address. This chapter suggests ways to evaluate the audience's concerns and strategies to reach different audiences.

Chapter 5 focuses on the organization of the argument essay by analyzing two basic types of arguments—positions and proposals. Outlining is reviewed as a tool to ensure effective organization. Chapter 6 considers the importance of evidence. We demonstrate that the effectiveness of a writer's argument largely depends on how well the writer uses evidence—facts, testimony, statistics, and observations— to support his or her ideas. Chapter 7 introduces the socially constructed Toulmin model of logic as a way of testing the premises of the writer's argument.

Chapter 8 explores the principles of visual argument in art, advertisements, editorial cartoons, photographs, and ancillary graphics such as charts and tables. Focusing on developing visual literacy skills, the chapter shows students how to apply the tools of critical analysis to the many visual arguments they encounter every day. Finally, Chapter 9 discusses research strategies, including locating and evaluating print and electronic sources, note-taking tips, and drafting and revising argument essays. The Documentation Guide provides documentation formats and annotated sample student papers for both MLA and APA styles.

Part 2: The Readings

With over eighty contemporary essays and visuals, the readings offer a wide range of challenging and stimulating issues that we think will be of interest both to students and instructors. The topics are selected to encourage discussion, and attempt to represent the diversity of opinion connected to some of the controversial issues we face today.

The first seven chapters of Part Two examine broad themes: "Advertising and Consumerism," "Gender Issues," "September 11, 2001," "Race and Ethnicity," "What Makes a Family," "Law and Order," and "Ethical Issues in Medicine." Each of these chapters is divided into two or three subtopics that take a closer look at the multiple viewpoints surrounding various controversial issues. The final chapter of readings is a casebook on the human cloning debate—a unit that explores the subject of human cloning in depth. The casebook provides students with the background necessary to understand the issue while presenting multiple points of view from politicians, scientists, and ethicists.

Study Apparatus

The study apparatus of the book is designed to help students thoughtfully consider the issues, their own opinions on these issues, and how they might engage in meaningful dialogue. Questions encourage critical thinking about each article's content and how it is written. Each chapter in Part Two features an introduction to the chapter theme and its subsections. A brief headnote to each reading in Part Two provides students with context and pertinent information regarding the reading, as well as biographical information about the author of the piece. "Before You Read" and "As You Read" questions help frame the reading. Following each reading are "Questions for Analysis and Discussion" that stimulate thinking on the content, argument, and writing strategies of the author. Some questions ask students to consider how other authors in the section would respond to a particular essay's argument or evidence, encouraging critical thinking across the theme or chapter. Several writing assignments follow the end of each subsection of readings, helping students to synthesize the information they have read and their own opinions.

New to This Edition

The first two editions of this text, titled *Crossfire*, focused on creating avenues for effective argument. In the last edition, we revised the text to focus more on promoting meaningful *dialogue*, and we changed the title to *Dialogues* to reflect this new direction. The intention was to move away from confrontation and dispute and work toward discussion and understanding. We have continued this approach in this fourth edition, incorporating the insights and suggestions of many instructors who used the last edition. Some changes to this edition include:

The Rhetoric

Each of the rhetoric chapters has been updated and they include new study and discussion questions and expanded apparatus. Furthermore, we have increased the number of readings in these chapters and have added two new sample student essays and analyses. The examples of documentation using electronic sources have been updated and expanded in the "Documentation Guide: MLA and APA Styles."

Perhaps the most conspicuous change to Part One is the addition of a visuals chapter, which considers how visual media such as art, photographs, advertising, editorial cartoons, and ancillary graphics are used to create arguments and persuade audiences. The chapter also advises students on how they can incorporate such visual devices into their own writing to help develop effective arguments.

The Reader

- Part Two contains over eighty essays and visuals, most of which are new to this edition, and written or created within the last five years, making this issue of *Dialogues* particularly current. New chapters cover recent issues that we feel are of particular interest to students.
- New major thematic changes examine recent issues that we feel are of particular interest to students:
  - "Advertising and Consumerism" includes new subthemes on how advertisers "hook" consumers and the American culture of excess.
  - "Gender Issues" includes a new section on how feminism is viewed in the twenty-first century.
  - "September 11, 2001" takes an in-depth look at some of the cultural changes effected by this tragic act of terrorism, including Patriotism and the Flag and Reacting to Terrorism.
  - "Race and Ethnicity" explores the role of race and ethnic culture in America today as it pertains to stereotypes, assimilation, and the controversial practice of racial profiling.
  - "What Makes a Family" examines the changing face of the American family.
  - "Ethical Issues in Medicine" introduces the topic of stem cell research, a subject of much debate in recent months.
- A new casebook—"The Human Cloning Debate"—gives students the opportunity to explore this topic in depth and helps them to understand the multiple points of view on this scientific and ethical issue.

- Writing assignments that follow each section encourage students to address issues further, prompting them to formulate critical responses to the different points of view expressed in the section. Some questions include suggestions for using the Internet to explore a topic more fully and to aid research.

Acknowledgments

Many people behind the scenes deserve much acknowledgment and gratitude. It would be impossible to thank all of them, but there are some for whose help we are particularly grateful. First, we would like to thank all the instructors and students who used the first three editions of *Crossfire* and *Dialogues*. Their continued support has made this latest edition possible. Also, we would like to thank those instructors who spent hours answering lengthy questionnaires on the effectiveness of the essays and who supplied many helpful comments and suggestions in the preparation of this new edition: Mike Cadden, Missouri Western Sate College; Clarence Hundley, Thomas Nelson Community College; Carolyn J. Kelly, Iowa State University; Iraj Omidvar, Iowa State University; Harold M. Snyder, East Carolina University; Meryl Soto-Schwartz, Lakeland Community College; Jonathan Taylor, Ferris State University; Karen Taylor, University of Texas, Pan American; and Mary Waguespack, Loyola University.

A very special thanks goes to Kathryn Goodfellow, for her assistance in locating articles and writing the study apparatus for Part Two, as well as for her help on the Instructor's Manual and Companion Website (www.ablongman.com/goshgarian). Always so bright, efficient, and full of good ideas, she actually made a rather onerous revision seem like a good time. Our thanks also to Darren Beals for his help in preparing the manuscript for submission.

Finally, our thanks to the people at Longman Publishers, especially our editor Susan Kunchandy, her ever-efficient Assistant Editor, Rebecca Gilpin, and our Development Editor, Karen Helfrich. We are very appreciative of their fine help.

GARY GOSHGARIAN
KATHLEEN KRUEGER
JANET BARNETT MINC

Strategies for Reading and Writing Arguments

Understanding Persuasion
Thinking Like a Negotiator

Think of all the times in the course of a week when someone tries to convince you of something. You listen to the radio on the way to school or work and are relentlessly bombarded by advertisements urging you to buy vitamins, watch a particular television show, or eat at the new Mexican restaurant in town. You open a newspaper and read about the latest proposals to lower the drinking age, to raise the age for retirement, and to provide tax relief for the poor. The phone rings and the caller tries to sell you a magazine subscription or to convince you to vote for candidate X. There's a knock on your bedroom door and your sister wants to borrow a CD and the keys to your car. Whether the issue is as small as a CD or as important as taxes, everywhere you turn you find yourself called on to make a decision and to exercise a choice.

If you think about all these instances, you'll discover that each decision you finally do make is heavily influenced by the ability of others to persuade you. People who have mastered the art of argument are able to influence others to do what they want. Your ability to understand how argument works and how to use it effectively will help you become aware of the ways in which you are influenced by the arguments of others, as well as become more persuasive yourself. Anyone can learn to argue effectively by learning the techniques needed to create successful arguments.

This book is designed to help you to achieve two goals: (1) to think critically about the power of other peoples' arguments and (2) to become persuasive in your own arguments.

Argument

Broadly speaking, *persuasion* means influencing someone to do something. It can take many forms: fast-paced glittering ads, high-flying promises from salespeople, emotional appeals from charity groups—even physical threats. What will concern us in this book is *argument*—the form of persuasion that relies on reasoning and logical thought to convince people. While glitter, promises, emotional appeals, and

3

even veiled threats may work, the real power of argument comes from the arguer's ability to convince others through language.

Because this is a book about writing, we will concentrate on the aspects of persuasion that most apply in writing, as opposed to those that work best in other forms (advertisements or oral appeals, for instance). Although written arguments can be passionate, emotional, or even hurtful, a good one demonstrates a firm foundation of clear thinking, logical development, and solid supporting evidence to persuade a reader that the view expressed is worth hearing. The ultimate goal might be to convince readers to change their thinking on an issue, but that does not always happen. A more realistic goal might be to have your listeners seriously consider your point of view and to win their respect through the logic and skill of your argument.

Most of what you write in college and beyond will attempt to persuade someone that what you have to say is worthy of consideration, whether it's a paper stating your views on immigration laws, an analysis of "madness" in *King Lear,* a letter to the editor of your school newspaper regarding women's varsity basketball, or a lab report on the solubility of salt. The same demands of persuasion and argument will carry over into your professional life. Such writing might be in the form of progress reports on students or colleagues, legal briefs, business reports, medical evaluations, memos to colleagues, results of a technical study or scientific experiment, proposals, maybe even a sales speech. In searching for a job or career, you might have to sell yourself in letters of inquiry.

The success or failure of those attempts will strongly depend on how well you argue your case. Therefore, it's important that as a college student, you learn the skills of writing persuasive arguments. Even if you never write another argument, you will read, hear, and make them the rest of your life.

What Makes an Argument?

Arguments, in a sense, underlie nearly all forms of writing. Whenever you express ideas, you are attempting to persuade somebody to agree with you. However, not every matter can be formally argued. Nor are some things worth the effort. So, before we go on to discuss the different strategies, we should make clear which subjects do and do not lend themselves to argument.

Facts Are Not Arguable

Because facts are readily verifiable, they can't be argued. Of course, people might dispute a fact. For instance, you might disagree with a friend's claim that Thomas Jefferson was the second president of the United States. But to settle your dispute, all you have to do is consult an encyclopedia. What makes a fact a fact and, thus, inarguable, is that it has only one answer. It occurs in time and space and cannot be disputed. A fact either *is* or *is not* something. Thomas Jefferson was the third president of the United States, not the second. John Adams was the second. Those are facts. So are the following statements:

- The distance between Boston and New York City is 214 miles.
- Martin Luther King, Jr.'s birthday is now celebrated in all 50 states.
- I got a 91 on my math test.
- The Washington Monument is 555 feet high.
- The Japanese smoke more cigarettes per capita than any other people on earth.
- My dog Fred died a year ago.
- George W. Bush was elected as the 43rd president of the United States.

All that is required to prove or disprove any of these statements is to check with some authority for the right answer. Sometimes facts are not easily verifiable, for instance, "Yesterday, 1,212,031 babies were born in the world" or "More people have black hair than any other color." These statements may be true, but it would be a daunting, if not impossible, challenge to prove them. And what would be the point?

Opinions Based on Personal Taste or Preference Are Not Arguable

Differing opinions are the basis of all argument. However, you must be careful to distinguish between opinions based on personal taste and opinions based on judgments. Someone who asks your "opinion" about which color shoes to buy is simply seeking your color preference—black versus brown, say. If someone asks your "opinion" of a certain movie, the matter could be more complicated.

Beyond whether or not you liked it, what might be sought is your aesthetic evaluation of the film: a judgment about the quality of acting, directing, cinematography, set design—all measured by critical standards you've developed over years of moviegoing. Should you be asked your "opinion" of voluntary euthanasia, your response would probably focus on moral and ethical questions: Is the quality of life more important than the duration of life? What, if any, circumstances justify the taking of a life? Who should make so weighty a decision—the patient, the patient's family, the attending physician, a health team?

The word *opinion* is commonly used to mean different things. As just illustrated, depending on the context, opinion can refer to personal preference, a reaction to or analysis of something, or an evaluation, belief, or judgment, all of which are different. In this text we categorize all these different possibilities as either opinions of taste or opinions of judgment.

Opinions of taste come down to personal preferences, based on subjective and, ultimately, unverifiable judgments. Each of the following statements is an opinion of taste:

- George looks good in blue.
- Pizza is my favorite food.
- Pat Metheny is the greatest living jazz guitarist.
- Video games are a waste of time.

Each of these statements is inarguable. Let's consider the first: "George looks good in blue." Is it a fact? Not really, since there is no objective way to measure its validity. You might like George in blue, whereas someone else might prefer him in red. Is the statement then debatable? No. Even if someone retorts, "George does *not* look good in blue," what would be the basis of argument but personal preference? And where would the counterargument go? Nowhere.

Even if a particular preference were backed by strong feelings, it would not be worth debating, nor might you sway someone to your opinion. For instance, let's say you make the statement that you never eat hamburger. You offer the following as reasons:

1. You're disgusted by the sight of ground-up red meat.
2. When the meat is cooked, its smell disgusts you.
3. Hamburgers remind you of the terrible argument that broke out at a family barbecue some years ago.
4. You once got very sick after eating meatloaf.
5. You think beef cattle are the dirtiest of farm animals.

Even with all these "reasons" to support your point of view, you have not constructed an argument that goes beyond your own personal preference. In fact, the "reasons" you cite are themselves grounded in personal preferences. They amount to explanations rather than an argument. The same is true of the statements about pizza, musicians, and video games.

Opinions Based on Judgments Are Arguable

An *opinion of judgment* is one that weighs the pros and cons of an issue and determines their relative worth. That "something" might be a book, a song, or a public issue, such as capital punishment. Such an opinion represents a position on an issue that is measured against standards other than those of personal taste—standards that are rooted in values and beliefs of our culture: what's true and false, right and wrong, good and bad, better and worse. Consequently, such an opinion is arguable.

In other words, personal opinions or personal preferences can be transformed into bona fide arguments. Let's return to the example of hamburger. Suppose you want to turn your own dislike for ground meat into a paper persuading others to give up eating beef. You can take several approaches to make a convincing argument. For one, you can take a health slant, arguing that vegetarians have lower mortality rates than people whose diets are high in animal fat and cholesterol; or that the ingestion of all the hormones in beef increases the risk of cancer. You might even take an environmental approach, pointing out that the more beef we eat, the more we encourage the conversion of woodlands and rain forests into grazing land, thus destroying countless animals and their habitats. You can even take an ethical stand, arguing from an animal-rights point of view that intensive farming practices create the inhumane treatment of animals—that is, crowding, force-feeding, and force-breeding. You might also argue that the killing of animals is morally wrong.

The point is that personal opinions can be starting points for viable arguments. But those opinions must be developed according to recognized standards of values and beliefs.

The Uses of Argument

Many arguments center on issues that are controversial. Controversial issues, by definition, create disagreement and debate because people hold opposing positions about them. And, most of the time, there are more than two sides. Depending on the issue, there may be multiple opinions and perspectives. Because these views are often strongly held, we tend to view argument only in the form of a *debate,* an encounter between two or more adversaries who battle with each other over who is right. The media does much to contribute to the way we picture argument, particularly in the area of politics.

Every four years or so the image returns to our television screens. Two candidates, dark-suited and conservatively dressed, hands tightly gripping their respective podiums, face off for all of America to watch. Each argues passionately for his or her solution to poverty, educational failings, high taxes, and countless other social and economic problems. Each tries desperately to undermine the arguments of the opponent in an effort to capture the votes of those watching. It's a winner-take-all debate, and it's often the image we see in our minds when we think of argument.

Argument *is* a form of persuasion that seeks to convince others to do what the arguer wants. Argument allows us to present our views and the reasons behind those views clearly and strongly. Yet argument can serve more productive purposes than the above illustration. Although argument can be a debate between two or more opponents who will never see eye-to-eye, in the world outside presidential debates and television sound bites argument can also begin a *dialogue* among opposing sides. It can enable them to listen to each others' concerns and to respond to them in a thoughtful way. Rather than attempt to demolish their opponents' arguments, these negotiators can often arrive at positions that are more valuable because they try to reconcile conflicting viewpoints by understanding and dealing directly with their opponents' concerns. Through the practice of *debate, dialogue,* and *deliberation,* real change can happen. In this chapter we explore these three essential elements of argument and explain how they will enable you to be more effective when you write to persuade others.

Debate

Think for a moment of all the associations the word *debate* suggests to you: winning, losing, taking sides, opposition, and competition. Debate is how we traditionally think of argument. It is a situation in which individuals or groups present their views as forcefully and persuasively as possible, often referring to their opponents' arguments only to attack or deride them. Practiced with just this goal in mind, debate can serve the purpose of presenting your position clearly in contrast to your opposition's, but it does little to resolve controversial issues. Focusing too much on the adversarial qualities of debate can prevent you from listening and considering other viewpoints. You can become so preoccupied with defeating opposing arguments that you fail to recognize the legitimacy of other opinions. This may lead you to ignore them as you fashion your own argument.

Consider the last time you debated an issue with someone. Perhaps it was an informal occasion in which you attempted to convince the other person of your point of view. It may have been about a job opportunity or the best place to spend spring break or what movie to see next weekend. Your aim was to persuade the other person to "see it your way," and, if it were a typical debate, you were successful only if the other individual acquiesced. Debates are traditionally won or lost, and losers often feel frustrated and disappointed. Even more important, reasonable concerns on the losing side are often overlooked or not addressed. Debate does not provide a mechanism for compromise. It is not intended to provide a path toward common ground or a resolution in which all parties achieve a degree of success and positive change is made. Although some issues are so highly contentious that true consensus can never be achieved, an effective argument must acknowledge and respond to opposition in a thoughtful and productive manner.

But debate is an important way to develop your arguments because it allows you to explore their strengths and weaknesses. It can be a starting point for argument rather than a conclusion. Debate contains some of the essential elements of argument: Someone with a strong opinion tries to demonstrate the effectiveness of that view, hoping to persuade others to change positions or to take a particular course of action. When we debate, we have two objectives: to state our views clearly and persuasively and to distinguish our views from those of our opponents. Debate can help us develop our arguments because it encourages us to *formulate* a *claim, create reasons to support it,* and *anticipate opposition.*

Formulating Claims

The claim is the heart of your argument. Whether you hope to protest a decision, change your readers' minds, or motivate your audience to take action, somewhere in your argument must be the assertion you hope to prove. In an argument essay this assertion or claim functions as the *thesis* of the paper, and it is vital to the argument. The claim states precisely what you believe. It is the *position* or opinion you want your readers to accept or the action you want them to take. Thus, it's very important to state your claim as clearly as possible. It will form the basis for the rest of your argument.

Claims often take the form of a single declarative statement. For example, a claim in an argument essay about homelessness might look like this:

> If we look further into the causes of homelessness, we will discover that in many cases it is not the homeless individual who is at fault but rather conditions that exist in our society that victimize certain individuals.

A claim for an essay about teen pregnancy might be stated even more simply:

> The current rhetoric that maintains that the sexual references in the lyrics of popular music are to blame for the rise in teenage parenthood in the United States ignores several crucial realities.

Sometimes writers signal their claims to their readers by certain words: *therefore, consequently, the real question is, the point is, it follows that, my suggestion is.* Here's an example:

Therefore, I believe that scientists can find other effective ways to test new medicines and surgical techniques other than relying on helpless laboratory animals.

Because some arguments make recommendations for solving problems, your claim might be framed as a conditional statement that indicates both the problem and the solution. This can be accomplished with split phrases such as *either . . . or, neither . . . nor, if . . . then.* For example,

> If we don't tighten our immigration laws, we will leave ourselves open for more terrorist attacks.

Claims must have support to convince a reader, so they are often followed by "because" statements—that is, statements that justify a claim by explaining why something is true or recommended or beneficial:

> Outlawing assisted suicide is wrong because it deprives individuals of their basic human right to die with dignity.

Formulating your claim when you debate is a first step for three basic reasons:

1. It establishes the subject of your argument.
2. It solidifies your own stand or position about the issue.
3. It sets up a strategy on which your argument can be structured.

There are no hard-and-fast rules for the location of your claim. It can appear anywhere in your essay: as your opening sentence, in the middle, or as your conclusion. However, many writers state their claim early in the essay to let their readers know their position and to use it as a basis for all the supporting reasons that follow. In later chapters we will look at strategies for arriving at a claim and ways to organize your reasons to effectively support it.

Creating Reasons

We have all seen a building under construction. Before the roof can be laid or the walls painted or the flooring installed, the support beams must be carefully placed and stabilized. Reasons are the support beams of an argument essay. Whether your claim will be considered correct, insightful, or reasonable will depend on the strength and persuasiveness of your reasons.

Reasons answer some basic questions about your claim:

> Why do you believe your claim to be true?
>
> On what information or assumptions do you base your claim?
>
> What evidence can you supply to support your claim?
>
> Do any authorities or experts concur with your claim?

You can derive reasons from personal experience, readings, and research. Your choices will depend on your claim and the information and evidence you need to make your reasons convincing. Let's use one of the examples from our discussion about claims to demonstrate what we mean:

Your Claim: Outlawing assisted suicide is wrong because it deprives individuals of the basic human right to die with dignity.

Question 1: Why do you believe your claim to be true?

Response: When individuals are terminally ill, they suffer many indignities: They can lose control of their bodily functions and must be dependent on others for their care. A prolonged illness with no hope of recovery causes the individual and family members to suffer needlessly. When death is imminent anyway, individuals should be given the right to decide when and how to end their lives.

Question 2: On what information or assumptions do you base your claim?

Response: I believe that no individual wants to suffer more than necessary. No one wants to lose his or her independence and have to rely on others. Everyone wants to be remembered as a whole human being, not as a dying invalid.

Question 3: What evidence can you supply to support your claim?

Response: This is based on personal examples and on readings about how terminal illness is dealt with in hospitals and clinics.

Question 4: Do any authorities or experts concur with your claim?

Response: Yes, many authorities in the field of medicine agree with my claim. I can use their statements and research to support it.

By examining the responses to the questions, you can see how reasons can be created to support your claim. The answer to the first question suggests several reasons why you might be opposed to outlawing assisted suicide: the indignities suffered by the terminally ill, unnecessary suffering, the right to control one's own fate. Question 2 explores your assumptions about what the terminally ill might experience and provides additional reasons to support your claim. The third and fourth questions suggest ways to support your claim through personal examples, references to ideas and examples found in readings related to your topic, and the support of experts in the field.

Credibility is an essential element in creating reasons. To be a successful debater, you must be believable; you must convince your audience that you are knowledgeable about your subject and that the facts, statistics, anecdotes, and whatever else you use to support your reasons are accurate and up-to-date. This means constructing your reasons through research and careful analysis of all the information available. For example, if you argue in an essay that there are better ways to run the U.S. welfare system, you will need to understand and explain how the current system operates. You can use the facts and statistics that you uncover in your research to analyze existing problems and to support your ideas for change. Being thoroughly informed helps you present and use your knowledge persuasively. Acquainting yourself with the information necessary for convincing reasons will make you appear believable and competent. In later chapters we will discuss how to formulate reasons to support your claim and how to evaluate evidence and use it effectively.

Another way to achieve credibility is to avoid logical fallacies, which will undermine the logic or persuasiveness of your argument. *Logical fallacies,* a term derived from the Latin *fallere* meaning "to deceive," are unintentional errors in logic or deliberate attempts to mislead the reader by exaggerating evidence or using methods of argument that appeal to prejudice or bias. In Chapter 2, we will review the most common forms of logical fallacies so you can recognize them in the arguments of others and avoid them in your own writing.

Anticipating Opposition

Because debate anticipates opposition, you need to be certain that your reasons can withstand the challenges that are sure to come. Your goal as a successful debater is not only to present your reasons clearly and persuasively, but also to be prepared for the ways in which those individuals holding other views will respond to them. For instance, in an essay on discrimination in women's collegiate sports, you may state that the operating budget of the women's varsity basketball team at your school is a fraction of that for the men's team. As evidence you might point to the comparative lack of advertising, lower attendance at games, and lesser coverage than for the men's team. Unless you anticipate other perspectives on your issue, however, your argument could fall apart should someone suggest that women's basketball teams have lower budgets simply because they have smaller paying audiences. Not anticipating such a rebuttal would weaken your position. Had you been prepared, you could have acknowledged that opposing point and then responded to it by reasoning that the low budget is the cause of the problem, not the result of it. Putting more money into advertising and coverage could boost attendance and, thus, revenue.

In short, it is not enough to simply present your own reasons, no matter how effectively you support them. Unless you are aware of and familiar with opposing reasons, you leave yourself open to being undermined. To make your case as effective as possible, you must acknowledge and respond to the strongest reasons that challenge your own. To present only the weakest points of those who disagree with you or to do so in a poor light would likely backfire on your own credibility.

The following are strategies we recommend to help you become more aware of views that are different from your own and ways you might respond to them.

"Yes, but . . ." Exchanges

One way to be aware of the reasons on the other side is to study and research your topic carefully. After you've done some reading, a useful method to explore the way others might respond to your ideas is to engage in a "Yes, but . . ." exchange. Imagine you are face to face with someone holding a different position and, as you run down the list of your own reasons, his or her response is "Yes, but . . . [something]." What might that "something" be? Your task is first to acknowledge the validity of the other individual's viewpoint, and then to respond to that idea with reasons of your own. Consider, for instance, how a debate about affirmative action programs might proceed. You begin:

> Affirmative action programs discriminate against white males by denying them employment for which they are qualified.

From what you've heard and read, your opponent might respond this way:

> Yes, there are probably instances in which white males have lost employment opportunities because of affirmative action programs, but without these programs minority candidates would never be considered for some job openings regardless of their qualifications.

Another reason might be:

> Race and gender should not be a consideration when hiring an applicant for a job.

From your readings, you may uncover this opposing reason:

> Yes, in an ideal society race and gender would never be a factor for employers, but since we don't live in such a society, affirmative action programs ensure that race and gender don't become negative considerations when an individual applies for a job.

Imagining your debate in a "Yes, but . . ." exchange will help you work through a number of possibilities to strengthen your reasons in the light of opposition and to become more aware of other viewpoints.

Pro/Con Checklists

Another method to help you become more aware of opposing viewpoints is to create a pro/con checklist. Making a pro/con checklist is useful for several reasons. First, it helps you solidify your own stand on the issue. It puts you in the position of having to formulate points on which to construct an argument. Second, by anticipating counterpoints, you can better test the validity and strength of your points. By listing potential resistance, you can determine the weak spots in your argument. Third, tabulating your own points will help you decide how to organize your reasons—which points to put at the beginning of your paper and which to put in the conclusion. Depending on the issue, you may decide, for the sake of impact, to begin with the strongest point and end with the weakest. This is the strategy of most advertisers—hitting the potential customer right off with the biggest sales pitch. Or you may decide to use a climactic effect by beginning with the weakest point and building to the strongest and most dramatic. Last, by ordering your key points, you can create a potential framework for constructing your argument. See the sample pro/con checklist on page 13.

Moving from Debate to Dialogue

Debate is an important step in constructing an argument. It propels us to find a strong position and to argue that position as effectively as possible. But if we define argument as only debate, we limit the potential power of argument in our society. One common misconception is that all arguments are won or lost. This may be

SAMPLE PRO/CON CHECKLIST

CLAIM: Human cloning should be outlawed because it is unnecessary and unethical.

PRO	CON
Human cloning is unnecessary because we have better ways to treat infertility.	Current fertility treatments are very expensive and are often unsuccessful.
Because we have too many unwanted children in the world already, we should not create more.	People have a right to have their own children.
Cloning is an unnatural process.	It is no more unnatural than many of the ways we currently treat infertility.
Human cloning will devalue the uniqueness of each individual.	A clone will be a unique and separate human being.

true in formalized debates, but in real life few arguments are decided so clearly, and when they are, the conflicting issues that lie at the heart of the debate can persist and continue to create dissension among individuals and groups. The prolonged tensions and sometimes violent confrontations that surround the issue of abortion may be the outcome of a debate that supposedly was resolved by a Supreme Court decision, *Roe* v. *Wade,* but remains a continuing problem because the debate did not engender a dialogue in which conflicting sides listened to each other and reconsidered their views from a more informed perspective. Argument must do more than provide an opportunity to present one's views against those of an opponent. We need to use it as a vehicle to explore other views as well and to help us shape a process in which change can happen and endure.

Dialogue

Take another moment to consider words that come to mind when you think of *dialogue:* discussion, listening, interaction, and understanding. By definition a dialogue includes more than one voice, and those voices are responsive to each other. When we have a dialogue with someone, we don't simply present our own views. We may disagree, but we take turns so that no one voice monopolizes the conversation. The object of a dialogue is not to win or lose; the object is to communicate our ideas and to listen to what the other person has to say in response.

For example, you may find a policy in a particular class regarding make-ups unfair. Since your instructor seems to be a reasonable person, you visit her office to discuss your objections. Your dialogue might proceed like this:

> **You:** Professor, your syllabus states that if a student misses a test, there are no make-ups. I think that this is unfair because if a student is genuinely ill or has an important conflict, the student will be penalized.
>
> **Professor:** I can understand your concern, but I have that policy because some students use make-ups to gain extra time to study. And, by asking other students about the questions on the test, they gain an advantage over students who take the test when it's scheduled. I don't think that's fair.
>
> **You:** I hadn't thought of that. That's a good reason, but I'm still worried that even if I have a legitimate excuse for missing a test, my grade in the course will suffer. What can I do if that happens?
>
> **Professor:** Let me think about your problem. Perhaps there's a way that I can be fair to you and still not jeopardize the integrity of my exams.
>
> **You:** What if a student provides a physician's note in case of illness or a few day's advance notice in case of a conflict? Would you be able to provide an alternative testing day if that should happen?
>
> **Professor:** That might be a good way to deal with the problem, as long as the make-up could be scheduled soon after. I'm going to give this more thought before I decide. I appreciate your suggestions. Stop by tomorrow and we can come to an agreement.

This hypothetical dialogue works because each participant listens and responds to the ideas of the other. Each has an important stake in the issue, but both focus on finding constructive ways to deal with it rather than trying to prove that the other is wrong. As a result, a compromise can be reached, and each person will have made a contribution to the solution.

When we move from debate to dialogue, we move from an arbitrary stance to one that allows for change and modification. Dialogue requires that both sides of the debate do more than simply present and react to each other's views in an adversarial fashion; it demands that each side respond to the other's points by attempting to understand them and the concerns they express. Often it is difficult for those participating in a debate to take this important step. In such cases it will be your task, as a student of argument, to create the dialogue between opposing sides that will enable you to recognize common concerns and, if possible, to achieve a middle ground.

Creating a dialogue between two arguments involves identifying the writers' claims and key reasons. This is a skill we discuss in Chapter 2, where we look at strategies for reading and analyzing argument essays.

Deliberation

Deliberate is a verb that we don't use very much and we probably don't practice enough. It means to carefully and fully consider our reasons for and against something before making up our minds. We often speak of a jury deliberating about its verdict. Jury members must methodically weigh all the evidence and testimony that have been presented and then reach a judgment. Deliberation is not a quick process. It takes time to become informed, to explore all the alternatives, and to feel comfortable with a decision.

Deliberation plays an important part in the process of developing arguments. *Debate* focuses our attention on opposition and the points on which we disagree. *Dialogue* creates an opportunity to listen and explore the arguments that conflict with our own. Deliberation, the careful consideration of all that we have learned through debate and dialogue, enables us to reach our own informed position on the conflict. Because we have participated in both debate and dialogue, we have a more complete understanding of the opposing arguments, as well as the common ground they may share. We are able to take the concerns of all sides into account.

Deliberation does not always resolve an issue in a way that is pleasing to all sides. Some issues remain contentious and irreconcilable, so that the parties are unable to move beyond debate. And, just as a jury sometimes reaches a verdict that is not what either the defense or the prosecution desires, deliberation does not ensure that all concerns or arguments will be considered equally valid. However, deliberation does ensure that you have given the arguments of all sides careful attention. And, unlike a jury, you have much broader parameters to determine your position. You do not have to decide *for* or *against* one side or the other. Your deliberations may result in an entirely new way of viewing a particular issue or of solving a problem.

Consider, for example, a debate about whether a new football stadium should be built in a city experiencing economic problems, such as high unemployment and a failing public school system. One side of the debate may argue that a new stadium would result in additional jobs and revenue for the city from the influx of people who would come to watch the games. Another side may argue that the millions of dollars intended to subsidize a new stadium would be better spent creating job-training programs and promoting remedial education for schoolchildren. Your deliberation would involve several steps:

1. Becoming informed about the issue by reading and researching the information available
2. Creating a dialogue by listening to the arguments of all sides in the debate and trying to understand the reasons behind their claims
3. Carefully weighing all the arguments and information
4. Determining your own position on the issue

Your position might agree with one side or the other, or it might propose an entirely different response to the situation—say, a smaller stadium with the extra funds available to the schools, or a delay in the construction of a stadium until the

nent problem is solved, or an additional tax to fund both, and so on. It
.en be your task to convince all sides of the value of your position.

    .iberation enables you to use argument productively. It allows you to con-
    .ll sides of a problem or issue and to use your own critical analysis to find a
way to respond.

    As you learn more about writing your own arguments, you'll find that debate,
dialogue, and deliberation can help you identify different perspectives, search for
shared concerns, and develop your own position on an issue.

REVIEW: BASIC TERMINOLOGY

Argument Essay	An essay that attempts to convince or persuade others through reason, logic, and evidence to do what the writer wants or believe as the writer wishes.
Claim	The statement in your essay that expresses your position or stand on a particular issue. The claim states precisely what you believe. It is the viewpoint you want your readers to accept or the action you want them to take.
Reasons	The explanation or justification behind your claim. To be effective, reasons must be supported by evidence and examples.
Debate	The act of presenting your claim and reasons and challenging and being challenged by someone who holds a different viewpoint. Debate often focuses on differences between opponents rather than shared concerns and values.
Dialogue	The act of listening and responding to those who hold viewpoints that are different from your own on a particular issue. The object of a dialogue is to find common ground by trying to understand other viewpoints while sharing your own. It is intended to reduce conflict rather than promote it.
Deliberation	The careful and informed consideration of all sides of an issue before reaching a conclusion or position on it. Deliberation can result in the resolution of a contentious issue.

Taking a "War of Words" Too Literally

Deborah Tannen

The following essay provides important insights into the ways in which we often approach argument in our society. The article by Deborah Tannen appeared in the weekly edition of the *Washington Post* on March 23, 1998. It is adapted from her book, *The Argument Culture: Moving from Debate to Dialogue,* which explores how U.S. culture promotes a warlike, adversarial approach to problem-solving. Tannen is a professor of linguistics at Georgetown University. She is the author of the best-sellers *You Just Don't Understand: Women and Men in Conversation* and *Talking from 9 to 5: Women and Men in the Workplace.* As you read Tannen's article, think about whether you have had experiences similar to those Tannen describes, when disagreements could have been settled more successfully through dialogue and thoughtful deliberation rather than conflict.

1   I was waiting to go on a television talk show a few years ago for a discussion about how men and women communicate, when a man walked in wearing a shirt and tie and a floor-length skirt, the top of which was brushed by his waist-length red hair. He politely introduced himself and told me that he'd read and liked my book *You Just Don't Understand,* which had just been published. Then he added, "When I get out there, I'm going to attack you. But don't take it personally. That's why they invite me on, so that's what I'm going to do."

2   We went on the set and the show began. I had hardly managed to finish a sentence or two before the man threw his arms out in gestures of anger, and began shrieking—briefly hurling accusations at me, and then railing at length against women. The strangest thing about his hysterical outburst was how the studio audience reacted: They turned vicious—not attacking me (I hadn't said anything substantive yet) or him (who wants to tangle with someone who screams at you?) but the other guests: women who had come to talk about problems they had communicating with their spouses.

3   My antagonist was nothing more than a dependable provocateur, brought on to ensure a lively show. The incident has stayed with me not because it was typical of the talk shows I have appeared on—it wasn't, I'm happy to say—but because it exemplifies the ritual nature of much of the opposition that pervades our public dialogue.

4   Everywhere we turn, there is evidence that, in public discourse, we prize contentiousness and aggression more than cooperation and conciliation. Headlines blare about the Star Wars, the Mommy Wars, the Baby Wars, the Mammography Wars; everything is posed in terms of battles and duels, winners and losers, conflicts and disputes. Biographies have metamorphosed into demonographies whose authors don't just portray their subjects warts and all, but set out to dig up as much dirt as possible, as if the story of a person's life is contained in the warts, only the warts, and nothing but the warts.

5   It's all part of what I call the argument culture, which rests on the assumption that opposition is the best way to get anything done: The best way to discuss an idea is to set up a debate. The best way to cover news is to find people who express the most extreme views and present them as "both sides." The best way to begin an essay is to attack someone. The best way to show you're really thoughtful is to criticize. The best way to settle disputes is to litigate them.

6   It is the automatic nature of this response that I am calling into question. This is not to say that passionate opposition and strong verbal attacks are never appropriate. In the words of Yugoslavian-born poet Charles Simic, "There are moments in life when true invective is called for, when it becomes an absolute necessity, out of a deep sense of justice, to denounce, mock, vituperate, lash out, in the strongest possible language." What I'm questioning is the ubiquity, the knee-jerk nature of approaching almost any issue, problem or public person in an adversarial way.

7   Smashing heads does not open minds. In this as in so many things, results are also causes, looping back and entrapping us. The pervasiveness of warlike formats and language grows out of, but also gives rise to, an ethic of aggression: We come to value aggressive tactics for their own sake—for the sake of argument. Compromise becomes a dirty word, and we often feel guilty if we are conciliatory rather than confrontational—even if we achieve the result we're seeking.

8   Here's one example. A woman called another talk show on which I was a guest. She told the following story: "I was in a place where a man was smoking, and there was a no-smoking sign. Instead of saying 'You aren't allowed to smoke in here. Put that out!' I said, 'I'm awfully sorry, but I have asthma, so your smoking makes it hard for me to breathe. Would you mind terribly not smoking?' When I said this, the man was extremely polite and solicitous, and he put his cigarette out, and I said, 'Oh, thank you, thank you!' as if he'd done a wonderful thing for me. Why did I do that?"

9   I think the woman expected me—the communications expert—to say she needs assertiveness training to confront smokers in a more aggressive manner. Instead, I told her that her approach was just fine. If she had tried to alter his behavior by reminding him of the rules, he might well have rebelled: "Who made you the enforcer? Mind your own business!" She had given the smoker a face-saving way of doing what she wanted, one that allowed him to feel chivalrous rather than chastised. This was kinder to him, but it was also kinder to herself, since it was more likely to lead to the result she desired.

10   Another caller disagreed with me, saying the first caller's style was "self-abasing." I persisted: There was nothing necessarily destructive about the way the woman handled the smoker. The mistake the second caller was making—a mistake many of us make—was to confuse ritual self-effacement with the literal kind. All human relations require us to find ways to get what we want from others without seeming to dominate them.

11   The opinions expressed by the two callers encapsulate the ethic of aggression that has us by our throats, particularly in public arenas such as politics and law. Issues are routinely approached by having two sides stake out opposing po-

sitions and do battle. This sometimes drives people to take positions that are more adversarial than they feel—and can get in the way of reaching a possible resolution. [. . .]

12   The same spirit drives the public discourse of politics and the press, which are increasingly being given over to ritual attacks. On Jan. 18, 1994, retired admiral Bobby Ray Inman withdrew as nominee for Secretary of Defense after several news stories raised questions about his business dealings and his finances. Inman, who had held high public office in both Democratic and Republican administrations, explained that he did not wish to serve again because of changes in the political climate—changes that resulted in public figures being subjected to relentless attack. Inman said he was told by one editor, "Bobby, you've just got to get thicker skin. We have to write a bad story about you every day. That's our job."

13   Everyone seemed to agree that Inman would have been confirmed. The news accounts about his withdrawal used words such as "bizarre," "mystified" and "extraordinary." A *New York Times* editorial reflected the news media's befuddlement: "In fact, with the exception of a few columns, . . . a few editorials and one or two news stories, the selection of Mr. Inman had been unusually well received in Washington." This evaluation dramatizes how run-of-the-mill systematic attacks have become. With a wave of a subordinate clause ("a few editorials . . ."), attacking someone personally and (from his point of view) distorting his record are dismissed as so insignificant as to be unworthy of notice.

14   The idea that all public figures should expect to be criticized ruthlessly testifies to the ritualized nature of such attack: It is not sparked by specific wrongdoing but is triggered automatically.

15   I once asked a reporter about the common journalistic practice of challenging interviewees by repeating criticism to them. She told me it was the hardest part of her job. "It makes me uncomfortable," she said. "I tell myself I'm someone else and force myself to do it." But, she said she had no trouble being combative if she felt someone was guilty of behavior she considered wrong. And that is the crucial difference between ritual fighting and literal fighting: opposition of the heart.

16   It is easy to find examples throughout history of journalistic attacks that make today's rhetoric seem tame. But in the past such vituperation was motivated by true political passion, in contrast with today's automatic, ritualized attacks—which seem to grow out of a belief that conflict is high-minded and good, a required and superior form of discourse.

17   The roots of our love for ritualized opposition lie in the educational system that we all pass through.

18   Here's a typical scene: The teacher sits at the head of the classroom, pleased with herself and her class. The students are engaged in a heated debate. The very noise level reassures the teacher that the students are participating. Learning is going on. The class is a success.

19   But look again, cautions Patricia Rosof, a high school history teacher who admits to having experienced just such a wave of satisfaction. On closer inspection, you notice that only a few students are participating in the debate; the ma-

jority of the class is sitting silently. And the students who are arguing are not addressing subtleties, nuances or complexities of the points they are making or disputing. They don't have that luxury because they want to win the argument—so they must go for the most dramatic statements they can muster. They will not concede an opponent's point—even if they see its validity—because that would weaken their position.

20   This aggressive intellectual style is cultivated and rewarded in our colleges and universities. The standard way to write an academic paper is to position your work in opposition to someone else's. This creates a need to prove others wrong, which is quite different from reading something with an open mind and discovering that you disagree with it. Graduate students learn that they must disprove others' arguments in order to be original, make a contribution and demonstrate intellectual ability. The temptation is great to oversimplify at best, and at worst to distort or even misrepresent other positions, the better to refute them.

21   I caught a glimpse of this when I put the question to someone who I felt had misrepresented my own work: "Why do you need to make others wrong for you to be right?" Her response: "It's an argument!" Aha, I thought, that explains it. If you're having an argument, you use every tactic you can think of—including distorting what your opponent just said—in order to win.

22   Staging everything in terms of polarized opposition limits the information we get rather than broadening it.

23   For one thing, when a certain kind of interaction is the norm, those who feel comfortable with that type of interaction are drawn to participate, and those who do not feel comfortable with it recoil and go elsewhere. If public discourse included a broad range of types, we would be making room for individuals with different temperaments. But when opposition and fights overwhelmingly predominate, only those who enjoy verbal sparring are likely to take part. Those who cannot comfortably take part in oppositional discourse—or choose not to—are likely to opt out.

24   But perhaps the most dangerous harvest of the ethic of aggression and ritual fighting is—as with the audience response to the screaming man on the television talk show—an atmosphere of animosity that spreads like a fever. In extreme forms, it rears its head in road rage and workplace shooting sprees. In more common forms, it leads to what is being decried everywhere as a lack of civility. It erodes our sense of human connection to those in public life—and to the strangers who cross our paths and people our private lives.

■ QUESTIONS FOR DISCUSSION AND WRITING

1. Do you agree with Tannen's assertion that our public discussions about controversial issues have been turned into "battles and duels" by the media? Explain why or why not. Look through several current newspapers or newsmagazines to see if you can find evidence of this trend. Do other forms of media, such as television and radio, also encourage this outlook?

2. How has the "argument culture" affected our ability to resolve controversial issues? Can you think of any examples of current controversies that have been negatively affected by the tendency of those involved to defend their own "turf" rather than listen and respond constructively to the ideas of others who hold differing views?

3. Tannen cites the example of a woman who called in to a talk show and questioned whether her conciliatory approach to a potential conflict was the best course of action (paragraphs 8 and 9). In your journal, discuss some of your own experiences in confronting someone else about behavior you find unacceptable. What approaches have been successful for you? Do you agree with Tannen that the woman was wise to avoid conflict?

4. In your own experience, have you found that schools and teachers promote and reward students who engage in heated debate with other students, as Tannen contends in paragraphs 18 to 20? Do you think this style of communication discourages students who may not be as comfortable with this confrontational behavior? Have you found that a "winner-take-all" approach to argument is a productive way to solve problems or disagreements? What problems can arise from this approach? Are there any benefits?

SAMPLE ARGUMENTS FOR ANALYSIS

Read the following two essays to find the basic components in writing arguments and to practice debate, dialogue, and deliberation. After you have read each essay carefully, respond to these questions about them:

1. Identify each writer's claim and restate it in your own words. What do you think is the writer's purpose in writing the essay?

2. What reasons does each writer use to support his claim? Make a list of the reasons you find in each essay. Are the reasons convincing?

3. Find examples of the ways each writer supports those reasons. How convincing is the evidence he presents? Is it pertinent? reliable? sufficient? Is it slanted or biased?

4. Does the writer acknowledge views about the subject that are different from his own? Where does he do this? What is the writer's attitude toward those who hold different views? Does he try to understand those views or does he respond only negatively toward them?

5. Using debate, dialogue, and deliberation, complete the following activities individually or in small groups:
   a. To become acquainted with opposing reasons, write a "yes, but . . ." exchange or a pro/con checklist.
   b. Using your checklist or exchange, create a dialogue between two or more opposing sides on the issue that attempts to find points of disagreement as well as common ground or shared concerns among them. Look for opportunities for each side to listen and respond constructively to the other.

    c. Deliberate. Review the reasons and examples from a number of perspectives. What reasons on either side do you find the most compelling? What concerns have particular merit? How can you balance the interests of all sides of the issue? Formulate a claim that takes into account what you have learned from listening and considering several perspectives and provide reasons to support it.

The Case Against Tipping
Michael Lewis

Many people have strong views about tipping. Some consider it an optional act of kindness to express appreciation for good service, an additional expense over what they have already paid. For others it is an essential part of their day's wages, and thus their income. The following essay by Michael Lewis explores this dichotomy. Lewis, a journalist, writes about economics, politics, international economic relations, and society. As you read this article, think about your own attitudes toward the practice of tipping. What motivates a tip? If you have ever been on the receiving end, did you find that relying on others' generosity for your income left you vulnerable to their whims?

1   No lawful behavior in the marketplace is as disturbing to me as the growing appeals for gratuities. Every gentle consumer of cappuccinos will know what I'm getting at: Just as you hand your money over to the man behind the counter, you notice a plastic beggar's cup beside the cash register. "We Appreciate Your Tips," it reads in blue ink scrawled across the side with calculated indifference. The young man or woman behind the counter has performed no especially noteworthy service. He or she has merely handed you a $2 muffin and perhaps a ruinous cup of coffee and then rung them up on the register. Yet the plastic cup waits impatiently for an expression of your gratitude. A dollar bill or two juts suggestively over the rim—no doubt placed there by the person behind the counter. Who would tip someone a dollar or more for pouring them a cup of coffee? But you can never be sure. The greenbacks might have been placed there by people who are more generous than yourself. People whose hearts are not made of flint.

2   If you are like most people (or at any rate like me), you are of two minds about this plastic cup. On the one hand, you do grasp the notion that people who serve you are more likely to do it well and promptly if they believe they will be rewarded for it. The prospect of a tip is, in theory at least, an important incentive for the person working behind the counter of the coffee bar. Surely, you don't want to be one of those people who benefit from the certain hop to the worker's step that the prospect of a tip has arguably induced without paying your fair share of the cost. You do not wish to be thought of as not doing your share, you cheapskate.

3   And these feelings of guilt are only compounded by the niggling suspicion that the men who run the corporation that runs the coffee shops might be figuring on a certain level of tipping per hour when they decide how generous a wage they should extend to the folks toiling at the counters. That is, if you fail to tip the person getting you that coffee, you may be directing and even substantially affecting that person's level of income.

4   That said, we are talking here about someone who has spent all of 40 seconds retrieving for you a hot drink and a muffin. When you agreed to buy the drink and the muffin you did not take into account the plastic-cup shakedown. In short, you can't help but feel you are being had.

5   There in a nutshell is the first problem with tipping: the more discretion you have in the matter the more unpleasant it is. Tipping is an aristocratic conceit—"There you go, my good man, buy your starving family a loaf"—best left to an aristocratic age. The practicing democrat would rather be told what he owes right up front. Offensively rich people may delight in peeling off hundred-dollar bills and tossing them out to groveling servants. But no sane, well-adjusted human being cares to sit around and evaluate the performance of some beleaguered coffee vendor.

6   This admirable reticence means that, in our democratic age at least, gratuities are inexorably transformed into something else. On most occasions where they might be conferred—at restaurants, hotels and the like—tips are as good as obligatory. "Tipping is customary," reads the sign in the back of a New York City taxi, and if anything, that is an understatement. Once, a long time ago, I tried to penalize a cabdriver for bad service and he rolled alongside me for two crowded city blocks, shouting obscenities through his car window. A friend of mine who undertipped had the message drummed home more perfectly: a few seconds after she stepped out of the cab, the cab knocked her over. She suffered a fracture in her right leg. But it could have been worse. She could have been killed for . . . undertipping! (The driver claimed it was an accident. Sure it was.)

7   There, in a nutshell, is the second problem with tipping: the less discretion you have in the matter, the more useless it is as an economic incentive. Our natural and admirable reluctance to enter into the spirit of the thing causes the thing to lose whatever value it had in the first place. It is no accident that the rudest and most inept service people in America—New York City cabdrivers—are also those most likely to receive their full 15 percent. A tip that isn't a sure thing is socially awkward. But a tip that is a sure thing is no longer a tip really. It's more like a tax.

8   Once you understand the impossibility of tipping in our culture, the plastic cup on the coffee-bar counter can be seen for what it is: a custom in the making. How long can it be before the side of the coffee cup reads "Tipping Is Customary"? I called Starbucks to talk this over, and a pleasant spokeswoman told me that this chain of coffee bars, at least, has no such designs on American mores. The official Starbucks line on their Plexiglas container is that it wasn't their idea but that of their customers. "People were leaving loose change on

the counter to show their gratitude," she said. "And so in 1990 it was decided to put a tasteful and discreet cup on the counter. It's a way for our customers to say thanks to our partners." (Partners are what Starbucks calls its employees.)

9   Perhaps. But you can be sure that our society will not long tolerate the uncertainty of the cup. People will demand to know what is expected of them, one way or the other. Either the dollar in the cup will become a routine that all civilized coffee buyers will endure. Or the tasteful and discreet cup will disappear altogether, in deference to the straightforward price hike.

10   A small matter, you might say. But if the person at the coffee-bar counter feels entitled to a tip for grabbing you a coffee and muffin, who won't eventually? I feel we are creeping slowly toward a kind of baksheesh economy in which everyone expects to be showered with coins simply for doing what they've already been paid to do. Let's band together and ignore the cup. And who knows? Someday, we may live in a world where a New York cabdriver simply thanks you for paying what it says on the meter.

■ QUESTIONS FOR DISCUSSION AND WRITING

1. Do you think Lewis has had much experience in a job that relies on tips? What evidence can you find to demonstrate this?

2. Do you agree with Lewis? In your journal, respond to Lewis's ideas by exploring your own views on tipping. What is your position on this topic? What experiences have you had that support your own view?

The Consequences of "Carnage as Entertainment"

John Ellis

Television has been blamed for a multitude of social problems: Johnny does poorly in school because he watches too much television. Families are falling apart because instead of communicating with each other, they spend their time in front of the TV. Violent and overt sexual behavior is also blamed on television. The following article by John Ellis probes this controversy. Ellis is a columnist for the *Boston Globe,* in which this article originally appeared. As you read Ellis's essay, reflect on your own television viewing habits. Do you believe people imitate what they see on television? Are children especially vulnerable to television's influence?

1   Read the roll, as compiled by the Associated Press.

2   On Oct. 1, 1997, a 16-year-old student in Pearl, Miss., allegedly killed his mother, then went to his high school and shot nine students, two of them dead.

3   On March 24, 1998, an 11-year-old boy and his 13-year-old friend allegedly opened fire on classmates at a middle school in Jonesboro, Ark. Four schoolchildren and a teacher were killed in the hail of gunfire. Ten more were wounded.

4   On April 24, 1998, a 14-year-old boy went to his eighth-grade graduation dance in Edinboro, Pa. He allegedly opened fire on the festivities almost imme-

diately thereafter, killing one teacher and wounding another. Two classmates were also injured in the shooting spree.

5   On May 19, 1998, a high school senior allegedly shot and killed a classmate in the parking lot of their Fayetteville, Tenn., school. Authorities said they had argued about a girl.

6   On May 21, 1998—the day before yesterday—a 15-year-old student allegedly opened fire in the Thurston High School cafeteria in Springfield, Ore., killing two, critically wounding eight others and injuring 14 more. Earlier in the day, the suspect allegedly shot and killed his parents. After the melee had ended, the suspect was quoted as saying: "Just shoot me, shoot me now."

7   We are inheriting a whirlwind. Television violence has come home to roost. Thirty years ago, Kipland Kinkel, the 15-year-old suspect in the Thurston High School massacre, would have been just another juvenile delinquent in need of counseling. It would never have occurred to him that he could walk into his high school's cafeteria with a semi-automatic weapon and start squeezing off rounds.

8   These days, children like Kinkel have seen this kind of violent behavior on television countless times. They know that if someone shoots up his school, he will become a celebrity. News media will want to interview him. Talk show hosts will want to have him on their shows. Network correspondents will vie for the "exclusive" rights to his "story."

9   By the end of next week, more people will know Kinkel's name than will know the names of the doctors at Harvard who are gaining on a cure for cancer. To say that our media culture is sick is to vastly understate the dimensions of the virus. Consider the following dispatch from the April 16 edition of *The Washington Post*.

10   "Researchers at four universities who examined 9,000 hours of TV programming found that the overall level of violence on broadcast and cable television has held steady over the three years of their study. In all, they found that 61 percent of the programs examined last year contained some violence, roughly the same as the preceding two years.

11   "Sixty-seven percent of the programs carried by the broadcast networks in prime time and 64 percent of prime-time shows on basic cable contained violence during the 1996–97 season, according to the study. For 'premium' cable networks such as HBO and Showtime, which tend to air uncut theatrical movies, 87 percent of programs had violence."

12   More important, the violence depicted on television and in the movies escalates with each passing year, as audiences grow inured to "routine" violence. According to the American Medical Association, "TV portrays violence in a way that increases the risk of learning aggressive attitudes. The AMA considers violence to be a major national health problem, and television to be an important contributing factor."

13   Sissela Bok, in her new book *Mayhem*, argues that media violence ("carnage as entertainment" as she calls it) is especially harmful to children, leading to "increased fearfulness, progressive desensitization, greater appetite for more frequent and more violent programming, and higher levels of aggression."

14   Incredibly, the entertainment industry continues to maintain that there is no correlation between violence as depicted in the media and violence in American life. Jack Valenti, president of the Motion Picture Association of America, which represents major TV producers as well as Hollywood studios, blasted the study cited above as "unwarranted assumptions jumping to a preconceived conclusion. These are blurred and ephemeral numbers."

15   This is irresponsible nonsense. We are at a crossroads here. The fact is that school massacres in America this spring are running at the rate of one a month. If the violence continues, then a minor massacre at some middle school in Massachusetts won't even be a news story in three or four years. In the not distant future, it is possible that someone will have to wipe out a whole class of kids to make the network news.

16   We can either do something about the excessive, gratuitous violence that permeates our national media or surrender a civilized society. The stakes are just that. What was once alarming is now chilling. Carnage as entertainment has consequences. The people of Springfield, Ore., can tell you that.

■ QUESTIONS FOR DISCUSSION AND WRITING

1. What are your own views about the effects of media violence on the actions of children and teenagers? Do you agree with Ellis's position?
2. How do you think our society could respond constructively to Ellis's concerns? Would simply cutting back on the amount of time children watch television have a significant impact on the problem of child violence? In your journal, suggest several ways this problem could be addressed.
3. In paragraph 16 Ellis states, "We can either do something about the excessive, gratuitous violence that permeates our national media or surrender a civilized society." Do you think these are two reasonable choices? In Chapter 2 we discuss a logical fallacy called a *false dilemma* in which the writer overstates the consequences of inaction or disagreement with his or her position. The reader is given a dramatic and often exaggerated choice. Do you think Ellis is guilty of this logical fallacy? If so, how would you restate his choices to avoid it?

■ EXERCISES

1. Try to determine from the following list which subjects are arguable and which are not.
   a. Letter grades in all college courses should be replaced by pass/fail grades.
   b. Capital punishment is no deterrent to crime.
   c. Lobster is my favorite seafood.
   d. Professor Greene is one of the best professors on campus.
   e. The university should install condom machines in all dormitories.
   f. Pornography poses a threat to women.
   g. Minorities make up only 9 percent of the upper management positions in corporate America.
   h. The earth's population will be 7.3 billion by the year 2010.
   i. Juveniles who commit serious crimes should be sent to adult prisons.

    j. Last night's sunset over the mountains was spectacular.

    k. Advertisers often mislead the public about the benefits of their products.

    l. AIDS testing for health care workers should be mandatory.

    m. Bilingual education programs fail to help non–English-speaking children become part of mainstream society.

    n. Abortion is a decision that should be left up to women, not the courts.

    o. I think women are better listeners than men.

    p. Couples should have to get a license before having children.

    q. Given all the billions of galaxies and billions of stars in each galaxy, there must be life elsewhere.

    r. Secondhand smoke causes cancer.

2. In your argument notebook, create a pro/con checklist for the following topics. Make two columns: pro on one side, con on the other. If possible, team up with other students to brainstorm opposing points on each issue. Try to come up with five or six solid points and counterpoints.

    a. I think women are better listeners than men.

    b. Capital punishment is no deterrent to crime.

    c. "Hard" sciences such as math are more difficult than "soft" sciences such as sociology.

    d. The production and sale of cigarettes must be outlawed for the health of the American public.

    e. The university should reduce tuition for those students who maintained an A average during the previous year.

    f. ROTC should be made available to all students in U.S. colleges and universities.

    g. The majority of American people support prayer in school.

3. Use one of these topics to construct a dialogue in which the object is not to oppose the other side but to respond constructively to its concerns. As a first step, analyze the reasons provided by both sides and make a list of their concerns, noting whether any are shared. Then create a dialogue that might take place between the two.

4. Write about a recent experience in which you tried to convince someone of something. What reasons did you use to make your claim convincing? Which were most successful? What were the opposing reasons? How did you respond?

CHAPTER 2

Reading Arguments
Thinking Like a Critic

We read for a variety of purposes. Sometimes it's to find information about when a particular event will take place or to check on the progress of a political candidate or to learn how to assemble a piece of furniture. Other times we read to be entertained by a favorite newspaper columnist or to discover the secrets behind making a pot of really good chili. But if you've ever picked up a book, a magazine article, a newspaper editorial, or a piece of advertising and found yourself questioning the ideas and claims of the authors, then you've engaged in a special kind of reading called *critical reading*. When you look beyond the surface of words and thoughts to think about the ideas and their meaning and significance, you are reading critically.

Critical reading is active reading. It involves asking questions and not necessarily accepting the writer's statements at face value. Critical readers ask questions of authors such as these:

- What do you mean by that phrase?
- Can you support that statement?
- How do you define that term?
- Why is this observation important?
- How did you arrive at that conclusion?
- Do other experts agree with you?
- Is this evidence up-to-date?

By asking such questions, you are weighing the writer's claims, asking for definitions, evaluating information, looking for proof, questioning assumptions, and making judgments. In short, you are actively engaged in thinking like a critic.

Why Read Critically?

When you read critically, you think critically. Instead of passively accepting what's written on a page, you separate yourself from the text and decide what is convincing to you and what is not. Critical reading is a process of discovery. You discover

28

where an author stands on an issue, and you discover the strengths and weaknesses of an author's argument. The result is that you have a better understanding of the issue. By asking questions of the author, by analyzing where the author stands with respect to others' views on the issue, you become more knowledgeable about the issue and more able to develop your own informed viewpoint on the subject.

Critical reading not only sharpens your focus on an issue. It also heightens your ability to construct and evaluate your own arguments. That will lead you to become a better writer because critical reading is the first step to critical writing. Good writers look at the written word the way a carpenter looks at a house—they study the fine details and how those details connect to create the whole. It's the same with critical reading. The better you become at analyzing and reacting to another's written work, the better you are at analyzing and reacting to your own: Is it logical? Are my points clearly stated? Do my examples really support my ideas? Have I explained this term clearly? Is my conclusion persuasive? In other words, critical reading will help you use that same critical eye with your own writing, making you both a better reader and a better writer.

Additionally, as you sharpen your skills as a reader and a writer, you will also develop your critical skills as an interpreter of arguments embodied not in words but in visual images. As you will see in Chapter 8, argumentation is not limited to verbal presentation. Photographs, political cartoons, and advertisements, among others, express potent and persuasive arguments in visual imagery.

Even though you may already employ many of the strategies of critical reading, we'd like to offer some suggestions and techniques to make you an even better critical reader.

Preview the Reading

Even before you begin reading, you can look for clues that may reveal valuable information about the subject of the article, the writer's attitude about the subject, the audience the writer is addressing, and the purpose of the article. As a prereading strategy, try to answer the following questions:

1. *Who is the writer?* Information about the writer is sometimes provided in a short biographical note on the first or last page of the reading. The writer's age, education, current profession, and professional background can tell you about his or her experience and perspective on the subject. For instance, a physician who is writing about assisted suicide may have a very different attitude toward that subject than an individual who has a degree in divinity. A writer who has held a high-ranking position in a government agency or a political appointment will bring that experience to bear in a discussion of a political issue. A writer's background and professional training can provide knowledge and credibility; you may be more inclined to believe an expert in a field than someone with little or no experience. However, direct experience can also limit the writer's perspective. A review of this information before you read can help you better evaluate the writer as an authority.

2. *Where was the article originally published?* Often the publication in which the article originally appeared will indicate the writer's audience and purpose. Some publications, such as scholarly journals, are intended to be read by other professionals in a particular field. Writers for such a journal assume that readers are familiar with the terminology of that profession and possess a certain level of education and experience. For example, an author writing about cancer research in a scholarly medical journal such as the *Journal of the American Medical Association (JAMA)* would assume a high degree of medical expertise on the part of the readers. An author writing about the same cancer research in *Newsweek* would provide a greatly simplified version with little medical terminology. Popular magazines you see at newsstands are designed to communicate to a larger, more general audience. Writers make an effort to explain difficult concepts in terms an inexperienced reader can understand. Knowing where the article was originally published will prepare you for the demands of the reading. It may also prepare you for the writer's point of view. Publications are usually designed for a specific audience. *The Wall Street Journal,* for example, has a readership largely comprising people interested in the economy, business, or investments. The articles in it reflect the concerns and interests of the business community. On the other hand, an article appearing in *High Times,* a publication that endorses the use and legalization of marijuana, has a very different set of readers. By familiarizing yourself with the publication in which the article originally appeared, you can learn much about the writer's likely political and professional opinions, knowledge you can use to judge the credibility of his or her argument.

3. *When was the article originally published?* The date of publication can also provide background about what was happening when the article was published. It will indicate factors that might have influenced the writer and whether the evidence used in the reading is current or historical. For instance, an article written about the economy during an earlier time of economic recession would be strongly influenced by factors of high unemployment and business failures. The writer's argument might not be as convincing during a period of growth and stability. Some readings are timeless in their consideration of basic truths about people and life; others can be challenged about whether their arguments can still be applied to current circumstances.

4. *What does the title reveal about the subject and the author's attitude toward it?* The title of an article often indicates both the subject of the article and the writer's attitude toward it. After you have identified the subject, look carefully at the words the writer has used to describe it. Are their connotations negative or positive? What other words do you associate with them? Does the title make reference to another written work or to a well-known slogan or familiar saying? Sometimes writers use their titles to suggest a parallel between their subject and a similar situation in recent times or a particular event in history. An article about the possibility of an annihilating nuclear attack in 2020 might be titled "Hiroshima in the Twenty-First Century." These choices are deliberate ways to inform readers about a writer's views and ideas on a subject. By considering the language in the title, you will be more aware of the writer's intent.

Let's try a preview of the first reading in this chapter. By carefully reading the introductory paragraph, you can learn the following information:

Preview Question 1: Who is the writer? As the introduction tells us, Henry Wechsler is the director of the College Alcohol Studies Program at the Harvard University School of Public Health. His professional title suggests that he is knowledgeable about alcohol use, particularly at the college level, because he directs a program that studies this area. You are about to read an essay, then, written by an expert in the field of alcohol research.

Preview Question 2: Where was the article originally published? By reading further in the paragraph, you find that the article was originally published in the *Boston Globe*. This is a widely circulated newspaper located in a major American city. The writer would expect the article to be read by a large cross-section of people with diverse economic and educational backgrounds. Because Boston is the city where Harvard and many other colleges are located, readers might have a special interest in issues that affect the college community.

Preview Question 3: When was the article originally published? The introduction tells you that the article first appeared on October 2, 1997. This is a fairly recent article, which makes it likely that it will be up-to-date and relevant to current concerns.

Preview Question 4: What does the title reveal about the subject and the author's attitude toward it? The title of the article, "Binge Drinking Must Be Stopped," suggests an emphatic and nonnegotiable attitude on the part of the author.

As you can see, your preview of the article has provided much valuable information that will help prepare you to begin the critical reading process.

Skim the Reading

Just as an athlete would never participate in a competitive event without first stretching his or her muscles and thoroughly warming up, you will find that successful critical reading is a process that benefits from a series of activities aimed at increasing your understanding of the writer's ideas. The first time through you may wish to skim the reading to get a general idea of its subject and intent. Further readings should be slower and more thoughtful so that each reason presented can be analyzed and evaluated and each idea judged and considered. Now that you have previewed the material about the author, the original publication and date, and the title, you are ready to skim the reading to find its basic features.

When you skim a reading, you are trying to discover the topic and the claim. Start by reading the first one or two paragraphs and the last paragraph. If the reading is a relatively short newspaper article, such as the following sample essay, this may be enough to give you a general idea of the writer's topic and point of view. If the reading is longer and more complex, you will also need to examine the first sentence or two of each paragraph to get a better sense of the writer's ideas.

SAMPLE ARGUMENT FOR ANALYSIS

For practice, let's skim the first reading in this chapter. To organize your impressions from skimming the reading, it's a good idea to write down some of them in your journal.

Binge Drinking Must Be Stopped

Henry Wechsler

"Binge" drinking is a problem on many college campuses. Away from home for the first time, many freshmen celebrate their new freedom by abusing alcohol at parties. But this behavior is not only confined to freshmen, as Henry Wechsler's research indicates. Henry Wechsler is the director of the College Alcohol Studies Program at the Harvard School of Public Health. He completed a survey focusing on the binge drinking practices of students at 140 colleges and universities. The survey revealed a high rate of binge drinking and a wide range of problems associated with this behavior, especially when connected to fraternity life. He wrote the following article in response to the death of MIT freshman Scott Krueger who died of alcohol poisoning after participating in binge drinking during a fraternity party. This essay was originally published in the *Boston Globe* on October 2, 1997.

1   We should be saddened and outraged by the tragic death of a young man just starting to fulfill his life promise.

2   This week's death from alcohol overdose of Scott Krueger, a freshman at the Massachusetts Institute of Technology, is an extreme and unfortunate consequence of a style of drinking that is deeply entrenched and widespread at American colleges. Binge drinking is a reality of college life in America and perhaps the central focus of fraternity-house life.

3   Since the Harvard School of Public Health study on college binge drinking was released almost three years ago, colleges have been deluged with reports on alcohol abuse. Even before our results became public, it was inconceivable that college administrators were unaware of the existence of alcohol problems at their institutions.

4   A quick ride in a security van on a Thursday, Friday, or Saturday night could provide all the information needed. A conversation with the chief of security could easily reveal where the binge drinking takes place and which students, fraternities, and alcohol outlets are violating college rules or local ordinances.

5   An incoming freshman learns during the first week of school where the alcohol and parties are and often has a binge drinking experience even before purchasing a text book. If students can find it so easily, so can college administrators. It is not that complicated: Drunken parties are usually at certain fraternity houses and housing complexes just off campus. The heaviest drinking

most likely takes place in a few bars near campus where large quantities of alcohol are sold cheaply.

6   If we know so much about the problem, why is it that we have not been able to do much about it? First, because colleges, like problem drinkers, do not recognize that they have a problem. It has been there for so long that they have adapted to it. They are lulled into complacency as long as the problem does not seem to increase or a tragedy does not occur.

7   Second, the solutions that are offered are usually only partial: a lecture, an awareness day, a new regulation in the dorms. The root of the problem is seldom touched. The supply of large quantities of cheap alcohol is viewed as outside the purview of college officials. "It's off campus" is a euphemism for "that's not my job." The bar or liquor store may be off campus, but it is controlled by licensing boards that city officials and colleges can substantially influence. The fraternity house may be off campus and not owned by the college, but it is affiliated with and depends on the college for its existence. Many colleges and universities simply wink at the activities of the fraternities and claim no responsibility.

8   Third, when new policies are established, they are often assumed to be in effect without proper verification. It is easy to say there is no drinking allowed in a dormitory or a fraternity, but enforcement is necessary to put the policy into effect. Legally, no alcohol can be sold to people under age 21, but 86 percent of college students drink.

9   We can no longer be shocked at what is happening on many college campuses and in many fraternities. This is no longer a time merely to form a committee to study the situation. It is time to act.

10   Action needs to be taken on many fronts: the college president's office, the fraternity and sorority system, the athletics department, community licensing boards and, foremost, those students who are sick of the drinking they see around them.

11   Parents who pay for college tuitions should demand a safe environment for their children. Binge drinking need not remain an integral part of college life. University presidents must make it their responsibility to produce change.

After skimming "Binge Drinking Must Be Stopped," you might record the following (we indicate in parentheses the paragraphs in which we found our ideas):

> Wechsler starts off with a reference to a young man who died from an alcohol overdose. He says we should be saddened and outraged by this. Then he suggests that binge drinking has become very common on college campuses, particularly in fraternities (*paragraphs 1 and 2*). Wechsler believes parents should insist that colleges provide a safe environment for their children by finding solutions for binge drinking. University presidents must take responsibility for solving this problem (*paragraph 11*).

By skimming the article, you now have some sense of what the reading will be about and the writer's position. Before beginning a closer reading of the text, you will want to take one additional step to prepare yourself to be an active and responsive reader: Consider your experience with the topic.

Consider Your Own Experience

Your next step in the reading process is to consider your own experience. Critical reading brings your own perspective, experience, education, and personal values to your reading. Sometimes you begin with very little knowledge about the subject of your reading. It may be a topic that you haven't given much thought or one that is unfamiliar and new. Other times you may start with some of your own ideas and opinions about the subject. By taking the time to consider what you know and how your own experiences and values relate to the author's ideas, you can add a dimension to your reading that enables you to question, analyze, and understand the writer's ideas more effectively. You will be a more active critical reader because you can respond to the writer's ideas with ideas of your own.

Before beginning a close reading, take the time to reflect on these questions:

- What do I know about this subject?
- What have I heard or read about it recently?
- What attitudes or opinions do I have about the subject?

Exploring what you already know or think about a subject can have several benefits: You can use your knowledge to better understand the situation or issue described in the reading; you can compare your own experience with that of the writer; you can formulate questions to keep in mind as you read; and you can become more aware of your own opinions about the subject. For instance, you may be reading an article about the benefits of the proposed plan for improving your state's welfare system. If you have some knowledge about this proposal from reading news stories or hearing discussions about it, you will begin your reading with some understanding of the issue. If you have had actual experience with the welfare system or know of others' experiences, you can provide examples of your own to challenge or support those of the writer. If you have taken the time to consider questions you have about the proposed plan, you will be actively seeking answers as you read. And, by exploring your own views on the subject before you read, you will find that the ideas in the article will enrich, inform, and possibly change your opinion.

After previewing and skimming the reading, John, a freshman composition student, wrote the following reflection on the topic of binge drinking in his journal:

> It would be hard to be a student at college and not notice the heavy drinking that goes on every weekend. Some people just can't have fun unless they drink too much. It's a fact of college life—for some people. And if you live in a small college community, sometimes that's all there is to do on Saturday night. I've seen some kids really ruin their lives with too much partying. They forget why they came to college in the first place—or maybe that is why they came. But not everybody drinks to excess. Most of us just like to get a little buzz and socialize and have fun. Most of us will just go just so far and stop, but there's always a few who can't seem to stop until they pass out or puke their guts out on

the sidewalk. Yeah, we've all been told the dangers of drinking too much, but some people aren't mature enough to see that they're hurting themselves. Binge drinking happens every weekend around here. It's not a pretty sight, but I'm not sure how the college president or anybody else could stop it. College students have always partied to relieve tension and to socialize. It's been going on for years. Why is college drinking suddenly such a big issue? And, if the drinking takes place outside of campus, how can the college stop it? If students want to get alcohol, even if they're underage, they'll find a way. Why should the college tell us whether we can drink or not?

John clearly has considerable experience with the topic and some strong opinions of his own. By considering them before he begins a close reading of the article, he is ready to explore and challenge the ideas he encounters in the reading.

Annotate the Reading

Annotating the text is the next stage of critical reading to help you become a thoughtful and careful reader. *Annotating* is responding to the ideas in the reading right on the pages of your text. (If you don't own the publication the essay appears in, make a photocopy.) There are many different ways to annotate a reading, but many readers use the following methods:

- Highlight or underline passages that you consider significant.
- Write questions in the margins that respond to the writer's ideas or that you wish to follow up with further investigation.
- Circle words or phrases that need to be defined or made clearer.
- Add comments or brief examples of your own that support or challenge the writer's.
- Draw lines between related ideas.
- Note the writer's use of transitions and qualifiers that subtly shade meaning.
- Point out with arrows or asterisks particularly persuasive examples.
- Mark difficult-to-understand sections of the text that need a closer look.

Annotation is a way to create an active dialogue between you and the writer by responding in writing to individual points in the reading. Your annotations become a personal record of your thoughts, questions, objections, comments, and agreements with the writer. Annotation can help you read like a critic because it makes you slow down and pay attention to each idea as you read. As an additional benefit, your written comments in the margin will serve as a reminder of your response to the ideas in the essay when you read it again. Figure 2.1 on pages 36–37 is an example of some of the ways you might annotate "Binge Drinking Must Be Stopped."

Summarize the Reading

Before you can begin to analyze and evaluate what you read, it's important to clearly understand what the writer is saying. *Summarizing* is a type of writing used to capture the essential meaning of a reading by focusing only on the writer's main points. When you summarize, you "tell back," in a straightforward way, the writer's

BINGE DRINKING MUST BE STOPPED

1   We should be saddened and outraged by the tragic death of a young man just starting to fulfill his life promise.

2   This week's death from alcohol overdose of Scott Krueger, a freshman at the Massachusetts Institute of Technology, is an extreme and unfortunate consequence of a style of drinking that is deeply entrenched and widespread in American colleges. Binge drinking is a reality of college life in America and perhaps the central focus of fraternity house life.

Does everyone at college drink?

claim

3   Since the Harvard School of Public Health study on college binge drinking was released almost three years ago, colleges have been (deluged) with reports on alcohol abuse. Even before our results became public, it was inconceivable that college administrators were unaware of the existence of alcohol problems at their institutions.

find out more info on this.

flooded

4   A quick ride in a security van on a Thursday, Friday, or Saturday night could provide all the information needed. A conversation with the chief of security could easily reveal where the binge drinking takes place and which students, fraternities, and alcohol outlets are violating college rules or local ordinances.

Is this the job of college administrators?

5   An incoming freshman learns during the first week of school where the alcohol and parties are and often has a binge drinking experience even before purchasing a textbook. If students can find it so easily, so can college administrators. It is not that complicated: Drunken parties are usually at certain fraternity houses and housing complexes just off campus. The heaviest drinking most likely takes place in a few bars near campus where large quantities of alcohol are sold cheaply.

qualifier
How does he know this?

qualifier

Who is "we"?

6   If we know so much about the problem, why is it that we have not been able to do much about it? First, because colleges, like problem drinkers, do not recognize that they have a problem. It has been there for so long that they have adapted to it. They are lulled into (complacency) as long as the problem does not seem to increase or a tragedy does not occur.

Is this contradicted by the next ¶? Don't colleges try to do something about binge drinking?

smug self-satisfaction

Figure 2.1

7   Second, the solutions that are offered are usually *(Agreed. These don't change behavior much.)* only partial: a lecture, an awareness day, a new regulation in the dorms. The root of the problem is seldom touched. The supply of large quantities of cheap alcohol is viewed as outside the purview of college officials. "It's off campus" is a (euphemism) for "that's not my job." The *(less offensive substitute word)* bar or liquor store may be off campus, but it is controlled by licensing boards that city officials and colleges can substantially influence. The fraternity house may be off campus and not owned by the college, but it is affiliated with and depends on the college for its existence. Many colleges and universities simply (wink) at the activities of the fraternities and claim no responsibility. *— What does he mean?*

8   Third, when new policies are established, they are often assumed to be in effect without proper (verification). *(proven to be true)* It is easy to say there is no drinking allowed in a dormitory or fraternity, but enforcement is necessary to put the policy into effect. Legally, no alcohol can be sold to people under age 21, but 86 percent of college students *(Impressive statistic.)* drink.

9   We can no longer be shocked at what is happening *(Who is "we"? Has it changed?)* on many college campuses and in many fraternities. This is no longer a time merely to form a committee to study the situation. It is time to act.

10   Action needs to be taken on many fronts: the college president's office, the fraternity and sorority system, the athletics department, community licencing boards, and foremost, those students who are sick of the drinking they see around them. *(his solution What should they do?)*

11   Parents who pay for college tuitions should demand *(Who is responsible?)* a safe environment for their (children.) Binge drinking *(Don't the drinkers have some responsibility?)* need not remain an (integral) part of college life. University presidents must make it their (responsibility) to produce change.

(essential)   *(Are college students "children"?)*

---

main ideas. Although summaries can vary in length depending on the length of the original reading, all summaries share these qualities:

- *A summary is considerably shorter than the original.* Because a summary is concerned only with the writer's main ideas, supporting details and examples are usually omitted. The length of a summary will vary depending on your purpose and the length and content of the original.

- *A summary is written in your own words.* Although it may be necessary to use certain of the writer's words for which there are no substitutes, a summary is written in your own words. If you find it necessary to include a short phrase from the original, then quotation marks must be used to set it off. (In Chapter 9, we discuss ways to use summary in a researched argument paper and the need to document the ideas in your summary with a citation.)
- *A summary is objective.* When you summarize, your job is to "tell back" the writer's main ideas with no comments or personal opinions of your own. Of course, once you have completed your summary, you are free to respond to it in any way you wish.
- *A summary is accurate.* It's a good idea to reread several times before you attempt to summarize a reading because it's important that you truly understand what the writer means. Sometimes it takes many tries to capture that exact meaning.
- *A summary is thorough.* Even though a summary is, as we've explained, much shorter than the original, a good summary contains each of the writer's main points.

Summarizing is an important step in critical reading because you need to thoroughly understand a writer's ideas before you can explain them, in writing, to others. Don't be discouraged when you first try to summarize a reading. Over time and with practice you will feel more comfortable writing summaries.

A good method to begin summarizing a reading is to write a one-sentence summary of the ideas in each paragraph. (Brief paragraphs that elaborate the same point can be summarized together.) By considering each paragraph separately, you will be sure to cover all the main ideas in the reading and be able to see at a glance how the ideas in the essay are connected to each other and how the writer has chosen to sequence them.

Let's go back to the essay "Binge Drinking Must Be Stopped" and try a one-sentence summary of each paragraph (we combine short paragraphs that are about the same idea):

> *Paragraphs 1 and 2:* The recent death of an MIT student was a terrible event that was caused by excessive drinking practices that are common on college campuses.
>
> *Paragraph 3:* Colleges should be aware of the problem of excessive drinking among their students because studies have been released about it.
>
> *Paragraph 4:* By speaking with law enforcement professionals in their own communities, colleges could become aware of where alcohol laws are being broken.
>
> *Paragraph 5:* Freshmen learn where to find alcohol when they first arrive on campus: fraternities, student housing, and bars close to campus.
>
> *Paragraph 6:* Colleges aren't doing anything about the problem because they have accepted it and don't want to admit it exists.
>
> *Paragraph 7:* Because the cause of the problem is the availability of alcohol off campus, colleges don't think it is their responsibility to act even though

they could exercise a strong influence over the places that sell alcohol to students.

Paragraph 8: Colleges don't check to see whether their own alcohol policies are being enforced.

Paragraphs 9 and 10: Rather than just talk about this problem, we need to do something about it at many different levels within the college and the community.

Paragraph 11: College presidents need to take responsibility for reducing the practice of excessive drinking at their colleges to provide a safe place for students.

Your one-sentence summary of each paragraph should reveal the essential parts of the essay: the claim and the main reasons the writer uses to support the claim. Once you have identified these important elements, you are ready to begin your summary. It might look something like this (note that we've added the name of the writer and the title of the article):

In his essay "Binge Drinking Must Be Stopped" Henry Wechsler expresses his concern about the common practice of excessive drinking on college campuses. He suggests that colleges are failing in their responsibility to deal with this problem adequately. Although colleges should be informed about the problem, they won't acknowledge its seriousness. Because it doesn't happen on their campuses, they don't feel that it is their responsibility. Wechsler thinks that colleges could exercise their influence off campus in ways that would help to solve the problem. And, even when colleges do have alcohol policies to restrict drinking, they don't check to see if their policies are being enforced. The problem of binge drinking needs to be dealt with now at many different levels within the college and the community. Wechsler thinks that college presidents need to take responsibility for dealing with binge drinking so that it is no longer an important part of college life.

In looking over this summary, you'll notice that we begin with a general sentence that presents the writer's topic and claim. Then, after reviewing our one-sentence paragraph summaries, we have chosen the writer's main reasons to include in the rest of our paragraph. We have tried to eliminate any ideas that are repeated in more than one paragraph, so we can focus on only the major points.

Summarizing a reading means taking all the separate ideas the writer presents, deciding which ones are important, and weaving them together to create a whole. Our next step in the critical reading process is to consider the ways in which the writer has presented those ideas.

Analyze and Evaluate the Reading

To *analyze* something means to break it down into its separate parts, examine those parts closely, and evaluate their significance and how they work together as a whole. You already began this process when you summarized the main idea in each paragraph of your reading. But analysis goes beyond identifying the ideas in the essay. When we analyze, we consider how each part of the essay functions. We are discovering and evaluating the assumptions and intentions of the writer, which lie below the surface of the writing and which we consider separately from the meaning of the essay itself. Analysis helps us consider how successfully and effectively the writer has argued.

Although there is no set formula for analyzing an argument, we can offer some specific questions you should explore when reading an essay that is meant to persuade you:

- What are the writer's assumptions? What does the writer take for granted about the readers' values, beliefs, or knowledge? What does the writer assume about the subject of the essay or the facts involved?
- What kind of audience is the writer addressing?
- What are the writer's purpose and intention?
- How well does the writer accomplish those purposes?
- What kinds of evidence has the writer used—personal experience or scientific data or outside authorities?
- How convincing is the evidence presented? Is it relevant? Is it reliable? Is it specific enough? Is it sufficient? Is it slanted or dated?
- Does the writer's logic seem reasonable?
- Did the writer address opposing views?
- Is the writer persuasive?

For the sake of illustration, let's apply these questions to our reading:

- *What are the writer's assumptions?*

  The writer assumes that the death of the MIT student indicates a widespread problem of binge drinking on college campuses. He thinks that colleges have a responsibility to control the behavior of their students. He assumes that college students will continue to binge drink without any such controls.

- *What kind of audience is the writer addressing?*

  He seems to be addressing college administrators, parents of college students, and readers who have a special interest in college life.

- *What are the writer's purpose and intention?*

  He wants to make his readers aware that a problem exists and that colleges are not effectively dealing with it.

- *How well does the writer accomplish this purpose?*

  He makes a strong argument that colleges refuse to acknowledge that there's a problem.

- *What kinds of evidence has the writer used?*

  He refers to a study by the Harvard School of Public Health and uses examples of student hangouts that he has heard about but not experienced personally. He seems familiar with college programs on alcohol awareness. He implies that he consulted with the campus security chief for some of his information.

- *How convincing is the evidence?*

Wechsler mentions a scientific study in paragraph 3 but never offers any details from it. Wechsler could provide more solid evidence that the problem is widespread. His examples of places where students can find alcohol seem convincing.

- *Does the writer's logic seem reasonable?*

Wechsler effectively links the evidence he presents to his claim that excessive drinking on college campuses is being ignored by college administrators.

- *Did the writer address opposing views?*

No. We never hear how college administrators respond to this criticism. We also don't know if college students agree with the description of their behavior.

- *Is the writer persuasive?*

The writer is persuasive if we assume that the problem is widespread and that colleges can have a major impact on students' behavior when they are not on campus.

Argue with the Reading

Asking questions and challenging assumptions are important ways to read critically. Although you may not feel qualified to pass judgment on a writer's views, especially if the writer is a professional or an expert on a particular subject, you should keep in mind that as a part of the writer's audience, you have every right to determine whether an argument is sound, logical, and convincing. Your questions about and objections to the writer's ideas will help you evaluate the effectiveness of his or her argument and form your own judgment about the issue.

You may wish to record some of these thoughts in your annotations in the margins of the text. However, a good strategy for beginning writers is to respond at greater length in a journal. You might start by jotting down any points in the essay that contradict your own experience or personal views. Note anything you are skeptical about. Write down any questions you have about the claims, reasons, or evidence. If some point or conclusion seems forced or unfounded, record it and briefly explain why. The more skeptical and questioning you are, the more closely you are reading the text and analyzing its ideas. In particular, be on the lookout for logical fallacies, those instances in which the writer—whether unintentionally or purposefully—distorts or exaggerates evidence or relies on faulty logic to make a point. We discuss these fallacies extensively, later in this chapter.

Likewise, make note of the features of the text that impress you—powerful points, interesting wording, original insights, clever or amusing phrases or allusions, well-chosen references, or the general structure of the essay. If you have heard or read different views on the issue, you might wish to record them as well.

As an example, let's consider some questions, challenges, and features that might have impressed you in our sample essay:

- Wechsler claims that binge drinking is a common practice at colleges across America. Is that true? Does binge drinking take place at all colleges or only on certain campuses? Do all students engage in this practice, or is it more common among certain age groups, gender, fraternity members as opposed to non-members, residential students? Do college students drink more than noncollege students in the same age group?
- The statistic about the percentage of college students who drink (paragraph 8) is convincing.
- Colleges exist to educate students. Are they responsible for monitoring students' behavior when they are not attending classes or socializing off campus? Is it realistic to expect colleges to do this?
- Are colleges really denying that the problem exists? Don't they have counseling services to help students with drinking problems? What else can they do?
- Wechsler's points about the influence that colleges have in their communities (paragraph 7) are persuasive.
- Mentioning the concerns of students who don't drink and the parents of college students is a clever strategy Wechsler uses to expand his audience and pressure colleges to act.

Create a Debate and Dialogue Between Two or More Readings

Few of us would expect to be experts on tennis or golf after watching one match or tournament. We know that it takes time and effort to really begin to understand even the fundamentals of a sport. Reading a single article on a particular subject is the first step in becoming educated about the issues at stake, but a single essay provides us with only one perspective on that subject. As we continue to read about the subject, each new article will offer a new perspective and new evidence to support that view. The more we read, the more complex and thorough our knowledge about the subject becomes. Creating a dialogue between two or more readings is the next step in the process of critical reading.

When you annotate a reading in the earlier stages of critical reading, you begin a dialogue between yourself and the writer. When you create a dialogue between two or more readings, you go one step further: You look at the ideas you find in them to see how they compare and contrast with each other, how they are interrelated, and how the information from one reading informs you as you read the next. By creating a dialogue between the ideas you encounter in several readings, you will be able to consider multiple viewpoints about the same subject.

SAMPLE ARGUMENT FOR ANALYSIS

Begin reading this second selection on binge drinking by following the steps we've outlined in this chapter:

1. Preview the information about the author, where the article first appeared, the date of publication, and the title.
2. Skim the reading to discover the writer's topic and claim.
3. Consider your own experience, values, and knowledge about the subject.
4. Annotate the reading.
5. Summarize the essay.
6. Analyze and evaluate the effectiveness of the reading.
7. Argue with the reading.

Child Care for College Students

Froma Harrop

Froma Harrop presents another viewpoint on the subject of binge drinking and college students in her essay "Child Care for College Students," which appeared in the *Tampa Tribune.* Harrop, an editorial writer and columnist for the *Providence Journal,* argues that college students should be the ones held responsible for their behavior, not businesses and educational institutions.

1   Anyone suspicious that the American university experience has become a four-year extension of childhood need look no farther than the colleges' latest response to the binge-drinking "problem." Now, in a grown-up world, college administrators would tell students who down four or five stiff drinks in a row that they are jerks.

2   If they commit violent acts as a result, the police get called. If they drive after drinking, they go to the slammer. If they die from alcohol poisoning, they have nothing but their own stupidity to blame.

3   But if they can drink responsibly, then let them have a good time.

4   Forget about hearing any such counsel, for that would turn students into self-directing adults. Better to blame the problem on all-purpose "cultural attitudes" and "societal pressures" abetted by the villainous alcohol industry.

5   Thus, demands grow for better policing of off-campus liquor outlets. That is, turn local businesses into babysitters. There are calls to ban sponsorship of college events by companies selling alcohol or the marketing of such beverages on campus. That is, protect their charges from evil influences and trample on free speech. (What should colleges do with the frequent references in Western literature to the glories of drink? Rabelais, for example, said, "There are more old drunkards than old physicians.")

6   One former college official has suggested that universities stop serving champagne at parents' weekend brunches or at fundraising events. Remove

the bad example for the sake of the children. (Somehow it is hard to believe that a college with any sense of self-preservation would insist that its big-check writers remain cold sober.)

7   The truth is, most Americans can drink without problem. Careful use of alcohol relaxes and warms the drinker with a sense of well-being. Winston Churchill and Franklin Roosevelt saved Western civilization without ever missing a cocktail hour. Students have long enjoyed their own drinking traditions. Brahms' Academic Overture, the stately piece heard over and over again at college commencements, took its melody from a student drinking song.

8   Where is there a campus drinking crisis, anyway? Six college students have supposedly died this year from excessive drinking. These cases are lamentable, but many more college students died from sports-related injuries or car accidents.

9   An even more interesting question is: How many noncollege people in their late teens or early 20s have died from alcohol poisoning? Take note that no one is memorizing this particular statistic—even though the majority of high school students do not go on to college. That number is not etched on our national worry list for the following strange reason: Our society considers the 19-year-old who has a job an adult, while universities see the 19-year-old pre-law student as a child. Working people who cause trouble because they drink are punished. College students are given others to blame.

10   College administrators should know that, from a purely practical point of view, playing hide-the-bottle does no good when dealing with an alcoholic. Indeed, anyone who has hung around Alcoholics Anonymous or Al-Anon can immediately identify such behavior as "enabling." Rather than allow the problem drinker to sink into the mire of his addiction until he can no longer stand it and takes steps to straighten out, the enabler tries to save him. Rest assured that students interested in getting smashed for the night will find the booze.

11   Let us end here with yet another proposition: that binge drinking is more about binge than drinking. It would seem that someone who gulps five glasses of Jim Beam in five minutes is not looking for a pleasant high. Binge drinking is a stunt that has more in common with diving off bridges or swallowing goldfish than the quest for inebriation.

12   What any increase in binge drinking probably indicates is that the students really don't know how to drink. Binging may just be the latest evidence of decline in our nation's table arts. Instead of savoring wine and spirits in the course of a civilized meal, young people are administering them. The colleges' response is to put condoms on bottles.

Construct a Debate

Now that you have a good understanding of Froma Harrop's views on binge drinking by college students, you are ready to consider the ideas in both the essays you read. Our first step will be to consider the differences between these two writers by constructing a debate. From your summaries of the readings, select the main ideas that seem directly opposed to each other. To highlight those differences, create two columns, one for each writer. Here are a few of the ideas Wechsler and Harrop debate in their essays:

Wechsler	*Harrop*
Binge drinking is a major problem on college campuses: A student has died.	Binge drinking is not a major problem on campuses: Few students have died.
Colleges have a responsibility to take action about this problem.	Students are responsible for their own drinking.
Colleges should prevent off-campus suppliers of alcohol from giving it to college students.	Colleges should not "police" off-campus suppliers of alcohol.
Colleges should provide a safe environment for students.	College students are adults and should take care of themselves.
Binge drinking continues because colleges aren't treating it as an important problem.	Binge drinking happens because some college students haven't learned to drink responsibly.

These are just a sampling of the many ideas that might be debated by these writers. You should be able to come up with several more.

By considering differences, you can see at a glance the ways in which these writers oppose each other. Your next step is to find the ideas they have in common. This may take more searching, but it's an important step in creating a dialogue between them. To get you started, we'll list a few of the ideas we found. See if you can come up with a few more:

1. Both writers acknowledge that drinking takes place on college campuses.
2. Both writers indicate that binge drinking can be a problem and that students have died as a result.
3. Both writers agree that colleges are aware that binge drinking takes place off campus.

Now that you have found both differences and common ideas, you are ready to create a dialogue. When you create a dialogue between two readings, you find ways for the writers to speak to each other that recognize their differences and points of agreement.

Your dialogue will reveal how the ideas in both readings interrelate. Let's try to create a dialogue using some of the ideas we found:

Wechsler: Binge drinking is a serious problem on college campuses. It's an activity that has become commonplace.

Harrop: I agree that college students engage in binge drinking, but six deaths this year don't necessarily indicate that this is a crisis.

Wechsler: Just because more students haven't died doesn't mean that it isn't a dangerous activity and should be ignored. Colleges need to take steps to ensure that more students aren't harmed by this common practice.

Harrop: It's unfortunate that students have died, but why should we think it is the college's responsibility to police student drinking? College students are adults and should suffer the consequences of their behavior. It's their choice whether to drink and how much.

Wechsler: Colleges are responsible for their students. They need to find ways to prevent students from getting alcohol. They are responsible to the parents who pay the tuition and to the other students who have to tolerate excessive drinking among their peers.

Harrop: Practically speaking, colleges can't prevent students from drinking. Students who want to drink will find a way because they are adults with drinking problems, not children in need of supervision.

Complete this dialogue by finding additional ways in which the writers' ideas speak to each other.

As you can see, the dialogue helps us explore the readings in far greater depth than if we had read both essays in isolation. Each writer's ideas help us to evaluate the ideas of the other. By interrelating them in a dialogue, we can better appreciate how the perspective of each writer changes the way similar facts and information are interpreted. For instance, Henry Wechsler is outraged by the death of one MIT student from a binge-drinking episode; on the other hand, Froma Harrop does not find the deaths of six college students from excessive drinking an alarming statistic when she compares it to the number of college students who have died from other accidental causes. It is up to us as readers to decide which writer's interpretation is more persuasive.

SAMPLE ARGUMENTS FOR ANALYSIS

To practice creating your own dialogue between readings, read the following two letters to the editor, which appeared in two newspapers before and after Henry Wechsler's article. Read them critically, going through the steps we outlined in this chapter, and add them to the dialogue already created between Wechsler and Harrop. We think you'll find that your understanding of the issue will increase and that you'll feel more confident about forming your own position on the question of college binge drinking.

Letter from the *Washington Post,* October 5, 1996

To the Editor:

1   When we saw the headline "Party Hardly" and the revolting picture of four bare-chested, probably underage fraternity brothers guzzling cheap beer, we thought, "Finally! Your paper is tackling an issue that affects every college stu-

dent." Much to our chagrin, however, the article wasted two pages of newsprint glorifying drunkenness and poor study habits.

2   Perhaps you need to be aware of some ugly facts before your next article on college drinking: One out of every four student deaths is related to alcohol use (research shows that as many as 360,000 of the nation's 12 million undergraduates will die as a result of alcohol abuse); alcohol is a factor in 66 percent of student suicides and 60 percent of all sexually transmitted diseases; studies show that between 33 percent and 59 percent of drinking college students drive while intoxicated at least once a year (with as many as 30 percent driving impaired three to 10 times per year); and alcohol consumption was a factor in at least half of the cases of a study of college women who had been raped by an acquaintance.

3   Alcohol affects not only those who drink it: Those students who do not drink are affected by their classmates or roommates who do. Students at schools with high levels of binge drinking are three times more likely to be pushed, hit or sexually assaulted than are students at schools with less drinking. Students who live with people who drink heavily often are kept awake by obnoxious behavior or the sound of their roommates vomiting in the trash can.

4   The shame does not lie solely with your paper, however. *The Princeton Review*, which ranks "party schools" based on how much students use alcohol and drugs, how few hours students study every day and the popularity of fraternities and sororities, should focus on what most feel is the real purpose of a college education: to learn—not to learn how to party.

Kathryn Stewart
Corina Sole

Letter from the *Times-Picayune*, October 24, 1997

To the Editor:

1   The entire nation is justifiably concerned about recent tragic deaths caused by alcohol abuse on our college campuses. College students everywhere know where to procure alcohol and where to consume it without being "hassled."

2   Public dialogue asks if institutions are doing enough to control the situation. Unfortunately, it must be stated that colleges and universities are doing all they can.

3   A typical university fosters an alcohol awareness program, provides the services of a substance abuse coordinator, disciplines students for infractions and provides an atmosphere in which young people can grow responsibly.

4   There is more that must be done. Parents at one time held their sons and daughters accountable for the company they kept. A student who deliberately associates with a group known for its excesses, or who joins an organization suspended or expelled by the institution, is choosing bad company. Peer pressure does the rest.

5   The courts restrict the ability of colleges to discipline students for off-campus behavior unless the activity in question has a fairly direct relationship with
institutional mission.

6   They require due process, including confrontation by witnesses, for any disciplinary action. Peer pressures in the college-age group are so strong that testimony of witnesses is frequently difficult to obtain.

7   Until we return to a system in which colleges can function, at least in part,
in loco parentis (in place of the parent), other agencies of society will have to
step in.

8   To be fully effective, a college would need the ability to impose severe sanctions, including dismissal, on the base of reasonable proof of misbehavior or association with bad elements. Advocates of unrestrained constitutional rights
will have difficulty with this, but the student enters a contractual relationship
with a college to pursue an education.

9   The educators, not the legal system, should do the educating. Colleges exist to form good citizens, conscious of their own rights and the rights of others.
Colleges and universities should be evaluated on the basis of the results of their
educational work.

James C. Carter, S.J.
Chancellor,
Loyola University,
New Orleans

Deliberate About the Readings

As we explained in Chapter 1, deliberation is a way to arrive at your own position
on a particular issue. You can't begin deliberation until you have really listened to
and reflected on the complexities each issue involves. Once you have engaged in all
the steps in the process of critical reading, you are ready to deliberate.

In your deliberation, first consider each of the writer's claims and main points.
Then, thinking like a critic, find a way to respond that defines your own position
on the issue. Using the four readings in this chapter, a deliberation in your journal
about college binge drinking might look like this:

> All the writers see binge drinking as a problem, although they differ about
> where they place the blame and how they plan to solve the problem. Wechsler
> thinks that binge drinking among college students occurs because colleges are
> indifferent to it and refuse to recognize its seriousness. He urges colleges to use
> their influence and power to prevent students from obtaining alcohol. He
> doesn't seem to think that the students who engage in binge drinking have a
> lot of control over their behavior. Carter, Sole, and Stewart all agree with
> Wechsler about the seriousness of the problem; however, they disagree about
> where to place the blame. Carter thinks that colleges are doing all they can
> and should be given more legal power to discipline students who binge drink.
> Sole and Stewart suggest that the media is to blame by endorsing values that
> encourage students to drink and party rather than concentrate on their stud-
> ies. Only Harrop places the blame squarely on the shoulders of the binge

drinkers themselves. She feels strongly that students need to be treated as adults with drinking problems and suffer the consequences of their actions.

After reading these writings, I am convinced that binge drinking is a problem worthy of our attention. The statistics that Wechsler, Stewart, and Sole cite are convincing and impressive. I also know from my own experience that many students drink excessively, and I think that six deaths are too many for us to ignore. I also think that binge drinking is a problem that affects the entire college community, not just the drinkers, as Stewart and Sole point out. However, I tend to agree with Harrop that students must be held responsible for their own actions. I disagree with Carter that schools should act like parents. College is about becoming an adult in all areas of our lives, not just academics.

Any solution to the problem of binge drinking needs to include the students who abuse alcohol. Unless those students also see their drinking habits as a problem, nothing the college or legal system can impose will affect their behavior. Perhaps a combination of actions, including broader and stronger efforts to educate students about alcohol abuse, greater enforcement and harsher penalties for underage drinking by the legal system, and efforts by colleges to restrict alcohol availability in the community and on the campus, would make a significant dent in this problem.

Now try writing your own deliberation, in which you consider the points you find most important in each reading to arrive at your own position on the issue of binge drinking.

Look for Logical Fallacies

When you read the arguments of others, you need to pay attention to the writer's strategies, assertions, and logic to decide if the argument is reasonable. Like the cross-examining attorney in a court case, you must examine the logical connections among the claim, the reasons, and the evidence to reveal the strengths and weaknesses of the writer's argument.

Sometimes writers make errors in logic. Such errors are called **logical fallacies,** a term derived from the Latin *fallere,* meaning "to deceive." Used unintentionally, these fallacies deceive writers into feeling that their arguments are more persuasive than they are. Even though an argument may be well developed and contain convincing evidence, a fallacy creates a flaw in the logic of an argument, thereby weakening its structure and persuasiveness.

Not all logical fallacies are unintentional. Sometimes a fallacy is deliberately employed—for example, when the writer's goal has more to do with persuading than with arriving at the truth. Every day we are confronted with fallacies in media commercials and advertisements. Likewise, every election year the airwaves are full of candidates' bloated claims and pronouncements rife with logical fallacies of all kinds.

Recognizing logical fallacies when they occur in a reading is an important step in assessing the effectiveness of the writer's argument. This final section of our chapter will acquaint you with some of the most common logical fallacies.

PREVIEW: LOGICAL FALLACIES

- Ad hominem argument
- Ad misericordiam argument
- Ad populum argument
- Bandwagon appeal
- Begging the question
- Circular reasoning
- False analogy
- False dilemma
- Faulty use of authority
- Hasty generalization
- Non sequitur
- Post hoc, ergo propter hoc
- Red herring
- Slippery slope
- Stacking the deck

Ad Hominem Argument

From the Latin "to the man," the **ad hominem** argument is a personal attack on an opponent rather than on the opponent's views. Certainly the integrity of an opponent may be important to readers. Nonetheless, writers are usually more persuasive and credible when they focus on issues rather than character flaws. If, for instance, you are reading a paper against the use of animals in medical research and the writer refers to the opposition as "cold-hearted scientists only interested in fame and fortune," you might question whether the writer objects to the scientists' views or to their personal prosperity. Name-calling and character assassination should make you suspicious of the writer's real motives or balanced judgment. Personal criticisms, even if true, can be overemphasized and therefore undercut the writer's credibility.

However, there may be cases in which an ad hominem argument is a legitimate rhetorical tool. When the special interests or associations of an individual or group appear to have a direct impact on their position on an issue, it is fair to raise ques-

EXAMPLES OF AD HOMINEM ARGUMENTS

- How could Tom accuse her of being careless? He's such a slob.
- Of course he doesn't see anything wrong with violent movies. The guy's a warmonger.
- We cannot expect Ms. Lucas to know what it means to feel oppressed; she is the president of a large bank.

tions about their lack of objectivity on that basis. For example, the organizer of a petition to build a state-supported recycling center may seem reasonably suspect if it is revealed that he owns the land on which the proposed recycling center would be built. While the property owner may be motivated by sincere environmental concerns, the direct relationship between his position and his personal life makes this fair game for a challenge.

Ad Misericordiam Argument

Its name also derived from Latin, the **ad misericordiam** argument is the appeal "to pity." This appeal to our emotions need not be fallacious or faulty. A writer, having argued several solid points logically, may make an emotional appeal for extra support. Your local humane society, for instance, might ask you to donate money so it can expand its facilities for abandoned animals. To convince you, the society might point out how, over the last few years, the number of strays and unwanted pets has tripled. And because of budget constraints, the society has been forced to appeal to the public. It may claim that a donation of $25 would house and feed a stray animal for a month. Any amount you give, they explain, will ultimately aid the construction of a new pet "dormitory" wing. To bolster the appeal, the humane society literature might then describe how the adorable puppy and kitten in the enclosed photo will have to be put to death unless the overcrowding of the society's facilities is relieved by donations such as yours.

When an argument is based solely on the exploitation of the reader's pity, however, the issue gets lost. There's an old joke about a man who murdered his parents and appealed to the court for leniency because he was an orphan. It's funny because it ludicrously illustrates how pity has nothing to do with murder. Let's take a more realistic example. If you were a lawyer whose client was charged with bank embezzlement, you would not get very far basing your defense solely on the fact that the defendant was abused as a child. Yes, you may touch the hearts of the jurors, even move them to pity. Yet that would not exonerate your client. The abuse the defendant suffered as a child, as woeful as it is, has nothing to do with his or her crime as an adult. Any intelligent prosecutor would point out the attempt to manipulate the court with a sob story while distracting it from more important factors such as justice.

EXAMPLES OF AD MISERICORDIAM ARGUMENTS

- It makes no difference if he was guilty of Nazi war crimes. The man is eighty years old and in frail health, so he should not be made to stand trial.
- Paula is fourteen years old and lives on welfare with her mother; she suffers serious depression and functions like a child half her age. She should not be sent to adult court, where she will be tried for armed robbery, so she can spend her formative years behind bars.

Ad Populum Argument

From the Latin "to the people," an **ad populum** argument is just that—an argument aimed at appealing to the supposed prejudices and emotions of the masses. Writers attempt to manipulate readers by using emotional and provocative language to add appeal to their claims. The problem with the ad populum argument, however, is that such language sometimes functions as a smoke screen hiding the lack of ideas in the argument. You'll find examples of this fallacy on the editorial pages of your local newspaper—for example, the letter from parents raising a furor because they don't want their child or the children of their friends and neighbors taught by teachers with foreign accents; or the columnist who makes the ad populum case against capital punishment by inflating the number of innocent people wrongfully executed by the state; or the writer who argues that if gays and lesbians are allowed to serve in the military, our national defense will be jeopardized by "sex maniacs."

EXAMPLES OF AD POPULUM ARGUMENTS

- High-school students don't learn anything these days. Today's teachers are academically underprepared.
- If you want to see the crime rate drop, tell Hollywood to stop making movies that glorify violence.
- Doctors oppose health reform because it will reduce their large incomes.

Bandwagon Appeal

This familiar strategy makes the claim that everybody is doing this and thinking that. If we don't want to be left out, we had better get on the **bandwagon** and do and think the same things. The basic appeal in this argument is that of belonging to the group, behaving like the majority. It plays on our fears of being different, of being excluded. Of course, the appeal is fallacious inasmuch as we are asked to "get with it" without weighing the evidence of what is being promoted: "Smart shoppers shop at Sears"; "America reads Stephen King."

EXAMPLES OF BANDWAGON APPEALS

- Everybody's going to the System of a Down concert.
- Nobody will go along with that proposal.
- The majority of the American people want a constitutional amendment outlawing flag burning.

Begging the Question

Similar to circular reasoning, **begging the question** passes off as true an assumption that needs to be proven. For instance, to say that the defendant is innocent because he passed a polygraph test begs the question: Does passing a polygraph test mean somebody is innocent? Sometimes the begged question is itself loaded in a bigger question: "Are you ever going to act like you are equal and pay for one of our dates?" The begged question here is whether paying the costs of a date is a measure of sexual equality.

EXAMPLES OF BEGGING THE QUESTION

- That foolish law should be repealed.
- She is compassionate because she's a woman.
- If you haven't written short stories, you shouldn't be criticizing them.

Circular Reasoning

Circular reasoning is another common fallacy into which many writers fall. In it, the conclusion of a deductive argument is hidden in the premise of that argument. Thus, the argument goes around in a circle. For instance: "Steroids are dangerous because they ruin your health." This translates: Steroids are dangerous because they are dangerous. Sometimes the circularity gets camouflaged in a tangle of words: "The high cost of living in today's America is a direct consequence of the exorbitant prices manufacturers and retailers are placing on their products and services." Cut away the excess, and this translates: The high cost of living is due to the high cost of living. Repetition of key terms or ideas is not evidence. Nor does it prove anything. Instead of simply restating your premise, find solid evidence to support it.

EXAMPLES OF CIRCULAR REASONING

- People who are happy with their work are cheerful because they enjoy what they're doing.
- Smoking is bad for you because it ruins your health.
- Bank robbers should be punished because they broke the law.

False Analogy

An analogy compares two things that are alike in one or more ways. In any form of writing analogies are very useful, as they expand meaning and demonstrate imagination. In arguments they can be wonderful tools for persuasion. Unfortunately, they can also lead the writer astray and make his or her argument vulnerable to attack.

The problem with **false analogies** arises when the two things compared do not match up feature for feature, and ideas being compared do not logically connect or are pressed beyond legitimacy. The result is a false analogy. For instance, a candidate for a high-powered job may ask to be employed because of his extraordinary heroics during the Persian Gulf War. He may even claim that being a CEO is like fighting a battle: He needs to be brave, tough in mind and body, and willing to take and deal out punishment. Although the argument might sound appealing, running a company involves more than combat skills. Certainly it is important for a corporate executive to be strong and tough-minded. However, an office full of five-star generals might not be expert at dealing with economic recession or product liability. The fallacy is that the analogy is imperfect. Business and soldiering overlap minimally.

A sound analogy will clarify a difficult or unfamiliar concept by comparing it with something easily understood or familiar.

EXAMPLES OF FALSE ANALOGY

- The Ship of State is about to wreck on the rocks of recession; we need a new pilot.
- This whole gun control issue is polarizing the nation the way slavery did people living above and below the Mason-Dixon line. Do we want another Civil War?
- Letting emerging nations have nuclear weapons is like giving loaded guns to children.

False Dilemma

A **false dilemma** involves the simplification of complex issues into an either/or choice. For example, "Either we legalize abortion or we send young women to back-alley butchers," "Love America or leave it," "Either we keep gun ownership legal or only criminals will have guns." Such sloganizing ultimatums, although full of dramatic impact, unfortunately appeal to people's ignorance and prejudices.

EXAMPLES OF FALSE DILEMMA

- English should be the official language of the United States, and anybody who doesn't like it can leave.
- Movies today are full of either violence or sex.
- Either we put warning labels on records and compact discs, or we'll see more and more teenage girls having babies.

Faulty Use of Authority

The **faulty use of authority** occurs when someone who is an expert in one area is used as an authority for another unrelated area. For instance, the opinions of a four-star general about the use of force against an uncooperative foreign tyrant carry great weight in a discussion of U.S. foreign policy options. However, the opinions of that same individual about the Supreme Court's ruling on the question of assisted suicide are less compelling. His military expertise does not guarantee that his views on euthanasia are particularly valuable.

Advertisers frequently resort to the faulty use of authority to promote their products. Celebrities are asked to endorse products they may have no special knowledge about or any interest in aside from the sizable check they will receive for their services. Another example occurs when well-known popular figures rely on their achievements in one area to lend credibility to their views in another. For instance, the late Benjamin Spock, famous for his work on child development, became a spokesperson for the nuclear disarmament movement. Because of his reputation, people were willing to listen more closely to his views than to others who were less well known, yet his expertise in child-rearing gave him no more authority in this area than any other well-educated person. While Dr. Spock may, indeed, have been knowledgeable about nuclear arms, his expertise in that area would have to be demonstrated before he could be used as an effective authority on the subject.

EXAMPLES OF FAULTY USE OF AUTHORITY

- You should buy these vitamins because Cindy Crawford recommended them on television last night.
- The American Bar Association states that second-hand smoke is a serious cancer threat to nonsmokers.
- Americans shouldn't find hunting objectionable because one of our most popular presidents, Theodore Roosevelt, was an avid hunter.

Hasty Generalization

As the name indicates, the **hasty generalization** occurs when a writer arrives at a conclusion based on too little evidence. It's one of the most frequently found fallacies. If the local newspaper's restaurant critic is served underdone chicken at Buster's Diner during her first and only visit, she would be making a hasty generalization to conclude that Buster's serves terrible food. Although this may be true, one visit is not enough to draw that conclusion. If, however, after three visits she is still dissatisfied with the food, she is entitled to warn her readers about eating at Buster's.

Hasty generalizations can also occur when the writer relies on evidence that is not factual or substantiated. A generalization can only be as sound as its supporting evidence. Writers should provide multiple and credible examples to support their points. Be wary of sweeping, uncritical statements and words such as *always, all, none, never, only,* and *most.* Note whether the writer qualifies the claim with words that are limiting, such as *many, some, often,* and *seldom.*

EXAMPLES OF HASTY GENERALIZATIONS

- That shopping mall is unsafe because there was a robbery there two weeks ago.
- I'm failing organic chemistry because the teaching assistant doesn't speak English well.
- This book was written by a Harvard professor, so it must be good.

Non Sequitur

From the Latin for "does not follow," a **non sequitur** draws a conclusion that does not follow logically from the premise. For instance, suppose you heard a classmate make the following claim: "Ms. Marshall is such a good teacher; it's hard to believe she wears such ugly clothes." The statement would be fallacious because the ability to teach has nothing to do with taste in clothing. Some of the worst teachers might be the best dressers. Although you might want to believe a good teacher would be a good dresser, there is no reason to think so. Writers must establish a clear connection between the premise and the conclusion. And unless one is made through well-reasoned explanations, readers will not accept the cause-and-effect relationship.

Political campaigns are notorious for non sequiturs: "Candidate Jones will be a great senator because she's been married for twenty years." Or, "Don't vote for Candidate Jones because she is rich and lives in an expensive neighborhood." Whether the voters decide to vote for Candidate Jones or not should not depend on the length of her marriage or the neighborhood in which she lives—neither qualifies or disqualifies her from public office. The non sequiturs attempt to suggest a relationship between her ability to be a successful senator and unrelated facts about her life.

EXAMPLES OF NON SEQUITURS

- Mr. Thompson has such bad breath that it's a wonder he sings so well.
- She's so pretty; she must not be smart.
- I supported his candidacy for president because his campaign was so efficiently run.

Post Hoc, Ergo Propter Hoc

The Latin **post hoc, ergo propter hoc** is translated as "after this, therefore because of this." A post hoc, ergo propter hoc argument is one that establishes a questionable cause-and-effect relationship between events. In other words, because event *Y* follows event *X,* event *X* causes event *Y.* For instance, you would be making a post hoc argument if you claimed, "Every time my brother Bill accompanies me to Jacob's Field, the Cleveland Indians lose." The reasoning here is fallacious because we all know that although the Indians lose whenever Bill joins you at Jacob's Field, his presence does not cause the team to lose. Experience tells us that there simply is no link between the two events. The only explanation is coincidence.

Our conversations are littered with these dubious claims: "Every time I plan a pool party, it rains"; "Whenever I drive to Chicago, I get a flat tire." "Every movie that Harry recommends turns out to be a dud." What they underscore is our pessimism or dismay, rather than any belief in the truth of such statements.

It's not surprising that post hoc reasoning is often found in arguments made by people prone to superstition—people looking for big, simple explanations. You would be committing such a fallacy if, for instance, you claimed that you got a C on your math test because a black cat crossed your path that morning or because you broke a mirror the night before. Post hoc fallacies are also practiced by those bent on proving conspiracies. Following the assassination of President Kennedy in 1963 there was considerable effort by some to link the deaths of many people involved in the investigation to a government cover-up, even though the evidence was scanty. Today we hear Democrats protest that America goes to war every time Republicans are in office and Republicans protest that America gets poorer when Democrats are in office.

You might also have heard people argue that since the women's liberation movement, the number of latchkey children has risen sharply. The claim essentially says that the women's movement is directly responsible for the rise in working mothers over the last thirty years. While it is true that the women's movement has made it more acceptable for mothers to return to the workforce, the prime reason is particular to the individual. For some, it is simple economics; for others, personal fulfillment; for others still, a combination of the two. The feminist movement is one among many factors linked with women in the workforce and the consequent rise in latchkey children.

EXAMPLES OF POST HOC, ERGO PROPTER HOC ARGUMENTS

- Just two weeks after they raised the speed limit, three people were killed on that road.
- I saw Ralph in the courthouse; he must have been arrested.
- It's no wonder the crime rate has shot up. The state legislature voted to lower the drinking age.

Red Herring

A **red herring,** as the name suggests, is evidence that is fallaciously used to distract the audience from the true issues of an argument. The term is derived from the practice of using the scent of a red herring to throw hunting dogs off the trail of their real prey. In modern life this fallacy is more often used to confuse the audience by providing irrelevant information or evidence. For instance, when the head coach of a major league team was accused of using team funds on personal expenses, he defended himself by pointing to the team's winning record under his leadership. While the team had undeniably performed well during this period, his response was irrelevant to the charges made against him. He had hoped to distract his accusers from the real issue, which involved his lack of honesty and abuse of power. A red herring may distract the audience momentarily, but once it is discovered, it indicates that the individual has little or no effective reasons or evidence to support his or her position.

EXAMPLES OF RED HERRINGS

- Even though that hockey player was convicted of vehicular homicide, he shouldn't go to jail because he is such a great athlete.
- Susan didn't hire John for the job because his wife is always late for meetings.
- The teacher gave me an F in the course because she doesn't like me.

Slippery Slope

The **slippery slope** presumes one event will inevitably lead to a chain of other events that end in a catastrophe—as one slip on a mountain top will cause a climber to tumble down and bring with him or her all those in tow. This domino-effect reasoning is fallacious because it depends more on presumption than hard evidence: "Censorship of obscene material will spell the end to freedom of the press"; "A ban on ethnic slurs will mean no more freedom of speech"; "If assault rifles are outlawed, handguns will be next." America's involvement in Vietnam was the result of a slippery slope argument: "If Vietnam falls to the Communists, all of Southeast

EXAMPLES OF SLIPPERY SLOPE ARGUMENTS

- Legalized abortion is a step toward creating an antilife society.
- A ban on ethnic slurs will mean no more freedom of speech.
- If we let them build those condos, the lake will end up polluted, the wildlife will die off, and the landscape will be scarred forever.

Asia, and eventually India and its neighbors, will fall under the sway of communism." Even though Vietnam did fall, the result has not been the widespread rise of communism in the region; on the contrary, communism has fallen on hard times.

Stacking the Deck

When writers give only the evidence that supports their premise, while disregarding or withholding contrary evidence, they are **stacking the deck**. (Science students may know this as "data beautification," the habit of recording only those results that match what an experiment is expected to predict.) A meat-packing manufacturer may advertise that its all-beef hot dogs "now contain 10 percent less fat." Although that may sound like good news, what we are not being told is that the hot dogs still contain 30 percent fat.

This stacking-the-deck fallacy is common not only in advertising but also in debates of controversial matters. The faculty of a college, for instance, may petition for the firing of its president for failing to grant needed raises while an expensive new football stadium is being built. The complaint would not be fair, however, if the faculty ignored mentioning that the stadium funds were specifically earmarked for athletic improvement by the billionaire benefactor. Also, if the complaint left unrecognized the many accomplishments of the president, such as the successful capital campaign, the plans for a new library, and the influx of notable scholars, it would be an example of stacking the deck.

As you progress through the chapters in this book, you will find that thinking like a critic is the key to understanding and responding to argument. It will make you a stronger reader and a more effective writer. In the next chapter we explore ways that you can think like a writer to find and develop topics for your own argument essays.

EXAMPLES OF STACKING THE DECK

- Parents should realize that private schools simply encourage elitism in young people.
- We cannot take four more years of her in office, given the way she voted against the death penalty.
- Dickens's *Bleak House* is six hundred pages of boring prose.

■ EXERCISES

1. In your journal, list examples of logical fallacies you find in essays, news articles, editorials, advertising, junk mail, and other persuasive materials that you confront on a daily basis. Based on the information you and other group members collect, draw some hypotheses about which fallacies are most prevalent to-

day and why. If your instructor asks you to do so, convert those hypotheses into an outline of an argument essay for your campus newspaper.

2. Explain the faulty logic of the following statements. Of what fallacy (or fallacies) is each an example?

   a. When did you stop hiring other people to take your exams for you?

   b. He's too smart to play football; besides he broke his leg ten years ago.

   c. If we don't stop the publication of this X-rated material now, it won't be long before our children will be reading it at school.

   d. Karen must be depressed; she wore dark clothes all weekend.

   e. How can you accuse me of being late? You're such a slowpoke.

   f. Rap music isn't music because it's just noise and words.

   g. He's at least 6 feet 6 inches tall, so he must be a terrific basketball player.

   h. WGBB is the most popular radio station on campus because it has more listeners than any other station.

   i. Indians living on reservations get the necessities of life at government expense, so they have no worries.

   j. Take Tummy Tops laxatives instead of Mellow Malt, because Tummy Tops contains calcium while Mellow Malt has aluminum and magnesium.

   k. Lite Cheese Popcorn contains 34 percent fewer calories!

   l. Any decent person will agree that Nazism has no place in modern society.

Finding Arguments
Thinking Like a Writer

When confronted with an issue we feel strongly about, most of us have no trouble offering an energetically delivered opinion. Yet when we're asked to *write* an argument, we feel paralyzed. To express our ideas in written form forces us to commit ourselves to some position or to endorse a particular action. We have to take a risk and make a public statement about what we think and feel and believe. Our written words can be scrutinized. That makes us vulnerable, and nobody likes to feel exposed.

It is helpful to think of writing an argument as one way to explore our ideas about a subject or issue. As such, writing can be a means of growth and discovery. Exploring new ideas can be intimidating, but it's also challenging. Who doesn't secretly want to be Indiana Jones, at least once in a while? This chapter will demonstrate how writers begin the process of exploring their ideas to write argument essays. As novelist E. M. Forster explained, "How will I know what I think until I've seen what I've said?"

Exploration, of course, takes time. We're not recommending a writing process that begins an hour before a paper is due; rather, we're recommending what successful writers do: Take time to think your writing through. This means starting assignments early, working through all the stages, and allowing time to revise and polish your work before you submit it. Learning to write well is the same as learning to perform any other skilled activity. You have to practice your strokes or your scales to be a good tennis player or pianist; likewise, you have to practice your craft to be a good writer. As you gain more experience, some of the stages of the writing process will go more quickly for you on most projects. Even when you become a polished logician, however, you may find yourself writing about a topic that requires you to work out the assumptions in your argument slowly and painstakingly. That's okay. All writers do that. Welcome to the club.

The Writing Process

Many rhetorical theorists have tried to describe the writing process, but that's a little like describing snowflakes: Each one is different. Each person has a different way of writing, especially depending on the job. Think about it. You can dash off a note to your roommate in a second; if you're writing a job application letter, you'll probably take a great deal more time. If you have only twenty minutes to answer an essay question on a history exam, you'll get it done somehow; but give you an entire semester to write a term paper on the same subject, and you'll probably spend several weeks (if not months) doing the job. The scope and length of the assignment dictate a different writing process.

What most people studying the writing process agree on is that almost everyone goes through four distinct stages when writing: incubating, framing, reshaping, and polishing.

Incubating

When something prompts you to write (your boss tells you to write a report, you get an assignment, a letter requires an answer, you feel strongly about a controversy and want to write a letter to the editor), you spend time either mentally or physically preparing to respond. You may make notes, go to the library, or stare out the window. You're *incubating* the ideas you'll use to respond to the writing stimulus. In this chapter we provide strategies you can use to make this early stage of writing work for you.

Framing

In the second stage you begin, however haltingly, to put words to paper. Some people make an outline; others write a bare-bones rough draft in an attempt to get some ideas down on paper. Many people like to start by sketching out their conclusions so that they can see where their writing must take them. Others prefer the linear, start-with-the-introduction system that moves them through the task. The first goal in the framing stage, as in building a house, is to get the framework of the writing in place so you can start adding material to fill it out. At some point in the framing process you also take your potential readers into account in order to get some idea of their expectations and receptivity.

Reshaping

Once you have a draft framed, you're ready to do the hard work of writing: *rewriting*. At this stage you may move parts of your paper around, or make a new outline, or add or cut material to fill in gaps or eliminate imbalances. You'll have your readers much more clearly in mind because your goal is to persuade them; what you know about their background, experiences, and values will help you decide on a final shape for your paper, even if it means throwing away nearly everything you have framed. (A bad paper that's finished is still a bad paper; that's why you need to allow time for flexibility. Writers who are pressed for time sometimes have to polish something that's not good and hope their readers won't notice, a technique that doesn't usually work.) At the reshaping stage most good writers like to obtain feedback from other writers to get a sense of what their prospective readers will think of their writing; in a classroom situation this practice usually involves exchanging drafts with classmates or having conferences with your instructor.

Polishing

To have the greatest chance of persuading your readers to consider your point of view, your writing needs to be as readable as possible. That's why, after you've re-shaped it, you need to work on your sentence structure so that words "flow" for your readers. Or you may need to change words here and there to heighten their impact. If others have read your paper and offered feedback, you may wish to act on some of their suggestions for improvement. You always need to edit and proof-read what you've written so that no careless errors distract your readers from getting the message you're trying to convey. And you have to produce a copy, whether by handwriting it, typing it, or convincing your computer printer to spit it out.

In a nutshell, that's the writing process. Now let's look at how you might ex-ploit the features of that process when you start writing arguments.

Finding Topics to Argue

Every writer knows the experience of being blocked, or of having a topic but not knowing what to say about it, or of having only one point to make about an issue. To help generate more ideas, writers need to tap both internal and external re-sources.

In Your Immediate Vicinity

The world around you is full of arguments; you just need to take a moment to see them. Look at the front page and editorial pages of your campus newspaper, for in-stance. What's going on? Look at billboards and bulletin boards. What are people having meetings about? What changes are coming up? Listen to the conversations of people on the bus, or waiting in line at the bookstore, or in the library. What's up? What have you been reading for a class that gets you thinking? You might want to know how a theory for the origin of the universe was derived, or what the results of a recent study of employment success for former welfare recipients were based on, or even why two experts in the field of early childhood learning draw different conclusions from the same evidence. The reading you do for your own enjoyment may also provide some interesting ideas. A science fiction novel may make you wonder about the plausibility of alien life. Reading a murder mystery may make you think about the value of forensic anthropology. Look through the magazines in your room, or at the ads on television, or at the junk mail that fills your mailbox. Even casually reading magazines and newspapers on a daily or weekly basis will turn up issues and controversies. What claims are people making? What are people ask-ing you to do, or think, or wear, or look like, or support? These are sources of po-tential arguments; all you have to do is become aware of them. As Thoreau put it, "Only that day dawns to which we are awake."

In Your Larger Worlds

Don't limit yourself to campus. Often there are debates and discussions going on in your workplace, in your place of worship, on your block, in your town. You belong to a number of communities; each has its issues of interest, and in those issues you can find plenty to write about. And those environments aren't the only places you'll find sources for arguments; the world turns on proposals, positions, and controversies. It's almost impossible to turn on the radio or television today without seeing someone presenting an opinion. Your computer (or the one available on your campus) can connect you to a global community engaged in debate and dialogue on every issue imaginable. On the Internet you can participate in a number of discussions about controversial issues through listservs, Usenet newsgroups, and chat rooms. Make a list of the issues that interest you. What are the headlines in the newspaper? What's Congress voting on? What are the hot spots around the globe (or in the larger universe)? Don't stick to the familiar; there is much experimental territory just waiting to be explored.

Keeping a Journal

You've probably noticed that we encourage recording ideas and observations in a journal, a technique used by many professional writers. The journal doesn't have to be fancy; the cheap supermarket variety works just as well as the $3,000 laptop. (If you're comfortable at a keyboard, a computer disk makes a great notebook and fits in your shirt pocket, too—although you might want to keep a backup copy.)

Writers use journals as portable file cabinets of ideas. In a journal we record anything in language that interests us, not just materials for current projects. We may copy down a word or phrase or sentence we hear that we like, or photocopy and staple in a piece by a writer we admire, or even add things that infuriate or amuse us. A journal becomes a supermarket of ideas and strategies, but there's something very positive about the simple act of copying words. Somehow, physically writing or typing them makes them yours; you learn something about technique in doing the physical work of copying. (That's why we don't recommend making too many photocopies; you don't mentally store the information in the same way you do when you copy a passage yourself.)

For the novice argument writer, a journal is invaluable. You can use yours to include notes on possible topics; examples of good introductions and conclusions; catchy words, phrases, and titles; examples of logical fallacies—just about anything a writer might need. A journal is also particularly helpful for creating *dialogues*, the voices and opinions of others who may hold views that are different from your own on particular issues. By keeping a record or notes on what people have to say in newspapers, magazine articles, television talk shows, and casual conversation about various controversial issues, you'll have a ready resource to consult when you begin to deliberate about your position on a particular issue.

When you begin keeping the journal, set yourself a formal goal: for example, adding 100 words a day or writing five days out of the week. Then *stick to it*. Journals don't fill themselves. It takes discipline to keep a journal, and discipline is a characteristic of good writers. If you don't do the groundwork, your creativity won't break through. Throughout this text we've scattered suggestions and exercises for using journals; if you want to fully master the power of argument, we encourage you to *do* the exercises. Don't just read them. Write!

Developing Argumentative Topics

Topics alone aren't arguments, and many inexperienced writers have trouble making the jump from subject to argument. For example, you may be interested in heavy metal music. That's a subject—a big one. What can you argue about it? You could ask yourself, "What are the facts about heavy metal? When did it start? How can it be defined? What differentiates it from the mainstream rock played on most commercial radio stations? Why are some groups played, it seems, once an hour, and others almost totally ignored?" You can ask functional questions, such as "Who is the most influential figure in heavy metal music? Is heavy metal more relevant than, say, techno music?" You might ask aesthetic questions about the importance of melody or lyrics or harmony, or ethical questions such as whether the industry should put parental advisory labels on albums. You could even consider moral questions such as whether heavy metal music videos encourage sexism or violence. In recognizing the multiple possibilities of issues, you may find you have more to say on a topic than you think.

Getting Started

Sometimes getting started can be the most difficult step in the writing process. Where do I begin? What should I include? What ideas will work best? How shall I organize it all? You may have a hundred ideas in your head about the topic or—even worse—none at all. When this happens, there are a number of tried-and-true techniques that professional writers use to redirect those anxious questions and concerns into productive writing. While you may not need to use all the strategies each time you begin to write, you'll find that trying out each one of them will help you discover what works best for you.

Brainstorming

Brainstorming can help you get your ideas on paper in an informal and unstructured way. When you brainstorm, you write down as many ideas as you can about your subject, usually in short phrases, questions, or single words. Don't worry about placing them in any special order or even about making complete sense. The one rule to observe while you're brainstorming is not to judge the ideas that pop into your head and spill out onto your paper. When you give yourself permission to write down anything that seems related to your subject, you'll be surprised at the number of ideas that will occur to you. By not rejecting anything, you'll find that one idea will naturally lead to another. Even an idea that you may throw out later can lead you to an idea that may be a real gem. And the more ideas you record in your brainstorm, the more choices you will have to consider later as you sift through this record of your thoughts and decide what is and is not useful.

After critically reading the essays in Chapter 2 of this text, John, our first-year composition student, decided to write his first paper on college binge drinking. He began his writing preparation by brainstorming about the subject. Here's what he came up with:

binge drinking	why drink to excess?
drinking until you feel sick	want to forget all about the week
getting together with friends for a good time	makes us feel grown up
	nothing better to do on Saturday
partying after a tough week at school	night
	why does the college care?
so many bars, so little time	people can really hurt themselves
half the people underage	prevention—how?
whose responsibility is it?	part of the college experience
nobody checks anyway	ignore it—will it go away?
feeling terrible the next morning	trying to act cool
smelling like a beer can	what starts as fun can lead to death
role of the college administration	definition of an adult
rite of passage	do other cultures experience this?
impact of peer pressure	

As you can see, John had many different ideas about binge drinking, and the more he brainstormed, the more he discovered what they were. After looking over his brainstorm, John chose a few of the ideas that especially interested him to explore further.

John was lucky to have a subject already chosen before he began his brainstorm. But what happens if your instructor doesn't assign a particular topic for your paper and you are left to choose one for yourself? You may find it difficult to come up with a topic. You're not alone. Students often comment that the hardest part of writing is deciding what to write about. To ease the selection task, we suggest a brainstorming strategy. Take out a piece of paper and jot down whatever comes to mind in response to these questions:

- What issues in print or TV news interest you?
- What issues make you angry?
- What problems in your dorm/on campus/in your town/in your country concern you?
- What political issue concerns you most?
- What aspects about the environment worry you?
- If you were professor/dean/college president/mayor/governor/senator/president, what would be the first thing you'd do?
- What policies/practices/regulations/laws would you like to see changed?
- What do you talk about or argue over with friends or classmates?
- What ideas from books or articles have challenged your thinking?
- What books/movies/music/fashions/art do you like, and why?
- What books/movies/music/fashions/art do you hate, and why?

- What personalities in politics/show business/the media/academia do you have strong feelings about?

Here's a quick brainstorming list one student developed:

Issues That Interest Me
1. The war on terrorism
2. Excessive salaries for athletes
3. People who protest movie violence but oppose bans on assault rifles
4. The benefits of stem cell research
5. Racial profiling
6. Social messages in rap music
7. Environmentally unfriendly vehicles

Once you have brainstormed a list, organize the issues according to categories—for example, political, social, environmental, educational issues, and so on. Then transfer the list to your journal. Now, whenever an assignment comes up, you'll have a database of ideas to consult.

Clustering

Some writers find that visualizing their ideas on a page helps them explore their subject in new ways. Clustering* is a technique you can use to do that. It involves choosing a key word, phrase, or even a short sentence, and placing it in the center of a blank page with a circle around it. Next you try to think of ideas, words, or other short phrases that you can associate or relate to your key word or phrase. As you do, write them in the blank area surrounding the center and circle them and draw lines linking them to your center circled word or phrase. As you accumulate more and more clusters, the words and phrases within them will generate ideas on their own; these can be linked to the words that inspired them. When you have exhausted your cluster, you will have a complex network of ideas that should provide many ways to begin to explore your subject. By choosing any one or a combination of these words or ideas as a starting point, you can move to freewriting to find ways of developing these ideas further.

Figure 3.1 on page 68 shows how Rebecca, another student, used clustering to find new ways of thinking about assisted suicide, a topic she had chosen for her paper. When Rebecca examined her cluster, she found a map of the many ideas she might explore further:

- What role should family play in this decision?
- Will the cost of medical care affect the patient's decision?
- If pain can be controlled, will the patient be less inclined to seek this alternative?
- Should assisted suicide be legalized?
- Does the right to die with dignity exist?

---

*Clustering is a technique explored by Gabriele L. Rico in her book *Writing the Natural Way: Using Right Brain Techniques to Release Your Expressive Powers* (Los Angeles: J. P. Tarcher, 1983).

Figure 3.1

Her cluster revealed the complexity of the issue and became a starting point for Rebecca to investigate the subject in greater depth.

Freewriting

Freewriting goes one step beyond brainstorming. Instead of simply listing phrases, questions, and words related to your subject, freewriting involves writing freely, and without stopping, whatever thoughts and ideas you have about your subject, without worrying about sentence structure, spelling, or grammar. As in brainstorming, when you freewrite, it's important not to censor your ideas. Your aim is to discover what you know about your subject, and the best way you can do that is by giving your mind permission to go wherever it pleases. Freewriting isn't intended to be a finished part of your paper; instead, it's a way to generate the ideas and focus that you can use later as you begin to draft the paper itself.

Freewriting can begin with anything: your topic, a particularly interesting idea you've read about, or an experience that you can connect with your subject. If you have used brainstorming or clustering before freewriting, these activities can provide you with a key word or phrase to get you started. For instance, John found a good idea from his brainstorm to begin his freewriting:

Getting together with friends for a good time. That's what everyone looks forward to every weekend. Throw away the books, get out of the dorm and party.

Four, five, sometimes more drinks. Feeling no pain. Binge drinking just seems to happen. It isn't something you plan to do. When you're having a good time, you don't think about how terrible you're going to feel the next day or about all the stupid things you're doing. It's easy to get alcohol in town. Nobody ever checks for proof and if they do, you just go to another place down the street. It's so easy to get phony proof anyway. And the crowds are so large, no one looks so carefully. If college students want to drink, who's to say they can't? We're old enough to vote, die for our country, sign a contract. Why not drinking? And how are you ever going to learn to drink if you don't? College students drink for lots of reasons. Why? Well, it gets them in a party mood. It's fun. It makes us feel like adults. It's so cool. Everyone does it. There's nothing wrong with drinking, but is it a problem if you drink too much? Every weekend. I've heard about students who have died. They let it get out of control. Drunk driving, alcohol poisoning, stupid accidents. Binge drinking is drinking gone overboard. Guess that's all I can think of right now.

John used his freewriting to think on paper. While he didn't come up with any conclusions about how he felt about binge drinking, he did produce a number of ideas that he explored later, when he worked on the first draft of his paper:

- College students binge drink for many reasons.
- Binge drinking can be a problem.
- Drinking is related to feeling adult.
- Binge drinking is not a planned behavior, but it can get to be a habit.

One of the best reasons for using freewriting before you begin the first draft of your paper is to avoid the most intimidating sight a writer can see: a blank page. Unfortunately, sometimes that blank page is the result of a blank mind and undue concern about how your writing and ideas will appear to others. When you freewrite, you write for yourself alone. It is a way to make your ideas flow. Freewriting generates ideas that will help you begin to think about your subject before worrying about polishing your writing for an audience.

Asking Questions

Once you have a subject in mind, a good strategy for generating ideas is to make a list of questions you have about the subject. Your questions can cover areas in which you need more information, as well as questions you might like to answer as you think and write about your topic. For instance, John tried this strategy for his topic of college binge drinking and came up with the following questions:

Why do college students binge drink?

How many college students actually binge drink?

Is binge drinking a result of peer pressure?

Do students binge drink to show they are adults?

Do most college students find binge drinking acceptable?

Is binge drinking strictly a college student activity or do other age and economic groups do this as well?

Do college students stop binge drinking once they leave college?

Who should be responsible for binge drinking? the drinkers? the college? the law?

Why do college administrations feel that they must respond to the problem of drinking if it's off campus?

Do colleges have a legal responsibility to protect their students?

Are the alcohol prevention programs on campus effective?

It's easy to see how one question can lead to another. By choosing one question or several related ones, John had real direction for exploring his topic and focusing his paper as he began his research and his first draft.

Engaging in Dialogue with Others

Talking to other people is a great source of ideas. None of the techniques we've discussed so far have to be lonely activities. You can brainstorm with others, read your freewriting to a friend and listen to the response, or interview classmates to find out their questions and concerns about your subject. By sharing your ideas and listening to the responses of others, you will find a wealth of new ideas and perspectives. In fact, you'll be engaging in the kind of *dialogue* we discussed in Chapter 1. You can do this in a number of ways: participate in either small peer groups in your class or larger class discussions; speak individually with your instructor; seek out members of your community, on campus or outside your school; share ideas with others electronically through Internet chat rooms, e-mail, or listservs; or talk with family and friends. As Larry King and other talk show hosts prove every day, people love to talk. So, take advantage of it—and take notes.

Refining Topics

Once you have found—through the strategies we've discussed—subjects that strike you as interesting, you have to begin narrowing down your topic to a manageable size. The next step, then, is to look over your list and reduce it to those topics that are legitimately arguable. (See Chapter 1 for a refresher.)

Reducing Your Options

Your first step is to determine whether your subject is manageable. You don't want a subject that is too broad or unwieldy or that requires prohibitive amounts of research. For example, you would not want to argue that "women have always been discriminated against in sports." You could write a book about that if you had time to do all the research. To write a short paper, you have to narrow your subject. "The women's basketball team at State U. should get more television coverage" is a manageable reduction of your first idea, and one that you can handle in an average-length paper (see Figure 3.2). The more narrow your topic, the more you restrict your research and tighten the focus of your argument.

Avoiding Overspecialized Topics

On the other hand, don't pick a topic that requires extensive specialized knowledge, such as how to reduce the trade deficit or the problems inherent in thermonuclear

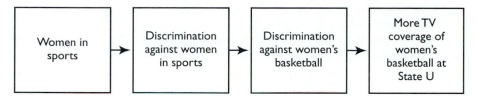

Figure 3.2

fusion. The issue you choose should be one you know a little something about and, to keep you interested, about which you have strong convictions. Also, it should be an issue you are willing to spend a reasonable amount of time exploring on your own or perhaps in the library. Aside from writing a convincing argument, a parallel goal of any project you research is to become better informed and more appreciative of the complexity of the issue. Therefore, select a topic on which you wish to be well informed and that you are willing to investigate and reflect on.

Formulating a Working Claim

Once you have decided on your topic and used some of the strategies we've discussed, you are ready to create a working claim. As we explained in Chapter 1, the claim is the heart of your essay. It functions as a thesis statement. It states what you believe or what action you'd like your readers to take. In Chapter 1 we provided examples of the different ways you can state your claim. However, at this early stage of your writing it would be difficult to create a claim that would be perfect for the paper you have yet to research and write. It's too early in the game to commit yourself. After all, your research may yield some surprising results, and you want to be open to all sides of the issue. At best, you can create a working claim—that is, a statement of your opinion or position on your topic that you can use temporarily to help you focus and organize your paper and limit your research.

After Rebecca, our first-year composition student, considered her subject of assisted suicide by clustering and freewriting, she realized what an enormous topic it was and that she needed to narrow it. She began by asking questions about assisted suicide. Should assisted suicide be legalized? Who should be allowed to commit suicide? anyone who wants to die? anyone in pain? just people who are terminally ill? For what reasons should assisted suicide be legalized? How can we determine when assisted suicide is appropriate? Who should make this decision? Is it morally wrong to end one's own life?

As Rebecca thought about the answers to these questions, she began to narrow the focus of her broad topic to one that she could explore in a paper of reasonable length. She decided that she would focus only on the issue of assisted suicide for the terminally ill. Her essay would consider the controversial issue of whether assisted suicide should be legalized. In particular, she was interested in the question of whether assisted suicide was morally wrong or a choice that each person had to make individually. Her working claim, then, both limited the range of her topic and very clearly expressed her point of view about it:

Assisted suicide
   Assisted suicide for the terminally ill
      Assisted suicide for the terminally ill should be legal.
      Assisted suicide allows people to die with dignity.
         Dying with dignity is a basic human right.
Working claim: Assisted suicide for the terminally ill should be legal because dying with dignity is a basic human right.

While Rebecca's views developed and changed as she investigated her topic further, her working claim helped her concentrate her research on those areas that pertained most directly to her ideas.

To arrive at a *working claim* for his paper on binge drinking, John also used some of the strategies illustrated earlier: brainstorming, freewriting, asking questions about the topic, and engaging in dialogue with others. When he sat down to create his working claim, he examined and reflected on his topic and decided on the following:

> Binge drinking is a serious problem on college campuses, and if we continue to ignore it or treat it as normal and acceptable student behavior, no one will ever find an effective way to eliminate it.

By creating a working claim early in his writing process, John benefited in a number of ways. He clearly took a position about his topic and expressed his point of view. While he had the opportunity to change his viewpoint as he thought further about his topic, his working claim served as a baseline. John's working claim also helped him organize the reasons he needed to support his position.

Let's take a look at John's working claim to see how it is organized. His claim can be divided into three parts:

1. Binge drinking is a problem on college campuses.
2. It is ignored or simply accepted as normal student behavior.
3. No one has yet found an effective way to solve this problem.

All these statements are arguable because, as we discussed in Chapter 1, they are based on judgment and interpretation, not on indisputable facts or personal opinion. As he developed his paper, John needed to decide on reasons to effectively convince his readers that these three parts of his working claim are true.

In addition, John's working claim helped him decide what he needed to investigate further. As John researched and became more knowledgeable about his topic, he revised his working claim to better reflect what he had learned. But at this stage of his paper, his working claim provided him with several specific areas that he needed to investigate in order to argue persuasively about them:

1. Is binge drinking really a problem on college campuses? How significant is it?
2. How is binge drinking ignored and by whom?
3. Is binge drinking regarded as normal student behavior and by whom?
4. What has been done to eliminate binge drinking?
5. What are some ways this problem can be dealt with?

In Chapter 9 we look at a number of ways available to John to research his topic. By using the questions suggested by his working claim as a guide, John had plenty of avenues to explore.

Thinking like a writer will help you make the jump from simply having an opinion on a subject to finding ways to express that opinion in an argument essay. In the next chapter we look at the way in which audience influences and affects the choices we make about what to include in an argument essay and how to present our arguments.

■ EXERCISES

1. Get together with a small group of students in your class and brainstorm possible topics for an argument essay concerning a controversial issue on your campus or in your community. Try to think of at least ten topics that are current and that most people in your group find interesting and arguable.

2. Make a visit to the periodicals section of your college library and look through current issues of periodicals and newspapers on the shelves to find out what issues and subjects are being debated in America and around the world. Find one or more topics that interest you and make copies of those articles for further reading and response in your journal.

3. Take some time to explore the Internet by doing a keyword search using a Web search engine (see page 212). In your journal, describe the results of your search. How many different sites devoted to your topic did you locate? What did you find surprising about the comments and opinions expressed by the participants?

4. Engage in a dialogue with other students, family members, friends, or people in the community who might have some interest and opinions on a potential topic. In your journal, record and respond to their diverse views.

5. Choose a topic that you might wish to investigate for an argument essay and use some of the strategies suggested in this chapter to get started: brainstorm, cluster, freewrite, question.

6. Formulate a list of questions about your potential topic.

7. After you have followed some of the strategies for exploring your topic, formulate a working claim. In your journal, identify which parts of your claim will need to be supported by reasons in your essay. Which parts of your claim will need to be investigated further?

CHAPTER 4

Addressing Audiences
Thinking Like a Reader

As we've discussed in previous chapters, the purpose of writing an argument is to prompt your listeners to consider seriously your point of view and for you to win their respect through the logic and skill of your thinking. When used productively, argument can be a way to resolve conflict and achieve common ground among adversaries. Thus, one of the primary ways to measure the success of your argument is to gauge how effectively it reaches and appeals to your audience. Knowing something about your audience will enable you to use that knowledge to make your arguments most effective.

Creating an argument would be a simple task if you could be guaranteed an audience of readers just like yourself. If everyone shared your cultural, educational, religious, and practical experiences, persuading them to accept your point of view would require very little effort. Clearly, however, this is not the case. A quick look around your classroom will reveal the many differences that make argument a challenging activity. Is everyone the same age? race? gender? ethnicity? Do you all listen to the same music? dress alike? live in the same neighborhood? vote for the same candidates? attend the same place of worship? Unless you attend a very unusual school, the answer to most of these questions will be a resounding "no." People are different; what interests you may bore the person behind you, whereas what puts you to sleep may inspire someone else to passionate activism. And what you see on the surface isn't the whole story about your classmates either. That rough-looking guy who works as a mechanic may write poetry in his spare time; that conservatively dressed woman may spend her weekends touring the countryside on a motorcycle. It's too easy to make assumptions about people's values and beliefs just by looking at them. If you want to persuade these people, you're going to have to assess them very carefully.

Knowing your audience will help you determine almost every aspect of the presentation of your case: the kind of language you use, the writing style (casual or formal, humorous or serious, technical or philosophical); the particular slant you take (appealing to the reader's reason, emotions, or ethics, or a combination of these); what emphasis to give the argument; the type of evidence you offer; and the kinds of authorities you cite. Also, this knowledge will let you better anticipate any objections to your position. In short, knowing your audience lets you adjust the shape of your argument the way you would refocus a camera after each photo you shoot.

If, for instance, you're writing for your economics professor, you would use technical vocabulary you would not use with your English professor. Likewise, in a newspaper article condemning alcohol abusers you would have to keep in mind that some of your readers or their family members might be recovering alcoholics; they may take exception to your opinions. A travel piece for an upscale international magazine would need to have a completely different slant and voice than one for the travel section of a small local newspaper.

Knowing your audience might make the difference between a convincing argument and a failing argument. Suppose, for instance, you decide to write an editorial for the student newspaper opposing a recently announced tuition hike. Chances are you would have a sympathetic audience in the student body because you share age, educational status, and interests. Most students do not like the idea of a higher tuition bill. That commonality might justify the blunt language and emotional slant of your appeal. It might even allow a few sarcastic comments directed at the administration. That same argument addressed to your school's board of trustees, however, would probably not win a round of applause. With them it would be wiser to adopt a more formal tone in painting a sympathetic picture of your financial strain; it's always smart to demonstrate an understanding of the opposition's needs, maybe even a compromise solution. In this case, your appeal to the trustees would be more credible if you acknowledged the university's plight while recommending alternative money-saving measures such as a new fund-raising program.

Or suppose you write an article with a religious thrust arguing against capital punishment. You argue that even in the case of confessed murderers, state execution is an immoral practice running counter to Christian doctrine; for supporting evidence you offer direct quotations from the New Testament. Were you to submit your article to a religious publication, your reliance on the authority of the scriptures would probably appeal to the editors. However, were you to submit that same article to the "My Turn" column for *Newsweek*, chances are it would be turned down, no matter how well written. The editors aren't necessarily an ungodly lot, but *Newsweek*, like most other large-circulation magazines, is published for an audience made up of people of every religious persuasion, as well as agnostics and atheists. *Newsweek* editors are not in the business of publishing material that excludes a large segment of its audience. Knowing your readers works in two ways: It helps you decide what materials to put into your argument, and it helps you decide where to publish your argument, whether it be on an electronic bulletin board, in a local paper, or on the op-ed page of *The Wall Street Journal*.

The Target Audience

The essays in this book come from a variety of publications, many of them magazines addressed to the "general" American readership. Others, however, come from publications directed to men or women, the political right or left, or from publications for people of particular ethnic, racial, and cultural identities. They're written for *target audiences*. When writers have a "target" audience in mind, particularly readers who share the same interests, opinions, and prejudices, they can take short-cuts with little risk of alienating anybody, because writer and readers have so many things in common. Consider the following excerpts concerning the use of animal testing in scientific research:

> Contrary to prevailing misperception, in vitro tests need not replace existing in vivo test procedures in order to be useful. They can contribute to chemical-safety evaluation right now. In vitro tests, for example, can be incorporated into the earliest stages of the risk-assessment process; they can be used to iden-tify chemicals having the lowest probability of toxicity so that animals need be exposed only to less noxious chemicals.

It is clear from the technical terminology (e.g., *in vitro, in vivo, toxicity*), profes-sional jargon (*test procedures, chemical-safety evaluation, risk-assessment process*), and the formal, detached tone, that the piece was intended for a scientifically educated readership. Not surprisingly, the article, "Alternatives to Animals in Toxicity Test-ing," was authored by two research scientists, Alan M. Goldberg and John M. Fra-zier, and published in *Scientific American* (August 1989). Contrast it with another approach to the topic:

> Almost 30 years ago, Queen had been a child herself, not quite two years old, living in Thailand under the care of her mother and another female elephant, the two who had tended to her needs every day since her birth. They taught her how to use her trunk, in work and play, and had given her a sense of fam-ily loyalty. But then Queen was captured, and her life was changed irrevocably by men with whips and guns. One man herded Queen by whipping and shouting at her while another shot her mother, who struggled after her baby until more bullets pulled her down forever.

What distinguishes this excerpt is the emotional appeal. This is not the kind of article you would find in *Scientific American* or most other scientific journals. Nor would you expect to see this kind of emotional appeal in a newsmagazine such as *Newsweek* or *Time*, or a general interest publication such as the Sunday magazine of many newspapers. The excerpt comes from an animal rights newsletter published by PETA, People for the Ethical Treatment of Animals. Given that particular audi-ence, the writer safely assumes immediate audience sympathy with the plight of ele-phants. There is no need for the author to qualify or apologize for such sentimen-talizing statements as "Queen had been a child herself" and "They taught her how to use her trunk, in work and play, and had given her a sense of family loyalty." In fact, given the context, the author is probably more interested in reminding readers of a shared cause than winning converts.

The General Audience

Unless you're convinced that your readers are in total agreement with you or share your philosophical or professional interests, you may have some trouble picturing just who you are persuading. It's tempting to say you're writing for a "general" audience; but, as we said at the beginning of this chapter, general audiences may include very different people with different backgrounds, expectations, and standards. Writing for such audiences, then, may put additional pressure on you.

In reality, of course, most of your college writing will be for your professors. This can be a little confusing because you may find yourself trying to determine just what audience your professor represents. You may even wonder why professors expect you to explain material with which they are familiar. You may feel that defining technical terms to your psychology instructor who covered them in class the week before, or summarizing a poem that you know your English professor can probably recite, is a waste of time. But they have a good reason: They assume the role of uninformed audience to let you show how much *you* know.

Of course, if you are arguing controversial issues, you may find yourself in the awkward position of trying to second-guess your instructor's stand on an issue. You may even be tempted to tone down your presentation so as not to risk offense and, thus, an undesirable grade. However, most instructors try not to let their biases affect their evaluation of a student's work. Their main concern is how well a student argues a position.

For some assignments your instructor may specify an audience for you: members of the city council, the readers of the campus newspaper, Rush Limbaugh's radio listeners, and so on. But if no audience is specified, one of your earliest decisions about writing should be in choosing an audience. If you pick "readers of *The National Review*," for instance, you'll know you're writing for mostly male, conservative, middle-aged, middle-class whites; the expectations of these readers are very different than for readers of *Jet* or *Vibes*. If you are constrained to (or want the challenge of) writing for the so-called general audience, construct a mental picture of who those people are so you'll be able to shape your argument accordingly. Here are some of the characteristics we think you might include in your definition.

The "general" audience includes those people who read *Newsweek, Time,* and your local newspaper. That means people whose average age is about thirty, whose educational level is high school plus two years of college, who make up the vast middle class of America, who politically stand in the middle of the road, and whose racial and ethnic origins span the world. You can assume that they read the daily newspaper and watch the evening news and are generally informed about what is going on in the country. You can assume a good comprehension of language nuances and a sense of humor. They are people who recognize who Shakespeare was, though they may not be able to quote passages or name ten of his plays. Nor will they necessarily be experts in the latest theory of black holes or be able to explain how photo emulsions work. However, you can expect them to be open to technical explanations and willing to listen to arguments on birth control, gun control, weight control, and the issue of homosexuals in the Boy Scouts. More importantly, you can look upon your audience members as people willing to hear what you have to say.

Guidelines for Knowing Your Audience

Before sitting down to write, think about your audience. Ask yourself the following questions: Will I be addressing other college students, or people of my parents' generation? Will my audience be of a particular political persuasion, or strongly identified with a specific cultural background? How might the age of my readers and their educational background influence the way they think about a given issue? On what criteria will they make their decisions about this issue? A good example of profiling your audience was evident in the 2000 presidential election. The Republicans gambled that "moral leadership" and "trust" were the chief criteria for voters. The Democrats, on the other hand, focused on more global issues such as the environment and world economy. As the election results showed, the Republicans assessed their audience more accurately than did the Republicans.

As the example above illustrates, an effective argument essay takes into account the values, beliefs, interests, and experiences of its audience. If you simply choose to argue what you feel is important without regard to your audience, the only person you persuade may be yourself! An effective argument tries to establish common ground with the audience. While this may be difficult at times, recognizing what you have in common with your audience will enable you to argue most persuasively.

Before you can do this, however, you will need to create a profile of your audience. You may find the checklist on the next page helpful in assessing an audience. If you like visual prompts, write the answers to these questions on a card or a slip of paper that you can hang over your desk or display in a window on your computer screen while you're working on your argument. Looking at these questions and answers occasionally will remind you to focus your arguments on these particular people.

Using Debate and Dialogue

Debate and dialogue, two of the methods of developing arguments discussed in Chapter 1, can also be used to sharpen your awareness of audience. For an example of how this can happen, let's revisit John, our first-year composition student who had decided to write his argument essay on the topic of binge drinking. After reading critically in his subject area (Chapter 2) and formulating a working claim (Chapter 3), John turned his attention to the question of audience. He found that using debate and dialogue helped him answer some of the questions in the audience checklist and provided essential information about how his audience might respond to his ideas.

John decided that his audience would be a general one comprised of people of all ages. He anticipated that most people in his audience would not endorse excessive drinking, but with such a diverse group of people he was unsure whether they would have similar reasons for their concern and how strongly they would agree or disagree with his reasons. John found that using two strategies, a "Yes, but . . ." exchange and creating a dialogue among different perspectives, helped to answer questions 2 and 3 on the audience checklist: Where do my readers stand on the issue? and How do I want my readers to view the issue? He used this information to develop ways to engage his readers in the essay.

Working with classmates in small peer groups, John found that a "Yes, but . . ." exchange revealed specific points that his audience might use to oppose his reasons. For instance, John began with the following statement:

AUDIENCE CHECKLIST

1. Who are the readers I will be addressing?
   a. What age group?
   b. Are they male, female, or both?
   c. What educational background?
   d. What socioeconomic status?
   e. What are their political, religious, occupational, or other affiliations?
   f. What values, assumptions, and prejudices do they have about life?
2. Where do my readers stand on the issue?
   a. Do they know anything about it?
   b. If so, how might they have learned about it?
   c. How do they interpret the issue?
   d. How does the issue affect them personally?
   e. Are they hostile to my stand on the issue?
3. How do I want my readers to view the issue?
   a. If they are hostile to my view, how can I persuade them to listen to me?
   b. If they are neutral, how can I persuade them to consider my viewpoint?
   c. If they are sympathetic to my views, what new light can I shed on the issue? How can I reinspire them to take action?
4. What do I have in common with my readers?
   a. What beliefs and values do we share?
   b. What concerns about the issue do we have in common?
   c. What common life experiences have we had?
   d. How can I make my readers aware of our connection?

College administrators have a responsibility to deter binge drinking by their students.

He received several responses from his peer group:

Yes, college administrators have a responsibility to their students, but that responsibility should be limited to academic matters.

Yes, binge drinking by students should be a concern to college administrators, but college administrators shouldn't interfere with the private lives or habits of their students.

Yes, college administrators should try to deter binge drinking by students, but they will be ineffective unless they receive support from the community and parents.

Although each of John's classmates agreed that college administrators had a valid interest in student binge drinking, there was considerable disagreement over how far that interest should extend and how effective any action taken by administrators would be. The "Yes, but . . ." exchange gave John greater insight into the ways others might respond to his ideas. As he developed his argument, he was able to acknowledge and address such concerns by his potential audience.

In a similar fashion, John used dialogue to gain insight into question 4 on the audience checklist: What do I have in common with my readers? In particular, John wanted to discover any shared concerns and values among himself and those who took different positions on solving the problem of binge drinking. To create a dialogue, John interviewed several of his classmates, his teachers, members of his family, and a few individuals from the community; he also read articles by health professionals concerned with alcohol abuse and young adults. His goal was to listen to a wide spectrum of views on the subject and to keep an open mind as he listened. He used his journal to record their comments and his own impressions. What emerged from this dialogue were several areas of shared concerns: Most agreed that binge drinking was an unhealthy practice that should be discouraged, and while there were many different suggestions about the measures that should be taken to eliminate it, all agreed that the students who engaged in binge drinking must ultimately accept responsibility for ending it. No solution would work, all agreed, unless the drinkers themselves were willing to stop. John found this information helpful because he knew that his audience would be more willing to listen to his argument if he could identify these shared values and concerns.

By engaging in both debate and dialogue, John gained knowledge that enabled him to appeal to his audience more effectively.

Adapting to Your Readers' Attitudes

Writing for a general audience is a challenge because in that faceless mass are three kinds of readers you'll be addressing:

1. People who agree with you
2. People who are neutral—those who are unconvinced or uninformed on the issue
3. People who don't share your views, and who might even be hostile to them

Each of these different subgroups will have different expectations of you and give you different obligations to meet if you are to present a convincing argument. Even readers sympathetic to your cause might not be familiar with special vocabulary, the latest developments around the issue, or some of the more subtle arguments from the opposition. Those hostile to your cause might be so committed to their own viewpoints that they might not take the time to discover that you share common concerns. And those neutral to the cause might simply need to be filled in on the issue and its background. If you're going to persuade your readers, you'll have to tailor your approach to suit their attitudes.

When addressing an audience, whether general or one of a particular persuasion, you must try to put yourself in its place. You must try to imagine the different needs and expectations these readers bring to your writing, always asking yourself what new information you can pass on and what new ways of viewing you can find for addressing the issue you're arguing. Let's look at some of the strategies you, as a writer, might use, depending on whether you anticipate a neutral, friendly, or unfriendly group of readers.

Addressing a Neutral Audience

Some writers think a neutral audience is the easiest to write for, but many others find this the most challenging group of readers. After all, they're *neutral*; you don't know which way they're leaning, or what may make them commit to your position. Your best role is the conveyor of knowledge: The information you bring, and the ways in which you present it, are the means by which you hope to persuade a neutral audience. Here are some of the ways to convey that information.

Fill in the Background

There are some issues about which few people are neutral: abortion, capital punishment, drug legalization, same-sex marriage, gun control. However, there are other issues about which some readers have not given a thought or made up their minds; or they may simply be uninformed. For instance, if you're part of a farming community, your concern about preserving good farmland might make you feel some urgency about unchecked industrial development in your area. To make a convincing case for readers from, say, Chicago or New York City, you first would have to tell them a little about the shortage of prime land for agriculture and why it is crucial to maintain the existing land. Similarly, as a resident of a large town, you might need to explain to readers from rural Vermont or Iowa why you think their community should be concerned with mandatory recycling in large cities. In both cases your task would be to provide your readers with the information they need to evaluate the issue by relating some of the history and background behind the controversy. All the while, you need to encourage them to weigh with an open mind the evidence you present.

Present a Balanced Picture

Part of educating a neutral audience about your position involves presenting a balanced picture of the issue by presenting multiple perspectives about the issue, not just one. Even though you are trying to help your readers understand why your position has value, you will be more persuasive if you treat *all* views fairly, including opposing views. You should clearly and accurately lay out the key arguments of all sides; then demonstrate why your position is superior. Your readers need to feel that you have looked at the total picture and reached your position after carefully weighing all views, a process you hope your readers will engage in as well. Let your readers make their decisions based on their own analysis of the information you have provided. Don't be guilty of stacking the deck, a logical fallacy we discuss in Chapter 2. Not representing the other sides at all, or representing them unfairly and inaccurately, can leave you open to criticisms of distortion, and it may make your readers feel that you're misleading them.

Personalize the Issues

One sure way of gaining readers' attention is to speak their language—that is, address their personal needs, hopes, and fears. (It's what skillful politicians do all the time on the campaign trail.) If you want to engage your readers' attention, demonstrate how the problem will affect them personally. On the matter of farmland, explain why if nothing is done to prevent its loss, the prices of corn and beans will triple over the next three years. On the recycling issue, explain how unrestricted trash dumping will mean that city dwellers will try to dump more trash in rural areas. However, although personalizing the issue is an effective way to make your readers aware of the importance of your issue, you should avoid creating an ad misericordiam argument. To be fully credible, you should be certain that the reasons and evidence you present to your readers are anchored in fact rather than emotion.

Show Respect

When you're an informed person talking about an issue to people with less knowledge than you, there's a dangerous tendency to speak down to them. Think how you feel when someone "talks down" to you. Do you like it? How persuasive do you think you can be if your readers think you're talking down to them? Don't condescend to or patronize them. Try not to simplify a complex issue so much that it is reduced to a false dilemma: "If we don't increase school taxes immediately, our children will no longer receive a quality education." Don't assume that your audience is so ill informed that it cannot envision a middle ground between the two alternatives. On the contrary, treat your readers as people who want to know what you know about the issue and who want you to demonstrate to them clearly and accurately why you think they should agree with you. Invite them into the discussion, encouraging them with sound reasons and strong evidence to consider the merits of your side. Although your audience may not be as informed as you, they are willing to listen and deserve respect.

Addressing a Friendly Audience

Writing an argument for the already converted is much easier than writing for a neutral audience or one that is hostile. In a sense, half the battle is won because no minds have to be changed. You need not brace yourself for opposing views or refutations. Your role is simply to provide readers with new information and to renew enthusiasm for and commitment to your shared position. Nonetheless, there are still steps you should take.

Avoid Appealing to Prejudices

One of the risks of addressing a sympathetic audience is appealing to prejudices rather than reasons and facts. Although it might be tempting to mock those who don't agree with you or to demean their views, don't. Stooping to that level only diminishes your own authority and undermines your credibility. Two of the logical fallacies we discuss in Chapter 2 address this problem. The first, an ad hominem argument, is a personal attack on those who disagree with your position. Unfortunately, this approach will reflect negatively on *you*. Use reason and hard evidence instead of insults and ridicule to underscore the weakness of other arguments while you make your readers aware of your mutual concerns. The second fallacy is an ad populum argument and involves using the presumed prejudices of your audience members to manipulate their responses to your argument. Once again, this approach will make you appear unreasonable and biased and may backfire if your audience does not share your prejudices. Instead, encourage your readers to respect different viewpoints, recognizing the merits of their arguments even though you ultimately disagree. It's simply a more reasonable approach, one that allows you and your readers to share informed agreement, and it will win the respect of friends and foes alike.

Offer New Information About the Issue

Even when your readers agree with you, they may need to have their memories refreshed regarding the history of the issue. In addition, you should provide readers with important new information on the issue. Such new developments might involve recent judiciary decisions, newly enacted legislation, or new scientific data that could serve to strengthen your position and their agreement or require a reconsideration of your views. Unless you are absolutely up-to-date about the progress of your issue, you will appear to be either ill informed or deliberately withholding information, seriously undermining your credibility with your audience, even a friendly one. Your willingness to share and educate your audience will enhance the persuasiveness of your views.

Addressing an Unfriendly Audience

As difficult as it may be to accept, some readers will be totally at odds with your views, even hostile to them. Writing for such a readership, of course, is especially challenging—far more than for neutral readers. So how do you present your argument to people you have little chance of winning over?

Seek Common Ground and Remind Your Audience About It

In this argumentative strategy, recommended by psychologist Carl Rogers, your goal is to find ways to connect with your audience through empathy and common experiences. For instance, let's say you are trying to persuade an audience of senior citizens to support a tax increase to fund local schools. After analyzing your audience, you might conclude that many are living on limited incomes and are concerned about the financial burden of additional taxes. This factor might make them a hostile audience, one not easily receptive to your position. A good strategy, then, to begin your argument might be to let them know that you are well acquainted with the difficulties of living on limited means. You might even refer to relatives or friends who are in a similar position. If you let your audience know that you empathize with and understand their difficulties, they will be more willing to listen to you.

Remind your audience of the beliefs and values you have in common. While it is unlikely that many of the senior citizens still have children attending the local schools, nonetheless, they may value education and understand its importance. You can let them know that you share this value, one that underlies your support for additional public school funding.

Recognize the concerns of your audience as legitimate and worthy of attention; you will demonstrate that you are aware of and respect their views. This means, of course, finding out what their concerns are. For instance, if you are trying to persuade your audience to support a tax increase to fund new programs in the public schools in your district, do some reading to find out the reasons why people would choose not to support the tax increase. By addressing those concerns, you will make your audience aware that you understand their position. This may make them more receptive to listening to yours.

REVIEW: ADDRESSING AUDIENCES

A Neutral Audience
- Fill in the background.
- Present a balanced picture.
- Personalize the issues.
- Show respect for your readers.

A Friendly Audience
- Avoid appealing to prejudices.
- Offer new information about the issue.

An Unfriendly Audience
- Seek common ground.
- Convey a positive attitude.
- Remember the Golden Rule.

To Improve Your Credibility with Your Audience, Avoid These Fallacies

Ad hominem argument	Leveling a personal attack against an opponent. A reliance on ad hominem arguments undercuts your credibility and may make you appear mean-spirited and desperate. Focus instead on the substance of an opponent's claim.
Ad misericordiam argument	Attempting to exploit the audience's emotions rather than appealing to logic and reason. Avoid using arguments that rely only on wrenching the reader's heart strings rather than logic and real evidence.

Ad populum argument	Appealing to the audience's presumed prejudices rather than proven facts. Even if you know the prejudices of your audience, such an appeal at best only persuades those already convinced. Rely on the force of logic and supporting evidence rather than bias and stereotyping.
Stacking the deck	Presenting only evidence that supports your points and withholding contrary evidence. Instead, acknowledge that conflicting evidence exists and respond to it.
False dilemma	Presenting an issue as an either-or choice and ignoring the possibility of a middle ground. Treat your audience as intelligent equals who are aware that at least several thoughtful alternatives are likely to exist.

Convey a Positive Attitude

Whether or not they know it, your audience will benefit from seeing the issue from another side. In other words, approach a hostile audience as someone who can shed a different light on the problem. View them as people who are potentially interested in learning something new. Without being defensive, arrogant, or apologetic, make your claim, enumerate your reasons, and lay out the evidence for your readers to evaluate on their own. Regard them as intelligent people capable of drawing their own conclusions. You may not win converts, but you might at least lead some to recognize the merits of your side. You might even convince a few people to reconsider their views.

Remember the Golden Rule

Even though they may not agree with you, treat the opposition with respect. Look upon them as reasonable people who just happen to disagree with you. Demonstrate your understanding of their side of the issue. Show that you have made the effort to research the opposition. Give credit where credit is due. If some of their counterpoints make sense, say so. In short, treat those from the other side and their views as you would want to be treated. You may just win a few converts.

SAMPLE ARGUMENTS FOR ANALYSIS

How a writer appeals to his or her audience can have a positive or a negative effect on the way the writer's message is received. The following three articles are concerned with the controversy regarding regulations on smoking and the resulting treatment of smokers by society. The writers address the audience in notably different ways. For the first essay, by C. Everett Koop, we have used annotation to illustrate some of the strategies Koop uses to appeal to his audience and the assumptions he makes about them. As a class exercise, read each of these essays and then consider the following questions:

■ QUESTIONS FOR ANALYSIS AND DISCUSSION

1. Locate the claim or thesis statement and summarize the main ideas in each essay.
2. What kind of audience is each writer addressing? neutral? friendly? hostile? What evidence can you find to support this?
3. Which writers attempt to present a balanced picture to the audience? Provide examples.
4. Do the writers convey a positive attitude toward the audience? Do any of the writers antagonize the audience? How is this done?
5. Have these writers committed any of the logical fallacies we've discussed? Where do these errors occur and how would you correct them?
6. How well does each writer establish common ground with the audience?
7. What is the purpose of each essay? How effectively does each writer accomplish this purpose?

Don't Forget the Smokers

C. Everett Koop

Dr. C. Everett Koop served as Surgeon General of the United States from 1981 until 1989. His duties in office were to advise the public on matters such as smoking, diet and nutrition, environmental health hazards, and disease prevention. Since leaving office, Dr. Koop has been a spokesperson and activist on issues of public health. This article appeared in the *Washington Post* on March 8, 1998.

1   To date, most of the tobacco control efforts of this administration have focused on preventing young people from taking up smoking. Everyone can agree that teenagers and younger children should not smoke. Even the tobacco industry can safely join in that refrain, and frequently does, with characteristic and clamorous hypocrisy as it turns its marketing machines loose on the young. But at exactly what age does the plight of American smokers lose its poignancy?

[margin note: Establishes common ground, shared views / charged language]

2   One-third of teenagers who experiment casually with cigarettes will become regular smokers, with one-half of these trying to quit, but failing, by age 18. In fact, the vast majority of current smokers were hooked in their teens or earlier. During the '80s, the tobacco industry mounted a public relations campaign maintaining that smoking was "an adult decision." It was a model of reverse psychology, tempting teens at the same time it offered false reassurance to their elders. The vast majority of smokers are captive to their addiction, so that most who "decide" to quit cannot—not without help or years of repeated tries.

[margin note: Assumes media-savvy reader familiar with ad campaigns]

3   If we pretend that adult smoking is a consumer choice like any other, we fall prey to the trap laid by Big Tobacco. Addiction makes the very notion of choice moot. Who would freely choose sickness and suffering, lost productivity or 50 percent chance of premature death? Yet cigarette smokers of all ages continue to die prematurely at the rate of more than 400,000 per year. If not one single young person started smoking from this day forward, these losses would still continue unabated for 30 years. Imagine 1,000 jumbo jets emblazoned with Marlboro and Winston and Camel insignia crashing each year for the next three decades. Should we accept such dramatic losses as par for the course?

Allusion to Big Brother assumes reader has literary background

Rhetorical question involves reader

4   We must not focus our efforts so narrowly on preventing tobacco use by youth that we send smokers the message that we have abandoned them—that their addiction is their own fault and that we don't care about them. This is exactly what the tobacco industry wants them to hear. Forget quitting, hedge the health bets instead. Responding to founded fears, tobacco companies unleashed so-called "low-tar" brands in an effort to hold on to their smokers and reduce the concerns of the uninitiated. But in their attempt to avoid becoming yet another statistic, smokers have only changed the form of their resultant lung cancers from the squamous cell cancers of the upper lung to the adenocarcinomas of the lower lung as they inhaled more deeply to extract the nicotine their bodies craved from such cigarettes. There is an alternative. We can combine tobacco prevention initiatives with efforts to ensure that those who are hooked can obtain effective treatments.

Addresses readers as adults who have power to shape public attitudes

Assumes readers are comfortable with medical terms

5   The facts are that quitting smoking at any age reduces the risk of premature death; current treatments can substantially increase the odds of quitting. It therefore seems logical that each decision to smoke should present an equal opportunity not to smoke and an equal opportunity to get help. The Food and Drug Administration's actions in 1996 to restrict tobacco marketing to minors and to approve over-the-counter marketing of nicotine gum and patches for adults were pioneering steps in the right direction. So are several pieces of congressional legislation currently under discussion that include provisions for tobacco addiction treatments.

Uses facts and reasons, not emotions

Assumes broad general knowledge

6   Nevertheless, much remains to be done if our nation is to make tobacco dependence treatment as acceptable and as readily available as tobacco itself. We must evaluate and approve potentially life-saving treatments for tobacco dependence at the level of priority we assign to treatments for diseases such as AIDS and cancer. Signaling such a course could help empower the private sector to meet these challenges in a way that will contribute to the health of our nation in the short and long run.

Suggests readers are in decision-making positions

7   Currently, the tobacco industry is lobbying Congress for its own solution to the needs of smokers. Under the guise of the new-found concern for the health of their consumers, these companies want incentives to market products that they claim will reduce the dangers of smoking. We do not want to stifle development of such products. Indeed, we should require reduced toxicity of tobacco products, as we now understand that they are unnecessarily dangerous and addictive. But such a course should not enable tobacco companies to undermine our efforts to reduce overall tobacco use by allowing them to advertise their products with claims such as "low tar" or "reduced delivery." Legitimate concern for the health of tobacco users should balance efforts to reduce the toxicity of tobacco products with the means to expedite the development of new treatments for those who are addicted. Under its existing authorities, including its designation of cigarettes and smokeless tobacco products as combination drug and device products, the FDA has many regulatory tools at its disposal to accomplish its goal of reducing the risk of death and disease in tobacco-addicted Americans. Congressional legislation that weakens the FDA's authority over tobacco reduces its ability to serve the public health.

Tone: serious

Sketches opposition's plan and shows weaknesses

Makes a direct appeal to knowledgeable readers

8   I strongly encourage any forthcoming congressional legislation or executive actions to strengthen, if not leave alone, the FDA's authority over tobacco, and to support the FDA's ability to evaluate new treatments and treatment approaches in a manner that is consistent with the devastation wrought by unremitting tobacco use. Moreover, in our battle with Big Tobacco, we should not hide behind our children. Instead, as we take every action to save our children from the ravages of tobacco, we should demonstrate our commitment to those who are already addicted, and those who will yet become addicted, will never expire.

Forceful language

Plays on connotation and denotation of word

What the Antismoking Zealots Really Crave

Jeff Jacoby

Jeff Jacoby, a founding director of the Pioneer Institute, a conservative public-policy think tank in Boston, writes a regular column for the *Boston Globe*, where this piece appeared on March 24, 1998.

1   A question for antitobacco militants: Why do you draw the line at private homes?

2   To protect nonsmokers, especially young ones, you've made it illegal to smoke in more and more places. You have banished smoking from tens of millions of private workplaces; from airplanes and buses; from most government buildings. You have gotten hundreds of cities—Boston is your latest conquest—to ban smoking in restaurants altogether. In California, you've even driven smokers from bars.

3   But smoking at home is OK.

4   Curious, no? You militants routinely justify your crusade by claiming to act for "the kids," yet in the one place a kid is likeliest to encounter cigarettes, smoking is wholly unregulated. Why? It can't be because you respect the rights of private property owners. After all, restaurants and bars are private property. And it can't be because the state never interferes in the way parents raise their children—the state interferes in everything from the commercials children see on television to the paint that goes on their walls. So why aren't you clamoring to take away parents' freedom to smoke at home?

5   Granted, that would just about outlaw *all* smoking. But isn't that what you want?

6   One of the nation's foremost antismoking activists, Stanton Glantz, compares cigarette manufacturers to Timothy McVeigh, the mass murderer of Oklahoma City. A *New York Times* reporter likens tobacco employees to "the guards and doctors in the Nazi death camps." Over a decade ago, the *Journal of the American Medical Association* was calling for "a declaration of all-out war" against the perpetrators of "the tobaccoism holocaust."

7   Such murderous rhetoric is typical. On taxpayer-funded billboards in California, a man about to light up asks, "Mind if I smoke?" The woman replies: "Care if I die?" Elizabeth Whelan of the American Council on Science and Health says smoking kills more people than "if every single day two filled-to-capacity jumbo jets crashed, killing all on board." A former director of the Centers for Disease Control has predicted that "the annual global death toll of tobacco will equal the total death toll of the Holocaust in Nazi Germany."

8   Such hysteria is more than repugnant, it is false. In *For Your Own Good* (Free Press), a lucid and superbly researched new book on the antitobacco jihad, journalist Jacob Sullum pinpoints the deceit:

9   "The rhetoric of tobacco's opponents implies a rough equivalence between a 65-year-old smoker who dies of lung cancer and a 40-year-old businessman killed in a plane crash, a 19-year-old soldier shot in the trenches of World War I, or a child murdered by the Nazis at Auschwitz. But there is a big difference between someone who dies suddenly at the hands of another person or in an accident and someone who dies as a result of a long-term, voluntarily assumed risk."

10   Maybe so, you antismoking activists might say, but the harm caused by smoking isn't limited to the smoker. His smoke poisons everyone he comes into contact with. They shouldn't be made to suffer because of his vile habit. Nonsmokers have a right to a smoke-free society.

11   In fact, the danger of secondhand smoke is more myth than science. Most epidemiological studies have found no statistically significant link between lung

cancer and secondhand smoke. Exposure to cigarette fumes may not be *good* for your health, but the medical fact is that secondhand smoke is not likely to do lasting harm to anyone.

12   Still—what about those kids growing up in smokers' homes? How can you sworn enemies of tobacco be so intent on criminalizing the smoke in smoky jazz bars, yet do nothing about the millions of children whose parents light up with abandon? Why don't you demand that cigarettes be outlawed in any house with kids? In other words, why don't you demand that cigarettes be outlawed—period!

13   Maybe the answer is that even zealots like you realize it wouldn't work. Alcohol Prohibition in the 1920s was a hideous failure, drenching the country in corruption, crime, and oceans of impure alcohol. In a nation with 45 million smokers, Tobacco Prohibition would be no less a disaster and most of you know it.

14   Or maybe the answer is that you couldn't *afford* to end smoking entirely. Ban all tobacco, and there'd be no tobacco taxes or (legal) tobacco profits. No profits or taxes, no hundreds of billions of dollars to fund a settlement. No gusher of dollars for new "health care" programs. No bonanza for plaintiffs' lawyers. No lavish budgets for all your antitobacco outfits. No goose. No golden eggs.

15   But I think the real answer is that you don't think you can get away with it—yet. Already some of you *are* targeting smokers' homes. At least one law review article has claimed that parents who expose their children to tobacco smoke "should be viewed as committing child abuse." A Pennsylvania legislator has proposed a ban on smoking in any vehicle carrying a minor. More intrusion is on its way.

16   Nicotine may be pleasurable, but it's nothing like the high of forcing others to behave the way you want them to. Power over other people's pleasures is very addicting, isn't it? "The true nature of the crusade for a smoke-free society," Sullum writes, is "an attempt by one group of people to impose their tastes and preferences on another." It's illiberal, it's vindictive, it's intolerant. It's you.

Media Have Fallen for Misguided Antismoking Campaign

Robert J. Samuelson

Robert J. Samuelson, the recipient of numerous journalism awards, is a nationally known columnist who focuses on political, economic, and social issues. This article was published in the *Boston Globe*.

1   The media are deeply sensitive to the rights of those we consider minorities: the poor, the disabled, blacks, gays, and immigrants, among others. But there is one minority much larger than any of these (at least 25 percent of the population) whose rights we deny or ignore: smokers. The debate over ciga-

rettes has been framed as if smokers are the unwitting victims of the tobacco industry. They lack free will and, therefore, their apparent desires and interests
don't count. They are to be pitied and saved, not respected.

2   This is pack journalism run amok. We media types fancy ourselves independent thinkers. Just the opposite is often true: We're patsies for the latest
crusade or fad. In this case, the major media have adopted the view of the public health community, which sees smoking as a scourge to be eradicated. The
"story" is the crusade; the villain is the tobacco industry. Lost are issues that
ought to inform this debate.

3   The simplest is whether, in trying to make Americans better off, the antismoking crusade would make many Americans worse off. Smokers would
clearly suffer from huge price and tax increases. The cost of the $368.5 billion
agreement between the tobacco industry and the state attorneys general is estimated at 62 cents a pack. President Clinton suggests raising that to $1.50 a
pack—about six times today's federal tax (24 cents). The cost would hit the
poor hardest. They smoke more than the rich.

4   Consider. About half (53 percent) of today's cigarette tax is paid by taxpayers with incomes of less than $30,000, estimates the congressional Joint Com-
mittee on Taxation. Higher prices will deter some people from smoking. But
for the rest, would siphoning billions away from poorer people be good policy?
Or fair?

5   The antismoking crusaders try to seem fair by arguing: (1) smoking has
been increasing among teenagers who, once they try cigarettes, may become
addicted for life; (2) tobacco ads cause much teenage smoking—teenagers are,
therefore, victims; and (3) passive smoking (nonsmokers inhaling smoke) in
public places is a serious health threat, justifying action against smokers. These
assumptions permeate media coverage, but the first two are open to question
and the third is untrue.

6   Start with teenage smoking. One survey from the University of Michigan
does show a rise. In 1996, 34 percent of 12th-graders reported smoking in the
past month—the highest since 1979 (34.4 percent). But the government's survey on drug abuse suggests the opposite: In 1996, only 18.3 percent of teenagers
between 12 and 17 had smoked in the past month, the lowest since 1985 (29
percent). It's hard to know which survey to believe, but neither depicts runaway
teenage smoking.

7   As for ads, teenagers do a lot of dangerous things (drugs, early sex) that
aren't advertised and are often illegal. The tobacco industry no doubt targets
teenagers, but the ads may affect brand choices more than they do the decision
to smoke. A new, comprehensive study—financed by the National Institutes of
Health—suggests that teenagers' home environment is more important in determining who smokes. "Children who report feeling connected to a parent are
protected against many different kinds of health risks including . . . cigarette,
alcohol, and marijuana use," it says.

8   And even teenagers who smoke do not necessarily become lifetime smokers. Among 12th-graders, the percentage of those who once smoked (63 per-

cent) is about twice as high as for those who currently do. The "addiction" isn't so great that millions haven't broken it.

9   Finally, passive smoking isn't a big public health risk, as many stories imply. The latest example of misreporting involved a study from Harvard Medical School. It purported to show that passive smoking doubled the risk of heart attacks, indicating a huge public health problem. That's how both the *New York Times* and *Washington Post* reported it. In fact, the study—at most—showed that passive smoking doubles a very tiny risk.

10   Here's why. The study followed 32,046 nonsmoking nurses between 1982 and 1992. Of these, four-fifths said they were exposed to passive smoking. But there were only 152 heart attacks (127 nonfatal) among all the nurses: a small number. Many heart attacks would have occurred even if no one was exposed to smoke. And most exposure to passive smoke is now private or voluntary, because public smoking has been barred in so many places. Will we outlaw husbands smoking in front of their wives—or vice versa?

11   You don't hear much of all this, because the press has an antismoking bias. The crusaders do have a case. Smoking is highly risky for smokers. But lots of things are risky, and don't smokers have a right to engage in behavior whose pleasures and pains are mainly theirs without being punished by the rest of society?

12   There is almost no one to make the smokers' case. They have been abandoned by the tobacco industry, politicians, and the press. Do smokers have rights? Apparently not.

Choosing Your Words

Whether addressing friends, foes, or the undecided, you must take care that your readers fully understand your case. In part this is accomplished by choosing your words carefully and by accurately defining any technical, unfamiliar, foreign, or abstract terms. Here are a few specific tips to follow to inform your readers without turning them off.

Distinguishing Denotation and Connotation

Many words, even the most common, carry special suggestions or associations, **connotations,** that differ from the precise dictionary definitions, **denotations.** For example, if you looked up the word *house* in the dictionary, one of the synonyms you'd find is *shelter.* Yet if you told people you live in a shelter, they would think that you live in a facility for the homeless or some kind of animal sanctuary. That is because *shelter* implies a covering or structure that protects those within from the elements or from danger. In other words, the term is not neutral, as is the word *house.* Likewise, dictionary synonyms for *horse* include *steed* and *nag,* but the former implies an elegant and high-spirited riding animal, while the latter suggests one that is old and worn out.

The denotations of words may be the same, but their connotations will almost always differ. And the reason is that dictionary denotations are essentially neutral and emotion-free, while connotations are most often associated with attitudes or charged feelings that can influence readers' responses. Therefore, it is important to be aware of the shades of differences when choosing your words. Consider the different meanings the connotations of the bracketed choices lend these statements:

> By the time I got home I was _____ [sleepy, exhausted, weary, beat, dead].
>
> My boyfriend drives around in a red _____ [car, vehicle, buggy, clunker, jalopy].
>
> I could hear him _____ [shout, yell, bellow, scream, shriek].

Connotations can also be personal and, thus, powerful tools for shaping readers' responses to what you say. Consider the word *pig*. The dictionary definition, or denotation, would read something like this: "A domestic farm animal with a long, broad snout and a thick, fat body covered with coarse bristles." However, the connotation of *pig* is far more provocative, for it suggests someone who looks or acts like a pig; someone who is greedy or filthy; someone who is sexually immoral. (Most dictionaries list the connotations of words, although some connotations might only be found in a dictionary of slang—e.g., *The New Dictionary of American Slang*, edited by Robert L. Chapman, or *Slang!* by Paul Dickson.)

There is nothing wrong with using a word because of its connotations, but you must be aware that connotations will have an emotional impact on readers. You don't want to say something unplanned. You don't want to offend readers by using words loaded with unintentional associations. For instance, you wouldn't suggest to advertisers that they "should be more creative when hawking their products" unless you intended to insult them. Although the term *hawking* refers to selling, it is unflattering and misleading because it connotes somebody moving up and down the streets peddling goods by shouting. Linguistically the word comes from the same root as the word *huckster*, which refers to an aggressive merchant known for haggling and questionable practices.

Connotatively loaded language can be used to create favorable as well as unfavorable reactions. If you are arguing against the use of animals in medical research, you will get a stronger response if you decry the sacrifice of "puppies and kittens" rather than the cooler, scientific, and less charged "laboratory animals."

You can understand why politicians, newspaper columnists, and anyone advocating a cause use connotative language. The loaded word is like a bullet for a writer making a strong argument. Consider the connotative impact of the italicized terms in the following excerpts taken from essays in this text:

> The bouncer who appeared to be in charge warned us that we would regret having ignored him. "You BOYS better stay right where you are!" *barked* the now seething bouncer. (Bryonn Bain, "The Bill of Rights for Black Men: Walking While Black")

> Such hysteria is more than repugnant, it is false. In *For Your Own Good* (Free Press), a lucid and superbly researched new book on the *antitobacco jihad*, journalist Jacob Sullum pinpoints the deceit. [. . .] (Jeff Jacoby, "What the Antismoking Zealots Really Crave")

Global consumer culture? *Supersize* it, baby. Pile on the wattage, horse-power, silicone, cholesterol and RAM until the lights *flicker,* the smoke alarms *shriek* and the cardiac paddles lurch to life. (Harry Flood, "Manufacturing Desire")

Each of the italicized words was selected not for its denotations but its negative connotations. In the first example, Byronn Bain could have chosen a more neutral word such as *said* to convey his denotative meaning; however, he deliberately selects *barked* to suggest doglike hostility and ignorance. Similarly, Jeff Jacoby describes the organized effort against smoking as a *jihad,* which evokes the image of a holy war waged by religious extremists. The final example could have read: ". . . human organs have been put on the auction block." And Harry Flood's description of the excesses of consumer culture features flickering lights and shrieking alarms—a jarring image of chaos and disorder.

Being Specific

To help readers better understand your argument, you need to use words that are precise enough to convey your exact meaning. If you simply say, "The weather last weekend was *terrible,*" your readers are left to come up with their own interpretations of what the weather was like. Was it hot and muggy? cold and rainy? overcast and very windy? some of each? Chances are your readers won't come up with the same weather conditions you had in mind. However, if you said, "Last weekend it rained day and night and never got above forty degrees," readers will have a more precise idea of the weekend's weather. And you will have accomplished your purpose of saying just what you meant.

The terms *general* and *specific* are opposites just as *abstract* and *concrete* are opposites. General words do not name individual things but classes or groups of things: animals, trees, women. Specific words refer to individuals in a group: your pet canary, the oak tree outside your bedroom window, the point guard. Of course, general and specific are themselves relative terms. Depending on the context or your frame of reference, a word that is specific in one context may be general in another. For instance, there is no need to warn a vegetarian that a restaurant serves veal Oscar and beef Wellington when simply *meat* will do. In other words, there are degrees of specificity appropriate to the situation. The following list illustrates just such a sliding scale, moving downward from the more general to the more specific:

General	Animal	Person	Book	Clothing	Food	Machine
	feline	female	novel	footwear	seafood	vehicle
	cat	singer	American	shoes	fish	fighter jet
Specific	Daisy, my pet	Tracy Chapman	*The Great Gatsby*	her Nikes	tuna	F-117

General words are useful in ordinary conversation when the people you're addressing understand your meaning and usually don't ask for clarification. The same is true in writing when you are addressing an audience familiar with your subject.

In such instances you can get away with occasional broad statements. For example, if you are running for class president, your campaign speeches would not require a great number of specifics as much as general statements of promise and principles:

> If elected, I intend to do what I can to ensure a comfortable classroom environment for each student at this college.

But when your audience is unfamiliar with your subject or when the context requires concrete details, generalities and abstract terms fall flat, leaving people wondering just exactly what you are trying to communicate. Let's say, for instance, you write a note to your dean explaining why you'd like to change the room where your English class meets. You wouldn't get very far on this appeal:

> Room 107 Richards is too small and uncomfortable for our class.

However, if you offer some specifics evoking a sense of the room's unpleasantness, you'd make a more persuasive case for changing the room:

> Room 107 Richards has 20 fixed seats for 27 students, leaving those who come in late to sit on windowsills or the floor. Worse still is the air quality. The radiators are fixed on high and the windows don't open. By the end of the hour it must be 90 degrees in there, leaving everybody sweaty and wilted including Professor Hazzard.

What distinguishes this paragraph is the use of concrete details: "20 fixed seats for 27 students"; latecomers forced to "sit on windowsills or on the floor"; radiators "fixed on high"; "the windows don't open"; "90 degrees"; and everybody was left "sweaty and wilted including Professor Hazzard." But more than simply conjuring up a vivid impression of the room's shortcomings, these specifics add substance to your argument for a room change.

Concrete language is specific language—words that have definite meaning. Concrete language names persons, places, and things: *Mother Teresa, Barry Bonds, New Zealand, Hartford, book, toothpaste.* Concrete terms conjure up vivid pictures in the minds of readers because they refer to particular things or qualities that can be perceived by the five senses—that is, they can be seen, smelled, tasted, felt, and heard. Abstract words, on the other hand, refer to qualities that do not have a definitive concrete meaning. They denote intangible qualities that cannot be perceived directly by the senses but are inferred from the senses—*powerful, foolish, talented, responsible, worthy.* Abstract words also denote concepts and ideas—*patriotism, beauty, victory, sorrow.* Although abstract terms can be useful depending on the context, writing that relies heavily on abstractions will fail to communicate clear meaning. Notice in the pairs below how concrete and specific details convert vague statements into vivid ones:

> **Abstract**   He was very nicely dressed.
>
> **Concrete**   He wore a dark gray Armani suit, white pinstriped shirt, and red paisley tie.

Abstract	Jim felt uncomfortable at Jean's celebration party.
Concrete	Jim's envy over Jean's promotion made him feel guilty.
Abstract	That was an incredible accident.
Concrete	A trailer truck jackknifed in the fog, causing seven cars to plow into each other, killing two, injuring eight, and leaving debris for a quarter mile along Route 17.

Abstract language is also relative. It depends on circumstances and the experience of the person using them. A *cold* December morning to someone living in Florida might mean temperatures in the forties or fifties. To residents of North Dakota, *cold* would designate air at subzero temperatures. It all depends on one's point of view. A *fair trial* might mean one thing to the prosecutor of a case, yet something completely different to the defense attorney. Likewise, what might be *offensive* language to your grandmother would probably not faze an average college student.

When employing abstract language, you need to be aware that readers may not share your point of view. Consequently, you should be careful to clarify your terms or simply select concrete alternatives. Below is an excerpt from a student paper as it appeared in the first draft. As you can see, it is lacking in details and specifics and has a rather dull impact.

> **Vague:** Last year my mother nearly died from medicine when she went to the hospital. The bad reaction sent her into a coma for weeks, requiring life-support systems around the clock. Thankfully, she came out of the coma and was released, but somebody should have at least asked what, if any, allergies she had.

Although the paragraph reads smoothly, it communicates very little of the dramatic crisis being described. Without specific details and concrete words, the reader misses both the trauma and the seriousness of the hospital staff's neglect, thus dulling the argument for stronger safeguards. What follows is the same paragraph revised with the intent of making it more concrete.

> **Revised:** Last year my mother nearly died from a codeine-based painkiller when she was rushed to the emergency room at Emerson Hospital. The severe allergic reaction sent her into a coma for six weeks, requiring daily blood transfusions, thrice weekly kidney dialysis, continuous intravenous medicines, a tracheotomy, and round-the-clock intensive care. Thankfully, she came out of the coma and was released, but the ER staff was negligent in not determining from her or her medical records that she was allergic to codeine.

Using Figurative Language

Words have their literal meaning, but they also can mean something beyond dictionary definitions, as we have seen. The sentence "Mrs. Jones is an angel" does not mean that Mrs. Jones is literally a supernatural winged creature, but a very kind and pleasant woman. What makes the literally impossible meaningful here is figurative language.

Figurative language (or a **figure of speech**) is comparative language. It is language that represents something in terms of something else—in figures, symbols, or likeness (Mrs. Jones and an angel). It functions to make the ordinary appear extraordinary and the unfamiliar appear familiar. It also adds richness and complexity to abstractions. Here, for instance, is a rather bland literal statement: "Yesterday it was 96 degrees and very humid." Here's that same sentence rendered in figurative language: "Yesterday the air was like warm glue." What this version does is equate yesterday's humid air to glue on a feature shared by each—stickiness. And the result is more interesting than the original statement.

The comparison of humid air to glue is linked by the words *like*. This example represents one of the most common figures of speech, the **simile.** Derived from the Latin *similis,* the term means similar. A simile makes an explicit comparison between dissimilar things (humid air and glue). It says that *A* is like *B* in one or more respects. The connectives used in similes are most often the words *like, as,* and *than:*

- A school of minnows shot by me like pelting rain.
- His arms are as big as hams.
- They're meaner than junkyard dogs.

When the connectives *like, as,* or *than* are omitted, then we have another common figure of speech, the **metaphor.** The term is from the Greek *meta* (over) + *pherin* ("to carry or ferry") meaning to carry over meaning from one thing to another. Instead of saying that *A* is like *B*, a metaphor equates them—*A is B*. For example, Mrs. Jones and an angel are said to be one and the same, although we all know that literally the two are separate entities.

- This calculus problem is a real pain in the neck.
- The crime in this city is a cancer out of control.
- The space shuttle was a flaming arrow in the sky.

Sometimes writers will carelessly combine metaphors that don't go with each other. Known as **mixed metaphors,** these often produce ludicrous results. For example:

- The heat of his expression froze them in their tracks.
- The experience left a bad taste in her eyes.
- The arm of the law has two strikes against it.

When a metaphor has lost its figurative value, it is called a **dead metaphor:** the *mouth* of a river, the *eye* of a needle, the *face* of a clock. Originally these expressions functioned as figures of speech, but their usage has become so common in our language that many have become **clichés** ("golden opportunity," "dirt cheap," "a clinging vine"). More will be said about clichés below, but our best advice is to avoid them. Because they have lost their freshness, they're unimaginative and they dull your writing.

Another common figure of speech is **personification,** in which human or animal characteristics or qualities are attributed to inanimate things or ideas. We hear it all the time: Trees *bow* in the wind; fear *grips* the heart; high pressure areas *sit* on the northeast. Such language is effective in making abstract concepts concrete and vivid and possibly more interesting:

- Graft and corruption walk hand in hand in this town.
- The state's new tax law threatens to gobble up our savings.
- Nature will give a sigh of relief the day they close down that factory.

As with other figures of speech, personification must be used appropriately and with restraint. If it's overdone, it ends up calling undue attention to itself while leaving readers baffled:

> Drugs have slouched their way into our schoolyards and playgrounds, laughing up their sleeves at the law and whispering vicious lies to innocent children.

For the sake of sounding literary, drugs here are personified as pushers slouching, laughing, and whispering. But such an exaggeration runs the risk of being rejected by readers as pretentious. If this happens, the vital message may well be lost. One must also be careful not to take shortcuts. Like dead metaphors, many once-imaginative personifications have become clichés: "justice is blind," "virtue triumphed," "walking death." While such may be handy catch phrases, they are trite and would probably be dismissed by critical readers as lazy writing.

Another figure of speech worth mentioning is the **euphemism,** which is a polite way of saying something blunt or offensive. Instead of toilets, restaurants have *restrooms.* Instead of a salesperson, furniture stores send us *mattress technicians.* Instead of false teeth, people in advertising wear *dentures.* The problem with euphemisms is that they conceal the true meaning of something. The result can be a kind of doubletalk—language inflated for the sake of deceiving the listener. Business and government are notorious for such practices. When workers are laid off, corporations talk about *restructuring* or *downsizing.* A few years ago the federal government announced *a revenue enhancement* when it really meant that taxes were going up; likewise, the Environmental Protection Agency referred to acid rain as *poorly buffered precipitation;* and when the CIA ordered a *nondiscernible microbinoculator,* it got a poison dart. Not only are such concoctions pretentious, they are dishonest. Fancy-sounding language camouflages hard truths.

Fancy-sounding language also has no place in good writing. When euphemisms are overdone, the result is a lot of verbiage and little meaning. Consider the example below before the euphemisms and pretentious language are reduced:

> **Overdone:** In the event that gaming industry establishments be rendered legal, law enforcement official spokespersons have identified a potential crisis situation as the result of influence exerted by the regional career-offender cartel.

Readers may have to review this a few times before they understand what's being said. Even if they don't give up, a reader's job is not to rewrite your words. Writing with clarity and brevity shows respect for your audience. Here is the same paragraph with its pretentious wordiness and euphemisms edited down:

Revised: Should casino gambling be legalized, police fear organized crime may take over.

Of course, not all euphemisms are double-talk concoctions. Some may be necessary to avoid sounding insensitive or causing pain. To show respect in a sympathy card to bereaved survivors, it might be more appropriate to use the expression *passed away* instead of the blunt *died*. Recently terms such as *handicapped* or *cripple* have given way to less derogatory replacements such as *a person with disabilities*. Likewise we hear *a person with AIDS* instead of "AIDS victim," which reduces the person to a disease or a label.

As with metaphors and personification, some euphemisms have passed into the language and become artifacts, making their usage potentially stale. People over age sixty-five are no longer "old" or "elderly," they're *senior citizens;* slums are *substandard housing;* the poor are *socially disadvantaged.* Although such euphemisms grew out of noble intentions, they tend to abstract reality. A Jules Feiffer cartoon from a few years ago captured the problem well. It showed a man talking to himself:

> I used to think I was poor. Then they told me I wasn't poor, I was needy. They told me it was self-defeating to think of myself as needy, I was deprived. Then they told me underprivileged was overused. I was disadvantaged. I still don't have a dime. But I have a great vocabulary.

Although euphemisms were created to take the bite off reality, they can also take the bite out of your writing if not used appropriately. As Feiffer implies, sometimes it's better to say it like it is; depending on the context, "poor" simply might have more bite than some sanitized cliché. Similarly, some old people resent being called "seniors" not just because the term is an overused label, but because it abstracts the condition of old age. Our advice regarding euphemisms is to know when they are appropriate and to use them sparingly. Good writing simply means knowing when the right expression will get the response you want.

Avoiding Clichés

A cliché (or trite expression) is a phrase that is old and overused to the point of being unoriginal and stale. At one time clichés were fresh and potent; overuse has left them flat. In speech we may resort to clichés for quick meaning. However, clichés can dull your writing and make you seem lazy for choosing a phrase on tap rather than trying to think of more original and colorful wording. Consider these familiar examples:

apple of his eye
bigger than both of us
climbing the walls
dead as a doornail
head over heels
last but not least
mind over matter
ripe old age

short but sweet

white as a ghost

The problem with clichés is that they fail to communicate anything unique. To say you were "climbing the walls," for example, is an expression that could fit a wide variety of contradictory meanings. Out of context, it could mean that you were in a state of high anxiety, anger, frustration, excitement, fear, happiness, or unhappiness. Even in context, the expression is dull. Furthermore, because such clichés are ready-made and instantly handy, they blot out the exact detail you intended to convey to your reader.

Clichés are the refuge of writers who don't make the effort to come up with fresh and original expressions. To avoid them, we recommend being alert for any phrases you have heard many times before and coming up with fresh substitutes. Consider the brief paragraph below, which is full of clichés marked in italics, and its revision:

> **Trite:** *In this day and age* a university ought to be concerned with ensuring that its women students take courses that will strengthen their understanding of their own past achievements and future *hopes and dreams.* At the same time any school *worth its salt* should be *ready and able* to provide *hands-on experience*, activities, and courses that reflect a commitment to diversity and inclusiveness. Education must *seize the opportunity* of leading us *onward and upward* so that we don't slide back to the male-only curriculum emphasis of the *days of old.*

> **Revised:** A university today ought to be concerned with ensuring that its women students take courses that will strengthen their understanding of their own past achievements and future possibilities. At the same time any decent school should provide experience, activities, and courses that reflect a commitment to diversity and inclusiveness. Education must lead us forward so that we don't revert to the male-only curriculum emphasis of the past.

Defining Technical Terms

Special or technical vocabulary that is not clear from the context can function as an instant roadblock to freely flowing communication between you and your readers—sympathetic to your views or not. You cannot expect a novice in political science to know the meaning of *hegemony* or a nonmedical person to know exactly what you mean by *nephrological necrosis.* To avoid alienating nonexpert readers, you'll have to define such uncommon terms.

You can do so without being obtrusive or disrupting the flow of your writing with "time-outs" here and there to define terms. Notice how smoothly definitions have been slipped into the following passages:

> State laws barring euthanasia (the administration of a lethal drug by a doctor) and assisted suicide for patients who are not terminally ill would not be affected. (Marcia Angell, "The Supreme Court and Physician-Assisted Suicide—The Ultimate Right")

> We used to learn in high school biology that "ontogeny recapitulates phylogeny": The development of each individual human being resembles the evo-

lution of the species. Apparently, these days that is regarded as unhelpful, if not inaccurate. (Michael Kingsley, "Reason, Faith and Stem Cells")

To think otherwise is to embrace a belief in genetic determinism—the view that genes determine everything about us, and that environmental factors or the random events in human development are utterly insignificant. (Robert Wachbroit, "Human Cloning Isn't As Scary As It Sounds")

Given what researchers have learned about Dolly, no one thinks the mechanics of cloning are very hard: take a donor egg, suck out the nucleus and hence the DNA, and fuse it with, say, a skin cell from the human being copied. Then, with the help of an electric current, the reconstituted cell should begin growing into a genetic duplicate. (Nancy Ross, "Baby, It's You and You and You . . .")

Clarifying Familiar Terms

Even some familiar terms can lead to misunderstanding because they are used in so many different ways with so many different meanings: *liberal, Native American, lifestyle, decent, active.* It all depends on who is using the word. For instance, to an environmentalist the expression *big business* might connote profit-hungry and sinister industrial conglomerates that pollute the elements; to a conservative, however, the phrase might mean the commercial and industrial establishment that drives our economy. Likewise, a *liberal* does not mean the same thing to a Democrat as it does to a Republican. Even if you're writing for a sympathetic audience, be as precise as you can about familiar terms. Remember the advice of novelist George Eliot: "We have all got to remain calm, and call things by the same names other people call them by."

Stipulating Definitions

For a word that doesn't have a fixed or standard meaning, writers often offer a *stipulative* definition that explains what they mean by the term. For instance, in his essay, "The Stuff of Life" (page 299), Scott Russell Sanders writes, "Medication, pilgrimage, and other forms of religious inquiry are only part of what I mean by *spiritual.*" In his statement he gives us traditional interpretations of the term. However, he immediately adds, "I also mean the nourishment that comes through art, literature, and science, through conversation, through skillful, useful work, through sharing bread and stories, through encounters with beauty and wilderness." With this stipulation, Sanders narrows the definition to the secular level, arguing that we spend more time seeking material rather than *spiritual* growth. Therefore, he justifies his "spiritual" suggestions that "[W]e might play more with our children, look after our elders, plant flowers, read books, make music, come to know the local birds and trees."

Like *spiritual,* the term *patriotism* is an abstraction with many possible definitions and interpretations. Since the terrorist attacks in New York and Washington on September 11, 2001, the term has undergone major consideration. In his essay, "The True Test of Patriotism Is Harder Than Just Waving a Flag" (page 415), Eugene Kane finds it necessary to look beyond mere flag-waving to stipulate a "true test of patriotism." Decrying the threats and unprovoked attacks on people from the Middle East and Muslims following the plane hijackings, Kane argues that one true test of patriotism is "continuing to hold firm to our bedrock ideals, the tolerance of different religions and backgrounds." Such a stipulation is integral to his claim that the strength of American patriotism is measured in the most trying times.

In their somewhat heated dialogue, "Revisionist Feminism" (page 394) Susan Faludi and Karen Lehrman take each other to task with stipulated terms. Faludi accuses Lehrman of yielding to "faux-feminism" (paragraph 6), women's liberation as defined by the advertising industry of the 1970s, that is, "feminism as reinterpreted through television commercials for pantyhose and marketing manuals for Dress for Success bow ties." In reply, Lehrman protests Faludi's practice of "leftist" "feminist theory" which she stipulates as a refusal "to acknowledge that [. . .] equality with men has to mean sameness to men, that until all aspects of traditional femininity are abolished, women will not be free" (paragraph 7).

Stipulating your terms is like making a contract with your reader. You set down in black and white the important terms and their limits. The result is that you eliminate any misunderstanding and reduce your own vulnerability. And, that can make the difference between a weak and potent argument.

Avoiding Overdefinition

Where do you stop explaining and begin assuming your reader knows what you mean? What terms are "technical" or "specialized" or "important" enough to warrant definition? You certainly don't want to define terms unnecessarily or to oversimplify. In so doing, you run the risk of dulling the thrust of your claims while insulting the intelligence of your readers. Just how to strike a balance is a matter of good judgment about the needs and capabilities of your audience.

A good rule of thumb is to assume that your readers are almost as knowledgeable as you. This way, you minimize the risk of patronizing them. Another rule of thumb is the synonym test. If you can think of a word or short phrase that is an exact synonym for some specialized or important term in your argument, you probably don't need to define it. On the other hand, if you need a long phrase or sentence to paraphrase the term, you may want to work in a definition; it could be needed. And don't introduce your definitions with clauses like "As I'm sure you know" or "You don't need to be told that. . . ." If the audience didn't need to know it, you wouldn't be telling them, and if they do know what the terms mean, you may insult their intelligence with such condescending introductions.

Using Sarcasm and Humor Sparingly

Although we caution you against using sarcasm or humor too often, there are times when they can be very effective techniques of persuasion. Writers will often bring out their barbs for the sake of drawing blood from the opposition and snickers from the sympathetic. But artful sarcasm must be done with care. Too strong, and you run the risk of trivializing the issue or alienating your audience with a bad joke. Too vague or esoteric, and nobody will catch the joke. It's probably safest to use these touches when you are writing for a sympathetic audience; they're most likely to appreciate your wit. There is no rule of thumb here. Like any writer, you'll have to decide when to use these techniques and how to artfully work them in.

■ EXERCISES

1. Let's say you were assigned to write a position paper defending the construction of a nuclear power plant in your state. What special appeals would you make were you to address your paper to the governor? to residents living next to the site where the proposed plant is to be built? to prospective construction workers and general contractors? to local environmentalists?

2. Choose one of the following claims, then list in sentence form three reasons supporting the argument. When you've finished, list in sentence form three reasons in opposition to the claim:
   a. Snowboarders are a menace to skiers.
   b. To save lives, a 55-mile per hour speed limit should be enforced nationwide.
   c. Condoms should be advertised on television.
   d. Students with drug convictions should be denied federally subsidized student aid.

3. Let's assume you have made up your mind on gun control. Write a brief letter to the editor of your local newspaper stating your views on the issue. In your letter, fairly and accurately represent arguments of the opposition while pointing out any logical weaknesses, flaws, impracticalities, and other problems you see. What different emphasis would your letter have were it to appear in a gun owner's newsletter? in a pro-gun control newsletter?

4. Write a letter to your parents explaining why you need an extra hundred dollars of spending money this month.

5. Each of the sentences below will take on a different meaning depending on the connotations of the words in brackets. Explain how each choice colors the writer's attitude and the reader's reaction to the statement.
   a. Sally's style of dress is really _____ [weird, exotic, unusual].
   b. If a factory is _____ [polluting, stinking up, fouling] the air over your house, you have a right to sue.
   c. Anyone who thinks that such words have no effect is _____ [unaware, ignorant, unconscious] of political history.
   d. Since September 11, 2001, the anti-immigration passion being stirred up in this country has become _____ [popular, trendy, common].
   e. It was clear from the way she _____ [stomped, marched, stepped] out of the room how she felt about the decision.

6. Identify the figures of speech used in the following sentences from essays in this book. In each example note the two things being compared and explain why you think the comparisons are appropriate or not:
   a. "Having the Old Country two hours away by jet, instead of across an ocean, means these new Americans don't have to slam the door on their place of origin as other immigrants have." (Ray Suarez, "Familiar Strangers")
   b. "Cops like Parks say that racial profiling is a sensible, statistically based tool." (Randall Kennedy, "You Can't Judge a Crook by His Color")
   c. "Karen, I enter into this conversation with you about feminism with some misgivings. Not because I don't want to talk to you. It is just that I suspect it will be like a phone conversation where the connection's so bad neither party can hear the other through the static." (Susan Faludi and Karen Lehrman, "Revisionist Feminism")
   d. "Of all the strange beasts that have come slouching into the 20th century, none has been more misunderstood, more criticized, and more important than materialism." (James Twitchell, "Two Cheers for Consumerism")
   e. "In the waning light the trees along the banks merged into a velvety blackness, and the froth of the creek shone like the Milky Way. Waves rose from the current, fleeting shapes that would eventually dissolve—like my own body, like the mountains, like the earth and stars." (Scott Russell Sanders, "The Stuff of Life")
   f. "My left hand scuttled over the concrete until it found my glasses." (Catharine Stimpson, "The Victim's Dilemma")
   g. "Inextinguishable subterranean fires belch smoke into the neighborhood, as if the ruin were an active volcano, spreading a stench whose source we do not care to think about." (Jonathan Schell, "A Letter from Ground Zero")
   h. "The counsel of realism advises me that my mugger will get off scot-free." (Catharine Stimpson, "The Victim's Dilemma")

7. Rewrite the following paragraph to eliminate the clichés and trite expressions:

It is not that we don't care about what goes on up in space; it's that the vast majority of red-blooded Americans are hard put to see what these untold billions of dollars can do. While great strides have been made in space research, we ask ourselves: Is life any safer? Are material goods all the more abundant? Are we living to a ripe old age because of these vast expenditures? Beyond the shadow of a doubt the answer is a resounding no. Those in Congress with a vested interest need to be brought back to reality, for the nation's pressing problems of crime, homelessness, and unemployment are right here on Mother Earth. Nothing is sacred including the budget for NASA, which should follow the footsteps of other programs and be slashed across the board. Yes, that will be a rude awakening to some who will have to bite the bullet, but there are just so many tax dollars to go around. And in the total scheme of things, wasting it on exploring the depths of outer space is not the way it should be.

CHAPTER 5

Shaping Arguments
Thinking Like an Architect

Just as there is no best way to build a house, there is no best structure for an argument. Some essays take an inductive approach. Such an essay begins with a specific circumstance and then presents reasons and evidence in support of, or in opposition to, that circumstance. Other essays adopt a deductive approach. These essays begin with an idea or philosophical principle, move to a specific circumstance, then conclude with why that circumstance is right and should be maintained, or wrong and should be changed. Some essays express their conclusions in the opening paragraphs. Others build up to them in the last paragraph. As an architect designing a blueprint will tell you, the structure of a building depends on the site, the construction crew, and the prospective owners. Arguments are the same. Depending on your topic, your goals, and your readers, you'll write very different kinds of arguments.

Although no two arguments look alike, every argument has three basic structural parts: a beginning, a middle, and an end. Each part performs certain basic functions. This isn't a simplistic definition. As in architecture, each part of a structure is there for a purpose; leave out one of the parts, and the whole collapses. So let's look at those parts and the jobs they do.

Components of an Argument

What follows is an organizational pattern for argument papers—a pattern to which, with some variations, most of the essays in this book conform. We offer it to help you plan your own argument papers. Although this model contains most of the components of arguments, it is not a formula written in stone. You should not feel bound to follow it every time you construct an argument. In fact, you might find it more effective to move blocks of writing around or to omit material. For instance, on issues unfamiliar to your readers, it might make sense to begin with background information so the context of your discussion will be understood. With familiar issues, it might be more persuasive to open with responses to opposing views. On especially controversial topics you might wish to reserve your responses for the main body of the paper. Or, for dramatic effect, you might decide to save them until the very end, thereby emphasizing your consideration of other perspectives. As a writer, you're free to modify this model any way you like; often you may want to try different models in different drafts of your paper to see which arrangement works best in each case. As with building houses, your choices in building arguments are numerous.

The Beginning

The beginning of your argument accomplishes, in a small space, three important goals.

- It introduces you, the writer. Here your audience meets you—senses your tone, your attitude toward your subject, and the general style of the piece.
- It appeals to your readers' reason, emotions, and/or sense of ethics. This can be done in a simple value statement, an anecdote, or some high-impact statistics intended to raise your readers' interest and concern.
- It identifies the topic and indicates your stand.

Depending on the issue and the audience, the beginning of an argument can be several paragraphs in length. In most arguments the beginning will end with a clear statement of the claim you are making—your thesis.

Although "Once upon a time . . ." is probably the most remembered introduction, it's not always the most effective; more ingenuity on your part is needed to "hook" your readers. For example, in *The Village Voice,* columnist Nat Hentoff began a column calling for eliminating duplication in the U.S. military by saying that he had telephoned the Pentagon press office for a comment on the subject. "Oh," said the officer with whom he spoke, "You want the *other* press office." As Hentoff remarked, he could have ended the column at that point; instead, he went on to develop his idea, confident that this introductory example would make his readers sympathetic to his point.

Composing good beginnings requires hard work. That's why many writers keep a journal in which they copy the strategies of writers they admire; that's how we happened to have a copy of Hentoff's introduction. As novice arguers, you may want to develop your own repertoire of start-up strategies by copying strategies you admire into your own argument journal.

The Middle

The middle portion of your argument is where you do the argumentative work: presenting your information, responding to other views, making your case. If you think of it in terms of building construction, here's where you pour a foundation and lay the framework; put in all the walls, floors, and systems; and have the building inspector examine your work. There are a number of substages.

Provide Background Information

Before you can begin presenting your reasons, you want to be sure that your audience has the information necessary to understand the issue. Background information should answer any of the following questions depending on your topic:

- How significant is the issue? How many people are affected by it? Who are the people most affected?

- What facts, statistics, or information do your readers need to know to follow your reasons?
- What terminology or key words need to be defined so your readers will understand your meaning?
- What factors have caused the problem or situation to develop?
- What will be the consequences if the situation is not corrected?

If handled correctly, this part of your essay can be the most persuasive and convincing because it lets your readers know why you are concerned and the reasons behind that concern. Moreover, it gives your readers the opportunity to share your concern. For example, in "The Supreme Court and Physician-Assisted Suicide—The Ultimate Right" (page 651), Marcia Angell begins her essay with a review of recent and impending court decisions as well as voter initiatives on assisted suicide. She includes statistics that indicate widespread public support for the legalization of this practice. This information is not only informative; it creates a sense of urgency about the U.S. public's concern with the prospect of prolonged and painful terminal illness, and sets the stage for the argument she will develop in her essay.

Respond to Other Points of View

As we discussed in Chapter 4, it is important to let your audience know that you have seriously deliberated other points of view before reaching your own position. By doing this, you appear informed and open-minded. In this part of your essay you should briefly review a number of viewpoints that are different from your own. If you've engaged in debate and dialogue, as we suggested in Chapter 1, you should be aware of opposing views and common concerns. Now is your opportunity to identify them and respond. You might even acknowledge the sincerity of those holding contrary views and cite the merits of their positions. Such acknowledgments help establish your authority as a writer. They will also help you define your own position more specifically for your readers by contrasting it with others. For example, in the essay "A Question of Life or Death," Kenneth Woodward states his awareness of the radically different views of frozen embryonic human cells as held by secularists and the Vatican. Woodward even quotes and paraphrases the editorial page of the secular *New York Times* and the official view of the Roman Catholic Church to provide the reader with a brief account of their opposing stands. In striking such a balance, he gains credibility while clarifying his own position.

Present Reasons in Support of Your Claim

The reasons supporting your claim comprise the heart of your essay and, therefore, its largest portion. Here you explain the reasons behind your claim and present supporting evidence—facts, statistics, data, testimony of authorities, examples—to convince your readers to agree with your position or take a particular course of action. Depending on the issue, this part of your essay usually takes several paragraphs, with each reason clearly delineated for your readers. Most of the essays in this book use this approach; Linda J. Collier's "Adult Crime, Adult Time: Outdated Juvenile Laws Thwart Justice" (page 553) is a good example.

Anticipate Possible Objections to Your Reasons

Even with a friendly audience, readers will have questions and concerns about your reasons. If you ignore these objections and leave them unanswered, you will weaken the effectiveness of your argument. Therefore, it is always wise to anticipate possible objections so you can respond to them in a constructive fashion that will strengthen and clarify your ideas. The kind of objections you anticipate, of course, will depend on your familiarity with your audience—their interests, values, beliefs, experiences, and so on. If you have carefully analyzed your audience, as we suggest in Chapter 4, you will be more aware of the objections likely to surface in response to your reasons. Raising objections and responding to them will once again demonstrate your awareness of alternative viewpoints. It will also give you an opportunity to strengthen your reasons and increase your credibility. One good example of the successful response to objections is T. Marcus Funk's "Young and Arrestless: The Case Against Expunging Juvenile Arrest Records" (page 558).

The End

The end is usually a short paragraph or two in which you conclude your argument. Essentially, your ending summarizes your argument by reaffirming your stand on the issue. It might also make an appeal to your readers to take action. Some writers include an anecdote, a passionate summation, or even a quiet but resonant sentence. Lincoln's "Gettysburg Address," for example, ends with the quiet "government of the people, by the people, and for the people," which is one of the most memorable phrases in American political history. Looking over the essays in this book, you will find that no two end quite alike. As a writer, you have many choices; experimentation is usually the best way to decide what will work for you. Many writers copy effective conclusions into their journals so they can refresh their memories when writing their own arguments.

SAMPLE ARGUMENT FOR ANALYSIS

To illustrate this three-part argument structure, we have included two sample argument essays for you to read. The first is "Indian Bones" by Clara Spotted Elk, a consultant for Native American interests. Although it is quite brief, the essay, originally published in the *New York Times,* contains all the essential components of an argument essay. It is followed by an analysis of its key structural features.

Indian Bones
Clara Spotted Elk

1   Millions of American Indians lived in this country when Columbus first landed on our shores. After the western expansion, only about 250,000 Indians survived. What happened to the remains of those people who were decimated by the advance of the white man? Many are gathering dust in American museums.

REVIEW: THE STRUCTURE OF AN ARGUMENT

The Beginning . . .
>   Introduces you as a writer
>   States the problem
>   Establishes your position and appeal
>   Presents your claim (thesis)

The Middle . . .
>   Provides background information
>   Responds to other points of view
>   Presents arguments supporting the claim
>   Anticipates possible objections

The End . . .
>   Summarizes your position and implications
>   Invites readers to share your conclusion and/or take action

2   In 1985, I and some Northern Cheyenne chiefs visited the attic of the Smithsonian's Natural History Museum in Washington to review the inventory of their Cheyenne collection. After a chance inquiry, a curator pulled out a drawer in one of the scores of cabinets that line the attic. There were the jumbled bones of an Indian. "A Kiowa," he said.

3   Subsequently, we found that 18,500 Indian remains—some consisting of a handful of bones, but mostly full skeletons—are unceremoniously stored in the Smithsonian's nooks and crannies. Other museums, individuals and Federal agencies such as the National Park Service also collect the bones of Indian warriors, women, and children. Some are on display as roadside tourist attractions. It is estimated that another 600,000 Indian remains are secreted away in locations across the country.

4   The museum community and forensic scientists vigorously defend these grisly collections. With few exceptions, they refuse to return remains to the tribes that wish to rebury them, even when grave robbing has been documented. They want to maintain adequate numbers of "specimens" for analysis and say they are dedicated to "the permanent curation of Indian skeletal remains."

     Indian people are tired of being "specimens." The Northern Cheyenne
5   word for ourselves is "tsistsistas"—human beings. Like people the world over, one of our greatest responsibilities is the proper care of the dead.

6   We are outraged that our religious views are not accepted by the scientific community and that the graves of our ancestors are desecrated. Many tribes are willing to accommodate some degree of study for a limited period of time—provided that it would help Indian people or mankind in general. But how many "specimens" are needed? We will not accept grave robbing and the continued hoarding of our ancestors' remains.

7   Would this nefarious collecting be tolerated if it were discovered that it affected other ethnic groups? (Incidentally, the Smithsonian also collects skeletons of blacks.) What would happen if the Smithsonian had 18,500 Holocaust victims in the attic? There would be a tremendous outcry in this country. Why is there no outcry about the Indian collection?

8   Indians are not exotic creatures for study. We are human begins who practice living religions. Our religion should be placed not only on a par with science when it comes to determining the disposition of our ancestors but on a par with every other religion practiced in this country.

9   To that end, Sen. Daniel K. Inouye will soon reintroduce the "Bones Bill" to aid Indians in retrieving the remains of their ancestors from museums. As in the past, the "Bones Bill" will most likely be staunchly resisted by the collectors of Indian skeletons—armed with slick lobbyists, lots of money and cloaked in the mystique of science.

10   Scientists have attempted to defuse this issue by characterizing their opponents as radical Indians, out of touch with the culture and with little appreciation of science. Armed only with a moral obligation to our ancestors, the Indians who support the bill have few resources and little money.

11   But, in my view, the issue should concern all Americans—for it raises very disturbing questions. American Indians want only to reclaim and rebury their dead. Is this too much to ask?

Analyzing the Structure

Now let's examine this essay according to the organizational features discussed so far.

The Beginning

Paragraph 1 clearly introduces the nature of the problem: The remains of the Indians "decimated by the advance of the white man" have wrongfully ended up "gathering dust in American museums." It isn't until paragraph 6 that Spotted Elk spells out her position: "We are outraged that our religious views are not accepted by the scientific community and that the graves of our ancestors are desecrated." (Because this essay was written for newspaper publication, the paragraphs are shorter than they might be in a formal essay; you may not want to delay your thesis until the sixth paragraph in a longer essay.) Notice, too, that in the introduction the author's persona begins to assert itself in the brief and pointed summation of the American Indian's fate. When Spotted Elk mentions the staggering decline in the population of her ancestors, we sense a note of controlled but righteous anger in her voice. Citation of the gruesome facts of history also appeals to the reader's ethical sense by prompting reflection on the Indians' demise.

The Middle

- **Background Information**   Paragraphs 2 and 3 establish the context of the author's complaint. Paragraph 2 is personal testimony to the problem—how she and other Native Americans viewed unceremonious "jumbled bones" in the museum drawer and were stunned by the representative insensitivity of their host curator, who treated the human remains as if they were a fossil. Paragraph 3 projects the problem to progressively larger contexts and magnitudes—from the single Kiowa in a drawer to the 18,500 in the Smithsonian at large; from that institution's collection to the estimated 600,000 remains in other museums, federal agencies and institutions, and "roadside tourist attractions." The broader scope of the problem is underscored here.

- **Response to Other Points of View**   In paragraph 4, Spotted Elk tersely sums up the opposing position of the "museum community and forensic scientists": "[. . .] they refuse to return remains to the tribes." She also states their reasoning: "They want to maintain adequate numbers of 'specimens' for analysis and say they are dedicated to the 'permanent curation of Indian skeletal remains.'"

- **Reasons in Support of the Claim**   Paragraphs 5 through 9 constitute the heart of Spotted Elk's argument. Here she most forcefully argues her objections and offers her reasons with supporting details: Indians resent being treated as specimens and want to bury their dead as do other religious people (paragraphs 5 and 6). She follows that with a concession that many Indians would accommodate some degree of anthropological study for a period of time, but do not approve of the huge permanent collections that now fill museums.

  In paragraph 7 the author continues to support her claim that American Indians have been discriminated against with regard to the disposition of ancestral remains. She writes that there would be a public outcry if the remains of other ethnic groups such as Holocaust victims were hoarded. Her proposal for change appears in paragraph 8: "Our religion should be placed not only on a par with science when it comes to determining the disposition of our ancestors but on a par with every other religion practiced in this country." This is the logical consequence of the problem she has addressed to this point. That proposal logically leads into paragraph 9, where she mentions efforts by Senator Daniel Inouye to see the "Bones Bill" passed into law. Throughout, Spotted Elk uses emotional words and phrases—*grisly, unceremoniously, slick lobbyists, cloaked in mystique*—to reinforce her points.

- **Anticipation of Possible Objections**   In paragraph 10, the author addresses objections of the opposition, in this case those "[s]cientists [who] have attempted to defuse this issue by characterizing their opponents as radical Indians, out of touch with the culture and with little appreciation of science." She refutes all three charges (of being "radical," as well as out of touch with Indian culture and science) with the phrase "[a]rmed only with a moral obligation to our ancestors"—a phrase that reaffirms her strong connection with her culture.

On the contrary, it is science that is out of touch with the "living religion" of Native Americans.

The End

The final paragraph brings closure to the argument. Briefly the author reaffirms her argument that Native Americans "want only to reclaim and rebury their dead." The question that makes up the final line of the essay is more than rhetorical, for it reminds us of the point introduced back in paragraph 5—that American Indians are no different than any other religious people with regard to the disposition of their ancestors. A powerful question brings the essay's conclusion into sharp focus.

As we stated in the beginning of this chapter, there is no best structure for an argument essay. As you develop your own essay, you may find it more effective to move certain structural features to locations that serve your purposes better. For instance, you may find that background information is more persuasive when you include it as support for a particular reason rather than provide it prior to your reasons. Possible objections might be raised along with each reason instead of saved for later. Ron Karpati's essay, "I Am the Enemy," provides a good example of a different approach to structuring an argument essay. Read the essay to see if you can pick out the structural elements he included and how he organized them. Following the essay, we've provided a brief analysis of its organization.

SAMPLE ARGUMENT FOR ANALYSIS

I Am the Enemy

Ron Karpati

Ron Karpati, a pediatrician and medical researcher of childhood illnesses, defends the use of animals in medical research. This article first appeared in *Newsweek*'s "My Turn" column.

1   I am the enemy! One of those vilified, inhumane physician-scientists involved in animal research. How strange, for I have never thought of myself as an evil person. I became a pediatrician because of my love for children and my desire to keep them healthy. During medical school and residency, however, I saw many children die of leukemia, prematurity and traumatic injury—circumstances against which medicine has made tremendous progress, but still has far to go. More important, I also saw children, alive and healthy, thanks to advances in medical science such as infant respirators, potent antibiotics, new surgical techniques and the entire field of organ transplantation. My desire to tip the scales in favor of the healthy, happy children drew me to medical research.

2   My accusers claim that I inflict torture on animals for the sole purpose of career advancement. My experiments supposedly have no relevance to medi-

cine and are easily replaced by computer simulation. Meanwhile, an apathetic public barely watches, convinced that the issue has no significance, and publicity-conscious politicians increasingly give way to the demands of the activists.

3   We in medical research have also been unconscionably apathetic. We have allowed the most extreme animal-rights protesters to seize the initiative and frame the issue as one of "animal fraud." We have been complacent in our belief that a knowledgeable public would sense the importance of animal research to the public health. Perhaps we have been mistaken in not responding to the emotional tone of the argument created by those sad posters of animals by waving equally sad posters of children dying of leukemia or cystic fibrosis.

4   Much is made of the pain inflicted on these animals in the name of medical science. The animal-rights activists contend that this is evidence of our malevolent and sadistic nature. A more reasonable argument, however, can be advanced in our defense. Life is often cruel, both to animals and human beings. Teenagers get thrown from the back of a pickup truck and suffer severe head injuries. Toddlers, barely able to walk, find themselves at the bottom of a swimming pool while a parent checks the mail. Physicians hoping to alleviate the pain and suffering these tragedies cause have but three choices: create an animal model of the injury or disease and use that model to understand the process and test new therapies; experiment on human beings—some experiments will succeed, most will fail—or finally, leave medical knowledge static, hoping that accidental discoveries will lead us to the advances.

5   Some animal-rights activists would suggest a fourth choice, claiming that computer models can simulate animal experiments, thus making the actual experiments unnecessary. Computers can simulate, reasonably well, the effects of well-understood principles on complex systems, as in the application of the laws of physics to airplane and automobile design. However, when the principles themselves are in question, as is the case with the complex biological systems under study, computer modeling alone is of little value.

6   One of the terrifying effects of the effort to restrict the use of animals in medical research is that the impact will not be felt for years and decades: drugs that might have been discovered will not be; surgical techniques that might have been developed will not be, and fundamental biological processes that might have been understood will remain mysteries. There is the danger that politically expedient solutions will be found to placate a vocal minority, while the consequences of these decisions will not be apparent until long after the decisions are made and the decision making forgotten.

7   Fortunately, most of us enjoy good health, and the trauma of watching one's child die has become a rare experience. Yet our good fortune should not make us unappreciative of the health we enjoy or the advances that make it possible. Vaccines, antibiotics, insulin and drugs to treat heart disease, hypertension and stroke are all based on animal research. Most complex surgical procedures, such as coronary-artery bypass and organ transplantation, are initially developed in animals. Presently undergoing animal studies are techniques to insert genes in humans in order to replace the defective ones found to be the cause of so much disease. These studies will effectively end if animal research is severely restricted.

8   In America today, death has become an event isolated from our daily existence—out of the sight and thoughts of most of us. As a doctor who has watched many children die, and their parents grieve, I am particularly angered by people capable of so much compassion for a dog or a cat, but with seemingly so little for a dying human being. These people seem so insulated from the reality of human life and death and what it means.

9   Make no mistake, however: I am not advocating the needlessly cruel treatment of animals. To the extent that the animal-rights movement has made us more aware of the needs of these animals, and made us search harder for suitable alternatives, they have made a significant contribution. But if the more radical members of this movement are successful in limiting further research, their efforts will bring about a tragedy that will cost many lives. The real question is whether an apathetic majority can be aroused to protect its future against a vocal, but misdirected, minority.

Analyzing the Structure

The Beginning

In paragraph 1, Karpati introduces himself to the reader as a scientist and a pediatrician with a personal and professional interest in his topic. While his first sentence proclaims, "I am the enemy," Karpati almost immediately lets his readers know that he is only an enemy to those who oppose his work; he describes himself as a caring doctor who wishes to help children stay healthy. His second sentence informs the reader that his topic will be the use of animals as research subjects; in the next sentences he strongly implies that the advances made in medicine are the results of research using animals. His claim, stated in paragraph 3, is that animal research is important to public health. By using the example of ill or injured children who might benefit from this work, Karpati makes a strong emotional appeal to his readers.

The Middle
Background Information

This information appears in several places in the essay. Paragraph 1 includes a list of advances in medicine that have come about, the reader assumes, through animal research. Later, in paragraph 7, Karpati lists specific drugs and surgical procedures that have resulted from using animals as research subjects. However, Karpati seems more interested in informing readers how he, a scientist who uses animals to conduct his research, is characterized negatively by animal-rights supporters.

Response to Other Points of View

Because Karpati's essay is largely a defense of his position on animal research, he focuses heavily on the views of those who oppose his position. In paragraph 2 he briefly summarizes the accusations made about him by animal-rights supporters. In paragraph 3 he suggests that these objections are voiced by extremists in that movement. Karpati goes on to indicate that he is aware of the reasons why others wish to eliminate animal research. In paragraph 4 he acknowledges that "pain [is] inflicted on these animals in the name of medical science." He agrees with the opposition that "life is often cruel," but suggests through his examples that human suffering is more compelling to physicians than is the suffering of animals. Later, in paragraph 9, Karpati refers back to this point and cites the contribution of the animal-rights movement in making researchers more sensitive to the issue of animal suffering.

Reasons in Support of the Claim
In paragraphs 4 through 8 Karpati presents his reasons to support his claim that medical research using animals should be continued for the benefit of human health. In paragraphs 4 and 5 he explains that the alternatives to animal research—experimenting on human subjects, relying on accidental discoveries, or using computer simulation—are not satisfactory. In paragraph 6 he warns that the impact of restricting animal research will have a far-reaching and negative impact on medical science. In paragraph 7 Karpati points to the results of animal research and its significant contributions to the healthy lives that most of his readers take for granted. Finally, in paragraph 8, he reasserts the importance of human life over the well-being of animals.

Possible Objections to Reasons
Karpati has included many of the objections to his reasons along with the reasons themselves. For instance, in paragraphs 4 and 5 he anticipates that his readers might wonder why humans and computers can't be substituted for animals in research. Karpati responds that experiments on humans will largely fail and computer simulations cannot duplicate complex biological processes.

The End
In the last paragraph Karpati summarizes his main point: The efforts of radical members of the animal-rights movement to limit the use of animals in research "will bring about a tragedy that will cost many lives." He makes a strong appeal to his readers to take action to prevent just that from happening.

Blueprints for Arguments
Our analysis of Karpati's essay gives some idea of its general organization, but it does not reflect fine subdivisions or the way the various parts of the essay are logically connected. That can be done by making an outline. Think of an outline as a blueprint of the argument you're building: It reveals structure and framework but leaves out the materials that cover the frame.

Opinions differ as to the value of making outlines before writing an essay. Some writers need to make formal outlines to organize their thoughts. Others simply scratch down a few key ideas. Still others write essays spontaneously without any preliminary writing. For the beginning writer an outline is a valuable aid because it demonstrates at a glance how the various parts of an essay are connected, whether the organization is logical and complete, whether the evidence is sequenced properly, and whether there are any omissions or lack of proportion. Your outline need not be elaborate. You might simply jot down your key reasons in a hierarchy from strongest to weakest:

Introduction

Reason 1

Reason 2

Reason 3

Reason 4

Conclusion

This blueprint might be useful if you want to capture your readers' attention immediately with your most powerful appeal. Or you might use a reverse hierarchy, beginning with your weakest argument and proceeding to your strongest, in order to achieve a climactic effect for an audience sympathetic to your cause. The outline will help you build your case.

You might prefer, as do some writers, to construct an outline after, rather than before, writing a rough draft. This lets you create a draft without restricting the free flow of ideas and helps you rewrite by determining where you need to fill in, cut out, or reorganize. You may discover where your line of reasoning is not logical; you may also reconsider whether you should arrange your reasons from the most important to the least or vice versa in order to create a more persuasive effect. Ultimately, outlining after the first draft can prove useful in producing subsequent drafts and a polished final effort.

Outlines are also useful when evaluating somebody else's writing. Reducing the argument of the opposition to the bare bones exposes holes in the reasoning process, scanty evidence, and logical fallacies. In writing this book, we used all three processes: We developed an outline to write the first draft and sway a publisher to accept it. Then experienced teachers read the draft and suggested changes to the outline to make it more effective. Finally, one of our collaborators took all the suggestions and her own ideas and created a new outline to help us revise the text. In our case, all three strategies were equally valuable.

The Formal Outline

Some teachers like students to submit *formal outlines* with their papers to show that the students have checked their structure carefully. This kind of outlining has several rules to follow:

- Identify main ideas with capital Roman numerals.
- Identify subsections of main ideas with capital letters, indented one set of spaces from the main ideas.
- Identify support for subsections with Arabic numerals, indented two sets of spaces from the main ideas.
- Identify the parts of the support with lowercase Roman numerals, indented three sets of spaces from the main ideas.
- Identify further subdivisions with lowercase letters and then italic numbers, each indented one set of spaces to the right of the previous subdivision.
- Make sure all items have at least two points; it's considered improper informal outlining to have only one point under any subdivision.

To demonstrate what a formal outline can look like, we have outlined Clara Spotted Elk's essay, "Indian Bones":

I. Hoarding of Indian remains
  A. At Smithsonian
    1. Single Kiowa at Smithsonian
    2. 18,500 others
  B. In other locations

II. Authorities' defense of collections
  A. Refusal to return grave-robbed remains
  B. Maintainence of "specimens"

III. Indians' response
  A. Outrage
    1. Desire to be seen as humans
    2. Desire to have religion accepted by science
    3. Nonacceptance of desecration of graves
    4. Resentment of lack of outcry by public
  B. Accommodation
    1. Limitation in time
    2. Service to Indians and mankind
  C. Demand equality with other religions

IV. "Bones Bill" legislation
  A. Resistance from scientific community
    1. Slick lobbyists
    2. Money
    3. Scientific mystique
    4. Characterization of Indians
      i. Radicals
      ii. Out of touch with culture
      iii. Little appreciation of science
  B. Indian counter-resistance
    1. Few resources
    2. Little money
    3. Moral obligation to ancestors

Keep in mind that an outline should not force your writing to conform to a rigid pattern and, thus, turn your essay into something stilted and uninspired. Follow the model as a map, taking detours when necessary or inspired.

Two Basic Shapes for Arguments

Consider the following claims for arguments:

1. Watching television helps to eliminate some traditional family rituals.
2. Pornography poses a threat to women.

3. *Lord of the Rings: The Fellowship of the Ring* is an imaginative and powerful movie.
4. Bilingual education programs fail to help non–English-speaking children become part of mainstream society.
5. Hate crime legislation is intended to allow certain people to have more protection under the law than others.
6. Cigarette advertising should be banned from billboards everywhere.
7. Medical doctors should not advertise.
8. Americans should be required to vote by law.
9. The production and sale of cigarettes ought to be outlawed.
10. Pass/fail grades have to be eliminated across the board if academic standards are to be maintained.

Looking over these statements, you might notice some patterns. The verbs in the first five are all in the present tense: *helps, poses, is, fail, is intended to.* However, each of the last five statements includes "should" words: *should, should not, ought to be, have to be.* These **obligation verbs** are found in almost all claims proposing solutions to a problem.

What distinguishes the first group from the second is more than the form of the verb. The first five claims are statements of the writer's stand on a controversial issue as it currently exists. The second group are proposals for what *should* be. Essentially, all the arguments in this book—and the ones you'll most likely write and read in your careers—fall into one of these two categories or a combination of each, for often a writer states his or her position on an issue, then follows it with proposals for changes. Later in this chapter we will discuss proposals. For the moment, let's take a look at position arguments.

Position Arguments

A *position argument* scrutinizes one side of a controversial issue. In such an argument the writer not only establishes his or her stand, but also argues vigorously in defense of it. Position arguments are less likely to point to a solution to a problem. Instead, they are philosophical in nature—the kinds of arguments on which political and social principles are founded, laws are written, and business and government policies are established. Position papers also tend to address themselves to the ethical and moral aspects of a controversy. If, for instance, you were opposed to the university's policy of mandatory testing for the AIDS virus, you might write a position paper protesting your school's infringement of individual rights and invasion of privacy.

As indicated by the present tense of the verbs in the first five claims, the position argument deals with the status quo—the way things are, the current state of affairs. Such an argument reminds the audience that something *currently* is good or bad, better or worse, right or wrong. Like all arguments, they tend to be aimed at changing the audience's feelings about an issue—euthanasia, abortion, capital punishment, and so on. That is why many position papers tend to direct their appeals to the reader's sense of ethics rather than to reason.

By contrast, proposal arguments identify a problem and recommend a likely solution. That's why their claims contain verbs that *obligate* the readers to take some action. In this sense they are practical rather than philosophical. For instance, if you were concerned about the spread of AIDS among college students, you might write a paper proposing that condom machines be installed in all dormitories. When you offer a proposal, you're trying to affect the future.

What to Look for in Position Arguments

What follows are some key features of position arguments. As a checklist, they can help you evaluate someone's stand on an issue and help guide you in writing your own position papers.

The writer deals with a controversial issue. The best kind of position paper is one that focuses on a debatable issue, one in which there is clear disagreement: abortion, capital punishment, euthanasia, affirmative action, sex in advertising, freedom of speech, gay rights, homelessness, gun control. These are the issues about which people have many different perspectives.

The writer clearly states a position. Readers should not be confused about where an author stands on an issue. Although the actual issue may be complex, the claim should be stated emphatically and straightforwardly. Don't waffle: "Using the death penalty in some situations and with some rights of appeal probably doesn't do much to lower crime anyway"; far better is an emphatic "Capital punishment is no deterrent to crime." In formulating your claim, be certain that your word choice is not ambiguous. Otherwise the argument will be muddled and, ultimately, unconvincing.

The writer recognizes other positions and potential objections. For every argument there are bound to be a number of other perspectives. Such is the nature of controversy. As a writer representing a position, you cannot assume that your readers are fully aware of or understand all the disagreement surrounding the issue you're arguing. Nor can you make a persuasive case without anticipating challenges. So in your argument you must spell out accurately and fairly the main points of the opposition and objections that might arise. We offer six reasons for doing this:

1. *You reduce your own vulnerability.* You don't want to appear ill informed or naive on an issue. Therefore, it makes sense to acknowledge opposing points of view to show how well you've investigated the topic and how sensitive you are to it. Suppose, for instance, you are writing a paper arguing that "anyone who commits suicide is insane." To avoid criticism, you would have to be prepared to answer objections that fully rational people with terminal illnesses often choose to take their own lives so as to avoid a painful demise and curtail the suffering of loved ones. Even if you strongly disagree with your opposition, recognizing views from the other side demonstrates that you are a person of responsibility and tolerance—two qualities for which most writers of argument strive.

2. *You distinguish your own position.* By citing opposing views, you distinguish your own position from that of others. This not only helps clarify the differences, but also lays out the specific points of the opposition to be refuted or discredited. Some writers do this at the outset of their arguments. Consider, for instance, how Ron Karpati sums up the views of the opposition in the opening paragraphs of his essay "I Am the Enemy."

3. *You can respond to opposing views.* A good response can challenge an opponent's ideas and examine the basis for the disagreement—whether personal, ideological, or moral. For instance, when Michael Kelley, in "Arguing for Infanticide" (page 167), responds to Steven Pinker's "Why They Kill Their Newborns" (page 158), he points out that Pinker's very logical argument for neonaticide ignores the moral and ethical values of our society regarding the relationship between mothers and their children. Kelley does not suggest that Pinker's reasons are incorrect; instead he challenges the basis for Pinker's argument.

4. *You might also challenge an opponent's logic, demonstrating where the reasoning suffers from flaws in logic.* For instance, the argument that Ms. Shazadi must be a wonderful mother because she's a great manager does not logically follow. While some qualities of a good manager might bear on successful motherhood, not all do. In fact, it can be argued that the very qualities that make a good manager—leadership, drive, ruthlessness, determination—might damage a parent-child relationship. This logical fallacy, called a false analogy, erroneously suggests that the two situations are comparable when they are not. An example of this can be found in Jeff Jacoby's "What the Antismoking Zealots Really Crave" (page 88) when he points out that a well-known antismoking activist has compared tobacco companies to mass murderers. While the dangers of cigarette smoking are widely accepted, the comparison between profit-driven corporations and murderous criminals cannot be supported with fact and reasonable evidence.

5. *You might challenge the evidence supporting an argument.* If possible, try to point out unreliable, unrealistic, or irrelevant evidence offered by the opposition; question the truth of counterarguments; or point to distortions. The realtor who boasts oceanside property is vulnerable to challenge if the house in question is actually half a mile from the beach. Look for instances of stacking the deck. For example, a writer might argue that supporting the building of a new sports complex will benefit the community by providing new jobs. However, if she fails to mention that workers at the old sports facility will then lose their jobs, she is misleading the audience about the benefits of this change. Challenge the evidence by looking for hasty generalizations. For example, a business degree from State U. may indeed guarantee a well-paying job after graduation, but the writer will need more than a few personal anecdotes to convince the reader that this is the case.

6. *You can gain strength through concessions.* Admitting weaknesses in your own stand shows that you are realistic, that you don't suffer from an inflated view of the virtues of your position. It also lends credibility to your argument while helping you project yourself as fair-minded. A successful example of this strategy is Ron Karpati's acknowledgment in paragraph 9 of "I Am the Enemy"

(page 113) that the animal-rights movement has sensitized scientists to the needs of animals.

The writer offers a well-reasoned argument to support the position. A position paper must do more than simply state your stand on an issue. It must try to persuade readers to accept your position as credible and convince them to adjust their thinking about the issue. Toward those ends, you should make every effort to demonstrate the best reasons for your beliefs and support the positions you hold. That means presenting honest and logically sound arguments.

Persuaders use three kinds of appeal: to *reason,* to *emotions,* and to readers' sense of *ethics.* You may have heard these described as the appeals of *logos, pathos,* and *ethos.* Although it is difficult to separate the emotional and ethical components from the rational or logical structure of an argument, the persuasive powers of a position argument may mean the proper combination of these three appeals. Not all arguments will cover all three appeals. Some will target logic alone and offer as support statistics and facts. Others centering around moral, religious, or personal values will appeal to a reader's emotions as well as reason. (These arguments are most successful for a readership that need not be convinced by force of reason alone.) Arguments based on emotion aim to reinforce and inspire followers to stand by their convictions. However, relying too heavily on an emotional appeal can result in an ad misericordiam argument, one that attempts to exploit the readers' pity. The most successful arguments are those that use multiple strategies to appeal to readers' hearts and minds.

When the issue centers on right-or-wrong or good-or-bad issues, position arguments make their appeals to the audience's ethical sense. In such papers your strategy has two intentions: one, to convince the reader that you are a person of good-will and moral character and thus enhance your credibility; and, two, to suggest that any decent and moral readers will share your position.

The writer's supporting evidence is convincing. A position paper does not end with an incontrovertible proof such as in a demonstration of a scientific law or mathematical theorem. No amount of logic can prove conclusively that your functional judgment is right or wrong; if that were the case, there would be few arguments. It is also impossible to prove that your aesthetic judgments are superior to another's or that a particular song, movie, or book is better than another. But your arguments have a greater chance of being persuasive if you can present evidence that convinces your readers that your argument is valid.

We'll say more about evidence in Chapter 6, but for now remember that a strong argument needs convincing evidence: facts, figures, personal observations, testimony of outside authorities, and specific examples. In general, the more facts supporting a position, the more reason there is for the reader to accept that position as valid. The same is true when refuting another position. An author needs to supply sound reasons and evidence to disprove or discredit an opponent's stand.

The writer projects a reasonable persona. Whenever we read an argument, we cannot help but be aware of the person behind the words. Whether it's in the choice of expressions, the tenacity of opinion, the kinds of examples, the force of the argument, the nature of the appeal, or the humor or sarcasm, we hear the author's voice and form an impression of the person. That impression, which is projected by the voice and tone of the writing, is the writer's *persona.*

Persona is communicated in a variety of ways: diction or the choice of words (formal, colloquial, slang, jargon, charged terms); the sentence style (long or short, simple or complex); and the kinds of evidence offered (from cool scientific data to inflammatory examples). As in face-to-face debates, a full range of feelings can be projected by the tone of a written argument: anger, irony, jest, sarcasm, seriousness.

Persona is the vital bond linking the writer to the reader. In fact, the success or failure of an argument might be measured by the extent to which the reader accepts the persona in an argument. If you like the voice you hear, then you have already begun to identify with the writer and are more likely to share in the writer's assumptions and opinions. If, however, that persona strikes you as harsh, distant, or arrogant, you might have difficulty subscribing to the author's argument even if it makes sense logically.

A good position argument projects a reasonable persona, one that is sincere and willing to consider opposing points of view. Steer clear of ad hominem arguments, which make personal attacks on those with whom you disagree rather than on their views. Although readers may not be convinced enough to change their stand or behavior, a writer with a reasonable persona can at least capture their respect and consideration. Remember, the success of your argument will largely depend on your audience's willingness to listen.

A word of warning. Not every persona has to be reasonable or pleasant, although for a beginner this works best. If an arrogant persona is fortified by wit and intelligence, readers may find it stimulating, even charming. A persona—whether outrageous, humorous, biting, or sarcastic—can be successful if it is executed with style and assurance. Some of the best arguments in Part Two of this book have biting edges.

CHECKLIST FOR WRITING A POSITION ARGUMENT

Have you:
- Chosen a controversial issue?
- Clearly stated a position?
- Recognized other positions and possible objections?
- Developed a well-reasoned argument?
- Provided convincing supporting evidence?
- Projected a reasonable persona?

When you read an argument with a memorable persona, jot down in your argument journal the details of how the writer created it; that way, you can turn back to this information when you're trying to create personas for the arguments you write.

SAMPLE ARGUMENT FOR ANALYSIS

What follows is an example of a position argument written by Robert Wachbroit on the issue of cloning. Ever since scientists in Scotland cloned an adult sheep by using the DNA in her cells to produce an identical replica, the world has been both fascinated and horrified by the prospect of genetic cloning. While many see the advantages of cloning livestock and plants, the possibility of cloning human beings is strongly debated. Wachbroit is a research scholar at the Institute for Philosophy and Public Policy at the University of Maryland. This essay first appeared in the *Washington Post*. As you read, consider how Wachbroit incorporates the six key points of position arguments into his essay.

Should We Cut This Out? Human Cloning Is Not as Scary as It Sounds

Robert Wachbroit

1   The recent news of the successful cloning of an adult sheep—in which the sheep's DNA was inserted into an unfertilized sheep egg to produce a lamb with identical DNA—has generated an outpouring of ethical concerns. These concerns are not about Dolly, the now famous sheep, nor even about the considerable impact cloning may have on the animal breeding industry, but rather about the possibility of cloning humans. For the most part, however, the ethical concerns being raised are exaggerated and misplaced, because they are based on erroneous views about what genes are and what they can do. The danger, therefore, lies not in the power of the technology, but in the misunderstanding of its significance.

2   Producing a clone of a human being would not amount to creating a "carbon copy"—an automaton of the sort familiar from science fiction. It would be more like producing a delayed identical twin. And just as identical twins are two separate people—biologically, psychologically, morally and legally, though not genetically—so a clone is a separate person from his or her non-contemporaneous twin. To think otherwise is to embrace a belief in genetic determinism—the view that genes determine everything about us, and that environmental factors or the random events in human development are utterly insignificant. The overwhelming consensus among geneticists is that genetic determinism is false.

3   As geneticists have come to understand the ways in which genes operate, they have also become aware of the myriad ways in which the environment affects their "expression." The genetic contribution to the simplest physical traits, such as height and hair color, is significantly mediated by environmental factors. And the genetic contribution to the traits we value most deeply, from intelligence to compassion, is conceded by even the most enthusiastic genetic

researchers to be limited and indirect. Indeed, we need only appeal to our ordinary experience with identical twins—that they are different people despite
their similarities—to appreciate that genetic determinism is false.

4   Furthermore, because of the extra steps involved, cloning will probably always be riskier—that is, less likely to result in a live birth—than in vitro fertilization (IVF) and embryo transfer. (It took more than 275 attempts before the researchers were able to obtain a successful sheep clone. While cloning methods
may improve, we should note that even standard IVF techniques typically have
a success rate of less than 20 percent.) So why would anyone go to the trouble
of cloning?

5   There are, of course, a few reasons people might go to the trouble, and so
it's worth pondering what they think they might accomplish, and what sort of
ethical quandaries they might engender. Consider the hypothetical example of
the couple who wants to replace a child who has died. The couple doesn't seek
to have another child the ordinary way because they feel that cloning would enable them to reproduce, as it were, the lost child. But the unavoidable truth is
that they would be producing an entirely different person, a delayed identical
twin of that child. Once they understood that, it is unlikely they would persist.

6   But suppose they were to persist? Of course we can't deny that possibility.
But a couple so persistent in refusing to acknowledge the genetic facts is not
likely to be daunted by ethical considerations or legal restrictions either. If our
fear is that there could be many couples with that sort of psychology, then we
have a great deal more than cloning to worry about.

7   Another disturbing possibility is the person who wants a clone in order to
have acceptable "spare parts" in case he or she needs an organ transplant later
in life. But regardless of the reason that someone has a clone produced, the result would nevertheless be a human being with all the rights and protections
that accompany that status. It truly would be a disaster if the results of human
cloning were seen as less than fully human. But there is certainly no moral justification for and little social danger of that happening; after all, we do not accord lesser status to children who have been created through IVF or embryo
transfer.

8   There are other possibilities we could spin out. Suppose a couple wants a
"designer child"—a clone of Cindy Crawford or Elizabeth Taylor—because they
want a daughter who will grow up to be as attractive as those women. Indeed,
suppose someone wants a clone, never mind of whom, simply to enjoy the noto-
riety of having one. We cannot rule out such cases as impossible. Some people
produce children for all sorts of frivolous or contemptible reasons. But we must
remember that cloning is not as easy as going to a video store or as engaging as
the traditional way of making babies. Given the physical and emotional burdens
that cloning would involve, it is likely that such cases would be exceedingly rare.

9   But if that is so, why object to a ban on human cloning? What is wrong with
placing a legal barrier in the path of those with desires perverse enough or
delusions recalcitrant enough to seek cloning despite its limited potential and
formidable costs? For one thing, these are just the people that a legal ban would

be least likely to deter. But more important, a legal barrier might well make cloning appear more promising than it is to a much larger group of people.

10   If there were significant interest in applying this technology to human beings, it would indicate a failure to educate people that genetic determinism is profoundly mistaken. Under those circumstances as well, however, a ban on human cloning would not only be ineffective but also most likely counterproductive. Ineffective because, as others have pointed out, the technology does not seem to require sophisticated and highly visible laboratory facilities; cloning could easily go underground. Counterproductive because a ban might encourage people to believe that there is a scientific basis for some of the popular fears associated with human cloning—that there is something to genetic determinism after all.

11   There is a consensus among both geneticists and those writing on ethical, legal and social aspects of genetic research, that genetic determinism is not only false, but pernicious; it invokes memories of pseudo-scientific racist and eugenic programs premised on the belief that what we value in people is entirely dependent on their genetic endowment or the color of their skin. Though most members of our society now eschew racial determinism, our culture still assumes that genes contain a person's destiny. It would be unfortunate if, by treating cloning as a terribly dangerous technology, we encouraged this cultural myth, even as we intrude on the broad freedom our society grants people regarding reproduction.

12   We should remember that most of us believe people should be allowed to decide with whom to reproduce, when to reproduce and how many children they should have. We do not criticize a woman who takes a fertility drug so that she can influence when she has children—or even how many. Why, then, would we object if a woman decides to give birth to a child who is, in effect, a non-contemporaneous identical twin of someone else?

13   By arguing against a ban, I am not claiming that there are no serious ethical concerns to the manipulation of human genes. Indeed there are. For example, if it turned out that certain desirable traits regarding intellectual abilities or character could be realized through the manipulation of human genes, which of these enhancements, if any, should be available? But such questions are about genetic engineering, which is a different issue than cloning. Cloning is a crude method of trait selection: It simply takes a pre-existing, unengineered genetic combination of traits and replicates it.

14   I do not wish to dismiss the ethical concerns people have raised regarding the broad range of assisted reproductive technologies. But we should acknowledge that those concerns will not be resolved by any determination we make regarding the specific acceptability of cloning.

Analysis of a Position Argument

The writer deals with a controversial issue. Ever since scientists announced they had cloned a sheep, the benefits and dangers of human cloning have been strongly debated by the general public, as well as by religious groups and scientists.

The writer clearly states a position. In paragraph 1 Wachbroit explains his position that ethical concerns about cloning "are exaggerated and misplaced" because people misunderstand "what genes are and what they can do. The danger, therefore, lies not in the power of the technology, but in the misunderstanding of its significance."

The writer recognizes other positions and possible objections. Throughout his essay, Wachbroit considers other positions and responds to possible objections to his ideas. In paragraph 2 he discusses the theory of genetic determinism, whose proponents share "the view that genes determine everything about us." In paragraphs 7 and 8 Wachbroit presents and responds to concerns about the abuses that may result from an acceptance of cloning, from harvesting organs for "spare parts" to creating "designer children." In paragraph 9 he raises a major objection to his position—"Why object to a ban on human cloning?"—and answers his question in the paragraphs that follow. By acknowledging and discussing a number of perspectives, Wachbroit demonstrates he has seriously considered all sides. The reader has the impression that his position and reasons take into account these other concerns.

The writer offers well-developed reasons to support the position. Each of Wachbroit's reasons addresses the central idea found in his claim: People fear cloning because they do not understand the limited power of genes to determine significant human qualities. As a result of this misunderstanding, cloning is seen as a potentially dangerous practice that should be banned. In particular, Wachbroit believes that once the myth of genetic determinism is revealed as unfounded, people will realize that cloning does not pose a threat to their ethical concerns.

Wachbroit presents his first reason in paragraph 2 when he confronts the popular belief in genetic determinism—"the view that genes determine everything about us"—advanced by those critical of cloning. He explains that producing a clone would be much "like producing a delayed identical twin" and not a science fiction "automaton." Because we all know that identical twins are distinct individuals, Wachbroit reasons that a clone would be "biologically, psychologically, morally and legally, though not genetically [. . .] a separate person from his or her non-contemporaneous twin." In paragraph 3 Wachbroit works to disprove the theory of genetic determinism based on the scientific evidence that genes only control a limited number of human characteristics, such as hair color and height. According to Wachbroit, those human qualities "that we value most deeply, from intelligence to compassion," are only indirectly influenced by our genetic structure. Thus, Wachbroit insists, a clone could not be a "carbon copy" of another person because those essential qualities cannot be duplicated in humans, even with identical genes.

In paragraphs 5 through 8 Wachbroit directly addresses the "ethical quandaries" (paragraph 5) that might develop if cloning is used inappropriately. To those concerned that a clone will be created for "spare parts" for organ transplants, Wachbroit asserts that regardless of the reasons for creating a clone, "the result would nevertheless be a human being with all the rights and protections that accompany that status" (paragraph 7). In other words, an individual created through cloning would be protected from such bodily harm. Moreover, since "we do not accord lesser status to children who have been created through IVF or embryo transfer," Wachbroit argues that there is "no moral justification for and little social danger of that happening." In the case of couples who desire a "designer child" resembling a particular celebrity, Wachbroit suggests in paragraph 8 that the "physical and emotional burdens" that accompany the cloning process would deter those with such "frivolous" reasons for wanting a child. Therefore, according to Wachbroit, a legal ban is unnecessary.

Wachbroit further argues in paragraph 9 that such a ban would not deter the very people it is intended to stop: "those with desires perverse enough or delusions recalcitrant enough to seek cloning despite its limited potential and formidable costs." Moreover, Wachbroit warns in paragraph 10, a legal ban on cloning would drive it "underground," which would give the government even less control over it and allow greater opportunity for abuse. Referring back to his first reason, Wachbroit points out that a ban on cloning "might encourage people to believe that there is a scientific basis for some of the popular fears associated with cloning—that there is something to genetic determinism after all."

Finally, in paragraph 12 Wachbroit reminds his audience members of their shared belief in human reproductive freedom: "most of us believe people should be allowed to decide with whom to reproduce, when to reproduce and how many children they should have." If we support this freedom, Wachbroit argues, then we cannot deny people the right to clone themselves.

Although Wachbroit provides several strong reasons to support his position, some of his reasons and examples have their weaknesses. For instance, in paragraph 5 he concludes that the hypothetical couple who wish to replace a deceased child will abandon their efforts once they understand they cannot "reproduce" an actual replica of the lost child. However, this might not deter them; perhaps they would in fact be willing to settle for outer resemblance alone. Similarly, Wachbroit's assumption in paragraph 8, that the difficulties of cloning will deter people from employing it as a method of reproduction, may also be unconvincing. Many couples go through considerable difficulties to conceive children; Wachbroit does not demonstrate how cloning could be more difficult. Finally, Wachbroit's assumption in paragraph 12 that his audience agrees with his statements about reproductive freedom may rest on shaky ground. Contrary to his example, women have been criticized for taking fertility drugs and, as recent legal and criminal cases have demonstrated, society does have an interest in women's reproductive choices.

The writer's supporting evidence is convincing. Wachbroit supports his reasons with references to scientific research that indicates he is knowledgeable about cloning. These appear in paragraph 3 in his explanation of the way genes work; in paragraphs 4 and 7 in his discussion of in vitro fertilization and embryo transfer; and in his reference to geneticists in paragraph 11.

In addition, Wachbroit's hypothetical examples are familiar to most readers: the couple who might wish to replace a child who has died (paragraph 5), the individual who wishes to create "spare parts" in case of a need for organ transplant (paragraph 7), and the people who want to have a celebrity look alike child (paragraph 8). By focusing on examples that illustrate common concerns, Wachbroit's responses are targeted and convincing.

The writer projects a reasonable persona. The persona Wachbroit projects is that of a concerned and thoughtful scholar. He seriously considers the perspectives of others and treats their views respectfully even as he disagrees. For example, in paragraph 14 he states that he does not "wish to dismiss the ethical concerns people have raised" about cloning. Moreover, Wachbroit is careful to avoid appearing inflexible in his position. Even at the end of his essay, in paragraph 13, he acknowledges that people have raised "serious ethical concerns" about this new technology.

Proposal Arguments

Position arguments examine existing conditions. *Proposal arguments,* however, look to the future. They make recommendations for changes in the status quo—namely, changes in a policy, practice, or attitude. Essentially, what every proposal writer says is this: "Here is the problem, and this is what I think should be done about it." The hoped-for result is a new course of action or way of thinking.

Proposals are the most common kind of argument. We hear them all the time: "There ought to be a law against that"; "The government should do something about these conditions." We're always making proposals of some kind: "Van should work out more"; "You ought to see that movie"; "We should recycle more of our trash." As pointed out earlier in this chapter, because proposals are aimed at correcting problems, they almost always make their claims in obligation verbs such as *ought to, needs to be,* and *must.*

Sometimes proposal arguments take up local problems and make practical recommendations for immediate solutions. For instance, to reduce the long lines at the photocopy machines in your campus library, you might propose that the school invest in more copiers and station them throughout the building. Proposal arguments also seek to correct or improve conditions with more far-reaching consequences. If, for example, too many of your classmates smoke, you might write a proposal to your school's administration to remove all cigarette machines from campus buildings or to limit smoking areas on campus.

Still other proposals address perennial social issues in an effort to change public behavior and government policy. A group of physicians might recommend that marijuana be legalized for medical use. An organization of concerned parents might ask the federal government to ban toys that contain toxic or flammable materials. Everyone has ideas about things that should be changed; proposals are the means we use to make those changes happen.

What to Look for in Proposal Arguments

Proposals have two basic functions: (1) They inform readers that there is a problem; and (2) they make recommendations about how to correct those problems. To help you sharpen your own critical ability to build and analyze proposal arguments, we offer some guidelines.

The writer states the problem clearly. Because a proposal argument seeks to change the reader's mind and/or behavior, you first must demonstrate that a problem exists. You do this for several reasons. Your audience may not be aware that the problem exists or they may have forgotten it or think that it has already been solved. Sympathetic audiences may need to be reinspired to take action. It is crucial, therefore, that proposals clearly define the problem and the undesirable or dangerous consequences if matters are not corrected.

For both uninformed and sympathetic audiences, writers often try to demonstrate how the problem personally affects the reader. An argument for greater measures against shoplifting can be more convincing when you illustrate how petty thefts inevitably lead to higher prices. A paper proposing the elimination of pesticides might interest the everyday gardener by demonstrating how much carcinogenic chemicals can contaminate local drinking water. To make the problem even more convincing, the claim should be supported by solid evidence—statistics, historical data, examples, testimony of witnesses and experts, maybe even personal experience.

The writer clearly proposes how to solve the problem. After defining the problem clearly, you need to tell your readers how to solve it. This is the heart of the proposal, the writer's plan of action. Besides a detailed explanation of what should be done and how, the proposal should supply reliable supporting evidence for the plan: testimony of others, ideas from authorities, statistics from studies.

The writer argues convincingly that this proposal will solve the problem. Perhaps the first question readers ask is "How will this solution solve the problem?" Writers usually address this question by identifying the forces behind the problem and demonstrating how their plan will counter those forces. Suppose, for instance, you propose putting condom machines in all college dorms as a means of combating the spread of AIDS. To build a convincing case, you would have to summon evidence documenting how condoms significantly reduce the spread of AIDS. To make the connection between the problem and your solution even stronger, you might go on to explain how readily available machines leave students little excuse for unsafe sex. Students cannot complain that they jeopardized their health because they couldn't make it to a drugstore.

The writer convincingly explains how the solution will work. Generally readers next ask how the plan will be put into action. Writers usually answer by detailing how their plan will work. They emphasize their plan's advantages and how efficiently (or cheaply, safely, conveniently) it can be carried out. For the condom machine proposal, that might mean explaining how and where the machines will be installed and how students can be encouraged to use them. You might cite advantages of your proposal, such as the easy installation of the machines and the low price of the contents.

The writer anticipates objections to the proposed solution. Writers expect disagreement and objections to proposal arguments: Proposals are aimed at changing the status quo, and many people are opposed to or are fearful of change. If you want to persuade readers, especially hostile ones, you must show that you respect their sides of the argument too. Most proposal writers anticipate audience response to fortify their case and establish credibility. (See Chapter 4 for more discussion of audience response.)

The writer explains why this solution is better than the alternatives. Although you may believe that your solution to the problem is best, you cannot expect readers automatically to share that sentiment. Nor can you expect readers not to wonder about other solutions. Good proposal writers investigate other solutions that have been tried to solve this problem so they can weigh alternative possibilities and attempt to demonstrate the superiority of their plan and the disadvantages of others. If you are knowledgeable about ways the problem has been dealt with in the past, you might be able to show how your plan combines the best features of other, less successful solutions. For instance, in the condom machine proposal you might explain to your readers that universities have attempted to make students more aware that unsafe sex promotes the spread of AIDS; however, without the easy availability of condom machines, students are more likely to continue to engage in unsafe sex. The promotion of AIDS awareness and the presence of condom machines might significantly reduce that problem.

The writer projects a reasonable persona. As in position arguments, your persona is an important factor in proposals, for it conveys your attitude toward the subject and the audience. Because a proposal is intended to win readers to your side, the best strategy is to project a persona that is fair-minded. Even if you dislike or are angry about somebody else's views on an issue, projecting a reasonable and knowledgeable tone will have a more persuasive effect than a tone of belligerence.

If you are arguing for condom machines in dormitories, you would be wise to recognize that some people might object to the proposal because availability might be interpreted as encouragement of sexual behavior. So as not to offend or antagonize such readers, adopting a serious, straightforward tone might be the best mode of presenting the case.

CHECKLIST FOR WRITING A PROPOSAL ARGUMENT

Have you:
- Clearly stated the problem?
- Clearly proposed a solution?
- Explained why the solution will work?
- Demonstrated how the solution will work?
- Addressed possible objections?
- Shown why the solution is better than alternatives?
- Projected a reasonable persona?

SAMPLE ARGUMENT FOR ANALYSIS

The following argument was written by Martha Balash, a first-year English composition student, whose assignment was to write a proposal argument. Read through Balash's essay and respond to the questions that follow. Note that Martha used research to support her ideas and documentation to acknowledge her sources. The style of documentation in this paper is MLA, which we discuss in detail in the Documentation Guide.

Schools Can Help to Prevent Teen Pregnancy
Martha Balash

1   The problem of teen pregnancy is one that has plagued our society for many years and continues to grow. According to research conducted by The National Campaign to Prevent Teen Pregnancy, over one million teenage girls in the United States between ages fourteen to nineteen will become pregnant this year. These numbers are astounding: it is estimated that every twenty-six seconds a teen becomes pregnant (Campaign).

2   Although teen pregnancy has been a problem for some time, no workable solution has had a major impact on reducing these overwhelming statistics. In the meantime, teenagers who become pregnant and have children are placing themselves at a higher risk for dropping out of high school and living in poverty and on public assistance (Rolling and Burnett 142). This is a problem that affects us all, not just the individual teen mother and her family. The Center for Population Options reports that "53 percent of outlays for Aid to Families with Dependent Children (AFDC), food stamps, and Medicaid are attributable to households begun by teen births" (Sylvester). As a mother of two soon-to-be teenagers and a taxpayer, I am concerned that we find effective strategies for dealing with this situation.

3   The causes of teen pregnancy are numerous, but I feel that a major cause is a lack of education, not only for teens, but also for adults and parents as well. Teens are misinformed about many aspects of sex. They are not taught the importance of abstaining from sex nor, at the very least, the proper use of effective birth control and protection from sexually transmitted diseases. What makes this problem even worse is that often the adults who interact with teenagers are no better informed than the teens. They avoid discussing sexual issues with teens because they don't know what to advise or because they are uncomfortable with the subject. These adults need to be educated about correct information about sexual matters and about the importance of their role in their children's education. I think that the public schools could develop programs and services to help make this happen.

4   At present, the educational programs on sex in our schools are limited. Often the first time the subject is introduced formally is in a Family Living class

during the last semester of fifth grade. In our school district a county health nurse came weekly for one hour to instruct the class over an eight-week period. Prior to the class, parents were invited to attend a meeting to hear about the program and to ask questions and voice concerns. This was a good start. However, after that initial meeting, parents were given no role to play. While students were encouraged to discuss the class at home with their parents, this kind of interaction could have been promoted more by having students complete homework assignments and projects which required parental participation. Detailed information about class topics could have been sent home to give parents and children an opportunity to communicate and become more aware of each others' ideas and attitudes about this important subject. By fostering open communication at this early age, the school could have helped to develop behaviors and habits that might continue into the teen years.

5   There are other ways that the schools can foster educational opportunities for parents and children. School districts need to have educators on their staffs who can be available for parents who seek information and guidance. Many parents don't know what is "normal" sexual behavior for children of a particular age. They may rely heavily on their memories of their own experiences when they were that age, and these may or may not be accurate or reliable. These educators could conduct regular workshops and parent discussion groups as well as be available for individual meetings with concerned parents.

6   There will be people who object to any interference from the schools regarding sex education. They feel strongly that children should learn about sex exclusively from their parents. I agree that this would be the ideal situation; sex education must be more than just learning about the mechanics of sex. Important values and attitudes about love and relationships must be transmitted as well. However, the depressing statistics about teen pregnancy seem to indicate that some parents have not been successful at educating their children about this area of life. While schools certainly can't do the whole job, they can provide an opportunity for parents and children to begin a discussion about sex and life that can continue beyond the classroom.

7   There have been successful programs instituted throughout communities in the United States which have involved state education funding. One such program, Young Adults for Positive Achievement, was initiated in approximately fifty schools in California and resulted in a significant drop in the teen pregnancy rate in those areas. This program consisted of pregnancy education and prevention for teens (Vaz 50). My plan builds on their idea of using education to prevent teen pregnancy. By including parents and educators, my proposal attacks the problem from two fronts rather than just one.

8   It is essential for parents to remain involved in their children's lives throughout childhood and adolescence. Children need to know what their parents expect of them and how their parents feel about sex and dating. The schools need to take an active role in making this happen by providing educational programs and services to promote communication and understanding between parents and children.

WORKS CITED

Campaign For Our Children. *The National Teen Pregnancy Clock.* 21 Apr. 1998 <http://www.cfoc.org/clock.html>.

The National Campaign to Prevent Teen Pregnancy. *Facts and Stats.* 14 Oct. 1998 <http://www.teenpregnancy.org>.

Rolling, Peggy C., and Michael F. Burnett. "The Influence of Open-Mindedness and Knowledge on Attitudes Toward Teen Pregnancy Among Family and Consumer Services Teachers." *Family and Consumer Services Research Journal* 26.2 (1997): 141–59.

Sylvester, Kathleen. "Preventable Calamity: How to Reduce Teenage Pregnancy." *USA Today* March 1997: 32[†]. Lexis-Nexis. 20 October 1998. <http://web.lexis-nexis.com/universe>.

Vaz, Valerie. "Programs That Work: Young Adults for Positive Achievement." *Essence* Oct. 1995: 50.

■ QUESTIONS FOR ANALYSIS AND DISCUSSION

Briefly summarize the main points of Martha Balash's essay. Then answer the following questions about the essay to see how it fulfills our guidelines for a proposal argument:

1. Where does Balash identify the problem? Explain how she demonstrates that the problem is significant. Does she explain how the problem might affect the reader? Where does she do this?
2. What does Balash propose to solve the problem? In what paragraph do you find the solution stated?
3. According to Balash's essay, how will her solution help to solve the problem? Where does she demonstrate this?
4. Does Balash explain how her solution will work? Where does she do this? Does she provide enough detail for you to understand how it will work?
5. Has Balash anticipated objections to her solution? in which paragraphs? Find an example of this. How does she respond to the objection? How does she acknowledge her audience's concerns?
6. Does Balash seem aware of other programs that have been tried to solve the problem? Where does she refer to them in her essay?
7. What attitude about her subject does Balash convey to her readers? Does she seem reasonable and balanced? If so, find some examples of how she conveys this.

■ EXERCISES

1. Look in several current issues of a local or national newspaper to find examples of essays written by columnists about controversial issues. You might find these in your college library or online through the Internet. Make a list in your journal of the strategies different writers use to begin their essays. Bring your examples to class and work in a group to share your findings. You may want to photocopy your examples so that each group member has a "catalogue" of good introductions to consider.

2. Repeat exercise 1, but this time collect examples of conclusions from argument essays. Your goal here is to compile a catalogue of endings to consult for examples.

3. Construct a formal outline for one of the essays other than "Indian Bones" in this chapter. Compare it with another student's. If there are places where your outlines differ, analyze how your readings are different.

4. Go back to the examples you found for exercise 1. Divide the essays you and the members of your group found into position and proposal arguments.

5. In your journal, respond to the ideas in Ron Karpati's or Robert Wachbroit's essay. With which of their reasons do you agree? How would you refute any of their reasons? Make a pro/con checklist that lists their reasons and points you might use to debate them.

6. Through the Internet or your library resources, do some reading on either Karpati's or Wachbroit's subject to find out how others view the issue. Create a dialogue among the various positions on the issue and explore their points of view to find common or shared concerns or values. With this knowledge, deliberate about how you stand on the issue.

7. If you were to write an argument essay of your own on either subject, how would you begin your essay? Experiment with a few introductions.

8. Write a first draft of your own essay on either topic.

CHAPTER 6

Using Evidence
Thinking Like an Advocate

◆

Because this is a democracy, there's a widespread conviction in our society that having opinions is our responsibility as citizens—a conviction supported by our fast-forward multimedia culture. You see it on the nightly news every time a reporter sticks a microphone in the face of somebody on the street, or whenever Oprah Winfrey or Montel Williams moves into the studio audience. It's the heart of talk radio and television programs. In newspapers and magazines it comes in the form of "opinion polls" that tally up our positions on all sorts of weighty issues:

"Should condoms be distributed in high schools?"
"Is the economy this year in better shape than it was last year at this time?"
"Do you think the American judicial system is just?"
"Can the government do more to prevent domestic terrorism?"
"Is capital punishment a deterrent to crime?"
"Is the president doing a good job fighting terrorism?"

All this on-the-spot opinion making encourages people to take an immediate stand on an issue, whether or not they have sufficient understanding and information about it. However, holding an opinion on a matter does not necessarily mean you have investigated the issue, or that you've carefully considered the views of others or that you've gathered enough information to support your position. If you want to make successful arguments, you need more than a gut reaction or simple reliance on yourself for the "truth."

This means thinking of yourself as an *advocate*—a prosecutor or defense attorney, if you like. You need a case to present to the jury of your readers, one that convinces them that your interpretation is plausible. Like an advocate, when you're constructing an argument, you look for support to put before your readers: facts, statistics, people's experiences—in a word, *evidence*. The jury judges your argument both on the evidence you bring forth and on the interpretation of that evidence that you present. So, like an advocate, to write successful arguments, you need to be able to understand and weigh the value of the *supporting evidence* for your case.

How Much Evidence Is Enough?

Like any advocate, you need to decide *how much* evidence to present to your readers. Your decision will vary from case to case, although with more practice you'll find it easier to judge. Common sense is a good predictor: If the evidence is enough to persuade you, it's probably enough to persuade like-minded readers. Unsympathetic readers may need more proof. The more unexpected or unorthodox your claim, the more evidence you need to convince skeptical readers. It's often as much a case of the *right* evidence as it is the *right amount* of evidence. One fact or statistic, if it touches on your readers' most valued standards and principles, may be enough to swing an argument for a particular group. Here's where outlining (Chapter 5) can help; an outline helps you make sure you present evidence for every assertion you make.

It's easier to gather too much evidence and winnow out the least effective than to have too little and try to expand it. One of our teachers used to call this the "Cecil B. DeMille strategy," after the great Hollywood producer. DeMille's theory was that if audiences were impressed by five dancers, they'd really be overwhelmed by five hundred—but just to be sure, he'd hire a thousand. That's a good strategy to have when writing arguments; you can always use a sentence such as "Of the 116 explosions in GMC trucks with side-mounted fuel tanks, four cases are most frequently cited" and then go on to discuss those four. You've let your readers know that another 112 are on record so they can weigh this fact when considering the four you examine in particular. You may never need a thousand pieces of evidence—or dancers—in an argument, but there's no harm in thinking big!

Why Arguments Need Supporting Evidence

Evidence is composed of facts and their interpretations. As we said in Chapter 1, facts are pieces of information that can be verified—that is, statistics, examples, testimony, historical details. For instance, it is a fact that SAT verbal scores across the nation have gone up for the last six years. One interpretation might be that students today are spending more time reading and less time watching television than students in the last decade. Another interpretation might be that secondary schools are putting more emphasis on language skills. A third might be that changes in the test or the prevalence of test-preparation courses has contributed to the higher scores.

In everyday conversation we make claims without offering supporting evidence: "Poverty is the reason why there is so much crime"; The president is doing a poor job handling the economy"; "Foreign cars are better than American cars." Although we may have good reasons to back up such statements, we're not often called upon to do so, at least not in casual conversation. In written arguments, however, presenting evidence is critical, and a failure to do so is glaring. Without supporting data and examples, an argument is hollow. It will bore the reader, fail to convince, and collapse under criticism. Moreover, you'll be in danger of making a hasty generalization by drawing a conclusion with too little evidence, as the following paragraph illustrates.

> Video games are a danger to the mental well-being of children. Some children play video games for hours on end, and the result is that their behavior and concentration are greatly affected. Many of them display bad behavior. Others have difficulty doing other, more important things. Parents with young children should be more strict about what video games their children play and how long they play them.

Chances are this paragraph has not convinced you that video games are a threat to children. The sample lacks the details that might persuade you. For instance, exactly what kind of bad behavior do children display? And what specific video games out of the hundreds on the market are the real culprits? How is concentration actually affected? What "more important things" does the author mean? And how many hours of video consumption need occur before signs of dangerous behavior begin to manifest themselves?

Consider how much sharper and more persuasive the following rewrite is with the addition of specific details, facts, and examples:

> Video games may be fun for children, but they can have detrimental effects on their behavior. They encourage violent behavior. A steady dose of some of the more violent games clearly results in more aggressive behavior. One study by the Department of Psychology at State University has shown that after two hours of "Urban Guerrilla," 60 percent of the 12 boys and 20 percent of the 12 girls tested began to mimic the street-fighting gestures—punching, kicking, karate-chopping each other. It was also shown that such games negatively affect concentration. Even half an hour after their game playing had lapsed, the boys had difficulty settling down to read or draw. Since my parents restricted my little brother's game playing to weekends, he concentrates when completing his homework and has fewer fights with his best friend.

The statistics from the academic study, as well as the concrete case of the writer's own brother, give readers something substantial to consider. Presenting supporting evidence puts meat on the bones of your argument. (In Chapter 9 we will go into greater depth about how to gather research evidence, particularly from the library.)

Forms of Evidence

We hope that when you begin to develop an argument, you utilize debate, dialogue, and deliberation, as we suggested in Chapter 1. As you do this, you need to expand and deepen your understanding of the issue by collecting useful evidence from both sides of the issue. Don't neglect this critical step: Remember, the bulk of your argument is composed of material supporting your claim.

Writers enlist four basic kinds of evidence to support their arguments: personal experience (theirs and others'), outside authorities, factual references and examples, and statistics. We'll examine each separately, but you'll probably want to use combinations of these kinds of evidence when building your arguments in order to convince a wide range of readers. *non-debateable*

Personal Experience—Yours and Others'

The power of personal testimony cannot be underestimated. Think of the number of movies that have failed at the box office in spite of huge and expensive ad campaigns. Think of the number of times you've read a book on the recommendation of friends— or taken a certain course or shopped at a particular store. You might have chosen the college you're attending based on the recommendation of someone you know. Many people find the word-of-mouth judgments that make up personal testimony the most persuasive kind of evidence.

In written arguments, the personal testimony of other people is used to affirm facts and support your claim. Essentially, their experiences provide you with eyewitness accounts of events that are not available to you. Such accounts may prove crucial in winning over an audience. Suppose you are writing about the rising abuse of alcohol among college students. In addition to statistics and hard facts, your argument can gain strength from quoting the experience of a first-year student who nearly died one night from alcoholic poisoning. Or, in an essay decrying discrimination against minorities in hiring, consider the authenticity provided by an interview of neighborhood residents who felt they were passed over for a job because of race or ethnic identity.

Your own eyewitness testimony can be a powerful tool of persuasion. Suppose, for example, that you are writing a paper in which you argue that the big teaching hospital in the city provides far better care and has a lower death rate than the small rural hospital in your town. The hard facts and statistics on the quality of care and comparative mortality rates you provide will certainly have a stark persuasiveness. But consider the dramatic impact on those figures were you to recount how your own trip to the rural emergency room nearly cost you your life because of understaffing or the lack of critical but expensive diagnostic equipment.

Personal observation is useful and valuable in arguments. However, you should be careful not to draw hasty generalizations from such testimony. The fact that you and three of your friends are staunchly in favor of replacing letter grades with a pass/fail system does not support the claim that the entire student body at your school is in favor of the conversion. You need a much greater sample. Likewise, the dislike most people in your class feel for a certain professor does not justify the claim that the university tenure system should be abolished. On such complex issues, you need more than personal testimony to make a case.

You also have to remember the "multiple-perspective" rule. As any police officer can tell you, there are as many versions of the "truth" of an incident as there are people who saw it. The people involved in a car accident see it one way (or more), yet witnesses in a car heading in the other direction may interpret events differently, as will people in an apartment six stories above the street on which the accident took place. Your job is to sort out the different testimonies and make sense of them. Personal experience—yours and that of people you know—is valuable. However, on bigger issues you need statistics and data, as well as the evidence provided by outside authorities.

Outside Authorities

Think of the number of times you've heard statements such as these:

> "Scientists have found that . . ."
>
> "Scholars inform us that . . ."
>
> "According to his biographer, President Lincoln decided that . . ."

What these statements have in common is the appeal to outside authorities—people recognized as experts in a given field, people who can speak knowledgeably about a subject. Because authoritative opinions are such powerful tools of persuasion, you hear them all the time in advertisements. Automobile manufacturers quote the opinions of professional race car drivers; the makers of toothpaste cite dentists' claims; famous basketball players push brand-name sneakers all the time. Similarly, a good trial lawyer will almost always rely on forensic experts or other such authorities to help sway a jury.

Outside authorities can provide convincing evidence to support your ideas. However, there are times when expert opinion can be used inappropriately. This faulty use of authority can undermine the effectiveness of your argument. For the most part, experts usually try to be objective and fair-minded when asked for opinions. But, an expert with a vested interest in an issue might slant the testimony in his or her favor. The dentist who has just purchased a huge number of shares in a new toothpaste company would not be an unbiased expert. You wouldn't turn for an unbiased opinion on lung cancer to scientists working for tobacco companies, or ask an employee facing the loss of his or her job to comment on the advisability of layoffs. When you cite authorities, you should be careful to note any possibility of bias so your readers can fairly weigh the contributions. (This is often done through *attribution*; see Chapter 9.) Knowing that Professor Brown's research will benefit from construction of the supercollider doesn't make her enthusiasm for its other potential benefits less credible, but it does help your readers see her contributions to your argument in their proper context.

Another faulty use of authority is the use of an expert to provide evidence in a subject area in which he or she possesses no expertise. If you are going to cite authorities, you must make sure that they are competent; they should have expertise in their fields. You wouldn't turn to a professional beekeeper for opinions on laser surgery any more that you would quote a civil engineer on macroeconomic theory. And yet, just that is done all the time in advertising. Although it makes better sense to ask a veterinarian for a professional opinion about what to feed your pet, advertisers hire known actors to push dog food (as well as yogurt and skin cream). Of course, in advertising, celebrity sells. But that's not the case in most written arguments. It would not impress a critical reader to cite Tom Cruise's views on the use of fetal tissue or the greenhouse effect. Again, think about the profile of your audience. Whose expertise would they respect on your topic? Those are the experts to cite.

Factual References and Examples

Facts do as much to inform as they do to persuade, as we mentioned in Chapter 1. If somebody wants to sell you something, they'll pour on the details. For instance, ask the used car salesperson about that red 1999 Ford Explorer in the lot and he or she will hold forth about what a "creampuff" it is: only 18,400 original miles, mint condition, five-speed transmission with overdrive, all-black leather interior, and loaded—AC, power brakes, cruise control, premium sound system, captain's chair, and so on. Or listen to how the cereal manufacturers inform you that their toasted Os now contain "all-natural oat bran, which has been found to prevent cancer." Information is not always neutral. The very selection process implies intent. By offering specific facts or examples about your claim, you can make a persuasive argument.

The strategy in using facts and examples is to get readers so absorbed in the information that they nearly forget they are being persuaded to buy or do something. So common is this strategy in television ads that some have been given the name "infomercials"—ads that give the impression of being a documentary on the benefits of a product. For instance, you might be familiar with the margarine commercial narrated by a man who announces that at thirty-three years of age he had a heart attack. He then recounts the advice of his doctor for avoiding coronary disease, beginning with the need for exercise and climaxing with the warning about cutting down on cholesterol. Not until the very end of the ad does the narrator inform us that, taking advantage of his second chance, the speaker has switched to a particular brand of margarine, which, of course, is cholesterol-free.

In less blatant form, this "informational" strategy can be found in newspaper columns and editorials, where authors give the impression that they are simply presenting the facts surrounding particular issues when in reality they may be attempting to persuade readers to see things their way. For instance, suppose in an apparently objective commentary a writer discusses how history is replete with people wrongfully executed for first-degree murder. Throughout the piece the author cites several specific cases in which it was learned too late that the defendant had been framed or that the real killer had confessed. On the surface the piece may appear to be simply presenting historical facts, but the more subtle intention may be to convince people that capital punishment is morally wrong. The old tagline from *Dragnet,* "Just the facts, ma'am," isn't quite the whole picture. How those facts are used is also part of their persuasive impact.

Often facts and examples are used to establish cause-and-effect relationships. It's very important, when both writing and reading arguments, to test the links the facts forge. While one event may indeed follow another, you can't automatically assume a causal relationship. This can result in a logical fallacy, in this case post hoc, ergo propter hoc. For instance, it may rain the day after every launch of the space shuttle, but does that prove that shuttle launches affect the weather in Florida? Similarly, we are all familiar with politicians who claim credit for improvements in the economy that have little to do with the legislation they have proposed. They hope to gain votes by having the public believe that there is a direct causal relationship between their actions and the economic improvement. Often this strategy backfires when opponents point out the lack of any actual connection.

Sometimes even experts disagree; one might see the rise in prostate cancer rates for vasectomy patients as reason to abolish the surgery; another might point to other contributing causes (diet, lack of exercise, hormonal imbalance). If you don't have the expertise to determine which of the conflicting experts is correct, you'll probably decide based on the *weight of the evidence*—whichever side has the most people or the most plausible reasons supporting it. This, in fact, is how most juries decide cases.

Statistics

People are impressed by numbers. Saying that 77 percent of the student body at your school supports a woman's right to choose is far more persuasive than saying that a lot of people on campus are pro-choice. **Statistics** have a special no-nonsense authority. Batting averages, medical statistics, polling results (election and otherwise), economic indicators, the stock market index, unemployment figures, scientific ratings, FBI statistics, percentages, demographic data—they all are reported in numbers. If they're accurate, statistics are difficult to argue against, though a skillful manipulator can use them to mislead.

The demand for statistics has made market research a huge business in America. During an election year, weekly and daily results on voters' opinions of candidates are released from various news organizations and TV networks, as well as independent polling companies such as the Harris and Gallup organizations. Most of the brand-name products you buy, the TV shows and movies you watch, or the CDs you listen to were made available after somebody did test studies on sample populations to determine the potential success of these items. Those same statistics are then used in promotional ads. Think of the number of times you've heard claims such as these:

> "Nine out of ten doctors recommend Zappo aspirin."
>
> "Our new Speed King copier turns out 24 percent more copies per minute."
>
> "Sixty-eight percent of those polled approve of women in military combat roles."

Of course, these claims bear further examination. If you polled only ten doctors, nine of whom recommended Zappo, that's not a big enough sample to imply that 90 percent of *all* doctors do. To avoid drawing a hasty generalization from too small a sample, avoid using sweeping words such as *all, always, never,* or *none*. Either be straightforward about the statistics supporting your claim, or limit your claim with qualifiers such as *some, many, often,* or *few*. As Mark Twain once observed, "There are lies, damned lies, and statistics."

Numbers don't lie, but they can be manipulated. Sometimes, to sway an audience, claim makers will cite figures that are inaccurate or dated, or they will intentionally misuse accurate figures to make a case. If, for instance, somebody claims that 139 students and professors protested the invitation of a certain controversial guest to your campus, it would be a distortion of the truth not to mention that another 1500 attended the talk and gave the speaker a standing ovation. Providing only those numbers or statistics that support the writer's claim and ignoring or concealing figures that might indicate otherwise is one way of stacking the deck. While this practice might deceive—at least temporarily—an uninformed audience, the writer risks damaging his or her credibility once the true figures are revealed.

Be on guard for the misleading use of statistics, a technique used all too frequently in advertising. The manufacturer that claims its flaked corn cereal is 100 percent cholesterol-free misleads the public because no breakfast cereal of any brand contains cholesterol (which is found only in animal fats). French fries prepared in pure vegetable oil are also cholesterol-free, but that doesn't mean that they're the best food for your health. Manufacturers that use terms like *cholesterol-free, light,* and *low-fat* are trying to get you to buy their products without really examining the basis for their nutritional claims. Although it's tempting to use such crowd-pleasing statistics, it's a good idea to avoid them in your own arguments because they are deceptive. If your readers discover your deception, your chances of persuading them to accept your position or proposal become unlikely.

PREVIEW: TO EVALUATE SUPPORTING EVIDENCE, ASK . . .

- Is the evidence sufficient?
- Is the evidence detailed enough?
- Is the evidence relevant?
- Does the evidence fit the claim?
- Is the evidence up-to-date and verifiable?
- Is the evidence biased?
- Is the evidence balanced and fairly presented?

Some Tips About Supporting Evidence

Because, as argument writers, you'll be using evidence on a routine basis, it will help you to develop a systematic approach to testing the evidence you want to use. Here are some questions to ask yourself about the evidence you enlist in an argument.

Do You Have a Sufficient Number of Examples to Support Your Claim?

You don't want to jump to conclusions based on too little evidence. Suppose you want to make the case that electric cars would be better for the environment than motor vehicles. If all you offer as evidence is the fact that electric vehicles don't pollute the air, your argument would be somewhat thin. Your argument would be much more convincing if you offered the following evidence: that in addition to zero emission at the tailpipe—which is good for the atmosphere—electric cars do not use engine fluids or internal combustion parts, all of which constitute wastes that contaminate our landfills and water supplies. Furthermore, because electric vehicles don't use gasoline or oil, the hazards associated with storage of such fluids are eliminated.

Likewise, you should avoid making hasty generalizations based on your own experience as evidence. For instance, if your Acme Airlines flight to Chattanooga was delayed last week, you shouldn't conclude that Acme Airlines always leaves late. However, you would have a persuasive case were you to demonstrate that over the last six months 47 percent of the frequent flyers you interviewed complained that Acme flights left late.

Is Your Evidence Detailed Enough?
The more specific the details, the more persuasive your argument. Instead of generalizations, cite figures, dates, and facts; instead of paraphrases, offer quotations from experts. Remember that your readers are subconsciously saying, "Show me! Prove it!" If you want to tell people how to bake bread, you wouldn't write, "Mix some flour with some yeast and water"; you'd say, "Dissolve one packet of yeast in 1 cup of warm water and let it sit for ten minutes. Then slowly mix in 3 cups of sifted whole wheat flour." Or, as in our electric car example above, instead of simply asserting that there would be none of the fluid or solid wastes associated with internal combustion vehicles, specify that in electric vehicles there would be no motor oil, engine coolants, transmission fluid or filters, spark plugs, ignition wires, and gaskets to end up in landfills. What your readers want are specifics—and that's what you should give them.

Is Your Evidence Relevant to the Claim You Make or Conclusion You Reach?
Select evidence based on how well it supports the point you are arguing, not on how interesting, novel, or humorous it is or how hard you had to work to find it. Recall that using evidence that is unrelated or irrelevant is a logical fallacy called a non sequitur. For instance, if you are arguing about whether John Lennon is the most influential songwriter in rock and roll history, you wouldn't mention that he had two sons or that he owned dairy cattle; those are facts, but they have nothing to do with the influence of his lyrics. Historian Barbara Tuchman relates that in writing *The Guns of August,* she discovered that the kaiser bought his wife the same birthday present every year: twelve hats of his choosing, which he required her to wear. Tuchman tried to use this detail in Chapter 1, then in Chapter 2, and so on, but was finally obligated to relegate the detail to a stack of notecards marked "Unused." It just didn't fit, even though for her it summarized his stubborn selfishness. (She did work it into a later essay, which is why we know about it.) Learn her lesson: Irrelevant evidence distracts an audience and weakens an argument's persuasive power.

Does Your Conclusion (or Claim) Exceed the Evidence?
Don't make generalizations about entire groups when your evidence points to select members. Baseball may be the national pastime, but it would be unwise to claim that *all* Americans love baseball. Experience tells you that some Americans prefer football or basketball, while others don't like any sports. Claims that are out of proportion to the evidence can result in a fallacy called the **bandwagon appeal.** The

bandwagon appeal suggests to the audience that they should agree with the writer because everyone else does, rather than because the writer has supplied compelling evidence to support the reasons and claim. This is a favorite strategy of advertisers, who work to convince us that we should buy a certain product because everyone else is doing so. While this strategy is in itself fallacious, these salespeople are often unable to produce adequate evidence to support their sweeping claims of nation-wide popularity for their product.

Is Your Evidence Up-to-Date and Verifiable?

You want to be sure that the evidence you enlist isn't so dated or vague that it fails to support your claim. For instance, figures demonstrating an increase in the rate of teen pregnancy will not persuade your audience if the numbers are ten years old. Similarly, it wouldn't be accurate to say that Candidate Oshawa fails to support the American worker because fifteen years ago he purchased a foreign car. His recent and current actions are far more relevant.

When you're citing evidence, your readers will expect you to be specific enough for them to verify what you say. A writer supporting animal rights may cite the example of rabbits whose eyes were burned by pharmacological testing, but such tests have been outlawed in the United States for many years. Another writer may point to medical research that appears to abuse its human subjects, but not name the researchers, the place where the testing took place, or the year in which it occurred. The readers have no way of verifying the claim and may become suspicious of the entire argument because the factual claims are so difficult to confirm.

Is Your Evidence Slanted?

Sometimes writers select evidence that supports their case while ignoring evidence that does not. Often referred to as stacking the deck, this practice makes for an unfair argument, and one that could be disastrous for the arguer. Even though some of your evidence has merit, your argument will be dismissed if your audience discovers that you slanted or suppressed evidence.

For example, suppose you heard a friend make the following statements: "If I were you, I'd avoid taking a course with Professor Gorman at all costs. He gives surprise quizzes, he assigns fifty pages a night, and he refuses to grade on a curve." Even if these reasons are true, that may not be the whole truth. Suppose you learned that Professor Gorman is, in fact, a very dynamic and talented teacher whose classes successfully stimulate the learning process. By holding back that information, your friend's argument is suspect.

Sometimes writers will take advantage of their readers' lack of information on a topic and offer evidence that really doesn't support their claims. Recently several newspapers reported that a study written up in the *Archives of Internal Medicine* proved that eating nuts prevents heart attacks. According to the study, some thirty thousand Seventh-Day Adventists were asked to rate the frequency with which they ate certain foods. Those claiming to eat nuts five or more times a week reported fewer heart attacks. What the newspapers failed to report was that all Seventh-Day Adventists are vegetarians, and that those who ate more nuts also ate fewer dairy products (which are high in cholesterol and saturated fat, both of which contribute to heart disease) and eggs (also high in cholesterol) than others in the study. Newspapers have failed to report that all the subsequent pro-nut publicity was distributed by a nut growers' association.*

It is to your benefit to present all relevant evidence so that you clearly weigh both sides of an issue. As we discussed in Chapter 4, you want to demonstrate to your readers that you have made an effort to consider other perspectives and that your conclusions are fair and balanced. Otherwise your argument might not be taken seriously. Let's return to the argument that electric cars are more beneficial to the environment than cars with internal combustion engines. Your key evidence is the fact that electric cars do not use petroleum products and various motor parts that contribute to the pollution of air, land, and waterways. If you left your argument at that, you would be guilty of suppressing an important concern regarding electric vehicles: the disposal of the great amounts of lead in the huge electric vehicles' batteries. Failure to acknowledge that opposing point reduces your credibility as a writer. Readers would wonder either about your attempt at deception or about your ignorance. Either way they would dismiss your argument.

TO TEST YOUR EVIDENCE FOR LOGICAL FALLACIES, ASK THESE QUESTIONS

Stacking the deck	Did I present evidence that only supports my point of view? Have I withheld evidence that might contradict it?
Non sequitur	Is my evidence related and relevant to the reasons or claim it is supporting?
Hasty generalization	Have I provided sufficient evidence to support my conclusions?
Red herring	Does all of my evidence pertain to the true issue? Have I tried to distract my audience's attention with irrelevant concerns?
Bandwagon appeal	Can my evidence stand on its own? Have I argued that my audience should support my ideas because they reflect a popular viewpoint?
Faulty use of authority	Are the authorities I cite actually experts in my subject area? Could my authorities be biased because of their background or their professional or political associations?

---

*Mirkin, Gabe, and Diana Rich. *Fat Free Flavor Full*. Boston: Little, Brown, 1995: 51.

A much better strategy would be to confront this concern and then try to overcome it. While acknowledging that lead is a dangerous pollutant, you could point out that more than 95 percent of battery lead is recycled. You could also point out that progress is being made to improve battery technology and create alternatives such as the kinds of fuel cells used in spacecraft.* The result is a balanced presentation that makes your own case stronger.

In summary, using evidence means putting yourself in an advocate's place. You'll probably do this while building your argument, and certainly when you revise; then you should see yourself as an advocate for the other side and scrutinize your evidence as if you were going to challenge it in court. As a reader, you need to keep that Missouri "show me!" attitude in mind at all times. A little healthy skepticism will help you test the information you're asked to believe. The next chapter will help you do so.

SAMPLE ARGUMENT FOR ANALYSIS

The following is a paper written by a student, Darren Beals. In it, Beals responds to the claims that the media coverage of juvenile violence and Internet accessibility to weapons influenced the behavior of Kipland Kinkel, the student convicted of murdering his parents and several of his classmates on May 21, 1998. Read the essay carefully and take notes about it in your argument journal. Then, either individually or in your peer group, answer the questions that follow.

Violent Culture: The Media, the Internet, and Placing Blame
Darren Beals

1   On May 21, 1998, a 15-year-old boy walked into his high school cafeteria and began shooting his classmates. Later, the public learned that he had already killed his parents, and had also placed explosive devices around the house, perhaps with the intention of taking out a few police officers who would later investigate the scene (*Associated Press* to *The Boston Globe*).

2   As I watched the media coverage on every channel, I was struck by how many different television programs presented their side of Kip Kinkel's shooting spree. Tabloid-type programs revealed the "shocking" warning signals that were "ignored." News programs reported the gruesome details and updated us on Kinkel's status. Kinkel was featured on shows from *Face the Nation* and *Dateline* to *Inside Edition* and *Extra*. Everyone, it seemed, had something to say about Kip Kinkel. And the big question everyone was asking was "why?"

---

*May, Thomas J. "Electric Cars Will Benefit the Environment and the Economy." *The Boston Globe* 10 Aug. 1994: 15.

3 "Yes, why?" asked my viewer-self. And as television has always been there with a ready answer, it did not fail me now. Was it his parents who failed to see the warning signs? Was it the police who did not lock him up when they found the first gun the day before? Was it the media exposure of similar high-profile school killings in West Paducah, Kentucky, and Jonesboro, Arkansas (Bragg)? No, said television. It was the Internet.

4 Although the details reported from program to program focused on different aspects of Kinkel and his horrible actions, few broadcasts failed to mention, however briefly, his connection to the Internet. The Internet showed him how to build bombs. The Internet allowed him to discuss explosives with other sickos. The Internet exposed him to violence. The Internet supplied the tools he needed. The Internet told him about guns and ammo. The Internet, one might assume from the reports, drove this 15-year-old to kill.

5 As a critical television viewer, I began to wonder about the Internet's role in this tragedy. Was it really to blame? Or was television pointing its finger to shift the blame away from itself? After all, wasn't all this media attention simply encouraging other psycho-teens to seize their own ten minutes of fame? At least they know what gets our attention. It may even seem logical that copy-cat killings are more frequent. Kill your classmates and get your face on TV.

6 TV, on the other hand, would naturally want to redirect the blame. The new kid on the block, the Internet, is the natural scapegoat. And don't forget, you can't be watching television if you are online, can you? Knock a rival and shift the blame at the same time. Seems pretty convenient. But what if television is right? What if the Internet really did play a role in all this tragedy? Is the Internet responsible in some way, or is it simply another component of our inherent culture of violence?

7 I decided to investigate the issue myself. If I was 15 years old, how much information could I tap into on the Internet? How would I find out how to build a bomb, buy a gun or ask questions on explosives? How much information is really out there? And how easy is it to get? I then embarked on a weekend exploration of Internet violence. I found out that there are definitely more Kip Kinkels out there, and plenty of people willing to teach them.

8 But who is Kip Kinkel? Before examining how he may have used the Internet to feed his twisted mind, it may be useful to try to profile him. Was Kip really that different from the average suburban kid? To answer this question, we need to find out exactly what is the average high school student. The answer would surprise most people. A quiz posted online by *Dateline NBC* the week of May 25, 1998, reports that "out of every 100 students . . . an estimated 71 [of them] have carried a weapon to school. Typically boys carry weapons four times more often than girls. Weapons include guns, razors, knives, and clubs" (*Dateline NBC*). This same quiz reports a more frightening statistic. Twenty out of every 100 suburban high schools boys are likely to own a gun. "A Justice Department report found that one in five own a gun and 45 percent of suburban high school boys have been threatened with a gun or shot at on the way to or from school" (*Dateline NBC*). Thus, the fact that Kinkel even had a gun isn't that unusual according to these statistics.

9   Other critics cite the National Rifle Association and its recent media campaign aimed at kids. Kristen Rand, the director of federal policy for the Violence Policy Center, attacks the NRA's recent advertising campaign featuring
movie star Charlton Heston in which he is surrounded by a group of children
with the caption "are gun rights lost on our kids?" Says Rand, "the motivation
for the NRA and firearms industry to create a generation of pro-gun kids is twofold—to future customers for the industry and political foot soldiers for the
NRA" (Violence Policy Center).

10   Despite some odd behavior such as stuffing firecrackers down gopher
holes, shooting at squirrels in the woods and tossing rocks at cars from over-
passes, many neighbors and friends felt that Kip was a regular kid. A *Boston
Globe* reporter relates that his strange antics were attributed to "phases" and typical male adolescent behavior (Jacoby). In a culture where violent movies and
television are the norm, who can blame a kid for boasting about his firearm
skills? After all, we admire such skills in Schwarzenegger, Stallone, Willis and
Segal.

11   But there is a big difference between boasting and acting, and Kinkel
acted. Many people point to the media as the reason. Extensive coverage of
other school shootings may encourage other students to do the same thing.
Even President Clinton believes there may be a connection—on the same day
as Kinkel's shooting spree, he ordered the Department of Justice to examine
school shootings and determine whether there may be a "copycat" phenomenon at work.

12   So assuming that Kinkel was not that different from many kids his age,
what separates him from his peers? Was it his access to the Internet and the information he gathered there? If Kinkel was born 20 years earlier before the Internet would he have acted the way he did on May 21st? If we are to believe the
television coverage, the Internet helped make Kip Kinkel a killer. The question
is, how?

13   Let's say you are a 15-year-old boy with an interest in guns. Just an interest—you're curious to find out what kind of guns there are, how they kill, and
maybe how you might buy one. A quick Altavista word search yields 121,470
matches to the word query "gun types." The query "killing with guns" returns
462,390 matches. Scanning the matches quickly reveals relevant pages such as a
site called "The Killing House" located in England where you can "test your
shooting skills." Another site provides information on handguns and how to
use them (Ultimate Weapons Systems, Handguns).

14   Instead of being satisfied, your interest is now raised—there is so much information out there. From guns and bullets you move to bombs. You haven't
given up on guns, you are merely increasing your "arsenal" of information. You
want to know more about explosive devices. How do you make one? How can
you share information with other people who know what they're talking about?
You go to a newsgroup and start reading. After trying simple words like "bomb"
you discover that many professions use the word—so you become more specific. You use the word "explosives" which yields successful results. After reading the postings there, your vocabulary has enlarged greatly, allowing you even

more detailed access to specific groups often linked to the topic, such as "anarchy." You note the e-mail names of some of the people posting on these sites, and you get in touch with them.

15   E-mail, like IRC, allows personal one-on-one correspondence. You can go to a chat room to discuss pyrotechnics. You can spill your guts to other crazies who hate the world on an IRC. If you don't mind waiting a bit, e-mail allows you to send messages to groups of people at a time, doubling your responses and information. There are many, many angry people out there, and they are happy to tell you how to get even. They may even live out their violent fantasies through a 15-year-old boy who "has the guts" to do what they only talk about.

16   After spending a great deal of time online. I began to formulate some conclusions. The first was that there are a lot of sickos out there. Information is easy to find on just about everything. And there are many people who don't hesitate to share their "knowledge" with anyone—child or adult—who will listen. The second thing I noticed was that there really is no regulation on the Internet. With the exception of controlled servers, anyone can post anything they want.

17   So where were Kip Kinkel's parents when he was gathering all his Internet information? Can a parent really not know what their child is up to? My guess is that they did have some idea, but it is easy to deceive. Set a bookmark to the Disney homepage and with a click of a button it is on the screen before Mom and Dad enter the room. Clever parents will hit the "back" button to see where their children were before. And the bottom line about Internet use is indeed parental control. Some people may argue that some parents don't even know how to use a computer, let alone monitor their child's activities on the Internet. My answer to this claim is if you don't know how to use a computer, learn. It is a parental responsibility when you purchase a machine for your home to know how to operate it. If you won't learn, don't provide online access. Or better yet, if your children are under 12, get "net nanny" software such as Patrol, Cybersitter, Cybersnoop or X-Stop (Monro).

18   Am I blaming Kinkel's parents? No. Likewise, I don't hold the Internet responsible, or television, or other media. We can keep pointing fingers, while avoiding the real issue—our national culture of violence. While the Internet (or a library, for that matter) can supply the details, we must remember that Kinkel had to first have an interest in violence. We would be hard pressed to prove that the Internet actually incited his interest in guns and bombs. It more likely provided information to his already hungry and violent brain. Our culture is more responsible for the evil seeds in his head. So who really is to blame? Why do we even ask "why?" Do we really want to know?

WORKS CITED

Associated Press. "Troubling Image of Troubled Youth." *The Boston Globe.* (22 May 1998.)

Bragg, Rick. "Past Victims Relive Pain As Tragedy Is Repeated." *New York Times.* 25 May 1998, natl.ed. (27 May 1998.)

Dateline NBC. With Stone Phillips and Jane Pauley. NBC. May 1998. Online. Internet. (26 May 1998.)

Jacoby, Jeff. "The Classroom Culture That Spawned Kip Kinkel." *The Boston Globe.* (28 May 1998.)

Johassen, Robert. *rjohnss@aol.com.* "Using Semi-automatic Weapons." Online posting. Newsgroupalt.firearms.semiautomatic.Usenet.(25 May 1998.)

"The Killing House." Online. Internet. (24 May 1998.)

(Alias name: kinderbomb). *kinder@mail.com.* E-mail to alias kinderbomb. (28 May 1998.)

Monro, Kathryn. "Parental Filtering Utilities: Net Nanny." *PC Magazine* Online. March 1998. Online. Internet. (27 May 1998.)

Ultimate Weapons Systems. "Tactical Weapons and Firearms Accessories for Law Enforcement Personal Protection—Security—Military—Defense." 1996. Online. Internet. (27 May 1998.)

Violence Policy Center. "Arkansas School Shooting Focuses New Attention on Youth Gun Culture." March 1998. Online. Internet. (27 May 1998.)

■ QUESTIONS FOR ANALYSIS AND DISCUSSION

1. What claim (Chapter 2) is Beals arguing? What are the reasons for his claim? What do you think the pros and cons he listed in developing this argument might have been?

2. Who is Beals's target audience? What clues does he give you? What values and prejudices might the readership hold?

3. What different forms of evidence (personal, outside authorities, factual references, statistics) does Beals provide? Which form(s) of evidence does he rely on most?

4. Evaluate the supporting evidence that Beals provides. Is it relevant? Is it detailed enough? Does it seem dated and verifiable? Does his claim exceed his evidence? Does his evidence strike you as slanted? If you were his reader, would you be persuaded by his reasons? What changes (if any) in evidence would you recommend to help him make his argument more persuasive?

5. Use debate, dialogue, and deliberation to respond to Beals's essay in your journal (see Chapter 1 to review this process):
   a. Make a pro/con checklist to identify the ideas with which you disagree—for example, the responsibility of the media, the Internet, parents regarding youth violence.
   b. Create a dialogue to help you understand and respond productively to Beals's ideas.
   c. Given what you've learned through debate and dialogue, write at least a page in which you deliberate about the conflicting issues that Beals raises in his essay. How does your understanding of Beals's position change or modify your own viewpoint? Is there a way to reconcile conflicting concerns about this subject?

Establishing Claims
Thinking Like a Skeptic

You have decided the issue you're going to argue. With the aid of debate and dialogue you've sharpened your ideas and considered alternative perspectives and common concerns. You've thought about your audience and determined what you have in common, where you might agree, and where you might disagree. After deliberating, you have formulated a working claim, and you have gathered solid evidence to support it. Now it's time to establish the logical structure of your argument and decide how best to arrange this material to persuade your readers.

If you've ever tried handing in a paper made up of slapped-together evidence and first-draft organization, you've probably discovered a blueprint for disaster. Perhaps you didn't test your work, didn't revise it, or didn't think about how it would appeal to a reader. You assumed that because *you* understood how the parts fit together, your readers would as well. To help you detect and correct these problems, this chapter focuses on thinking like a *skeptic*—a skeptical building inspector, to be exact—because a skeptical attitude works best.

To construct a persuasive argument, one that has a chance of convincing your readers, you have to pay careful attention to the logical structure you are building. You can't take anything for granted; you have to question every step you take, every joist and joint. You have to ask yourself if you're using the right material for the right purpose, the right tool at the right time. In other words, you have to think like a building inspector examining a half-built two-story house—one whose builder is notoriously crafty at compromising quality. A healthy skepticism—and a logical system—help uncover flaws before they create a disaster.

The Toulmin Model

Stephen Toulmin, a British philosopher and logician, analyzed hundreds of arguments from various fields of politics and law.* He concluded that nearly every argu-

---

*Toulmin, Stephen. *The Uses of Argument.* Cambridge: Cambridge University Press, 1958.

ment has certain patterns and parts. The best arguments, Toulmin found, are those addressed to a skeptical audience, one eager to question the reasoning where it seems faulty, to demand support for wobbly assumptions, and to raise opposing reasons.

The slightly retooled version of the Toulmin model we describe below encourages you to become a skeptical audience. It provides useful everyday terms to help you unearth, weigh, and, if necessary, fix an argument's logical structures. It lets you verify that the major premises in your argument or those of your opposition are clear and accurate, helps you determine whether repairs to your claims are needed and whether counterarguments are addressed. It shows you where supporting evidence may be needed and helps you avoid logical fallacies. And, since Toulmin's terms are designed to be broadly practical, they allow you to present your case to a wide variety of readers.

Toulmin's Terms

According to Toulmin, a fully developed argument has six parts. They are the *claim,* the *grounds,* the *warrant,* the *backing,* the *qualifiers,* and the *rebuttals.*

The Claim

The **claim** is the assertion you are trying to prove. It is the position you take in your argument, often as a proposal with which you are asking your reader to agree. In a well-constructed argument, each part makes its ultimate claim, its conclusion, seem inevitable.

The Grounds Proof

Just as every argument contains a claim, every claim needs supporting evidence. The **grounds** are the statistics, research studies, facts, and examples that bolster your claim and that your audience accepts without requiring further proof.

The Warrant

The claim is usually stated explicitly. However, underlying the claim are a number of assumptions and principles that are also critical to the success of your argument. These are the **warrants** that implicitly support your argument by connecting your claim to the grounds. They enable your audience to follow the reasoning in your argument. The success of your argument depends on whether the audience accepts the often half-buried assumptions, commonly held values, legal or moral principles, laws of nature, commonsense knowledge, or shared beliefs.

Visualizing how arguments are built and work can help you understand their structure. Imagine, then, an Amish barn raising—or the way a lot of very un-Amish suburban houses are constructed these days. After the foundation is dug and laid, prefabricated walls are erected. They're then stabilized by buttressing boards that are jammed diagonally between the walls and the ground. Think of the warrant as an argument's half-buried foundation. Everything is based on this foundation—including the argument's walls, its claims. The grounds are like those buttressing boards: They are lines of evidence that hold the walls up and together. The conclusion is the roof. The difference between arguments and buildings is that these buttressing boards, the grounds for your argument, aren't taken away when the argument's structure is complete.

The Backing

Because your warrant is an assumption, you cannot be certain that it will always be accepted by your readers. So you must provide reasons to back it up. These reasons, called **backing,** indicate that the warrant is reliable in a particular argument, though it doesn't have to be true in all cases at all times.

The Qualifiers

Qualifiers provide a way to indicate when, why, and how your claim and warrant are reliable. They're words or phrases such as *often, probably, possibly, almost always;* verbs like *may* and *might, can* and *could;* or adjectives and adverbs that yoke your claim to some condition. The subtlest kind of qualifier is an adjective that acknowledges that your claim is true to a degree: "Coming from a dysfunctional family *often* makes it *harder* to resist the angry lure of crime." The qualifiers *often* and *harder* imply that the statement is conditional and not absolute. They allow for exceptions.

You need to consider a few qualifications about using qualifiers; like antibiotics, they're too powerful to use unwisely. Using too few qualifiers can indicate that you're exaggerating your argument's validity. As we've mentioned in previous chapters, common fallacies, such as *hasty generalizations,* are often potentially valid arguments that go astray by not qualifying their claims enough, if at all. Using *no* qualifiers can result in a claim that is too general and sweeping. Although many students think a qualified claim is a weak claim, in fact, the qualified claim is often the most persuasive. Few truths are *completely* true; few claims are *always* right. A well-qualified claim, then, shows that the writer respects both the difficulty of the issue and the intelligence of the reader.

Nevertheless, qualifiers alone cannot substitute for reasoning your way to the tough, subtle distinctions on which the most persuasive arguments depend. For example, look at the claim that "Innocent people have an inviolable right to life." It's wisely qualified with the word "innocent" since just saying "People have an inviolable right to life" wouldn't hold up. Hitler, after all, was a human. Did he too have "an inviolable right to life"? But even *innocent* is not qualification enough. It raises too many tough, troubling questions. "Innocent" of what? "Innocent" by whose judgment, and why? What if killing a few innocent people were the only way to end a war that is killing *many* innocent people?

Using a lot of qualifiers, therefore, is no guarantee that your argument is carefully reasoned. In fact, strongly qualifying your argument's claim may be a sign that you doubt your argument's validity. But such doubt can itself be encouraging. Misusing or overusing qualifiers can indicate that your instinct of anxiety is right—that you've discovered better reasons to doubt your initial argument than to defend it. In fact, acknowledging the appeal of a flawed claim—and describing how you only discovered its flaws once you tried trumpeting its strengths—is an effective way of earning the reader's respect. It shows you to be an honest arguer capable of learning from errors—and thus worth learning *from*.

Deciding what to state and what to imply is a large part of writing any good argument. Just as a building's cross-beams don't have to be visible to be working, not everything important in an argument has to be stated. For example, if someone were to claim that winters in Minnesota are "mostly long and cold," we probably wouldn't stop the flow of argument to ask him to define the qualifier *mostly*. We'd instead keep the qualifier in mind, and let the Minnesotan's definition of "mostly" emerge, implied, from the rest of the story. Similarly, it's sometimes wise to leave your argument's qualifiers implied.

Still, it's often better to risk belaboring the obvious. To minimize the chances that your reader will misunderstand (or altogether miss) your meaning, qualify your claims as clearly and explicitly as possible. "Reading" the argument you're writing like a skeptical reader will help you decide which qualifiers are needed, where they are needed, and how explicitly they need to be stated.

The Rebuttals

Reading your argument skeptically also allows you to participate, answer, and even preempt rebuttals. **Rebuttals** represent the exceptions to the claim. There are many different kinds of rebuttals, and any persuasive argument ought to acknowledge and incorporate the most important ones. Rebuttals are like large-scale qualifiers. They acknowledge and explain the conditions or situations in which your claim would not be true—while still proving how your claim *is* true under other conditions. It's wise, then, to anticipate such rebuttals by regularly acknowledging all your argument's limits. This acknowledgment will prompt you to craft your claims more carefully.

Let's say, for example, that a sportswriter argues that allowing big-market baseball teams to monopolize talent ruins competition by perpetuating dynasties. Your rebuttal might be to cite the overlooked grounds of ignored evidence—grounds

REVIEW: SIX PARTS OF AN ARGUMENT

Claim	The assertion you are trying to prove
Grounds	The supporting evidence for the claim
Warrant	A generalization that explains why the evidence supports the claim
Backing	The reasons that show the warrant is reliable
Qualifiers	The words that show when, how, and why your claim is reliable
Rebuttal	The exceptions to the claim

that complicate, if not contradict, the writer's claim: "Then why have small-market teams won four of the last ten World Series?" Had the sportswriter anticipated and integrated this rebuttal, she could have improved the argument—from her warrant on up. Her argument could have taken into account this rebuttal in the form of more careful qualifications. "While the rule of money doesn't guarantee that the richer teams will always win the World Series, it does make it more difficult for hard-pressed teams to compete for available talent." This is now, of course, a less sweeping claim—and, therefore, more precise and persuasive.

Of course, no writer can anticipate their readers' every rebuttal, nor should the writer even try. But you should test your argument by trying to rebut it yourself or working with classmates in small groups. Then revise your arguments with those rebuttals in mind.

Field Work: Excavating Warrants

Excavating your warrants in order to explicate your argument can help you in several ways: You persuade your reader more effectively, detect flaws in your own argument, and identify the cause of otherwise confusing debates more quickly.

For example, let's say you want to argue that all students in American schools should be taught in English rather than in the students' native or family languages. The grounds that you use to support this claim are that fluency in English is essential for success in American society. For your audience to accept the connection between your claim and your grounds, you and they must agree on several warrants that underlie it. The first might be the assumption that schools prepare students for success in U.S. society. Since one of the purposes of an education is to develop skills such as reading, writing, and thinking critically that are considered basic requirements for success, most of your audience would likely accept this assumption. Therefore, it can be left implied and unstated.

The next two warrants implied by your claim may not be as readily acceptable to your audience as the one above and will need to be explicitly supported in your essay. The first is that our English language skills affect whether we are successful. The second warrant, implied by the first, is that individuals who are not fluent in English will not be successful members of society. These warrants will need considerable backing to show that they are reliable. First of all, you will have to define *success*. Are you thinking of financial success, career success, or social success? Without a clear explanation of what you mean by success, your argument will be weakened. Second, once you have defined success, you will need to provide backing to support your warrants. How do English language skills enable individuals to succeed, as you have defined it? How are individuals who lack fluency in English adversely affected? You will want to provide additional backing in the form of evidence, examples, and statistics to demonstrate that English language skills have a significant impact on an individual's chances for success.

Your last warrant is particularly important because it establishes a critical link between your claim that all students should be taught in English and the need for

TO AVOID ERRORS IN LOGIC, CHECK FOR THESE LOGICAL FALLACIES

Post hoc, ergo propter hoc	Be certain to demonstrate a cause-effect relationship between events by uncovering all warrants that underlie your claim.
Slippery slope argument	Make explicit the chain of events that link a situation to its possible outcome. Provide proof that this progression will inevitably occur.

fluency to succeed. This warrant assumes non-native speaking students will achieve greater fluency in English in the English-only classroom. You will need additional backing to prove this warrant, especially when you take into account possible rebuttals. For instance, what about students who enter U.S. schools with no English skills at all? How can they learn the required curriculum with no fluency in English? Will English-only classrooms fail to teach them language skills as well as subject matter? Will this approach alienate them from the American educational system and, thus, from success in our society? Making your responses to these rebuttals explicit will strengthen your argument.

Using Toulmin's approach to analyze your argument allows you to dig beneath the surface of your claim to find the underlying assumptions that form its foundation. It also allows your audience to see that even if they disagree with your claim, they may agree with many of the principles and assumptions that support it. Revealing this common ground, however hidden it lies, can provide opportunities to begin a dialogue that emerges from the recognition of shared values and beliefs. For instance, take the notoriously divisive issue of capital punishment. Those who support capital punishment say, in essence, "A human life is so precious that anyone who is guilty of depriving another of it should forfeit his or her own life." The opposing side says, in effect, "Human life is so precious that we have no right to deprive another of it no matter what the cause." By digging down to the warrants that underlie these positions, we may be surprised to find that the two sides have much in common: a respect for and appreciation of the value of human life. This discovery, of course, is no guarantee that we can reconcile dramatically opposing views on a particular issue. But the recognition of commonality might provide a first step toward increasing understanding—if not consensus—between opposing sides.

Digging deeply to excavate your warrants can also help you avoid two common logical fallacies: post hoc, ergo propter hoc and slippery slope arguments. A post hoc, ergo propter hoc fallacy occurs when the writer mistakenly draws a casual relationship between two or more events or situations that are unrelated or simply coincidental. Similarly, a slippery slope argument is based on an assumption that a particular outcome is inevitable if certain events happen or if a situation is allowed

WARRANTS

Notice the many layers of warrants that can underlie a single claim:

Claim	All students in American public schools should be taught in English-only classrooms.
Grounds	Fluency in English is essential for success in American society.
Warrant	Schools prepare students for success in our society.
Warrant	Success in American society can be determined by our English language skills.
Warrant	Individuals who are not fluent in English will not succeed in our society.
Warrant	Teaching classes only in the English language will ensure that students will be fluent in English.

to continue. In both cases, the writer fails to identify and support the underlying warrants that would create a convincing logical link.

SAMPLE ARGUMENTS FOR ANALYSIS

Now let's turn to two sample arguments to see how our version of the Toulmin model can help you test your own arguments more effectively. The first piece, originally published in the *New York Times Magazine,* provides a very logical but highly provocative argument about a crime that has received considerable media attention: infanticide. The author, Steven Pinker, is the director of the Center for Cognitive Neuroscience at the Massachusetts Institute of Technology and author of *How the Mind Works* (1997). His essay explains his interpretation of why mothers kill their newborn babies and argues that society should reconsider its response to their crime.

Why They Kill Their Newborns
Steven Pinker

1   Killing your baby. What could be more depraved? For a woman to destroy the fruit of her womb would seem like an ultimate violation of the natural order. But every year, hundreds of women commit neonaticide: they kill their newborns or let them die. Most neonaticides remain undiscovered, but every once in a while a janitor follows a trail of blood to a tiny body in a trash bin, or a woman faints and doctors find the remains of a placenta inside her.

2   Two cases have recently riveted the American public. Last November, Amy Grossberg and Brian Peterson, 18-year-old college sweethearts, delivered their baby in a motel room and, according to prosecutors, killed him and left his body in a dumpster. They will go on trial for murder next year and, if convicted, could be sentenced to death. In June, another 18-year-old, Melissa Drexler, arrived at her high-school prom, locked herself in a bathroom stall, gave birth to a boy and left him dead in a garbage can. Everyone knows what happened next: she touched herself up and returned to the dance floor. In September, a grand jury indicted her for murder.

3   How could they do it? Nothing melts the heart like a helpless baby. Even a biologist's cold calculations tell us that nurturing an offspring that carries our genes is the whole point of our existence. Neonaticide, many think, could be only a product of pathology. The psychiatrists uncover childhood trauma. The defense lawyers argue temporary psychosis. The pundits blame a throwaway society, permissive sex education and, of course, rock lyrics.

4   But it's hard to maintain that neonaticide is an illness when we learn that it has been practiced and accepted in most cultures throughout history. And that neonaticidal women do not commonly show signs of psychopathology. In a classic 1970 study of statistics of child killing, a psychiatrist, Phillip Resnick, found that mothers who kill their *older* children are frequently psychotic, depressed or suicidal, but mothers who kill their newborns are usually not. (It was this difference that led Resnick to argue that the category infanticide be split into neonaticide, the killing of a baby on the day of its birth, and filicide, the killing of a child older than one day.)

5   Killing a baby is an immoral act, and we often express our outrage at the immoral by calling it a sickness. But normal human motives are not always moral, and neonaticide does not have to be a product of malfunctioning neural circuitry or a dysfunctional upbringing. We can try to understand what would lead a mother to kill her newborn, remembering that to understand is not necessarily to forgive.

6   Martin Daly and Margo Wilson, both psychologists, argue that a capacity for neonaticide is built into the biological design of our parental emotions. Mammals are extreme among animals in the amount of time, energy and food they invest in their young, and humans are extreme among mammals. Parental investment is a limited resource, and mammalian mothers must "decide" whether to allot it to their newborn or to their current and future offspring. If a newborn is sickly, or if its survival is not promising, they may cut their losses and favor the healthiest in the litter or try again later on.

7   In most cultures, neonaticide is a form of this triage. Until very recently in human evolutionary history, mothers nursed their children for two to four years before becoming fertile again. Many children died, especially in the perilous first year. Most women saw no more than two or three of their children survive to adulthood, and many did not see any survive. To become a grandmother, a woman had to make hard choices. In most societies documented by anthropologists, including those of hunter-gatherers (our best glimpse into our ancestors' way of life), a woman lets a newborn die when its prospects for sur-

vival to adulthood are poor. The forecast might be based on abnormal signs in the infant, or on bad circumstances for successful motherhood at the time— she might be burdened with older children, beset by war or famine or without a husband or social support. Moreover, she might be young enough to try again.

8   We are all descendants of women who made the difficult decisions that allowed them to become grandmothers in that unforgiving world, and we inherited that brain circuitry that led to those decisions. Daly and Wilson have shown that the statistics on neonaticide in contemporary North America parallel those in the anthropological literature. The women who sacrifice their offspring tend to be young, poor, unmarried and socially isolated.

9   Natural selection cannot push the buttons of behavior directly; it affects our behavior by endowing us with emotions that coax us toward adaptive choices. New mothers have always faced a choice between a definite tragedy now and the possibility of an even greater tragedy months or years later, and that choice is not to be taken lightly. Even today, the typical rumination of a depressed new mother—how will I cope with this burden?—is a legitimate concern. The emotional response called bonding is also far more complex than the popular view, in which a woman is imprinted with a lifelong attachment to her baby if they interact in a critical period immediately following the baby's birth. A new mother will first coolly assess the infant and her current situation and only in the next few days begin to see it as a unique and wonderful individual. Her love will gradually deepen in ensuing years, in a trajectory that tracks the increasing biological value of a child (the chance that it will live to produce grandchildren) as the child proceeds through the mine field of early development.

10   Even when a mother in a hunter-gatherer society hardens her heart to sacrifice a newborn, her heart has not turned to stone. Anthropologists who interview these women (or their relatives, since the event is often too painful for the woman to discuss) discover that the women see the death as an unavoidable tragedy, grieve at the time and remember the child with pain all their lives. Even the supposedly callous Melissa Drexler agonized over a name for her dead son and wept at his funeral. (Initial reports that, after giving birth, she requested a Metallica song from the deejay and danced with her boyfriend turned out to be false.)

11   Many cultural practices are designed to distance people's emotions from a newborn until its survival seems probable. Full personhood is often not automatically granted at birth, as we see in our rituals of christening and the Jewish bris. And yet the recent neonaticides will seem puzzling. These are middle-class girls whose babies would have been kept far from starvation by the girl's parents or by any of thousands of eager adoptive couples. But our emotions, fashioned by the slow hand of natural selection, respond to the signals of the long-vanished tribal environment in which we spent 99 percent of our evolutionary history. Being young and single are two bad omens for successful motherhood, and the girl who conceals her pregnancy and procrastinates over its consequences will soon be disquieted by a third omen. She will give birth in circumstances that are particularly unpromising for a human mother: alone.

12   In hunter-gatherer societies, births are virtually always assisted because human anatomy makes birth (especially the first one) long, difficult and risky. Older women act as midwives, emotional supports and experienced appraisers who help decide whether the infant should live. Wenda Trevathan, an anthropologist and trained midwife, has studied pelvises of human fossils and concluded that childbirth has been physically tortuous, and therefore probably assisted, for millions of years. Maternal feelings may be adapted to a world in which a promising newborn is heralded with waves of cooing and clucking and congratulating. Those reassuring signals are absent from a secret birth in a motel room or a bathroom stall.

13   So what is the mental state of a teen-age mother who has kept her pregnancy secret? She is immature enough to have hoped that her pregnancy would go away by itself, her maternal feelings have been set at zero and she suddenly realizes she is in big trouble.

14   Sometimes she continues to procrastinate. In September, 17-year-old Shanta Clark gave birth to a premature boy and kept him hidden in her bedroom closet, as if he were E.T., for 17 days. She fed him before and after she went to school until her mother discovered him. The weak cry of the preemie kept him from being discovered earlier. (In other cases, girls have panicked over the crying and, in stifling the cry, killed the baby.)

15   Most observers sense the desperation that drives a woman to neonaticide. Prosecutors sometimes don't prosecute; juries rarely convict; those found guilty almost never go to jail. Barbara Kirwin, a forensic psychologist, reports that in nearly 300 cases of women charged with neonaticide in the United States and Britain, no woman spent more than a night in jail. In Europe, the laws of several countries prescribed less-severe penalties for neonaticide than for adult homicides. The fascination with the Grossberg-Peterson case comes from the unusual threat of the death penalty. Even those in favor of capital punishment might shudder at the thought of two reportedly nice kids being strapped to gurneys and put to death.

16   But our compassion hinges on the child, not just on the mother. Killers of older children, no matter how desperate, evoke little mercy. Susan Smith, the South Carolina woman who sent her two sons, 14 months and 3 years old, to watery deaths, is in jail, unmourned, serving a life sentence. The leniency shown to neonaticidal mothers forces us to think the unthinkable and ask if we, like many societies and like the mothers themselves, are not completely sure whether a neonate is a full person.

17   It seems obvious that we need a clear boundary to confer personhood on a human being and grant it a right to life. Otherwise, we approach a slippery slope that ends in the disposal of inconvenient people or in grotesque deliberations on the value of individual lives. But the endless abortion debate shows how hard it is to locate the boundary. Anti-abortionists draw the line at conception, but that implies we should shed tears every time an invisible conceptus fails to implant in the uterus—and, to carry the argument to its logical conclusion, that we should prosecute for murder anyone who uses an IUD. Those in favor of abortion draw the line at viability, but viability is a fuzzy gradient that

depends on how great a risk of an impaired child the parents are willing to tolerate. The only thing both sides agree on is that the line must be drawn at some point before birth.

18   Neonaticide forces us to examine even that boundary. To a biologist, birth is as arbitrary a milestone as any other. Many mammals bear offspring that see and walk as soon as they hit the ground. But the incomplete 9-month-old human fetus must be evicted from the womb before its outsize head gets too big to fit through its mother's pelvis. The usual primate assembly process spills into the first years in the world. And that complicates our definition of personhood.

19   What makes a living being a person with a right not to be killed? Animal-rights extremists would seem to have the easiest argument to make: that all sentient beings have a right to life. But champions of that argument must conclude that delousing a child is akin to mass murder; the rest of us must look for an argument that draws a small circle. Perhaps only the members of our own species, Homo sapiens, have a right to life? But that is simply chauvinism; a person of one race could just as easily say that people of another race have no right to life.

20   No, the right to life must come, the moral philosophers say, from morally significant traits that we humans happen to possess. One such trait is having a unique sequence of experiences that defines us as individuals and connects us to other people. Other traits include an ability to reflect upon ourselves as a continuous locus of consciousness, to form and savor plans for the future, to dread death and to express the choice not to die. And there's the rub: our immature neonates don't possess these traits any more than mice do.

21   Several moral philosophers have concluded that neonates are not persons, and thus neonaticide should not be classified as murder. Michael Tooley has gone so far as to say that neonaticide ought to be permitted during an interval after birth. Most philosophers (to say nothing of nonphilosophers) recoil from that last step, but the very fact that there can be a debate about the personhood of neonates, but no debate about the personhood of older children, makes it clearer why we feel more sympathy for an Amy Grossberg than for a Susan Smith.

22   So how do you provide grounds for outlawing neonaticide? The facts don't make it easy. Some philosophers suggest that people intuitively see neonates as so similar to older babies that you couldn't allow neonaticide without coarsening the way people treat children and other people in general. Again, the facts say otherwise. Studies in both modern and hunter-gatherer societies have found that neonaticidal women don't kill anyone but their newborns, and when they give birth later under better conditions, they can be devoted, loving mothers.

23   The laws of biology were not kind to Amy Grossberg and Melissa Drexler, and they are not kind to us as we struggle to make moral sense of the teenagers' actions. One predicament is that our moral system needs a crisp inauguration of personhood, but the assembly process for Homo sapiens is gradual, piecemeal and uncertain. Another problem is that the emotional circuitry of mothers has evolved to cope with this uncertain process, so the baby killers

turn out to be not moral monsters but nice, normal (and sometimes religious) young women. These are dilemmas we will probably never resolve, and any policy will leave us with uncomfortable cases. We will most likely muddle through, keeping birth as a conspicuous legal boundary but showing mercy to the anguished girls who feel they had no choice but to run afoul of it.

An Analysis Based on the Toulmin Model

Clearly Steven Pinker has taken a controversial stance on a disturbing social issue. In fact, in light of civilized society's attitudes toward the sacredness of the mother-infant bond, his position is one that many people might find shocking and repugnant. How could he propose that neonaticide, the murder of one's newborn infant, be viewed as an acceptable form of behavior, one that we have inherited from our evolutionary ancestors? As Pinker readily admits in the first three paragraphs of his essay, neonaticide seems alien to most of the values we as civilized people cherish. Nevertheless, Pinker argues that while it may be regarded as immoral, neonaticide is not necessarily the act of a mentally deranged woman, but rather a difficult decision guided by an instinct for survival handed down to a mother by generations of women before her. While he does not condone or endorse this practice, Pinker urges his readers to try to understand a context that might drive women to commit such an act.

Your first reaction to Pinker's ideas may be to dismiss them as outrageous and unworthy of serious consideration. Yet by closely analyzing Pinker's argument using the Toulmin method, you will be able to see how carefully Pinker has crafted his argument to challenge many of our assumptions about human behavior and, in particular, motherhood.

Claims and Grounds

Pinker presents the first part of his claim in paragraph 4 of his essay: Neonaticide is not an abnormal behavior but one that has been practiced "in most cultures throughout history." This statement seems to contradict the popular notion of neonaticide. Because our society regards neonaticide as an immoral act, many people likely assume that it is a rare occurrence. However, Pinker anticipates this assumption in paragraph 1 by reminding us that neonaticide *does* occur in our own society. It is, he claims, more common than we realize, since most murders of newborn babies go undetected. Only "every once in a while" do we discover that this act has taken place because some physical evidence is found. While Pinker offers no grounds for his assertion that "every year, hundreds of women commit neonaticide," his audience's familiarity with newspaper accounts of newborns abandoned in dumpsters and public restrooms lends credibility to his statement. This point is important because it establishes a link between contemporary women's behavior and the practices of our "long-vanished tribal environment."

Pinker develops this idea further in paragraphs 6 through 8 by suggesting that this behavior has been programmed into our "biological design" through human evolutionary development. He provides the grounds to support this part of his claim by citing two scholarly sources: Philip Resnick's study of child-killing statistics, which indicates that women who kill their newborn babies are typically not mentally ill, and research by Martin Daly and Margo Wilson that suggests neonaticide may be an intrinsic part of our "biological design," a necessity for human beings with limited resources to invest in their offspring. Relying on these grounds, Pinker goes on to argue in paragraph 9 that neonaticide is an "adaptive choice," one that is preferable to nurturing an infant whose continued survival is in doubt because of either the physical condition of the child or environmental difficulties for the mother.

So far, then, we have found two of the essential parts of the Toulmin model in Pinker's essay:

Claim	Neonaticide is not a pathologic behavior but can be, rather, the result of evolutionary development.
Grounds	Various anthropological studies indicate that neonaticide is a common and accepted practice in many contemporary societies; studies by psychologists argue that neonaticide is a normal part of our parenting emotions; research by psychologists demonstrates that women who commit neonaticide are not mentally ill.

Warrants, Backing, and Rebuttals

Now let's move on to Pinker's warrants, which work to support his claim. Pinker never directly states, yet he strongly implies as a *warrant*, that "biology is destiny." It is clear from his claim and the grounds used to support it that Pinker believes the biological impulses of a new mother who commits neonaticide may overwhelm her civilized sense of what is morally or even emotionally right. Human beings, according to Pinker, are at the mercy of their neurological programming. Pinker offers *backing* for this *warrant* in paragraph 10 when he relates interviews by anthropologists with women who have killed their newborn babies and who appear to grieve sincerely for their children, regarding their actions as "an unavoidable tragedy." These women, according to Pinker, were compelled to make a difficult choice, which each did in spite of her maternal feelings toward the newborn. Pinker reinforces this point later in the essay when he states in paragraph 23 that "the laws of biology were not kind to Amy Grossberg and Melissa Drexler," two young women who killed their infants just after birth. Pinker strongly implies that biological forces were at work when these women made their decisions.

Pinker's warrant provides plenty of opportunity for *rebuttal* because even if the reader accepts the idea that human beings, despite the teachings of civilized society, are still subject to the dictates of more primitive and instinctive urges, Pinker asserts that the urge to kill one's baby is stronger than, say, the maternal instinct to nurture that infant. We have all heard of situations in which a mother has risked or sacrificed her own life to save that of her child. Why, we might ask, wouldn't this emotion dominate the behavior of a new mother? Pinker acknowledges this rebuttal in paragraph 11 when he points out that the neonaticides we read about in newspapers are often committed by middle-class girls who have the resources to support a child or the option to give the baby up for adoption.

Pinker responds to this rebuttal in two ways: First, he reiterates his claim that the internal forces of our evolutionary background are stronger than the individual's own sense of right and wrong. These young women are responding to the "signals of the long-vanished tribal environment in which we spent 99 percent of our evolutionary history." Moreover, Pinker goes on to suggest, neonaticide is triggered by environmental and social factors, specifically, the age, marital status, and isolation of the new mother, that work to suppress more positive maternal responses. As he explains in paragraph 12, maternal feelings are more likely to emerge in an atmosphere of "cooing and clucking and congratulating" than in a "motel room or bathroom stall."

Pinker goes on to support his argument with several additional layers of warrants: If human behavior is controlled by deeply ingrained biological forces, then we can't be held legally responsible for these actions. In other words, while we may deeply deplore the act of neonaticide, we cannot fault these women for acting on an impulse they may not completely understand or feel able to control. In paragraph 15 Pinker provides backing for this claim by observing that few women in the United States are actually incarcerated for this crime and several European countries treat neonaticide less severely than other forms of homicide. Thus, although the killing of one's baby generates strong moral outrage in our society, we treat it less severely than most other offenses in the same category.

Logically, then, the next question must be "Why is this the case?" When older children are murdered by their mothers, as in Pinker's example of Susan Smith in paragraph 16, we waste little sympathy on the plight of the mother. We can agree with Pinker that "our compassion hinges on the child." Why do we react, according to Pinker, in a very different way to the death of a newborn? Pinker has very carefully brought us to his next warrant, which even he admits is the "unthinkable": Our reaction to the killing of a newborn and the killing of an older child is different because a newborn is not yet a "full person."

Pinker provides backing for his warrant in paragraphs 18 through 20. In paragraph 18 he points out a fact most readers would agree with: Unlike other mammals, human babies are helpless at birth. They are "incomplete." It will take an infant several years to achieve the level of physical development that some mammals enjoy at birth. Thus, a newborn baby cannot claim its rights as a person based on its physical completeness. Then, Pinker asks, on what basis can a newborn be seen as possessing "a right not to be killed"? By what traits do we define a person with a right to life? In paragraph 20 Pinker calls on the *backing* of "moral philosophers" who describe the traits human beings must possess to be considered fully human. Pinker concludes that newborn babies "don't possess these traits any more than mice do."

Anticipating that most readers will have a strong negative response to these ideas, Pinker acknowledges several rebuttals to this warrant. In paragraph 17 he recognizes that neither side of the abortion debate would agree with his assertion that birth should not be a marker to determine when a human being is given a right to life. To antiabortionists, who maintain that "personhood" begins at conception,

Pinker responds that if we adopt this viewpoint, the destruction of any fertilized human egg would be considered murder. To those in favor of abortion rights, who consider personhood to begin when the baby is capable of living outside the protection of the mother's body, Pinker counters that this depends on the condition of the infant and the willingness of the parents to accept the risks inherent in a premature birth. In paragraph 19 Pinker also rejects the position that all life deserves to be preserved. If this were practiced, Pinker reasons, then "delousing a child is akin to mass murder." Pinker's stance forces us to reexamine how we define a "person" and how we can determine at what point the right to live unharmed begins.

We can briefly summarize Pinker's warrants and backing as follows:

Warrant 1	Biology is destiny. We are at the mercy of our neurological programming, which has been handed down from our evolutionary ancestors.
Backing	Examples of women who grieve for the newborns they killed; references to Melissa Drexler and Amy Grossberg, who killed their newborn infants.
Warrant 2	If human behavior is controlled by deeply ingrained biological forces, then women can't be held legally responsible for following their natural impulses.
Backing	Examples of lenient criminal treatment of women who commit neonaticide; examples of less severe penalties for women who kill newborns, as opposed to those given for the murder of older children or adults.
Warrant 3	A newborn infant is not a full person. Neonates do not yet possess those human qualities that bestow on them the right to life.
Backing	A description of a newborn infant's physical helplessness; a definition of a "full person" according to some moral philosophers; a comparison of the intellectual and moral awareness of a newborn infant with that of a mouse.

Qualifiers

Throughout his essay Pinker is careful to use *qualifiers* that limit and clarify his claim. There are many examples of these; we will point out a few that appear early in the essay along with our emphasis and comments:

Paragraph 4	"But it's *hard* [difficult but not impossible] to maintain that neonaticide is an illness when we learn that it has been practiced and accepted in *most* [but not all] cultures throughout history. And that neonaticidal women do not *commonly* [typical but not in all cases] show signs of psychopathology."
Paragraph 5	"But normal human motives are *not always* [happens some of the time] moral, and neonaticide *does not have to be* [but it could be] a product of malfunctioning neural circuitry or a dysfunctional upbringing."

By using qualifiers, Pinker demonstrates his awareness that his claim may not always be true under all circumstances and accounts for the differing experiences of his audience.

As we stated at the beginning of this chapter, to construct a persuasive argument, you must pay careful attention to the logical structure you are building. As the Toulmin method illustrates, unless your claim is supported by a firm foundation (your warrants) and well buttressed by convincing grounds and backing, your structure will not withstand the rebuttals that will test its strength.

Pinker's view on neonaticide is disturbing, to say the least. For his essay to be persuasive, the reader must be willing to accept each of his warrants and the backing he uses to support them. Four days after Pinker's essay appeared in the *New York Times,* the following article was published in the *Washington Post.* As you read the article, notice how author Michael Kelley, a senior writer at the *National Journal,* attacks Pinker's claim by questioning each of his warrants and their backing. Calling Pinker's premise one of the "most thoroughly dishonest constructs anyone has ever attempted to pass off as science," Kelley also levels severe criticism at one of Pinker's sources, Michael Tooley. Kelley comments that Pinker's citation of Tooley's radical views, even though he may not directly agree with them, makes him "guilty by association." Kelley's accusation demonstrates why you should choose your sources carefully. Your audience will associate your views with the company they keep.

Arguing for Infanticide
Michael Kelley

1   Of all the arguments advanced against the legalization of abortion, the one that always struck me as the most questionable is the most consequential: that the widespread acceptance of abortion would lead to a profound moral shift in our culture, a great devaluing of human life. This seemed to me dubious on general principle: Projections of this sort almost always turn out to be wrong because they fail to grasp that, in matters of human behavior, there is not really any such thing as a trendline. People change to meet new realities and thereby change reality.

2   Thus, for the environmental hysterics of the 1970s, the nuclear freezers of the 1980s and the Perovian budget doomsayers of the 1990s, the end that was nigh never came. So, with abortions, why should a tolerance for ending human life under one, very limited, set of conditions necessarily lead to an acceptance of ending human life under other, broader terms?

3   This time, it seems, the pessimists were right. On Sunday, Nov. 2, an article in the *New York Times,* the closest thing we have to the voice of the intellectual establishment, came out for killing babies. I am afraid that I am sensationalizing only slightly. The article by Steven Pinker in the *Times Magazine* did not go

quite so far as to openly recommend the murder of infants, and printing the article did not constitute the *Times'* endorsement of the idea. But close enough, close enough.

4   What Pinker, a professor of psychology at the Massachusetts Institute of Technology, wrote and what the *Times* treated as a legitimate argument, was a thoroughly sympathetic treatment of this modest proposal: Mothers who kill their newborn infants should not be judged as harshly as people who take human life in its later stages because newborn infants are not persons in the full sense of the word, and therefore do not enjoy a right to life. Who says that life begins at birth?

5   "To a biologist, birth is as arbitrary a milestone as any other," Pinker breezily writes. "No, the right to life must come, the moral philosophers say, from morally significant traits that we humans happen to possess. One such trait is having a unique sequence of experiences that defines us as individuals and connects us to other people. Other traits include an ability to reflect upon ourselves as a continuous locus of consciousness, to form and savor plans for the future, to dread death and to express the choice not to die. And there's the rub: our immature neonates don't possess these traits any more than mice do."

6   Pinker notes that "several moral philosophers have concluded that neonates are not persons, and thus neonaticide should not be classified as murder," and he suggests his acceptance of this view, arguing that "the facts don't make it easy" to legitimately outlaw the killing of infants.

7   Pinker's causally authoritative mention of "the facts" is important. Because Pinker is no mere ranter from the crackpot fringe but a scientist. He is, in fact, a respected explicator of the entirely mainstream and currently hot theory of evolutionary psychology, and the author of *How the Mind Works,* a just-published, doubtlessly seminal, exceedingly fat book on the subject.

8   How the mind works, says Pinker, is that people are more or less hard-wired to behave as they do by the cumulative effects of the human experience. First cousins to the old Marxist economic determinists, the evolutionary psychologists are behavioral determinists. They believe in a sort of Popeye's theory of human behavior: I do what I do because I yam what I yam because I wuz what I wuz.

9   This view is radical; it seeks to supplant both traditional Judeo-Christian morality and liberal humanism with a new "scientific" philosophy that denies the idea that all humans are possessed of a quality that sets them apart from the lower species, and that this quality gives humans the capacity and responsibility to choose freely between right and wrong. And it is monstrous. And, judging from the writings of Pinker and his fellow determinists on the subject of infanticide, it may be the most thoroughly dishonest construct anyone has ever attempted to pass off as science.

10   Pinker's argument was a euphemized one. The more blunt argument is made by Michael Tooley, a philosophy professor at the University of Colorado, whom Pinker quotes. In this 1972 essay "Abortion and Infanticide," Tooley makes what he calls "an extremely plausible answer" to the question: "What

makes it morally permissible to destroy a baby, but wrong to kill an adult?" Simple enough: Personhood does not begin at birth. Rather, "an organism possesses a serious right to life only if it possesses the concept of a self as a continuing subject of experiences and other mental states, and believes that it is itself such a continuing entity."

11   Some would permit the killing of infants "up to the time an organism learned how to use certain expressions," but Tooley finds this cumbersome and would simply establish "some period of time, such as a week after birth, as the interval during which infanticide will be permitted."

12   And Tooley does not bother with Pinker's pretense that what is under discussion here is only a rare act of desperation, the killing of an unwanted child by a frightened, troubled mother. No, no, no. If it is moral to kill a baby for one, it is moral for all. Indeed, the systematic, professionalized use of infanticide would be a great benefit to humanity. "Most people would prefer to raise children who do not suffer from gross deformities or from severe physical, emotional, or intellectual handicaps," writes eugenicist Tooley. "If it could be shown that there is no moral objection to infanticide the happiness of society could be significantly and justifiably increased."

13   To defend such an unnatural idea, the determinists argue that infanticide is in fact natural: In Pinker's words, "it has been practiced and accepted in most cultures throughout history." This surprising claim is critical to the argument that the act of a mother killing a child is a programmed response to signals that the child might not fare well in life (because of poverty, illegitimacy or other factors). And it is a lie.

14   In fact, although millions of mothers give birth every year under the sort of adverse conditions that Pinker says trigger the "natural" urge to kill the baby, infanticide is extremely rare in all modern societies, and is universally treated as a greatly aberrant act, the very definition of a moral horror. The only cultures that Pinker can point to in which infanticide is widely "practiced and accepted" are those that are outside the mores of Western civilization: ancient cultures and the remnants of ancient cultures today, tribal hunter-gatherer societies.

15   And so goes the entire argument, a great chain of dishonesty, palpable untruth piled upon palpable untruth. "A new mother," asserts Pinker, "will first coolly assess the infant and her situation and only in the next few days begin to see it as a unique and wonderful individual." Yes, that was my wife all over: cool as a cucumber as she assessed whether to keep her first-born child or toss him out the window. As George Orwell said once of another vast lie, "You have to be an intellectual to believe such nonsense. No ordinary man could be such a fool."

■ QUESTIONS FOR ANALYSIS AND DISCUSSION

1. Briefly outline the basic Toulmin components of Kelley's argument: What is his claim? What grounds does he use to support it? Then find and identify Kelley's warrants and the backing he provides to demonstrate their reliability.

2. To what aspects of Pinker's claim and warrants does Kelley object? On what grounds does he object?

3. Pinker limits his discussion of neonaticide to the behavior of "depressed new mothers" (paragraph 9). Does Kelley ignore this distinction in his response to Pinker? How does Kelley shift the discussion from Pinker's "anguished girls" (paragraph 23) to "millions of mothers" (paragraph 14 in Kelley)? Do you think this is a fair interpretation of Pinker's intent?

4. Kelley begins his essay with a reference to the legalization of abortion. On what basis does he suggest a link between the "widespread acceptance of abortion" and Pinker's theories about neonaticide?

5. In paragraph 3 of his essay Kelley states that Pinker "did not go quite so far as to openly recommend the murder of infants." Discuss the implications of Kelley's use of the qualifiers *quite* and *openly*. What do you think he intends to imply about Pinker's objectives?

6. In paragraph 10, what does Kelley mean by describing Pinker's argument as "euphemized"? What connection does Kelley make between Pinker's views and the theories expressed by Michael Tooley in his 1972 essay? Does your analysis of Pinker's claim and warrants lead you to believe that Pinker endorses Tooley's theories, as Kelley asserts?

7. In your journal, discuss your own response to Kelley's essay. Which reasons do you find particularly persuasive? With which reasons do you disagree, and why?

8. In paragraph 9, Kelley criticizes Pinker's attempt to take a "scientific" approach to a serious moral issue by suggesting that humans lack "the capacity and responsibility to choose freely between right and wrong." In your journal, consider how Pinker might respond to that statement. Would he agree with Kelley's interpretation of his ideas? How would Pinker suggest that society should deal with the problem of neonaticide?

SAMPLE STUDENT ARGUMENT FOR ANALYSIS

Given the fact that half of all children will see their parents' marriage terminate by the time they turn eighteen, divorce has become an American way of life. While society may shake its collective head at such a statistic, lamenting the loss of the traditional family, not all children of divorce see it as a problem. In the following essay, Lowell Putnam explores the effect of his parents' divorce on his development, arguing that divorce should not be a taboo topic, and that children of broken homes are not always damaged.

Lowell Putnam is a sophomore at Harvard. When he is not living on campus, he splits his time between his mother's home in New York and his father's home in Massachusetts.

Read through Putnam's essay and make notes in your journal. Notice whether and how its parts work together—and, if possible, where some of the parts may need to be reworked. Then respond to the questions that follow.

Did I Miss Something?

Lowell Putnam

1   The subject of divorce turns heads in our society. It is responsible for bitten tongues, lowered voices, and an almost pious reverence saved only for life threatening illness or uncontrolled catastrophe. Having grown up in a "broken home," I am always shocked to be treated as a victim of some social disease. When a class assignment required that I write an essay concerning my feelings about or my personal experiences with divorce, my first reaction was complete surprise. An essay on aspects of my life affected by divorce seems completely superfluous, because I cannot differentiate between the "normal" part of my youth and the supposed angst and confusion that apparently come with all divorces. The separation of my parents over sixteen years ago (when I was three years old) has either saturated every last pore of my developmental epidermis to a point where I cannot sense it or has not affected me at all. Eugene Ehrlich's *Highly Selective Dictionary for the Extraordinarily Literate* (1997) defines divorce as a "breach"; however, I cannot sense any schism in my life resulting from the event to which other people seem to attribute so much importance. My parents' divorce is a ubiquitous part of who I am, and the only "breach" that could arrive from my present familial arrangement would be to tear me away from what I consider my normal living conditions.

2   Though there is no doubt in my mind that many unfortunate people have had their lives torn apart by the divorce of their parents, I do not feel any real sense of regret for my situation. In my opinion, the paramount role of a parent is to love his or her child. Providing food, shelter, education, and video games are of course other necessary elements of successful child rearing, but these secondary concerns stem from the most fundamental ideal of parenting, which is love. A loving parent will be a successful one even if he or she cannot afford to furnish his or her child with the best clothes or the most sophisticated gourmet delicacies. With love as the driving force in a parent's mind, he or she will almost invariably make the correct decisions. When my mother and father found that they were no longer in love with each other after nine years of marriage, their love for me forced them to take the precipitous step to separate. The safest environment for me was to be with one happy parent at a time, instead of two miserable ones all the time. The sacrifice that they both made to relinquish control over me for half the year was at least as painful for them as it was for me (probably even more so), but in the end I was not deprived of a parent's love, but merely of one parent's presence for a few weeks at a time. My father and mother's love for me has not dwindled even slightly over the past fifteen years, and I can hardly imagine a more well-adjusted and contented family.

3   As I reread the first section of this essay, I realize that it is perhaps too optimistic and cheerful regarding my life as a child of divorced parents. In all truthfulness, there have been some decidedly negative ramifications stemming from

our family separation. My first memory is actually of a fight between my mother and father. I vaguely remember standing in the end of the upstairs hallway of our Philadelphia house when I was about three years old, and seeing shadows moving back and forth in the light coming from under the door of my father's study, accompanied by raised voices. It would be naïve of me to say that I have not been at all affected by divorce, since it has permeated my most primal and basic memories; however, I am grateful that I can only recall one such incident, instead of having parental conflicts become so quotidian that they leave no mark whatsoever on my mind. Also, I find that having to divide my time equally between both parents leads to alienation from either side of my family. Invariably, at every holiday occasion, there is one half of my family (either my mother's side or my father's) that has to explain that "Lowell is with his [mother/father] this year," while aunts, cousins, and grandparents collectively arch eyebrows or avert eyes. Again, though, I should not be hasty to lament my distance from loved ones, since there are many families with "normal" marriages where the children never even meet their cousins, let alone get to spend every other Thanksgiving with them. Though divorce has certainly thrown some proverbial monkey wrenches into some proverbial gears, in general my otherwise strong familial ties have overshadowed any minor blemishes.

4   Perhaps one of the most important reasons for my absence of "trauma" (for lack of a better word) stemming from my parents' divorce is that I am by no means alone in my trials and tribulations. The foreboding statistic that sixty percent of marriages end in divorce is no myth to me, indeed many of my friends come from similar situations. The argument could be made that "birds of a feather flock together" and that my friends and I form a tight support network for each other, but I strongly doubt that any of us need or look for that kind of buttress. The fact of the matter is that divorce happens a lot in today's society, and as a result our culture has evolved to accommodate these new family arrangements, making the overall conditions more hospitable for me and my broken brothers and shattered sisters.

5   I am well aware that divorce can often lead to issues of abandonment and familial proximity among children of separated parents, but in my case I see very little evidence to support the claim that my parents should have stayed married "for the sake of the child." In many ways, my life is enriched by the division of my time with my father and my time with my mother. I get to live in New York City for half of the year, and in a small suburb of Boston for the other half. I have friends who envy me, since I get "the best of both worlds." I never get double-teamed by parents during arguments, and I cherish my time with each one more since it only lasts half the year.

6   In my opinion, there is no such thing as a perfect life or a "normal" life, and any small blips on our karmic radar screen have to be dealt with appropriately but without any trepidation or self-pity. Do I miss my father when I live with my mother (and vice versa)? Of course I do. However, I know young boys and girls who have lost parents to illness or accidental injury, so my pitiable position is relative. As I look back on the last nineteen years from the relative in-

dependence of college, I can safely say that my childhood has not been at all marred by having two different houses to call home.

■ QUESTIONS FOR ANALYSIS AND DISCUSSION

1. Identify Putnam's claim. Where does he state it in his essay? From your experience, do you agree with him? Do you agree that people discuss divorce "in an almost pious reverence saved only for life threatening illness"?
2. On what grounds does Putnam base his claim? Find specific evidence he presents to support his claim. Do you find it convincing and supportive?
3. Do you agree with Putnam's definition of what makes a good parent?
4. Putnam has several warrants, some of them stated explicitly and some implied. In paragraph 2 he states: "A loving parent will be a successful one even if he or she cannot afford to furnish his or her child with the best clothes or the most sophisticated gourmet delicacies." Do you agree with his warrant? On what commonly shared values or beliefs does he base this warrant? Are there any aspects of his warrant with which you disagree? What backing does Putnam provide to support his warrant? Is it sufficient?
5. What other warrants underlie Putnam's claim? In a small peer group, identify several layers of warrants and discuss whether these need additional backing to be convincing.
6. Notice the qualifier Putnam uses in paragraph 3 when he says, "In all truthfulness, there have been *some* decidedly negative ramifications stemming from our family separation" (emphasis added). What limitations does this qualifying statement put on his argument? Does this limitation weaken his argument at all?
7. Does Putnam acknowledge and address anticipated rebuttals to his argument? Can you locate any in his essay? What rebuttals can you make in response to his argument?
8. If you are a child of divorced parents, write about the experience as it affected your emotional and psychological outlook. How did it impact your life growing up, and how did it affect your adult view of marriage? Answer the same questions if your parents remained married, considering in your response how your life may have been different if your parents had divorced while you were young.
9. In your peer group, discuss the effects of divorce on children. Further develop Putnam's idea that it is just another way of life. Compare notes with classmates to assemble a complete list. Based on this list, develop your own argument about the effects of divorce on children.

Using Visual Arguments
Thinking Like an Illustrator

Ours is a visual world. From the first cave paintings of prehistoric France to the complicated photomosaic posters that adorn dorm walls today, we are inspired, compelled, and persuaded by visual stimuli. Everywhere we look there are images vying for our attention—magazine ads, T-shirt logos, movie billboards, artwork, traffic signs, political cartoons, statues, and storefront windows. Glanced at only briefly, visuals communicate information and ideas. They may project commonly held values, ideals, and fantasies. They can relay opinion, inspire reaction, and influence emotion. And because the competition for our attention today is so great, and the time available for communication is so scarce, images must compete to make an impression or risk being lost in a blur of visual information.

Because the goal of a calculated visual is to persuade, coax, intimidate, or otherwise subliminally influence its viewer, it is important that its audience can discern the strategies or technique it employs. In other words, to be a literate reader of visuals, one must be a literate reader of arguments.

Consider the instant messages projected by brand names, company logos, or even the American flag. Such images may influence us consciously and unconsciously. Some visual images, such as advertisements, may target our emotions, while others, such as graphics, may appeal to our intellect. Just as we approach writing with the tools of critical analysis, we should carefully consider the many ways visuals influence us.

Common Forms of Visual Arguments

Visual arguments come in many different forms and use many different media. Artists, photographers, advertisers, cartoonists, and designers approach their work with the same intentions that authors of written material do—they want to share a point of view, present an idea, inspire or evoke a reaction. For example, think back to when you had your high-school yearbook photo taken. The photographer didn't simply sit you down and start snapping pictures. More likely, the photographer told you how to sit, tilt your head, and where to gaze. You selected your clothing for the picture carefully and probably spent more time on your hair that day. Lighting, shadow, and setting were also thoughtfully considered. You and your photographer crafted an image of how you wanted the world to see you—an image of importance because it would be forever recorded in your yearbook, as well as distributed to family and friends as the remembrance of a milestone in your life. In effect, you were creating a visual argument.

While there are many different kinds of visual arguments, the most common ones take the form of artwork, advertisements, editorial cartoons, and news photos. These visuals often do not rely on an image alone to tell their story, although it is certainly possible for a thoughtfully designed visual to do so. More often, however, advertisements are accompanied by ad copy, editorial cartoons feature comments or statements, and news photos are placed near the stories they enhance.

Ancillary visuals—that is, graphs, charts, and tables—have great potential for enhancing written arguments and influencing the audience. They provide snapshots of information and are usually used to provide factual support to written information. We will discuss these types of visuals, and how you can use them to enhance your own written arguments, later in this chapter. But first, let us examine some powerful visual images and the ways they capture our attention, impact our sensibilities, and evoke our responses.

Analyzing Visual Arguments

As critical readers of written arguments, we do not take the author simply at face value. We consider the author's purpose and intent, audience, style, tone, and supporting evidence. We must apply these same analytical tools to effectively "read" visual arguments. As with written language, understanding the persuasive power of "visual language" requires a close examination and interpretation of the premise, claims, details, supporting evidence, and stylistic touches embedded in any visual piece. We should ask ourselves the following four questions when examining visual arguments:

- Who is the target *audience?*
- What are the *claims* made in the images?
- What shared history or cultural *assumptions*—or warrants—does the image make?
- What is the supporting *evidence?*

Like works of art, visuals often employ color, shape, line, texture, depth, and point of view to create their effect. Therefore, to understand how visuals work and to analyze the way visuals persuade, we must also ask questions about specific aspects of form and design. For example, some questions to ask about print images such as those in newspaper and magazine ads include:

- What in the frame catches your attention immediately?
- What is the central image? What is the background image? foreground images? What are the surrounding images? What is significant in the placement of these images? Their relationship to one another?

- What verbal information is included? How is it made prominent? How does it relate to the other graphics or images?
- What specific details (people, objects, locale) are emphasized? Which are exaggerated or idealized?
- What is the effect of color and lighting?
- What emotional effect is created by the images—pleasure? longing? anxiety? nostalgia?
- Do the graphics and images make you want to know more about the subject or product?
- What special significance might objects in the image have?
- Is there any symbolism imbedded in the images?

Considering these questions helps us to critically survey a visual argument and enables us to formulate reasoned assessments of its message and intent. In the next pages of this chapter, we will analyze in greater detail some visual arguments presented in art, advertising, editorial cartoons, and photographs. Part Two of this book continues the investigation of visual arguments as they connect to the topics of each chapter.

Art

The French artist Georges Braque (1882–1963) once said, "In art, there can be no effect without twisting the truth." While not all artists would agree with him, Braque, who with Pablo Picasso originated the cubist style, "saw" things from a different perspective than the rest of us, and he expressed his vision in his paintings. All art is an interpretation of what the artist sees. It is filtered through the eyes of the artist and influenced by his or her own perceptions.

Throughout history, artists have applied their craft to advance religious, social, and political visual arguments. Portraits of kings and queens present how the monarchs wanted their people to see them, with symbolic tools of power such as scepters, crowns, and rich vestments. Art in churches and cathedrals was used as a means of visual instruction for people who could not read. Much of modern art reveals impressions, feelings, and emotions without remaining faithful to the actual thing depicted. While entire books are written about the meaning and function of art, let's examine how one particular artist, Pablo Picasso (1881–1973), created a visual argument.

Pablo Picasso's "Guernica"

Pablo Picasso, with fellow artist Georges Braque, invented a style of painting known as **cubism**. Cubism is based on the idea that the eye observes things from continually changing viewpoints, as fragments of a whole. Cubism aims to represent the essential reality of forms from multiple perspectives and angles. Thus, cubist paintings don't show reality as we see it. Rather, they depict pieces of people, places, and things in an unstable field of vision.

Picasso's painting "Guernica" (Figure 8.1) represents the essence of cubism. During the Spanish Civil War, the German air force bombed the town of Guernica,

Figure 8.1

the cultural center of the Basque region in northern Spain and a Loyalist stronghold. In only a few minutes on April 26, 1937, hundreds of men, women, and children were massacred in the deadly air strike. Two months later, Picasso expressed his outrage at the attack in a mural he titled simply, "Guernica."

The mural is Picasso's statement about the horror and devastation of war. The painting is dynamic and full of action, yet its figures seem flat and static. It is balanced while still presenting distorted images and impressions. It is ordered while still evoking a sense of chaos and panic. To better understand Picasso's "statement," let's apply some of the questions about visual arguments described earlier in the chapter to this painting.

Who Is Picasso's Target Audience?

Knowing the history of the painting can help us understand whom Picasso was trying to reach. In January 1937, Picasso was commissioned to paint a mural for the 1937 *Exposition Internationale Arts et Techniques des dans la Vie Moderne,* an art exhibition to open in France in May of that same year. While he had never been a political person, the atrocity of Guernica in April compelled him to express his anger and appeal to the world.

Before the mural went on display, some politicians tried to replace it with a less "offensive" piece of art. When the picture was unveiled at the opening of the expo, it was received poorly. One critic described it as "the work of a madman." Picasso had hoped that his work would shock people. He wanted the outside world to care about what happened at Guernica. However, Picasso may have misjudged his first audience. In 1937, Europe was on the brink of world war. Many people were in denial that the war could touch them and preferred to ignore the possibility that it was imminent. It was this audience who first viewed "Guernica"—an audience that didn't want to see a mural about war, an audience that was trying to avoid the inevitable. Years later, the mural would become one of the most critically acclaimed works of art of the twentieth century.

What Claims Is Picasso Making in the Images?

Picasso's painting comprises many images that make up an entire scene. It depicts simultaneously events that happened over a period of time. The overall claim is that war itself is horrible. The smaller claims address the injustice of Guernica more directly. A mother wails in grief over her dead infant, a reminder that the bombing of Guernica was a massacre of innocents. Picasso also chose to paint his mural in black and white, giving it the aura of a newspaper, especially in the body of the horse. He could be saying, "This is news" or "This is a current event that you should think about."

It should be mentioned that Picasso created many versions of the images in the mural, carefully considering their position, placement, and expression, sometimes drawing eight or nine versions of a single subject. He thoughtfully considered how the images would convey his message before he painted them in the mural.

What Shared History of Cultural Assumptions Does Picasso Make?

The assumptions in any argument are the principles or beliefs that the audience takes for granted. These assumptions implicitly connect the claim to the evidence. By naming his mural "Guernica," Picasso knew that people would make an immediate connection between the chaos on the wall and the events of April 26, 1937. He also assumed that the people viewing the painting would be upset by it. In addition, there are symbols in the painting that would have been recognized by people at the time—such as the figure of the bull in the upper-left-hand corner of the mural, a long-time symbol for Spain.

What Is Picasso's Supporting Evidence?

Although Picasso was illustrating a real event, cubism allowed him to paint "truth" rather than "reality." If Picasso was trying to depict the horror of Guernica, and by extension, the terror and chaos of war, all the components of his mural serve as supporting evidence. The wailing figures, panicked faces, the darkness contrasted by jumbled images of light all project the horror of war. Even the horse looks terrified. Overall, "Guernica" captures the emotional spirit of the horror of war. Picasso wasn't just trying to say, "War is hell." He was also trying to impress upon his audience that such atrocities should never happen again. In essence, Picasso was making an appeal for peace by showing its opposite, the carnage of war.

■ QUESTIONS FOR ANALYSIS AND DISCUSSION

Referring to the more specific questions regarding visual arguments discussed earlier in the chapter, apply them to Picasso's painting.

1. What images in the painting catch your attention, and why?
2. What is the central image? Is there a central image? What appears in the foreground? What is significant about the placement of the images? How do they relate to one another?
3. What verbal information, if any, is included, and why? (Remember that Picasso did title his painting "Guernica." What might have happened if he had named it something more abstract?)

4. What specific details are emphasized? What is exaggerated or idealized?
5. What is the effect of color and light?
6. Does the image make you want to know more?
7. What symbolism is imbedded in the image?

Norman Rockwell's "Freedom of Speech"

Picasso's mural was designed to be displayed in a large hall at the World Exposition, and later, presumably, in a museum. Other artists had less grand aspirations for their work. Norman Rockwell (1894–1978) was an artist who featured most of his work on the covers of magazines, most notably *The Saturday Evening Post,* a publication he considered "the greatest show window in America." In 47 years, Rockwell contributed 321 paintings to the magazine and became an American icon.

On January 6, 1941, President Franklin Delano Roosevelt addressed Congress, delivering his famous "Four Freedoms" speech. Against the background of the Nazi domination of Europe and the Japanese oppression of China, Roosevelt described the four essential human freedoms—freedom of speech, freedom of worship, freedom from want, and freedom from fear. Viewing these freedoms as the fundamental basis on which our society was formed, Roosevelt called upon Americans to uphold these liberties at all costs. Two years later, Rockwell, inspired by Roosevelt's speech, created his famous series of paintings on these "Four Freedoms," reproduced in four consecutive issues of *The Saturday Evening Post.* So popular were the images that they were used by the U.S. government to sell war bonds, to inspire public support for the war effort, and to remind people of the ideals for which they were fighting. The paintings serve as an example of how art can sometimes extend into advertising.

Let's take a closer look at one of the four paintings, "Freedom of Speech" (Figure 8.2 on page 180). When the war department adopted the painting for the war bond effort, it added two slogans to the image. The command "Save Freedom of Speech" was printed at the top of the painting in large, capital letters and, in even larger typeface, "Buy War Bonds" was printed at the bottom. As we analyze this painting, we will also make references to its later use as part of the effort to sell war bonds.

Before he took a brush to his canvas, Rockwell consciously or unconsciously asked himself some of the same questions writers do when they stare at a blank piece of paper while preparing to create a written argument. After determining that he would use the American small-town vehicle of democracy, the town meeting, as the means to express the theme of freedom of speech, he then painted his "argument."

Who Is Rockwell's Audience?

The Saturday Evening Post was widely read in America in the 1930s and 40s. Rockwell would have wanted his work to appeal to a wide audience, readers of the magazine. If we examine the people in the painting—presumably based on Rockwell's Arlington, Vermont, friends and neighbors—we can deduce the kind of audience the artist was hoping to touch: small-town citizens from a middle-income, working-class environment. Like the language of an argument written for a "general audience," the figures represent what Rockwell considered all-American townsfolk.

The venue is a meetinghouse or town hall because people are sitting on benches. The figures represent a generational cross-section of men and women, from the elderly

Figure 8.2

white-haired man to the left of the central standing figure to the young woman behind him. Style of dress reinforces the notion of class diversity, from the standing man in work clothes to the two men dressed in white shirts, ties, and suit jackets. The formality of the seated figures also opens audience identity to life beyond a small, rural community. That is, some of the men's formal attire and the woman in a stylish hat broaden the depiction to include white-collar urban America. While diversity in age and class is suggested, diversity of race is not. There are no Asians, African Americans, or other nonwhites in the scene. This exclusion might be a reflection of the times and, perhaps, the popular notion of what constituted small-town America sixty years ago. While such exclusion would be unacceptable today, it should be noted that in the years following this painting's completion, Rockwell used his considerable talent and fame to champion the civil rights struggle.

What Is Rockwell's Claim?

When the government adopted Rockwell's Painting for their World War II effort campaign to sell war bonds, they added the caption: "Save Freedom of Speech. Buy

War Bonds." When we consider the poster as an advertising piece, this essentially becomes the poster's claim. And we know the artist's intention, to illustrate the theme of freedom of speech. Rockwell's challenge was in how he makes his claim—how he dramatizes it on canvas. Just as a writer uses words to persuade, the artist makes his claim in symbolic details of the brush.

It has been said that Norman Rockwell's paintings appeal to a dreamy-eyed American nostalgia and at the same time project a world where the simple acts of common folk express high American ideals. In this painting we have one of the sacred liberties dramatized by a working-class man raised to the figure of a political spokesman in the assembly of others. Clearly expressing his opinion as freely as anybody else, he becomes both the illustration and defender of the democratic principles of freedom and equality.

What Are Rockwell's Assumptions?

As with written arguments, the success of a visual argument depends on whether the audience accepts the assumptions (the values, legal or moral principles, commonsense knowledge, or shared beliefs) projected in the image. One assumption underlying Rockwell's illustration is that freedom of speech is desirable for Americans regardless of gender, class, or position in society. We know this instantly from the facial expressions and body language of the figures in the canvas. For instance, the face of the man standing seems more prominent because it is painted against a dark blank background and is brighter than any others, immediately capturing our attention. His face tilts upward with a look of pride, lit as if by the inspiration of the ideals he represents—freedom of expression. One might even see suggestions of divine inspiration on his face as it rises in the light and against the night-blackened window in the background. The lighting and man's posture are reminiscent of religious paintings of past centuries. Additionally, the man's body is angular and rough, while his facial characteristics strongly resemble those of a young Abraham Lincoln—which suggests a subtle fusion of the patriotic with the divine. The implied message is that freedom of speech is a divine right.

As for the surrounding audience, we take special note of the two men looking up at the speaker. The older man appears impressed and looks on with a warm smile of approval, while the other man on the right gazes up expectantly. In fact, the entire audience supports the standing man with reasonable, friendly, and respectful gazes. The speaker is "Everyman." And he has the support and respect of his community. Rockwell's audience, subscribers of *The Saturday Evening Post,* saw themselves in this image—an image that mirrored the values of honest, decent, middle America.

What Is Rockwell's Supporting Evidence?

The key supporting image in Rockwell's painting is the sharp contrast between the standing man with those sitting around him. Not only is he the only one standing in the room, he is also the only working-class person clearly depicted. He stands out from the other people in the room. It is significant that those around him look up to him—a dramatic illustration of what it means to give the common man his say. Were the scene reversed—with the central figure formally dressed and those looking up approvingly attired in work clothes—we would have a completely different message: That is, a representative of the upper class perhaps "explaining" higher concepts to a less educated class of people. The message would be all wrong. In the painting, class barriers are transcended as the "common man" has risen to speak his mind with a face full of conviction, while upper-class people look on in support. That's the American ideal in action.

Because this is a painting instead of a newspaper photograph, every detail is selected purposely and, thus, is open to interpretation. One such detail is the fold of papers sticking out of the man's jacket pocket. What might those papers represent? And what's the point of such a detail? What associations might we make with it? There are words printed on the paper, but we cannot read them, so we're left to speculate. The only other paper in the painting is in the hand of the man on the right. The words "report" and "town" are visible. So, we might conclude that the speaker's pocket contains the same pamphlet, perhaps a summary report of the evening's agenda or possibly a resolution to be voted on. Whatever the documentation is, it is clear that the man doesn't need it, that his remarks transcend whatever is written on that paper. And here lies more evidence of Rockwell's claim and celebration of the unaided articulation of one man's views out of many—the essence of freedom of speech.

■ QUESTIONS FOR ANALYSIS AND DISCUSSION

Referring to the more specific questions regarding visual arguments discussed earlier in the chapter, apply them to Rockwell's painting.

1. What images in the painting catch your attention, and why?
2. What is the central image? Is there a central image? What appears in the foreground? What is significant about the placement of the images? How do they relate to one another?
3. What verbal information, if any, is included, and why?
4. What specific details are emphasized? What is exaggerated or idealized?
5. What is the effect of color and light?
6. Does the image make you want to know more?
7. What symbolism is imbedded in the image?

Advertisements

Norman Rockwell sought to embody a concept through his art, and, as a result, his painting tries to prompt reflection and self-awareness. In other words, his visuals serve to open the mind to a new discovery or idea. Advertising also selects and crafts visual images. However, advertising has a different objective. Its goal is not to stimulate expansive and enlightened thought but to direct the viewer to a single basic response: Buy this product!

Images have clout, and none are so obvious or so craftily designed as those that come from the world of advertising. Advertising images are everywhere—television, newspapers, the Internet, magazines, the sides of buses, and on highway billboards. Each year, companies collectively spend more than $150 billion on print ads and television commercials (more than the gross national product of many countries). Advertisements comprise at least a quarter of each television hour and form the bulk of most newspapers and magazines. Tapping into our most basic emotions, their appeal goes right to the quick of our fantasies: happiness, material wealth, eternal youth, social acceptance, sexual fulfillment, and power.

Yet, most of us are so accustomed to the onslaught of such images that we see them without looking and hear them without listening. But if we stopped to examine how the images work, we might be amazed at their powerful and complex psychological force. And we might be surprised at how much effort goes into the crafting of such images—an effort solely intended to make us spend our money.

Like a written argument, every print ad or commercial has an *audience, claims, assumptions,* and *evidence.* Sometimes these elements are obvious; sometimes they are understated; sometimes they are implied. They may boast testimonials by average folk or celebrities, or cite hard scientific evidence. And sometimes they simply manipulate our desire to be happy or socially accepted. But common to every ad and commercial, no matter what the medium, is the *claim* that you should buy this product.

Print ads are potentially complex mixtures of images, graphics, and text. So in analyzing an ad, you should be aware of the use of photography, the placement of those images, and the use of text, company logos, and other graphics such as illustrations, drawings, side bar boxes, additional logos, etc. And you should keep in mind that every aspect of the image has been thought about and carefully designed. Let's take a look at how a recent magazine ad for Altoids breath mints uses some of these elements, including emotional appeal, the use of color and light, and text placement to convince us that Altoids is better than other brands.

Altoids Ad

When analyzing a print ad, we should try to determine what first catches our attention. In the Altoids ad (Figure 8.3 on page 184) the image of the soldier, featured floating on a pale green (the original is in color) solid background, jumps out from the page. This is a calculated move on the part of the ad's designers, of course. The soldier fills the ad. The image is arresting—and we stop and look. Ad images are staged and manipulated for maximum attention and effect. The uncluttered minimalist nature of this advertisement with the surrounding blank space draws us to the soldier, and to the little tin he is holding in his hand.

The soldier himself cuts a comic figure. He is wearing an ill-fitted uniform, he sports thick glasses, and he lacks the glamorous chiseled quality of many male models commonly used in advertising. Also, from his expression, he looks fairly keyed up. This comic quality coupled with the text at the bottom appeals to the viewer's sense of humor.

Who Is the Audience for the Ad?

The Altoids ads for years have featured males and females, young adult and old. So it could be said that the target audience is the general adult population. Because the ad does not specify that Altoids are breath mints, the audience is broadened to include those people who like mints, for taste and/or as a solution to bad breath.

Figure 8.3

What Is the Claim?

Because advertisers are vying for our attention, they must project their claim as efficiently as possible in order to discourage us from turning the page. The stated or implied claim of all advertising is that product *X* will make life better for you. Most ads aren't so bald in their claims, of course. But the promise is there by inference.

Likewise, the claim is here in the Altoids ad in the form of two bold, simple statements at the bottom. The first two sentences (in large, dark capitals) are clearly exclamations from the soldier: "Thank you sir! May I have another!" The second statement (in smaller white letters below) is from the advertiser who tells us specifically what the soldier wants: "The curiously strong mints." It is interesting to note that the actual name of the product, Altoids, appears only on the little tin held in the soldier's right hand. That fact suggests the success of brand-name recognition as well as, perhaps, British understatement.

But let's take a closer look at the intention of framing the claim in two statements and at how the layout subtly directs us. The first statement is intended to tap into our shared cultural expectations of what we know about military service.

Soldiers must shout responses to their superiors and thank them *even* for punishments. For instance, after being assigned, say, twenty pushups as disciplinary action, a soldier is expected to not only thank his drill sergeant for the punishment, but to actually ask for more. The ad twists this expectation by having Altoids be the "punishment." In this ad, the soldier is actually getting a treat. He wants more.

The indirect claim is that the reader should also want these "curiously strong mints." (If it's good enough for the recruit, it's good enough for us!) The word "curiously" is designed to set the product apart from its competitors. "Curiously" is a common usage in British English, and the parent company for Altoids, Callard & Bowser-Suchard Inc. has its roots in England. Viewers familiar with the mint will enjoy the ad for its comic appeal. Those unfamiliar with the product may wonder just what makes these mints "curiously strong." And curiosity is an effective hook. The British "curiously" also softens the tough U.S. soldier image, suggesting that while this is one strong mint, it's not so strong to offend the British—a people who Americans traditionally have associated with cultural refinement.

Another possible claim—again indirect—could be aimed at breath mint users. We know that soldiers are supposed to shout back responses to their commanding officer, often at close range—face-to-face. Perhaps his commanding officer was appalled at his recruit's bad breath and gave him an Altoid. So, the claim is doubled: It tastes good and cures bad breath.

What Is the Evidence?

Altoids' tag line, "The curiously strong mints," implies that other mints are simply ordinary and unremarkable. Altoids are different—they are "curiously strong" and thus, presumably, superior to their bland competition. And referring back to the possible scenario that led to the soldier's first mint, viewers might presume that if a commanding officer would "treat" his company's bad breath with this mint, it must be good.

What Are the Assumptions?

The creators of this ad made several assumptions about us, the audience: (1) that we are familiar with the phrase "Thank you sir, may I have another"; (2) that we understand who is depicted in the ad—a soldier at boot camp; (3) that we like mints; and (4) that we want to have fresh breath because we care about being socially acceptable.

■ QUESTIONS FOR ANALYSIS AND DISCUSSION

Apply the principles of critical analysis described in the above section on advertising, as well as the elements of form and design discussed earlier in the chapter, to the ads that appear in the following pages. First take a look at the Shreve, Crump & Low ad in Figure 8.4 on page 186.

1. Shreve, Crump & Low is a prestigious jewelry and fine gift store located in Boston. Consider the text at the bottom of the ad. How does the text encour-

Save your will power for things
like hot fudge sundaes.

Every woman needs 18k white gold and diamond jewelry from DiLaro to add an icy sparkle to her
wardrobe. Not to mention a sparkle to her eye. Come to Shreve's to make
your selection. Resistance is not only futile, it is foolish.

330 Boylston Street, Boston • The Mall at Chestnut Hill • (617) 267-9100
For information, call 800-324-0222

SHREVE,CRUMP & LOW

Figure 8.4

age the reader to purchase the jewelry? What message does it leave the reader who chooses to "resist"?

2. Evaluate how the model is used to sell the jewelry in the ad. Consider the use of lighting, shading, and so on in your response. Would this ad be as effective if the model were looking out of the photo? If she were clothed? What conclusions, if any, can you make about her? Explain.

3. In what type of magazine would you expect to see this ad? Who is the target audience? How does the text in the advertisement appeal to this target audience?

4. The lead text states that the viewer should "Save your will power for things like hot fudge sundaes." How does this affect the cost of the product? How might this purchase be ironic to some readers? Explain.

Now refer to the Timberland ad in Figure 8.5.

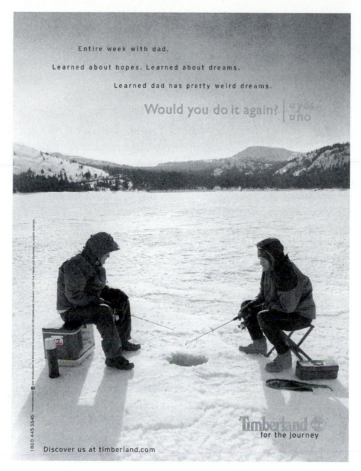

Figure 8.5

1. This ad was originally published in black and white rather than in color. Does this contribute to or detract from its effectiveness?
2. What verbal information is included with the images? How is it made prominent? How does this information relate to the other graphics or images?
3. Describe the nature of the father-son relationship depicted here. What might have just been said? What might each be thinking?
4. If you were the son, which box would you check? Explain. What is the point of the statement, "Learned dad has pretty weird dreams."
5. Why do you suppose the advertisers decided on ice fishing as the father-son activity here? Why not surf-casting on a tropical beach, yachting, golf, or tennis? Explain.
6. Discuss the product placement in this ad. How do you know what is being sold? What is the claim of this ad?

7. What type of person does this image appeal to? Is this ad targeting males only? What assumptions does the image make about fathers and sons?
8. What specific details in the photograph are emphasized? Which are exaggerated? idealized? understated?

Editorial or Political Cartoons

Editorial cartoons have been a part of American life for over a century. They are a mainstay feature on the editorial pages in most newspapers—those pages reserved for columnists, contributing editors, and illustrators to present their views in words and pen and ink. As in the nineteenth century when they first started to appear, such editorial cartoons are political in nature, holding up political and social issues for public scrutiny and sometimes ridicule.

A stand-alone editorial cartoon—as opposed to a strip of multiple frames—is a powerful and terse form of communication that combines pen-and-ink drawings with dialogue balloons and captions. They're not just visual jokes, but visual humor that comments on social/political issues while drawing on viewers' experience and knowledge.

The editorial cartoon is the story of a moment in the flow of familiar current events. And the key words here are *moment* and *familiar*. Although a cartoon captures a split instant in time, it also infers what came before and, perhaps, what may happen next—either in the next moment or in some indefinite future. And usually the cartoon depicts a specific moment in time. One of the most famous cartoons of the last forty years is the late Bill Mauldin's Pulitzer–Prize winning drawing of the figure of Abraham Lincoln with his head in his hands. It appeared the morning after the assassination of President John Kennedy in 1963. There was no caption nor was there a need for one. The image represented the profound grief of a nation that had lost its leader to an assassin's bullet. But to capture the enormity of the event, Mauldin brilliantly chose to represent a woeful America by using the figure of Abraham Lincoln as depicted in the sculpture of the Lincoln Memorial in Washington, D.C. In so doing, the message implied that so profound was the loss that it even reduced to tears the marble figure of a man considered to be our greatest president, himself assassinated a century before.

For a cartoon to be effective, it must make the issue clear at a glance and it must establish where it stands on the argument. As in the Mauldin illustration, we instantly recognize Lincoln and identify with the emotions. We need not be told the circumstances, since by the time the cartoon appeared the next day, all the world knew the horrible news, that the President had been assassinated. To convey less obvious issues and figures at a glance, cartoonists resort to images that are instantly recognizable, that we don't have to work hard to grasp. Locales are determined by give-away props: An airplane out the window suggests an airport, a cactus and cattle skull a desert, an overstuffed armchair and TV the standard living room. Likewise, human emotions are instantly conveyed: Pleasure is a huge toothy grin, fury is steam blowing out of a figure's ears, love is two figures making goo-goo eyes with floating hearts overhead. People themselves may have exaggerated features to emphasize a point or emotion.

In his essay "What Is a Cartoon?" Mort Gerberg says that editorial cartoons rely on such visual clichés to instantly convey their messages. That is, they employ stock figures for their representation—images instantly recognizable from cultural stereotypes like the fat-cat tycoon, the mobster thug, and the sexy female movie star. And these come to us in familiar outfits and props that give away their identities and profession. The cartoon judge has a black robe and gavel; the prisoner wears striped overalls and a ball and chain; the physician dons a smock and holds a stethoscope; the doomsayer is a scrawny long-haired guy carrying a sign saying, "The end is near." These are visual clichés known by the culture at large, and we instantly recognize them.

The visual cliché may be what catches our eye in the editorial cartoon, but the message lies in what the cartoonist does with it. As Gerberg observes, "The message is in twisting it, in turning the cliché around."

Jack Ohman's "Cloned Embryo Department" Cartoon

Consider Jack Ohman's cartoon (from *The Oregonian*) in Figure 8.6 that addresses the issue of human cloning (this issue is explored in detail in Chapter 17 of Part Two). The visual cliché is a woman shopping in a supermarket. We know that

Figure 8.6

from the familiar props: the shopping cart, the meat display unit, the department banner, and hint of shelving in the background. Even the shopper is a familiar figure, an elderly woman in an overcoat pushing her cart. The twist, of course, is that instead of a refrigeration unit displaying lamb, beef, and poultry, we see trays of neatly arranged embryonic clones with their genetic specialties indicated by pop-up signs.

The issue, of course, is the debate on human cloning. The cartoon was published on December 10, 2001, shortly after the announcement by the genetics firm Advanced Cell Technology in Worcester, Massachusetts, that they had cloned the first human embryo. (The embryos only survived a few cell divisions before they perished.) Although the lab claimed that the intention of cloning was not to create human beings but to treat particular human ailments such as Parkinson's disease, cancer, and strokes, the publicity fanned the flames of debate over the ethics and morality of cloning. Some people view such breakthroughs as medically promising; others fear we are crossing the line and playing God.

The cartoon's joke is in the twist—the gap between the familiar and the unexpected. The familiar is the supermarket cliché; the unexpected is the casual display of embryos flagged for desirable traits in a supermarket's "Cloned Embryo Department." Of course, the scene depicts some indefinite future time when cloning is permitted by law and widely practiced.

What Is the Cartoon's Claim?

The claim in this cartoon is that natural birth is better than genetic engineering. That is implicit in the satirical image of the human talents and traits quantified and commercialized in the meat section of the supermarket. And it is explicit in the woman's thoughts, "I miss the stork. . . ."

What Are the Cartoon's Assumptions?

This cartoon makes the assumptions that people see human beings as more complex and elusive than particular traits and talents, and that purchasing babies according to desired traits is perverse and unnatural. It also presumes that readers are familiar with the recent developments in cloning. Although the cartoon appeared shortly after the statement by Advanced Cell Technology, its success is not necessarily dependent on the audience's knowledge of that announcement.

What Is the Cartoon's Evidence?

The cartoon presents the darkly satirical notion that instead of relying on natural procreation, we would someday shop for scientifically perfected babies in a supermarket. Next to more "serious" preferences such as embryos cloned from donors with "1600 SAT" scores and "20/20 vision" are the embryos cloned from people good at juggling and ear wiggling. It is in these juxtapositions that the cartoonist reveals where he stands on the issue. He is mocking our society by reducing the aspirations of would-be parents to having kids with narrowly specific talents.

Ohman's stand is then clearly and more powerfully conveyed by the older woman's private thought—"I miss the stork. . . ." The message is that in the imagined new world where we can shop for our ideal babies, there will be those who yearn for the good old days. Of course, "the stork" is a polite metaphorical reference to sexual reproduction—a term appropriate for the shopper in the drawing, an elderly woman conservatively dressed. However, the term is another cliché, and in a curious twist it plays off the standard supermarket meat department display—as if *stork* were another kind of meat or poultry option.

■ QUESTIONS FOR ANALYSIS AND DISCUSSION

Apply the principles of critical analysis described in the above section on editorial cartoons, as well as the elements of form and design discussed earlier in the chapter, to the cartoons that appear below. First take a look at Figure 8.7.

1. What is the cliché in this picture? How does the cliché contrast with the unexpected?
2. Is this cartoon funny? Why or why not? How would parents react to it? students?
3. What assumptions does the cartoon make? What do we need to know in order to understand its point?

Figure 8.7

Figure 8.8

4. Based on the cartoonist's "argument," what do you think he is advocating? Is he for or against gun control? Can you tell? Does it matter? Explain your answers.

Now refer to the cartoon in Figure 8.8.

1. What is happening in this cartoon? Whom does the first kid "hate"? Does the cartoon make more sense when we know that it appeared shortly after September 11, 2001? Why or why not?
2. Consider the comment made by the middle kid in the cartoon, who agrees at first, but then asks a clarifying question. Is this significant? Why doesn't the first kid ask the same thing?
3. What is the cartoonist's claim in this cartoon? What evidence does he provide? Explain.
4. Although this cartoon was drawn in the context of the events following September 11, 2001, would it have been equally effective ten years ago? Ten years into the future? Would the previous cartoon be as timeless? Explain.

News Photographs

Although editorial cartoons can stand on their own, they are frequently featured on editorial pages in newspapers that include commentary on the topic they depict. Photographs are another vehicle used to augment commentary in newspapers, journals, and magazines. Indeed, sometimes the photograph *tells* the story better than words ever could, because they have the ability to instantly touch our deepest emotions.

At first glance, you may think that photos are simply snapshots of an event or moment. But most photographs presented in leading newspapers and journals are the result of effort and planning. Photojournalists are constantly making editorial decisions when they take a picture. They think about where to take the photo, the right moment, whom to include, the angle, the lighting, depth, and speed of film. They consider the subject matter and how it might affect an audience. In some cases, they think about why they are taking the picture and what argument they want to present on film. Some of the most compelling photographs in history come from photojournalists capturing one moment. These photos are not posed, but they still tell a story. Some famous photos include the shot of a sailor kissing a nurse in New York City's Time's Square when victory was declared at the end of World War II. Or, who can forget the Pulitzer Prize–winning photo of firefighter Chris Fields carrying the lifeless body of one-year-old Baylee Almon from the wreckage of the federal office building after the Oklahoma City bombing? While we might not recall the names of the people involved, the image itself remains stamped upon our memory.

As a unit, the news story and the photo work together to tell a story. The best photos often tell a story without using any words. But knowing the context in which the photo was taken is important as well. At the very least, the date and location establish the circumstances. Consider Figure 8.9, a photo taken on January 19, 2002, in Afghanistan.

Figure 8.9

Who Is the Target Audience?

This photo, taken by Spanish photographer Enric Morti, appeared in *Time* magazine in January 2002 and was selected as one of the best photos of the week for its
Web page photo collage. The photo is rather nonpolitical considering the moment
in which it was taken, with American troops occupying Ahghanistan and actively
searching that country for Osama Bin Laden and his Al Queda network.

What Is the Purpose of the Image?

The image captures a moment in time, a moment the photographer felt was important to save. The boys play on top of disabled tanks, a stark contrast to what
Americans expect to see when viewing children at play. We associate ball playing
with green fields and soft grass. But for these two boys, the muddy brown metal of
the tank tops forms their playing field. What happens if one of them should fall?
Parents viewing this photo may be thankful that their own children are so much
better off.

What Are the Claims Made in the Image?

While the photo is not directly political, it does make a comment. The photo may
garner sympathy for children who live in such a harsh environment. It also puts human faces on the Afghanistan conflict, but is not overly sentimental. Another claim
could be the unbreakable spirit of children—that they will play wherever they are
and under whatever conditions they face. Finally, it may make viewers, at home safe
in their living rooms reading a magazine, grateful that they live in America.

What Assumptions Does the Image Make?

The photographer assumes that most people will find this photo somewhat arresting and stop to take a longer look at it. Notice how the shot uses the outline of a
windshield to further frame the boys at play. Would this photo be as startling if it
were intended for a publication in Afghanistan? Probably not, because it might not
seem that out of the ordinary. Even for people who do not have children, the surprise of seeing children playing on top of tanks would strike a chord.

■ QUESTIONS FOR ANALYSIS AND DISCUSSION

Consider the photograph in Figure 8.10 taken by *Boston Globe* photojournalist
Suzanne Kreiter. It shows two panhandlers on a Boston street. The photograph accompanied a 2002 article, "A Street to Call Home," which reports on how some
homeless people panhandle on the very spot where they live.

1. This photograph accompanied an article about homelessness in an urban area
   of the Northeast. What assumptions about the audience does the photographer
   make?
2. What details in the photograph convey homelessness to the viewer? Consider
   objects, location, and background.
3. A close examination of the two main figures in this photograph makes a strong
   statement about their character. Consider their position, posture, relationship

Figure 8.10

to one another, the direction of their gazes, the facial expressions, their clothing and describe the character of these individuals.

4. Would you describe these people as heroic? downtrodden? defiant? helpless victims? noble survivors? Explain why.
5. What argument about homelessness in embedded in this photograph? In other words, what is the claim?
6. Does the background of the photograph detract from or add to the meaning of the photograph?
7. How do you expect to see the homeless depicted? Is this expectation based on stereotype? Does this image of the homeless reinforce or contradict the stereotypical view of the homeless? Explain your answer. Does this photograph change your idea of urban poverty? Why or why not?

8. Do you see any similarities in style or content between this photograph and Norman Rockwell's "Freedom of Speech"?

Ancillary Graphics: Tables, Charts, and Graphs

Art, advertisements, editorial cartoons, and news photos all present interesting visual ways to persuade, and knowing how they do this improves your critical thinking and analytical skills. Ancillary graphics, however, such as tables, charts, and graphs, are some visual tools you can use in your own persuasive essays. In Chapter 6, we discussed how numerical data and statistics are very persuasive in bolstering an argument. But a simple table, chart, or graph can convey information at a glance while conveying trends that support your argument. In fact, such visuals are preferable to long, complicated paragraphs that confuse the reader and may detract from your argument.

Ancillary graphics usually take the form of tables, charts, graphs (including line, bar, and pie graphs), and illustrations such as maps and line drawings (of a piece of equipment, for example).

Numerical Tables

There are many ways of representing statistical data. As you know from courses you've taken in math or chemistry, the simplest presentation of numerical data is the table. Tables are useful in demonstrating relationships among data. They present numerical information in tabular fashion arranged in rows or columns so that data elements may be referenced and compared. Tables also facilitate the interpretation of data without the expense of several paragraphs of description.

Suppose you are writing a paper in which you argue that part-time faculty at your institution teach more hours, but are underpaid and undersupported when it comes to benefits. Your research reveals that most part-time faculty receive less than $3,000 per course, and nearly one-third earn $2,000 or less per course—which is little more than the minimum wage. You also discover that the treatment of part-timers at your own school reflects a national trend—faced with rising enrollments and skyrocketing costs, colleges and universities have come to rely more on part-time instructors. Moreover, while they may carry heavier teaching loads, these part-time faculty do not receive the same benefits as full professors. Your claim is that such lack of support is not only unfair to the instructors, but also that it compromises the nature of higher education since low compensation drives instructors to take on other jobs to meet the cost of living.

Presenting this information in a table will allow you to demonstrate your point while saving space for your discussion. The tables below provide the results of a survey conducted by the Coalition on the Academic Work Force (CAW), describing how history faculty are facing this situation.

As the title indicates, the table reproduced in Figure 8.11 shows the percentage of history courses taught by full- and part-time faculty. The table intends to help readers understand how much institutions have come to depend on part-time instructors, especially graduate teaching assistants and part-time nontenure-track

Percentage of History Courses Taught, by Faculty Type

	Intro Courses	Other Courses	All Courses
Full-Time Tenure Track	49%	72%	59%
Full-Time Nontenure Track	9%	5%	7%
Part-Time Tenure Track	1%	1%	1%
Part-Time Nontenure Track	23%	15%	19%
Graduate Teaching Assistants	17%	8%	13%
Percentage of All Courses Taught	55%	45%	
Number of Courses Taught	5,825	4,759	10,584

Source: AHA Surveys.

Figure 8.11

teachers—people who are paid the least and often denied the benefits enjoyed by full-time faculty. The horizontal rows break down faculty types into five discrete categories—from "Full-Time Tenure Track" at the top to "Graduate Teaching Assistants" on the bottom. The three vertical columns tabulate the percentages according to categories: "Intro Courses," "Other Courses," and "All Courses," which is the median—the calculated halfway point between the other two categories.

Reading from left to right along the first row, we see that 49 percent of the introductory history courses and 72 percent of the "other courses" were taught by full-time tenure-track faculty. This compares with 41 percent of the introductory courses taught by part-timers (part-time tenure track [1%] + part-time nontenure-track faculty [23%] + graduate teaching assistants [17%]). The last column, which represents the median percentage of intro and other courses, tells us that part-timers taught 33 percent or a third of all history courses. That is a compelling figure when tabulated for comparison to full-time faculty.

The second table (Figure 8.12 on page 198) presents the reported benefits for nontenure-track and part-time faculty. Here nine categories of benefits are tabulated according to three categories of faculty. (Presumably nearly 100 percent of history departments provide full-time tenure-track faculty the kinds of support and benefits listed.) The first line shows the comparative institutional support for travel to professional meetings for the three categories of instructors: 76.9 percent for full-time nontenure track, 46.4 for part-time faculty paid by a fraction of full-time salary, and 15.2 for part-time faculty paid by the course.

The fifth line down tabulates the copaid health plan for the three categories of faculty. As we can see at a glance, 72 percent of the institutions with full-time non-tenure-track faculty and 63 percent of the departments with part-time faculty paid a fraction of full-time salaries provide some kind of health plan copaid by the

History Departments, Benefits

	% for Full-Time Nontenure-Track Faculty	% for Part-Time Faculty (Paid by semester)	% for Part-Time Faculty (Paid by course)
Support Travel to Prof. Mtgs.	76.9	46.4	15.2
Support Attendance at Prof. Mtgs.	41.0	28.6	22.9
Provide Regular Salary Increases	68.4	53.6	28.1
Access to Research Grants	52.1	39.3	13.3
Health Plan Paid by Both	72.17	62.96	12.99
Health Plan Paid by School	32.17	22.22	2.26
Health Plan Paid by Employee	1.74	7.41	3.95
Retirement Plan	73.91	55.56	10.17
Life Insurance	76.52	44.44	5.65

Source: AHA Surveys.

Figure 8.12

school and faculty member. This compares with just 13 percent of institutions providing such a benefit to part-time faculty paid on a per-course basis. Similarly, 32 percent of the institutions with full-time nontenure-track faculty provided a health plan paid for by the school, as compared to 2.26 percent of those with faculty paid by the course. Reading across the other benefits categories reveals how much more generous institutions were to full-time nontenure-track faculty than to part-timers—including retirement plans and insurance.

As the above paragraphs demonstrate, explaining all this information in the body of your text can be complicated and confusing. And when you are trying to prepare a compelling argument, simplicity of style and clarity of text are essential. Using tables helps you clearly depict data while you move forward with your discussion.

Line Graphs
Line graphs show the relationship between two or more sets of numerical data by plotting points in relation to two axes. The vertical axis is usually used to represent

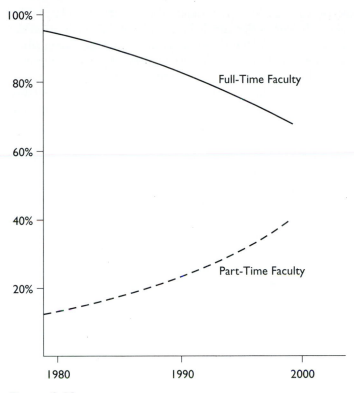

Figure 8.13

amounts, and the horizontal axis normally represents increments of time, although this is not always the case. Line graphs are probably easier for most people to read than tables, and they are especially useful when depicting trends or changes over time. Consider the graph in Figure 8.13.

This graph plots the comparative increase and decrease of full- and part-time faculty over a twenty-year period (based on data from AHA surveys). The vertical or y-axis represents the percentage of part-time faculty and the horizontal or x-axis represents the time starting from 1980. There are two lines on the graph: The upper line represents the decreasing percentage of full-time history faculty of the colleges and universities surveyed, while the lower line represents the increase in part-time history faculty over the same twenty-year period. The declining slope of the upper line instantly captures the decreasing dependence on full-time faculty, whereas the rising slope of the lower line illustrates the increasing dependence on part-time hires. Because the data are plotted on the same graph, we understand how the two are interrelated.

We also notice that neither line is straight but slightly curving. The upper line (full-time faculty) curves downward, while the lower line (part-time faculty) curves upward. Should the trend continue, at some point the lines will cross approximately around the 50th percentile level on the y-axis—that is, when half the college history courses surveyed are taught by part-timers. Also, if we extrapolate both lines toward the right along the curves they are defining, we will eventually arrive at some hypothetical future date when 100 percent of all history courses are taught by part-time faculty and none by full-timers. While we presume that most colleges and universities would not allow this to happen, the trend suggests just how the increased dependence on part-timers is changing the nature of higher education, as fewer courses are taught by full-time faculty. The graphs indeed make a persuasive argument.

Bar Graphs and Pie Charts

Bar graphs and pie charts often are used to compare parts and enable readers to grasp complex data and the relationships among variables at a glance. A bar graph uses horizontal or vertical bars and is commonly used to show either quantities of the same item at different times, quantities of different items at the same time, or quantities of the different parts of an item that make up the whole. They are usually differentiated by contrasting colors, shades, or textures, with a legend explaining what these colors, shades, or textures mean.

The bar graph in Figure 8.14 shows the increase of part-time and adjunct faculty in history departments over a twenty-year period as broken down by type of employment and gender (based on data from the AHA survey of the historical profession and unpublished data from AHA departmental surveys). As indicated, the graph demonstrates a dramatic increase in that time period. In 1980, only 4.3 percent of male and 2.0 percent of female history faculty were part-time—a total of 6.3 percent. Two decades later, part-time male and female faculty increased to over 24 percent. This number could be even larger if graduate teaching assistants were included. As this graph shows, the appeal of bar graphs is that they take comparative amounts of data and transform them into instant no-nonsense images.

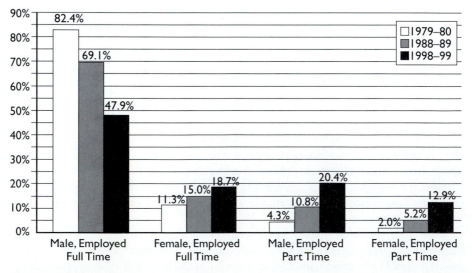

Figure 8.14

Pie Charts

Pie charts present data as wedge-shaped sections of a circle or "pie." The total amount of all the pieces of the pie must equal 100 percent. They are an efficient way of demonstrating the relative proportion of the whole something occupies—an instant way to visualize "percentages" without thinking in numbers. But when using pie charts, it is best to include six or fewer slices. If more pieces than that are used, the chart becomes messy and its impact is muted. Figure 8.15 dramatically demonstrates the portion of all history courses in the CAW survey that were taught by part-time faculty, including graduate students.

This pie chart clearly reveals that the combined wedges of graduate teaching assistants and part-time instructors form a substantial portion of the pie. In fact, they comprise almost half of the teaching population. This image quickly and powerfully demonstrates the point of your argument that part-time faculty make up a disproportionately large part of history faculty while enjoying a disproportionately small percentage of the benefits. The chart allows readers to visualize the information as they read it.

Used together, these visuals can play an invaluable role in bolstering a written argument on behalf of part-time faculty. Instead of blinding readers with reams of raw data, these pictorials organize numbers and bring their significance to life. Comparative benefits and changing dependencies are transformed into easy-to-understand tables, graphs, and charts. At a glance, complex ideas and confusing numbers are organized into memorable images.

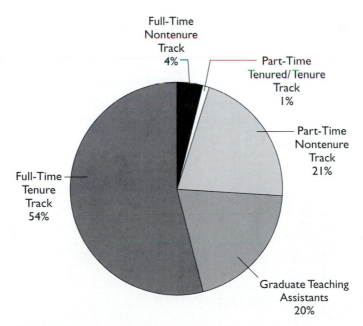

Figure 8.15

Tips for Using Ancillary Graphics

While understanding the types of ancillary graphics at your disposal is important, it is also important to know how to properly use them. Here are a few guidelines to consider when using graphics in your persuasive essays:

- Include only the data you need to demonstrate your point.
- Make a reference to the chart or graphic in the body of your text.
- Try to keep the graphic on the same page as your discussion.
- Present only one type of information in each graph or chart.
- Label everything in your graph and provide legends where appropriate.
- Assign a figure number to each graphic for easy reference.
- Don't crowd your text too closely around the graphic.
- Remember to document the sources used to create the graphics.

As you begin to incorporate visuals into your own papers, consider the discussion provided earlier in this chapter regarding visual arguments. Consider why you wish to use the graphic and what you want it to do. Think about your audience's needs.

■ QUESTIONS FOR ANALYSIS AND DISCUSSION

Select an essay from Part Two and make recommendations for how graphics could help enhance and support the author's argument. Some pieces to consider include:

- "Buy This 21-Year-Old and Get All His Friends Absolutely Free"
- "The Bully in the Mirror"
- "Will Boys Be Boys?"
- "The New Nostalgia"
- "Adult Crime, Adult Time: Outdated Juvenile Laws Thwart Justice"
- "You Can't Judge a Crook by His Color"
- "The Maximum Security Adolescent"
- "Should Human Cloning Be Permitted?"

Research the topic the essay covers and locate statistical information that the author could have used to support his or her argument. Develop some charts and graphs and determine where they would be most effective.

CHAPTER 9

Researching Arguments
Thinking Like an Investigator

Most arguments derive their success from the evidence they contain, so good argumentative writers learn to find evidence in many sources and present the best evidence to support their claims. In the academic world, much of that evidence is gathered through *research,* either conducted in a lab or field or through examination of the previously published work of other investigators and scholars. The research paper you may be asked to write challenges you to learn how more experienced writers find and present evidence that meets the standards of the academic community.

When you walk through the library, you are surrounded with researched arguments. The book claiming that the Kennedy assassination was part of a CIA conspiracy is a researched argument. So are the journal articles asserting that Shakespeare's plays were written by Sir Francis Bacon, and the research report that claims AZT is an effective treatment for some AIDS patients. The article in *Fortune* on the need for changes in the capital gains tax is one, too, as is the review claiming that Nirvana was the most important band of the 1990s. All these arguments have something in common: To back up their claims, their authors have brought in supporting evidence that they gathered through a focused research effort. That evidence gives you and readers like you grounds by which to decide whether you will agree with the authors' claims. Libraries, then, aren't just storehouses for history; they provide good writers with valuable information to support their ideas.

In the previous chapters we've stressed the importance of finding evidence that will impress readers of your argument's merits. To review, researched evidence plays an important role in convincing readers of the following:

- Expert, unbiased authorities agree with your position in whole or in part, adding to your credibility.
- Your position or proposal is based on facts, statistics, and real-life examples, not mere personal opinion.
- You understand different viewpoints about your subject as well as your own.
- Your sources of information are verifiable, since researched evidence is always accompanied by documentation.

A good analogy to use, once again, is that of the lawyer presenting a case to a jury. When you write a researched argument, you're making a case to a group of people who will make a decision about a subject. Not only do you present your arguments in the case, but you call on witnesses to offer evidence and expert opinion, which you then interpret and clarify for the jury. In a researched argument, your sources are your witnesses.

Writing an argumentative research paper isn't different from writing any other kind of argument, except in scale. You will need more time to write the paper in order to conduct and assimilate your research, the paper is usually longer than nonresearched papers, and the formal presentation (including documentation) must be addressed in more detail. The argumentative research paper is an extension and refinement of the essays you've been writing. It's not a different species of argument.

Sources of Information

There are two basic kinds of research sources, and depending partly on the type of issue you've picked to research, one may prove more helpful than the other. The first kind is *primary sources,* which include firsthand accounts of events (interviews, diaries, court records, letters, manuscripts). The second is *secondary sources,* which interpret, comment on, critique, explain, or evaluate events or primary sources. Secondary sources include most reference works and any books or articles that expand on primary sources. Depending on whether you choose a local or a more global issue to write about, you may decide to focus more on primary or more on secondary sources; but in most research, you'll want to consider both.

Primary Sources

If you choose a topic of local concern to write about, your chief challenge will be finding enough research material; very current controversies or issues won't yet have books written about them, so you may have to rely more heavily on electronic databases, which you can access through a computer, or interviews and other primary research methods to find information. If you choose a local issue to argue, consider the following questions.

- Which experts on campus or in the community might you interview to find out the pros and cons of the debated issue? an administrator at your college? a professor? the town manager? Think of at least two local experts who could provide an overview of the issue from different angles or perspectives.
- What local resources—such as a local newspaper, radio station, TV station, or political group—are available for gathering printed or broadcast information? If one of your topics is a campus issue, for example, the student newspaper, student committees or groups, university on-line discussion groups, or the student government body might be places to search for information.

Once you determine that you have several possible sources of information available locally, your next step is to set up interviews or make arrangements to read or view related materials. Most students find that experts are eager to talk about lo-

PREPARING INTERVIEW QUESTIONS

Consider the following guidelines as you prepare questions for an interview:

- Find out as much information as you can about the issue and about the expert's stand on the issue before the interview. Then you won't waste interview time on general details you could have found in the newspaper or on the local TV news.
- Ask open-ended questions that allow the authority to respond freely, rather than questions requiring only "yes" or "no" answers.
- Prepare more questions than you think you need and rank them in order of priority according to your purpose. Using the most important points as a guide, sequence the list in a logical progression.

cal issues and have little problem setting up interviews. However, you'll need to allow plenty of time in your research schedule to gather background information, phone for interviews, prepare your questions, and write up your notes afterward. If you're depending on primary research for the bulk of your information, get started as soon as the paper is assigned.

Preparing for Interviews

A few common courtesies apply when preparing for interviews. First, be ready to discuss the purpose of your interview when setting up an appointment. Second, go into the interview with a list of questions that show you have already thought about the issue. Be on time and have a notebook and pen to record important points. If you think you may want to quote people directly, ask their permission to do so and read the quotation back to them to check it for accuracy.

Conducting Interviews

Be prepared to jot down only key words or ideas during the interview, reserving time afterward to take more detailed notes. Keep the interview on track by asking focused questions if the interviewee wanders while responding to your question. When you are leaving, ask if it would be okay to call if you find you have other questions later.

Writing Up Interviews

As soon as possible after the interview, review the notes you jotted down and flesh out the details of the conversation. Think about what you learned. How does the information you gathered relate to your main topic or question? Did you gather any information that surprised or intrigued you? What questions remain? Record the date of your interview in your notes as you may need this information to document your source when you write the paper.

Secondary Sources

Although many primary sources—published interviews, public documents, results of experiments, and first-person accounts of historical events, for example—are available in the college library, the library is also a vast repository of secondary source material. If your topic is regional, national, or international in scope, you'll want to consider both of these kinds of sources. For example, if your topic is proposed changes to the Social Security System, you might find information in the *Congressional Record* on committee deliberations, a primary source, and also read editorials on the op-ed page of the *New York Times* for interpretive commentary, a secondary source.

A Search Strategy

Because the sheer amount of information in the library can be daunting, plan how you will find information before you start your search. Always consult a reference librarian if you get stuck in planning your search or if you can't find the information you need.

Choosing Your Topic

Your argument journal may remind you of potential topics, and Chapter 3 covered how to develop a topic. But what if you still can't think of a topic? You might try browsing through two print sources that contain information on current issues:

> *Facts on File* (1940 to the present). A weekly digest of current news.
>
> *Editorials on File* (1970 to the present). Selected editorials from U.S. and Canadian newspapers reprinted in their entirety.

If you have access to the Internet, the *Political Junkie* Web site will provide you with ideas from the latest news stories in national and regional newspapers and magazines, columnists' viewpoints on current issues, up-to-the-minute reports on public figures, and links to the Web sites of numerous political and social organizations. You can access this site at <http://www.politicaljunkie.com>. Also, think about which subjects you find interesting from the essays in Part Two of this book. These four sources should give you a wealth of ideas to draw on.

PREVIEW: A SEARCH STRATEGY

- Choose your topic.
- Get an overview of your topic.
- Compile a working bibliography.
- Locate sources.
- Evaluate sources.
- Take notes.

Getting an Overview of Your Topic

If you know little about your topic, encyclopedias can give you general background information. Just as important, encyclopedia articles often end with bibliographies on their subjects—bibliographies prepared by experts in the field. Using such bibliographies can save you hours in the library.

If your library houses specialized encyclopedias, either in print or through computer, related to your topic, check them first. If not, go to the general encyclopedias. Following is a list of general and specialized encyclopedias you may find helpful.

General Encyclopedias

Academic American Encyclopedia. Written for high-school and college students.

New Encyclopedia Britannica and *Britannica Online. Micropaedia* is a ten-volume index of the *New Encyclopedia Britannica.*

Encyclopedia Americana. Extensive coverage of science and technology and excellent on American history.

Specialized Encyclopedias

Encyclopedia of American Economic History (1980). Overview of U.S. economic history and aspects of American social history related to economics.

Encyclopedia of Bioethics (1995). Covers life sciences and health care.

Encyclopedia of Philosophy (1972). Scholarly articles on philosophy and philosophers.

Encyclopedia of Psychology (1994). Covers topics in the field of psychology.

Encyclopedia of Religion (1993). Covers theoretical, practical, and sociological aspects of religion worldwide.

Encyclopedia of Social Work (1995). Covers social work issues including minorities and women.

Encyclopedia of World Art (1959–1983). Covers artists and art works and contains many reproductions of art works.

McGraw-Hill Encyclopedia of Science and Technology (1997). Covers physical, natural, and applied sciences.

This is just a brief listing of the many encyclopedias available in areas that range from marriage and the family to folklore and social history. Your librarian can assist you in finding the encyclopedia you need. Be sure to check the dates of encyclopedias so you locate the most current information available.

Compiling a Working Bibliography

Because you don't know at the beginning of your search which sources will prove most relevant to your narrowed topic, keep track of every source you consult. Record complete publication information about each source in your notebook, on 3" × 5" index cards, or on printouts of on-line sources. The list that follows describes the information you'll need for particular kinds of sources.

For a Book
Authors' and/or editors' names
Full title, including subtitle
Place of publication (city, state, country)
Date of publication (from the copyright page)
Name of publisher
Volume or edition numbers
Library call number

For an Article
Authors' names
Title and subtitle of article
Title of periodical (magazine, journal, newspaper)
Volume number and issue number, if any
Date of the issue
All page numbers on which the article appears
Library location

For an Electronic Source
Authors' names, if given
Title of material accessed
Name of periodical (if applicable)
Volume and issue numbers (if applicable)
Date of material, if given
Page numbers or numbers of paragraphs (if indicated)
Title of the database
Publication medium (e.g., CD-ROM, diskette, microfiche, online)
Name of the vendor, if relevant
Electronic publication date
Date of access to the material, if relevant
Path specification for online media (e.g., FTP information; directory; file name)

Note that for electronic sources, which come in many different formats, you should record all the information that would allow another researcher to retrieve the documents you used. This will vary from source to source, but the important point is to give as much information as you can.

Your instructor may ask you to prepare an *annotated bibliography,* in which you briefly summarize the main ideas in each source and note its potential usefulness. You will also want to evaluate each source for accuracy, currency, or bias.

Jenny, a first-year composition student, decided to write her argument essay on book banning in the public schools. Here are some sample entries from her annotated bibliography.

Sample Entries for an Annotated Bibliography

Frequently Asked Questions: Parental Rights. Family Research Council. 13 Oct. 1998 <http://www.frc.org:80/faq22.html>. This is a Web site created by a politically conservative organization that actively supports parental rights. This site provides the group's rationale for endorsing passage of a Parental Freedom of Information Act, which would give parents greater power over their children's education in the public schools. This site clearly states a political position against government interference in the exercise of parental rights, and it is not free of bias. However, it is informative and well supported and it provides persuasive information about this viewpoint.

May, Timothy. "The Case for Not Letting Kids Read" *Catcher in the Rye.* *Sacramento Bee* 4 May 1997: F-3. *Lexis-Nexis.* 28 Oct. 1998 <http://web .lexis-nexis.com/universe>. May agrees with a local high-school district's decision to remove *Catcher in the Rye* from the approved reading list because he thinks it is too difficult for high-school students to understand. He suggests that students should be assigned classic literature before reading contemporary fiction. May does not really address the issue for censorship; he is more concerned with proving that high-school students lack sufficient background to appreciate *Catcher in the Rye.* Even though he claims that he does not approve of censorship, he supports the board's action. This does not seem to be a useful source for my paper.

People for the American Way. *Attacks on the Freedom to Learn.* Washington: People for the American Way, 1996. This is an annual survey taken by a 300,000-member civil liberties organization that documents and analyzes national statistics on censorship attempts directed toward public education. It includes short descriptions of specific censorship incidents on a state-by-state basis. This survey is intended to demonstrate that censorship attempts are on the rise. There is a strong bias against any attempts to censor or limit educational materials, but the statistics seem reliable and they are supported by examples of actual attempts at censorship.

A working bibliography (as opposed to an annotated bibliography) would include the complete publication information for each source, but not the evaluation of its usefulness to the paper.

Locating Sources

Your college library offers a range of methods and materials for finding the precise information you need. Here is a brief guide to locating periodicals, books, and electronic sources.

Finding Periodicals

Instead of going to the periodicals room and leafing page by page through magazines, journals, and newspapers to find information pertinent to your topic, use periodical indexes to locate the articles you need. Your college library will have these indexes available in print, CD-ROM, or online databases. The form you choose will depend on what is available and how current your information must be. When deciding whether to use the printed or electronic versions, carefully note the dates of the material the indexes reference. For example, you cannot use the CD-ROM version of *The Readers' Guide to Periodical Literature* to find a source from 1979. However, for a more current source (from 1983 to present), use the CD-ROM version since it provides abstracts of articles. These will allow you to decide whether locating the full article is worth your time and effort. Here is a list of some of the periodical indexes often available in college libraries. If your library does not have these indexes, ask the reference librarian the best way to find periodical articles in your library.

Periodical Indexes
General

Readers' Guide to Periodical Literature. 1915 to present. Print. Indexes popular journals and magazines and some reviews of movies, plays, books, and television.

Readers' Guide Abstracts. 1983 to present. Same content as *Readers' Guide* but with abstracts.

Newspaper Abstracts. 1985 to present. Abstracts to articles in national and regional newspapers.

New York Times. 1851 to present. Extensive coverage is national and international.

Periodical Abstracts. 1986 to present. Abstracts and full-text articles from more than 950 general periodicals.

ABI/Inform. August 1971 to present. About eight hundred thousand citations to articles in 1,400 periodicals. Good source for business-related topics. Complete text of articles from five hundred publications since 1991.

Lexis-Nexis Universe. Full-text access to newspapers, magazines, directories, legal and financial publications, and medical journals.

Specialized

Applied Science and Technology Index/Applied Science and Technology Abstracts. 1913 to present. Covers all areas of science and technology.

Art Index/Art Abstracts. 1929 to present. Wide coverage of art and allied fields.

Business Periodicals Index. 1958 to present. Covers all areas of business.

Education Index/Education Abstracts. 1929 to present. June 1983 to present. Covers elementary, secondary, and higher education.

PAIS International in Print/PAIS Database (formerly *Public Affairs Information Service Bulletin*). 1915 to present. Excellent index to journals, books, and reports in economics, social conditions, government, and law.

Ethnic Newswatch. 1990 to present. Indexes news publications by various ethnic groups. Includes full texts of most articles.

Social Sciences Index (*International Index* 1907–1965; *Social Sciences and Humanities* 1965–1974; *Social Sciences Index* 1974 to present). 1907 to present. Indexes scholarly journals in political science, sociology, psychology, and related fields.

Humanities Index. (See *Social Sciences Index* entry for name changes.) 1907 to present. Covers scholarly journals in literature, history, philosophy, folklore, and other fields in the humanities.

America: History and Life. 1964 to present. Index and abstracts to articles in more than 2,000 journals. Covers the histories and cultures of the United States and Canada from prehistory to the present.

SPORT Discus. 1975 to present. Covers sports, physical education, physical fitness, and sports medicine.

Social Issues Researcher (*SIRS*). Full-text articles from newspapers, journals, and government publications related to the social sciences.

Congressional Universe. Offers a legislative perspective on congressional bills, hearings, public laws, and information on members of Congress.

Sociofile. 1974 to present. Coverage includes family and socialization, culture, social differentiation, social problems, and social psychology.

Essay and General Literature Index. 1900 to present. Indexes essays and chapters in collected works. Emphasis is on social sciences and humanities.

Finding Books

Your library catalog, whether available in printed (card), electronic, or microform format, indexes the books your library holds. (You may be able to access other kinds of sources using the catalog as well, for example, government documents or maps.) Every catalog provides access to books in three basic ways: by author, title, and general subject. If the catalog is electronic, you can also use keyword searching to locate books. In a keyword search on a computer terminal, you type in a word related to your topic, and the catalog lists all the sources that include that word in the title.

To make keyword searching more efficient, you can often combine two or more search terms. For example, if you know that you want information on "violence" and can narrow that to "violence and music not rap music," the catalog will give you a much shorter list of sources than if you had typed only "violence," which is a very broad topic. This is called Boolean searching, and the typical ways you can combine terms are to use "and" to combine search terms; "or" to substitute search terms (e.g., "violent crime" or "assault"); and "not" to exclude terms. For example, suppose you are looking for information on cigarette smoking by teenagers. In a Boolean search, you could use the search phrase: *teenager or youth and smoking not marijuana.*

If you are searching by subject rather than author or title, it's useful to know that libraries organize subject headings according to the *Library of Congress Subject Headings* (*LCSH*). These are large red books, usually located near the library's catalog. You will save time and be more successful if you look up your subject in the *LCSH*. For example, if you search the catalog using the term "movies," you won't find a single source. If you look up "movies" in the *LCSH,* it will tell you that the subject heading is "motion pictures." Type in "motion pictures," and you'll find the sources you need.

Listed below are other useful sources of information.

Biographies

There are so many different biographical sources it is difficult to know which one has the information you need. The following titles will save you a lot of time:

Biography and Genealogy Master Index. (Spans from B.C. to the present.) Index to more than one million biographical sources.

Biographical Index. 1947 to present. International and all occupations. Guide to sources in books, periodicals, letters, diaries, etc.

Contemporary Authors. 1962 to present. Contains biographical information about authors and lists of their works.

Almanacs

World Almanac and Book of Facts. 1968 to present. Facts about government, business, society, etc. International in scope.

Statistical Abstract of the United States. 1879 to present. Published by the U.S. Bureau of the Census. Good source for statistics about all aspects of the United States including economics, education, society, and politics.

Statistical Masterfile. 1984 to present. State and national government statistics and private and international.

Reviews, Editorials

Book Review Digest. 1905 to present. Index to book reviews with excerpts from the reviews.

Book Review Index. 1965 to present. Indexes to more books than the above but doesn't have excerpts from reviews.

Bibliographies

Look for these in journal articles, books, encyclopedia articles, biographical sources, etc.

Finding Internet Sources

The Internet offers countless possibilities for research using government documents, newspapers and electronic journals, Web sites, business publications, and much more. You may have access to the Internet through either campus computer labs or your own computer. The easiest way to access the Net is by using the World Wide Web (WWW), a point-and-click system in which related documents are linked.

To make your search easier and more efficient, you can rely on several of the powerful search engines available for exploring the World Wide Web. Each of the search engines we've listed below uses keyword searches to find material on your topic. These words can specify your topic, supply the title of a book or article about your topic, name a person associated with your topic, and so on. It's important to try out a number of keyword combinations when you are searching for resources. For instance, if your topic is assisted suicide, you might also search under *euthanasia* and *physician-assisted suicide.* By adding additional terms such as *terminal illness, legalization,* and *patient's rights,* you may be able to both narrow your search and find material filed under different topic headings that is related to your subject.

Here is a list of the more popular search engines. You'll find them useful for locating information on the Internet:

Google <http://www.google.com>

This search engine will give you a lot of options. Keywords can be used for subject searches or to find a phrase that appears in the sources. You may also supply the name of a person or a title to prompt your search. It will search for each of your keywords separately or as a unit. You can also limit or expand the time parameters of your search from the current date to up to two years.

Yahoo! <http://www.yahoo.com>

Yahoo! works just like *Google.* It will also expand your search by linking you to two other search engines, *AltaVista* and *Infoseek,* if you request them.

AltaVista <http://www.altavista.com>

AltaVista will give you the choice of searching the Web or Usenet groups, which are discussion groups on particular topics. Unlike *Yahoo!* and *Google,* this engine will not give you the option of limiting your search to a certain time period.

Excite <http://www.excite.com>

Excite has a unique feature that suggests a list of words related to your keywords to help you focus more specifically on your topic. It also supplies a list of newspaper articles about your topic.

Infoseek <http://www.infoseek.com>

Infoseek can search the Web, news articles, newsgroups (personal essays by individuals), and information about private companies with services related to your topic. It also can supply maps and e-mail addresses.

Lycos <http://www.lycos.com>

Lycos offers full texts of some journal and news articles, as well as access to Web sites, personal home pages, and a dictionary of keywords.

When you are using any search engine, be sure to check the instructions so you can use it as effectively as possible. Also, don't rely on only one search engine. Use several to give yourself access to the broadest range of materials.

Three additional Web sites that may help you if you are searching for information related to government, politics, legislation, or statistics are the following:

Library of Congress <http://www.loc.gov>
This Web site provides information about the U.S. Congress and the legislative process. It will search for past legislative bills by topic, bill number, or title; allow you to read the *Congressional Record* from the current and past year's Congresses; find committee reports by topic or committee name; and provide full-text access to current bills under consideration in the House of Representatives and the Senate.

U.S. Census Bureau <http://www.census.gov>
You can find facts, figures, and statistics derived from the last census at this site. There is also some information about world population.

White House <http://www.whitehouse.gov>
At this site you can find current and past White House press briefings and news releases, as well as a full range of statistics and information produced by federal agencies for public use.

Remember that the Internet is constantly changing, so no book will be completely up to date on how to access its information. Check to see if your college has workshops or courses on using the Internet—it's an important research tool and it's worth your time to learn how to navigate in cyberspace.

Evaluating Sources

The first examination of your sources isn't intended to find the precise information you'll use in your final paper; rather, it is a preliminary assessment to help you decide whether the material is *relevant* and *reliable* for your purposes.

Print Sources

You can often sense a print source's relevance by skimming its preface, introduction, table of contents, conclusion, and index (for books) or abstract and headings (for articles) to see whether your topic appears and how often. Many students mark their bibliography cards with numbers (1 = most relevant, 2 = somewhat relevant, 3 = not very relevant) to help them remember which sources they most want to examine. If a source contains no relevant material, mark the bibliography card "unusable" but don't discard it; if you refine your topic or claim later, you may want to go back to that source.

The reliability of a printed source is judged in a number of ways:

- Check the date: Is it recent or timely for your topic?
- Look at the citations: Is the author's evidence recent or timely?
- Is the author an expert in the field? To find out, use the biographical sources listed earlier in this chapter or find book reviews in the reference section.

- Where does the author work? A source's credentials may influence your readers. You may also find out what biases the author may have; for example, if the author is the founder of Scientists Against Animal Research, you'll have a good idea about his or her personal beliefs on that subject.

Electronic Sources

Using material that you find on the Internet will present special challenges in determining the value of a source. Unlike most printed journal and newspaper articles and books, Internet materials are not necessarily reviewed by editors or professional colleagues to determine whether the facts are correct and the conclusions reliable. Anyone who has (or knows someone who has) the technical skills can develop a Web site and post opinions for the world to read. Sometimes it's difficult to determine whether the information you find on the Web is worth using. While there are no hard-and-fast rules to indicate whether an Internet source is reliable, here are a few suggestions that will help you evaluate whether you have found a credible source:

- **Domain address.** Each Internet host computer is assigned a domain indicating the type of organization that created the site. This domain indicator appears at the end of the address. Most sites will be labeled one of the following:

  edu for an educational site
  gov for a government site
  com for a commercial site
  org for an organizational site

  While we can't vouch for the quality of all the material at these different domains, it is more likely that sites affiliated with an educational institution or a government office will provide information that has been carefully researched and prepared. Although commercial sites and sites sponsored by organizations may also provide valid information, it is important to check carefully for bias or misinformation that might be made available to further the interests of the business or organization.
- **Author of the site.** Try to identity the author or authors of the material published at the site. Is the author a professional or an authority in a field relevant to the topic? The director of a public health clinic may have opinions worth considering on the medical use of marijuana; he may or may not have the same level of credibility in a discussion about punishment for juvenile criminals.
- **Identity of the organization.** If the site is maintained by an organization, find out what interests, if any, the organization represents. Who created the organization? A government-appointed committee investigating public support of family planning will have a very different agenda from a committee organized by private interest groups. While both groups may be scrupulously honest in their presentation of the facts, each may interpret those facts with a particular bias. Your awareness of their "slant" will help you decide how to use the information. The reference section of most libraries can provide directories of associations and organizations.

- **Date of posting.** Check the date when the site was posted. Has the site been updated recently? If not, is the material still current and relevant?
- **Quality of references.** Are sources provided to support the information posted on the site? Most credible sites will document their facts, research studies, and statistics. Many articles and essays will be followed by a bibliography. It's always a good idea to double-check these references to determine whether the information is accurate. The absence of any references to support statements of fact and statistics may indicate that the site is unreliable.
- **Quality of material.** Look for indications that the material has been written or assembled by an educated, well-informed individual who offers a balanced and thoughtful perspective on the issue. Is the written text free of obvious grammatical mistakes, spelling errors, problems with sentence structure, and so on? Does the author indicate awareness and respect for other views even while disagreeing with them? Is the coverage of material thorough and well supported? Although poorly written and executed Web sites can be obvious indications of low reliability, don't be fooled by slick, attractive presentations either. You need to investigate beneath the surface to determine whether the content of the site meets academic standards of fairness and thoroughness.
- **Intended use.** Consider how you will use the material at the site. If you are looking for reliable statistics and factual information, then checking the author's credentials and the status of the organization or company will be important to maintaining your own credibility. However, there are times when personal examples and experiences of individuals who are not professionally qualified may still be of value. For example, a student writing a paper on Alzheimer's disease came across a site in which an Alzheimer's victim kept a diary of the progression of her illness. Even though she was not qualified to give expert medical opinion on the disease itself, her diary provided a unique insight into the feelings and perceptions of someone experiencing the loss of her intellectual capabilities. In her paper, the student writer was able to incorporate some of this compelling personal testimony.

Let's see how this advice works in practice. Jenny decided to do an Internet search to find background information for her argument essay on book banning in the public schools. (Sample entries from her annotated bibliography appear earlier in this chapter.) Using several search engines and a keyword search, Jenny had no trouble finding a large number of sites concerned with this subject. However, before relying on the information she found at the sites, Jenny had to determine which sites were reliable. To do this, she examined several features of each site, as recommended above.

The first site Jenny found was called *The On-Line Books Page: Banned Books On-Line* <http://www.cs.cmu.edu/People/spok/banned-books.html>. Using the criteria from the list we've provided, Jenny made the following evaluation of the site (see Figure 9.1):

- **Domain address.** Jenny noted that the domain address contained "edu," indicating an educational institution. As she read through the information on the

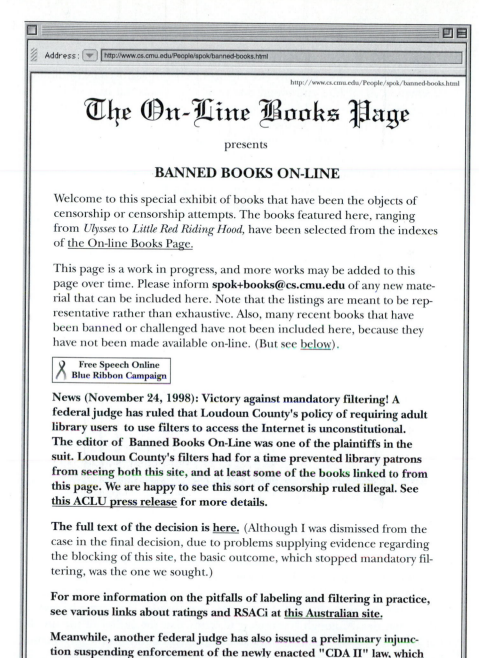

http://www.cs.cmu.edu/People/spok/banned-books.html

The On-Line Books Page

presents

BANNED BOOKS ON-LINE

Welcome to this special exhibit of books that have been the objects of censorship or censorship attempts. The books featured here, ranging from *Ulysses* to *Little Red Riding Hood,* have been selected from the indexes of the On-line Books Page.

This page is a work in progress, and more works may be added to this page over time. Please inform **spok+books@cs.cmu.edu** of any new material that can be included here. Note that the listings are meant to be representative rather than exhaustive. Also, many recent books that have been banned or challenged have not been included here, because they have not been made available on-line. (But see below).

Free Speech Online
Blue Ribbon Campaign

News (November 24, 1998): Victory against mandatory filtering! A federal judge has ruled that Loudoun County's policy of requiring adult library users to use filters to access the Internet is unconstitutional. The editor of Banned Books On-Line was one of the plaintiffs in the suit. Loudoun County's filters had for a time prevented library patrons from seeing both this site, and at least some of the books linked to from this page. We are happy to see this sort of censorship ruled illegal. See this ACLU press release for more details.

The full text of the decision is here. (Although I was dismissed from the case in the final decision, due to problems supplying evidence regarding the blocking of this site, the basic outcome, which stopped mandatory filtering, was the one we sought.)

For more information on the pitfalls of labeling and filtering in practice, see various links about ratings and RSACi at this Australian site.

Meanwhile, another federal judge has also issued a preliminary injunction suspending enforcement of the newly enacted "CDA II" law, which made it a crime to knowingly communicate "for commercial purposes" material considered "harmful to minors." For more information, see the EFF Blue Ribbon Campaign site.

Figure 9.1

Web site, she learned that the site was based at Carnegie Mellon University, a well-known and reputable school.

- **Author of the site.** At the end of the site, the author identified himself by name. Using the home page link (see Figure 9.2), Jenny searched for additional information about him and found that he is a post-doctoral student in computer science at Carnegie Mellon University. Since this description didn't indicate any special expertise on the subject of banned books, Jenny needed to investigate more. An *AltaVista* keyword search using the author's name produced more information about his recent Ph.D. from Carnegie Mellon in computer science and his other professional activities related to banned books.

- **Identity of the organization.** The links provided on the home page allowed Jenny to gather more information about *The On-Line Books Page* and its author. By clicking on The University Library Project link, Jenny found that the author was associated with a Carnegie Mellon project intended to make all authored works available on the Internet. She also learned that the Web space and computing support for the site were provided by the School of Computer Science at Carnegie Mellon. Another link specified the criteria used to determine which books were placed on the banned book list. Still other links provided further background information about the goals of the site and its association with the Library of Congress. This information and the support of well-known and credible organizations and projects made Jenny feel confident about the value of this site.

- **Date of posting.** Jenny noted that the material on the Web site was current, having last been updated in the very month in which she was doing her research. The site itself contained information about both recent attempts to limit public library Internet access and historical accounts of book banning.

- **Quality of references.** The author provided frequent references to other Web sites on banned books, as well as to printed books on censorship. Checking through the Internet and the college library, Jenny confirmed that these references were used reliably and even decided to incorporate some of them into her research.

- **Quality of material.** Jenny found the text well written and the entire site organized and thorough. To evaluate whether the author's perspective was well balanced, Jenny checked to see if books from all ends of the political spectrum were included in the list. She discovered that the list included a group of diverse books, from the Bible to Qur'an to works of nineteenth-century poetry to contemporary books that had been criminalized under "hate speech" laws in other countries. Although it was clear to Jenny that the author of the site did not approve of book banning, this bias did not seem to distort the information he provided.

- **Intended use.** Jenny was interested in finding out the titles of books that were banned, those responsible for the banning, and the reasons behind the decisions. She found *The On-Line Books Page* very useful. Jenny was particularly impressed by its range of titles. The site's list covered classic and historical works, as well as more modern ones. The explanations that accompanied each

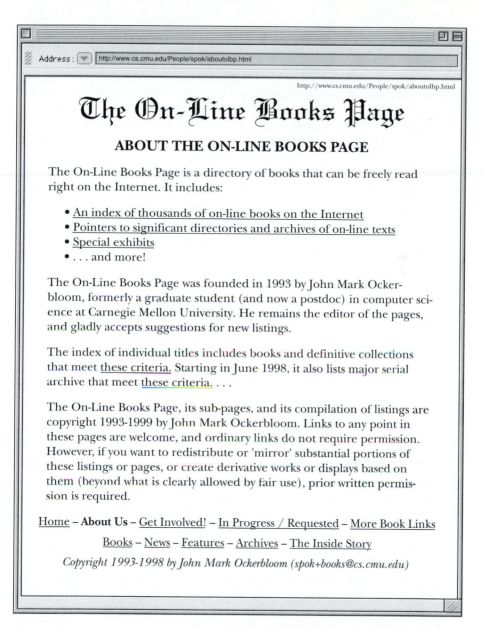

http://www.cs.cmu.edu/People/spok/aboutolbp.html

The On-Line Books Page

ABOUT THE ON-LINE BOOKS PAGE

The On-Line Books Page is a directory of books that can be freely read right on the Internet. It includes:

- An index of thousands of on-line books on the Internet
- Pointers to significant directories and archives of on-line texts
- Special exhibits
- . . . and more!

The On-Line Books Page was founded in 1993 by John Mark Ocker-bloom, formerly a graduate student (and now a postdoc) in computer science at Carnegie Mellon University. He remains the editor of the pages, and gladly accepts suggestions for new listings.

The index of individual titles includes books and definitive collections that meet these criteria. Starting in June 1998, it also lists major serial archive that meet these criteria. . . .

The On-Line Books Page, its sub-pages, and its compilation of listings are copyright 1993-1999 by John Mark Ockerbloom. Links to any point in these pages are welcome, and ordinary links do not require permission. However, if you want to redistribute or 'mirror' substantial portions of these listings or pages, or create derivative works or displays based on them (beyond what is clearly allowed by fair use), prior written permission is required.

Home – **About Us** – Get Involved! – In Progress / Requested – More Book Links

Books – News – Features – Archives – The Inside Story

Copyright 1993-1998 by John Mark Ockerbloom (spok+books@cs.cmu.edu)

Figure 9.2

listing briefly explained the circumstances surrounding the book's censorship and provided specific dates and information about it.

After carefully evaluating *The On-Line Books Page: Banned Books On-Line,* Jenny concluded that it was a reliable source that might supply her with valuable information for her argument essay.

Jenny found three other Web sites that were also concerned with the issue of banned books. However, after using the criteria outlined above to evaluate the three, Jenny decided not to use them. Here are some of the reasons why:

- **Domain address.** Two of the sites had addresses that indicated that they had no association with any educational institution, government, business, or organization; the Web sites were developed by individuals for their own personal use. Jenny decided that the materials on these sites were more likely to reflect personal opinion than careful research. The third site was maintained by an organization that Jenny decided to investigate further.
- **Author of the site.** By using the links provided in each site, Jenny discovered that one author was a student writing a paper for an Internet course; another was an individual who supplied some personal information about his life (as well as family photographs), but nothing that indicated expertise on book banning; and the third was identified as a news editor for a newspaper published in California. Jenny needed more information before she could conclude that any of these authors was a reliable source.
- **Identity of the organization.** Only the site authored by the newspaper editor indicated an association with an organization. Using links in the site, Jenny found that he was affiliated with a religious group that strongly advocated the elimination of different races and religions in American life. After reading several articles on the group's Web site, Jenny concluded that the material contained strong political and racial bias that made her question the reliability of the newspaper editor.
- **Date of posting.** None of the sites had been updated within the past year. Although Jenny was interested in both historical and current information on book banning, she was concerned that the authors had made no attempts to keep the information in the sites current and timely.
- **Quality of references.** Only one site contained a list of related readings, and none of the sites used references to support statements of fact or opinion.
- **Quality of material.** Jenny immediately noticed the poor writing quality of the student paper. It was filled with misspellings and grammatical errors, and was poorly organized. The second site demonstrated better quality writing, but the author did not develop or support his ideas sufficiently. For instance, he based much of his claim on an "informal survey" without specifying the details of how the survey was conducted. The site authored by the newspaper editor did not reflect respect for other viewpoints or any attempt to present a balanced perspective on the issue of book banning.
- **Intended use.** Jenny wanted to be sure that the information she used in her argument essay was accurate. The absence of information about two of the authors and the political affiliations of the third caused her to doubt that any of these sites could be relied on for accuracy.

As Jenny discovered, the Internet can offer a wide array of source material to research, but it does take additional effort to determine which sources will meet the academic standards required for research. If you remember to think like an investigator and examine your findings carefully, you'll discover reliable and valuable information and ideas for your argument essays.

Taking Notes

There are as many different styles of note taking as there are writers. Some people like to use 4" × 6" cards, recording one idea on each card. This is useful because you can easily shift cards around as you change your outline; you don't have to re-copy material as often. Other students take their notes in their argument journals or on sheets of wide computer paper so they can make notes or copy bibliographic references in the margins. If you decide to use note cards, we offer two words of advice: First, mark every note card in some way to identify the source. You might want to use the author's name, a short abbreviation of the title, or some kind of numbering system tying your note cards and bibliography together. Don't neglect this or you'll find yourself desperately searching for a reference at 2 A.M. on the day your paper is due, with no way to track it down. Second, on each note card indicate whether it's a summary, paraphrase, or direct quote; some people use different-colored cards, pens, or highlighters to distinguish the three kinds of notes. Other people use the initials *S, P,* and *Q* to make the cards. This designation proves useful when deciding on how and when to *document* your sources (see the Documentation Guide).

Most research notes fall into three categories: summary, paraphrase, and quotation.

Summary

Summary is most useful when you want to record the author's main idea without the background or supporting evidence. To summarize accurately, you condense an extended idea into a sentence or more in your own words. Your goal is to record the *essence* of the idea as accurately as possible in your own words.

Here's Jenny's summary of a passage from one of her sources.

Original
During the 1995–96 school year, there were more attempts to remove or restrict educational materials, censor school programs, stifle student expression, pass harmful, anti–public education legislation and inject coercive religious doctrine into the school day than ever before in the 14-year history of this report. Researchers confirmed 475 incidents in 44 states in all regions of the country. Those 475 incidents include both outright attempts to censor materials, as well as efforts to impose an ideological or sectarian agenda through other means. States with the highest number of incidents were California, Pennsylvania and Florida. No incidents, however, were reported in Arkansas, Delaware, Hawaii, North Dakota, Vermont, West Virginia, or Wyoming. (From People for the American Way, *Attacks on the Freedom to Learn,* p. 6.)

Jenny's Summary
People for the American Way reports that attempts to affect public school education through the censorship or control of educational materials or programs increased in 1995–96 more than in any other year since their report was

published. Four hundred and seventy-five incidents were recorded in 44 states across the country.

For more on writing summaries, see Chapter 2.

Paraphrase

Paraphrasing is useful when you want to preserve an author's line of reasoning or specific ideas, but don't want or need to use the original words. When you paraphrase, you restate the original in your own words and sentence structure as accurately as possible.

Here is an excerpt from another source that Jenny used in her paper:

Original

The past century has witnessed a subtle shift in the role of child-rearing from a private matter to a matter of increasingly public concern. Government bureaucrats display an arrogant, "we know best" attitude that manifests itself in such things as value-free sex education classes for elementary schoolchildren, education agendas that encourage children to question the authority of their parents, and the refusal to allow parents to view the curricula and testing materials used by their children's schools. (From Family Research Council, *Frequently Asked Questions: Parental Rights* <http://www.frc.org:80/faq22.html>.)

Jenny's Paraphrase

According to the Family Research Council, the responsibility of bringing up children has changed during this century from a reliance on the individual family unit to one in which the public plays an important part. The government thinks it knows better about child raising than a child's parents do. As a result, sex education classes in the schools ignore issues of morality, and schools teach children that their parents aren't always right. In addition, schools are unwilling to permit parents access to teaching and testing instruments.

Quotation

Direct quotation should be used only when the author's words are particularly memorable or succinct, or when the author presents factual or numerical evidence that can't be easily paraphrased. You must copy the author's *exact* wording, spelling, capitalization, and punctuation, *as you find it* (even if it contains an obvious mistake). Proofread every direct quotation at least twice; it's easier than you think to leave something out, change a verb tense, or add a word or two. If you want to add words for grammatical completeness or clarity, put them in square brackets such as these [ ]. If you want to eliminate words, mark the omission with three spaced periods, called *ellipsis points* (if the omission comes at the end of a sentence, the ellipsis is typed with four spaced periods), and put them within square brackets. If you find a source you are certain to quote from, it might be worthwhile to photocopy it to avoid errors when rewriting the words.

Here is an example of the effective use of quotation, based on another of Jenny's sources:

Original

Congress shall make no law respecting an establishment of religion, or prohibiting the free exercise thereof; or abridging the freedom of speech, or of the press, or the right of the people peaceably to assemble, and to petition the government for a redress of grievances. (From the First Amendment of the Constitution of the United States.)

Jenny's Effective Use of Quotation

Most Americans agree with the rights granted by the First Amendment of the Constitution, which stipulates that "Congress shall make no law [. . .] abridging the freedom of speech, or of the press."

Drafting Your Paper

Sometimes the sheer size of a researched argument paper can be intimidating. As a result, some writers suffer from "writer's block" when they start composing the paper. Here are several strategies for starting your draft.

1. **Write a five-minute summary.** The five-minute summary asks you to write a quick, one- or two-paragraph description of what your final paper will say. Basically you're creating a thumbnail sketch of the paper to clarify in your own mind how the paper will come together. The summary doesn't have to be formal; some people don't even use complete sentences. Almost always these summaries dispel writer's block and get your creativity flowing.
2. **Divide the paper into sections.** Dividing the paper into sections makes the task of writing a long paper more manageable. Most writers divide a paper, as we did in Chapter 5, into beginning, middle, and end, and further subdivide the middle.
3. **First, draft the sections you're confident about.** Drafting the sections you feel most confident about first builds momentum for drafting other parts of the paper. As reported by many students, this strategy might also lead you to alter the slant or emphasis of the final paper, thereby resulting in a better outcome.
4. **Use a simple code to indicate sources.** Using a simple code to indicate sources will save you a great deal of time in revising your paper. As you write your draft, you may not want to interrupt the flow of your ideas to copy quotations or summaries from note cards; instead, you can insert into your draft the author's or source's name and a quick reference to the content so that you'll know on a later draft what you intended to include. Here's an example of how Jenny used coded references in her first draft:

Attempts to ban books in public schools is on the rise. [People, Attacks 6] John Steinbeck's *Of Mice and Men* is a frequent target of protest for parents. [Mitchell, NYT B17]

Here you can see Jenny's code at work as she refers to notes from a report published by People for the American Way and an article from page B17 of the *New York Times*. Later she will have to incorporate these sources into the draft and provide parenthetical citations; for the time being she simply lists in shorthand the evidence to support her general statements.

Incorporating Your Research

Because the effort in finding sources and taking notes is so time-consuming, some writers think that their work will be "wasted" if they don't somehow cram all the notes they've taken into their final papers. Unfortunately, the results of such cramming often look less like a paper and more like note cards stapled together in a long string with an occasional sentence wedged between to provide transitions. Every successful writer ends up gathering more research data than is needed for a paper. But isn't it better to have plenty of material to pick and choose from than not have enough to make a persuasive case? The five tests we explained at the end of Chapter 6 (sufficiency, detail, relevance, avoidance of excess, and appropriateness) should determine which notes to incorporate into the final draft. Here, too, the flexibility of having one note per card may help you because you can shuffle and change the sequence of sources to see which order of presentation will have the most impact on your readers. If you're working with a computer, you may find yourself marking and moving blocks of text around as you judge the arrangement of your evidence. The first arrangement you come up with may not always be the best. Allow yourself some flexibility!

When incorporating sources into your paper, you don't want the "seams" to show between your own writing and the summaries, paraphrases, and quotations from your sources. So it's worth the effort to spend some time writing sentences and phrases that smoothly introduce sources into the text. Consider these two examples:

Awkward   The Anaheim school board decided to ban *Beloved,* and this was "not an example of censorship, but an isolated incident."

Revised   The school board in the Anaheim, California, school system stated that their decision to ban *Beloved* was "not an example of censorship, but an isolated incident."

Remember that while *you,* the writer, may understand how a particular source supports your points, your *readers* may miss the connections unless you provide them. "But I know what I meant!" isn't much of a defense when your readers can't follow your chain of thought. Again we fall back on the analogy of making a case to a jury: A good attorney not only presents a witness's testimony but also helps the jury understand what that testimony means.

Attribution

Many students fail to understand the importance of introducing their sources when they incorporate them into a paper. This introduction is called **attribution,** and it is an important part of the process of documentation. Attribution shows your readers that your evidence comes from identifiable, reliable sources. When the attribution contains the name of a book or the author's professional affiliation or other credentials, it also suggests to your readers how reliable the source may be. For instance, if you present a statistic on divorce and attribute it to the book *How to Pick Up Women,* your readers are less likely to respect that statistic than if it came from the U.S. Census Bureau. Likewise, if you cite evidence that eating rutabagas prevents colon cancer, your readers will treat the evidence differently if it comes from an unbiased researcher at the Mayo Clinic rather than from one at the American Rutabaga Institute. In neither case is the evidence less likely to be true, but the attribution in both cases makes the difference in plausibility.

ATTRIBUTION VERBS

Source Is Neutral

comments	observes	says
describes	points out	sees
explains	records	thinks
illustrates	reports	writes
notes		

Source Infers or Suggests, But Doesn't Actually Say So

analyzes	asks	assesses
concludes	considers	finds
predicts	proposes	reveals
shows	speculates	suggests
supposes	infers	implies

Source Argues

alleges	claims	contends
defends	disagrees	holds
insists	maintains	argues

Source Agrees with Someone/Something Else

admits	agrees	concedes
concurs	grants	allows

Source Is Uneasy or Disagrees

belittles	bemoans	complains
condemns	deplores	deprecates
derides	laments	warns

Many students have only one phrase in their repertoires for attribution: "According to. . . ." This works, but it is not very informative. By choosing a more connotative argumentative verb, as you do when you state a position or proposal, you can signal to your readers the source's attitude toward the statement. For instance, consider this sentence:

Senator Smith ____ that the change is needed.

Look how changing the verb can change the way your audience regards Smith's position (not all these verbs will work in this sentence structure).

If you're not sure of the connotations of any of these verbs, or you're not sure that the sentence you created works with a particular choice, consult an unabridged dictionary or your instructor. Clumsy attribution can distract readers in the same way typos and grammatical errors can, so you want to make your attributions as smooth as possible. (For placement of a bibliographic reference after attributed material, see the next section on documentation.)

Revising and Editing Your Paper

After you have worked your source material into a draft, it's time to look at your writing skeptically, as your readers will. Start by testing all the parts of your argument. This may not be easy to do because you've been living with this topic for several weeks and may have lost your objectivity and ability to see the gaps. (If you're working in writing groups, ask another member to read your paper and offer you some feedback on it.) Then change, delete, add, or reorganize material to make your case more effectively.

To help you revise your argument, we recommend making an outline of the draft *as you've written it*—not as you intended to write it. This will serve as an x-ray of the paper, helping you detect any holes or imbalances. Moreover, it will show you the actual order in which points are presented so that you can consider reorganizing or changing your argumentative strategy. The strategies explained in Chapters 6 and 7 for assessing evidence and considering claims ought to help you at this stage; apply them as stringently to your own writing as you would to an essay you're reading.

If you made notes in your argument journal at an earlier date about connections you wanted to make in your final paper, now is the time to include those connections if, in fact, they fit into the paper's final shape. You might also consider other kinds of evidence to include. Can you think of personal experiences or those of other people to support the evidence of your outside authorities? Have you found facts and statistics to buttress the opinions you present? What are your readers' criteria for judging an issue? Have you presented claims that meet those criteria and phrased them in that manner? It's also time to make sure that all transitions between points are included and are accurate. For instance, if you switch points around, make sure that the point you can "second" is actually the second, not the third or fourth. Also, check to be sure you've included documentation for all your sources and that you have bibliographic note cards or other records of documentation information to prepare the notes in your final copy. Then polish your prose so that your sentences are smooth, your paragraphs are complete, and your grammar and punctuation are precise. Many students "let down" their efforts when they sense their papers are nearing completion; as a result, their final grades suffer. The revising and editing stage requires sharp attention. Don't undercut all your hard research efforts by presenting your argument in anything but its best form.

Preparing and Proofreading Your Final Manuscript

Once you have polished the draft to your satisfaction, it is time to attend to the presentation of your paper. Flawless presentation is important in research, not only because of the appreciation it will win from your instructor and readers, but also because it will reinforce your credibility with your readers. A sloppy paper with typographical or grammatical errors, missing documentation, or illegible print makes your readers think that your argument might be sloppy as well. A well-prepared paper suggests to your readers that you have taken extra care to ensure that everything is correct—not only the presentation, but the content as well. This good impression may make readers more inclined to accept your arguments.

Most instructors expect research papers to be neatly and legibly typed with clear titles, double spacing, standard margins (1-inch) and type sizes (10- or 12-point), and minimal handwritten corrections. Your last name and the page number should appear in the upper-right-hand corner of every page after the title page. For English courses the standard guide to manuscript format is the *MLA Handbook for Writers of Research Papers,* 5th edition. MLA requirements are spelled out in most college composition handbooks and illustrated in Jenny's final paper (see the Documentation Guide). Before you submit your paper, proofread it carefully for typographical errors, misspellings, omitted words, and other minor errors. If possible, let several hours elapse before your final proofreading so you can see what you've actually typed instead of what you *think* you typed. Never let the pressure of a deadline keep you from proofreading your paper. Readers get annoyed by minor errors, and annoyed readers are less likely to be persuaded by the content of your argument.

Plagiarism

Plagiarism is a crime in the academic community. The scholarly world operates by exchanging information and acknowledging the sources of this information. If you fail to acknowledge your sources or make it appear that someone else's work is actually your own, you are sabotaging the exchange of scholarly information. You're blocking the channels. Perhaps it doesn't seem important to you now, but you should know that plagiarism has very serious consequences. It can earn you a failing grade on an assignment or for a course, a suspension or even expulsion from school, and/or a permanent notation on the transcripts that future employers and graduate schools will see. Even if you are never caught, you've still stolen ideas and words from someone.

Plagiarism falls into two categories: intentional and accidental. Intentional plagiarism includes copying a phrase, a sentence, or a longer passage from a source and passing it off as your own; summarizing or paraphrasing someone else's ideas without acknowledgment; and buying or borrowing a paper written by someone else and submitting it as your own. Accidental plagiarism includes forgetting to place quotation marks around someone else's words and not acknowledging a source because you were ignorant of the need to document it. Carelessness and ignorance are not defenses against plagiarism.

Many questions about plagiarism involve the tricky subject of *common knowledge*—that is, standard information in a field of study, as well as commonsense observations and proverbial wisdom. Standard information includes the major facts in a discipline—for example, the chemical formula for water is H_2O or the Seneca Falls Convention for Women's Rights took place in 1848. If most of your sources accept such a fact without acknowledgment, you can assume it is common knowledge to readers in that field. However, if you're dealing with lesser-known facts (the numbers of soldiers at the Battle of Hastings), interpretations of those facts (assessments of the importance of the Seneca Falls meeting), or a specialist's observation (a scholar's analysis of Susan B. Anthony's rhetoric), you'll need to provide documentation.

Commonsense information, such as the notions that politicians are concerned with getting votes or that icy roads make driving dangerous, need not be documented. Proverbs and clichés don't need documentation either, although proverbs taken from recognized poems or literary works do. (Thus, "A stitch in time" needs no documentation, but "To be or not to be" should carry a reference to *Hamlet*.)

Here are four simple rules to help you avoid plagiarism.

1. *Take your research notes carefully.* Write down (or print out) a full bibliographical reference for each source (the forms for these appear in the Documentation Guide). Also, note whether you are quoting, paraphrasing, or summarizing what you find in your source (see earlier discussion in this chapter). If your notes are clear and thorough, you'll never have to worry about which words and ideas are yours and which are your sources'.

2. *Always introduce your source carefully so that your audience knows to whom they're listening.* Proper attribution is a signal to your readers that you're switching from your own work to someone else's. It also is a signal to you to check that a source is represented accurately (with no exaggeration) and that a bibliographic citation appears in your list of Works Cited or References.

3. *When in doubt, document.* While it is possible to overdocument, it is not an intellectual crime to do so. Rather, it reveals a lack of self-confidence in your own argument or your determination to prove to your instructor and readers that you've seen every source ever published on your subject. However, overdocumenting is a less serious academic sin than plagiarizing!

4. *Enter the documentation right after the use of the source; it doesn't "carry over" between paragraphs or pages.* It is tempting, especially when using one source for an extended period, to leave all the documentation until the end of a large passage of text (which might be several paragraphs or several pages in length). But even if you weave attribution skillfully throughout the whole passage, the convention in academics is that you document a source in each paragraph in which you use it. If another source intervenes, it is twice as important that the main source be documented in every paragraph of use. So if you use the same article in four successive paragraphs, each of those paragraphs must have some parenthetical source reference. With skillful attribution the parenthetical reference can be reduced to a simple page number, which won't interrupt the "flow" of your text.

To understand how plagiarism works, let's look at some of the ways writers might handle, or mishandle, this passage from Dennis Baron's article "English in a Multicultural Society," which appeared in the Spring 1991 issue of *Social Policy.* Here's the original passage from page 8:

> The notion of a national language sometimes wears the disguise of inclusion: we must all speak English to participate meaningfully in the democratic process.

Sometimes it argues unity: we must speak one language to understand one another and share both culture and country. Those who insist on English often equate bilingualism with lack of patriotism. Their intention to legislate official English often masks racism and certainly fails to appreciate cultural difference: it is a thinly veiled measure to disenfranchise anyone not like "us."

Plagiarized Use

Supporters of U.S. English argue we must all speak one language to understand one another and share both culture and country. But Dennis Baron argues that "[t]heir intention to legislate official English often masks racism and certainly fails to appreciate cultural difference" (8). English-only legislation really intends to exclude anyone who is not like "us."

This is plagiarism because the writer has copied Baron's words in the first sentence and paraphrased them in the last, but made it appear as though only the middle sentence were actually taken from Baron's article.

Plagiarized Use

Calls for a national language sometimes wear the disguise of inclusion, according to linguist Dennis Baron. When U.S. English argues that we must all speak English to participate meaningfully in the democratic process, or that we must speak one language to understand one another and share both culture and country, Baron says they are masking racism and failing to appreciate cultural difference (8).

Here the plagiarism comes in presenting Baron's actual words without quotation marks, so it looks as if the writer is paraphrasing rather than quoting. Even with the attribution and the citation of the source, this paragraph is still an example of plagiarism because the direct quotations are disguised as the writer's paraphrase.

Acceptable Use

Linguist Dennis Baron argues that supporters of official English legislation use the reasons of inclusions, unity, and patriotism to justify these laws, but that their efforts may hide racist and culturally intolerant positions. Baron says that sometimes English-only laws are "thinly-veiled measure[s] to disenfranchise anyone not like 'us.'" (8).

Here the source is properly handled. The writer paraphrases most of the original text in the first sentence, then skillfully incorporates a direct quotation in the second (note the use of square brackets to make the noun agree in number with the verb, and the conversion of double quotation marks from the original into single quotation marks in the quote). The attribution clearly says that both points are taken from Baron, but the quotation marks show where Baron's actual words, rather than the writer's, are used.

Documentation Guide
MLA and APA Styles

Almost every academic discipline has developed its own system of *documentation,* a sort of code for indicating where the writer's evidence may be found. A good way to think of the rules of documentation is by analogy to a sport, for example, basketball: Academic readers expect you to play by the established rules (what to document, how to avoid plagiarism, how to attribute sources). If you want to play the game, you have to observe the rules. At the same time—as you probably know—there are accepted variations on the rules (e.g., 30- or 45-second shot clocks, the dimensions of the 3-point line) in certain basketball leagues. The various styles of documentation used in the humanities, social sciences, and natural sciences are the equivalent of these acceptable variations.

You must document any idea or words you *summarize, paraphrase,* or *quote directly* from a source. The two most common variations on documentation used in colleges and universities are the Modern Language Association (MLA) style, used widely in the humanities, and the American Psychological Association (APA) style, used widely in the social sciences. We will explain them in detail later in this chapter. (Some of your courses may also require you to use CSE [Council of Science Editors] style; *The Chicago Manual of Style,* which you might know as Turabian style; or a journalistic style guide such as *The Associated Press Style Book.*) Think of these systems not as annoyances for you as a writer, but as rule books for playing the game of researched writing on different courts. Your instructor will tell you which rules to follow.

Where Does the Documentation Go?

Fortunately, both MLA and APA styles have abandoned footnotes in favor of parenthetical citations within the paper and a source list at the end of the paper, a much neater format to work with. In both styles you put a brief reference or attribution to your source in parentheses within the body of the paper, and a full bibliographical citation in a list of *Works Cited* (MLA) or *References* (APA). (These are the equivalents of what you probably called a "Bibliography" in high school.) Documenting your sources, if performed properly, will help you avoid plagiarism. The shape that citations take in the two systems, however, is a little different, so make sure you observe the forms carefully.

230

Documentation Style

Let's look at how both systems handle documentation for some of the most commonly used information sources. Suppose you want to quote from Charles Siebert's article, "The DNA We've Been Dealt," which appeared in the September 17, 1995, issue of the *New York Times Magazine.* Here's how it would appear in your list of sources:

> **MLA**   Siebert, Charles. "The DNA We've Been Dealt." *New York Times Magazine* 17 Sept. 1995: 50–64.

> **APA**   Siebert, C. (1995, September 17). The DNA we've been dealt. *New York Times Magazine,* pp. 50–64.

As you can see, each style orders information differently.* Likewise, both styles use a parenthetical reference in the paper to show where the evidence comes from, but again they do it differently. Note that while the italizing and underlining of publications are both acceptable methods, check with your instructor on a preferred method.

> **MLA**   One author reports that "the Genome Project is expected to leave us with a complete readout of our biological blueprint by the year 2005 (at an estimated cost of $3 billion)" (Siebert 53).

If the author's name appears in your attribution, only the page number needs to go in the parentheses:

> **MLA**   Charles Siebert reports that "the Genome Project is expected to leave us with a complete readout of our biological blueprint by the year 2005 (at an estimated cost of $3 billion)" (53).

Both references tell your readers that they can find this source in your Works Cited list, alphabetized by the last name, "Siebert." If you had more than one reference to Siebert in your Works Cited list, then you would add a shortened form of the title in the parentheses so readers would know to which Siebert article you were referring (Siebert, *DNA* 53).

The APA style references for the same situations would be

> **APA**   One author reports that "the Genome Project is expected to leave us with a complete readout of our biological blueprint by the year 2005 (at an estimated cost of $3 billion)" (Siebert, 1995).

> or

> **APA**   Charles Siebert (1995) reports that "the Genome Project is expected to leave us with a complete readout of our biological blueprint by the year 2005 (at an estimated cost of $3 billion)."

---

*Note that both MLA and APA begin the entry flush with the left margin; subsequent lines are indented 1/2" or five typewriter spaces. All entries should be double-spaced.

When you use more than one work by an author in your paper, APA style distinguishes them by date of publication. For example, if you cited two Siebert articles from 1995, the earlier one is designated 1995a, and the second is referred to as 1995b.

Using parenthetical citations for electronic sources can be much trickier because such sources typically have no page numbers. In MLA style, if your source uses paragraph numbers, provide the paragraph number preceded by *par* or *pars*. In APA style, if your source uses paragraph numbers, provide the paragraph number preceded by *para.* or *paras.,* or use the symbol ¶. If you need to include the author's name or a brief title, place a comma after the name or title. If another type of designation is used in the source to delineate its parts (such as *screens* or *Part II*), write out the word used for that part:

MLA	Between 1992 and 1996, the message delivered by political advertisements changed dramatically (Edwards, par. 15).
APA	Between 1992 and 1996, the message delivered by political advertisements changed dramatically (Edwards, 1998, para. 15).

If your source has no numbering, then no page or paragraph numbers should appear in your parenthetical reference unless your instructor indicates otherwise. Some instructors ask students to number the paragraphs of electronic sources to make references easier to locate.

A Brief Guide to MLA and APA Styles

The handbooks for MLA and APA documentation are available in most college libraries. If you don't find the information you need in the following brief guide, look for these books or Web sites:

MLA	Gibaldi, Joseph. *MLA Handbook for Writers of Research Papers.* 5th edition. New York: MLA, 1999.

The Web site of the Modern Language Association is: <http://www.mla.org>.

APA	*Publication Manual of the American Psychological Association* (5th ed.). (2001). Washington, D.C.: APA.

The Web site for APA is <http://www.apastyle.org>. The American Psychological Association provides updates to documentation on its Web site; the Purdue University Online Writing Lab also provides a useful guide to APA documentation: <http://owl.english.purdue.edu/Files/34.html>.

General Format for Books

MLA	Author. *Title.* Edition. City of Publication: Publisher, Year.
APA	Author. (Year of Publication). *Title.* City of Publication, State: Publisher.

One Author

> **MLA**   Kozol, Jonathan. *Savage Inequalities: Children in America's Schools.*
> New York: Crown, 1991.

> **APA**   Kozol, J. (1991). *Savage inequalities: Children in America's schools.*
> New York: Crown.

MLA uses the author's full first name plus middle initial, whereas APA uses the initial of the first name (unless more initials are needed to distinguish among people with the same initials). APA capitalizes only first words and proper nouns in titles and subtitles; MLA capitalizes all words except prepositions, conjunctions, and articles. MLA lists only the city; APA lists the city but also includes the state if the city is unfamiliar or could be confused with another. Finally, MLA permits the abbreviation of certain publishers' names, whereas APA drops unnecessary words such as *Co., Inc.,* and *Publishers.*

Two or More Authors

> **MLA**   Pyles, Thomas, and John Algeo. *History and Development of the*
> *English Language.* 4th ed. Fort Worth: Harcourt, 1993.

> **APA**   Pyles, T., & Algeo, J. (1993). *History and development of the English*
> *language* (4th ed.). Fort Worth, TX: Harcourt, Brace, Jo-
> vanovich.

In MLA style, only the first author's name is given last name first. In APA style, the ampersand (&) is used to join authors' names. The ampersand is also used in parenthetical references (e.g., "[Pyles & Algeo, 1993, p. 23]") but not in attributions (e.g., "According to Pyles and Algeo"). In MLA style, for works with four or more authors, you may replace all but the first author's name by the abbreviation *et al.* You may use that abbreviation in APA style if there are six or more authors.

More Than One Work by an Author

> **MLA**   Baron, Dennis. *Grammar and Gender.* New Haven: Yale UP, 1986.
>
> ---. *Grammar and Good Taste.* New Haven: Yale UP, 1982.

In MLA style, if you cite more than one work by a particular author, the individual works are listed in alphabetical order. For the second and any additional entries, type three hyphens and a period instead of the author's name; then skip a space and type the title, underlined or in italics.

In APA style, when citing more than one work by an author, the author's name is repeated and the entries are listed chronologically (first published to most recent) rather than in alphabetical order. If two works by one author are published in the same year, then the works are listed alphabetically by title, with a lowercase "a" following the year of the first work, "b" following the year in the second work, and so on.

Anthology with an Editor

MLA   Shapiro, Michael, ed. *Language and Politics*. New York: New York UP, 1984.

APA   Shapiro, M. (Ed.). (1984). *Language and politics*. New York: New York University Press.

Essay in a Collection or Anthology

MLA   Davis, Vivian I. "Paranoia in Language Politics." *Not Only English: Reaffirming America's Multilingual Heritage*. Ed. Harvey A. Daniels. Urbana: NCTE, 1990. 71–76.

APA   Davis, V. (1990). Paranoia in language politics. In H. Daniels (Ed.), *Not only English: Reaffirming America's multilingual heritage* (pp. 71–76). Urbana, IL: NCTE.

Book in a Later Edition

MLA   Zinn, Howard. *The Politics of History*. 2nd ed. Urbana: Illinois UP, 1990.

APA   Zinn, H. (1990). *The politics of history* (2nd ed.). Urbana, IL: University of Illinois Press.

Multivolume Work

MLA   Lincoln, Abraham. *The Collected Works of Abraham Lincoln*. Ed. Roy P. Basler. 5 vols. New Brunswick: Rutgers UP, 1953.

APA   Basler, R. P. (Ed.). (1953). *The collected works of Abraham Lincoln*. (Vol. 5). New Brunswick, NJ: Rutgers University Press.

Book with a Group or Corporate Author

MLA   National Council of Teachers of English Committee on Classroom Practices. *Non-native and Nonstandard Dialect Students*. Urbana: NCTE, 1982.

APA   National Council of Teachers of English Committee on Classroom Practices. (1982). *Non-native and nonstandard dialect students*. Urbana, IL: NCTE.

Begin the entry with the corporate or group name alphabetized by the first letter of the main word (not including *a, an,* or *the*).

Reference Works

MLA   Risanowsky, A. "Language." *The New Columbia Encyclopedia*. 1975 ed.

APA   Risanowsky, A. (1975). Language. In *The new Columbia encyclopedia* (Vol. 11, pp. 143–148). New York: Columbia.

If the reference book is widely available (such as a major encyclopedia or bibliography), a short bibliography form as shown here is acceptable in MLA; APA recommends including more information rather than less. For a less widely known reference book, MLA recommends using the form for a book, multiple-authored book, or series, depending on what the book is.

Editor's Preparation of a Previous Work

MLA   Austen, Jane. *Pride and Prejudice*. Ed. R. W. Chapman. Oxford: Oxford UP, 1988.

APA   Austen, J. (1988). *Pride and prejudice* (R. W. Chapman, Ed.). Oxford: Oxford University Press. (Original work published 1813)

Translated Work

MLA   Calvino, Italo. *Italian Folktales*. Trans. George Martin. New York: Harcourt, 1980.

APA   Calvino, I. (1980). *Italian folktales* (G. Martin, Trans.). New York: Harcourt. (Original work published 1956)

In APA style the date of the translation is placed after the author's name. The date of the original publication of the work appears in parentheses at the end of the citation. This text would be cited in an essay as (Calvino 1956/1980). Note there is no period after the final parenthesis.

Anonymous Work

MLA   *Microsoft Windows*. Vers. 3.1. Belleville: Microsoft, 1992.

APA   *Microsoft Windows 3.1*. [Computer software]. (1992). Belleville, WA: Microsoft.

Articles

MLA format and APA format for articles are similar to the formats for books. One of the few differences concerns the "volume number" of each issue. Volume numbers for any magazine or journal found in a library or acquired by subscription (these usually appear six times a year or less frequently) should be included in your entry. If a journal appears monthly or more frequently, or can be acquired on newsstands, you can usually omit the volume number. If the journal has continuous pagination (i.e., if the January volume ends on page 88 and the February volume begins on page 89), you don't need to include the month or season of the issue in your citation. If the journal starts over with page 1 in each issue, then you must include the month or season in your citation.

Magazines and newspapers (unlike scholarly journals) often dispense articles over several pages (for instance, pages 35–37, then continuing on 114–115). MLA permits using the form "35+" instead of typing out all the pages on which such articles appear; in APA references to newspaper articles, all page numbers must be noted.

MLA	Author. "Article Title." *Journal or Magazine Title* volume number (Date): inclusive pages.

APA	Author. (Date). Article title. *Journal or Magazine Title, volume number,* inclusive pages.

Scholarly Journal with Continuous Pagination

MLA	Madrid, Arturo. "Official English: A False Policy Issue." *Annals of the American Association of Political and Social Sciences* 508 (1990): 62–65.

APA	Madrid, A. (1990). Official English: A false policy issue. *Annals of the American Association of Political and Social Sciences, 508,* 62–65.

Scholarly Journal with Each Issue Paged Separately

MLA	Baron, Dennis. "English in a Multicultural America." *Social Policy* 31 (Spring 1991): 5–14.

If this journal used issue numbers instead of seasons, the form would be *Social Policy* 31.1 (1991): 5–14.

APA	Baron, D. (1991). English in a multicultural America. *Social Policy, 31,* 5–14.

Magazine Article

MLA	Joelson, J. R. "English: The Language of Liberty." *The Humanist* July/Aug. 1989: 35+.

APA	Joelson, J. R. (1989, July/August). English: The language of liberty. *The Humanist, 35,* 37.

This is the form for a magazine that appears monthly. For a magazine that appears bimonthly or weekly, see the examples under "Anonymous Article."

Anonymous Article

MLA	"Lessons from the U.S. Army." *Fortune* 22 Mar. 1993: 68+.
APA	Lessons from the U.S. army. (1993, March 22). *Fortune,* 68–74.

Review

MLA	Estrada, Alfred J. "Divided Over a Common Language." Rev. of *Hold Your Tongue: Bilingualism and the Politics of "English Only,"* by James Crawford. *Washington Post* 4 Oct. 1992: WBK4+.

APA	Estrada, A. (1992, October 4). Divided over a common language [Review of the book *Hold your tongue: Bilingualism and the politics of "English Only"*]. *The Washington Post,* pp. WBK4, WBK8.

When newspapers designate sections with identifying letters (e.g., A, B, or here, WBK), that information is included in the reference. The "4+" indicates that the review begins on page 4 and continues on other nonadjacent pages in the newspaper. APA includes initial articles such as "The" in a newspaper title; MLA omits them. If the reviewer's name does not appear, begin with "Rev. of *Title*" in the MLA system or [Review of the book *Title*]" in the APA system. If the reviewer's name does not appear, but the review has a title, begin with the title of the review in both systems.

Newspaper Article

MLA	Maliconico, Joseph. "New Influx of Immigrants." *New Jersey News-Tribune* 17 Mar. 1991: A1.

APA	Maliconico, J. (1991, March 17). New influx of immigrants. *The New Jersey News-Tribune,* p. A1.

Newspaper Editorial

MLA	Gilmar, Sybil T. "Language Foreign to U.S. Schools." Editorial. *Philadelphia Inquirer* 25 Apr. 1990: 17A.

APA	Gilmar, S. (1990, April 25). Language foreign to U.S. schools [Editorial]. *The Philadelphia Inquirer,* p. 17A.

Letter to the Editor of a Magazine or Newspaper

MLA	Shumway, Norman D. "Make English the Official Language." *Chicago Tribune* 30 Aug. 1992, sec. 4: 2.

APA	Shumway, N. (1992, August 30). Make English the official language [Letter to the editor]. *Chicago Tribune,* sec. 4, p. 2.

If the newspaper or magazine doesn't give a title to the letter, for MLA style add the word *Letter* followed by a period after the author's name. Do not underline or use quotation marks. For APA style skip that information and use the rest of the citation form.

Electronic Sources
Editorial or Letter to the Editor

> **MLA**   Baker, Stewart. Editorial. "The New Escape Censorship? Ha!" *Wired* 3.09. 1 Apr. 1998 <http://www.wired.com/wired/3.09/departments/baker.if.html>.

If this were a letter to the editor, *Editorial* would be replaced by *Letter.*

> **APA**   Baker, S. (1998, April 1). The net escape censorship? Ha! [Letter to the Editor]. *Wired* [Electronic version]. *3.09*. Retrieved February 7, 2002, from http://www.wired.com/wired/3.09/departments/baker.if.html

Electronic Mail

> **MLA**   Mendez, Michael R. "Re: Solar power." E-mail to Edgar V. Atamian. 11 Sept. 1996.

> **APA**   In APA, electronic correspondence via e-mail, listservs, and newsgroups typically does not appear in the reference list. It is cited only in an intext reference: (M. Mendez, personal communication, September 11, 1996).

Electronic Mailing List

> **MLA**   Kosten, Arthur. "Major Update of the WWWVL Migration and Ethnic Relations." Online posting. 7 Apr. 1998. ERCOMER News. 7 May 1998 <http://www.ercomer.org/archive/ercomernews/0002.html>.

Magazine Article

> **MLA**   Pitta, Julie. "Un-Wired." *Forbes* 20 Apr. 1998. 6 Apr. 1998 <http://www.forbes.com/Forbes/98/020/6108045a.htm>.

> **APA**   Pitta, J. (1998, April 20). Un-wired? *Forbes, 65*, 25–30. Retrieved February 7, 2002, from http://www.forbes.com/Forbes/98/020/6108045a.htm

Note that MLA uses angle brackets to enclose the online address; APA does not.

Electronic Journal

> **MLA**   Rumsey, Deborah J. "Cooperative Teaching Approach to Introductory Statistics." *Journal of Statistics Education* 6.1 (1998): 77 pars. 21 July 1998 <http://www. stat.ncsu.edu/info/jse/v6n1/rumsey.html>.

> **APA**   Rumsey, D. (1998, May). A cooperative teaching approach to introductory statistics. *Journal of Statistics Education, 6*(1). Retrieved February 7, 2002, from http://www.stat.ncsu.edu/info/jse/v6n1/rumsey.html

CD-ROM

MLA	"Euthanasia." *The American Heritage Dictionary of the English Language.* 3rd ed. CD-ROM. Boston: Houghton Mifflin Co., 1992.
APA	Euthanasia. (1992). In *The American heritage dictionary of the English language.* [CD-ROM]. Boston: Houghton Mifflin.

Online Book

MLA	Clark, Rufus W. *The African Slave Trade.* Boston: American Tract Society: 1860. 19 June 1998 <http://moa.umdl.umich.edu/cgi/bin/moa/idx?notisid=AHL6707>.
APA	Clark, R. W. (1860). *The African slave trade.* Retrieved February 7, 2002, from http://moa.umdl.umich.edu/cgi-bin/moa/idx?notisid=AHL6707

Web Page

MLA	*Using Modern Language Association (MLA) Format.* Purdue University Online Writing Lab. 1 August 1998 <http://owl.english.purdue.edu/files/33.html>.
APA	Using Modern Language Association (MLA) Format. (1998, April 15). Purdue University Online Writing Lab. Retrieved August 1, 1998, from http://owl.english.purdue.edu/files/33.html

For MLA, begin the entry with the name of the individual who created the Web site (last name first), if available, and then a period. Follow with the title of the site (underlined); the name of the organization associated with the site, if available; the date of access; and the electronic address.

For APA, begin with the last name of the author, then initials, then a period. Follow with the date of publication or latest update. If there is no individual author, then begin with the title of the site, then date of publication or update. Follow with the name of the organization associated with the site, if available, and the retrieval date.

Miscellaneous Sources
Film, Filmstrip, Slide Program, and Videotape

MLA	Lee, Spike, dir. *Do the Right Thing.* Perf. Lee, Danny Aiello, Ossie Davis, Ruby Dee, and Richard Edson. Paramount, 1989.
APA	Lee, S. (Director). (1989). *Do the right thing.* [Motion Picture]. Hollywood, CA: Paramount.

To cite a filmstrip, slide program, or videotape in MLA style, include the name of the medium after the title without underlining (italicizing) or using quotation marks, and add the running time to the end. If you are citing the work as a whole, rather than the work of one of the creative artists involved in the project, start with the title instead. For instance:

> **MLA** *Do the Right Thing.* Dir. Spike Lee. Videocassette. Paramount, 1989.

In APA style, substitute the name of the medium for *Film:* [Videotape].

Television or Radio Program

> **MLA** *The Bilingual Battle.* Dir. Steve Adubato, Jr. PBS, Secaucus. 25 March 1996.

> **APA** Adubato Jr., S. (Director). (1996, March 25). *The bilingual battle* [Television broadcast]. Secaucus, NJ: PBS.

Interview

> **MLA** Pennington, Professor Linda Beth. Personal interview. 20 April 1993.

> **APA** In APA, personal communications including interviews do not appear in the reference list. They are cited only in an intext reference: (L. Pennington, personal communication, April 20, 1993).

The APA doesn't offer formal forms for "unrecoverable" materials such as personal letters or e-mail messages, lectures, and speeches, and in professional practice these are not included in reference listings. However, in collegiate writing assignments, most instructors will ask you to include them. You may, therefore, have to design a hybrid citation form based on these more standard forms. Remember that the APA encourages you to provide more, rather than less, information in your citations. The MLA has forms for almost any kind of communication, even nonrecoverable ones. Consult the *MLA Handbook for Writers of Research Papers,* 5th edition, to find additional forms.

Sample Research Papers

Following are two sample student research papers, the first in MLA format and the second in APA format. As you read them, notice the margins and other format requirements of the two different styles, such as the use of running heads, the placement of titles, and the different citation forms. We have added marginal annotations to highlight these special features and to demonstrate the structural elements of the arguments.

As these research papers demonstrate, the researched argument is different from the other arguments you've written only in quantity and format, not in quality. You still must make a claim and find evidence to support it, tailor your presentation to your readers, and use a logical structure that considers the various sides of an issue. As you progress in your academic life and, later, in your professional life, you will find that variations on the researched argument can become successful senior projects, theses, sales proposals, journal articles, grant proposals—even books—so mastering the skills of argumentative writing will serve you well.

1/2"
Benson 1

1"

Jenny Benson

Professor Johnson

English 112

November 22, 2001

Censorship: A Threat to Public Education

Nearly fifty years ago, Ray Bradbury published the novel <u>Fahrenheit 451</u>, the story of a society so fearful of knowledge and uncensored thought that it chooses to burn all the books that exist. In this futuristic society, fire fighters no longer extinguish fires; they set them in a determined effort to control what people know and think. Books and the knowledge they hold are seen as evil and must be destroyed. While Bradbury's novel can be found in the science fiction section of most libraries, the plot of his book is not so farfetched as some people might believe. The danger of censorship continues to threaten our basic freedom to choose for ourselves what to read and to make our own judgments about its value.

In recent years, the public schools have been the battleground upon which individuals who wish to limit our access to knowledge and information have focused their efforts. According to the 1996 People for the American Way annual survey of censorship challenges to public education, there were 300 attempts in 1995-96 to restrict or remove books used in public school classrooms or libraries. The success rate for these

Heading appears on first page

Double-space between title and first line and throughout paper

1"
One-inch margin on each side and at bottom

Introduces general topic and position

Narrows topic to censorship in public schools

Provides background information

Last name and page number at right-hand corner of each page

1"

challenges was 41% (6). Each successful challenge directly limited the rights of many schoolchildren. These incidents included attempts to censor health and history textbooks; literature collections, novels,

Specific page number of source in parenthetical reference; author already cited in text

and films; school newspapers and literary magazines; and numerous other types of publications (12). They occurred across the entire country; the survey documents forty-four states reporting censorship attempts (6).

Most Americans agree with the rights granted by the First Amendment, which stipulates that "Congress shall make no law

Bracketed ellipsis indicates words omitted from quotation

[. . .] abridging the freedom of speech, or of the press" ("Constitution"). A 1997 survey of 1,001 adults conducted by Market Shares Corporation for the Chicago Tribune confirmed that over half of those surveyed support the First Amendment rights guaranteed by the

Abbreviated title of source in parenthetical reference; no page number because source is a single page

Constitution ("Speech Right"). However, recent controversies in public schools across the country over the choices of books for school reading and library use indicate that a small but vocal group of Americans think that censorship is appropriate when parents object to the subject matter of the books chosen for school use. In these cases, parents often demand that their son or daughter not be required to read a particular book or that the book be removed from the school reading list or library. As the statistics above

Statistics used as evidence

indicate, 41% of the time, they are effective. While parents do have the right to control the reading material of their own

Benson 3

children, the decision by schoolboards or
school administrators to remove a book from
a school in response to a protest by one or
more parents is wrong. Parents should not
have the right to censor or control the   Claim
books used in the public schools.

James L. Payne of the <u>National Review</u>
correctly points out that parents have a   Acknowledges
constitutional right to question the schools   other positions
about what their own children are reading
and learning (58). If they have a personal
objection to this material, they also have a
right to request that the school seriously
consider their complaints. It is important
for parents to become involved with their
children's education. As the Family Research
Council, a conservative political
organization, asserts in its position on
parental rights, parents should have the
right to "direct the upbringing and   Direct quotation
education of their children." However, this   from electronic
                                              source with no
control should be limited to their own   page numbers
children. When parents decide that the
entire school curriculum should reflect   Restates claim
their personal values, they are affecting
the education of every child in the school,
not just their own.

While schools need to be aware of the
concerns of parents in their district, this
should not be a primary consideration when
they are deciding upon the books children
should read as part of their studies. These   Reason
choices should be based upon solid academic   supporting
                                              claim
principles and established learning

Benson 4

objectives rather than on the religious, social, or moral beliefs of particular individuals or groups. If the schools try to accommodate these narrow concerns, they will find that they are sacrificing great works of literature for minor and sometimes foolish reasons. For example, The On-Line Books Page Web site indicates that in 1996, Shakespeare's Twelfth Night was removed from the curriculum of a New Hampshire school

Specific evidence

district because some felt that it encouraged alternative lifestyle choices. In addition, "Little Red Riding Hood" was banned in two California school districts because the heroine is described as taking food and wine to her grandmother

Web site source, no page number

(Ockerbloom). It is difficult to believe that any student would begin cross-dressing after reading Twelfth Night, nor does it seem likely that children would be tempted to use alcohol after reading "Little Red Riding Hood." Yet, school districts banned these books as a result of these complaints.

Reason supporting claim

Even schoolboards may not be the best judges of the value or lack of value in a literary work. Sometimes these groups overreact to parents' complaints without having the knowledge needed to judge these books on their educational merits. In

Specific evidence

Anaheim, California, the schoolboard voted 4-1 to remove Toni Morrison's Beloved from the Advanced Placement curriculum after one anonymous individual in the community

Benson 5

objected to its contents. The board took
this action despite the recommendation of a
joint parent-school committee appointed to
study the book and the approval of an
Instructional Materials Review Committee.
What is even more revealing is that two of
the four board members who voted against the
book did not even read the entire text
(Manfredi).

Many parents want to protect their
children from ideas that they believe are
dangerous or frightening. While these
individuals are well intentioned, their
concerns are misplaced. What these parents
fail to realize is that reading about these
ideas in the controlled setting of a
classroom gives children the opportunity
to ask questions and receive answers that
may help them better understand troubling
issues. Class discussion with their peers
can help them examine their own beliefs and
values. It may also reassure them that their
fears or fantasies are normal and shared by
others. For instance, One Fat Summer, a
well-respected book by Robert Lipsyte, was
assigned in a seventh-grade developmental
reading class in Levittown, New York. It is
the story of an overweight boy who learns
how to deal with his tormentors and feel
self-confident. According to the teachers in
that district, students enjoyed reading and
discussing this story because it was about
the difficulties of growing up. However, this
book was removed from the class because one

Acknowledges possible objection

Responds to objection

Specific evidence

parent complained about its treatment of
adolescent sexuality (Vinciguerra). Now all
of the children will be deprived of these
discussions. Moreover, often these
"dangerous" ideas are ones that children have
encountered or will be exposed to at some
point in their lives. Teen pregnancy, rape,
child abuse, gangs, and drugs are all a part
of our world. Trying to protect children from
being exposed to them is futile and may make
them unprepared to face these problems later
in life.

It is fair for parents to expect the
school district to establish clear academic
guidelines for choosing the books used in the
classroom. Books should be age-appropriate,
Acknowledges possess literary merit, and relate to the
possible rest of the curriculum. Parents have the
objection and right to question whether the school's
responds choices fulfill these standards. But,
especially in the case of library books, the
school also has the right to expect parents
to monitor their own children's reading. If
parents do not wish their child to borrow a
certain book from the school library, it is
their responsibility to enforce this, not the
school's. Removing the book from the school
library because a parent finds it
objectionable unfairly deprives other
children of the opportunity to read it.

Reason But the strongest reason to prevent the
supporting banning of books in the public schools by
claim individuals or special interest groups is
that it undermines the basic reason for

Benson 7

public education: the free and open
exchange of ideas and access to knowledge
and information. By limiting students'
exposure to ideas, we limit their ability
to think critically, to make informed
judgments based on a broad range of
information, and to express those ideas as
the First Amendment guarantees. We prevent
them from exercising the full rights of
their citizenship. By catering to the
concerns of a few, we violate the freedom
of the majority. In the U.S. Supreme Court
decision <u>Board of Education</u> v. <u>Pico</u> in   Use of authority
1982, a case which involved the banning of
nine books from a school library, the
majority opinion stated:

> Just as access to ideas makes it   Long quotation
> possible for citizens [. . .] to   (more than four
>   lines); left
> exercise their right of free speech   margin indented
> and press in a meaningful manner,   one inch
> such access prepares students for   (10 spaces),
>   double-spaced
> active and effective participation
> in the pluralistic, often
> contentious society in which they
> will soon be adult members. The
> special circumstances of the school
> library make that environment
> especially appropriate for the
> recognition of the First Amendment
> rights of students. (U.S. Supreme   Parenthetical
> Court)   reference
>   appears after
    This statement makes it clear that the   final
Justices understood the connection between   punctuation
knowledge and freedom, and recognized that
students are entitled to both.

Barbara Dority, an activist with the
Washington Coalition Against Censorship,
points out that even though attempts to
censor public school materials are not
successful most of the time, the threat of
censorship negatively affects the choices
that school personnel make. Teachers and
librarians don't choose books that they might
otherwise choose because they are afraid of
stirring up controversy. School principals
restrict student newspapers because they
worry that students' ideas might offend
others (52). Even the possibility of
censorship is enough to stifle creativity and
free thought.

There are always people, sometimes well
intentioned, who think that the suppression
of ideas will result in a better, more moral
environment. Unless we keep careful watch
over these attempts to censor and limit the
flow of knowledge, they will overwhelm and
consume the rights of everyone else.

Benson 9

Works Cited

Bradbury, Ray. <u>Fahrenheit 451</u>. New York:
    Ballantine, 1953.

"Constitution of the United States."
    <u>Britannica Online</u>. Vers. 97.1.1. Mar.
    1997. Encyclopedia Britannica. 14 Oct.
    1998 <http://www.eb.com:180>.

Dority, Barbara. "Public Education Under
    Siege." <u>The Humanist</u> July 1994: 36+.

"Frequently Asked Questions: Parental
    Rights." Family Research Council. 13 Oct.
    1998 <http://www.frc.org:80/faq22.html>.

Manfredi, Richard. "District Removes Morrison
    Novel." <u>Orange County Register</u> 16 May
    1998: B-1.

Ockerbloom, John Mark. <u>The On-Line Books
    Page: Banned Books On-Line</u>. 11 Oct. 1998
    <http://www.cs.cmu.edu/People/spok/
    banned-books.html>.

Payne, James L. "Education Versus the
    American Way: People for the American
    Way's Censorship Allegations." <u>National
    Review</u> 25 Sept. 1995: 58+.

People for the American Way. <u>Attacks on the
    Freedom to Learn</u>. Washington: People for
    the American Way, 1996.

"Speech Right Goes Too Far, Some Say."
    <u>Houston Chronicle</u> 5 July 1997: A-13.

<u>U.S. Supreme Court: Board of Education</u> v.
    <u>Pico 457 U.S. 853 (1982)</u>. Findlaw. 12
    Nov. 1998 <http://laws.findlaw.com/us/
    457/853.html>.

Vinciguerra, Thomas. "A 1977 Novel Comes
    Under Scrutiny." <u>New York Times</u> 8 June
    1997, LI ed., sec. 13:8.

List is alphabetized by author's last name. Use title if no author. Double-space throughout.

Online encyclopedia

Web sites are constantly updated. Include date of access. This Web address is no longer available

Web site with individual author

Titles of books, journals, and newspapers are underlined

↕ 1/2"
Television Desensitizes   1

Abbreviated title and page number appear on each page, including the title page

Television Desensitizes Children to Violence

Amber Sifritt

English 112

March 8, 2002

If your instructor requires an abstract of your paper, locate it on the second page of your paper

Double-space
between title
and first line
and through-
out paper

1"

Identifies
issue and
significance

Presents other
positions

Television Desensitizes   2

Television Desensitizes Children
to Violence

   Kids killing kids. It seems to be all
over the news these days. The acts of
violence have a depressing similarity: kids
bring weapons to school and gun down
classmates and teachers. The reasons behind
these actions are shockingly simple: for
instance, in Arkansas, one of the pre-teen
murderers was upset because his girlfriend
had ended their relationship. He took
revenge by slaughtering four girls and a
teacher, who used her body to shield another
child. If this was a rare occurrence, we
could attribute it to one disturbed child.
But it's not. There have been incidents in
Pennsylvania, Oregon, Kentucky, Colorado,
and other communities all across the
country. There is a problem occurring with
this generation of children which we can't
ignore. We must take action immediately to
prevent any more child violence. Otherwise,
our greatest fear will not be of wars or
natural disasters; it will be of our own
children.

   There have been many theories advanced
about the causes of these incidents. Some
experts blame them on the availability of
guns and the children's experience with
firearms for target-shooting or hunting.
Certainly, having relatively easy access to
guns made these violent acts more likely to
occur. But this theory does not explain *why*
these children chose to commit these acts.

Television Desensitizes   3

Many children, particularly in rural areas, are familiar with guns from an early age; this has been true since the early pioneer days. But these children do not use guns to fatally attack others. The question we must ask goes deeper than this theory: what makes it possible for a child to commit murder? I think that one answer is that children have become desensitized toward violence by excessive television viewing. Parents need to become aware of this potential danger and begin to curtail the amount of time that their children spend viewing television and supervise the shows that they do watch.

Claim

From early childhood on, children are saturated with scenes of violence during television viewing. According to Louise Brown (1997), American children spend an average of 4 hours a day glued to the television screen. By the time they reach the age of eighteen, they have watched 8,000 television murders. In Brown's article, she refers to George Gerbner, an analyst who conducted a 30-year study of television violence. Gerbner suggests that viewers who watch television excessively develop a "Mean World Syndrome." These individuals perceive the world as more violent than it actually is. For children this may result in the expectation that difficulties in relationships and everyday problems should naturally be resolved by violent solutions.

Reason
supporting claim

Statistics

Use of authority

However, watching a daily dose of violent murders and terrorism on the

Television Desensitizes   4

Reason supporting claim

television screen may have additional negative effects on children. Sissela Bok (1998), a philosopher who studies the impact of modern culture on our values and actions, suggests that "desensitization in response to media violence . . . actually helps to counteract the fear and anxiety that such violence might otherwise provoke" (p. 69). In other words, rather than live in continual fear of being the victim of a violent act, children become numb to the violence they see depicted on television, treating it casually as part of their everyday world. Bok asks whether this

Page number cited immediately after quotation

"numbing of feeling" (p. 69) may make children less sensitive to the pain of others. Given the casual way that the latest child murderers have planned and executed their crimes, it appears that these children are quite insensitive to the suffering they are causing.

Penelope Leach (1994), a well-known child psychologist and expert on parenting, reinforces this point in her book *Children First*:

Long quotation (over 40 words) indented five spaces from left margin, no quotation marks

Two generations ago only a few unfortunate children ever saw anyone hit over the head with a brick, shot, rammed by a car, blown up, immolated, raped or tortured. Now all children, along with their elders, see such images every day of their lives and are expected to enjoy them. . . . The seven-year-old who hides his eyes in the family cops-and-robbers drama is

Television Desensitizes   5

Page reference
appears at end,
outside final
punctuation

desensitized four years later to a
point where he crunches potato chips
through the latest video nasty.
(p. 152)

Leach's point is that this is a gradual
process. One encounter with television
violence will not make a child grow callous
to the effects of violence; however, years
of repeated and constant exposure will have
a detrimental effect on a child's awareness
of the real consequences of a violent act.

Lt. Col. Dave Grossman, a former West
Point psychology professor and Army Ranger,
agrees that this repeated exposure to
violent acts can make them seem more
acceptable. He compares the exposure of
children to violence on television with
basic training in the military in which
trainees are conditioned to overcome their
aversion to killing other human beings by
"psychological conditioning techniques"
(McCain, 1998, p. 37). While violence is an
unfortunate reality during times of war, it
is alarming that so many children accept
this as part of their daily lives through
their television viewing.

Words right from children's mouths
confirm the effect television has on them,
according to Louise Brown: "I like watching
shows with fights because I learn moves to
beat up my cousins," one child asserts.
Another child says, "Sometimes it might get
into your head that TV is your life." Still
another child is quoted as stating that she

enjoys watching cartoons that show her how to "kick butt" (Brown, 1997). As these statements indicate, children take the violence that they see on television quite seriously. And, because children often can't distinguish between make-believe and reality, they are more likely to try to imitate the violence they see in cartoons or other programming, according to Barbara Wilson, a senior researcher and professor of communications at the University of California at Santa Barbara (Stamper, 1998). When children become comfortable with violence, they aren't aware of its true effect or outcome.

Even more disturbing are the results of a $3.5 million dollar study of over 6,000 hours of television on 23 channels that indicate that the "good guys" commit 40% of the violence on television. This means that children see their positive role models engaging in violent behavior. Moreover, this study finds that most of the violence depicted on television "goes unpunished, is unjustified, [and] has no lasting effect on the victim" (Stamper, 1998). The consequence of this is that children will emulate this behavior and imitate it, thinking that it is acceptable because of the way it is treated on television.

While other forms of electronic media, such as movies and rock music, may also be responsible for desensitizing our children, television is a medium to which every child

Margin notes:

Author is not cited in text, so name and date appear in parenthetical citation

Statistics

Brackets are used to indicate insertion of word not found in source

Acknowledges possible objections and responds

Television Desensitizes   7

has easy access. Children often need
transportation to go to the movies as well
as money to buy a ticket or CD; television,
however, is free and available in their own
homes. Unless parents make a special point
of supervising each and every television
show their children watch, children are free
to watch whatever looks interesting.
Unfortunately, violence and bloodshed often
attract young viewers. What makes this even
worse is that many of the talk shows and
cartoons containing violence are on at
convenient times for children to watch. For
instance, *The Jerry Springer Show, The Ricki*   Examples
Lake Show, X-Men, and *Spider-Man* are all
shown at times when children are home from
school. Since many parents work outside of
the home, children can spend the afternoon
watching and absorbing this violent
material.

    Some people don't agree that television   Acknowledges
violence has a great impact on the young,   possible
impressionable minds of children. When they   objections and
see shows such as *The Jerry Springer Show*   responds
and *South Park,* they comment that these
shows are not any more violent than what
children are used to in the school yard or
see on other television programs. However,
they are missing the point. Just because
violence is seen regularly at school or on
television does not make it acceptable. And
the more often children see this, the more
familiar it becomes. We cannot use the

Television Desensitizes   8

current standards for television to measure
its acceptability.

The most effective and universal
solution to this problem would be to have
the television industry establish a new set
of rules and regulations regarding subject
matter that is permitted on television shows
designed for children and for those that
will be aired at times when children will be
watching. However, it seems unlikely that
this will happen soon because unless
pressure is applied by financial interests,
such as corporate sponsors, television
executives will not feel compelled to
change. Television will probably not be
cleaning up its act in the near future
unless there is a powerful, organized effort
on the part of the public to make it happen.
We cannot wait for this to occur because we
are paying too high a price in youth
violence in the meantime.

Proposes
solution

The responsibility to protect children
from excessive television violence must rest
with parents. Parents must assume an active
role in monitoring their children's
television consumption. It seems that too
many parents fail to undertake this
responsibility. Parents rely upon the
television to be their children's baby-
sitter, leaving them with free time to do
other tasks. While this is reasonable for
short periods of time, the 4 hours a day that
the average child spends watching television
indicates that many parents use the

Television Desensitizes   9

television to avoid interacting with their
children. Parents need to sit down with their
children during television viewing time and
explain that what their children see on the
screen is not real and that violence is not
the best solution for a problem. Better yet,
parents need to turn off the television and
encourage their children to engage in other
activities. Hobbies, sports, reading, chores
around the house, and homework will be more
productive uses of their children's
intelligence and energies than staring
passively at the television absorbing violent
ways to deal with human relationships.

Turning off the television won't
completely eliminate the terrible violence
that children are committing. However, it
will eliminate one of the ways that children
become desensitized to violence and the pain
that it causes others. It may restore some
meaning to that Biblical admonition "Do unto
others as you would have them do unto you."

Television Desensitizes   10

References

Begin first
line of each
citation at
the left
margin.
Indent all
subsequent
lines five
spaces from
the left margin.

Capitalize
the first
letter of
titles and
subtitles.

Newspaper
article from
online
database

Bok, S. (1998). *Mayhem: Violence as public entertainment.* Reading, MA: Addison-Wesley.

Brown, L. (1997, December 13). The tube that rocks the cradle. *The Toronto Star,* p SW6. Retrieved February 15, 1999, from Lexis-Nexis: http://web.lexis-nexis.com/universe

Leach, P. (1994). *Children first: What our society must do—and is not doing—for our children today.* New York: Alfred Knopf.

McCain, R. S. (1998, December 21). Television's bloody hands. *Insight on the News, 14,* 37.

Stamper, J. (1998, April 17). TV fantasy land warps children. *The Orlando Sentinel,* p. A1. Retrieved February 28, 1999, from Lexis-Nexis: http://web.lexis-nexis.com/universe

PART 2

Dialogues

Advertising and Consumerism

The clock radio wakes us, blaring advertisements for vitamins, banks, and automobiles. Our coffee cups announce the brand we drink, and the logos on our clothing reveal the psychology of our fashion choices. As we wait for the bus or drive our cars, billboards display lounging vacationers in exotic locations. Reading a magazine, clothing ads tell us what we should wear, cigarette ads depict a life of clean refreshment, and alcohol ads warn us to drink their product responsibly. We open the newspaper and shuffle through pages of department store advertisements. And as we sit down at our desks to work, the Internet browser flashes a banner for a camcorder, and it's not even 9:00 A.M.!

Every single day of our lives, we are bombarded with advertising images and messages. Advertising is so pervasive, few of us really notice it, or consider its enormous influence on our lives. This chapter examines the many different ways advertising weaves its web of influence—how it hooks consumers, how it creates feelings of need, and how it manipulates our language to convince us to buy.

The first section of readings, "Hooking the Consumer," addresses the ways advertisers influence our thinking to get us to buy their products. We begin with "Targeting a New World," in which Joseph Turow discusses the ways in which advertisers exploit rips in the American social fabric to "target market" their products. Jean Kilbourne then explores the deep connection between advertising and the mass media, and the insidious ways in which the two manipulate consumers in "Buy This 24-Year-Old and Get All His Friends Absolutely Free." John Fraim reviews how advertising has changed from marketing a product based on its merits, to marketing a product based on social feelings and impressions in "Friendly Persuasion: The Growing Ubiquity of Advertising." The section concludes with "Hey Kids, Buy This!" in which David Leonhardt and Kathleen Kerwin explain how marketers now directly target children, often circumventing parents' wishes by appealing to children's desires and insecurities.

From luring consumers, we move to the psychology of consumer desire. What drives consumerism in this country? Why do we want what we want, and is it really so bad that we want it all? In "Two Cheers for Consumerism," professor James Twitchell wonders why we don't admit that we are all basically consumers at heart. Harry Flood takes a different view, comparing the decadence of current consumer taste to that of the fallen civilizations of ancient Rome and prerevolutionary France in "Manufacturing Desire." The final two authors in this section long for more tempered consumerism. In "The Stuff of Life," Scott Russell Sanders marvels that Americans are "swamped with stuff" despite the fact that we can't seem to stop accumulating. And Bill McKibben proposes the radical idea that we observe $100 holiday seasons, a concept that many merchandisers find both disturbing and un-American.

The chapter closes with a group of readings exploring the language of advertising, one of the most pervasive forms of persuasion in American life. The language used in advertising is a special form of communication, one that combines words and fantasies for the sole purpose of separating consumers from their money. In "With These Words, I Can Sell You Anything," language-watcher William Lutz demonstrates how advertisers twist words that carry no true meanings yet still convince us that their product is better or more desirable. However, professional ad writer Charles A. O'Neill makes a persuasive argument that even though the language of ads might be appealing, no advertisement can force consumers to lay their money down. The last essay in this section, John Leo's "The Selling of Rebellion," examines how advertisers rely on popular cultural messages not necessarily related to their products to create consumer identification and interest. Sample advertisements then provide an opportunity to analyze how advertisers use language and visual images to sell their products.

HOOKING THE CONSUMER

Targeting a New World

Joseph Turow

Advertisers do not pitch their marketing campaigns to a universal audience. Rather, they target specific audiences to market specific products. This "divide and conquer" approach is called **target marketing.** In the following article, communications professor Joseph Turow explores how the techniques of target marketing exploit and even encourage rips in the American social fabric.

Turow is a professor at the Annenberg School for Communication at the University of Pennsylvania. He is the author of five books, including *Playing Doctor: Television, Storytelling, and Medical Power* (1989) and *Media Systems in Society: Understanding Industries, Strategies, and Power* (revised 1997). The following article is excerpted from his latest book, *Breaking Up America: Advertisers and the New Media World* (revised 1998).

■ **BEFORE YOU READ**

The following piece discusses how marketers use target marketing, based on demo-graphic profiling to sell specific products to particular groups of people. How would you describe the consumer target group to which you belong? What values define your group, and why?

■ **AS YOU READ**

How can exploiting Americans' social and cultural divisions help advertisers market their products? Is there anything unethical about this approach?

> "Advertisers will have their choice of horizontal demographic groups and vertical psychographic program types."
>
> "Our judgment as to the enhanced quality of our subscriber base has been confirmed by the advertisers."
>
> "Unfortunately, most media plans are based on exposure opportuni-ties. This is particularly true for television because G.R.P. analysis is usually based on television ratings and ratings do not measure actual exposure."

1   Most Americans would likely have a hard time conceiving the meaning of these quotations. The words would clearly be understood as English, but the jargon would seem quite mysterious. They might be surprised to learn that they have heard a specialized language that advertisers use about them. Rooted in various kinds of research, the language has a straightforward purpose. The aim is to package individuals, or groups of people, in ways that make them useful targets for the advertisers of certain products through certain types of media.

2   Clearly, the way the advertising industry talks about us is not the way we talk about ourselves. Yet when we look at the advertisements that emerge from the cauldron of marketing strategies and strange terminology, we see pictures of our surroundings that we can understand, even recognize. The pictures re-mind us that the advertising industry does far more than sell goods and services through the mass media. With budgets that add up to hundreds of billions of dollars, the industry exceeds the church and the school in its ability to promote images about our place in society—where we belong, why, and how we should act toward others.

3   A revolutionary shift is taking place in the way advertisers talk about Amer-ica and the way they create ads and shape media to reflect that talk. The shift has been influenced by, and has been influencing, major changes in the audio-visual options available to the home. But it most importantly has been driven by, and has been driving, a profound sense of division in American society.

4   The era we are entering is one in which advertisers will work with media firms to create the electronic equivalents of gated communities. Marketers are aware that the U.S. population sees itself marked by enormous economic and cultural tensions. Marketers don't feel, though, that it benefits them to encour-age Americans to deal with these tensions head-on through a media brew of

discussion, entertainment, and argumentation aimed at broadly diverse audiences. Rather, new approaches to marketing make it increasingly worthwhile for even the largest media companies to separate audiences into different worlds according to distinctions that ad people feel make the audiences feel secure and comfortable. The impact of these activities on Americans' views of themselves and others will be profound, enduring, and often disturbing.

5   The changes have begun only recently. The hallmark is the way marketers and media practitioners have been approaching the development of new audiovisual technology. Before the late 1970s, most people in the United States could view without charge three commercial broadcast stations, a public (noncommercial) TV station, and possibly an independent commercial station (one not affiliated with a network). By the mid-1990s, several independent broadcast TV stations, scores of cable and satellite television channels, videocassettes, video games, home computer programs, online computer services, and the beginnings of two-way ("interactive") television had become available to major segments of the population with an interest and a budget to match.

6   People in the advertising industry are working to integrate the new media channels into the broader world of print and electronic media to maximize the entire system's potential for selling. They see these developments as signifying not just the breakup of the traditional broadcast network domain, but as indicating a breakdown in social cohesion, as well. Advertisers' most public talk about America—in trade magazine interviews, trade magazine ads, convention speeches, and interviews for this book—consistently features a nation that is breaking up. Their vision is of a fractured population of self-indulgent, frenetic, and suspicious individuals who increasingly reach out only to people like themselves.

7   Advertising practitioners do not view these distinctions along primarily racial or ethnic lines, though race and ethnicity certainly play a part, provoking turf battles among marketers. Rather, the new portraits of society that advertisers and media personnel invoke involve the blending of income, generation, marital status, and gender into a soup of geographical and psychological profiles they call "lifestyles."

8   At the business level, what is driving all this is a major shift in the balance between targeting and mass marketing in U.S. media. Mass marketing involves aiming a home-based medium or outdoor event at people irrespective of their background or patterns of activities (their lifestyles). Targeting, by contrast, involves the intentional pursuit of specific segments of society—groups and even individuals. The Underground [radio] Network, the Comedy Central cable channel, and *Details* magazine are far more targeted than the ABC Television Network, the Sony Jumbotron Screen on Times Square, and the Super Bowl. Yet even these examples of targeting are far from close to the pinpointing of audiences that many ad people expect is possible.

9   The ultimate aim of this new wave of marketing is to reach different groups with specific messages about how certain products tie into their lifestyles. Target-minded media firms are helping advertisers do that by building *primary media*

communities. These are formed when viewers or readers feel that a magazine, TV channel, newspaper, radio station, or other medium reaches people like them, resonates with their personal beliefs, and helps them chart their position in the larger world. For advertisers, tying into those communities means gaining consumer loyalties that are nearly impossible to establish in today's mass market.

10   Nickelodeon and MTV were pioneer attempts to establish this sort of ad-sponsored communion on cable television. While they started as cable channels, they have become something more. Owned by media giant Viacom, they are lifestyle parades that invite their target audiences (relatively upscale children and young adults, respectively) into a sense of belonging that goes far beyond the coaxial wire into books, magazines, videotapes, and outdoor events that Viacom controls or licenses.

11   The idea of these sorts of "programming services" is to cultivate a must-see, must-read, must-share mentality that makes the audience feel part of a family, attached to the program hosts, other viewers, and sponsors. It is a strategy that extends across a wide spectrum of marketing vehicles, from cable TV to catalogs, from direct mailings to online computer services, from outdoor events to in-store clubs. In all these areas, national advertisers make it clear that they prefer to conduct their targeting with the huge media firms they had gotten to know in earlier years. But the giants don't always let their offspring operate on huge production budgets. To keep costs low enough to satisfy advertisers' demands for efficient targeting, much of ad-supported cable television is based on recycled materials created or distributed by media conglomerates. What makes MTV, ESPN, Nickelodeon, A&E, and other such "program services" distinctive is not the uniqueness of the programs but the special character created by their *formats:* the flow of their programs, packaged to attract the right audience at a price that will draw advertisers.

12   But media firms have come to believe that simply attracting groups to specialized formats is often not enough. Urging people who do not fit the desired lifestyle profile *not* to be part of the audience is sometimes also an aim, since it makes the community more pure and thereby more efficient for advertisers. So in the highly competitive media environment of the 1980s and early 1990s, cable companies aiming to lure desirable types to specialized formats felt the need to create "signature" materials that both drew the "right" people and signaled the "wrong" people that they ought to go away. It is no accident that the producers of certain signature programs on Nickelodeon (for example, *Ren and Stimpy*) and MTV (such as *Beavis and Butt-head*) in the early 1990s acknowledge that they chase away irrelevant viewers as much as they attract desirable ones.

13   An even more effective form of targeting, ad people believe, is a type that goes beyond chasing undesirables away. It simply excludes them in the first place. Using computer models based on zip codes and a variety of databases, it is economically feasible to tailor materials for small groups, even individuals. That is already taking place in the direct mail, telemarketing, and magazine industries. With certain forms of interactive television, it is technologically quite

possible to send some TV programs and commercials only to neighborhoods, census blocks, and households that advertisers want to reach. Media firms are working toward a time when people will be able to choose the news, information, and entertainment they want when they want it. Advertisers who back these developments will be able to offer different product messages—and variable discounts—to individuals based on what they know about them.

14   Clearly, not all these technologies are widespread. Clearly, too, there is a lot of hype around them. Many companies that stand to benefit from the spread of target marketing have doubtless exaggerated the short time it will take to get there and the low costs that will confront advertisers once they do. Moreover, as will be seen, some marketers have been slower than others to buy into the usefulness of a media system that encourages the partitioning of people with different lifestyles.

15   Nevertheless, the trajectory is clear. A desire to label people so that they may be separated into primary media communities is transforming the way television is programmed, the way newspapers are "zoned," the way magazines are printed, and the way cultural events are produced and promoted. Most critically, advertisers' interest in exploiting lifestyle differences is woven into the basic assumptions about media models for the next century—the so-called 500 Channel Environment or the future Information Superhighway.

16   For me and you—individual readers and viewers—this segmentation and targeting can portend terrific things. If we can afford to pay, or if we're important to sponsors who will pick up the tab, we will be able to receive immediately the news, information, and entertainment we order. In a world pressing us with high-speed concerns, we will surely welcome media and sponsors that offer to surround us with exactly what we want when we want it.

17   As an entirety, though, society in the United States will lose out.

18   One of the consequences of turning the U.S. into a pastiche of market-driven labels is that such a multitude of categories makes it impossible for a person to directly overlap with more than a tiny portion of them. If primary media communities continue to take hold, their large numbers will diminish the chance that individuals who identify with certain social categories will even have an opportunity to learn about others. Off-putting signature programs such as *Beavis and Butt-head* may make the situation worse, causing individuals annoyed by the shows or what they read about them to feel alienated from groups that appear to enjoy them. If you are told over and over again that different kinds of people are not part of your world, you will be less and less likely to want to deal with those people.

19   The creation of customized media materials will likely take this lifestyle segregation further. It will allow, even encourage, individuals to live in their own personally constructed worlds, separated from people and issues they don't care about or don't want to be bothered with. The desire to do that may accelerate when, as is the case in the late-twentieth-century United States, seemingly intractable antagonisms based on age, income, ethnicity, geography, and more result from competition over jobs and political muscle. In these circumstances, market segmentation and

targeting may accelerate an erosion of the tolerance and mutual dependence between diverse groups that enable a society to work. Ironically, the one common
message across media will be that a common center for sharing ideas and feelings
is more and more difficult to find—or even to care about.

■ QUESTIONS FOR ANALYSIS AND DISCUSSION

1. Turow uses three quotations to begin his essay. How do these quotations contribute to the points he makes in his article? Are they an effective way to reach
   his audience? Explain.
2. How does packaging individuals, or groups of people, make them "useful targets" for advertisers? Give some examples of ways advertisers "package" people
   or groups of people.
3. According to Turow, what social impact does target marketing have on America? Do you agree with his perspective? Explain.
4. Evaluate Turow's tone in this essay. What phrases or words reveal his tone?
   Who is his audience? How does this tone connect to his intended audience?
5. What point is the author trying to make in this article? What is his own particular opinion of targeted marketing? Cite examples from the text in your response.
6. Why would producers of certain television programs actually want to "chase
   away" certain viewers? How can audience exclusion help improve a target market for advertisers? Is this practice damaging to our society? Why or why not?

Buy This 24-Year-Old and Get All His Friends Absolutely Free
Jean Kilbourne

Have you ever stopped to think about how much advertising permeates our world?
You may be surprised to discover that advertising now supports almost every communication medium, from newspapers and magazines, to television, radio, and the
Internet. Advertising sponsors most sporting events, and even schools receive larges
sums from companies for their product loyalty. In fact, the average person views
over 3,000 advertisements each and every day! In the next article, Jean Kilbourne
describes the subtle ways advertisers influence consumers, and how much they are
willing to spend just for a chance to entice us.

Jean Kilbourne, Ed.D, is the author of *Deadly Persuasion: Why Women and
Girls Must Fight the Addictive Power of Advertising* (1999). She has produced several
award-winning documentaries, including *Killing Us Softly, Slim Hope,* and *Pack of
Lies.* The next article is an excerpt from the first chapter of *Can't Buy Me Love: How
Advertising Changes the Way We Think and Feel* (2000), a revised edition of her 1999
book, *Deadly Persuasion.*

■ BEFORE YOU READ

When you read a magazine or newspaper, or watch a television program, how aware are you of the products that are pitched to you? Do you think these advertisements influence you as a consumer?

■ AS YOU READ

What populations does the author identify as the most vulnerable to advertising, and how does she feel about the exploitation of these groups?

1   If you're like most people, you think that advertising has no influence on you. This is what advertisers want you to believe. But, if that were true, why would companies spend over $200 billion a year on advertising? Why would they be willing to spend over $250,000 to produce an average television commercial and another $250,000 to air it? If they want to broadcast their commercial during the Super Bowl, they will gladly spend over a million dollars to produce it and over one and a half million to air it. After all, they might have the kind of success that Victoria's Secret did during the 1999 Super Bowl. When they paraded bra-and-panty-clad models across TV screens for a mere thirty seconds, one million people turned away from the game to log on to the Website promoted in the ad. No influence?

2   Ad agency Arnold Communications of Boston kicked off an ad campaign for a financial services group during the 1999 Super Bowl that represented eleven months of planning and twelve thousand "man-hours" of work. Thirty hours of footage were edited into a thirty-second spot. An employee flew to Los Angeles with the ad in a lead-lined bag, like a diplomat carrying state secrets or a courier with crown jewels. Why? Because the Super Bowl is one of the few sure sources of big audiences—especially male audiences, the most precious commodity for advertisers. Indeed, the Super Bowl is more about advertising than football: The four hours it takes include only about twelve minutes of actually moving the ball.

3   Three of the four television programs that draw the largest audiences every year are football games. And these games have coattails: twelve prime-time shows that attracted bigger male audiences in 1999 than those in the same time slots the previous year were heavily pushed during football games. No wonder the networks can sell this prized Super Bowl audience to advertisers for almost any price they want. The Oscar ceremony, known as the Super Bowl for women, is able to command one million dollars for a thirty-second spot because it can deliver over 60 percent of the nation's women to advertisers. Make no mistake: The primary purpose of the mass media is to sell audiences to advertisers. We are the product. Although people are much more sophisticated about advertising now than even a few years ago, most are still shocked to learn this.

4   Magazines, newspapers, and radio and television programs round us up, rather like cattle, and producers and publishers then sell us to advertisers, usu-

ally through ads placed in advertising and industry publications. "The people you want, we've got all wrapped up for you," declares *The Chicago Tribune* in an ad placed in *Advertising Age,* the major publication of the advertising industry, which pictures several people, all neatly boxed according to income level.

5   Although we like to think of advertising as unimportant, it is in fact the most important aspect of the mass media. It *is* the point. Advertising supports more than 60 percent of magazine and newspaper production and almost 100 percent of the electronic media. Over $40 billion a year in ad revenue is generated for television and radio and over $30 billion for magazines and newspapers. As one ABC executive said, "The network is paying affiliates to carry network commercials, not programs. What we are is a distribution system for Procter & Gamble." And the CEO of Westinghouse Electric, owner of CBS, said, "We're here to serve advertisers. That's our raison d'être."

6   The media know that television and radio programs are simply fillers for the space between commercials. They know that the programs that succeed are the ones that deliver the highest number of people to the advertisers. But not just any people. Advertisers are interested in people aged eighteen to forty-nine who live in or near a city. *Dr. Quinn, Medicine Woman,* a program that was number one in its time slot and immensely popular with older, more rural viewers, was canceled in 1998 because it couldn't command the higher advertising rates paid for younger, richer audiences. This is not new: the *Daily Herald,* a British newspaper with 47 million readers, double the combined readership of *The Times, The Financial Times, The Guardian,* and *The Telegraph,* folded in the 1960s because its readers were mostly elderly and working class and had little appeal to advertisers. The target audience that appeals to advertisers is becoming more narrow all the time. According to Dean Valentine, the head of United Paramount Network, most networks have abandoned the middle class and want "very chic shows that talk to affluent, urban, unmarried, huge-disposable-income 18-to-34-year-olds because the theory is, from advertisers, that the earlier you get them, the sooner you imprint the brand name."

7   Newspapers are more in the business of selling audiences than in the business of giving people news, especially as more and more newspapers are owned by fewer and fewer chains. They exist primarily to support local advertisers, such as car dealers, realtors, and department store owners. A full-page ad in *The New York Times* says, "A funny thing happens when people put down a newspaper. They start spending money." The ad continues, "Nothing puts people in the mood to buy like a newspaper. In fact, most people consider it almost a prerequisite to any spending spree." It concludes, "Newspaper. It's the best way to close a sale." It is especially disconcerting to realize that our newspapers, even the illustrious *New York Times,* are hucksters at heart.

8   The Internet advertisers target the wealthy too, of course. "They give you Dick," says an ad in *Advertising Age* for an Internet news network. "We give you Richard." The ad continues, "That's the Senior V.P. Richard who lives in L.A., drives a BMW and wants to buy a DVD player and a kayak." Not surprisingly, there are no magazines or Internet sites or television programs for the poor or

for people on welfare. They might not be able to afford the magazines or computers but, more importantly, they are of no use to advertisers.

9   This emphasis on the affluent surely has something to do with the invisibility of the poor in our society. Since advertisers have no interest in them, they are not reflected in the media. We know so much about the rich and famous that it becomes a problem for many who seek to emulate them, but we know very little about the lifestyles of the poor and desperate. It is difficult to feel compassion for people we don't know.

10   Ethnic minorities will soon account for 30 percent of all consumer purchases. No wonder they are increasingly important to advertisers. Nearly half of all Fortune 1000 companies have some kind of ethnic marketing campaign. Nonetheless, minorities are still underrepresented in advertising agencies. African-Americans, who are over 10 percent of the total workforce, are only 5 percent of the advertising industry. Minorities are underrepresented in ads as well—about 87 percent of people in mainstream magazine ads are white, about 3 percent are African-American (most likely appearing as athletes or musicians), and less than 1 percent are Hispanic or Asian. As the spending power of minorities increases, so does marketing segmentation. Mass marketing aimed at a universal audience doesn't work so well in a multicultural society, but cable television, the Internet, custom publishing, and direct marketing lend themselves very well to this segmentation. The multiculturalism that we see in advertising is about money, of course, not about social justice.

11   Many companies these days are hiring anthropologists and psychologists to examine consumers' product choices, verbal responses, even body language for deeper meanings. They spend time in consumers' homes, listening to their conversations and exploring their closets and bathroom cabinets. Ad agency Leo Burnett's director of planning calls these techniques "getting in under the radar." Robert Deutsch, a neuroscientist and anthropologist who works for ad agency DDB Needham, likens himself to a vampire—"I suck information out of people, and they love it."

12   One new market research technique involves monitoring brain-wave signals to measure how "engaged" viewers are in what they are watching. According to the president of the company doing this research, "We are the only company in the industry reading people's thoughts and emotions. Someone's going to be a billionaire doing this. I think it will be us."

13   Through focus groups and in-depth interviews, psychological researchers can zero in on very specific target audiences—and their leaders. "Buy this 24-year-old and get all his friends absolutely free," proclaims an ad for MTV directed to advertisers. MTV presents itself publicly as a place for rebels and nonconformists. Behind the scenes, however, it tells potential advertisers that its viewers are lemmings who will buy whatever they are told to buy.

14   The MTV ad gives us a somewhat different perspective on the concept of "peer pressure." Advertisers, especially those who advertise tobacco and alcohol, are forever claiming that advertising doesn't influence anyone, that kids smoke and drink because of peer pressure. Sure, such pressure exists and is an

important influence, but a lot of it is created by advertising. Kids who exert peer pressure don't drop into high schools like Martians. They are kids who tend to be leaders, whom other kids follow for good or for bad. And they themselves are mightily influenced by advertising, sometimes very deliberately as in the MTV ad. As an ad for *Seventeen* magazine, picturing a group of attractive young people, says, "Hip doesn't just happen. It starts at the source: *Seventeen*." In the global village, the "peers" are very much the same, regardless of nationality, ethnicity, culture. In the eyes of the media, the youths of the world are becoming a single, seamless, soulless target audience—often cynically labeled "Generation X," or, for the newest wave of teens, "Generation Y." "We're helping a soft drink company reach them, even if their parents can't," says an ad for newspapers featuring a group of young people. The ad continues, "If you think authority figures have a hard time talking to Generation X, you should try being an advertiser," and goes on to suggest placing ads in the television sections of newspapers.

15   Direct-marketing techniques make it possible for advertisers to customize ads for subscribers of the same magazine according to what a particular subscriber has previously bought. In 1994 the direct-marketing firm Bronner Slosberg Humphrey Inc. customized a print campaign for L. L. Bean by comparing the company's customer base to the subscription lists of about twenty national magazines. Different ads were tailored to specific customers. Thus if two New Yorker subscribers lived next door to each other, the same edition of the magazine could contain two different L. L. Bean ads. According to Mike Slosberg, vice-chairman of the company, "In essence, the ad becomes direct mail, and the magazine is the envelope."

16   Perhaps we are not surprised that magazines are only envelopes. But many of us had higher hopes for cable television and the Internet. However, these new technologies have mostly become sophisticated targeting devices. "Now you can turn your target market into a captive audience," says an ad for an Internet news and information service that features a man roped into his office chair.

17   "Capture your audience," says another, featuring a bunch of eyeballs dripping in a net. This ad is selling software that "allows you to track the clicks and mouse-over activities of every single user interacting with your banner ad." Another company recently launched a massive data-collection effort, with the goal of getting at least one million consumers to fill out surveys. It will use the data to deliver ads it claims can be targeted right down to the individual. "Sorry. We can't target by shoesize. YET," says an ad for Yahoo!, a very successful Internet company, which goes on to tell advertisers, "You're wondering . . . what do our 35 million registered users offer you? Well, information. A lot of it. About who they are. What they're interested in. What kind of job they hold. How old they are. Get the picture?" As a writer for *Advertising Age* said, "What was once a neutral platform for global communication and vast information gathering is now seen as a virtual playground for marketers seeking new and better ways to reach consumers."

18   Home pages on the World Wide Web hawk everything from potato chips to cereal to fast food—to drugs. Alcohol and tobacco companies, chafing under advertising restrictions in other media, have discovered they can find and woo young people without any problem on the Web. Indeed, children are especially vulnerable on the Internet, where advertising manipulates them, invades their privacy, and transforms them into customers without their knowledge. Although there are various initiatives pending, there are as yet no regulations against targeting children online. Marketers attract children to Websites with games and contests and then extract from them information that can be used in future sales pitches to the child and the child's family. They should be aware that this information might be misleading. My daughter recently checked the "less than $20,000" household income box because she was thinking of her allowance.

19   Some sites offer prizes to lure children into giving up the e-mail addresses of their friends too. Online advertising targets children as young as four in an attempt to develop "brand loyalty" as early as possible. Companies unrelated to children's products have Websites for children, such as Chevron's site, which features games, toys, and videos touting the importance of—surprise!—the oil industry. In this way, companies can create an image early on and can also gather marketing data. As one ad says to advertisers, "Beginning this August, Kidstar will be able to reach every kid on the planet. And you can, too."

20   Children are easily influenced. Most little children can't tell the difference between the shows and the commercials (which basically means they are smarter than the rest of us). The toys sold during children's programs are often based on characters in the programs. Recently the Center for Media Education asked the Federal Trade Commission to examine "kidola," a television marketing strategy in which toy companies promise to buy blocks of commercial time if a local broadcast station airs programs associated with their toys.

21   Perhaps most troubling, advertising is increasingly showing up in our schools, where ads are emblazoned on school buses, scoreboards, and book covers, where corporations provide "free" material for teachers, and where many children are a captive audience for the commercials on Channel One, a marketing program that gives video equipment to desperate schools in exchange for the right to broadcast a "news" program studded with commercials to all students every morning. Channel One is hardly free, however—it is estimated that it costs taxpayers $1.8 billion in lost classroom time. But it certainly is profitable for the owners who promise advertisers "the largest teen audience around" and "the undivided attention of millions of teenagers for 12 minutes a day." Another ad for Channel One boasts, "Our relationship with 8.1 million teenagers lasts for six years [rather remarkable considering most of theirs last for . . . like six days]." Imagine the public outcry if a political or religious group offered schools an information package with ten minutes of news and two minutes of political or religious persuasion. Yet we tend to think of commercial persuasion as somehow neutral, although it certainly promotes beliefs and behavior that have significant and sometimes harmful effects on the individual, the family, the society, and the environment.

22   "Reach him at the office," says an ad featuring a small boy in a business suit, which continues, "His first day job is kindergarten. Modern can put your sponsored educational materials in the lesson plan." Advertisers are reaching nearly 8 million public-school students each day.

23   According to the Council for Aid to Education, the total amount corporations spend on "educational" programs from kindergarten through high school has increased from $5 million in 1965 to about $500 million today. The Seattle School Board recently voted to aggressively pursue advertising and corporate sponsorship. "There can be a Nike concert series and a Boeing valedictorian," said the head of the task force. We already have market-driven educational materials in our schools, such as Exxon's documentary on the beauty of the Alaskan coastline or the McDonald's Nutrition Chart and a kindergarten curriculum that teaches children to "Learn to Read through Recognizing Corporate Logos."

24   There are penalties for young people who resist this commercialization. In the spring of 1998 Mike Cameron, a senior at Greenbrier High School in Evans, Georgia, was suspended from school. Why? Did he bring a gun to school? Was he smoking in the boys' room? Did he assault a teacher? No. He wore a Pepsi shirt on a school-sponsored Coke day, an entire school day dedicated to an attempt to win ten thousand dollars in a national contest run by Coca-Cola.

25   Coke has several "partnerships" with schools around the country in which the company gives several million dollars to the school in exchange for a long-term contract giving Coke exclusive rights to school vending machines. John Bushey, an area superintendent for thirteen schools in Colorado Springs who signs his correspondence "The Coke Dude," urged school officials to "get next year's volume up to 70,000 cases" and suggested letting students buy Coke throughout the day and putting vending machines "where they are accessible all day." Twenty years ago, teens drank almost twice as much milk as soda. Today they drink twice as much soda as milk. Some data suggest this contributes to broken bones while they are still teenagers and to osteoporosis in later life.

26   Just as children are sold to the toy industry and junk food industry by programs, video games, and films, women are sold to the diet industry by the magazines we read and the television programs we watch, almost all of which make us feel anxious about our weight. "Hey, Coke," proclaims an ad placed by *The Ladies' Home Journal,* "want 17-1/2 million very interested women to think Diet?" It goes on to promise executives of Coca-Cola a "very healthy environment for your ads." What's being sold here isn't Diet Coke—or even *The Ladies' Home Journal.* What's really being sold are the readers of *The Ladies' Home Journal,* first made to feel anxious about their weight and then delivered to the diet industry. Once there, they can be sold again—*Weight Watchers Magazine* sells its readers to the advertisers by promising that they "reward themselves with $4 billion in beauty and fashion expenditures annually."

27   No wonder women's magazines so often have covers that feature luscious cakes and pies juxtaposed with articles about diets. "85 Ways to Lose Weight," *Woman's Day* tells us—but probably one of them isn't the "10-minute ice cream

pie" on the cover. This is an invitation to pathology, fueling the paradoxical obsession with food and weight control that is one of the hallmarks of eating disorders.

28   It can be shocking to look at the front and back covers of magazines. Often there are ironic juxtapositions. A typical woman's magazine has a photo of some rich food on the front cover, a cheesecake covered with luscious cherries or a huge slice of apple pie with ice cream melting on top. On the back cover, there is usually a cigarette ad, often one implying that smoking will keep women thin. Inside the magazine are recipes, more photos of fattening foods, articles about dieting—and lots of advertising featuring very thin models. There usually also is at least one article about an uncommon disease or trivial health hazard, which can seem very ironic in light of the truly dangerous product being glamorized on the back cover.

29   In February 1999, *Family Circle* featured on its front cover a luscious photo of "gingham mini-cakes," while promoting articles entitled "New! Lose-Weight, Stay-Young Diet," "Super Foods That Act Like Medicine," and "The Healing Power of Love." On the back cover was an ad for Virginia Slims cigarettes. The same week, *For Women First* featured a chocolate cake on its cover along with one article entitled "Accelerate Fat Loss" and another promising "Breakthrough Cures" for varicose veins, cellulite, PMS, stress, tiredness, and dry skin. On the back cover, an ad for Doral cigarettes said, "Imagine getting more." *The Ladies' Home Journal* that same month offered on its cover "The Best Chocolate Cake You Ever Ate," along with its antidote, "Want to Lose 10 lbs? Re-program Your Body." Concern for their readers' health was reflected in two articles highlighted on the cover, "12 Symptoms You Must Not Ignore" and "De-Stressors for Really Crazy Workdays"—and then undermined by the ad for Basic cigarettes on the back cover (which added to the general confusion by picturing the pack surrounded by chocolate candies).

30   Dr. Holly Atkinson, a health writer for *New Woman* between 1985 and 1990, recalled that she was barred from covering smoking-related issues, and that her editor struck any reference to cigarettes in articles on topics ranging from wrinkles to cancer. When Atkinson confronted the editor, a shouting match ensued. "Holly, who do you think supports this magazine?" demanded the editor. As Helen Gurley Brown, former editor of *Cosmopolitan,* said: "Having come from the advertising world myself, I think, 'Who needs somebody you're paying millions of dollars a year to come back and bite you on the ankle?'"

31   Today we export a popular culture that promotes escapism, consumerism, violence, and greed. Half the planet lusts for Cindy Crawford, lines up for blockbuster films like *Die Hard 12* with a minimum of dialogue and a maximum of violence (which travels well, needing no translation), and dances to the monotonous beat of the Backstreet Boys. *Baywatch,* a moronic television series starring Ken and Barbie, has been seen by more people in the world than any other television show in history. And at the heart of all this "entertainment" is advertising. As Simon Anholt, an English consultant specializing in global brand development, said, "The world's most powerful brand is the U.S. This is because it has

Hollywood, the world's best advertising agency. For nearly a century, Hollywood has been pumping out two-hour cinema ads for Brand U.S.A., which audiences around the world flock to see." When a group of German advertising agencies placed an ad in *Advertising Age* that said, "Let's make America great again," they left no doubt about what they had in mind. The ad featured cola, jeans, burgers, cigarettes, and alcohol—an advertiser's idea of what makes America great.

32   Some people might wonder what's wrong with this. On the most obvious level, as multinational chains replace local stores, local products, and local character, we end up in a world in which everything looks the same and everyone is Gapped and Starbucked. Shopping malls kill vibrant downtown centers locally and create a universe of uniformity internationally. Worse, we end up in a world ruled by, in John Maynard Keynes's phrase, the values of the casino. On this deeper level, rampant commercialism undermines our physical and psychological health, our environment, and our civic life and creates a toxic society. Advertising corrupts us and, I will argue, promotes a dissociative state that exploits trauma and can lead to addiction. To add insult to injury, it then co-opts our attempts at resistance and rebellion.

33   Although it is virtually impossible to measure the influence of advertising on a culture, we can learn something by looking at cultures only recently exposed to it. In 1980 the Gwich'in tribe of Alaska got television, and therefore massive advertising, for the first time. Satellite dishes, video games, and VCRs were not far behind. Before this, the Gwich'in lived much the way their ancestors had for a thousand generations. Within ten years, the young members of the tribe were so drawn by television they no longer had time to learn ancient hunting methods, their parents' language, or their oral history. Legends told around campfires could not compete with *Beverly Hills 90210*. Beaded moccasins gave way to Nike sneakers, sled dogs to gas-powered skimobiles, and "tundra tea" to Folger's instant coffee.

34   Human beings used to be influenced primarily by the stories of our particular tribe or community, not by stories that are mass-produced and market-driven. As George Gerbner, one of the world's most respected researchers on the influence of the media, said, "For the first time in human history, most of the stories about people, life, and values are told not by parents, schools, churches, or others in the community who have something to tell, but by a group of distant conglomerates that have something to sell." The stories that most influence our children these days are the stories told by advertisers.

■ QUESTIONS FOR ANALYSIS AND DISCUSSION

1. According to Kilbourne, why don't advertisers want consumers to be aware of the influence of advertising? Evaluate how Kilbourne supports this assertion. How do you think advertising agencies would respond to her statement? Explain.

2. How do advertisers use "peer pressure" to target young adults? How effective is this tactic, and why?

3. Kilbourne describes how some schools make deals with advertisers in exchange for free educational materials and/or funding. How does she feel about this practice? What is your own position on the situation? Explain.

4. What mixed messages do advertisers send to women? How do these mixed messages help promote their marketing agenda?

5. How does Kilbourne's example of the influence of advertising in the Gwich'in tribe in Alaska support her points regarding the influence of advertising in our own culture? Are the examples parallel? Explain.

Friendly Persuasion: The Growing Ubiquity of Advertising, or What Happens When Everyone Becomes an Ad?

John Fraim

> *"Ubiquity: Existence or apparent existence everywhere at the same time; omnipresence."*
> —*American Heritage Dictionary*

Only fifty years ago, Americans knew where they could expect to see advertisements. And advertisements, and the products they pitched, were obvious. But this innocent style of marketing is a thing of the past, explains media critic John Fraim. Advertising is everywhere and in everything. From product placement in movies, to marketing pitches that masquerade as newspaper editorials, to invisible Internet transaction fees, the day is rapidly approaching, says Fraim, that we will no longer be able to determine what is, and isn't, an ad.

Fraim is a California-based writer and publisher. He is the president of GreatHouse Company, a research firm specializing in the study of symbolism in popular culture. He is the author of the award-winning book *Spirit Catcher* (1997), a biography of John Coltrane. This article appeared in the 2000 edition of *M/C: A Journal of Media and Culture.*

■ BEFORE YOU READ

When you read an article in a magazine or newspaper, do you expect it to be uninfluenced by advertising or marketing agendas? How important is it that the media keep the reporting information and advertising separate?

■ AS YOU READ

Is the "growing ubiquity of advertising" Fraim describes disturbing? Or is it simply a accepted fact that advertising is "everywhere"?

1   Once upon a time, not very long ago, advertisements were easy to recognize. They had simple personalities with goals not much more complicated than selling you a bar of soap or a box of cereal. And they possessed the reas-

suring familiarity of old friends or relatives you've known all your life. They were Pilgrims who smiled at you from Quaker Oats boxes or little tablets named "Speedy" who joyfully danced into a glass of water with the sole purpose of giving up their short life to help lessen your indigestion from overindulgence. Yes, sometimes they could be a little obnoxious but, hey, it was a predictable annoyance.

2   And once, not very long ago, advertisements also knew their place in the landscape of popular culture, their boundaries were the ad space of magazines or the commercial time of television programs. When the ads got too annoying, you could toss the magazine aside or change the TV channel. The ease and quickness of their dispatch had the abruptness of slamming your front door in the face of an old door-to-door salesman.

3   This all began to change around the 1950s when advertisements acquired a more complex and subtle personality and began straying outside of their familiar media neighborhoods. The social observer Vance Packard wrote a best-selling book in the late 50s called *The Hidden Persuaders* which identified this change in advertising's personality as coming from hanging around Professor Freud's psychoanalysis and learning his hidden, subliminal methods of trickery.

The Evolution of Subliminal Techniques

4   The book *Hidden Persuaders* made quite a stir at the time, bringing about congressional hearings and even the introduction of legislation. Prominent motivation researchers Louis Cheskin and Ernest Dichter utilized the new ad methods and were publicly admonished as traitors to their profession. The life of the new subliminal advertising seemed short indeed. Even Vance Packard predicted its coming demise. "Eventually, say by AD 2000," he wrote in the preface to the paperback edition of his book, "all this depth manipulation of the psychological variety will seem amusingly old-fashioned."

5   Yet, 40 years later, any half-awake observer of popular culture knows that things haven't exactly worked out the way Packard predicted. In fact what seems old-fashioned today is the belief that ads are those simpletons they once were before the 50s and that products are sold for features and benefits rather than for images. Even Vance Packard expresses an amazement at the evolution of advertising since the 50s, noting that today ads for watches have nothing to do with watches or that ads for shoes scarcely mention shoes. Packard remarks "it used to be the brand identified the product. In today's advertising the brand is the product." Modern advertising, he notes, has an almost total obsession with images and feelings and an almost total lack of any concrete claims about the product and why anyone should buy it. Packard admits puzzlement. "Commercials seem totally unrelated to selling any product at all." Jeff DeJoseph of the J. Walter Thompson firm underlines Packard's comments. "We are just trying to convey a sensory impression of the brand, and we're out of there."

6   Subliminal advertising techniques have today infiltrated the heart of corporate America. As Ruth Shalit notes in her article "The Return of the Hidden Persuaders" from the 27 September 1999 issue of *Salon* magazine, "far from be-

ing consigned to the maverick fringe, the new psycho-persuaders of corporate America have colonized the marketing departments of mainstream conglomerates. At companies like Kraft, Coca-Cola, Proctor & Gamble and Daimler-Chrysler, the most sought-after consultants hail not from McKinsey & Company, but from brand consultancies with names like Archetype Discoveries, PsychoLogics and Semiotic Solutions."

The Growing Ubiquity of Advertising

7   Yet pervasive as the subliminal techniques of advertising have become, the emerging power of modern advertising ultimately centers around "where" it is rather than "what" it is or "how" it works. The power of modern advertising is within this growing ubiquity or "everywhereness" of advertising rather than the technology and methodology of advertising. The ultimate power of advertising will be arrived at when ads cannot be distinguished from their background environment. When this happens, the environment will become a great continuous ad.

8   In the process, ads have wandered away from their well-known hangouts in magazines and TV shows. Like alien-infected pod-people of early science fiction movies, they have stumbled out of these familiar media playgrounds and suddenly sprouted up everywhere. The ubiquity of advertising is not being driven by corporations searching for new ways to sell products but by media searching for new ways to make money.

9   Traditionally, media made money by selling subscriptions and advertising space. But these two key income sources are quickly drying up in the new world of online media. Journalist Mike France wisely takes notice of this change in an important article "Journalism's Online Credibility Gap" from the 11 October 1999 issue of *Business Week*. France notes that subscription fees have not worked because "Web surfers are used to getting content for free, and they have been reluctant to shell out any money for it." Advertising sales and their Internet incarnation in banner ads have also been a failure so far, France observes, because companies don't like paying a flat fee for online advertising since it's difficult to track the effectiveness of their marketing dollars. Instead, they only want to pay for actual sales leads, which can be easily monitored on the Web as readers click from site to site.

10   Faced with the above situation, media companies have gone on the prowl for new ways to make money. This search underpins the emerging ubiquity of advertising: the fact that it is increasingly appearing everywhere. In the process, traditional boundaries between advertising and other societal institutions are being overrun by these media forces on the prowl for new "territory" to exploit.

11   That time when advertisements knew their place in the landscape of popular culture and confined themselves to just magazines or TV commercials is a fading memory. And today, as each of us is bombarded by thousands of ads each day, it is impossible to "slam" the door and keep them out of our house as we could once slam the door in the face of the old door-to-door salesmen.

12   Of course you can find them on the matchbook cover of your favorite bar, on t-shirts sold at some roadside tourist trap or on those logo baseball caps you

always pick up at trade shows. But now they have got a little more personal and stare at you over urinals in the men's room. They have even wedged themselves onto the narrow little bars at the check-out counter conveyer belts of supermarkets or onto the handles of gasoline pumps at filling stations. The list goes on and on. (No, this article is not an ad.)

Advertising and Entertainment

13   In advertising's march to ubiquity, two major boundaries have been crossed. They are crucial boundaries which greatly enhance advertising's search for the invisibility of ubiquity. Yet they are also largely invisible themselves. These are the boundaries separating advertising from entertainment and those separating advertising from journalism.

14   Once, not long ago, when ads were simple and confined, entertainment was also simple and its purpose was to entertain rather than to sell. There was money enough in packed movie houses or full theme parks to make a healthy profit. But all this has changed with advertising's ubiquity.

15   Like media corporations searching for new revenue streams, the entertainment industry has responded to flat growth by finding new ways to squeeze money out of entertainment content. Films now feature products in paid for scenes and most forms of entertainment use product tie-ins to other areas such as retail stores or fast-food restaurants. Also popular with the entertainment industry is what might be termed the "versioning" of entertainment products into various subspecies where entertainment content is transformed into other media so it can be sold more than once. A film may not make a profit on just the theatrical release but there is a good chance it doesn't matter because it stands to make a profit in video rentals.

Advertising and Journalism

16   The merger of advertising and entertainment goes a long way towards a world of ubiquitous advertising. Yet the merger of advertising and journalism is the real "promised land" in the evolution of ubiquitous advertising. This fundamental shift in the way news media make money provides the final frontier to be conquered by advertising, a final "promised land" for advertising. As Mike France observes in *Business Week,* this merger "could potentially change the way they cover the news. The more the press gets in the business of hawking products, the harder it will be to criticize those goods—and the companies making them."

17   Of course, there is that persistent myth, perpetuated by news organizations that they attempt to preserve editorial independence by keeping the institutions they cover and their advertisers at arm's length. But this is proving more and more difficult, particularly for online media. Observers like France have pointed out a number of reasons for this. One is the growth of ads in news media that look more like editorial content than ads. While long-standing ethical rules bar magazines and newspapers from printing advertisements that look like editorial copy, these rules become fuzzy for many online publications. Another reason making it difficult to separate advertising from journalism is the

growing merger and consolidation of media corporations. Fewer and fewer corporations control more and more entertainment, news and ultimately advertising. It becomes difficult for a journalist to criticize a product when it has a connection to the large media conglomerate the journalist works for.

18   Traditionally, it has been rare for media corporations to make direct investments in the corporations they cover. However, as Mike France notes, CNBC crossed this line when it acquired a stake in Archipelago in September 1999. CNBC, which runs a business-news Website, acquired a 12.4% stake in Archipelago Holdings, an electronic communications network for trading stock. Long-term plans are likely to include allowing visitors to cnbc.com to link directly to Archipelago. That means CNBC could be in the awkward position of both providing coverage of online trading and profiting from it. France adds that other business news outlets, such as Dow Jones (DJ), Reuters, and Bloomberg, already have indirect ties to their own electronic stock-trading networks.

19   And, in news organizations, a popular method of cutting down on the expense of paying journalists for content is the growing practice of accepting advertiser written content or "sponsored edit" stories. The confusion to readers violates the spirit of a long-standing American Society of Magazine Editors (ASME) rule prohibiting advertisements with "an editorial appearance." But as France notes, this practice is thriving online. This xchange happens in ever so subtle ways. "A bit of puffery inserted here," notes France, "a negative adjective deleted there—it doesn't take a lot to turn a review or story about, say, smart phones, into something approaching highbrow ad copy." He offers an example in forbes.com whose Microsoft ads could easily be mistaken for staff-written articles.

20   France reminds us that journalism is built on trust. In the age of the Internet, though, trust is quickly becoming an elusive quality. He writes "as magazines, newspapers, radio stations, and television networks rush to colonize the Internet, the Great Wall between content and commerce is beginning to erode." In the end, he ponders whether there is an irrevocable conflict between e-commerce and ethical journalism. When you can't trust journalists to be ethical, just who can you trust?

Transaction Fees & Affiliate Programs—Advertising's Final Promised Land?

21   The engine driving the growing ubiquity of advertising, though, is not the increasing merger of advertising with other industries (like entertainment and journalism) but rather a new business model of online commerce and Internet technology called transaction fees.

22   This emerging and potentially dominant Internet e-commerce technology provides for the ability to track transactions electronically on Websites and to garner transaction fees. Through these fees, many media Websites take a percentage of payment through online product sales. In effect, a media site becomes one pervasive direct mail ad for every product mentioned on its site.

This of course puts them in a much closer economic partnership with advertisers than is the case with traditional fixed-rate ads where there is little connection between product sales and the advertising media carrying them.

23   Transaction fees are the new online version of direct marketing; the emerging Internet technology for their application is one of the great economic driving forces of the entire Internet commerce apparatus. The promise of transaction fees is that a number of people, besides product manufacturers and advertisers, might gain a percentage of profit from selling products via hypertext links. Once upon a time, the manufacturer of a product was the one that gained (or lost) from marketing it. Now, however, there is the possibility that journalists, news organizations and entertainment companies might also gain from marketing via transaction fees.

24   Given this scenario, it is not surprising that advertisers are most likely to increasingly pressure media Websites to support themselves with e-commerce transaction fees. Charles Li, Senior Analyst for New Media at Forrester Research, estimates that by the year 2003, media sites will receive $25 billion in revenue from transaction fees, compared with $17 billion from ads and $5 billion from subscriptions.

25   The possibility is great that all media will become like great direct response advertisements taking a transaction fee percentage for anything sold on their sites. And there is the more dangerous possibility that all of us will become the new "promised land" for a ubiquitous advertising. All of us will have some cut in selling somebody else's product.

26   When this happens and there is a direct economic incentive for all of us to say nice things about products, what is the need and importance of subliminal techniques and methods creating advertising based on images which try to trick us into buying things?

A Society Without Critics?

27   It is for these reasons that criticism and straight news are becoming an increasingly endangered species. Everyone has to eat but what happens when one can no longer make meal money by criticizing current culture?

28   Cultural critics become a dying breed. There is no money in criticism because it is based around disconnection rather than connection to products. No links to products or Websites are involved here. Critics are becoming lonely icebergs floating in the middle of a cyber-sea of transaction fees, watching everyone else (except themselves) make money on transaction fees. The subliminal focus of the current consultancies is little more than a repackaging of an old theme discovered long ago by Vance Packard. But the growing "everywhereness" and "everyoneness" of modern advertising through transaction fees may mark the beginning of a revolutionary new era. Everyone might become their own "brand," a point well made in Tim Peters's article "A Brand Called You."

29   Orville Schell, dean of the Graduate School of Journalism at the University of California at Berkeley, has summarized this growing ubiquity of advertising in a rather simple and elegant manner saying "at a certain point, people won't

be able to differentiate between what's trustworthy and what isn't." Over the long run, this loss of credibility could have a corrosive effect on society in general—especially given the media's importance as a political, cultural, and economic watchdog. Schell warns, "if people don't trust their information, it's not much better than a Marxist-Leninist society."

30   Yet, will we be able to realize this simple fact when we all become types of Marxists and Leninists? Still, there is the great challenge to America to learn how to utilize transaction fees in a democratic manner. In effect, a combination of the technological promise of the new economy with that old promise, and perhaps even myth, of a democratic America. America stands on the verge of a great threshold and challenge in the growing ubiquity of advertising. In a way, as with most great opportunities or threats, this challenge centers on a peculiar paradox. On the one hand, there is the promise of the emerging Internet business model and its center around the technology of transaction fees. At the same time, there is the threat posed by transaction fees to America's democratic society in the early years of the new millennium.

31   Yes, once upon a time, not very long ago, advertisements were easy to recognize and also knew their place in the landscape of popular culture. Their greatest, yet silent, evolution (especially in the age of the Internet) has really been in their spread into all areas of culture rather than in methods of trickery and deceit. Now, it is more difficult to slam that front door in the face of that old door-to-door salesman. Or toss that magazine and its ad aside, or switch off commercials on television. We have become that door-to-door salesman, that magazine ad, that television commercial. The current cultural landscape takes on some of the characteristics of the theme of that old science fiction movie "The Invasion of the Body Snatchers." A current advertising campaign from RJ Reynolds has a humorous take on the current zeitgeist fad of alien abduction with copy reading "if aliens are smart enough to travel through space then why do they keep abducting the dumbest people on earth?"

32   One might add that when Americans allow advertising to travel through all our space, perhaps we all become the dumbest people on earth, abducted by a new alien culture so far away from a simplistic nostalgia of yesterday.

REFERENCES

France, Mike. "Journalism's Online Credibility Gap." *Business Week* 11 Oct. 1999.

Packard, Vance. *The Hidden Persuaders.* Out of Print, 1957. Pine, Joseph, and James Gilmore. *The Experience Economy.* Harvard Business School, 1999.

Shalit, Ruth. "The Return of the Hidden Persuaders." *Salon* Magazine 27 Sep. 1999. <http://www.salon.com/media/col/shal/1999/09/27/persuaders/index.html>.

Wolf, Michael. *Entertainment Economy.* Times Books, 1999.

■ **QUESTIONS FOR ANALYSIS AND DISCUSSION**

1. Fraim locates the shift in advertising technique as occurring in the 1950s when advertisements began to apply psychoanalysis and "subliminal methods of

trickery." In what ways is this shift still apparent in advertising today? Cite some examples.

2. In paragraph 7, Fraim comments that "the ultimate power of advertising will be arrived at when ads cannot be distinguished from their background environment." What examples does he provide that this has already happened? Can you think of other venues that he may have left out, such as video games or fashion logos?

3. Fraim states that on a daily basis, we are "bombarded by thousands of ads each day" (paragraph 11). Does this number seem excessive? Does it need more supporting evidence, or is it an accepted fact? Explain.

4. In paragraph 16, Fraim notes that the merger of advertising and journalism is the real "promised land" in the evolution of ubiquitous advertising. "This fundamental shift in the way news media make money provides the final frontier to be conquered by advertising.[. . .]" How would Kilbourne respond to this statement? Explain.

5. What are transaction fees? How could they make "everyone an ad"? Explain.

6. Evaluate Fraim's closing paragraphs. How do they connect to the points he makes in his essay? Are they an effective way to end his article? Why or why not?

Hey Kids, Buy This!

David Leonhardt and Kathleen Kerwin

There was a time when ads aimed at children were slotted between Saturday morning cartoons. But that has all changed. Marketers have discovered this eager and impressionable segment of the population and have turned kids into consumers of brand-name products practically from birth. Children today have more money to spend and more products to choose from, making them very attractive targets for advertising pitches. Today, the sole purpose of some television programs is to promote toys and games for children. In addition, Internet Web sites lure youngsters with promises of games, e-mail, and free merchandise while subtly pitching their products. Has Madison Avenue gone too far? Journalists David Leonhardt and Kathleen Kerwin think that they have.

David Leonhardt is a staff editor for *Business Week* and Kathleen Kerwin is the Detroit division bureau manager of that publication. This article first appeared as the cover story for the June 30, 1997, issue of *Business Week*.

■ BEFORE YOU READ

Think about your consumer habits as a child. What did you want to buy and how did you learn about the product? What made you want the product, and why?

■ AS YOU READ

Consider how the authors use statistics to support their points. Do you find one kind of evidence more credible than another?

1   At 1:58 p.m. on Wednesday, May 5, in Houston's St. Luke's Episcopal Hospital, a consumer was born. Her name was Alyssa J. Nedell, and by the time she went home three days later, some of America's biggest marketers were pursuing her with samples, coupons, and assorted freebies. Procter & Gamble hoped its Pampers brand would win the battle for Alyssa's bottom. Johnson & Johnson offered up a tiny sample of its baby soap. Bristol-Myers Squibb Co. sent along some of its Enfamil baby formula.

2   Like no generation before, Alyssa's enters a consumer culture, surrounded by logos, labels, and ads almost from the moment of birth. As an infant, Alyssa may wear Sesame Street diapers and miniature pro basketball jerseys. By the time she's 20 months old, she will start to recognize some of the thousands of brands flashed in front of her each day. At age 7, if she's anything like the typical kid, she will see some 20,000 TV commercials a year. By the time she's 12, she will have her own entry in the massive data banks of marketers.

3   Multiply Alyssa by 30 million—the number of babies born in this country since 1990—and you have the largest generation to flood the market since their baby boom parents. More impressive than their numbers, though, is their wealth. The increase in single-parent and dual-earner households means kids are making shopping decisions once left to mom. Combining allowance, earnings, and gifts, kids 14 and under will directly spend an estimated $20 billion this year, and they will influence another $200 billion. No wonder they have become the target of marketing campaigns so sophisticated as to make the kid-aimed pitches of yore look like, well, Mickey Mouse.

4   Forget, for now, the hullabaloo over alcohol and tobacco ads that attract kids well under the age of consent. Yes, the makers of such "sin products" are under fire for the cartoon characters they used to sell their wares, as are trend-setting designers such as Calvin Klein, whose ads feature sexualized waifs barely out of puberty. But what goes on in the name of more legitimate children's fare is far more pervasive—and in many ways just as insidious.

5   Marketers that had long ignored children now systematically pursue them—even when the tykes are years away from being able to buy their products. "Ten years ago, it was cereal, candy, and toys. Today, it's also computers and airlines and hotels and banks," says Julie Halpin, general manager of Saatchi & Saatchi Advertising's Kid Connection division. "A lot of people are turning to a whole segment of the population they haven't been talking to before."

6   Those that have always targeted kids, such as fast-food restaurants and toy makers, have stepped up their pitches, hoping to reach kids earlier and bind them more tightly. Movies, T-shirts, hamburger wrappers, and dolls—all are part of the cross-promotional blitz aimed at convincing kids to spend.

7   Together, the new efforts represent a quantitative and qualitative change in the marketing aimed at children. As any parent who has struggled to find kids' underwear without a licensed cartoon character on it knows, virtually no space is free of logos. And traditional ads have more venues than ever, with a gaggle of new magazines, dozens of Web sites, and entire TV channels aimed at kids.

From 1993 to 1996 alone, advertising in kid-specific media grew more than 50 percent, to $1.5 billion, according to *Competitive Media Reporting.*

8   The cumulative effect of initiating our children into a consumerist ethos at an ever earlier age may be profound. As kids drink in the world around them, many of their cultural encounters—from books to movies to TV—have become little more than sales pitches, devoid of any moral beyond a plea for a purchase. Even their classrooms are filled with corporate logos. Instead of transmitting a sense of who we are and what we hold important, today's marketing-driven culture is instilling in them the sense that little exists without a sales pitch attached and that self-worth is something you buy at a shopping mall.

9   "No one ad is so bad," says Mary Pipher, a clinical psychologist and author of *The Shelter of Each Other,* a current best-seller about family life. "But the combination of 400 ads a day creates in children a combination of narcissism, entitlement, and dissatisfaction."

Brand Barrage

10 It also can leave parents feeling as if Madison Avenue were raising their kid. Paula Goedert, a tax attorney in Chicago with two sons, ages 15 and 6, has noticed big changes in kids' marketing over the past decade. "Brand awareness has become an incredibly abusive experience—the relentless requests to go to McDonald's, to see movies that are inappropriate for 6-year-olds that are advertised on kids' shows," Goedert says.

11   In the end, the barrage may hurt the marketers themselves. Parents and policymakers are increasingly unnerved by the notion of marketers gathering information about children's preferences and then hiring psychologists to analyze it. In the last year, the federal government has shown a new interest in regulating advertising, be it commercials over the Internet or those for tobacco and alcohol. Meanwhile, some parents, unwilling to expose their children to the unceasing ad blitz, are trying to shield them from consumer culture altogether. "We have deliberately tried to keep Madeline from becoming brand-aware," says Nancy Brophy, an Arlington Heights (Ill.) mother of three, including 5-year-old Madeline. "If something's hot, like Beanie Babies or Power Rangers, I'll avoid it."

12   Marketers, for the most part, say the concerns are overblown—and that critics don't give kids and their parents enough credit. "I have a high regard for the intelligence of kids," says Tom Kalinske, president of Knowledge Universe, a new education company, and the former CEO of Sega of America and Mattel Inc. Kalinske and others in the industry believe that kids today are more sophisticated consumers than the generations that preceded them, well able to recognize hype and impervious to crude manipulation. But at least a few worry about the effects of what they do. "As more companies go after kids, the more pressure on kids there will be," says Tom Harbeck, Nickelodeon's senior vice-president for marketing.

13   For better or worse, the marketing barrage has created a generation hypersensitive to the power of brands. For teens, insecure as ever about fitting in, the

barrage of brand names offers the irresistible promise of instant cool. The onslaught begins so early—and continues so consistently—that even children who recognize it have trouble putting it aside. "My father always tells me that I could buy two pairs of jeans for what you pay for Calvin Klein," laughs Leydiana Reyes, an eighth-grader in Brooklyn, N.Y. "I know that. But I still want Calvin Klein."

14   Helping to create that lust for brands is a plethora of new ad vehicles. Walt Disney Co. is launching a 24-hour kids' radio network. At Time Warner, *Time, Sports Illustrated,* and *People* have all started or are about to start new editions for kids and teens. In addition, there are Nickelodeon, the Cartoon Network, and a bevy of new girls' magazines.

15   Underlying much of the new kid advertising is an implicit challenge to one of society's basic assumptions: that there is a fundamental difference between kids and grown-ups in judgment and taste. At one time, marketers pitched their children's wares mainly to parents, who would decide what their kids ate, wore, and played with. To appeal to the immature judgment of children was to take unfair advantage.

Cars, Too

16   But today that reticence is gone. "We're relying on the kid to pester the mom to buy the product, rather than going straight to the mom," says Barbara A. Martino, a vice-president in Grey Advertising Inc.'s 18 & Under division. Why? In part because it's harder for advertisers to eke out domestic sales growth and in part because busy parents no longer act as filters between their kids and the outside world.

17   Kids are being tempted with more than just toys. In an era when children are seen, heard, and catered to as if they were smaller versions of grown-ups, some nontraditional kid marketers are figuring out that the fastest way to mom and dad may well be through junior. In the May issue of *Sports Illustrated for Kids,* which attracts mostly 8- to 14-year-old boys, the inside cover featured a brightly colored two-page spread for the Chevy Venture minivan.

18   This is General Motor's first attempt to woo the group that Karen Francis, the Venture's brand manager, calls "back-seat consumers." Francis is sending the minivan into malls and showing previews of Disney's *Hercules* on a VCR inside. "We're kidding ourselves when we think kids aren't aware of brands," says Francis, adding that even she was surprised by how often parents told her their kids played a tie-breaking role in deciding which car to buy.

19   Marketers of other big-ticket items are also pursuing kids. Delta Airlines Inc. publishes an in-flight magazine for kids, while United Airlines serves McDonald's Happy Meals. Stein Roe & Farnham, Inc., a Chicago money-management firm, runs a mutual fund for child investors consisting largely of favorites such as Disney and Nike Inc. And IBM has teamed up with the National Basketball Association, hoping sports-crazed kids will sway their parents to choose its Aptiva when they shop for a personal computer.

Marlboro Kids

20   Kid marketers have also recognized the power of nontraditional marketing such as loyalty programs. Last year, PepsiCo launched its enormously successful Pepsi Stuff, which lets customers trade bottle caps for merchandise, including mountain bikes and phone cards. This year, it's aiming the program even more directly at teenagers, increasing the trade-in value of the 20-ounce bottles they favor and using endorsers with kid appeal, such as basketball's Lisa Leslie and baseball's Derek Jeter. "It's more important for us to be successful with teens," says Dave Burwick, vice-president for marketing. "If there are 12 million people out there with our stuff, let's have them be 12 million 18-year-olds."

21   Tobacco companies have also seized on the giveaway programs. Philip Morris Co. denies that Marlboro Gear, largely made up of cowboy-like outerwear, is aimed at teens. To get the gear, participants must mail in a form stating they are over 21. But Marlboro is now the brand of choice for 60 percent of teen smokers, according to the Centers for Disease Control. Camel has a similar program called Camel Cash, which features Joe Camel on its "dollars." Despite talk of a legal settlement with tobacco companies that could ban such programs, new initiatives that appeal to teens are appearing. U.S. Tobacco Co.'s Skoal brand and Philip Morris' Virginia Slims are both sponsoring rock concert tours.

22   Other tobacco and alcohol ads appeal to even younger kids. Close to 90 percent of 10- to 17-year-olds recognize Joe Camel as a cigarette booster, studies show. The California-based Center on Alcohol Advertising recently found that 9- to 11-year-old children were more apt to recognize the Budweiser frogs and be able to recite the beer's slogan than they were to remember that Tony the Tiger says, "They're grrr-eat." On the fringes, there are even brasher efforts to woo kids with questionable products. A California candy company called Hotlix markets a line of cocktail-flavored lollipops, including a margarita version that comes with salt and a tequila-flavored pop with an edible worm inside of it.

23   Ad campaigns that blur the line between adulthood and childhood are especially troubling—and especially effective—because parents have largely lost their role as "gatekeeper." Just take a look at the grocery-store aisle, where kids are confronted with plenty of messages on their level—literally. Frito Lay Inc. last year rolled out a display called Chip City that allows kids to measure themselves, look at themselves in a funhouse mirror, and press a button to hear Chester Cheetah, spokescharacter for its Chee-tos. Since kids want their chips now, the display includes plenty of one-ounce packages on sale for a quarter.

24   Everywhere, the target is younger. Companies that have already saturated the grade school market are turning toward the crib. Overall sales of licensed sports gear are flat, but the National Football League saw 37 percent growth last year in sales of clothing for tots. Across all lines, sales of licensed products for infants grew 32 percent, to $2.5 billion, in 1996. That means that even before kids can recognize symbols, they are surrounded by the brands that will soon beckon. "Kids are the most pure consumers you could have," says Debra McMahon, a vice-president who follows media for Mercer Management Consulting. "They tend to interpret your ad literally. They are infinitely open."

25   That description fits Nicholas Rouillard, a 9-year-old from Westfield, Mass. The difference between an ad and a TV show is simple, he says: "Commercials are shorter. A commercial is one minute long, but a cartoon can last up to two hours."

26   He's right. The line between the sponsor and the sponsored has all but disappeared. Much of kids' entertainment, featuring characters whose licensed images are immediately stamped on toys, sheets, clothes, even food packages, is almost indistinguishable from the commercials that support it. Amid the media clutter, commercials try to entertain, focusing less on the product and more on creating an image. At the same time, movies and TV shows are more intricately linked to the selling of toys than ever before. Hasbro Inc., for example, helped design the car in Warner Bros. new *Batman* flick. New, long-term licensing deals between studios and master marketers such as Mattel and McDonald's mean the trend will continue.

Built-in Scripts

27   "Toy companies used to be a font of creativity," says Seth M. Seigel, co-chairman of Beanstalk Group, a licensing company that represents the latest craze, Tamagotchi dolls. "Now, what they sell is little more than three-dimensional celluloid." Indeed, Louis Marx Toy Co., the largest in the country back in the 1950s, never signed a single license. Last year, 38 percent of all dollars spent on toys went to licensed toys. Thanks to *Star Wars,* the *Jurassic Park* sequel, *Hercules,* and the next *Batman* installment, that number could near 50 percent this year.

28   The slew of licensed toys leaves less time for imaginative play, and that, too, is causing worries. When toys come with built-in scripts, there's less room for creativity. "You learn flexibility when you play imaginatively. You learn self-control and how to delay impulses," says Dorothy G. Singer, a child psychologist at Yale University and the co-author of *House of Make Believe.* "If the toy comes from TV, a kid tends to follow the story line."

29   Of course, making a toy appeal to a kid isn't as simple as slapping a licensed character on it. Figuring out which hero is the right one brings in the market researchers. "Twenty years ago, you had maybe a dozen companies" researching kids, says Deborah Roedder John, a University of Minnesota professor who specializes in kid marketing, adding that back then she knew practically everybody in the field. "Now, there are many firms out there I've never heard of."

30   Their goal is to know more about children's preferences than even parents do. Researchers host online chats, where kids are more apt to talk openly about personal matters. They hire toddlers to play with new toys and then watch from behind a two-way mirror, often joined by psychologists. Nickelodeon alone surveys 4,000 children every week in its offices, at schools, over the phone, and on the Internet.

31   Thanks in part to recent academic studies, marketers now know more than ever about the child psyche. That has helped them translate the urges and obsessions of different age groups into bigger sales. By limiting the number of

each new Beanie Baby and announcing on its Web site which dolls it had discontinued, Ty Inc. in Oak Brook, Ill., for example, cashed in on the desire of 7-year-olds to collect. That urge used to be satisfied by sea shells or baseball cards, back before the latter became an investment opportunity.

Backlash?

32 At the same time, the new research has allowed some companies to shatter long-held assumptions about kids' behavior—such as the belief that female images work with girls but alienate boys. Nickelodeon discovered that kids were changing and didn't hesitate to launch a series of live-action shows with girls as the protagonists. One, *The Secret World of Alex Mack,* now has an audience that is 53 percent male.

33 Some of the new kid marketing draws on more troubling trends. It's no secret that images of sexuality and other forbidden pursuits appeal to many teenagers. And marketers, fighting to be noticed, are increasingly calling upon such symbols. Think about the current controversy over "heroin chic" images in fashion magazines. Or last year's Calvin Klein campaign that mimicked cheesy child pornography videos. That may have been the most egregious example of sexualizing children in order to sell to them, but it's not unique.

34 In fact, there are already signs of a backlash against the constant marketing assault facing kids. In Massachusetts, the Boston Children's Museum is running an exhibit that teaches children to understand commercials by allowing them to experiment with lighting and backdrops to change the look of an object. The purpose, says the museum's director of cultural programs, Joanne Rizzi, is "to show the manipulative aspect of commercials." In California, meanwhile, the state government is investigating Anheuser-Busch Cos. Inc.'s new giveaway program—called "Buy the Beer, Get the Gear"—in part out of concern over its appeal on college campuses. And in Washington, the Federal Trade Commission has proposed banning Joe Camel, while Bill Clinton has used the bully pulpit of the White House to chastise alcohol and tobacco companies for targeting kids.

35 None of those efforts, however, is likely to deflect the massive sales machine now directed at children. As long as kids have money to spend, marketers will fight to reach them. "Every 10 years, we begin to ask these questions, and no one has come up with a satisfactory answer," says Minnesota's John. The solution probably lies where it always has: with parents. They will simply have to be more vigilant than ever, knowing that wherever their children go—from day care to the Internet—there's now a marketer close behind.

■ QUESTIONS FOR ANALYSIS AND DISCUSSION

1. How does the opening anecdote about Alyssa J. Nedell establish the authors' main point about consumerism among children? Explain.
2. According to the article, what problems has the barrage of brand-name products directed at young children created for parents?

3. The authors are particularly critical of how tobacco and alcohol companies have indirectly marketed their products to young people. List several examples from the essay of how these companies, and others from your own experience, indirectly target children. What is your opinion of their strategies?
4. What are the authors' conclusions regarding the trend toward marketing to children? Do you feel this trend is inevitable? Should it be controlled? If so, how?

■ WRITING ASSIGNMENTS

1. Locate some advertisements for some popular products. Who is the audience for each advertisement? Discuss the ways the ads are, or are not, targeted to a specific demographic group. Assess how well the ads appeal to the shared lifestyle and desires of this group.
2. Write an essay in which you explore the connection between social diversification, product targeting, and audience packaging. Explore some of the reasons why the "divide and conquer" method of marketing works, and if it is an ethical approach to advertising.
3. Leonhardt and Kerwin suggest that the changing nature of family structure—that is, more two-income households and more children left on their own—has contributed to kids having more money and parents failing to act as "gatekeepers" of their purchases. Write an essay discussing the role you feel parents should play in shaping their children's behavior as consumers. How can they influence their children's buying habits, and how can they educate their children to be smart consumers?
4. Advertisers might argue that corporate sponsorship in schools makes students' educational quality of life better, from supporting athletic events, to outfitting a new computer lab, to providing expensive scientific equipment. Is this the trade-off for sponsorship? Should schools allow companies exclusive rights to market products to students in school? Write an essay in which you support or question this practice.
5. Write an essay evaluating advertising techniques in the last half of the twentieth century. How have ads changed, and why? Has advertising become more, or less, ethical? creative? focused? You may wish to refer to the references John Fraim provides at the end of his article for resources on the history of advertising.

THE QUEST FOR STUFF

Two Cheers for Consumerism

James Twitchell

While media and social critics question the methods of advertising agencies and lament the loss of basic values in the name of consumerism, professor James Twitchell openly embraces the media-driven world of advertising. In the next piece,

Twitchell explores the joys of consumerism, and the social criticism that condemns our "quest for stuff" as materialistic and self-centered.

Twichell is a professor of English and advertising at the University of Florida. He switched from teaching poetry to the study of mass culture and advertising after discovering that his students could complete more ad jingles than they could lines of poetry. Since then, he has written several books on the subject, including *Twenty Ads That Shook the World* (1998) and *Lead Us into Temptation: The Triumph of American Materialism* (1999). This essay originally appeared in the August/September 2000 issue of *Reason Magazine* as an excerpt from his 1999 book.

■ BEFORE YOU READ

Why is materialism so criticized, yet so wholeheartedly embraced by American society? If we are basically consumers at heart, as the next piece argues, why are we so quick to condemn advertising?

■ AS YOU READ

How does the perspective of the author of the next essay differ from others in this section in his attitude toward advertising? What can you surmise from his tone and use of language? How well does Twitchell convince his readers that his position is reasonable and correct?

1   Of all the strange beasts that have come slouching into the 20th century, none has been more misunderstood, more criticized, and more important than materialism. Who but fools, toadies, hacks, and occasional loopy libertarians have ever risen to its defense? Yet the fact remains that while materialism may be the most shallow of the 20th century's variousisms, it has been the one that has ultimately triumphed. The world of commodities appears so antithetical to the world of ideas that it seems almost heresy to point out the obvious: Most of the world most of the time spends most of its energy producing and consuming more and more stuff. The really interesting question may be not why we are so materialistic, but why we are so unwilling to acknowledge and explore what seems the central characteristic of modern life.

2   And why is the consumer so often depicted as powerless? From Thomas Hobbes in the mid-17th century ("As in other things, so in men, not the seller but the buyer determines the price") to Edwin S. Gingham in the mid-20th century ("Consumers with dollars in their pockets are not, by any stretch of the imagination, weak. To the contrary, they are the most merciless, meanest, toughest market disciplinarians I know"), the consumer was seen as participating in the meaning-making of the material world. How and why did the consumer get dumbed down and phased out so quickly? Why has the hypodermic metaphor (false needs injected into a docile populace) become the unchallenged explanation of consumerism?

3   Much of our current refusal to consider the liberating role of consumption is the result of who has been doing the describing. Since the 1960s, the primary

"readers" of the commercial "text" have been the well-tended and tenured members of the academy. For any number of reasons—the most obvious being their low levels of disposable income, average age, and the fact that these critics are selling a competing product, "high culture" (which is also coated with its own dream values)—the academy has casually passed off as "hegemonic brain-washing" what seems to me, at least, a self-evident truth about human nature: We like having stuff.

4   In place of the obvious, they have substituted an interpretation that they themselves often call vulgar Marxism. It is supposedly vulgar in the sense that it is not as sophisticated as the real stuff, but it has enough spin on it to be more appropriately called Marxism lite. Go into almost any cultural studies course in this country and you will hear consumerism condemned: What we see in the marketplace is the result of the manipulation of the many for the profit of the few. Consumers are led around by the nose. We live in a squirrel cage. Left alone, we would read Wordsworth, eat lots of salad, and meet to discuss Really Important Subjects.

5   The idea that consumerism creates artificial desires rests on a wistful igno-rance of history and human nature, on the hazy, romantic feeling that there ex-isted some halcyon era of noble savages with purely natural needs. Once we're fed and sheltered, our needs have always been cultural, not natural. Until there is some other system to identify and satisfy those needs and yearnings, capital-ism—and the culture it carries with it—will continue not just to thrive, but to triumph.

6   In the way we live now, it is simply impossible to consume objects without consuming meaning. Meaning is pumped and drawn everywhere throughout the modern commercial world, into the farthest reaches of space and into the smallest divisions of time. Commercialism is the water we all swim in, the air we breathe, our sunlight and shade. Currents of desire flow around objects like smoke in a wind tunnel.

7   This isn't to say that I'm sanguine about material culture. It has many prob-lems that I have glossed over. Consumerism is wasteful; it is devoid of other-wordly concerns. It is heedless of the truly poor, who cannot gain access to the loop of meaningful information that is carried through its ceaseless exchanges. On a personal level, I struggle daily to keep it at bay. For instance, I fight to keep Chris Whittle's Channel One TV and all place-based advertising from en-tering the classroom; I contribute to PBS in the hope that they will stop slip-ping down the slope of commercialism (although I know better); I am annoyed that Coke has bought all the "pouring rights" at my school and is now trying to do the same to the world; and I just go nuts at Christmas.

8   But I also realize that while you don't have to like it, it doesn't hurt to un-derstand it and our part in it. We have not been led astray. To some degree, the triumph of consumerism is the triumph of the popular will. You may not like what is manufactured, advertised, packaged, branded, and broadcast, but it is far closer to what most people want most of the time than at any other period of modern history.

9   We have not been led into this world of material closeness against our better judgment. For many of us, especially when we're young, consumerism is not against our better judgment. It *is* our better judgment. And this is true regardless of class or culture. We have not just asked to go this way, we have demanded. Now most of the world is lining up, pushing and shoving, eager to elbow into the mall. Woe to the government or religion that says no.

10   Getting and spending have been the most passionate, and often the most imaginative, endeavors of modern life. We have done more than acknowledge that the good life starts with the material life, as the ancients did. We have made stuff the dominant prerequisite of organized society. Things "R" Us. Consumption has become production. While this is dreary and depressing to some, as doubtless it should be, it is liberating and democratic to many more.

■ QUESTIONS FOR ANALYSIS AND DISCUSSION

1. In his first paragraph, Twitchell asks, "The really interesting question may be not why we are so materialistic, but why we are so unwilling to acknowledge and explore what seems the central characteristic of modern life." Answer his question drawing from information presented in this chapter and your own personal experience.

2. Why, according to Twitchell, is consumption "liberating"? Why do we, as a society, seem to want to refuse this role, but secretly embrace it?

3. What is the attitude of academia toward consumerism? How does Twitchell feel about this attitude? Because he is a professor of English, how do you think his colleagues would respond to his study of consumerism and advertising?

4. Critics of advertising assert that consumerism creates artificial desires. On what is this idea based? How does Twitchell respond to this idea?

5. Why is it impossible, according to the author, to "consume objects without consuming meaning"? Do you agree? Explain.

Manufacturing Desire
Harry Flood

"Welcome to the factory floor. The product? Things that are not essential, but hard to live without. What is being supplied here is demand. Want. Craving. All you could desire. All you can imagine. Maybe more than you can handle." So reads the clip leading into Harry Flood's article on "manufacturing desire" in *Adbusters Magazine.* The final decade of the twentieth century was one of the most prosperous in American history. Unemployment fell to new national lows, salaries reached new highs, and Americans with money to spend kept the economy humming. In the next article, Flood explores some of the social forces driving the "decadence" of the '90s, what it reveals about us as consumers, and what it might foreshadow in our future.

Adbusters Magazine, a nonprofit magazine published by the Adbusters Media Foundation based in Vancouver, Canada, is concerned with the ways in which commercial forces "erode our physical and cultural environment." Its articles have been featured in *The Wall Street Journal* and hundreds of other newspapers, magazines, and television and radio shows around the world. This article first appeared in the Winter 2000 issue of *Adbusters Magazine.*

■ BEFORE YOU READ

What things do you want that money can buy? Do you want a luxury automobile? a designer wardrobe? a signature watch? What makes these items more desirable than their less expensive, but equally functional counterparts? What makes you want these things?

■ AS YOU READ

How does the "culture of celebrity" contribute to our desire for decadence? Explain.

1   "WHY IS THIS CHILD SMILING?" asks a recent print ad of a cute tot blissfully snoozing. "Because he has lived his whole life in the biggest bull market in history." Cue the smug nods, the flush of pride. For here, swaddled in Baby Gap and lying in a Morigeau crib, is the immaculate American kid, born in the best damn place and time there has ever been. A child wanting for nothing.

2   He will soon learn, of course, to want everything.

3   Americans are beyond apologizing for their lifestyle of scorched-earth consumerism. To the strange little cabal of moralists who have recently questioned the official program, the response has mostly been to crank up the volume and drown the doubt out. Global consumer culture? Supersize it, baby. Pile on the wattage, horsepower, silicone, cholesterol and RAM until the lights flicker, the smoke-alarms shriek and the cardiac paddles lurch to life. Give us marbled steaks and sport-utes, please, and put it all on our tab—we're good for it. Because we are working dogs. And we have worked out the formula for millennial prosperity: keep your head down and your wallet open, and watch the economy roll. Enjoy the rollicking good times while building "the America we deserve."

4   Time was, decadence on this scale was something to fear. If one group of people was gobbling up resources out of all proportion to its needs, consuming at thirty times the rate of other groups of people, at everyone's expense, well . . . that was bad karma, to say the least. Their society was surely soft, cancerous and doomed.

5   But somehow, the First World has managed to give it all a happy spin. We have decided not to avoid decadence but to embrace it. Crave it. Buy it. Sell it. What's decadent? Ice cream with the density of plutonium, a bubblebath with a barley-flour chaser, that great new Gucci scent called "Envy." Decadence is just the celebration of universal human appetites, fully expressed—and any premium wiener who'd object to that idea must already be half-dead.

6   There's no mistaking contemporary America for Versailles-era France or Rome in the time of the Caesars. Decadence has grown up, grown cool, grown systematic in its excess. It's an indoor trout stream in the tasteful lakeside mansion of a software magnate. It's leasing, rather than owning, a fine German automobile so you can exchange it for a new one in ten months. You don't see the new deci-billionaires of Silicon Valley splashing their wealth around wantonly, like the '80s Wall Street crowd. What you see is specific, laser-guided generosity—like cutting friends and relatives into the IPO, or buying a tax-deductible painting by your boss' kid. Keeping the money in the family. The new design aesthetic, as seen in *Wallpaper* magazine, is sexily minimalist, with high design and hyperattention to every detail. Labor-intensive and expensive as hell, but worth it.

7   See how much we're grown up? Can you understand now why the rest of the world has its nose to the glass, wanting a piece of this?

8   Perhaps decadence isn't a thing but a behavior. Or maybe decadence goes deeper than a behavior, as deep as the emotion that hatched it. The Motion Picture Association of America fixes an R rating on films that include profanity, nudity, sex, violence or "decadent situations." So understanding decadence may simply involve renting a few saucy blockbuster action pictures and monitoring the responses they provoke. As the beloved stars appear on the screen, predictable thoughts materialize in the primitive hindbrain of the viewer: I want your hair. I want your money. I want to see you naked on the Internet.

9   Not every American lives a decadent life, of course. But decadence, as the marketers say, has great penetration. Those who aren't themselves trashing hotel rooms or being photographed in their swimming pools for *InStyle* magazine, end up thinking a lot about those who are—because the culture of celebrity (or the culture of "ornament," as Susan Faludi calls it) is the water we're all swimming in. Refracted through the glass of the tank, the contours of the world outside tend to distort.

10   A Canadian newspaper recently quoted a Toronto woman who had taken a leave from her law practice to stay home with the baby. She was grumbling that the family was now forced to get by on her husband's $37,000 salary. "I love to live in poverty," she said, sardonically. "It's my favorite thing in life." The story was supposed to be about the social trend of professional women making domestic choices. But it was really about a different social trend altogether: the hyper-inflation of the concept of "enough."

11   Decadence is self-delusion on a massive scale. Like the motto of the new gadget-packed magalog Sony Style—"things that are not essential, yet hard to live without"—it's about convincing yourself of the value of this lifestyle, because to question it would force choices we're not prepared to make.

12   "How much do I deserve?" we all ask ourselves, if only implicitly. "Not just money, but adventure, sex, fizzy water, educational opportunities, time on the beach, peace of mind—the package. How much do I deserve?"

13   A thoughtful answer might be, "I don't deserve anything. The notion that some people are just naturally more entitled than others is for Calvinists,

Monarchists and Donald Trump. It simply doesn't feel right to claim more than a modest reasonable allotment. If I've happened to stake a claim on a rich crook of the river, that's my good luck. The guy upstream has worked just as hard as I have. So I share."

14   But that view now seems downright un-American. "How much do I deserve? All I can cram in my mouth, brain, glove-box and daytimer," says the hard-charging capitalist. "I've earned it. And you haven't earned the right to tell me differently." That's why, when the Australian ethicist Peter Singer wonders, "What is our charitable burden?" it strikes so many Americans as unusual, controversial, bizarre. For a lot of folks, the calculation of an acceptable level of personal sacrifice is easy: It's zero. No other answer computes. I think that partly explains the extreme responses Singer evokes. He touches people in a place they don't like to be touched.

15   It's tempting to think of decadence as a personal act with personal consequences (namely, to the soul). If that were true, it would all come down to a matter of taste, and we could agree to live and let live with our own strange preoccupations. But decadence is really a political act. Americans aren't living large in a vacuum; they're living large at the expense of things and people: the growing underclass, the stability of the economy, the texture of mental environment, the planet itself. Every mile we log alone in the car, every sweat-shop-made sneaker we buy, every porn site we visit, every tobacco stock we day-trade in, is a brick in the wall of the new world we're creating. Not everyone got a vote in this process; yet everyone pays the price. Eventually, everyone pays an incredible price.

16   "In a new way, America's decadence has made it vulnerable," a friend offers. Today, all is well, so keep your eye on today. Ten years ago the average personal savings rate in North America was about ten percent. Now it's zero. "If the Dow tumbles, people literally will not be able to tolerate a diminishment in their lifestyle. You'll see consumer rage, deeper and deeper debt problems as consumption patterns hold constant but income falls." Because, the thing is, the desire doesn't go away. The manufacture of desire won't slow down, even if the manufacture of everything else does.

■ QUESTIONS FOR ANALYSIS AND DISCUSSION

1. According to Flood, what was America's cultural attitude toward "decadence"? How has this attitude changed, and why?
2. According to Flood, how does contemporary America compare to Versailles-era France and imperial Rome? Explain the similarities and differences between the cultures.
3. In paragraph 10, Flood gives an example of a Toronto woman lamenting her single-family income. How does this example support his point?
4. Flood concludes his article with the ominous warning that "America's decadence has made it vulnerable." A year after he wrote this article, America entered a recession. From your own perspective, discuss whether Flood's concerns carry merit.

5. Go to the Adbusters Web site at <http://www.adbusters.com>. How would you define the political stance of this magazine? What leads you to this conclusion? How is Flood's piece compatible with the political and cultural position of the magazine?

The Stuff of Life
Scott Russell Sanders

As a whole, Americans own more things than the people of any other nation on earth. They represent the most powerful purchasing population in modern culture, and yet many complain that they don't make enough money to buy the things they need and want. What drives this desire for more stuff? Will we ever have enough? In the next essay, Scott Russell Sanders examines the rising tide of consumerism in the United States. He argues that our drive to accumulate is damaging to both ourselves and to our society. But are we willing to sacrifice our desire for individual gain in favor of the public good?

Sanders is the author of many books focusing on personal relationships and connections to our social and natural world. He is the author of *Staying Put: Making a Home in a Restless World* (1994) and *Hunting for Hope: A Father's Journeys* (1999). He is the winner of the Lannan Literary Award and The Great Lakes Book Award. The next article was first published in the July/August 1998 issue of *Audubon*.

▦ BEFORE YOU READ

It seems to be an economic truth that the more we earn, the more we spend. Think back to a time when you had less money than you have now. How did your spending habits at that time differ from your purchasing habits now? Could you ever go back to living on less? Why or why not?

▦ AS YOU READ

What implications does materialism have for the ecology of our planet? Should we be concerned?

1   On our last night in Rocky Mountain National Park, after a week of backpacking, my son, Jesse, and I sat on a granite ledge overlooking a creek just below our campsite. The water crashed through a jumble of boulders, churning up an icy mist.

2   Though it was June, glacial air poured down the creek from snow fields higher up. I pulled up the hood of my jacket, stuffed hands into pockets, and hunkered down to soak in the spray. Still I trembled. I couldn't tell whether my

shivering was from the cold or from the spell of moving water. After a while, Jesse murmured, "This is a good place."

3   "It is."

4   In the waning light the trees along the banks merged into a velvety blackness, and the froth of the creek shone like the Milky Way. Waves rose from the current, fleeting shapes that would eventually dissolve—like my own body, like the mountains, like the earth and stars. I blinked at my son, who rode the same current. Our time in the mountains had left me feeling cleansed and clarified.

5   The spell of the high country began to evaporate as soon as we climbed into our rental car the next day. The ignition key, steering wheel, and sunfried upholstery chafed my skin; the thrum of pavement under the wheels and the press of traffic chafed my brain. Everything moved too fast.

6   Never one to stare at scenery through windows, my son dived into his book. At 17 and 49, both of us moody, Jesse and I had learned that keeping quiet was less wearisome than shouting at each other. We'd quarreled at the start of our trip, but the mountains had calmed us, and we had made peace. In the morning we would fly home to Indiana.

7   The truce began to evaporate as soon as we returned to the land of electricity, money, and clocks. His first act when we entered our motel room was to switch on the television; the sound was like a file scraping my nerves. "Does that have to be so loud?" I snapped.

8   "If you want it off, why don't you say so?" He jabbed the remote control, and the picture blinked out. "It's all trash anyhow."

9   I didn't argue, because I could feel tension rising between us. Now that we'd left the trail, I was once again in charge of budget and schedule, and that alone would have irked him. Back in the city, where much of what I saw struck me as wasteful, ugly, or mad, I was also prone to the ranting that so disturbed Jesse. In our quarrels he had accused me of casting a shadow over his life, because my grief over the fate of the earth filled him with despair. For his sake, I would have to find a way back through this confusion to the sanity I had felt in the mountains.

10   Whenever I return from a sojourn in the woods or waters or mountains, I'm dismayed by the noise and jumble of the workaday world. One moment I can lay everything I need on the corner of a poncho, tally my responsibilities on the fingers of one hand. The next moment, it seems, I couldn't fit all my furniture and tasks into a warehouse. Time in the wild reminds me how much of what I ordinarily do is mere dithering, how much of what I own is mere encumbrance. Coming home, I can see that there are too many appliances in my cupboards, too many clothes in my closet, too many strings of duty jerking me in too many directions. The opposite of simplicity, as I understand it, is not complexity but clutter.

11   Returning from a backcountry trip, I vow to purchase nothing that I don't really need, give away everything that is excess, refuse all chores that don't arise from central concerns. The simplicity I seek is not the enforced austerity of the poor. I seek instead the richness of a gathered and deliberate life, which comes

from letting one's belongings and commitments be few in number and high in quality.

12   As our plane banked after takeoff, we caught one last glimpse of the Front Range shining to the west. Viewed from the air, Denver seemed to be blundering outward in every direction. No doubt many who lived there felt the city was already large enough. But more people were eagerly joining the sprawl, and who was going to stop them? Like other American cities, Denver swells on a blind faith in abundance, a faith that there will always be enough water, land, metal, wood, and oil that is cheap.

13   I realized that nothing will prevent us from extending our sway over every last inch of earth—nothing except outward disaster or inward conversion. Since I couldn't root for disaster, I'd have to work for a change of heart and mind. If we hope to survive on this planet, we must learn restraint. We need to say "Enough!" with relish and conviction.

14   But how, when we seem mindlessly devoted to growth? Like birds and bees and bacteria, we yearn to propagate our kind. Nothing could be more natural. We're unusual among species only in being able to escape, for the short run, the natural constraints on our population or appetites, and in being able to magnify our hungers through the lens of technology.

15   It seems that our evolutionary history has shaped us to equate well-being with increase, to yearn not merely for more offspring but also more of everything: shoes, meat, horsepower, loot. In a hunting and gathering society, the fruits of an individual's search for more food, better tools, and richer land were shared with the tribe. The more relentless the search, the more likely the tribe would flourish.

16   How much any group can accumulate or use is limited, of course, by its level of technology. Hunters on foot armed with stone-tipped weapons can wipe out woolly mammoths and giant beavers; they can open up grasslands by burning or alter the mix of plants in their home territory, but they can't turn a mountain inside out in search of glittering metal or erase a forest or poison the sea. The harnessing of mechanical power dramatically increased our ability to make the world over; the rise of towns enabled us to pile up wealth. I suspect that we're no more greedy than our ancestors, just far more potent in pursuing our desires.

17   The constant hankering for more has become a menace. Our devotion to growth exhausts resources, accelerates pollution, and drives other species to extinction; it upsets community by swelling the scale of institutions and settlements, and it harms the individual by encouraging a scramble for possessions and nagging discontent in the midst of plenty.

18   What are we poor ravenous creatures to do? We may keep riding the exponential curves higher on every graph—widgets produced, hamburgers sold, acres paved—until nature jerks us back toward the zero point. Or we may choose to live more sustainably. Biology, I'm afraid, is on the side of gluttony and compulsive growth. Restraint will have to come from culture, that shared conversation by which we govern our appetites.

19   Animal rights activists protest, but elephants are being culled in a southern African park. Rangers insist that the elephants have multiplied beyond the land's capacity; they're uprooting trees, trampling vegetation, exposing soil to erosion. In the absence of predators, beavers also can devastate a woods, and deer can graze fragile plants beyond the point of recovery. These animals possess no inborn curb to prevent them from destroying their own habitat. Their growth is checked only by the water or food supply, predators, or disease.

20   Anthropologists now believe that early humans behaved much like these animals, degrading one habitat after another, then moving on. North America is dotted with sites of ancient social experiments that failed, from the Maya to the mound-builders. Even now some indigenous peoples in the rainforests of Asia and South America pursue slash-and-burn agriculture at a pace the forests cannot sustain. Such evidence suggests that the ecological wisdom surviving today had to be learned over long periods of time, through trial and error. Only gradually did humans develop cultural practices—stories, taboos, birth control methods, hunting rituals, rules about the use of common land—that curbed our instinct to follow hunger wherever it leads.

21   The capacity for restraint based on knowledge and compassion is a genuine, though embattled, source of hope. Whenever the Environmental Protection Agency proposes higher standards for emissions from smokestacks and cars, for example, critics attack the standards as too expensive, claiming that the richest country in the world can't afford to pay the real price of energy, nor cut back on the use of electricity and gasoline in exchange for breathable air. For every voice that echoes Thoreau's famous plea, "Simplify, simplify," a dozen cry, "Amplify, amplify!"

22   The present scale of human destructiveness is unprecedented, but the impulse to eat whatever's in reach is entirely natural. What is unnatural, what comes only from culture, is reflection and regard for other life forms. We're the only species capable of acting, through love and reason, to preserve our fellow creatures.

23   If our addiction to growth is rooted in evolutionary history, we can't just decide to feel good about living with less. We can, however, shift the focus of our expansive desires. We can change the standard by which we measure prosperity. We can choose to lead a materially simpler life not as a sacrifice but as a path toward fulfillment. In ancient terms, we can learn to seek spiritual rather than material growth.

24   Meditation, pilgrimage, and other forms of religious inquiry are only part of what I mean by spiritual. I also mean the nourishment that comes through art, literature, and science, through conversation, through skillful, useful work, through sharing bread and stories, through encounters with beauty and wildness. I mean slowing down and focusing on the present moment, with its inexhaustible depths, rather than dashing through life toward some ever-retreating goal.

25   If we imagine that the fullness we yearn for can be reckoned in dollars or yen or purchased in stores, there will be no end to our craving. Every time we

browse store aisles without needing a thing, or switch on the television to banish silence, or pump ourselves full of chemicals in search of a jolt, we are hunting for a freshness that we're far more likely to find in the place from which we set out, had we but eyes to see.

26   We could cut back dramatically on our food and fuel consumption, wood and metal use, and size of houses and wardrobes without suffering any deprivation. We could free this surplus for others to use, and free ourselves from the burden of lugging it around. As we increase the likelihood of strife by scrambling for more wealth, so we may increase the likelihood of peace by living modestly and sharing what we have. Thus our needs and the needs of the planet coincide.

27   Less burdened by possessions, less frenzied by activities, we might play more with our children, look after our elders, plant flowers, read books, make music, come to know the local birds and trees. We might take better care of the land. We might lie down at night and rise up in the morning without feeling the cramp of anxiety. Instead of leaping around like grasshoppers from notion to notion, we might sit still and think in a connected way about our families, our communities, and the meaning of life.

28   For days after returning home, I felt oppressed by the glut of things. My desk was mounded with mail. Lights blinked on the answering machine, messages lurked in the computer. Meanwhile, the kitchen faucet had sprung a leak, the car's engine was tapping ominously, and our wildflower patch had all but disappeared under a surf of weeds.

29   "You don't have to do everything your first day home," my wife, Ruth, pointed out. Though I knew better, I kept imagining that if I could first answer every request, fix every broken thing, *then* I would simplify my life. But trying to catch up once and for all is like digging a hole in sand. Unable to make any headway, missing the mountains and the company of my son, I began to slide down the slope toward gloom.

30   Familiar with my moods, Ruth kept an eye on me to make sure I didn't slide too far—or throw out any crucial mail, junk the car, or put up a FOR SALE sign in the front yard.

31   One evening that first week home, friends called to invite us out to their farm for a look at the stars. Ruth covered the mouthpiece and said she thought it would be a shame to squander this clear night.

32   "I've got too much work to do," I told her, pausing on my way upstairs with an armload of papers. Ruth looked at me hard, then said into the phone, "We'll be there in half an hour."

33   On our drive into the country, whenever I began to speak about fixing the car or balancing the checkbook, Ruth asked me about my time in the Rockies. So I told her of snowshoeing with Jesse up into avalanche country; of meeting hummingbird, coyote, and elk; of watching sunlight pour through lodgepole pines. By the time we rolled down John and Beth's gravel drive, the memories had steadied me. We could see our friends walking to meet us, their silhouettes tall and thin against a background of stars.

34   I climbed out of the car with a greeting on my lips, but the sky hushed me. From the black bowl of space countless fiery lights shone down, each one a sun or swirl of suns, the whole brilliant host of them enough to strike me dumb. The Milky Way arced overhead, reminding me of froth glimmering on the dark surface of a mountain creek. I know the names of a dozen constellations, but I wasn't thinking in words right then. I was too busy feeling brimful of joy, without need of any props except the universe. The deep night drew my scattered pieces back to the center, stripped away clutter and weight, and set me free.

■ QUESTIONS FOR ANALYSIS AND DISCUSSION

1. What is the author's attitude toward consumerism? What bothers him about it, and why? How do you think he would respond to James Twitchell's argument at the beginning of this section?
2. In what ways is our current "quest for stuff" connected to the earliest roots of civilization? Explain.
3. Sanders states that "[consumer] restraint will have to come from culture." In your opinion, how likely is American culture to embrace such an ideology of restraint? Explain.
4. How, according to Sanders, would our lives improve by simplifying and rejecting the current trend of consumerism? Do you agree with his position?
5. Evaluate Sanders' argument. How well does he defend his position? Is his logic convincing? How effective is his use of supporting evidence? Explain.

The $100 Christmas

Bill McKibben

For many of us, the December holidays are a time of gift lists and flurried shopping. Christmas sales begin the day after Thanksgiving and stores stay open until midnight on Christmas Eve, hoping to get the last dollar out of holiday shoppers. Many department stores generate almost one-third of their annual revenue during the holiday season. But is the spirit of giving getting out of hand? Has it been corrupted by advertisers weaving the "powerful dark magic" of greed? In the next essay, Bill McKibben describes how his church promoted the radical idea that people spend only $100 on gifts *per family* during the holidays. And he proposes that other churches, mosques, and synagogues consider making the same recommendation.

McKibben is a former staff writer for *The New Yorker* and the author of numerous books, including *The End of Nature* and *Long Distance: A Year of Living Strenuously* (2000). He wrote the following article for the November/December 1997 issue of *Mother Jones* magazine. The article later spawned a longer version of his Christmas experience, with the book *Hundred Dollar Holiday: A Case for a Joyful Christmas*.

■ BEFORE YOU READ

How do you approach the holiday season? Do you anticipate it with excitement? stress? depression? Do you plan, decorate, and shop? Are your memories warm, lonely, comforting, happy? Explain.

■ AS YOU READ

How is McKibben's proposal both conservative and radical at the same time?

1   I know what I'll be doing on Christmas Eve. My wife, my 4-year-old daughter, my dad, my brother, and I will snowshoe out into the woods in late afternoon, ready to choose a hemlock or a balsam fir and saw it down—I've had my eye on three or four likely candidates all year. We'll bring it home, shake off the snow, decorate it, and then head for church, where the Sunday school class I help teach will gamely perform this year's pageant. (Last year, along with the usual shepherds and wise people, it featured a lost star talking on a cell phone.) And then it's home to hang stockings, stoke the fire, and off to bed. As traditional as it gets, except that there's no sprawling pile of presents under the tree.

2   Several years ago, a few of us in the northern New York and Vermont conference of the United Methodist Church started a campaign for what we called "Hundred Dollar Holidays." The church leadership voted to urge parishioners not to spend more than $100 per family on presents, to rely instead on simple homemade gifts and on presents of services—a back rub, stacking a cord of firewood. That first year I made walking sticks for everyone. Last year I made spicy chicken sausage. My mother has embraced the idea by making calendars illustrated with snapshots she's taken.

3   The $100 figure was a useful anchor against the constant seductions of the advertisers, a way to explain to children why they weren't getting everything on their list. So far, our daughter, Sophie, does fine at Christmas. Her stocking is exciting to her, the tree is exciting; skating on the pond is exciting. It's worth mentioning, however, that we don't have a television, so she may not understand the degree of her impoverishment. This holiday idea may sound modest. It is modest. And yet at the same time it's pretty radical. Christmas, it turns out, is a bulwark of the nation's economy. Many businesses—bookstores, for instance, where I make my living—do one-third of their volume in the months just before December 25th. And so it hits a nerve to question whether it all makes sense, whether we should celebrate the birth of a man who said we should give all that we have to the poor by showering each other with motorized tie racks.

4   It's radical for another reason, too. If you believe that our consumer addiction represents our deepest problem—the force that keeps us from reaching out to others, from building a fair society, the force that drives so much of our environmental degradation—then Christmas is the nadir. Sure, advertising works its powerful dark magic year-round. But on Christmas morning, with everyone pil-

ing downstairs to mounds of presents, consumption is made literally sacred. Here, under a tree with roots going far back into prehistory, here next to a crèche with a figure of the infant child of God, we press stuff on each other, stuff that becomes powerfully connected in our heads to love, to family, and even to salvation. The 12 days of Christmas—and in many homes the eight nights of Hanukkah—are a cram course in consumption, a kind of brainwashing.

5   When we began the $100 campaign, merchants, who wrote letters to the local papers, made it clear to us what a threatening idea it was. Newspaper columnists thought it was pretty extreme, too—one said church people should stick to religion and leave the economy alone. Another said that while our message had merit, it would do too much damage to business.

6   And he was right, or at least not wrong. If we all backed out of Christmas excess this year, we would sink many a gift shop; if we threw less lavish office parties, caterers would suffer—and florists and liquor wholesalers and on down the feeding chain. But we have to start somewhere, if we're ever to climb down from the unsustainable heights we've reached, and Christmas might as well be it.

7   When we first began to spread this idea about celebrating Christmas in a new way, we were earnest and sober. Big-time Christmas was an environmental disgrace—all that wrapping paper, all those batteries. The money could be so much better spent: The price of one silk necktie could feed a village for a day; the cost of a big-screen television could vaccinate more than 60 kids. And struggling to create a proper Christmas drives poor families into debt. Where I live, which is a poor and cold place, January finds many people cutting back on heat to pay off their bills. Those were all good reasons to scale back. But as we continued our campaign, we found we weren't really interested in changing Christmas because we wanted fewer batteries. We wanted more joy. We felt cheated by the Christmases we were having—so rushed, so busy, so full of mercantile fantasy and catalog hype that we couldn't relax and enjoy the season.

8   Our growing need to emphasize joy over guilt says a great deal about the chances for Christian radicalism, for religious radicalism in general. At its truest, religion represents the one force in our society that can postulate some goal other than accumulation. In an I-dolatrous culture, religion can play a subversive role. Churches, mosques, and synagogues almost alone among our official institutions can say, It's not the economy, stupid. It's your life. It's learning that there's some other center to the universe.

9   Having that other center can change the way we see the world around us. It's why devoted clergy and laypeople occasionally work small miracles in inner cities and prisons; it's why alcoholics talk about a Higher Power. If we're too big, then perhaps the solution lies in somehow making ourselves a little smaller.

10   You may be too late for this Christmas. You may already have bought your pile of stuff, or perhaps it's too late to broach the subject with relatives who will gather with you for the holidays, bearing (and therefore expecting) great stacks of loot. Our local Methodist ministers begin in September, preaching a skit sermon about the coming holiday. Many in our church community now participate. So do some of our neighbors and friends around the country. None of us

are under any illusions; we know that turning the focus of Christmas back to Christ is a long and patient effort, one that works against every force that consumer culture can muster. But to judge from our own holidays in recent years, it's well worth the effort. I know what we'll be doing Christmas morning: After we open our stockings and exchange our few homemade gifts, we'll go out for a hike. Following the advice of St. Francis of Assisi, who said that even the birds deserve to celebrate this happy day, we'll spread seed hither and yon—and for one morning the chickadees and the jays will have it easy. And then we'll head back inside to the warm and fragrant kitchen and start basting the turkey, shaping the rolls, mashing the potatoes.

■ QUESTIONS FOR ANALYSIS AND DISCUSSION

1. Is a $100 holiday possible in your family? realistic? good in principle but impossible in practice? Is it fair? Explain.
2. McKibben defines the current materialistic traditions of Christmas and Hanukkah as the result of advertisers who have exploited the spirit of these holidays and brainwashed consumers. "The 12 days of Christmas—and in many homes the eight nights of Hanukkah—are a cram course in consumption. [. . .]" Do you agree? Why or why not?
3. McKibben states that his daughter, Sophie, is happy with her modest gifts because she finds the entire holiday experience exciting. He comments, however, that "it's worth mentioning, however, that we don't have a television, so she may not understand the degree of her impoverishment." What connection is McKibben making between television and our desire for things? Does he have a point?
4. How did merchants react to the proposal of a $100 holiday? Why is one columnist's comment that "church people should stick to religion and leave the economy alone" ironic? Explain.

■ WRITING ASSIGNMENTS

1. In his article "The Stuff of Life," Scott Russell Sanders comments that the roots of materialism are deeply connected to the beginnings of civilization. If materialism is an important element of civilization, why do so many critics of consumerism imply that our desire for things is bad for our culture and our society?
2. With a group of classmates, make a list of at least 15 to 20 appliances and equipment that people have in their homes—refrigerators, microwave ovens, DVD players, computers, VCRs, televisions, stereos (include components), etc. Individually, rank each item as a necessity, a desirable object, or a luxury item. For example, you may decide a refrigerator is a necessary item, but that an air conditioner is a luxury item. Compare your list with others in your

group. How do the lists compare? What accounts for the discrepancies? Write an essay detailing your discussion and conclusions.

3. Access the Web sites for several similar soft or sports drinks, such as <http://www.pepsi.com>, <http://www.coke.com>, <http://www.gatorade.com>, and <http://www.powerade.com>. How do the Web sites promote their products? Who is the target audience, and how do their sites reflect this audience? What techniques do they use to sell? Write an essay evaluating how these drinks sell their products. Address the fact that the products are essentially the same. How do they convince consumers to part with their money?

4. Adbusters addresses the unethical ways advertisers manipulate consumers to "need" products. However, if we study ads long enough, we can determine for ourselves the ways we may be manipulated. Select several printed or television advertisements and analyze how they manipulate consumers to increase their "quest for stuff." Is there anything wrong with this manipulation? Why or why not?

THE LANGUAGE OF ADVERTISING

With These Words, I Can Sell You Anything

William Lutz

William Lutz has been called the "George Orwell of the 1990's." He teaches English at Rutgers University and is the author of several books, including *Beyond Nineteen Eighty-Four* (1984) and *Doublespeak Defined* (1999). The following article is an excerpt from Lutz's book *Doublespeak* (1990).

■ BEFORE YOU READ

Consider the phrase "like magic" as it might be used in an ad—for example, "Zappo dish detergent works like magic." What does the phrase suggest at a quick glance? What does it mean upon detailed analysis? Make a list of other such words used in advertising to make "big promises."

■ AS YOU READ

A "weasel word" is a word so hollow it has no meaning. As you read Lutz's article, consider your own reaction to such words when you hear them. Have they ever motivated you to make a purchase?

1   One problem advertisers have when they try to convince you that the product they are pushing is really different from other, similar products is that their claims are subject to some laws. Not a lot of laws, but there are some designed to prevent fraudulent or untruthful claims in advertising. Even during the

happy years of nonregulation under President Ronald Reagan, the FTC did crack down on the more blatant abuses in advertising claims. Generally speaking, advertisers have to be careful in what they say in their ads, in the claims they make for the products they advertise. Parity claims are safe because they are legal and supported by a number of court decisions. But beyond parity claims there are weasel words.

2   Advertisers use weasel words to appear to be making a claim for a product when in fact they are making no claim at all. Weasel words get their name from the way weasels eat the eggs they find in the nests of other animals. A weasel will make a small hole in the egg, suck out the insides, then place the egg back in the nest. Only when the egg is examined closely is it found to be hollow. That's the way it is with weasel words in advertising: Examine weasel words closely and you'll find that they're as hollow as any egg sucked by a weasel. Weasel words appear to say one thing when in fact they say the opposite, or nothing at all.

"Help"—The Number One Weasel Word

3 The biggest weasel word used in advertising doublespeak is "help." Now "help" only means to aid or assist, nothing more. It does not mean to conquer, stop, eliminate, solve, heal, cure, or anything else. But once the ad says "help," it can say just about anything after that because "help" qualifies everything coming after it. The trick is that the claim that comes after the weasel word is usually so strong and so dramatic that you forget the word "help" and concentrate only on the dramatic claim. You read into the ad a message that the ad does not contain. More importantly, the advertiser is not responsible for the claim that you read into the ad, even though the advertiser wrote the ad so you would read that claim into it.

4   The next time you see an ad for a cold medicine that promises that it "helps relieve cold symptoms fast," don't rush out to buy it. Ask yourself what this claim is really saying. Remember, "helps" means only that the medicine will aid or assist. What will it aid or assist in doing? Why, "relieve" your cold "symptoms." "Relieve" only means to ease, alleviate, or mitigate, not to stop, end, or cure. Nor does the claim say how much relieving this medicine will do. Nowhere does this ad claim it *will cure anything.* In fact, the ad doesn't even claim it will *do* anything at all. The *ad only claims* that it will aid in relieving (not curing) your cold symptoms, which are probably a runny nose, watery eyes, and a headache. In other words, this medicine probably contains a standard decongestant and some aspirin. By the way, what does "fast" mean? Ten minutes, one hour, one day? What is fast to one person can be very slow to another. Fast is another weasel word. *[SUBJECTIVE]*

5   Ad claims using "help" are among the most popular ads. One says, "Helps keep you young looking," but then a lot of things will help keep you young looking, including exercise, rest, good nutrition, and a facelift. More importantly, this ad doesn't say the product will keep you young, only "young *looking.*" Someone may look young to one person and old to another.

6   A toothpaste ad says, "Helps prevent cavities," but it doesn't say it will actually prevent cavities. Brushing your teeth regularly, avoiding sugars in foods,

and flossing daily will also help prevent cavities. A liquid cleaner ad says, "Helps keep your home germ free," but it doesn't say it actually kills germs, nor does it even specify which germs it might kill.

7   "Help" is such a useful weasel word that it is often combined with other action-verb weasel words such as "fight" and "control." Consider the claim, "Helps control dandruff symptoms with regular use." What does it really say? It will assist in controlling (not eliminating, stopping, ending, or curing) the *symptoms* of dandruff, not the cause of dandruff nor the dandruff itself. What are the symptoms of dandruff? The ad deliberately leaves that undefined, but assume that the symptoms referred to in the ad are the flaking and itching commonly associated with dandruff. But just shampooing with *any* shampoo will temporarily eliminate these symptoms, so this shampoo isn't any different from any other. Finally, in order to benefit from this product, you must use it regularly. What is "regular use"—daily, weekly, hourly? Using another shampoo "regularly" will have the same effect. Nowhere does this advertising claim say this particular shampoo stops, eliminates, or cures dandruff. In fact, this claim says nothing at all, thanks to all the weasel words.

8   Look at ads in magazines and newspapers, listen to ads on radio and television, and you'll find the word "help" in ads for all kinds of products. How often do you read or hear such phrases as "helps stop . . . ," "helps overcome . . . ," "helps eliminate . . . ," "helps you feel . . . ," or "helps you look . . ."? If you start looking for this weasel word in advertising, you'll be amazed at how often it occurs. Analyze the claims in the ads using "help," and you will discover that these ads are really saying nothing.

9   There are plenty of other weasel words used in advertising. In fact, there are so many that to list them all would fill the rest of this book. But, in order to identify the doublespeak of advertising and understand the real meaning of an ad, you have to be aware of the most popular weasel words in advertising today.

Virtually Spotless

10   One of the most powerful weasel words is "virtually," a word so innocent that most people don't pay any attention to it when it is used in an advertising claim. But watch out. "Virtually" is used in advertising claims that appear to make specific, definite promises when there is no promise. After all, what does "virtually" mean? It means "in essence of effect, although not in fact." Look at that definition again. "Virtually" means *not in fact*. It does *not* mean "almost" or "just about the same as," or anything else. And before you dismiss all this concern over such a small word, remember that small words can have big consequences.

11   In 1971 a federal court rendered its decision on a case brought by a woman who became pregnant while taking birth control pills. She sued the manufacturer, Eli Lilly and Company, for breach of warranty. The woman lost her case. Basing its ruling on a statement in the pamphlet accompanying the pills, which stated that, "When taken as directed, the tablets offer virtually 100 percent protection," the court ruled that there was no warranty, expressed or implied, that the pills were absolutely effective. In its ruling, the court pointed out that, ac-

cording to *Webster's Third New International Dictionary,* "virtually" means "almost entirely" and clearly does not mean "absolute" (*Whittington* v. *Eli Lilly and Company,* 333 F. Supp. 98). In other words, the Eli Lilly company was really saying that its birth control pill, even when taken as directed, *did not in fact* provide 100 percent protection against pregnancy. But Eli Lilly didn't want to put it that way because then many women might not have bought Lilly's birth control pills.

12   The next time you see the ad that says that this dishwasher detergent "leaves dishes virtually spotless," just remember how advertisers twist the meaning of the weasel word "virtually." You can have lots of spots on your dishes after using this detergent and the ad claim will still be true, because what this claim really means is that this detergent does not *in fact* leave your dishes spotless. Whenever you see or hear an ad claim that uses the word "virtually," just translate that claim into its real meaning. So the television set that is "virtually trouble free" becomes the television set that is not in fact trouble free, the "virtually foolproof operation" of any appliance becomes an operation that is in fact not foolproof, and the product that "virtually never needs service" becomes the product that is not in fact service free.

New and Improved

13 If "new" is the most frequently used word on a product package, "improved" is the second most frequent. In fact, the two words are almost always used together. It seems just about everything sold these days is "new and improved." The next time you're in the supermarket, try counting the number of times you see these words on products. But you'd better do it while you're walking down just one aisle, otherwise you'll need a calculator to keep track of your counting.

14   Just what do these words mean? The use of the word "new" is restricted by regulations, so an advertiser can't just use the word on a product or in an ad without meeting certain requirements. For example, a product is considered new for about six months during a national advertising campaign. If the product is being advertised only in a limited test market area, the word can be used longer, and in some instances has been used for as long as two years.

15   What makes a product "new"? Some products have been around for a long time, yet every once in a while you discover that they are being advertised as "new." Well, an advertiser can call a product new if there has been "a material functional change" in the product. What is "a material functional change," you ask? Good question. In fact it's such a good question it's being asked all the time. It's up to the manufacturer to prove that the product has undergone such a change. And if the manufacturer isn't challenged on the claim, then there's no one to stop it. Moreover, the change does not have to be an improvement in the product. One manufacturer added an artificial lemon scent to a cleaning product and called it "new and improved," even though the product did not clean any better than without the lemon scent. The manufacturer defended the use of the word "new" on the grounds that the artificial scent changed the chemical formula of the product and therefore constituted "a material functional change."

16   Which brings up the word "improved." When used in advertising, "improved" does not mean "made better." It only means "changed" or "different from before." So, if the detergent maker puts a plastic pour spout on the box of detergent, the product has been "improved," and away we go with a whole new advertising campaign. Or, if the cereal maker adds more fruit or a different kind of fruit to the cereal, there's an improved product. Now you know why manufacturers are constantly making little changes in their products. Whole new advertising campaigns, designed to convince you that the product has been changed for the better, are based on small changes in superficial aspects of a product. The next time you see an ad for an "improved" product, ask yourself what was wrong with the old one. Ask yourself just how "improved" the product is. Finally, you might check to see whether the "improved" version costs more than the unimproved one. After all, someone has to pay for the millions of dollars spent advertising the improved product.

17   Of course, advertisers really like to run ads that claim a product is "new and improved." While what constitutes a "new" product may be subject to some regulation, "improved" is a subjective judgment. A manufacturer changes the shape of its stick deodorant, but the shape doesn't improve the function of the deodorant. That is, changing the shape doesn't affect the deodorizing ability of the deodorant, so the manufacturer calls it "improved." Another manufacturer adds ammonia to its liquid cleaner and calls it "new and improved." Since adding ammonia does affect the cleaning ability of the product, there has been a "material functional change" in the product, and the manufacturer can now call its cleaner "new," and "improved" as well. Now the weasel words, "new and improved" are plastered all over the package and are the basis for a multimillion-dollar ad campaign. But after six months the word "new" will have to go, until someone can dream up another change in the product. Perhaps it will be adding color to the liquid, or changing the shape of the package, or maybe adding a new dripless pour spout, or perhaps a _____. The "improvements" are endless, and so are the new advertising claims and campaigns.

18   "New" is just too useful and powerful a word in advertising for advertisers to pass it up easily. So they use weasel words that say "new" without really saying it. One of their favorites is "introducing," as in, "Introducing improved Tide," or "Introducing the satin remover." The first is simply saying, here's our improved soap; the second, here's our new advertising campaign for our detergent. Another favorite is "now," as in "Now there's Sinex," which simply means that Sinex is available. Then there are phrases like "Today's Chevrolet," "Presenting Dristan," and "A fresh way to start the day." The list is really endless because advertisers are always finding new ways to say "new" without really saying it. If there is a second edition of this book, I'll just call it the "new and improved" edition. Wouldn't you really rather have a "new and improved" edition of this book rather than a "second" edition?

Acts Fast

19   "Acts" and "works" are two popular weasel words in advertising because they bring action to the product and to the advertising claim. When you see the ad

for the cough syrup that "Acts on the cough control center," ask yourself what this cough syrup is claiming to do. Well, it's just claiming to "act," to do something, to perform an action. What is it that the cough syrup does? The ad doesn't say. It only claims to perform an action or do something on your "cough control center." By the way, what and where is our "cough control center"? I don't remember learning about that part of the body in human biology class.

20   Ads that use such phrases as "acts fast," "acts against," "acts to prevent," and the like are saying essentially nothing, because "act" is a word empty of any specific meaning. The ads are always careful not to specify exactly what "act" the product performs. Just because a brand of aspirin claims to "act fast" for headache relief doesn't mean this aspirin is any better than any other aspirin. What is the "act" that this aspirin performs? You're never told. Maybe it just dissolves quickly. Since aspirin is a parity product, all aspirin is the same and therefore functions the same.

Works Like Anything Else

21   If you don't find the word "acts" in an ad, you will probably find the weasel word "works." In fact, the two words are almost interchangeable in advertising. Watch out for ads that say a product "works against," "works like," "works for," or "works longer." As with "acts," "works" is the same meaningless verb used to make you think that this product really does something, and maybe even something special or unique. But "works," like "acts," is basically a word empty of any specific meaning.

Like Magic

22   Whenever advertisers want you to stop thinking about the product and to start thinking about something bigger, better, or more attractive than the product, they use that very popular weasel word, "like." The word "like" is the advertiser's equivalent of a magician's use of misdirection. "Like" gets you to ignore the product and concentrate on the claim the advertiser is making about it. "For skin like peaches and cream" claims the ad for a skin cream. What is this ad really claiming? It doesn't say this cream will give you peaches-and-cream skin. There is no verb in this claim, so it doesn't even mention using the product. How is skin ever like "peaches and cream"? Remember, ads must be read literally and exactly, according to the dictionary definition of words. (Remember "virtually" in the Eli Lilly case.) The ad is making absolutely no promise or claim whatsoever for this skin cream. If you think this cream will give you soft, smooth, youthful-looking skin, you are the one who has read that meaning into the ad.

23   The wine that claims "It's like taking a trip to France" wants you to think about a romantic evening in Paris as you walk along the boulevard after a wonderful meal in an intimate little bistro. Of course, you don't really believe that a wine can take you to France, but the goal of the ad is to get you to think pleasant, romantic thoughts about France and not about how the wine tastes or how expensive it may be. That little word "like" has taken you away from crushed grapes into a world of your own imaginative making. Who knows, maybe the

next time you buy wine, you'll think those pleasant thoughts when you see this brand of wine, and you'll buy it. Or, maybe you weren't even thinking about buying wine at all, but now you just might pick up a bottle the next time you're shopping. Ah, the power of "like" in advertising.

24   How about the most famous "like" claim of all, "Winston tastes good like a cigarette should"? Ignoring the grammatical error here, you might want to know what this claim is saying. Whether a cigarette tastes good or bad is a subjective judgment because what tastes good to one person may well taste horrible to another. Not everyone likes fried snails, even if they are called escargot. (*De gustibus non est disputandum,* which was probably the Roman rule for advertising as well as for defending the games in the Colosseum.) There are many people who say all cigarettes taste terrible, other people who say only some cigarettes taste all right, and still others who say all cigarettes taste good. Who's right? Everyone, because taste is a matter of personal judgment.

25   Moreover, note the use of the conditional, "should." The complete claim is, "Winston tastes good like a cigarette should taste." But should cigarettes taste good? Again, this is a matter of personal judgment and probably depends mostly on one's experiences with smoking. So, the Winston ad is simply saying that Winston cigarettes are just like any other cigarette: Some people like them and some people don't. On that statement, R. J. Reynolds conducted a very successful multimillion-dollar advertising campaign that helped keep Winston the number-two-selling cigarette in the United States, close behind number one, Marlboro.

Can't It Be Up to the Claim?

26 Analyzing ads for doublespeak requires that you pay attention to every word in the ad and determine what each word really means. Advertisers try to wrap their claims in language that sounds concrete, specific, and objective, when in fact the language of advertising is anything but. Your job is to read carefully and listen critically so that when the announcer says that "Crest can be of significant value . . . ," you know immediately that this claim says absolutely nothing. Where is the doublespeak in this ad? Start with the second word.

27   Once again, you have to look at what words really mean, not what you think they mean or what the advertiser wants you to think they mean. The ad for Crest only says that using Crest "can be" of "significant value." What really throws you off in this ad is the brilliant use of "significant." It draws your attention to the word "value" and makes you forget that the ad only claims that Crest "can be." The ad doesn't say that Crest *is* of value, only that it is "able" or "possible" to be of value, because that's all that "can" means.

28   It's so easy to miss the importance of those little words, "can be." Almost as easy as missing the importance of the words "up to" in an ad. These words are very popular in sales ads. You know, the ones that say, "Up to 50 percent Off!" Now, what does that claim mean? Not much, because the store or manufacturer has to reduce the price of only a few items by 50 percent. Everything else can be reduced a lot less, or not even reduced. Moreover, don't you want to know

50 percent off of what? Is it 50 percent off the "manufacturer's suggested list price," which is the highest possible price? Was the price artificially inflated and then reduced? In other ads, "up to" expresses an ideal situation. The medicine that works "up to ten times faster," the battery that lasts "up to twice as long," and the soap that gets you "up to twice as clean" all are based on ideal situations for using these products, situations in which you can be sure you will never find yourself.

Unfinished Words

29   Unfinished words are a kind of "up to" claim in advertising. The claim that a battery lasts "up to twice as long" usually doesn't finish the comparison—twice as long as what? A birthday candle? A tank of gas? A cheap battery made in a country not noted for its technological achievements? The implication is that the battery lasts twice as long as batteries made by other battery makers, or twice as long as earlier model batteries made by the advertiser, but the ad doesn't really make these claims. You read these claims into the ad, aided by the visual images the advertiser so carefully provides.

30   Unfinished words depend on you to finish them, to provide the words the advertisers so thoughtfully left out of the ad. Pall Mall cigarettes were once advertised as "A longer, finer and milder smoke." The question is, longer, finer, and milder than what? The aspirin that claims it contains "Twice as much of the pain reliever doctors recommend most" doesn't tell you what pain reliever it contains twice as much of. (By the way, it's aspirin. That's right; it just contains twice the amount of aspirin. And how much is twice the amount? Twice of what amount?) Panadol boasts that "nobody reduces fever faster," but, since Panadol is a parity product, this claim simply means that Panadol isn't any better than any other product in its parity class. "You can be sure if it's Westinghouse," you're told, but just exactly what it is you can be sure of is never mentioned. "Magnavox gives you more" doesn't tell you what you get more of. More value? More television? More than they gave you before? It sounds nice, but it means nothing, until you fill in the claim with your own words, the words the advertisers didn't use. Since each of us fills in the claim differently, the ad and the product can become all things to all people, and not promise a single thing.

31   Unfinished words abound in advertising because they appear to promise so much. More importantly, they can be joined with powerful visual images on television to appear to be making significant promises about a product's effectiveness without really making any promises. In a television ad, the aspirin product that claims fast relief can show a person with a headache taking the product and then, in what appears to be a matter of minutes, claiming complete relief. This visual image is far more powerful than any claim made in unfinished words. Indeed, the visual image completes the unfinished words for you, filling in with pictures what the words leave out. And you thought that ads didn't affect you. What brand of aspirin do you use?

32   Some years ago, Ford's advertisements proclaimed "Ford LTD—700 percent quieter." Now, what do you think Ford was claiming with these unfinished

words? What was the Ford LTD quieter than? A Cadillac? A Mercedes Benz? A BMW? Well, when the FTC asked Ford to substantiate this unfinished claim, Ford replied that it meant that the inside of the LTD was 700 percent quieter than the outside. How did you finish those unfinished words when you first read them? Did you even come close to Ford's meaning?

Combining Weasel Words

33   A lot of ads don't fall neatly into one category or another because they use a variety of different devices and words. Different weasel words are often combined to make an ad claim. The claim, "Coffee-Mate gives coffee more body, more flavor," uses Unfinished Words ("more" than what?) and also uses words that have no specific meaning ("body" and "flavor"). Along with "taste" (remember the Winston ad and its claim to taste good), "body" and "flavor" mean nothing because their meaning is entirely subjective. To you, "body" in coffee might mean thick, black, almost bitter coffee, while I might take it to mean a light brown, delicate coffee. Now, if you think you understood that last sentence, read it again, because it said nothing of objective value; it was filled with weasel words of no specific meaning: "thick," "black," "bitter," "light brown," and "delicate." Each of those words has no specific, objective meaning, because each of us can interpret them differently.

34   Try this slogan: "Looks, smells, tastes like ground-roast coffee." So, are you now going to buy Taster's Choice instant coffee because of this ad? "Looks," "smells," and "tastes" are all words with no specific meaning and depend on your interpretation of them for any meaning. Then there's that great weasel word "like," which simply suggests a comparison but does not make the actual connection between the product and the quality. Besides, do you know what "ground-roast" coffee is? I don't, but it sure sounds good. So, out of seven words in this ad, four are definite weasel words, two are quite meaningless, and only one has any clear meaning.

35   Remember the Anacin ad—"Twice as much of the pain reliever doctors recommend most"? There's a whole lot of weaseling going on in this ad. First, what's the pain reliever they're talking about in this ad? Aspirin, of course. In fact, any time you see or hear an ad using those words "pain reliever," you can automatically substitute the word "aspirin" for them. (Makers of acetaminophen and ibuprofen pain relievers are careful in their advertising to identify their products as nonaspirin products.) So, now we know that Anacin has aspirin in it. Moreover, we know that Anacin has twice as much aspirin in it, but we don't know twice as much as what. Does it have twice as much aspirin as an ordinary aspirin tablet? If so, what is an ordinary aspirin tablet, and how much aspirin does it contain? Twice as much as Excedrin or Bufferin? Twice as much as a chocolate chip cookie? Remember those Unfinished Words and how they lead you on without saying anything.

36   Finally, what about those doctors who are doing all that recommending? Who are they? How many of them are there? What kind of doctors are they? What are their qualifications? Who asked them about recommending pain re-

lievers? What other pain relievers did they recommend? And there are a whole lot more questions about this "poll" of doctors to which I'd like to know the answers, but you get the point. Sometimes, when I call my doctor, she tells me to take two aspirin and call her office in the morning. Is that where Anacin got this ad?

Read the Label, or the Brochure

37   Weasel words aren't just found on television, on the radio, or in newspaper and magazine ads. Just about any language associated with a product will contain the doublespeak of advertising. Remember the Eli Lilly case and the double-speak on the information sheet that came with the birth control pills. Here's another example.

38   In 1983, the Estée Lauder cosmetics company announced a new product called "Night Repair." A small brochure distributed with the product stated that "Night Repair was scientifically formulated in Estée Lauder's U.S. laboratories as part of the Swiss Age-Controlling Skincare Program. Although only nature controls the aging process, this program helps control the signs of aging and encourages skin to look and feel younger." You might want to read these two sentences again, because they sound great but say nothing.

39   First, note that the product was "scientifically formulated" in the company's laboratories. What does that mean? What constitutes a scientific formulation? You wouldn't expect the company to say that the product was casually, mechanically, or carelessly formulated, or just thrown together one day when the people in the white coats didn't have anything better to do. But the word "scientifically" lends an air of precision and promise that just isn't there.

40   It is the second sentence, however, that's really weasely, both syntactically and semantically. The only factual part of this sentence is the introductory dependent clause—"only nature controls the aging process." Thus, the only fact in the ad is relegated to a dependent clause, a clause dependent on the main clause, which contains no factual or definite information at all and indeed purports to contradict the independent clause. The new "skincare program" (notice it's not a skin cream but a "program") does not claim to stop or even retard the aging process. What, then, does Night Repair, at a price of over $35 (in 1983 dollars) for a .87-ounce bottle do? According to this brochure, nothing. It only "helps," and the brochure does not say how much it helps. Moreover, it only "helps control," and then it only helps control the "*signs* of aging," not the aging itself. Also, it "encourages" skin not to *be* younger but only to "look and feel" younger. The brochure does not say younger than what. Of the sixteen words in the main clause of this second sentence, nine are weasel words. So, before you spend all that money for Night Repair, or any other cosmetic product, read the words carefully, and then decide if you're getting what you think you're paying for.

Other Tricks of the Trade

41   Advertisers' use of doublespeak is endless. The best way advertisers can make something out of nothing is through words. Although there are a lot of visual

images used on television and in magazines and newspapers, every advertiser wants to create that memorable line that will stick in the public consciousness. I am sure pure joy reigned in one advertising agency when a study found that children who were asked to spell the world "relief" promptly and proudly responded "r-o-l-a-i-d-s."

42   The variations, combinations, and permutations of doublespeak used in advertising go on and on, running from the use of rhetorical questions ("Wouldn't you really rather have a Buick?" "If you can't trust Prestone, who can you trust?") to flattering you with compliments ("The lady has taste." "We think a cigar smoker is someone special." "You've come a long way baby."). You know, of course, how you're *supposed* to answer those questions, and you know that those compliments are just leading up to the sales pitches for the products. Before you dismiss such tricks of the trade as obvious, however, just remember that all of these statements and questions were part of very successful advertising campaigns.

43   A more subtle approach is the ad that proclaims a supposedly unique quality for a product, a quality that really isn't unique. "If it doesn't say Goodyear, it can't be Polyglas." Sounds good, doesn't it? Polyglas is available only from Goodyear because Goodyear copyrighted that trade name. Any other tire manufacturer could make exactly the same tire but could not call it "Polyglas," because that would be copyright infringement. "Polyglas" is simply Goodyear's name for its fiberglass-reinforced tire.

44   Since we like to think of ourselves as living in a technologically advanced country, science and technology have a great appeal in selling products. Advertisers are quick to use scientific doublespeak to push their products. There are all kinds of elixirs, additives, scientific potions, and mysterious mixtures added to all kinds of products. Gasoline contains "HTA," "F-130," "Platformate," and other chemical-sounding additives, but nowhere does an advertisement give any real information about the additive.

45   Shampoo, deodorant, mouthwash, cold medicine, sleeping pills, and any number of other products all seem to contain some special chemical ingredient that allows them to work wonders. "Certs contains a sparkling drop of Retsyn." So what? What's "Retsyn"? What's it do? What's so special about it? When they don't have a secret ingredient in their product, advertisers still find a way to claim scientific validity. There's "Sinarest. Created by a research scientist who actually gets sinus headaches." Sounds nice, but what kind of research does this scientist do? How do you know if she is any kind of expert on sinus medicine? Besides, this ad doesn't tell you a thing about the medicine itself and what it does.

Advertising Doublespeak Quick Quiz

46   Now it's time to test your awareness of advertising doublespeak. (You didn't think I would just let you read this and forget it, did you?) The following is a list of statements from some recent ads. Your job is to figure out what each of these ads really says.

DOMINO'S PIZZA: "Because nobody delivers better."

SINUTAB: "It can stop the pain."

TUMS: "The stronger acid neutralizer."

MAXIMUM STRENGTH DRISTAN: "Strong medicine for tough sinus colds."

LISTERMINT: "Making your mouth a cleaner place."

CASCADE: "For virtually spotless dishes nothing beats Cascade."

NUPRIN: "Little. Yellow. Different. Better."

ANACIN: "Better relief."

SUDAFED: "Fast sinus relief that won't put you fast asleep."

ADVIL: "Better relief."

PONDS COLD CREAM: "Ponds cleans like no soap can."

MILLER LITE BEER: "Tastes great. Less filling."

PHILIPS MILK OF MAGNESIA: "Nobody treats you better than MOM (Philips Milk of Magnesia)."

BAYER: "The wonder drug that works wonders."

CRACKER BARREL: "Judged to be the best."

KNORR: "Where taste is everything."

ANUSOL: "Anusol is the word to remember for relief."

DIMETAPP: "It relieves kids as well as colds."

LIQUID DRÁNO: "The liquid strong enough to be called Dráno."

JOHNSON & JOHNSON BABY POWDER: "Like magic for your skin."

PURITAN: "Make it your oil for life."

PAM: "Pam, because how you cook is as important as what you cook."

IVORY SHAMPOO AND CONDITIONER: "Leave your hair feeling Ivory clean."

TYLENOL GEL-CAPS: "It's not a capsule. It's better."

ALKA-SELTZER PLUS: "Fast, effective relief for winter colds."

The World of Advertising

47   In the world of advertising, people wear "dentures," not false teeth; they suffer from "occasional irregularity," not constipation; they need deodorants for their "nervous wetness," not for sweat; they use "bathroom tissue," not toilet paper; and they don't dye their hair, they "tint" or "rinse" it. Advertisements offer "real counterfeit diamonds" without the slightest hint of embarrassment, or boast of goods made out of "genuine imitation leather" or "virgin vinyl."

48   In the world of advertising, the girdle becomes a "body shaper," "form persuader," "control garment," "controller," "outerwear enhancer," "body garment," or "anti-gravity panties," and is sold with such trade names as "The Instead," "The Free Spirit," and "The Body Briefer."

49   A study some years ago found the following words to be among the most popular used in U.S. television advertisements: "new," "improved," "better," "extra," "fresh," "clean," "beautiful," "free," "good," "great," and "light." At the

same time, the following words were found to be among the most frequent on British television: "new," "good-better-best," "free," "fresh," "delicious," "full," "sure," "clean," "wonderful," and "special." While these words may occur most frequently in ads, and while ads may be filled with weasel words, you have to watch out for all the words used in advertising, not just the words mentioned here.

50   Every word in an ad is there for a reason; no word is wasted. Your job is to figure out exactly what each word is doing in an ad—what each word really means, not what the advertiser wants you to think it means. Remember, the ad is trying to get you to buy a product, so it will put the product in the best possible light, using any device, trick, or means legally allowed. Your own defense against advertising (besides taking up permanent residence on the moon) is to develop and use a strong critical reading, listening, and looking ability. Always ask yourself what the ad is *really* saying. When you see ads on television, don't be misled by the pictures, the visual images. What does the ad say about the product? What does the ad *not* say? What information is missing from the ad? Only by becoming an active, critical consumer of the doublespeak of advertising will you ever be able to cut through the doublespeak and discover what the ad is really saying.

51   Professor Del Kehl of Arizona State University has updated the Twenty-third Psalm to reflect the power of advertising to meet our needs and solve our problems. It seems fitting that this chapter close with this new Psalm.

> **The Adman's 23rd**
> The Adman is my shepherd;
> I shall ever want.
> He maketh me to walk a mile for a Camel;
> He leadeth me beside Crystal Waters
>   In the High Country of Coors;
> He restoreth my soul with Perrier.
> He guideth me in Marlboro Country
> For Mammon's sake.
> Yea, though I walk through the Valley of the
>   Jolly Green Giant,
> In the shadow of B.O., halitosis, indigestion,
>   headache pain, and hemorrhoidal tissue,
> I will fear no evil,
> For I am in Good Hands with Allstate;
> Thy Arid, Scope, Tums, Tylenol, and Preparation H—
> They comfort me.
> Stouffer's preparest a table before the TV
> In the presence of all my appetites;
> Thou anointest my head with Brylcream;
> My Decaffeinated Cup runneth over.
> Surely surfeit and security shall follow me
> All the days of Metropolitan Life,

And I shall dwell in a Continental Home
With a mortgage forever and ever.
Amen.

■ QUESTIONS FOR ANALYSIS AND DISCUSSION

1. How would a copywriter for an advertising agency respond to this article? Would he or she agree with the way Lutz characterizes all advertisements as trying to trick consumers with false claims into buying a product?
2. When you see the word "new" on a product, do you think twice about buying that product? What regulations restrict use of the word "new"? How can manufacturers make a product "new" to sidestep these regulations? Do these regulations serve the interests of the advertiser or the consumer?
3. Review Lutz's "Advertising Doublespeak Quick Quiz." Choose five items and analyze them using dictionary meanings to explain what the ads are really saying.
4. What tone does Lutz use throughout the article? Is his writing style humorous, informal, or academic? What strategies does he use to involve the reader in the piece?
5. What do you think of Lutz's ending his article with a parody of the Twenty-third Psalm? Do you find it appropriate or funny? Is it offensive? Does it suit the theme of the essay?
6. In paragraph 43 Lutz describes how manufacturers claim for their products unique properties that are not in fact unique after all. Could these claims be considered circular reasoning? Explain.

The Language of Advertising
Charles A. O'Neill

In this essay, marketing executive Charles A. O'Neill disputes William Lutz's criticism of advertising doublespeak. While admitting to some of the craftiness of his profession, O'Neill defends the huckster's language—both verbal and visual—against claims that it distorts reality. Examining some familiar television commercials and magazine ads, he explains why the language may be charming and seductive but far from brainwashing.

O'Neill is an independent marketing and advertising consultant in Boston. This essay first appeared in the textbook *Exploring Language* in 1998.

■ BEFORE YOU READ

O'Neill makes several generalizations that characterize the language of advertising. Think about ads you have recently seen or read and make a list of your own generalizations about the language of advertising.

■ AS YOU READ

Does the fact that O'Neill is a professional advertising consultant influence your reception of his essay? Does it make his argument more or less persuasive?

1   The figure on the billboard and in the magazine ads looked like a rock singer, perhaps photographed in the midst of a music video taping session. He was poised, confident, shown leaning against a railing or playing pool with his friends. His personal geometry was always just right. He often wore a white suit, dark shirt, sunglasses. Cigarette in hand, wry smile on his lips, his attitude was distinctly confident, urbane.

2   He was so successful, this full-lipped, ubiquitous dromedary, that his success quite literally killed him. By mid-1997, with such people and agencies as President Clinton and the Federal Trade Commission harassing him at every turn, his masters had no choice. Camel market share reportedly climbed from 3.9 percent in 1989 to 4.4 percent by 1990. According to the FTC, six years after Joe was introduced, more than 13 percent of all smokers under the age of 18 chose Camels as their nicotine delivery system of choice. Finally, the president lent his weight to what had already become a raging debate. "Let's stop pretending that a cartoon camel in a funny costume is trying to sell to adults, not children." New rules, introduced largely as a result of the debate about Joe, prohibit the use of cartoon characters in advertisements.

3   The obvious topic of the debate that finally killed Joe is cigarette advertising, but beneath the surface it signals something more interesting and broad based: the rather uncomfortable, tentative acceptance of advertising in our society. We recognize the legitimacy—even the value—of advertising, but on some level we can't quite fully embrace it as a "normal" part of our experience. At best, we view it as distracting. At worst, we view it as dangerous to our health and a pernicious threat to our social values. Also lending moral support to the debate about advertising is no less an authority than the Vatican. In 1997, the Vatican issued a document prepared by the Pontifical Council, titled "Ethics in Advertising." Along with acknowledgment of the positive contribution of advertising (e.g., provides information, supports worthy causes, encourages competition and innovation), the report states, as reported by the *Boston Globe*, "In the competition to attract ever larger audiences . . . communicators can find themselves pressured . . . to set aside high artistic and moral standards and lapse into superficiality, tawdriness and moral squalor."

4   How does advertising work? Why is it so powerful? Why does it raise such concern? What case can be made for and against the advertising business? In order to understand advertising, you must accept that it is not about truth, virtue, love, or positive social values. It is about money. Ads play a role in moving customers through the sales process. This process begins with an effort to build awareness of a product, typically achieved by tactics designed to break through the clutter of competitive messages. By presenting a description of

product benefits, ads convince the customer to buy the product. Once prospects have become purchasers, advertising is used to sustain brand loyalty, reminding customers of all the good reasons for their original decision to buy.

5   But this does not sufficiently explain the ultimate, unique power of advertising. Whatever the product or creative strategy, advertisements derive their power from a purposeful, directed combination of images. Images can take the form of words, sounds, or visuals, used individually or together. The combination of images is the language of advertising, a language unlike any other.

6   Everyone who grows up in the Western world soon learns that advertising language is different from other languages. Most children would be unable to explain how such lines as "With Nice 'n Easy, it's color so natural, the closer he gets the better you look!" (the once-famous ad for Clairol's Nice 'n Easy hair coloring) differed from ordinary language, but they would say, "It sounds like an ad." Whether printed on a page, blended with music on the radio, or whispered on the sound track of a television commercial, advertising language is "different."

7   Over the years, the texture of advertising language has frequently changed. Styles and creative concepts come and go. But there are at least four distinct, general characteristics of the language of advertising that make it different from other languages. They lend advertising its persuasive power:

1. The language of advertising is edited and purposeful.
2. The language of advertising is rich and arresting; it is specifically intended to attract and hold our attention.
3. The language of advertising involves us; in effect, *we* complete the message.
4. The language of advertising is a simple language; it holds no secrets from us.

Edited and Purposeful

8   In his famous book *Future Shock,* Alvin Toffler describes various types of messages we receive from the world around us each day. As he sees it, there is a difference between normal "coded" messages and "engineered" messages. Much of normal, human experience is "uncoded"; it is merely sensory. For example, Toffler describes a man walking down a street. Toffler notes that the man's sensory perceptions of this experience may form a mental image, but the message is not "designed by anyone to communicate anything, and the man's understanding of it does not depend directly on a social code—a set of agreed-upon signs and definitions."[1] In contrast, Toffler describes a talk show conversation as "coded"; the speaker's ability to exchange information with their host, and our ability to understand it, depend upon social conventions.

9   The language of advertising is coded. It is also a language of carefully engineered, ruthlessly purposeful messages. When Toffler wrote *Future Shock,* he estimated that the average adult was exposed to 560 advertising messages each day. Now, with the advent of 200-channel, direct-broadcast satellite television,

the Internet, and other new forms of mass media Toffler could not have contemplated, this figure is surely exponentially higher today. None of these messages would reach us, to attract and hold our attention, if it were completely unstructured. Advertising messages have a clear purpose; they are intended to trigger a specific response.

Rich and Arresting

10   Advertisements—no matter how carefully "engineered"—cannot succeed unless they capture our attention. Of the hundreds of advertising messages in store for us each day, very few will actually command our conscious attention. The rest are screened out. The people who design and write ads know about this screening process; they anticipate and accept it as a premise of their business.

11   The classic, all-time favorite device used to breach the barrier is sex. The desire to be sexually attractive to others is an ancient instinct, and few drives are more powerful. A magazine ad for Ultima II, a line of cosmetics, invites readers to "find everything you need for the sexxxxiest look around. . . ." The ad goes on to offer other "Sexxxy goodies," including "Lipsexxxxy lip color, naked eye color . . . Sunsexxxy liquid bronzer." No one will accuse Ultima's marketing tacticians of subtlety. In fact, this ad is merely a current example of an approach that is as old as advertising. After countless years of using images of women in various stages of undress to sell products, ads are now displaying men's bodies as well. A magazine ad for Brut, a men's cologne, declares in bold letters, "MEN ARE BACK"; in the background, a photograph shows a muscular, shirtless young man preparing to enter the boxing ring—a "manly" image indeed; an image of man as breeding stock.

12   Every successful advertisement uses a creative strategy based on an idea that will attract and hold the attention of the targeted consumer audience. The strategy may include strong creative execution or a straightforward presentation of product features and customer benefits.

- An ad for Clif Bars, an "energy bar," is clearly directed to people who want to snack but wouldn't be caught dead in a coffee house eating ginger spice cake with delicate frosting, much less ordinary energy bars—the kind often associated with the veggie and granola set: The central photograph shows a gristled cowboy-character, holding a Clif Bar, and asking, in the headline, "What 'n the hell's a carbohydrate?" Nosiree. This here energy bar is "bound to satisfy cantankerous folk like you."
- Recent cigar ads attract attention through the use of unexpected imagery. An ad for Don Diego cigars, for example, shows a bejeweled woman in an evening dress smoking a cigar, while through the half-open door her male companion asks, "Agnes, have you seen my Don Diegos?"
- A two-page ad for Diesel clothing includes a photo showing the principal participants in the famous Yalta conference in 1945 (Churchill, Roosevelt,

and Stalin) with one important difference: Young models in Diesel clothing have been cleverly added and appear to be flirting with the dignitaries. The ad is presented as a "Diesel historical moment" and "the birth of the modern conference." This unexpected imagery is engaging and amusing, appealing to the product's youthful target audience.

Even if the text contains no incongruity and does not rely on a pun for its impact, ads typically use a creative strategy based on some striking concept or idea. In fact, the concept and execution are often so good that many successful ads entertain while they sell.

13   Consider, for example, the campaigns created for Federal Express. A campaign was developed to position Federal Express as the company that would deliver packages, not just "overnight," but "by 10:30 A.M." the next day. The plight of the junior executive in "Presentation," one TV ad in the campaign, is stretched for dramatic purposes, but it is, nonetheless, all too real: The young executive, who is presumably trying to climb his way up the corporate ladder, is shown calling another parcel delivery service and all but begging for assurance that he will have his slides in hand by 10:30 the next morning. "No slides, no presentation," he pleads. Only a viewer with a heart of stone can watch without feeling sympathetic as the next morning our junior executive struggles to make his presentation *sans* slides. He is so lost without them that he is reduced to using his hands to perform imitations of birds and animals in shadows on the movie screen. What does the junior executive *viewer* think when he or she sees the ad?

1. Federal Express guarantees to deliver packages "absolutely, positively overnight."
2. Federal Express packages arrive early in the day.
3. What happened to that fellow in the commercial will absolutely not happen to me, now that I know what package delivery service to call.

14   A sound, creative strategy supporting an innovative service idea sold Federal Express. But the quality and objective "value" of execution doesn't matter. A magazine ad for Merit Ultra Lights made use of one word in its headline: "Yo!" This was, one hopes, not the single most powerful idea generated by the agency's creative team that particular month—but it probably sold cigarettes.

15   Soft drink and fast-food companies often take another approach. "Slice of life" ads (so-called because they purport to show people in "real-life" situations) created to sell Coke or Pepsi have often placed their characters in Fourth of July parades or other family events. The archetypical version of this approach is filled-to-overflowing with babies frolicking with puppies in the sunlit foreground while their youthful parents play touch football. On the porch, Grandma and Pops are seen quietly smiling as they wait for all of this affection to transform itself in a climax of warmth, harmony, and joy. Beneath the veneer, these ads work through repetition: How-many-times-can-you-spot-the-logo-in-this-commercial?

16   More subtly, these ads seduce us into feeling that if we drink the right combination of sugar, preservatives, caramel coloring, and a few secret ingredients, we'll fulfill our yearning for a world where young folks and old folks live together in perfect bliss.

17   If you don't buy this version of the American Dream, search long enough and you are sure to find an ad designed to sell you what it takes to gain prestige within whatever posse you do happen to run with. As reported by *The Boston Globe,* "the malt liquor industry relies heavily on rap stars in delivering its message to inner-city youths, while Black Death Vodka, which features a top-hatted skull and a coffin on its label, has been using Guns N' Roses guitarist Slash to endorse the product in magazine advertising." A malt liquor company reportedly promotes its 40-ounce size with rapper King T singing, "I usually drink it when I'm just out clowning, me and the home boys, you know, be like downing it . . . I grab me a 40 when I want to act a fool." A recent ad for Sasson jeans is a long way from Black Death in execution, but a second cousin in spirit. A photograph of a young, blonde (they do have more fun, right?) actress appears with this text: "Baywatch actress Gena Lee Nolin Puts On Sasson OO-LA-LA. Sasson. Don't put it on unless it's Sasson."

18   Ads do not often emerge like Botticelli's Venus from the sea, flawless and fully grown. Most often, the creative strategy is developed only after extensive research. "Who will be interested in our product? How old are they? Where do they live? How much money do they earn? What problem will our product solve?" Answers to these questions provide the foundation on which the creative strategy is built.

Involving

19   We have seen that the language of advertising is carefully engineered; we have discovered a few of the devices it uses to get our attention. R. J. Reynolds has us identifying with Joe in one of his many uptown poses. Coke and Pepsi have caught our eye with visions of peace and love. An actress offers a winsome smile. Now that they have our attention, advertisers present information intended to show us that their product fills a need and differs from the competition. It is the copywriter's responsibility to express, exploit, and intensify such product differences.

20   When product differences do not exist, the writer must glamorize the superficial differences—for example, differences in packaging. As long as the ad is trying to get our attention, the "action" is mostly in the ad itself, in the words and visual images. But as we read an ad or watch it on television, we become more deeply involved. The action starts to take place in us. Our imagination is set in motion, and our individual fears and aspirations, quirks, and insecurities, superimpose themselves on that tightly engineered, attractively packaged message.

21   Consider, once again, the running battle among the low-calorie soft drinks. The cola wars have spawned many "look-alike" advertisements, because the product features and consumer benefits are generic, applying to all products in the category. Substitute one cola brand name for another, and the messages are often identical, right down to the way the cans are photographed in the closing sequence. This strategy relies upon mass saturation and exposure for impact.

22   Some companies have set themselves apart from their competitors by making use of bold, even disturbing, themes and images. For example, it was not uncommon not long ago for advertisers in the fashion industry to make use of gaunt, languid models—models who, in the interpretation of some observers, displayed a certain form of "heroin chic." Something was most certainly unusual about the models appearing in ads for Prada and Calvin Klein products. A young woman in a Prada ad projects no emotion whatsoever, she is slightly hunched forward, her posture suggesting that she is in a trance or drug-induced stupor. In a Calvin Klein ad, a young man, like the woman in the Prada ad, is gaunt beyond reason. He is shirtless. As if to draw more attention to his peculiar posture and "zero body fat" status, he is shown pinching the skin next to his navel.

23   Just as he publicly attacked Joe Camel, President Clinton took an aggressive position against the depiction of heroin chic. In a speech in Washington, D.C., the president commented on the increasing use of heroin on college campuses, noting that "part of this has to do with the images that are finding their way to our young people." One industry observer agreed, asserting that "people got carried away by the glamour of decadence."

24   Do such advertisers as Prada and Calvin Klein bear responsibility—morally, if not legally—for the rise of heroin use on college campuses? Emergency room visits connected with heroin use reportedly grew from 63,200 in 1993 to 76,000 by 1995, echoing a strong rise in heroin addiction. Is this a coincidence? Does heroin chic and its depiction of a decadent lifestyle exploit certain elements of our society—the young and uncertain, for example? Or did these ads, and others of their ilk, simply reflect profound bad taste? In fact, on one level, all advertising is about exploitation; the systematic, deliberate identification of our needs and wants, followed by the delivery of a carefully constructed promise that Brand X will satisfy them.

25   Symbols offer an important tool for involving consumers in advertisements. Symbols have become important elements in the language of advertising, not so much because they carry meanings of their own, but because we bring meaning to them. One example is provided by the campaign begun in 1978 by Somerset Importers for Johnnie Walker Red Scotch. Sales of Johnnie Walker Red had been trailing sales of Johnnie Walker Black, and Somerset Importers needed to position Red as a fine product in its own right. Their agency produced ads that made heavy use of the color red. One magazine ad, often printed as a two-page spread, is dominated by a close-up photo of red autumn leaves. At lower right, the copy reads, "When their work is done, even the leaves

turn Red." Another ad—also suitably dominated by a photograph in the appropriate color—reads: "When it's time to quiet down at the end of the day, even a fire turns Red." Red. Warm. Experienced. Seductive.

26   As we have seen, advertisers make use of a great variety of techniques and devices to engage us in the delivery of their messages. Some are subtle, making use of warm, entertaining or comforting images or symbols. Others, like Black Death Vodka and Ultima II, are about as subtle as MTV's "Beavis and Butthead." Another common device used to engage our attention is old but still effective: the use of famous or notorious personalities as product spokespeople or models. Advertising writers did not invent the human tendency to admire or otherwise identify themselves with famous people. Once we have seen a famous person in an ad, we associate the product with the person: "Joe DiMaggio is a good guy. He likes Mr. Coffee. If I buy a Mr. Coffee coffee maker and I use it when I have the boss over for dinner, then maybe she'll think I'm a good guy, too." "Guns N' Roses rule my world, so I will definitely make the scene with a bottle of Black Death stuck into the waistband of my sweat pants." "Gena Lee Nolin is totally sexy. She wears Sasson. If I wear Sasson, I'll be sexy, too." The logic is faulty, but we fall under the spell just the same. Advertising works, not because Joe DiMaggio is a coffee expert, Slash has discriminating taste, or Gena knows her jeans, but because we participate in it. In fact, we charge ads with most of their power.

A Simple Language

27   Advertising language differs from other types of language in another important respect; it is a simple language. To determine how the copy of a typical advertisement rates on a "simplicity index" in comparison with text in a magazine article, for example, try this exercise: Clip a typical story from the publication you read most frequently. Calculate the number of words in an average sentence. Count the number of words of three or more syllables in a typical 100-word passage, omitting words that are capitalized, combinations of two simple words, or verb forms made into three-syllable words by the addition of *-ed* or *-es*. Add the two figures (the average number of words per sentence and the number of three-syllable words per 100 words), then multiply the result by .4. According to Robert Gunning, if the resulting number is 7, there is a good chance that you are reading *True Confessions*.[2] He developed this formula, the "Fog Index," to determine the comparative ease with which any given piece of written communication can be read. Here is the complex text of a typical cigarette endorsement:

> I demand two things from my cigarette. I want a cigarette with low tar and nicotine. But I also want taste. That's why I smoke Winston Lights. I get a lighter cigarette, but I still get a real taste. And real pleasure. Only one cigarette gives me that: Winston Lights.

The average sentence in this ad runs 7 words. *Cigarette* and *nicotine* are three syllable words, with *cigarette* appearing four times; *nicotine*, once. Consider *that's* as two words, the ad is exactly 50 words long, so the average number of three-syllable words per 100 is ten.

$$
\begin{array}{rl}
7 & \text{words per sentence} \\
+ 10 & \text{three-syllable words/100} \\
\hline
17 & \\
\times .4 & \\
\hline
6.8 & \text{Fog Index}
\end{array}
$$

According to Gunning's scale, this ad—which has now been consigned to the dustbin of advertising history thanks to government regulations—is written at about the seventh-grade level, comparable to most of the ads found in mass-circulation magazines.

28   It's about as sophisticated as *True Confessions;* that is, harder to read than a comic book, but easier than *Ladies Home Journal.* Of course, the Fog Index cannot evaluate the visual aspect of an ad—another component of advertising language. The headline, "I demand two things from my cigarette," works with the picture (that of an attractive woman) to arouse consumer interest. The text reinforces the image. Old Joe's simple plea, "Try New Camel Lights," is too short to move the needle on the Fog Index meter, but in every respect it represents perhaps the simplest language possible, a not-distant cousin of Merit Ultra Lights' groundbreaking and succinct utterance, "Yo!"

29   Why do advertisers generally favor simple language? The answer lies with the consumer: Consider Toffler's speculation that the average American adult is subject to some 560 advertising or commercial messages each day. As a practical matter, we would not notice many of these messages if length or eloquence were counted among their virtues. Today's consumer cannot take the time to focus on anything for long, much less blatant advertising messages. In effect, Toffler's "future" is here now, and it is perhaps more "shocking" than he could have foreseen at the time. Every aspect of modern life runs at an accelerated pace. Overnight mail has moved in less than ten years from a novelty to a common business necessity. Voice mail, pagers, cellular phones, e-mail, the Internet—the world is always awake, always switched on, and hungry for more information, now. Time generally, and TV-commercial time in particular, is now dissected into increasingly smaller segments. Fifteen-second commercials are no longer unusual.

30   Toffler views the evolution toward shorter language as a natural progression: three-syllable words are simply harder to read than one- or two-syllable words. Simple ideas are more readily transferred from one person to another than complex ideas. Therefore, advertising copy uses increasingly simple language, as does society at large. In *Future Shock,* Toffler speculates:

> If the [English] language had the same number of words in Shakespeare's time as it does today, at least 200,000 words—perhaps several times that many—have dropped out and been replaced in the intervening four centuries. The high turnover rate reflects changes in things, processes, and qualities in the environment from the world of consumer products and technology.

It is no accident that the first terms Toffler uses to illustrate his point ("fast-back," "wash-and-wear," and "flashcube") were invented not by engineers, or journalists, but by advertising copywriters.

31   Advertising language is simple language; in the ad's engineering process, difficult words or images—which in other forms of communication may be used to lend color or find shades of meaning—are edited out and replaced by simple words or images not open to misinterpretation. You don't have to ask whether King T likes to "grab a 40" when he wants to "act a fool," or whether Gena wears her Sassons when she wants to do whatever it is she does.

Who Is Responsible?

32   Some critics view the advertising business as a cranky, unwelcomed child of the free enterprise system—a noisy, whining, brash kid who must somehow be kept in line, but can't just yet be thrown out of the house. In reality, advertising mirrors the fears, quirks, and aspirations of the society that creates it (and is, in turn, sold by it). This factor alone exposes advertising to parody and ridicule. The overall level of acceptance and respect for advertising is also influenced by the varied quality of the ads themselves. Some ads, including a few of the examples cited here, seem deliberately designed to provoke controversy. For example, it is easy—as President Clinton and others charged—to conclude that Joe Camel represented a deliberate, calculated effort by R. J. Reynolds to encourage children to smoke cigarettes. But this is only one of the many charges frequently levied against advertising:

1. Advertising encourages unhealthy habits.
2. Advertising feeds on human weaknesses and exaggerates the importance of material things, encouraging "impure" emotions and vanities.
3. Advertising sells daydreams—distracting, purposeless visions of lifestyles beyond the reach of the majority of the people who are most exposed to advertising.
4. Advertising warps our vision of reality, implanting in us groundless fears and insecurities.
5. Advertising downgrades the intelligence of the public.
6. Advertising debases English.
7. Advertising perpetuates racial and sexual stereotypes.

33   What can be said in advertising's defense? Advertising is only a reflection of society. A case can be made for the concept that advertising language is an ac-

ceptable stimulus for the natural evolution of language. Is "proper English" the language most Americans actually speak and write, or is it the language we are told we should speak and write?

34   What about the charge that advertising debases the intelligence of the public? Those who support this particular criticism would do well to ask themselves another question: Exactly how intelligent is the public? Sadly, evidence abounds that "the public" at large is not particularly intelligent, after all. Johnny can't read. Susie can't write. And the entire family spends the night in front of the television, channel surfing for the latest scandal—hopefully, one involving a sports hero or political figure said to be a killer or a frequent participant in perverse sexual acts.

35   Ads are effective because they sell products. They would not succeed if they did not reflect the values and motivations of the real world. Advertising both reflects and shapes our perception of reality. Consider several brand names and the impressions they create: Ivory Snow is pure. Federal Express won't let you down. Absolut is cool. Sasson is sexxy. Mercedes represents quality. Our sense of what these brand names stand for may have as much to do with advertising as with the objective "truth."

36   Advertising shapes our perception of the world as surely as architecture shapes our impression of a city. Good, responsible advertising can serve as a positive influence for change, while generating profits. Of course, the problem is that the obverse is also true: Advertising, like any form of mass communication, can be a force for both "good" and "bad." It can just as readily reinforce or encourage irresponsible behavior, ageism, sexism, ethnocentrism, racism, homophobia, heterophobia—you name it—as it can encourage support for diversity and social progress. People living in society create advertising. Society isn't perfect. In the end, advertising simply attempts to change behavior. Do advertisements sell distracting, purposeless visions? Occasionally. But perhaps such visions are necessary components of the process through which our society changes and improves.

37   Joe's days as Camel's spokesman are over. His very success in reaching new smokers was the source of his undoing. But standing nearby and waiting to take his place is another campaign; another character, real or imagined; another product for sale. Perhaps, by learning how advertising works, we can become better equipped to sort out content from hype, product values from emotions, and salesmanship from propaganda.

NOTES

1. Alvin Toffler, *Future Shock* (New York: Random House, 1970), p. 146.

2. Curtis D. MacDougall, *Interpretive Reporting* (New York: Macmillan, 1968), p. 94.

■ QUESTIONS FOR ANALYSIS AND DISCUSSION

1. O'Neill opens his essay with a discussion of the controversial figure Joe Camel. What are your views on the Joe Camel controversy? Do you think the FTC and the former president were justified in expressing their concerns about the character? Should ads that target young people for products that are bad for them be outlawed? Explain.
2. Do you think it is ethical for advertisers to create a sense of product difference when there really isn't any? Consider advertisements for products such as gasoline, beer, or coffee.
3. In the last section of the essay, O'Neill anticipates potential objections to his defense of advertising. What are some of these objections? What effect does his anticipation of these objections have on the essay as a whole?
4. In paragraph 25 O'Neill writes, "Symbols offer an important tool for involving consumers in advertisements." Can you think of specific symbols from the advertising world that you associate with your own life? Are they effective symbols for advertising?
5. O'Neill is an advertising professional. How does his writing style reflect the advertising techniques he describes? Cite examples to support your answer.
6. Can you think of any recent advertising campaigns that created controversy? What made them controversial?

The Selling of Rebellion

John Leo

What motivates a person to purchase one product over another? Sometimes it is simply the associations consumers make with a product that convince them to buy it. In this essay, John Leo examines the theme of rebellion in advertising. Why do people like to buy products that are associated with breaking rules? How do advertising gurus tap into this desire?

Columnist Leo is a contributing editor at *U.S. News & World Report* in which this essay appeared on October 12, 1998. His work has appeared in many major magazines and newspapers, including the *New York Times, McCall's, Newsweek,* and *Time.*

■ BEFORE YOU READ

Think of current ads that feature "rebellious" themes. What markets are these commercials targeting? How do such ads motivate their target markets to buy?

■ AS YOU READ

Consider what motivates you personally to purchase a product. What do you think are the chief advertising themes advertisers apply to your age group?

1   Most TV viewers turn off their brains when the commercials come on. But they're worth paying attention to. Some of the worst cultural propaganda is jammed into these 60-second and 30-second spots.

2   Consider the recent ad for the Isuzu Rodeo. A grotesque giant in a business suit stomps into a beautiful field, startling a deer and jamming skycrapers, factories, and signs into the ground. (I get it: Nature is good; civilization and business are bad.) One of the giant's signs says "Obey," but the narrator says, "The world has boundaries. Ignore them." Trying to trample the Rodeo, the hapless giant trips over his own fence. The Isuzu zips past him, toppling a huge sign that says "Rules."

3   Presumably we are meant to react to this ad with a wink and a nudge, because the message is unusually flat-footed and self-satirical. After all, Isuzus are not manufactured in serene fields by adorable lower mammals. The maddened giant makes them in his factories. He also hires hip ad writers and stuffs them in his skyscrapers, forcing them to write drivel all day, when they really should be working on novels and frolicking with deer.

4   But the central message here is very serious and strongly antisocial: We should all rebel against authority, social order, propriety, and rules of any kind. "Obey" and "Rules" are bad. Breaking rules, with or without your Isuzu, is good. Auto makers have been pushing this idea in various ways since "The Dodge Rebellion" of the mid-1960s. Isuzu has worked the theme especially hard, including a TV ad showing a bald and repressive grade-school teacher barking at kids to "stay within the lines" while coloring pictures, because "the lines are our friends."

Away with Standards

5 A great many advertisers now routinely appeal to the so-called postmodern sensibility, which is heavy on irony (wink, nudge) and attuned to the message that rules, boundaries, standards, and authorities are either gone or should be gone. Foster Grant sunglasses has used the "no limits" refrain. So have Prince Matchabelli perfume ("Life without limits"), Showtime TV (its "No Limits" campaign) and AT&T's Olympics ads in 1996 ("Imagine a world without limits"). No Limits is an outdoor-adventure company, and No Limit is the name of a successful rap record label. Even the U.S. Army used the theme in a TV recruitment ad. "When I'm in this uniform I know no limits," says a soldier—a scary thought if you remember Lt. William Calley in Vietnam or the Serbian Army today.

6   Among the ads that have used "no boundaries" almost as a mantra are Ralph Lauren's Safari cologne, Johnnie Walker scotch ("It's not trespassing when you cross your own boundaries"), Merrill Lynch ("Know no boundaries"), and the movie *The English Patient* ("In love, there are no boundaries").

7   Some "no boundaries" ads are legitimate—the Internet and financial markets, after all, aim at crossing or erasing old boundaries. The antisocial message

is clearer in most of the "no rules" and "antirules" ads, starting with Burger King's "Sometimes, you gotta break the rules." These include Outback steakhouses ("No rules. Just right"), Don Q rum ("Break all the rules"), the theatrical troupe De La Guarda ("No rules"), Neiman Marcus ("No rules here"), Columbia House Music Club ("We broke the rules"), Comedy Central ("See comedy that breaks rules"), Red Kamel cigarettes ("This baby don't play by the rules"), and even Woolite (wool used to be associated with decorum, but now "All the rules have changed," an ad says under a photo of a young woman groping or being groped by two guys). "No rules" also turns up as the name of a book and a CD and a tag line for an NFL video game ("no refs, no rules, no mercy"). The message is everywhere—"the rules are for breaking," says a Spice Girls lyric.

8   What is this all about? Why is the ad industry working so hard to use rule-breaking as a way of selling cars, steaks, and Woolite? In his book *The Conquest of Cool*, Thomas Frank points to the Sixties counterculture. He says it has become "a more or less permanent part of the American scene, a symbolic and musical language for the endless cycles of rebellion and transgression that make up so much of our mass culture . . . rebellion is both the high- and mass-cultural motif of the age; order is its great bogeyman."

9   The pollster-analysts at Yankelovich Partners Inc. have a different view. In their book *Rocking the Ages: The Yankelovich Report in Generational Marketing,* J. Walker Smith and Ann Clurman say rule-breaking is simply a hallmark of the baby boom generation: "Boomers always have broken the rules. . . . The drugs, sex, and rock 'n roll of the '60s and '70s only foreshadowed the really radical rule-breaking to come in the consumer marketplace of the '80s and '90s."

10   This may pass—Smith says the post-boomers of generation X are much more likely to embrace traditional standards than boomers were at the same age. On the other hand, maybe it won't. Pop culture is dominated by in-your-face transgression now and the damage is severe. The peculiar thing is that so much of the rule-breaking propaganda is largely funded by businessmen who say they hate it, but can't resist promoting it in ads as a way of pushing their products. Isuzu, please come to your senses.

■ QUESTIONS FOR ANALYSIS AND DISCUSSION

1. Summarize the argument Leo makes about the relationship between rebellion and American society. Do you agree with his argument? Explain.
2. Evaluate America's current obsession with rebellion. Is it indeed a new phenomenon, or is there a historical connection between Americans and the spirit of rebellion?
3. In paragraph 9 Leo quotes pollsters who say that "rule-breaking is simply a hallmark of the baby boom generation." Do you agree? Are these advertisements targeting baby boomers' desire to keep breaking the rules? Is there a connection between the types of products using this theme and the target audience?

4. Leo mentions that advertisers are appealing to the "so-called postmodern sensibility." What is the "postmodern sensibility"? How does it connect to the concept of rule breaking? Do you agree with Leo's evaluation?
5. How might this "rule-breaking" approach to marketing backfire?

Sample Ads and Study Questions

The following section features three recently published magazine advertisements.
Diverse in content and style, some ads use words to promote the product, while
others depend on emotion, name recognition, visual appeal, or association. They
present a variety of sales pitches and marketing techniques.

Corresponding to each ad is a list of questions to help you analyze how the ad
works its appeal to promote a product. When studying the advertisements, approach each as a consumer, an artist, a social scientist, and a critic with an eye for
detail.

Need is the opposite of luxury.
It's what's left when everything else is stripped away.
Need is where you begin. In cars, it's about things
like reliability, durability and, of course, safety.
That's where we started when developing our newest
line of cars. And it wasn't until we were satisfied that we
added things. Things that have less to do with practicality, and
more to do with having fun. Like a powerful engine, a sport-tuned
suspension, even alloy wheels. The result is the Saturn L-Series.
A line of cars that has what you need,
as well as what you want.

SATURN.

Saturn

1. Would you know what this ad was selling if the logo and the copy were not in the ad? Would there be any ambiguity about what was being sold in the advertisement? Explain.
2. This advertisement features a great deal of printed material under the picture. Does the copy detract from the simplicity of the photograph, or complement it?
3. Who do you think is the target audience for this advertisement? How do you think a married woman would respond to it? a single young adult male? a teenage girl? Explain.
4. Apply the Fog Index from Charles O'Neill's article "The Language of Advertising" to the blurb at the bottom of the page. What is the grade level of the language? What does this tell you about the intended purchasing audience?
5. What "values" do the people in the photograph convey? What subtle cues in the photograph promote an image of who buys Saturn vehicles? Consider the use of lighting, shadow, and setting in your response.

Project Y

1. If you were leafing through a magazine and saw this ad for Project Y, what would you think the ad was promoting? Does this impression change on close inspection of the text?
2. Project Y focuses on ways to improve marketing tactics to young consumers. Through the words and images used in this ad, what can you determine about this company's impression of Generation Y consumers? Explain.
3. In what ways does the young man in the photograph represent his generation? Do you agree with this representation? Explain.
4. Who is the target audience for this ad? In what magazines would you expect to see it? Is it an effective ad? Explain.

SafeWeb.com

1. Consider how the people and their billboards are placed in this ad. How do the people, the billboards, the buildings, and the setting all work together to promote the concept of the product?
2. If you were reading a magazine and saw this ad, would you stop to examine it further? Can you tell what the ad is selling without reading the print at the top of the page? Explain.
3. What does this ad imply about the world of the Internet? In what ways could their message be considered ironic?
4. Where are the people in the ad looking? What are their facial expressions? Would this ad be more effective if the people were looking at each other or if they displayed more emotion? Why or why not?

◼ WRITING ASSIGNMENTS

1. You are an advertising executive. Select one of the products featured in the sample ads section and write a new advertising campaign for it. Do you tap into popular consciousness? Do you use "weasel words"? How do you hook your audience, and how do you create a need for the product? Defend your campaign to your supervisors by explaining the motivation behind your creative decisions.
2. Write a paper in which you consider advertising strategies. Support your evaluation with examples of advertising campaigns with which you are familiar. Make an argument for the appropriateness or exploitativeness of such campaigns. You may draw support from the articles written by William Lutz, John Leo, and Charles A. O'Neill.

CHAPTER 11

Gender Matters

In the past century, we have witnessed enormous changes in the roles of both women and men at home, in the workplace, and in society. Traditional ways of defining the self in terms of gender have been challenged and irrevocably altered. The essays in this chapter examine how these changes have affected men and women as they continue to redefine themselves, their relationships with each other, and with society.

Perceptions of gender begin at an early age, and it seems as if children are growing up faster than ever. A media-driven culture exposes them to social and cultural pressures their parents' generation never experienced. The first section of readings in this chapter addresses some of the gender issues children and teenagers face at the beginning of the third millennium. In "Saplings in the Storm," Mary Pipher discusses the trauma girls experience in early adolescence when they become aware that society seems to place more value on female attractiveness and passivity over intelligence and independence. In "Will Boys Be Boys?" John Leo describes a disturbing trend in American society that views boys as troublemakers by nature, more easily prescribed Ritalin than questioned directly about any disruptive behaviors. The next three articles examine how pop culture pressures children to dress and act older than they are. Susanna Rodell describes the influence of fashion on little girls in "Bump and Grind: Little Girls Strut Their Stuff." Stephen S. Hall examines how boys face similar pressures in "The Bully in the Mirror." As Hall explains, boys are learning what girls have long known: It isn't easy growing up in a "*Baywatch*" world.

The readings in the next section, "Gender Communication," address how our sense of gender identity affects the way we communicate. In "Women Have More to Say on Everything," Tony Kornheiser describes the differences in the way the sexes communicate. Linguist Deborah Tannen looks at why "real men don't say they're sorry" and the frustration this creates for the women in their lives in "I'm Sorry, I Won't Apologize." And Herbert Gold and Anna Quindlen offer insights into the assumptions and understandings that underlie friendships within the genders.

The last section explores how feminism has—or hasn't—changed the way women perceive themselves in the new century. Katie Roiphe says that even though her own life is a "model of modern female independence," with a well-paying job and a successful career, she secretly longs for a confident and financially secure man to take care of her. The confusing messages about women's roles can have even more dangerous consequences, as Leslie Marmon Silko argues in "In the Combat Zone." She asserts that women are easy victims of male violence because they are "taught to be self-sacrificing, passive victims." We conclude with two perspectives on feminism today. Susan Faludi and Karen Lehrman argue about what it means to be a "feminist" and discuss the phenomenon known as "revisionist feminism."

GENDER AND SELF-PERCEPTION

Saplings in the Storm
Mary Pipher

With the onset of adolescence children are faced with a multitude of gender-related issues. In addition to dealing with physical and emotional changes, many adolescents must try to adapt to shifting social roles. Changing social expectations can be overwhelming, says psychologist Mary Pipher, especially for girls. In this excerpt taken from the introduction to her best-selling book *Reviving Ophelia*, Pipher is concerned that girls may be losing their true selves in an effort to conform to what they believe society expects from them.

Psychologist and family therapist Pipher is the author of several books, including *The Shelter of Each Other* (1997) and *Another Country: Navigating the Emotional Terrain of Our Elders* (1999), which examines the difficulties older adults face in American culture.

■ BEFORE YOU READ

Did the way you fit into your social groups change when you reached adolescence? If so, in what ways? What do you think accounts for such changes?

■ AS YOU READ

According to Pipher, what social constraints do girls alone face with the onset of adolescence? Why do these cultural pressures exist?

1   When my cousin Polly was a girl, she was energy in motion. She danced, did cartwheels and splits, played football, basketball and baseball with the neighborhood boys, wrestled with my brothers, biked, climbed trees and rode horses. She was as lithe and as resilient as a willow branch and as unrestrained

as a lion cub. Polly talked as much as she moved. She yelled out orders and advice, shrieked for joy when she won a bet or heard a good joke, laughed with her mouth wide open, argued with kids and grown-ups and insulted her foes in the language of a construction worker.

2   We formed the Marauders, a secret club that met over her garage. Polly was the Tom Sawyer of the club. She planned the initiations, led the spying expeditions and hikes to haunted houses. She showed us the rituals to become blood "brothers" and taught us card tricks and how to smoke.

3   Then Polly had her first period and started junior high. She tried to keep up her old ways, but she was called a tomboy and chided for not acting more ladylike. She was excluded by her boy pals and by the girls, who were moving into makeup and romances.

4   This left Polly confused and shaky. She had temper tantrums and withdrew from both the boys' and girls' groups. Later she quieted down and reentered as Becky Thatcher. She wore stylish clothes and watched from the sidelines as the boys acted and spoke. Once again she was accepted and popular. She glided smoothly through our small society. No one spoke of the changes or mourned the loss of our town's most dynamic citizen. I was the only one who felt that a tragedy had transpired.

5   Girls in what Freud called the latency period, roughly age six or seven through puberty, are anything but latent. I think of my daughter Sara during those years—performing chemistry experiments and magic tricks, playing her violin, starring in her own plays, rescuing wild animals and biking all over town. I think of her friend Tamara, who wrote a 300-page novel the summer of her sixth-grade year. I remember myself, reading every children's book in the library of my town. One week I planned to be a great doctor like Albert Schweitzer. The next week I wanted to write like Louisa May Alcott or dance in Paris like Isadora Duncan. I have never since had as much confidence or ambition.

6   Most preadolescent girls are marvelous company because they are interested in everything—sports, nature, people, music and books. Almost all the heroines of girls' literature come from this age group—Anne of Green Gables, Heidi, Pippi Longstocking and Caddie Woodlawn. Girls this age bake pies, solve mysteries and go on quests. They can take care of themselves and are not yet burdened with caring for others. They have a brief respite from the female role and can be tomboys, a word that conveys courage, competency and irreverence.

7   They can be androgynous, having the ability to act adaptively in any situation regardless of gender role constraints. An androgynous person can comfort a baby or change a tire, cook a meal or chair a meeting. Research has shown that, since they are free to act without worrying if their behavior is feminine or masculine, androgynous adults are the most well adjusted.

8   Girls between seven and eleven rarely come to therapy. They don't need it. I can count on my fingers the girls this age whom I have seen: Coreen, who was physically abused; Anna, whose parents were divorcing; and Brenda, whose father killed himself. These girls were courageous and resilient. Brenda said, "If

my father didn't want to stick around, that's his loss." Coreen and Anna were angry, not at themselves, but rather at the grown-ups, who they felt were making mistakes. It's amazing how little help these girls needed from me to heal and move on.

9   A horticulturist told me a revealing story. She led a tour of junior-high girls who were attending a math and science fair on her campus. She showed them side oats grama, bluestem, Indian grass and trees—redbud, maple, walnut and willow. The younger girls interrupted each other with their questions and tumbled forward to see, touch and smell everything. The older girls, the ninth-graders, were different. They hung back. They didn't touch plants or shout out questions. They stood primly to the side, looking bored and even a little disgusted by the enthusiasm of their younger classmates. My friend asked herself, What's happened to these girls? What's gone wrong? She told me, "I wanted to shake them, to say, 'Wake up, come back. Is anybody home at your house?'"

10   Recently I sat sunning on a bench outside my favorite ice-cream store. A mother and her teenage daughter stopped in front of me and waited for the light to change. I heard the mother say, "You have got to stop blackmailing your father and me. Every time you don't get what you want, you tell us that you want to run away from home or kill yourself. What's happened to you? You used to be able to handle not getting your way."

11   The daughter stared straight ahead, barely acknowledging her mother's words. The light changed. I licked my ice-cream cone. Another mother approached the same light with her preadolescent daughter in tow. They were holding hands. The daughter said to her mother, "This is fun. Let's do this all afternoon."

12   Something dramatic happens to girls in early adolescence. Just as planes and ships disappear mysteriously into the Bermuda Triangle, so do the selves of girls go down in droves. They crash and burn in a social and developmental Bermuda Triangle. In early adolescence, studies show that girls' IQ scores drop and their math and science scores plummet. They lose their resiliency and optimism and become less curious and inclined to take risks. They lose their assertive, energetic and "tomboyish" personalities and become more deferential, self-critical and depressed. They report great unhappiness with their own bodies.

13   Psychology documents but does not explain the crashes. Girls who rushed to drink in experiences in enormous gulps sit quietly in the corner. Writers such as Sylvia Plath, Margaret Atwood and Olive Schreiner have described the wreckage. Diderot, in writing to his young friend Sophie Volland, described his observations harshly: "You all die at 15."

14   Fairy tales capture the essence of this phenomenon. Young women eat poisoned apples or prick their fingers with poisoned needles and fall asleep for a hundred years. They wander away from home, encounter great dangers, are rescued by princes and are transformed into passive and docile creatures.

15   The story of Ophelia, from Shakespeare's *Hamlet,* shows the destructive forces that affect young women. As a girl, Ophelia is happy and free, but with adolescence she loses herself. When she falls in love with Hamlet, she lives only

for his approval. She has no inner direction; rather she struggles to meet the demands of Hamlet and her father. Her value is determined utterly by their approval. Ophelia is torn apart by her efforts to please. When Hamlet spurns her because she is an obedient daughter, she goes mad with grief. Dressed in elegant clothes that weigh her down, she drowns in a stream filled with flowers.

16   Girls know they are losing themselves. One girl said, "Everything good in me died in junior high." Wholeness is shattered by the chaos of adolescence. Girls become fragmented, their selves split into mysterious contradictions. They are sensitive and tenderhearted, mean and competitive, superficial and idealistic. They are confident in the morning and overwhelmed with anxiety by nightfall. They rush through their days with wild energy and then collapse into lethargy. They try on new roles every week—this week the good student, next week the delinquent and the next, the artist. And they expect their families to keep up with these changes.

17   My clients in early adolescence are elusive and slow to trust adults. They are easily offended by a glance, a clearing of the throat, a silence, a lack of sufficient enthusiasm or a sentence that doesn't meet their immediate needs. Their voices have gone underground—their speech is more tentative and less articulate. Their moods swing widely. One week they love their world and their families, the next they are critical of everyone. Much of their behavior is unreadable. Their problems are complicated and metaphorical—eating disorders, school phobias and self-inflicted injuries. I need to ask again and again in a dozen different ways, "What are you trying to tell me?"

18   Michelle, for example, was a beautiful, intelligent seventeen-year-old. Her mother brought her in after she became pregnant for the third time in three years. I tried to talk about why this was happening. She smiled a Mona Lisa smile to all my questions. "No, I don't care all that much for sex." "No, I didn't plan this. It just happened." When Michelle left a session, I felt like I'd been talking in the wrong language to someone far away.

19   Holly was another mystery. She was shy, soft-spoken and slow-moving, pretty under all her makeup and teased red hair. She was a Prince fan and wore only purple. Her father brought her in after a suicide attempt. She wouldn't study, do chores, join any school activities or find a job. Holly answered questions in patient, polite monosyllables. She really talked only when the topic was Prince. For several weeks we talked about him. She played me his tapes. Prince somehow spoke for her and to her.

20   Gail burned and cut herself when she was unhappy. Dressed in black, thin as a straw, she sat silently before me, her hair a mess, her ears, lips and nose all pierced with rings. She spoke about Bosnia and the hole in the ozone layer and asked me if I liked rave music. When I asked about her life, she fingered her earrings and sat silently.

21   My clients are not different from girls who are not seen in therapy. I teach at a small liberal arts college and the young women in my classes have essentially the same experiences as my therapy clients. One student worried about her best friend who'd been sexually assaulted. Another student missed class

after being beaten by her boyfriend. Another asked what she should do about crank calls from a man threatening to rape her. When stressed, another student stabbed her hand with paper clips until she drew blood. Many students have wanted advice on eating disorders.

22   After I speak at high schools, girls approach me to say that they have been raped, or they want to run away from home, or that they have a friend who is anorexic or alcoholic. At first all this trauma surprised me. Now I expect it.

23   Psychology has a long history of ignoring girls this age. Until recently adolescent girls haven't been studied by academics, and they have long baffled therapists. Because they are secretive with adults and full of contradictions, they are difficult to study. So much is happening internally that's not communicated on the surface.

24   Simone de Beauvoir believed adolescence is when girls realize that men have the power and that their only power comes from consenting to become submissive adored objects. They do not suffer from the penis envy Freud postulated, but from power envy.

25   She described the Bermuda Triangle this way: Girls who were the subjects of their own lives become the objects of other's lives. "Young girls slowly bury their childhood, put away their independent and imperious selves and submissively enter adult existence." Adolescent girls experience a conflict between their autonomous selves and their need to be feminine, between their status as human beings and their vocation as females. De Beauvoir says, "Girls stop being and start seeming."

26   Girls become "female impersonators" who fit their whole selves into small, crowded spaces. Vibrant, confident girls become shy, doubting young women. Girls stop thinking, "Who am I? What do I want?" and start thinking, "What must I do to please others?"

27   This gap between girls' true selves and cultural prescriptions for what is properly female creates enormous problems. To paraphrase a Stevie Smith poem about swimming in the sea, "they are not waving, they are drowning." And just when they most need help, they are unable to take their parents' hands.

28   Olive Schreiner wrote of her experiences as a young girl in *The Story of an African Farm*. "The world tells us what we are to be and shapes us by the ends it sets before us. To men it says, work. To us, it says, seem. The less a woman has in her head the lighter she is for carrying." She described the finishing school that she attended in this way: "It was a machine for condensing the soul into the smallest possible area. I have seen some souls so compressed that they would have filled a small thimble."

29   Margaret Mead believed that the ideal culture is one in which there is a place for every human gift. By her standards, our Western culture is far from ideal for women. So many gifts are unused and unappreciated. So many voices are stilled. Stendhal wrote: "All geniuses born women are lost to the public good."

30   Alice Miller wrote of the pressures on some young children to deny their true selves and assume selves to please their parents. *Reviving Ophelia* suggests that adolescent girls experience a similar pressure to split into true and false

selves, but this time the pressure comes not from parents but from the culture. Adolescence is when girls experience social pressure to put aside their authentic selves and to display only a small portion of their gifts.

31   This pressure disorients and depresses most girls. They sense the pressure to be someone they are not. They fight back, but they are fighting a "problem with no name." One girl put it this way: "I'm a perfectly good carrot that everyone is trying to turn into a rose. As a carrot, I have good color and a nice leafy top. When I'm carved into a rose, I turn brown and wither."

32   Adolescent girls are saplings in a hurricane. They are young and vulnerable trees that the winds blow with gale strength. Three factors make young women vulnerable to the hurricane. One is their developmental level. Everything is changing—body shape, hormones, skin and hair. Calmness is replaced by anxiety. Their way of thinking is changing. Far below the surface they are struggling with the most basic of human questions: What is my place in the universe, what is my meaning?

33   Second, American culture has always smacked girls on the head in early adolescence. This is when they move into a broader culture that is rife with girl-hurting "isms," such as sexism, capitalism and lookism, which is the evaluation of a person solely on the basis of appearance.

34   Third, American girls are expected to distance from parents just at the time when they most need their support. As they struggle with countless new pressures, they must relinquish the protection and closeness they've felt with their families in childhood. They turn to their none-too-constant peers for support.

35   Parents know only too well that something is happening to their daughters. Calm, considerate daughters grow moody, demanding and distant. Girls who loved to talk are sullen and secretive. Girls who liked to hug now bristle when touched. Mothers complain that they can do nothing right in the eyes of their daughters. Involved fathers bemoan their sudden banishment from their daughters' lives. But few parents realize how universal their experiences are. Their daughters are entering a new land, a dangerous place that parents can scarcely comprehend. Just when they most need a home base, they cut themselves loose without radio communications.

36   Most parents of adolescent girls have the goal of keeping their daughters safe while they grow up and explore the world. The parents' job is to protect. The daughters' job is to explore. Always these different tasks have created tension in parent-daughter relationships, but now it's even harder. Generally parents are more protective of their daughters than is corporate America. Parents aren't trying to make money off their daughters by selling them designer jeans or cigarettes, they just want them to be well adjusted. They don't see their daughters as sex objects or consumers but as real people with talents and interests. But daughters turn away from their parents as they enter the new land. They befriend their peers, who are their fellow inhabitants of the strange country and who share a common language and set of customs. They often embrace the junk values of mass culture.

37   This turning away from parents is partly for developmental reasons. Early adolescence is a time of physical and psychological change, self-absorption, preoccupation with peer approval and identity formation. It's a time when girls focus inward on their own fascinating changes.

38   It's partly for cultural reasons. In America we define adulthood as a moving away from families into broader culture. Adolescence is the time for cutting bonds and breaking free. Adolescents may claim great independence from parents, but they are aware and ashamed of their parents' smallest deviation from the norm. They don't like to be seen with them and find their imperfections upsetting. A mother's haircut or a father's joke can ruin their day. Teenagers are furious at parents who say the wrong things or do not respond with perfect answers. Adolescents claim not to hear their parents, but with their friends they discuss endlessly all parental attitudes. With amazing acuity, they sense nuances, doubt, shades of ambiguity, discrepancy and hypocrisy.

39   Adolescents still have some of the magical thinking of childhood and believe that parents have the power to keep them safe and happy. They blame their parents for their misery, yet they make a point of not telling their parents how they think and feel; they have secrets, so things can get crazy. For example, girls who are raped may not tell their parents. Instead, they become hostile and rebellious. Parents bring girls in because of their anger and out-of-control behavior. When I hear about this unexplainable anger, I ask about rape. Ironically, girls are often angrier at their parents than at the rapists. They feel their parents should have known about the danger and been more protective; afterward, they should have sensed the pain and helped.

40   Most parents feel like failures during this time. They feel shut out, impotent and misunderstood. They often attribute the difficulties of this time to their daughters and their own failings. They don't understand that these problems go with the developmental stage, the culture and the times.

41   Parents experience an enormous sense of loss when their girls enter this new land. They miss the daughters who sang in the kitchen, who read them school papers, who accompanied them on fishing trips and to ball games. They miss the daughters who liked to bake cookies, play Pictionary and be kissed good-night. In place of their lively, affectionate daughters they have changelings—new girls who are sadder, angrier and more complicated. Everyone is grieving.

42   Fortunately adolescence is time-limited. By late high school most girls are stronger and the winds are dying down. Some of the worst problems—cliques, a total focus on looks and struggles with parents—are on the wane. But the way girls handle the problems of adolescence can have implications for their adult lives. Without some help, the loss of wholeness, self-confidence and self-direction can last well into adulthood. Many adult clients struggle with the same issues that overwhelmed them as adolescent girls. Thirty-year-old accountants and realtors, forty-year-old homemakers and doctors, and thirty-five-year-old nurses and schoolteachers ask the same questions and struggle with the same problems as their teenage daughters.

43   Even sadder are the women who are not struggling, who have forgotten that they have selves worth defending. They have repressed the pain of their adolescence, the betrayals of self in order to be pleasing. These women come to therapy with the goal of becoming even more pleasing to others. They come to lose weight, to save their marriages or to rescue their children. When I ask them about their own needs, they are confused by the question.

44   Most women struggled alone with the trauma of adolescence and have led decades of adult life with their adolescent experiences unexamined. The lessons learned in adolescence are forgotten and their memories of pain are minimized. They come into therapy because their marriage is in trouble, or they hate their job, or their own daughter is giving them fits. Maybe their daughter's pain awakens their own pain. Some are depressed or chemically addicted or have stress-related illnesses—ulcers, colitis, migraines or psoriasis. Many have tried to be perfect women and failed. Even though they followed the rules and did as they were told, the world has not rewarded them. They feel angry and betrayed. They feel miserable and taken for granted, used rather than loved.

45   Women often know how everyone in their family thinks and feels except themselves. They are great at balancing the needs of their coworkers, husbands, children and friends, but they forget to put themselves into the equation. They struggle with adolescent questions still unresolved: How important are looks and popularity? How do I care for myself and not be selfish? How can I be honest and still be loved? How can I achieve and not threaten others? How can I be sexual and not a sex object? How can I be responsive but not responsible for everyone?

46   As we talk, the years fall away. We are back in junior high with the cliques, the shame, the embarrassment about bodies, the desire to be accepted and the doubts about ability. So many adult women think they are stupid and ugly. Many feel guilty if they take time for themselves. They do not express anger or ask for help.

47   We talk about childhood—what the woman was like at ten and at fifteen. We piece together a picture of childhood lost. We review her own particular story, her own time in the hurricane. Memories flood in. Often there are tears, angry outbursts, sadness for what has been lost. So much time has been wasted pretending to be who others wanted. But also, there's a new energy that comes from making connections, from choosing awareness over denial and from the telling of secrets.

48   We work now, twenty years behind schedule. We reestablish each woman as the subject of her life, not as the object of others' lives. We answer Freud's patronizing question "What do women want?" Each woman wants something different and particular and yet each woman wants the same thing—to be who she truly is, to become who she can become.

49   Many women regain their preadolescent authenticity with menopause. Because they are no longer beautiful objects occupied primarily with caring for others, they are free once again to become the subjects of their own lives. They

become more confident, self-directed and energetic. Margaret Mead noticed this phenomenon in cultures all over the world and called it "pmz," post-menopausal zest. She noted that some cultures revere these older women. Others burn them at the stake.

50   Before I studied psychology, I studied cultural anthropology. I have always been interested in that place where culture and individual psychology intersect, in why cultures create certain personalities and not others, in how they pull for certain strengths in their members, in how certain talents are utilized while others atrophy from lack of attention. I'm interested in the role cultures play in the development of individual pathology.

51   For a student of culture and personality, adolescence is fascinating. It's an extraordinary time when individual, developmental and cultural factors combine in ways that shape adulthood. It's a time of marked internal development and massive cultural indoctrination.

52   I want to try in this book to connect each girl's story with larger cultural issues—to examine the intersection of the personal and the political. It's a murky place; the personal and political are intertwined in all of our lives. Our minds, which are shaped by the society in which we live, can oppress us. And yet our minds can also analyze and work to change the culture.

53   An analysis of the culture cannot ignore individual differences in women. Some women blossom and grow under the most hostile conditions while others wither after the smallest storms. And yet we are more alike than different in the issues that face us. The important question is, Under what conditions do most young women flower and grow?

54   Adolescent clients intrigue me as they struggle to sort themselves out. But I wouldn't have written this book had it not been for these last few years when my office has been filled with girls—girls with eating disorders, alcohol problems, posttraumatic stress reactions to sexual or physical assaults, sexually transmitted diseases (STDs), self-inflicted injuries and strange phobias, and girls who have tried to kill themselves or run away. A health department survey showed that 40 percent of all girls in my midwestern city considered suicide last year. The Centers for Disease Control in Atlanta reports that the suicide rate among children age ten to fourteen rose 75 percent between 1979 and 1988. Something dramatic is happening to adolescent girls in America, something unnoticed by those not on the front lines.

55   At first I was surprised that girls were having more trouble now. After all, we have had a consciousness-raising women's movement since the sixties. Women are working in traditionally male professions and going out for sports. Some fathers help with the housework and child care. It seems that these changes would count for something. And of course they do, but in some ways the progress is confusing. The Equal Rights Amendment was not ratified, feminism is a pejorative term to many people and, while some women have high-powered jobs, most women work hard for low wages and do most of the "second shift" work. The lip service paid to equality makes the reality of discrimination even more confusing.

56   Many of the pressures girls have always faced are intensified in the 1990s. Many things contribute to this intensification: more divorced families, chemical addictions, casual sex and violence against women. Because of the media, which Clarence Page calls "electronic wallpaper," girls all live in one big town—a sleazy, dangerous tinsel town with lots of liquor stores and few protected spaces. Increasingly women have been sexualized and objectified, their bodies marketed to sell tractors and toothpaste. Soft- and hard-core pornography are everywhere. Sexual and physical assaults on girls are at an all-time high. Now girls are more vulnerable and fearful, more likely to have been traumatized and less free to roam about alone. This combination of old stresses and new is poison for our young women.

57   Parents have unprecedented stress as well. For the last half-century, parents worried about their sixteen-year-old daughters driving, but now, in a time of drive-by shootings and car-jackings, parents can be panicked. Parents have always worried about their daughters' sexual behavior, but now, in a time of date rapes, herpes and AIDS, they can be sex-phobic. Traditionally parents have wondered what their teens were doing, but now teens are much more likely to be doing things that can get them killed.

58   This book will tell stories from the front lines. It's about girls because I know about girls. I was one, I see them in therapy, I have a teenage daughter and I teach primarily young women. I am not writing about boys because I have limited experience with them. I'm not saying that girls and boys are radically different, only that they have different experiences.

59   I am saying that girls are having more trouble now than they had thirty years ago, when I was a girl, and more trouble than even ten years ago. Something new is happening. Adolescence has always been hard, but it's harder now because of cultural changes in the last decade. The protected place in space and time that we once called childhood has grown shorter. There is an African saying, "It takes a village to raise a child." Most girls no longer have a village.

60   Parents, teachers, counselors and nurses see that girls are in trouble, but they do not realize how universal and extreme the suffering is. This book is an attempt to share what I have seen and heard. It's a hurricane warning, a message to the culture that something important is happening. This is a National Weather Service bulletin from the storm center.

■ **QUESTIONS FOR ANALYSIS AND DISCUSSION**

1. What does Pipher mean when she says that girls "disappear mysteriously into the Bermuda Triangle" in early adolescence? Why do you think she uses this analogy repeatedly?

2. How do girls change with the onset of adolescence? To what extent are these changes physical and to what extent are they cultural? Do you think girls must make sacrifices to "fit in"? Explain.

3. What is the benefit of androgyny to girls? Can the same benefits be applied to boys?

4. Pipher's essay focuses on what happens to girls when they reach adolescence. Do you think she feels boys face similar issues? Do you think Pipher thinks society is harder on girls than on boys? Explain.

5. Is audience important to the success of this essay? Why or why not? How could this essay apply to issues that face both men and women?

6. Place Pipher's essay in different historical contexts. For example, do you think the problems she describes faced girls in the 1930s or the 1950s? Are the underlying social pressures facing teenage girls the same today? Explain.

Will Boys Be Boys?

John Leo

In the preceding article, Mary Pipher described the way America may be short-changing girls. In the next article, John Leo argues that boys are the true victims. "Pathologized" by society and the feminist movement, they are being treated as diseased creatures who must be administered drugs such as Ritalin in order to stop their misbehaving. In our effort to be fair to girls, are we turning against boys?

Leo is a columnist and contributing editor for *U.S. News & World Report.* Before joining *U.S. News* in 1988, he covered the social sciences and intellectual trends for *Time* magazine and the *New York Times.* This article first appeared in the July 7, 2000, issue of *U.S. News & World Report.*

■ BEFORE YOU READ

In elementary school, did you notice a difference between the way teachers treated boys and the way they treated girls? Did they favor one sex over another? Did they hold them to different sets of expectations?

■ AS YOU READ

Consider what evidence Leo uses to support his point of view. How valid is his evidence? What persuasive techniques does he use to convince his audience of the validity of his claims?

1   In my first daughter's prekindergarten class, run by parents in Greenwich Village, the children were from all sorts of ethnic and class backgrounds, but they always sorted themselves out by sex. The girls sat quietly at tables, drawing and talking. The boys all ran around screaming like maniacs, bouncing off the walls, raising so much ear-splitting commotion that my first reaction each day was a fleeting urge to strangle them all.

2   I do not believe that these male tots were acting out their assigned masculine gender roles in the patriarchical order. I think the obvious is true: Boys are different from girls. They like rough-and-tumble play. When they alight some-

where, they build something, then knock it down. They are not much interested in sitting quietly, talking about their feelings, or working on relationships. They like action, preferably something involving noise, conflict, and triumph.

3   Teachers know that girls are better suited to schooling. So if you want to teach boys, allowances must be made. One of the tragedies of the last 20 years or so is that school systems are increasingly unwilling to make those allowances. Instead, in the wake of the feminist movement, they have absorbed anti-male attitudes almost without controversy. They are now more likely to see ordinary boy behavior as something dangerous that must be reined in. Or they may tighten the screws on boys by drafting extraordinarily broad zero-tolerance and sexual-harassment policies. Worse, they may simply decide that the most active boys are suffering from attention deficit disorder and dope them up with Ritalin.

4   Two straws in the wind: Four kindergarten boys in New Jersey were suspended from school for playing cops and robbers at recess with "guns" (their hands, with one finger pointed out). Teasing, ridicule, and making unflattering remarks are now listed as sexual harassment violations for 4-year-olds and up in public schools in Manhattan's Chelsea neighborhood.

5   Boys are good. "It's a bad time to be a boy in America," Christina Hoff Sommers says in her important new book, *The War Against Boys.* "We are turning against boys," she writes. "Boys need discipline, respect, and moral guidance. . . . They do not need to be pathologized." Sommers's book is packed with examples of the anti-male attitudes that pervade the public schools. At University High School in Pacific Heights, Calif., boys must sit quietly though a "Women's Assembly," in which women are celebrated and men are blamed. Boys in one San Francisco class are regularly put through feminist paces, made to enjoy quilting and forced to listen as girls vent their anger at males. When Barbara Wilder-Smith, a teacher and researcher in the Boston area, made "Boys Are Good" T-shirts for her class, all 10 female teachers under her supervision strongly objected to the message. One of the 10 was wearing a button saying "So many men, so little intelligence." Some schools use the Bem Androgyny Scale, named for feminist psychologist Sandra Bem, to measure success in getting rid of those pesky masculine traits in boys.

6   In his book, *The Decline of Males,* anthropologist Lionel Tiger says women have taken charge of the public dialogue on gender and decisively bent it to their advantage. That is certainly true of dialogue about the schools. We spent most of the 1990s fretting about bogus research claiming that the schools were shortchanging and damaging girls, when the truth is that boys are the ones in trouble.

7   Boys are much more likely than girls to have problems with schoolwork, repeat a grade, get suspended, and develop learning difficulties. In some schools boys account for up to three fourths of special-education classes. They are five times more likely than girls to commit suicide and four to nine times more likely to be drugged with Ritalin. Student polls show that both girls and boys say their teachers like the girls more and punish the boys more often.

8   Girls get better grades than boys, take more rigorous courses, and now attend college in much greater numbers. While the traditional advantage of boys over girls in math and science has narrowed (girls take as least as many upper-level math courses as boys, and more biology and chemistry), the advantage of girls over boys in reading and writing is large and stable. In writing achievement, 11th-grade boys score at the level of eighth-grade girls. The Department of Education reported this year: "There is evidence that the female advantage in school performance is real and persistent."

9   The school failure of so many boys, magnified and fanned by anti-male hostility, is a severe social problem. Women now account for 56 percent of American college students and the male-female gap is still widening. It is 60–40 in Canada and 63–37 among American blacks. These numbers, always overlooked in media laments about "underrepresentation," have several ominous implications. One is for much more fatherlessness. College women who can't find college-educated mates won't marry down, they will likely just have their babies alone.

10   It's time to discuss some remedies, including vouchers, single-sex schools, and programs targeted at specific problems of boys. Save the males.

■ QUESTIONS FOR ANALYSIS AND DISCUSSION

1. Leo states, "Teachers know that girls are better suited to schooling" (paragraph 3). Is this true? How does he support this statement? Do you think that most teachers would agree? Why or why not?
2. What is the specific problem Leo is addressing in this essay? Is it boys' behavior? School apathy? Unfair treatment based on gender? Explain.
3. Leo connects the current trend in school systems to no longer make "allowances" for boys' bad behavior as occurring in the "wake of the feminist movement." In what ways is the feminist movement connected to this "anti-male attitude" in schools? What evidence does Leo provide to support his view? Explain.
4. Evaluate the solutions Leo offers at the end of his essay to solve the problem of society "turning against boys." How will vouchers and single-sex schools remedy the problem?

Bump and Grind: Little Girls Strut Their Stuff

Susanna Rodell

While many parents worry that their children are growing up too fast, few realize just how strong the influence of pop culture can be on kids to act and dress a certain way. Childhood is no longer a time of innocence, but fraught with its own social anxieties and pressures. In the next article, Susanna Rodell, a journalist and mother of two girls, describes how little girls, trying to emulate pop stars such as

Britney Spears, end up looking like "little trollops." The peer pressure to conform is great, and the author fears her own child might give in to third-grade "fashion fascists."

Rodell is a columnist and reporter for the Raleigh *News and Observer.* This article first appeared online as a column in MSN's *UnderWire.*

■ **BEFORE YOU READ**

How did you dress when you were a child? Did you feel any social pressure to dress a certain way? Did social acceptance depend on how you dressed? Do you think kids today face peer pressure at a younger age?

■ **AS YOU READ**

Evaluate the author's tone in this essay. Is she angry? worried? sarcastic? What personal issues could she have that influence her view of the essay's subject matter? Explain.

1   It's a stinking hot May afternoon. It also happens to be Community Pride Day in Hillsborough, North Carolina, one of those raggedy events in a small town where organizations like 4-H and the local electric co-op set up booths in the shopping center, and the health department does free dental check-ups.

2   My kid's school band has been asked to play; but before that happens, there's a dance performance. The staticky PA system kicks in and the show begins. When it's time for the older kids, elementary-school age, the music pumps up and it's disco city. The costumes turn raunchy: little black skin-tight hip-hugger clingy bell-bottoms, bare midriffs, little bra tops covering nonexistent bosoms. But you'd never know that to see how these children move. My, oh my.

3   Little pelvises thrust and gyrate. Little butts shake and roll. Little eyelids, heavily fringed with false lashes, flutter knowingly.

4   Following this display comes the Solo Act, in which the kid obviously deemed to be the most talented gets to shine all alone. She is, oh, say 11 or so. She is dressed like some macabre mini-drag-queen parody of Marilyn Monroe, complete with blond wig. She vamps excruciatingly through a lip-sync rendition of "Diamonds Are a Girl's Best Friend," interspersed with enough gymnastic tricks that eventually (inevitably) the wig flies off and lands on the hot blacktop while the little trollop soldiers on, finishing her number to damp applause from the thin crowd.

5   Anyone who wants to see pedophilia alive and well in these United States need only attend a small-town dance-school performance. And anyone who wants to experience the outrage of such a community need only point out that there is something sexual going on here. I know, because I did that, writing a column in my local paper saying I thought the whole thing was embarrassing and inappropriate. I got so many outraged letters from good Christian parents

accusing me of perverse and satanic tendencies, you'd think I'd invited them to join a coven.

6   My discomfort with all this is not disinterested, as you may have guessed. I have daughters, the youngest of whom was 8 at the time, and she was pretty miserable at school. Reason: She did not wish to try to look anything at all like Britney Spears when she showed up each day for her dose of education. She thought jeans and scuffed riding boots were just fine. So did I. But her peers did not.

7   My confident tomboy, with the aid of the kids in her class and the collusion of her teacher, was approaching school phobia because, as she tearfully related, each day when she arrived she would be inspected by the self-appointed Fashion Police, and always she would be pronounced inadequate. One young thing had appointed herself the Uber-enforcer of the class, and had picked my kid as sacrificial meat.

8   Ruby described the wardrobe of this child as follows: "She wears those funny plastic see-through sandals, you know, with the high heels? And she has these little outfits where everything matches, like these little pants that fit her really tight and a vest that goes with them, and then she has stuff in her hair and it's all the same color."

9   At 8, the really cool little girls are wearing lip gloss and eye shadow to school.

10   Another awful day, on the way home, Ruby squirms with embarrassment before finally asking, "Mama, can I get some deodorant?"

11   "Deodorant?" I ask in astonishment. "Whatever for?"

12   "The other kids use it," she quavers. "They say I stink."

13   Now I know there are kids out there who might need deodorant at 8, but Roo's little body is years away from the hormonal shifts that would produce anything approaching BO. No, here's what bothers the third-grade fashion fascists: She's simply not a good consumer.

14   She's not totally oblivious; she does favor flares with embroidered daisies, and she loves her thick-soled Doc Marten Mary Janes. But she lacks true commitment. At my prompting she'll run a brush through her hair before leaving the house. That's the extent of her attention to grooming. And dammit, I like her that way.

15   Unlike many of her classmates, she has no interest in learning disco routines and wishes with all her heart that she could just be friends with the boys. Britney Spears videos embarrass her.

16   It's bad enough that so many grown women get skunked into self-conscious insecurity about their appearances and their bodies, and that female adolescence consists so much of obsession over bodily conformity. Now they're scheming to take away childhood itself.

17   I try to support Ruby however I can. I give her the tools available to the underdog: sarcasm (which works in some instances) and encouragement in the things she excels at, such as riding her pony and climbing trees and running fast.

18   But I can't provide for her escape from one grim fact: She's the odd kid out, because she doesn't want to grow up too soon and too tacky. Maybe it'll produce character. I don't care. I hate it. She's right, and they're wrong. And she's too young to have to fight this battle.

■ QUESTIONS FOR ANALYSIS AND DISCUSSION

1. Rodell describes the costumes of some little girls in a dance performance as "raunchy." In your own opinion, is there anything wrong with the outfits these children are wearing? How would you respond to Rodell's pronouncement that such costumes border on the pedophilic?

2. After writing a column in which she comments that "bump and grind" dance school performances were "embarrassing and inappropriate," Rodell received many outraged letters. What do you think accounts for this parental outrage? Explain.

3. Rodell describes how her daughter, a "confident tomboy," faces peer pressure to dress more "fashionably." What advice would you give Rodell in this situation, and why?

4. Rodell comments, "It's bad enough that so many grown women get skunked into self-conscious insecurity about their appearances and their bodies. [. . .] Now they're scheming to take away childhood itself." Who is the "they" of this last sentence? Does she support her statement with evidence? Is such evidence necessary to make her argument? Explain.

The Bully in the Mirror
Stephen S. Hall

The expression goes "vanity, thy name is woman," and most people think of body obsessive behavior as a female trait. Women still account for 90 percent of cosmetic surgical procedures, and roughly the same number is true for teenagers being treated for eating disorders. But boys are becoming just as obsessed with their bodies, say psychiatrists Harrison Pope, Katharine Phillips, and Roberto Olivardia. Their research reveals a disturbing trend—teenage boys are spending more time in the gym in quest of steroid-boosted buff bodies. Cultural messages reinforce this viewpoint, from the action heroes they play with as children, to the images they view on television, to the peer pressure they receive at school. In America today, young men are constantly faced with "the bully in the mirror."

Stephen S. Hall is a science writer and author of several books, including *Invisible Frontiers* (1987), a book that describes the origins of biotechnology, and *Mapping the Next Millennium* (1992) describing cartographic approaches to scientific knowledge. He is a contributing writer to the *New York Times Magazine,* in which this article first appeared on August 22, 1999.

■ BEFORE YOU READ

What is the "perfect" male physique? What does it look like? Is your image influenced by outside forces, such as the media, your gender, or your age? How do the real men you know compare to the image you have in your mind?

■ AS YOU READ

The young man featured in this article, Alexander, comments that people judge others on physical appearance. What do you want people to notice about you? How do your feelings compare to those Alexander expresses in this article?

1   On an insufferably muggy afternoon in July, with the thermometer pushing 90 degrees and ozone alerts filling the airwaves, Alexander Bregstein was in a foul mood. He was furious, in fact, for reasons that would become clear only later. Working on just three hours of sleep, and having spent the last eight hours minding a bunch of preschool kids in his summer job as a camp counselor, Alexander was itching to kick back and relax. So there he was, lying on his back in the weight room of his gym, head down on an incline bench, earphones pitching three-figure decibels of the rock band Finger Eleven into his ears as he gripped an 85-pound weight in each hand and then, after a brief pause to gather himself, muscled them into the air with focused bursts of energy. Each lift was accompanied by a sharp exhalation, like the quick, short stroke of a piston.

2   The first thing you need to know about Alexander is that he is 16 years old, bright, articulate and funny in that self-deprecating and almost wise teen-age way. However, about a year ago, Alexander made a conscious decision that those weren't the qualities he wanted people to recognize in him, at least not at first. He wanted people to see him first, and what they see these days are thick neck muscles, shoulders so massive that he can't scratch his back, a powerful bulge in his arms and a chest that has been deliberately chiseled for the two-button look—what Alexander now calls "my most endearing feature." He walks with a kind of cocky gravity-testing bounce in his step that derives in part from his muscular build but also from the confidence of knowing he looks good in his tank top and baggy shorts. As his spotter, Aaron Anavim, looked on, Alexander lifted the 85-pound weights three more times, arms quivering, face reddening with effort. Each dumbbell, I realized as I watched, weighed more than I did when I entered high school. Another half-dozen teen-agers milled around the weight room, casting glances at themselves and one another in the mirror. They talked of looking "cut," with sharp definition to their muscles, and of developing "six-packs," crisp divisions of the abdominals, but of all the muscles that get a workout in rooms like these, the most important may be the ones that move the eyes in restless sweeping arcs of comparison and appraisal. "Once you're in this game to manipulate your body," Alexander said, "you want to be the best," likening the friendly competition in the room to a form of "whipping

out the ruler." While we talked between sets of Alexander's 90-minute routine, his eyes wandered to the mirror again and again, searching for flaws, looking for areas of improvement. "The more you lift," he admitted, "the more you look in the mirror."

3   In this weight room, in a gym in a northern New Jersey suburb, the gym rats have a nickname for Alexander: Mirror Boy. That's a vast improvement over the nicknames he endured at school not long ago. "I know it sounds kind of odd to have favorite insults," he told me with a wry smile, munching on a protein bar before moving on to his next set of lifts, "but Chunk Style always was kind of funny." And kind of appropriate. Until recently, Alexander carried nearly 210 pounds on a 5-foot-6 frame, and when I asked if he was teased about his weight, he practically dropped a dumbbell on my feet. "Oh! Oh, man, was I teased? Are you kidding?" he said in his rapid, agreeable patter. "When I was fat, people must have gone home and thought of nothing else except coming in with new material the next day. They must have had study groups just to make fun of people who were overweight." He even got an earful at home. "My parents—God bless them, but they would make comments all the time. My father would say, 'If you eat all that, you'll be as big as a house.' And I'm, like: 'Dad, it's a little late for that. What am I now? A mobile home?'"

4   The day of reckoning came in April 1998, during a spring-break vacation in Boca Raton, Fla. As his family was about to leave its hotel room to go to the beach, Alexander, then 15, stood in front of a mirror and just stared at the spectacle of his shirtless torso. "I remember the exact, like, moment in my mind," he said. "Everything about that room is burned into my head, every little thing. I can tell you where every lamp was, where my father was standing, my mother was sitting. We were about to go out, and I'm looking in this mirror—me, with my gut hanging over my bathing suit—and it was, like: Who would want to look at this? It's part of me, and I'm disgusted! That moment, I realized that nobody was giving me a chance to find out who I was because of the way I looked."

5   And so Alexander decided to do something about it, something drastic.

6   There is a kind of timeless, archetypal trajectory to a teen-ager's battle with body image, but in most accounts the teen-ager is female and the issue is anorexia or bulimia. As any psychologist knows, however, and as any sufficiently evolved adult male could tell you, boys have body-image problems, too. Traditionally, they have felt pressure to look not thin, but rather strong and virile, which increasingly seems to mean looking bulked up and muscular, and that is why I was interested in talking to Alexander.

7   No one can quite cite any data, any scientific studies proving that things are different, but a number of psychologists with whom I spoke returned to the same point again and again: the cultural messages about an ideal male body, if not new, have grown more insistent, more aggressive, more widespread and more explicit in recent years.

8   Since roughly 90 percent of teen-agers who are treated for eating disorders are female, boys still have a way to go. Young girls have suffered greatly from insecurity about appearance and body image, and the scientific literature on

anorexia and related body-image disorders depicts a widespread and serious health problem in adolescent females. But to hear some psychologists tell it, boys may be catching up in terms of insecurity and even psychological pathology. An avalanche of recent books on men and boys underlines the precarious nature of contemporary boyhood in America. A number of studies in the past decade—of men, not boys—have suggested that "body-image disturbances," as researchers sometimes call them, may be more prevalent in men than previously believed and almost always begin in the teen-age years. Katharine Phillips, a psychiatrist at the Brown University School of Medicine, has specialized in "body dysmorphic disorder," a psychiatric illness in which patients become obsessively preoccupied with perceived flaws in their appearance—receding hairlines, facial imperfections, small penises, inadequate musculature. In a study of "30 cases of imagined ugliness," Phillips and colleagues described a surprisingly common condition in males whose symptoms include excessive checking of mirrors and attempts to camouflage imagined deformities, most often of the hair, nose and skin. The average age of onset, Phillips says, is 15.

9   Two years ago, Harrison G. Pope Jr., of Harvard Medical School, and his colleagues published a modest paper called "Muscle Dysmorphia: An Under-recognized Form of Body Dysmorphic Disorder" in a relatively obscure journal called *Psychosomatics*. The study described a group of men and women who had become "pathologically preoccupied" by their body image and were convinced that they looked small and puny, even though they were bulging with muscles. The paper got a lot of attention, and it led to an even more widely publicized study earlier this year from the same lab reporting how male action-figure toys like G.I. Joe and the "Star Wars" characters have bulked up over the years.

10   When you visit the office of Harrison (Skip) Pope, in a grim institutional building on the rolling grounds of McLean Hospital in Belmont, Mass., the first thing you notice are the calipers hanging on the wall—partly as objets d'art, but partly as a reminder that what we subjectively consider attractive can sometimes yield to objective measurement. Pope, after all, was one of the scientists who devised what might be called the Buff Equation, or: $FFMI = W \times (1 - BF/100) \times h - 2 + 6.1 \times (1.8 - H)$.

11   The formula is ostensibly used to calculate a person's Fat-free Mass Index; it has sniffed out presumed steroid use by Mr. America winners, professional bodybuilders and men whose unhealthy preoccupation with looking muscular has induced them to use drugs.

12   Pope is a wiry, compact psychiatrist who can squat 400 pounds in his spare time. ("You can reach me pretty much all day except from 11 A.M. to 2 P.M.," he told me, "when I'm at the gym.") I had gone to see him and his colleague Roberto Olivardia not only because they were the lead authors on the G.I. Joe study, but also because their studies of body-image disorders in slightly older postadolescent men may be the best indicator yet of where male body-image issues are headed.

13   Shortly after I arrived, Olivardia emptied a shopping bag full of male action dolls onto a coffee table in the office. The loot lay in a heap, a plastic orgy

of superhero beefcake—three versions of G.I. Joe (Hasbro's original 1964 version plus two others) and one G.I. Joe Extreme, Luke Skywalker and Han Solo in their 1978 and mid-90's versions, Mighty Morphin Power Rangers, Batman, Superman, Iron Man and Wolverine. The inspiration for the whole study came from an adolescent girl. Pope's 13-year-old daughter, Courtney, was surfing the Web one night, working on a school project on how Barbie's body had radically changed over the years, and Pope thought to himself, There's got to be the male equivalent of that.

14   Once Pope and Olivardia gathered new and "vintage" action figures, they measured their waist, chest and biceps dimensions and projected them onto a 5-foot-10 male. Where the original G.I. Joe projected to a man of average height with a 32-inch waist, 44-inch chest and 12-inch biceps, the more recent figures have not only bulked up, but also show much more definition. Batman has the equivalent of a 30-inch waist, 57-inch chest and 27-inch biceps. "If he was your height," Pope told me, holding up Wolverine, "he would have 32-inch biceps." Larger, that is, than any bodybuilder in history.

15   Now let it be said that measuring the styrene hamstrings of G.I. Joe does not represent 20th-century science at its most glorious. But Pope says it's a way to get at what he calls "evolving American cultural ideals of male body image." Those ideals, he maintains, create "cultural expectations" that may contribute to body-image disorders in men. "People misinterpreted our findings to assume that playing with toys, in and of itself, caused kids to develop into neurotic people as they grew up who abused anabolic steroids," Pope said. "Of course that was not our conclusion. We simply chose the toys because they were symptomatic of what we think is a much more general trend in our society."

16   Leaving such extreme pathology aside, the point remains that a boy's body image is shaped, if not determined, by the cruelest, most unforgiving and meanest group of judges imaginable: other boys. And even if you outgrow, physically and emotionally, the body image that oppressed you as an adolescent, it stays with you in adult life as a kind of subdermal emotional skin that can never be shed, only incorporated into the larger person you try to become. I think that's what Garry Trudeau, the formerly small cartoonist, had in mind when he described life as a tall adult as that of a "recovering short person."

17   It was during his sophomore year, getting "the daylights pounded out of him" in wrestling and gaining even more weight, that Alexander began what he calls, with justification, his "drastic transformation." He started by losing 30 pounds in one month. For a time, he consumed only 900 calories a day, and ultimately got down to 152 pounds. He began to lift weights seriously, every day for three months straight. He started to read magazines like *Flex* and *Men's Fitness*. He briefly dabbled with muscle-building supplements like creatine. He got buff, and then beyond buff.

18   By the time his sophomore year in high school began, Alexander had packaged his old self in a phenomenally new body, and it has had the desired effect. "My quality of social life changed dramatically when I changed my image," he said. He still maintained friendships with the guys in the computer lab, still pro-

grammed, still played Quake with dozens of others. But he worked out at the gym at least five times a week. He shifted his diet to heavy protein. He pushed himself to lift ever-heavier weights. Until an injury curtailed his season, he brought new strength to his wrestling. Still, he wasn't satisfied. When I asked him if he ever felt tempted to try steroids during his effort to remake his physical image, he denied using them, and I believe him. But he wasn't coy about the temptation.

19   "When someone offers you a shortcut," he replied, "and it's a shortcut you want so bad, you're willing to ignore what it might be doing to your insides. I wanted to look better. Who cares if it's going to clog up my kidneys? Who cares if it'll destroy my liver? There was so much peer pressure that I didn't care."

20   Alexander was especially pleased by the good shape he was in—although he didn't care for aerobics, his resting heart rate was low, he ran a mile under six minutes and seemed to have boundless energy. But fitness was only part of what he was after. As he put it: "No one's looking for a natural look, of being thin and in shape. It's more of looking toward a level beyond that." He added that "guys who work out, especially guys who have six-packs and are really cut up, are the ones girls go after."

21   To be honest, I was a little dubious about this until I spoke with an admittedly unscientific sampling of teen-age girls. It turned out that they not only agreed with the sentiment, but also spoke the same lingo. "If you're going swimming or something like that, girls like the stomach best," said Elizabeth, a 14-year-old. "Girls like it if they have a six-pack, or if they're really ripped, as they say. That's the most important thing. And arms too."

22   "But not too much," added her friend Kate, also 14. "You don't like it if the muscles are too huge."

23   "It changes your perspective on them if they have a flabby stomach," Elizabeth continued. "And the chest is important too."

24   After Alexander finished his workout that hot July day, we stopped to get something to drink at the gym's cafe. "I feel pretty good right now," Alexander admitted, "and I was furious when I went in there." It turned out that the night before, he had a conversation with a girl that took a decidedly unsatisfying turn at the end.

25   At a time when the collective amount of American body fat is enough to stretch the jaws of Skip Pope's calipers from coast to coast, when so many adults amble about like fatted calves and so many children are little more than couch potatoes in training, it's hard to find fault with disciplined, drug-free efforts by teen-age boys to add a bit of muscle; weight lifting is not a sport with shortcuts, and it has become an essential adjunct to contemporary athletic performance. But there is a psychological side to all this heavy lifting that may be as unhealthy and undermining on the inside as it seems fit on the outside. And it resides not in that telltale mirror, but in how we see ourselves.

26   "I look in the mirror and I don't see what other people see," Alexander told me. "I look in the mirror, and I see my flaws. People go, 'Oh, you're narcissistic.' I go, 'No, I was looking at how uneven my pecs are,' although I know

that in reality, they're, like, a nanometer off. And I have three friends who do exactly the same thing. They look and they go, 'Look how uneven I am, man!' And I go: 'What are you talking about! They look pretty even to me.' It's not narcissism—it's lack of self-esteem."

27   I'm not so worried about kids like Alexander—he clearly has demonstrated both the discipline to remake his appearance and the psychological distance not to take it, or himself, too seriously. But there will be many other boys out there who cannot hope to match the impossibly raised bar of idealized male body image without resorting to the physically corrosive effects of steroids or the psychologically corrosive effects of self-doubt. Either way, the majority of boys will be diminished by chasing after the golden few.

28   Moreover, this male preoccupation with appearance seems to herald a dubious, regressive form of equality—now boys can become as psychologically and physically debilitated by body-image concerns as girls have been for decades. After all, this vast expenditure of teen-age male energy, both psychic and kinetic, is based on the premise that members of the opposite sex are attracted to a retro, rough-hewn, muscular look, and it's a premise that psychologists who study boys have noticed, too. "While girls and women say one thing, some of them continue to do another," Pollack says. "Some of them are still intrigued by the old male images, and are attracted to them."

29   Because he's a perceptive kid, Alexander recognizes how feckless, how disturbing, how crazy this all is. "I tell you, it's definitely distressing," he said, "the fact that as much as girls get this anorexic thing and they're going through these image things with dolls and stuff, guys are definitely doing the same." True, he admitted, his social life has never been better. "But in a way it depresses me," he said, before heading off to a party, "that I had to do this for people to get to know me."

■ QUESTIONS FOR ANALYSIS AND DISCUSSION

1. Alexander states that he suffered from cruel comments about his weight for most of his life. Even his parents would make comments about his weight. What motivated Alexander to change his physique? Is it an extreme response, or a reasonable one? Does Alexander think he is better off now? Does Hall? Explain.

2. Alexander comments that he had an epiphany in a hotel room when he was 15: "I realized that nobody was giving me a chance to find out who I was because of the way I looked." What is ironic about this statement? Is the "ripped" Alexander the real person? Explain.

3. In your opinion, do the "jacked-up" muscles on action figures influence the way boys feel about their own bodies? If possible, go to a toy store or online and examine some of these figures. Do they reflect, as Pope claims, "evolving American cultural ideals of male body image"?

4. What cultural messages tell boys that steroid use is permissible? Describe some of the ways children receive these messages.

5. Analyze the author's use of statistics, facts, and supporting information to reinforce the points he makes in his essay. Do his conclusions seem reasonable based on the data he cites? Why or why not?

Restroom Symbols

Symbols have been used throughout history to convey meaning without words. More and more signs are minimizing the use of words and using symbols. They help us make snap decisions that could save our lives, such as in the case of stop or hazard signs. And they enable people who don't speak the language to get around in a different country. Consider the standard symbols for men's and women's rooms on this page. Do they symbolize more than meets the eye?

■ QUESTIONS FOR ANALYSIS AND DISCUSSION

1. How are the people "dressed"? Does this depiction of attire make certain assumptions about men and women? Are they dated? insulting? simply accepted symbols? Explain.
2. Many establishments now provide "unisex" bathrooms serving both men and women. What symbol would you expect to see on such a facility?
3. A euphemism substitutes a mild or even pleasant expression for an uncomfortable or blunt one. The more uncomfortable we are with a subject, the more euphemisms we construct. Euphemisms are often used when discussing sex, death, or bodily functions. In what ways are the symbols on men's and women's restrooms pictorial euphemisms?
4. If you were traveling from another country, such as Italy or China, and saw one of these symbols on the door, would you know what was behind the door? What if the doors were not next to each other? Explain.

■ **WRITING ASSIGNMENTS**

1. Write a detailed description of your ideal male image, or ideal female image (what you desire or what you would most like to look like yourself). Now record the personality traits you would want in this person. How does your description compare with the conclusions drawn by the psychologists in this section? Did outside cultural influences influence your description? Explain.

2. Several of the authors in this section attribute youth's desire to act, dress, and look a certain way to media pressure. Write an essay discussing whether this is true or not true. Support your perspective using examples from Pipher, Rodell, and Hall, and your own experiences and observations.

3. Is it harder to grow up male or female in America today? Using information from the articles in this section, as well as outside resources, write an essay explaining which gender faces the greatest and most daunting challenges, and why. Will this situation grow worse? Offer suggestions to help ease the gender-related challenges children face growing up in today's culture.

4. Write an essay in which you consider your own sense of cultural conditioning. Do you feel your behavior has been conditioned by sex-role expectations? In what ways? Is there a difference between the "real" you and the person you present to the world? If there is a difference, is it the result of cultural pressure? Explain.

5. Columnist John Leo writes that young men are suffering from an overzealous application of politically correct feminism in which boys are vilified and teachers view them as less intelligent and cooperative than girls. Write a response column addressing Leo's concerns. Identify the weaknesses in his argument and elect to either correct them with better, reinforcing evidence, or challenge them with alternative information.

6. Write an essay examining the connection between self-esteem and body image. How important are body image and social acceptance to personal self-esteem? Is self-esteem affected by cultural influences and social expectations of males and females? Explain.

GENDER COMMUNICATION

Women Have More to Say on Everything

Tony Kornheiser

A common complaint between the sexes is that men and women just don't speak the same language. In the next piece, columnist and humorist Tony Kornheiser observes the differences in the communication styles of his daughter and son, and by extension, women and men. His conclusion is that "women have more to say on everything."

Kornheiser is a columnist and sportswriter for the *Washington Post.* He also hosts *The Tony Kornheiser Show* on ESPN radio and cohosts *Pardon the Interruption* with fellow *Post* sports columnist Mike Wilbon on ESPN2. He is the author of several books, including *Pumping Irony* and *Bald as I Want to Be.*

■ BEFORE YOU READ

In the next article, columnist Tony Kornheiser describes the differences between the way his children, one boy and one girl, communicate. What stereotypes exist regarding the differences between the way men and women communicate?

■ AS YOU READ

How would you characterize Kornheiser's tone and style? What assumptions does he make about his audience? Does his article appeal to both sexes? Why or why not?

1   The last time I ventured into my favorite column area—differences between men and **women**—was when the infamous Teen Talk Barbie doll came out. Barbie was given 270 things to say, and one of them was "Math class is tough!" This, of course, is infuriating, because it plays into the damaging sexual stereotype that girls are stupid in math.

2   Well, I got cute and wrote how everyone knows girls are stupid in math. I gave an example of my own daughter, whom I love dearly, and who is a sensitive and caring soul, and how when I ask her, "If a bus leaves Cleveland at 7 p.m. heading for Pittsburgh, 200 miles away, and traveling 50 miles per hour, when will it arrive?" she answers, "Do all the children have seat belts, Daddy?" I thought it was a pretty good line. But I received all kinds of nasty mail, much of it—so help me—from female mathematicians, and female actuaries and female physicists specializing in subatomic particle acceleration. In that same column, I wrote that boys are stupid in English, yet I didn't get a single letter of protest from boys. Obviously, they couldn't read the column.

3   Anyway . . . here we go again.

4   My daughter recently came home from sleep-away camp, where she'd spent five weeks. She looked great. And I was so proud of her, going away by herself.

5   The first question I asked her was "How was camp?"

6   She began by saying, "Well, the day I left, I got on the bus, and I sat next to Ashley, and she brought Goldfish, which was good because I forgot my Now and Laters, and then Shannon came over, and she's from Baltimore, and she gets her clothes at the Gap, and she had a Game Boy, but all she had was Tetris, which I have, so we asked Jenny, who was the counselor, if anybody had Sonic the Hedgehog, but. . . ."

7   She went on like this for a few minutes, still talking about the bus ride up to camp five weeks ago, and I came to the horrifying realization that she was actually going to tell me how camp was, minute by minute. Because this is what girls do (and when they grow up and become women, they do it, too, as any man can vouch for). They gather information and dispense it without discrimina-

tion. Everything counts the same! It is not that women lack the ability to prioritize information, it is that they don't think life is as simple as men do, and so they are fascinated by the multiplicity of choices that they see.

8   This is why you have to be very specific with what you ask women. If, for example, you missed a Rams game, and you know a woman who saw it, never, ever ask, "What happened?" Unless you have nowhere to go until Thursday.

9   Ask:

10   1. Who won?

11   2. What was the score?

12   3. Was anyone carried out on a stretcher?

13   You must get them to fast-forward.

14   Left to their own devices, girls go through life volubly answering essay questions. And boys? Multiple choice is way too complicated. Boys restrict themselves to true/false.

15   Boys do not gather and retain information, they focus on results.

16   My son went to camp for six weeks—one week longer than my daughter. As I had with my daughter, I asked him, "How was camp?"

17   He said, "Good. I busted Jason's nose." Short and to the point.

18   This was followed by, "Can we go to McDonald's?"

19   Did I mention the cheers? My daughter came back with cheers. About 187,640 musical cheers, all of which are accompanied by an intricate series of hand, feet and hip movements. She went to camp a 10-year-old, she came back a Vandella.

20   It's amazing, the affinity of girls and cheers. If you've ever been to camp, you know that girls have a special gene for cheers and that even girls who have never been to camp before—or, for that matter, been to America or spoken English before—automatically know all the cheers the moment they step off the bus. As a boy at camp, I used to look at girls in amazement, wondering why they would waste their time like that, when they could be doing useful things like me—memorizing Willie Mays' doubles and sacrifice flies during an entire decade.

21   Boys don't do musical cheers.

22   Even during "color war," that traditional camp competition when cheering is supposed to result in points, here's how boys cheer on the way to the dining hall: They look at the other team and say, "Yo, Green Team, drop dead."

■ QUESTIONS FOR ANALYSIS AND DISCUSSION

1. Kornheiser, in the context of his daughter's communication style, states that women "gather information and dispense it without discrimination." Respond to Kornheiser's assertion. Is there truth to his stereotypical description of the way men and women relay information? Explain.

2. In his introduction, Kornheiser relates how his joking about girls and math resulted in angry letters from many women, yet his comments about boys and English received no such response. What accounts for this difference? Is it more important to dispel one stereotype than the other? Why or why not?

3. Based on his essay, can you determine which communication style Kornheiser prefers? As a writer and columnist, is Kornheiser more "male" or "female" in his communication style? Explain.

I'm Sorry, I Won't Apologize

Deborah Tannen

Do women apologize too much? Are men afraid to say "I'm sorry"? In this essay Tannen comments that even when men know they are wrong, they can't seem to bring themselves to honestly apologize, and even when women aren't wrong, they feel obliged to admit fault. Is this difficulty a result of socialization?

Tannen is a professor of linguistics at Georgetown University. She is the author of many best-selling books on linguistics, including *I Only Say This Because I Love You* (2001), *The Argument Culture* (1999), and *You Just Don't Understand* (1997). She has been a guest on *20/20, 48 Hours,* CNN, and the *NewsHour with Jim Lehrer.* This article first appeared in the *New York Times* in July 1996.

■ BEFORE YOU READ

What do the words "I'm sorry" really mean? What motivates you to apologize? Do you think these two words can help avoid conflicts?

■ AS YOU READ

Have you ever wanted to say you were sorry for something but didn't because you were afraid to admit you were wrong? Did any difficulties arise because you didn't apologize?

1   Almost daily, news reports include accounts of public figures or heads of companies being forced to say they're sorry. In a recent case, Marge Schott, managing partner of the Cincinnati Reds, at first did not want to apologize for her remark that Hitler "was good at the beginning but he just went too far." Under pressure, she finally said that she regretted her remarks "offended many people." Predictably—and especially given her history with such comments— many were not satisfied with this response and successfully lobbied for her resignation.

2   This particular use of "I'm sorry" has a familiar ring. The other day my husband said to me, "I'm sorry I hurt your feelings." I knew he was really trying. He has learned, through our years together, that apologies are important to me. But he was grinning, because he also knew that "I'm sorry I hurt your feelings" left open the possibility—indeed, strongly suggested—that he regretted not what he did but my emotional reaction. It sometimes seems that he thinks the earth will open up and swallow him if he admits fault.

3   It may appear that insisting someone admit fault is like wanting him to humiliate himself. But I don't see it that way, since it's no big deal for me to say I

made a mistake and apologize. The problem is that it becomes a big deal when he won't.

4   This turns out to be similar to the Japanese view. Following a fender bender, according to a *Times* article, the Japanese typically get out of their cars and bow, each claiming responsibility. In contrast, Americans are instructed by their insurance companies to avoid admitting fault. When an American living in Japan did just that—even though he knew he was to blame—the Japanese driver "was so incensed by the American's failure to show contrition that he took the highly unusual step of suing him."

5   The Japanese driver and I are not the only ones who are offended when someone obviously at fault doesn't just fess up and apologize. A woman who lives in the country told me of a similar reaction. One day she gave her husband something to mail when he went into town. She stressed that it was essential the letter be mailed that day, and he assured her it would. But the next day, when they left the house together, she found her unmailed letter in the car. He said, "Oh, I forgot to mail your letter." She was furious—not because he had forgotten, but because he didn't apologize. "If I had done that," she said, "I would have fallen all over myself saying how sorry I was. And if he had said he was sorry, I would have been upset about the letter, but I would have forgiven him. After all, anyone can forget something. But I couldn't stop being angry, because he didn't seem to care that much that he'd let me down. I know he felt bad about it, but he wouldn't say so. Is that just him," she asked, "or is it something about men?"

6   I think it's something about men—not all men, of course. There are plenty of men who apologize easily and often, and plenty of women who—like Marge Schott—avoid it at all costs. But there are many women, seemingly more than men, who easily say they're sorry and can't understand why it's such a big deal for others. Indeed, many women say "I'm sorry" as a conversational ritual—an automatic tip of the verbal hat to acknowledge that something regrettable happened. And others sometimes take this too literally.

7   One woman, for example, was talking on the phone when she got an interrupting call that she had to take immediately. When she rang the first caller back, she began by acknowledging that she had inconvenienced him and possibly been rude. "This is Sharon," she said. "I'm sorry." He responded, "You're sorry you're Sharon?" He may well have intended this retort as a good-natured tease, but it irritated her because it implied there was something odd about what she had said, while she felt it was run-of-the-mill, even required. I suspect it struck him as odd because he would avoid saying "sorry" if he could. One C.E.O. found that he could avoid it entirely: his deputy told me that part of his job was to make the rounds after the boss had lost his temper and apologize for him.

8   It's as if there's a tenet that real men don't say they're sorry. Take the closing scene in "Crimson Tide." Gene Hackman plays an unyieldingly authoritarian Navy captain in charge of a submarine carrying nuclear warheads. When he gets an unconfirmed order to launch, he is determined to comply, but is

thwarted by his lieutenant commander, played by Denzel Washington, who defies his commanding officer, sparks a mutiny and averts nuclear war. The order to launch turns out to have been an error. The final scene is one of those exhilarating, dramatic moments when justice is served. Standing at attention before a panel that has investigated the mutiny without hearing his side, the lieutenant commander expects to be court-martialed. Instead he is promoted—on the recommendation of his captain. As the film ends, the captain turns to his deputy and says, "You were right and I was wrong. . . ." The audience gasps: this icon of authoritarian rigidity is admitting error. Then he grins mischievously and finishes the sentence, ". . . about the horses—the Lipizzaners. They *are* from Spain, not Portugal." Never mind that they're really from Austria; the two men exchange a look of intense rapport, and the audience heaves a sigh of satisfying relief.

9   Not me. I felt frustrated. Why couldn't he just say it? "I made a mistake. You were right. I was wrong about starting that nuclear war."

10   And saying you're sorry isn't enough in itself. You have to seem sorry: your face should look dejected, your voice should sound apologetic. Describing how bad you feel is also a plus. Furthermore, the depth of remorse should be commensurate with the significance of the offense. An offhand "Sorry about that" might be fine for an insignificant error like dropping a piece of paper, but if you drop a glass of red wine on your host's brand new white couch, a fleeting "Sorry about that" will not suffice.

11   The same people who resist displaying contrition may be eager to see it in others. Nowhere is this more evident than in court. Judges and juries are widely believed to give milder sentences to defendants who seem contrite. Prisons used to be called "penitentiaries" because inmates were expected not only to serve their time but also to repent. Nowadays many offenders seem to regard prison sentences as contractual: I served my time, I paid my debt. No apologies.

12   Apologies seem to come most easily from those who know their error was not intentional. The Japanese Government, for example, quickly apologized for the obviously accidental downing of an American plane during joint military exercises. But they have been much more reluctant to apologize for offenses committed during World War II, like forcing Korean, Chinese, and Filipina girls to serve as "comfort women" to Japanese soldiers.

13   Sometimes, though, people react negatively to an apology from a public figure. The First Lady discovered this last year when she met with a group of female columnists—off the record, she thought—and talked about how she had been portrayed in the press. "I regret very much that the efforts on health care were badly misunderstood, taken out of context and used politically against the Administration. I take responsibility for that, and I'm very sorry for that," she said.

14   The first part of this quote clearly indicates that the fault was not with her actions—"the efforts on health care"—but rather with the way they were received and distorted by others. But because she went on to say the big, bad "S" word, all hell broke loose. One newspaper article quoted a political scientist as

saying, "To apologize for substantive things you've done raises the white flag. There's a school of thought in politics that you never say you're sorry. The best defense is a good offense." A Republican woman in the Florida state cabinet was quoted as saying: "I've seen women who overapologize, but I don't do that. I believe you negotiate through strength."

15   And there's the rub—apologizing is seen as a sign of weakness. This explains why more men than women might resist apologizing, since most boys learn early on that their peers will take advantage of them if they appear weak. Girls, in contrast, tend to reward other girls who talk in ways that show they don't think they're better than their peers.

16   Hillary Clinton's experience also explains why those who resist saying "I apologize" may find it more palatable to say "I'm sorry," because I'm sorry is not necessarily an apology. It can be—and in the First Lady's statement it clearly was—an expression of regret. It means "I'm sorry that happened." Her experience shows how easily this expression of regret can be mistaken for an apology.

17   Given this ambiguity, shouldn't we all strike the phrase "I'm sorry" from our vocabularies? Not necessarily. I think we'd do better as a society if more people said "I'm sorry" rather than fewer. Instead of all the railing against Hillary Clinton for apologizing when she expressed regret, how come no one thought that either Newt Gingrich or his mother should apologize when the latter quoted her son as uttering an irrefutable insult against the First Lady? The problem seems to be not a surfeit of apologies but a dearth of them. One business manager told me he has discovered that apologies can be a powerful tool: subordinates so appreciate his admitting fault that they not only forgive his errors but also become ever more loyal employees.

18   History includes many examples of apologies that were not weak but highly potent. Following the calamitous Bay of Pigs invasion, John F. Kennedy demonstrated the power not only of "taking responsibility" but also of actually taking blame. For someone that high up to admit fault was shocking—and effective. People forgave the President, and his Administration, for the colossal error.

19   I think those brave enough to admit fault would find a similar power at home: it's amazing how an apology, if it seems sincere, can dissipate another's anger, calm the roiling waters. Erich Segal got it exactly wrong. Love doesn't mean never having to say you're sorry. Love means being able to say you're sorry—and, like J.F.K., being strong enough to admit you were at fault.

■ QUESTIONS FOR ANALYSIS AND DISCUSSION

1. In your own experience, which gender tends to apologize more often? Does your answer match Tannen's observations? What do you think accounts for the difference, if any?

2. Explore the culture of "no fault" in American society. Can American resistance to apology affect foreign relations? What does Tannen imply could be the far-reaching problems for our society if we don't learn to apologize more often?

3. In 1998 President Bill Clinton publicly admitted his role in the Monica Lewinsky scandal. Many people said he waited too long to apologize. Others stated that his apology didn't go far enough, and that it was insincere. Can you apply Clinton's apology to some of the points Tannen makes in her article? Explain.

4. Do you think apologizing means you are of weak character or encourages others to take advantage of you? Support your response with examples from your own experience.

5. What do you think writer Erich Segal meant when he said, "Love means never having to say you're sorry"? Do you agree? Do you approve of Tannen's revision of the phrase?

In Each Other's Company
Herbert Gold

Several years ago, ABC introduced the short-lived sitcom *The Secret Lives of Men* about "what guys really talk about with each other behind closed doors." A female critic dryly commented that the show was doomed to a short run because the writers would quickly run out of material. Did the critic have a point? Are men's friendships based more on action rather than on open communication? In this essay, Herbert Gold explores his own friendships and what holds them together.

Gold is an award-winning author and the author of many novels, including *She Took My Arm As If She Loved Me* (1997) and *The Man Who Was Not With It* (1987). He has taught creative writing at such prestigious universities as Stanford, Cornell, and Harvard. This article first appeared in the *New York Times Magazine*'s "About Men" column.

■ BEFORE YOU READ

Are men's friendships with each other different from women's with other women? If so, in what ways?

■ AS YOU READ

Note the adjectives Gold uses to describe different situations. How does his choice of words complement his essay and influence its tone?

1   These days, in California at least, the men I know seem to drink less and spend more time in coffeehouses telling each other how young they look. The child-custody fathers can bring their kids and find others of their species. The kids drink hot chocolate and eat oatmeal-raisin cookies. The fathers say: "Well, I didn't think it would work out like this. But it's working out okay." I sit there and guess that we are all in this thing together. Yes, we are getting older. No, we're not alone. We have our friendships.

2   Twisting and diving, loping and attacking—plainly grunting and sweat-ing—a young textile tycoon and I play racquetball. With devout concentration, we hunt and roam in a closed arena. Evenly matched, we have learned not to be too cast down when we lose, although we chortle with joy when we win.

3   My partner's metabolism requires risk and the expense of inventive agility. I am struggling to understand why this fast play with a hard rubber ball and a short-handled racquet seems to rank with love, children and art as one of the great pleasures of life even if I lose—in fact, a pleasure without grief, which I can't say for love, children or art.

4   The tycoon and I are not intimate friends, but the game has made a bond between us. The racquet is a weapon, like the gun or the bow and arrow. Hunters also know this comradeship that springs up between men who share the ancient rituals of exertion, risk, competition. There are women in the club, but my partner and I share a bit of disdain for those who treat it merely as a sin-gles' meeting spa. For the moment, we are content in each other's company.

5   A few years ago I was interviewed for a book about "male bonding," which is a pompous way to say "friendship between men." The writer and I discussed how old friends are the dearest, perhaps because of self-love: they have wit-nessed one's life. And then we speculated that sometimes new friends are the best, because one is free to proclaim any self-inventions one likes, and the new infatuation makes credence easy and agreeable. So those occasional new friend-ships also imply self-love. You are whatever you seem to be at the moment, whatever the friend sees in you.

6   We were enjoying a meeting of minds about the deep matter of friendship, and I thought we understood each other. Then he asked, "Do you kiss your friend?"

7   "What?"

8   "On the lips?" he asked.

9   I began to laugh, and he looked hurt. I was laughing because I had thought we understood each other and we didn't; he was hurt because he had in mind a model for friendship based on a credo of his former wife's women's group, and evidently I didn't have that in mind.

10   So that other mode of association between men began to assert itself: hos-tile banter. I accused him of not attending to friendship, not listening to me, but merely going by the current politically correct feminist notion. He replied that women have a lot to teach men about friendship. We parted in mutual sus-picion.

11   Now when we meet, a few years later, we recall the incident with a sense of the shared past, irritation and disappointment—emotions!—which amount to a curious friendship. We went through something together. Talk may not be as true as racquetball, but discussion can sometimes arrive at understanding.

12   My concert promoter friend, Bill, seems to live with telephones stuck in his ears. To get his attention, one must participate in his current deals, his angers, his frantic triumphs. Mostly this is a lonely sharing. Yet we are friends. I had the idea of hiking with him in the California woods and suggested to this obsessed

talker that we take a vow of silence as we walked to the Tassajara Zen Monastery. He agreed, but before we could go he telephoned to say, "Something has come up."

13   "Something always comes up," I said.

14   Shamed, he put our hike back on his schedule. Our vow of silence lasted ten minutes, until the first bug bite. Then came his steady stream of cursing—un-broken-in boots, insect nips, poison oak for sure. So we talked. Then we were silent. We climbed and panted and forded streams. We learned something it was unnecessary to discuss: a difficult sharing affirms friendship. Planned and formal as a cross-country hike might be, fitted into a schedule, it nevertheless serves to define and establish the facts of feeling.

15   The great model for friendship is the lifeboat. Classically, war has occasioned these moments of unscheduled danger and sacrifice. No matter what good company I find in a man in a bar or on a commuter train, there remains that secret need to know: Will he pull me into the lifeboat when I am in danger of swamping at sea? Playing games, competing, confiding, long sharing of work or opinions, even the borrowing of money, provide only a shadow of the test. Is this a friendship that would survive the ship's going down, one of us in the lifeboat, the other in the sea and reaching out? Will he carry me back to safety under fire? These urban palships of mind don't put this ultimate ideal to the test.

16   In Just Desserts, a San Francisco coffeehouse, there is, nevertheless, a sense of shared risk among single men—or men only delaying their return to the marital bed. Yes, finally the ship is going down. But meanwhile there are talk, compassion, jokes along the way.

17   And raising a child demands almost as much concentration as climbing into that half-swamped lifeboat. Now that my sons are old enough, they try and try to beat me at racquetball. One day soon they will. I'll try to take it good-naturedly, garrulous afterward, hoping they will be philosophical with me, as gentle in the ancient round of things, as the hunter appreciating the prey slung over his shoulders for the trek homeward.

■ QUESTIONS FOR ANALYSIS AND DISCUSSION

1. What obvious differences, if any, can you think of between friendships within genders? Are these differences based on socialization or biology?
2. Consider Gold's story about his concert promoter friend Bill. He wants to spend time with Bill, but he comes up with the proposal that will prevent them from talking. Why does he do this? What do you think of his request? Would two women make a similar pact?
3. What evidence does Gold use to support his views? Do you think his evidence is solid? How might you dispute some of his views regarding male friendships?
4. What upsets Gold about the writer's question about kissing on the lips (paragraph 6)? Why do you think he is surprised by the question?
5. Why is talk not as "true as racquetball" (paragraph 11)?

The Comfort of Friends

Anna Quindlen

According to Anna Quindlen, despite the many social changes women have undergone over the last one hundred years in the spheres of family, career, education, and economics, the nature of their friendships remains timeless. The things that bonded women together in the past still unite them in the present. And much of the foundation of their friendship, she explains, is based on communication and empathetic understanding. Says Quindlen, "We talk, therefore I am."

Quindlen is an award-winning columnist and novelist. The recipient of a Pulitzer Prize, Quindlen's most recent books are *Short Guide to a Happy Life* (2000) and *Black and Blue* (1998).

■ BEFORE YOU READ

Think about the things that cement friendships. How can you tell your true friends from your acquaintances?

■ AS YOU READ

Consider Quindlen's analogy that women's friendships are like a quilt. How can a quilt represent friendship? How does this comparison set the tone for her essay?

1   I collect quilts not only because of their beauty but because of their history, or what I imagine their history to be. There is one here, lying on the couch, a satin crazy quilt with spiky silken stitches holding its parts together. In one corner is a flower and the initials EK in purple embroidery floss, in another a whimsical owl done in green crewel work, in another the name Sara in silky red script. When I look at it, I see a circle of women, building it bit by bit, block by block, and as they do so, talking to one another, about their days and their disappointments, their husbands and their children, the food they cook and the houses they furnish and the dreams they dream. There is a kind of quilt called a friendship quilt, but I imagine all of mine, no matter what their pattern, are emblems of female friendship, that essential thread that has so often kept the pieces of my own life together and from time to time kept me from falling apart.

2   I can imagine my own circle in these pieces of bright fabric. The striped patches are the West Coast friend who called today to ask about my work and to tell me about hers, to compare notes on our adolescent sons and our burgeoning books. The bits of deep purple represent the Washington friend who danced at my wedding and held my babies, as I did hers, and with whom I can always pick up as though we talk every day instead of every other month. That patch of bright color is my closest friend in elementary school, and that one my matron of honor, and another is my doctor friend, who checks in from her car

phone, static punctuating our plans. And all through is my closest friend, to whom I talk every day. "Where were you?" she says if she gets my machine, and "Where were you?" I say if I get hers, and when we find one another, we move on to gossip and news, soul-searching and support. I can tell her anything, and she me, but most of the time we don't have to. Most of the time we already know everything we need to know.

3   "Write about what you and your friends are talking about on the telephone," an editor told me when I was given the assignment of writing a personal column a decade ago. That wasn't all I wrote about over the years, but I probably could have gotten a column out of nearly every phone conversation. On the other hand, if my husband had to rely on his phone conversations with friends for column ideas—well, you finish the sentence. Whenever I've used that particular comparison, whether I was talking to female friends at lunch or speaking to a group of women in public, they've always burst out laughing before I got to the end of the subordinate clause. It was an immediate, visceral recognition of what seems to be a central fact of human attachment: that what men call friendship is often skin deep, while what we women make of it is something probing and intimate, an emotional undressing, something akin to an essay every time we sit down to lunch or pick up the phone. As Anaïs Nin wrote, "Each friend represents a world in us, a world possibly not born until they arrive, and it is only by this meeting that a new world is born."

4   Simple gender distinctions are probably too broad a brush for these more egalitarian days, in which more men have intimate friendships, more women have less time for them, and more men and women have relationships that transcend both sex and romance. But the truth is that most of the women I know, in the midst of hectic, confusing and sometimes disappointing lives, find one of their greatest sources of strength in a circle of female friends. It's why the movies "Waiting To Exhale" and "The First Wives Club" did so well at the box office—not because they were about women trashing men but because they were about women finding their greatest solace in the love and support of other women.

5   Harvard professor Carol Gilligan, an authority on the behavior of girls, says that the emotional connections that make intimate friendships possible begin early. "People used to look out on the playground and say that the boys were playing soccer and the girls were doing nothing," Gilligan says. "But the girls weren't doing nothing—they were talking. They were talking about the world to one another. And they become very expert about that in a way the boys did not."

6   Naturally, this is not always so. There is a kind of woman, usually called a "man's woman," who always seems to see other women as competition or furniture, whose orientation is always toward the XY chromosomes in the room. Maybe all of us become that kind of woman for a time; I can certainly remember years, stretching from puberty until I knew better, when I would have blown off any of my girlfriends for a guy. And sometimes it is only maturity that allows us to be vulnerable, to trust and confide in the way real friendship requires; we

can all remember the cruel vicissitudes of elementary school friendship, which often seemed like a game of musical chairs—four bars of tinny music and then suddenly no place for you in the magic circle.

7   Perhaps that's why, in the diary she received for her 13th birthday, Anne Frank wrote, "On the surface I seem to have everything, except my one true friend. All I think about when I'm with my friends is having a good time. I can't bring myself to talk about anything but ordinary everyday things." Instead, she told her diary what many of us tell our friends—about her romantic yearnings, her self-doubts, the differences with those closest to her. It's a model of female confidences, the immortal diary. "Dearest Kitty," begins one entry, "Mother and I had a so-called 'discussion' today." But there's a certain poignancy in the fact that Anne's closest confidant is paper and cardboard, incapable of reciprocal conversation. Of course, the diary is in many ways a vehicle, a way for Anne to know herself, which seems to be the end result of our closest friendships after all.

8   There were times, particularly when I found myself in a new and difficult role, when I practically went trolling for "one true friend": in the largely male newsrooms where I learned to be a reporter, the playgrounds where I first took my toddlers while trying to figure out how to be a mother, the hallways at school. Book groups and play groups: we cleave together. I only really understand myself, what I'm really thinking and feeling, when I've talked it over with my circle of female friends. When days go by without that connection, I feel like a radio playing in an empty room.

9   By circle of friends I don't mean a group of women all connected to each other—but all connected to me. It's the same with most of us, I think. Last month I went to a birthday lunch for one of my close friends; ranged around the table was a group of women, many of whom I'd never met before but all of whom I'd heard about many times. It was a meal of discovery—"Oh, that's her, and her, and her, too." They were friends of my friend from different times of her life, as I have mine, from school and work and my children's schools and my husband's work. In our constantly shifting lives, our female friends may be the greatest constant and the touchstone not only of who we are but who we once were, the people who, taken together, know us whole, from girlfriend to wife and mother and even to widow. Children grow and go; even beloved men sometimes seem to be beaming their perceptions and responses in from a different planet. But our female friends are forever.

10   Professor Gilligan says she thinks the women's movement had something to do with this, that it was when we began to value what it meant to us to be female that we were most able to be open with one another about our real lives, not the Hallmark card version, to reveal the aches beneath the apron, the bruises beneath the business suit. "For a long time our conversations focused on relationships with men," says Gilligan of her own circle. "But soon we were talking about everything: our love lives, our work, our angst. Times of crisis but also just ordinary times and good times. It's true closeness, true intimacy. The conversation lays the groundwork for a deeper connection."

11   But I suspect that sort of intimacy predates the newest wave of feminism, going back far further than we think. I remember my mother and her cousin Gloria, my grandmother and her friend Marion. I remember as a child thinking, seeing those women in conversation with one another, that it was like seeing an iceberg, knowing that so much was going on, had gone on beneath the surface of that moment, the years, the tears, the confidences. I read the letters of Victorian women, who, unencumbered by the sexual subtext that would accompany it today, spoke the language of love to one another and even shared the same bed in what was most often a gesture of emotional, not physical, intimacy. The historian Carroll Smith-Rosenberg says that close female friendships were taken for granted a century ago as a source of succor superior to the joining of two disparate parts in marriage. "Women," she wrote, "who had little status or power in the larger world of male concerns, possessed status and power in the lives of other women."

12   The first time I met Hillary Rodham Clinton, during the 1992 presidential campaign, she showed me a bracelet that she had just been given for her birthday. Her nine closest women friends had bought it for her, and the initials of each were engraved on the links. Later, during the president's first term, I asked how she managed to survive the maelstrom and continual scrutiny of life in the White House, and she showed me the bracelet once again. It was her circle of friends that kept her equilibrium constant. They were the people, she has said, to whom she sent the manuscript of her book to figure out how it could be improved. "Hillary," one said, "this is like a beautiful garden with some weeds." In a world in which she could never tell whom to trust, or how much, she knew her circle of friends would be honest. She also knew they would be kind. And she knew that when the going got rough and tough, she could call one of those women and get, not an instant analysis of how she should remake her image, but first and foremost a sympathetic ear.

13   Joanna Bull, who runs Gilda's Club, the support organization for people living with cancer and their families, says many of her support groups try to teach the men who participate to learn intimacy and openness in a way that is intuitive for many women and that comes from, and feeds, female friendships. "When I was diagnosed with leukemia," Bull recalls, "it meant everything in the world to me that there came from across the country 10 women who just nurtured me for the weekend. Some of them I rarely saw in person and mainly kept in touch with me by telephone. Most of them had never met one another. But all of them wanted to come right away, and they came to my house in California and we sat in the hot tub and we ate and drank and laughed and cried and talked and talked and talked. I don't think 10 men would do that. Which is sad for them."

14   As the mother of two sons, I wonder if our world of increasing gender equality will change that. My daughter has already begun to repeat the patterns I remember so well from my own girlhood: the little knot of girls in one corner of the schoolyard, trading sentences as though conversation were a contact sport; the cycle of best friends and betrayal, complete with tumultuous tears

and favorite possessions gladly given away; the constant analysis of classroom personal relations, as though between math and reading she had also studied group dynamics. And my boys? Well, when the eldest is on the phone for a long, long time these days, chances are that he's talking to a girl friend. Maybe the friendship circles of years to come will be more polyglot than those of my friends. Maybe he will never say to his wife, "What do you two find to talk about every day?" because he will have learned what there is to talk about from his own circle of female friends.

15   What do we find to talk about? Well, let's see: Kids. Hormones. Living room drapes. O. J. Simpson. Madonna. Movies. Books. Clothes. Politics. Men. "Melrose Place." Sadness. Happiness. Aging. Loss. Breast cancer. Cosmetic surgery. Black bean soup. Pot pie. Love. Piece by piece, we stitch the world together into something we can work with, something with which we can cover ourselves against the cold nights. I don't know what in the world I would do without them, for advice, for comfort, for simply knowing that there is someone out there who knows me as I am and loves me despite and because of it. I've never been in therapy, and maybe they are the reason why. We talk, therefore I am.

■ QUESTIONS FOR ANALYSIS AND DISCUSSION

1. How important is verbal communication to the success of women's relationships? Do the things that bond women's friendships differ from those that link men?

2. Quindlen's editor told her, "Write about what you and your friends are talking about on the telephone." Write about a recent conversation you had on the phone with a friend and analyze its content. What could a transcript of your conversation tell others about your relationship with that person?

3. What is a "man's woman"? Explain.

4. Analyze Quindlen's "circle of friends." Are all her friendships the same? How do you think she feels about her friends? What do her friends provide her with?

5. Quindlen recalls the behaviors of boys and girls on the playground when she was a child. She ends her article with an observation of boys and girls on the playground today. What conclusions does she draw from her comparison? Do you agree?

6. What does Quindlen's friend say is "sad" about men's friendships (paragraph 13)? Why does she feel this way? Drawing from your own experience, do you agree or disagree with Quindlen's friend?

Stopping for Directions

This cartoon by Don Reilly first appeared in *The New Yorker* magazine.

■ QUESTIONS FOR ANALYSIS AND DISCUSSION

1. It has been a long-held adage that men don't stop to ask for directions. Is it self-reliance? independence? Or are men simply unwilling to admit that they need help? What social impressions may influence their reluctance? Explain.

"Because my genetic programming prevents me from stopping to ask directions—that's why!"

2. Are women more likely to stop and ask for directions or other assistance? Or more importantly, why does this stereotype exist?
3. In the cartoon, the man tells the woman that it is his "genetic programming" that prevents him from stopping. How do you think the authors in this section would respond to this cartoon?
4. Explain why, in your opinion, the cartoon is—or isn't—true. Is this an American comedic situation, or does is it hold true for other cultures? Show this cartoon to some international students and ask for their reactions. Report your results in class for discussion.

■ WRITING ASSIGNMENTS

1. Do you think language itself can be "gendered"? For example, are there certain words that seem "male" and others that seem "female"? Review the essays by Gold and Quindlen and evaluate the words they use to convey their ideas. Write an argument essay that considers the idea of gendered language.

2. In the 1986 movie *When Harry Met Sally,* Harry (Billy Crystal) says to Sally (Meg Ryan) that men and women cannot be friends. Much of the movie is then spent trying to prove his statement wrong. Watch the movie. Support or refute Harry's statement. Can men and women be friends? Why or why not? Is there a middle ground? Support your view with examples from both the movie and your own experience.

3. Have you ever found yourself at an impasse with a member of the opposite sex because your communication styles were different? For example, did you think the person with whom you were arguing "just didn't get it" solely because of his or her sex? Explain what accounted for the miscommunication and how you solved it.

4. Margaret Atwood wrote a short poem "[You fit into me]" about women's ways of knowing. Locate a copy of this poem and analyze its meaning. Many women find the poem's second stanza more shocking than the first, because their interpretation of "hook" and "eye" is different from most men's understanding of these words. How are gender and language important to this poem and its interpretation?

5. Several of the authors in this section seem to advocate their own gender's communication style. Write an essay in which you support your gender's communication style, or advocate or analyze the style of the opposite sex. Is one better than the other? Why or why not? Remember to support your perspective with examples.

FEMINISM IN THE TWENTY-FIRST CENTURY

The Independent Woman and Other Lies

Katie Roiphe

Although traditional gender roles have greatly changed over the past 50 years, some preconceived notions remain, especially concerning money, sending conflicting messages to both men and women, says writer Katie Roiphe. On the one hand, men are expected to view women as economic equals. On the other hand, they are still expected to pick up the check and earn more than their female companions. And while many women may say that they want economic equality, they send a very different message when they insist that the men whom they marry earn a higher salary.

Self-proclaimed "postfeminist" Roiphe earned her Ph.D. from Princeton University and is the author of the non-fiction books *The Morning After: Sex, Fear, and Feminism* (1993) and *Last Night in Paradise: Sex and Morals at the Century's End* (1997), and the novel *Still She Haunts Me* (2001). She has contributed to articles appearing in many newspapers and magazines, including *Harpers,* the *New York Times,* and *Esquire,* where this essay first appeared in February 1997.

■ **BEFORE YOU READ**

Who should pay for the date when a man and a woman go out? Does it matter? Do the circumstances change if they are married? Do you think that society as a whole feels that men should be the primary breadwinners?

■ **AS YOU READ**

What does Roiphe identify as "traditional" gender roles for men and women? Do you agree with her perspective?

1   I was out to drinks with a man I'd recently met. "I'll take care of that," he said, sweeping up the check, and as he said it, I felt a warm glow of security, as if everything in my life was suddenly going to be taken care of. As the pink cosmopolitans glided smoothly across the bar, I thought for a moment of how nice it would be to live in an era when men always took care of the cosmopolitans. I pictured a lawyer with a creamy leather briefcase going off to work in the mornings and coming back home in the evenings to the townhouse he has bought for me, where I have been ordering flowers, soaking in the bath, reading a nineteenth-century novel, and working idly on my next book. This fantasy of a Man in a Gray Flannel Suit is one that independent, strong-minded women of the nineties are distinctly not supposed to have, but I find myself having it all the same. And many of the women I know are having it also.

2   Seen from the outside, my life is the model of modern female independence. I live alone, pay my own bills, and fix my stereo when it breaks down. But it sometimes seems like my independence is in part an elaborately constructed facade that hides a more traditional feminine desire to be protected and provided for. I admitted this once to my mother, an ardent seventies feminist, over Caesar salads at lunch, and she was shocked. I saw it on her face: How could a daughter of mine say something like this? I rushed to reassure her that I wouldn't dream of giving up my career, and it's true that I wouldn't. But when I think about marriage, somewhere deep in the irrational layers of my psyche, I still think of the man as the breadwinner. I feel as though I am working for "fulfillment," for "reward," for the richness of life promised by feminism, and that mundane things such as rent and mortgages and college tuitions are, ultimately, the man's responsibility—even though I know that they shouldn't be. "I just don't want to have to think about money," one of my most competent female friends said to me recently, and I knew exactly what she meant. Our liberated, postfeminist world seems to be filled with women who don't want to think about money and men who feel that they have to.

3   There are plenty of well-adjusted, independent women who never fantasize about the Man in the Gray Flannel Suit, but there are also a surprising number who do. Of course, there is a well-established tradition of women looking for men to provide for them that spans from Edith Wharton's *The House of Mirth* to Helen Gurley Brown's *Sex and the Single Girl* to Mona Simpson's *A Regular Guy*.

You could almost say that this is the American dream for women: Find a man who can lift you out of your circumstances, whisk you away to Venice, and give you a new life.

4   In my mother's generation, a woman felt she had to marry a man with a successful career, whereas today she is supposed to focus on her own. Consider that in 1990, women received 42 percent of law degrees (up from 2.5 percent in 1960) and that as of 1992, women held 47 percent of lucrative jobs in the professions and management. And now that American women are more economically independent than ever before, now that we don't need to attach ourselves to successful men, many of us still seem to want to. I don't think, in the end, that this attraction is about bank accounts or trips to Paris or hundred dollar haircuts, I think it's about the reassuring feeling of being protected and provided for, a feeling that mingles with love and attraction on the deepest level. It's strange to think of professional women in the nineties drinking cafe lattes and talking about men in the same way as characters in Jane Austen novels, appraising their prospects and fortunes, but many of us actually do.

5   A friend of mine, an editor at a women's magazine, said about a recent breakup, "I just hated having to say, 'My boyfriend is a dog walker.' I hated the fact that he didn't have a job." And then immediately afterward, she said, "I feel really awful admitting all of this." It was as if she had just told me something shameful, as if she had confessed to some terrible perversion. And I understand why she felt guilty. She was admitting to a sort of 1950s worldview that seemed as odd and unfashionable as walking down the street in a poodle skirt. But she is struggling with what defines masculinity and femininity in a supposedly equal society, with what draws us to men, what attracts us, what keeps us interested. She has no more reason to feel guilty than a man who says he likes tall blonds.

6   I've heard many women say that they wouldn't want to go out with a man who is much less successful than they are because "he would feel uncomfortable." But, of course, he's not the only one who would feel uncomfortable. What most of these women are really saying is that they themselves would feel uncomfortable. But why? Why can't the magazine editor be happy with the dog walker? Why does the woman at Salomon Brothers feel unhappy with the banker who isn't doing as well as she is? Part of it may have to do with the way we were raised. Even though I grew up in a liberal household in the seventies, I perceived early on that my father was the one who actually paid for things. As a little girl, I watched my father put his credit card down in restaurants and write checks and go to work every morning in a suit and tie, and it may be that this model of masculinity is still imprinted in my mind. It may be that there is a picture of our fathers that many of us carry like silver lockets around our necks: Why shouldn't we find a man who will take care of us the way our fathers did?

7   I've seen the various destructive ways in which this expectation can affect people's lives. Sam and Anna met at Brown. After they graduated, Anna went to Hollywood and started making nearly a million dollars a year in television production, and Sam became an aspiring novelist who has never even filed a tax return. At first, the disparity in their styles of life manifested itself in trivial ways.

"She would want to go to an expensive bistro," Sam, who is now twenty-seven, remembers, "and I would want to get a burrito for $4.25. We would go to the bistro, and either she'd pay, which was bad, or I'd just eat salad and lots of bread, which was also bad." In college, they had been the kind of couple who stayed up until three in the morning talking about art and beauty and *The Brothers Karamazov*, but now they seemed to be spending a lot of time arguing about money and burritos. One night, when they went out with some of Anna's Hollywood friends, she slipped him eighty dollars under the table so that he could pretend to pay for dinner. Anna felt guilty. Sam was confused. He had grown up with a feminist mother who'd drummed the ideal of strong, independent women into his head, but now that he'd fallen in love with Anna, probably the strongest and most independent woman he'd ever met, she wanted him to pay for her dinner so badly she gave him money to do it. Anna, I should say, is not a particularly materialistic person. She is not someone who cares about Chanel suits and Prada bags. It's just that to her, money had become a luminous symbol of functionality and power.

8   The five-year relationship began to fall apart. Sam was not fulfilling the role of romantic lead in the script Anna had in her head. In a moment of desperation, Sam blurted out that he had made a lot of money on the stock market. He hadn't. Shortly afterward, they broke up. Anna started dating her boss, and she and Sam had agonizing long-distance phone calls about what had happened. "She kept telling me that she wanted me to be more of a man," Sam says. "She kept saying that she wanted to be taken care of." There was a certain irony to this situation, to this woman who was making almost a million dollars a year, sitting in her Santa Monica house, looking out at the ocean, saying that she just wanted a man who could take care of her.

9   There is also something appalling in this story, something cruel and hard and infinitely understandable. The strain of Anna's success and Sam's as of yet unrewarded talent was too much for the relationship. When Anna told Sam that she wanted him to be more masculine, part of what she was saying was that she wanted to feel more feminine. It's like the plight of the too-tall teenage girl who's anxiously scanning the dance floor for a fifteen-year-old boy who is taller than she is. A romantic might say, What about love? Love isn't supposed to be about dollars and cents and who puts their Visa card down at an expensive Beverly Hills restaurant. But this is a story about love in its more tarnished, worldly forms, it's about the balance of power, what men and women really want from one another, and the hidden mechanics of romance and attraction. In a way, what happened between my friends Sam and Anna is a parable of our times, of a generation of strong women who are looking for even stronger men.

10   I've said the same thing as Anna—"I need a man who can take care of me"—to more than one boyfriend, and I hear how it sounds. I recognize how shallow and unreasonable it seems. But I say it anyway. And, even worse, I actually feel it.

11   The mood passes. I realize that I can take care of myself. The relationship returns to normal, the boyfriend jokes that I should go to the bar at the plaza to meet bankers, and we both laugh because we know that I don't really want to,

but there is an undercurrent of resentment, eddies of tension and disappoint-ment that remain between us. This is a secret refrain that runs through conver-sations in bedrooms late at night, through phone wires, and in restaurants over drinks. One has to wonder, why, at a moment in history when women can so patently take care of themselves, do so many of us want so much to be taken care of?

12   The fantasy of a man who pays the bills, who works when you want to take time off to be with your kids or read *War and Peace,* who is in the end responsi-ble, is one that many women have but fairly few admit to. It is one of those fan-tasies, like rape fantasies, that have been forbidden to us by our politics. But it's also deeply ingrained in our imaginations. All of girl culture tells us to find a man who will provide for us, a Prince Charming, a Mr. Rochester, a Mr. Darcy, a Rhett Butler. These are the objects of our earliest romantic yearnings, the pri-vate desires of a whole country of little girls, the fairy tales that actually end up affecting our real lives. As the feminist film critic Molly Haskell says, "We never really escape the old-fashioned roles. They get inside our heads. Dependence has always been eroticized."

13   Many of the men I know seem understandably bewildered by the fact that women want to be independent only sometimes, only sort of, and only selec-tively. The same women who give eloquent speeches at dinner parties on the subject of "glass ceilings" still want men to pay for first dates, and this can be sort of perplexing for the men around them who are still trying to fit into the puzzle that the feminism of the seventies has created for them. For a long time, women have been saying that we don't want a double standard, but it some-times seems that what many women want is simply a more subtle and refined version of a double standard: We want men to be the providers and to regard us as equals. This slightly unreasonable expectation is not exactly new. In 1963, a reporter asked Mary McCarthy what women really wanted, and she answered, "They want everything. That's the trouble—they can't have everything. They can't possibly have all the prerogatives of being a woman and the privileges of being a man at the same time."

14   "We're spoiled," says Helen Gurley Brown, one of the world's foremost the-orists on dating. "We just don't want to give up any of the good stuff." And she may have a point. In a world in which women compete with men, in which all of us are feeling the same drive to succeed, there is something reassuring about falling—if only for the length of a dinner—into traditional sex roles. You can just relax. You can take a rest from yourself. You can let the pressures and am-bitions melt away and give in to the archaic fantasy: For just half an hour, you are just a pretty girl smiling at a man over a drink. I think that old-fashioned rituals, such as men paying for dates, endure precisely because of how much has actually changed; they cover up the fact that men and women are equal and that equality is not always, in all contexts and situations, comfortable or even desirable.

15   This may explain why I have been so ungratefully day-dreaming about the Man in the Gray Flannel Suit thirty years after Betty Friedan published *The Fem-*

inine Mystique. The truth is, the knowledge that I can take care of myself, that I don't really need a man, is not without its own accompanying terrors. The idea that I could make myself into a sleek, self-sufficient androgyne is not all that appealing. Now that we have all of the rooms of our own that we need, we begin to look for that shared and crowded space. And it is this fear of independence, this fear of not needing a man, that explains the voices of more competent, accomplished corporate types than me saying to the men around them, "Provide for me, protect me." It may be one of the bad jokes that history occasionally plays on us: that the independence my mother's generation wanted so much for their daughters was something we could not entirely appreciate or want. It was like a birthday present from a distant relative—wrong size, wrong color, wrong style. And so women are left struggling with the desire to submit and not submit, to be dependent and independent, to take care of ourselves and be taken care of, and it's in the confusion of this struggle that most of us love and are loved.

16   For myself, I continue to go out with poets and novelists and writers, with men who don't pay for dates or buy me dresses at Bergdorf's or go off to their offices in the morning, but the Man in the Gray Flannel Suit lives on in my imagination, perplexing, irrational, revealing of some dark and unsettling truth.

■ QUESTIONS FOR ANALYSIS AND DISCUSSION

1. What does Roiphe say is the "lie" of the independent woman? Why is it a "lie"? Do you agree with her perspective?
2. On what premises does Roiphe base her argument? What evidence does she use to support it? Is her support sound? What assumptions, if any, does the argument make? Explain.
3. In paragraph 12 Roiphe likens the illicit nature of the "Man in the Gray Flannel Suit" fantasy to other fantasies women have including the "rape fantasy." What do you think she means by the "rape fantasy"? Does this analogy contribute to her argument? Why are these fantasies "forbidden to us by our politics"?
4. Have you ever experienced relationship difficulties stemming from earnings or income differences between the sexes? Explain.
5. In paragraph 13 Roiphe discusses what women really want. What do *you* think women really want? How does your analysis compare to Roiphe's conclusions?

In the Combat Zone

Leslie Marmon Silko

Safety experts warn women not to walk alone at night, to park where it is well-lit, and to avoid areas that could conceal muggers or rapists. Self-defense classes for women stress avoidance tactics rather than ways to actively confront violence. This approach, says Leslie Marmon Silko, creates a cultural consciousness of women as victims and targets. In this essay, Silko relates how her childhood hunting experiences helped empower her in a society that tends to view women as prey.

A recipient of a MacArthur Foundation Fellowship, Silko is one of America's best-known Native-American writers. A former professor of English and creative writing, she is the author of many short stories, essays, poetry, plays, articles, and books, including *Almanac of the Dead* (1991) and *Gardens in the Dunes* (1999).

■ BEFORE YOU READ

Have you ever found yourself planning your activities based on personal safety? For example, did you do without something because you were afraid of going to the store at night by yourself? Or have you skipped taking a shortcut when it was dark out? If not, why don't you fear these situations?

■ AS YOU READ

Note Silko's references to hunting throughout the essay. How does the theme of hunting unify the piece?

1   Women seldom discuss our wariness or the precautions we take after dark each time we leave the apartment, car, or office to go on the most brief errand. We take for granted that we are targeted as easy prey by muggers, rapists, and serial killers. This is our lot as women in the United States. We try to avoid going anywhere alone after dark, although economic necessity sends women out night after night. We do what must be done, but always we are alert, on guard and ready. We have to be aware of persons walking on the sidewalk behind us; we have to pay attention to others who board an elevator we're on. We try to avoid all staircases and deserted parking garages when we are alone. Constant vigilance requires considerable energy and concentration seldom required of men.

2   I used to assume that most men were aware of this fact of women's lives, but I was wrong. They may notice our reluctance to drive at night to the convenience store alone, but they don't know or don't want to know the experience of a woman out alone at night. Men who have been in combat know the feeling of being a predator's target, but it is difficult for men to admit that we women live our entire lives in a combat zone. Men have the power to end violence against women in the home, but they feel helpless to protect women from violent strangers. Because men feel guilt and anger at their inability to shoulder responsibility for the safety of their wives, sisters, and daughters, we don't often discuss random acts of violence against women.

3   When we were children, my sisters and I used to go to Albuquerque with my father. Sometimes strangers would tell my father it was too bad that he had three girls and no sons. My father, who has always preferred the company of women, used to reply that he was glad to have girls and not boys, because he

might not get along as well with boys. Furthermore, he'd say, "My girls can do anything your boys can do, and my girls can do it better." He had in mind, of course, shooting and hunting.

4   When I was six years old, my father took me along as he hunted deer; he showed me how to walk quietly, to move along and then to stop and listen carefully before taking another step. A year later, he traded a pistol for a little single shot .22 rifle just my size.

5   He took me and my younger sisters down to the dump by the river and taught us how to shoot. We rummaged through the trash for bottles and glass jars; it was great fun to take aim at a pickle jar and watch it shatter. If the Rio San Jose had water running in it, we threw bottles for moving targets in the muddy current. My father told us that a .22 bullet can travel a mile, so we had to be careful where we aimed. The river was a good place because it was below the villages and away from the houses; the high clay riverbanks wouldn't let any bullets stray. Gun safety was drilled into us. We were cautioned about other children whose parents might not teach them properly; if we ever saw another child with a gun, we knew to get away. Guns were not toys. My father did not approve of BB guns because they were classified as toys. I had a .22 rifle when I was seven years old. If I felt like shooting, all I had to do was tell my parents where I was going, take my rifle and a box of 12 shells and go. I was never tempted to shoot at birds or animals because whatever was killed had to be eaten. Now, I realize how odd this must seem; a seven-year-old with a little .22 rifle and a box of ammunition, target shooting alone at the river. But that was how people lived at Laguna when I was growing up; children were given responsibility from an early age.

6   Laguna Pueblo people hunted deer for winter meat. When I was thirteen I carried George Pearl's saddle carbine, a .30–30, and hunted deer for the first time. When I was fourteen, I killed my first mule deer buck with one shot through the heart.

7   Guns were for target shooting and guns were for hunting, but also I knew that Grandma Lily carried a little purse gun with her whenever she drove alone to Albuquerque or Los Lunas. One night my mother and my grandmother were driving the fifty miles from Albuquerque to Laguna down Route 66 when three men in a car tried to force my grandmother's car off the highway. Route 66 was not so heavily traveled as Interstate 40 is now, and there were many long stretches of highway where no other car passed for minutes on end. Payrolls at the Jackpile Uranium Mine were large in the 1950s, and my mother or my grandmother had to bring home thousands from the bank in Albuquerque to cash the miners' checks on paydays.

8   After that night, my father bought my mother a pink nickel-plated snubnose .22 revolver with a white bone grip. Grandma Lily carried a tiny Beretta as black as her prayer book. As my sisters and I got older, my father taught us to handle and shoot handguns, revolvers mostly, because back then, semiautomatic pistols were not as reliable—they frequently jammed. I will never forget the day my father told us three girls that we never had to let a man hit us or ter-

rorize us because no matter how big and strong the man was, a gun in our hand equalized all differences of size and strength.

9   Much has been written about violence in the home and spousal abuse. I wish to focus instead on violence from strangers toward women because this form of violence terrifies women more, despite the fact that most women are murdered by a spouse, relative, fellow employee, or next-door neighbor, not a stranger. Domestic violence kills many more women and children than strangers kill, but domestic violence also follows more predictable patterns and is more familiar—he comes home drunk and she knows what comes next. A good deal of the terror of a stranger's attack comes from its suddenness and unexpectedness. Attacks by strangers occur with enough frequency that battered women and children often cite their fears of such attacks as reasons for remaining in abusive domestic situations. They fear the violence they imagine strangers will inflict upon them more than they fear the abusive home. More than one feminist has pointed out that rapists and serial killers help keep the patriarchy in place.

10   An individual woman may be terrorized by her spouse, but women are not sufficiently terrorized that we avoid marriage. Yet many women I know, including myself, try to avoid going outside of their homes alone after dark. Big deal, you say; well yes, it is a big deal since most lectures, performances, and films are presented at night; so are dinners and other social events. Women out alone at night who are assaulted by strangers are put on trial by public opinion: Any woman out alone after dark is asking for trouble. Presently, for millions of women of all socioeconomic backgrounds, sundown is lockdown. We are prisoners of violent strangers.

11   Daylight doesn't necessarily make the streets safe for women. In the early 1980s, a rapist operated in Tucson in the afternoon near the University of Arizona campus. He often accosted two women at once, forced them into residential alleys, then raped each one with a knife to her throat and forced the other to watch. Afterward the women said that part of the horror of their attack was that all around them, everything appeared normal. They could see people inside their houses and cars going down the street—all around them life was going on as usual while their lives were being changed forever.

12   The afternoon rapist was not the only rapist in Tucson at that time; there was the prime-time rapist, the potbellied rapist, and the apologetic rapist all operating in Tucson in the 1980s. The prime-time rapist was actually two men who invaded comfortable foothills homes during television prime time when residents were preoccupied with television and eating dinner. The prime-time rapists terrorized entire families; they raped the women and sometimes they raped the men. Family members were forced to go to automatic bank machines, to bring back cash to end the ordeal. Potbelly rapist and apologetic rapist need little comment, except to note that the apologetic rapist was good looking, well educated, and smart enough to break out of jail for one last rape followed by profuse apologies and his capture in the University of Arizona li-

brary. Local papers recounted details about Tucson's last notorious rapist, the red bandanna rapist. In the late 1970s this rapist attacked more than twenty women over a three-year period, and Tucson police were powerless to stop him. Then one night, the rapist broke into a midtown home where the lone resident, a woman, shot him four times in the chest with a .38 caliber revolver.

13   In midtown Tucson, on a weekday afternoon, I was driving down Campbell Avenue to the pet store. Suddenly the vehicle behind me began to weave into my lane, so I beeped the horn politely. The vehicle swerved back to its lane, but then in my rearview mirror I saw the small late-model truck change lanes and begin to follow my car very closely. I drove a few blocks without looking in the rearview mirror, but in my sideview mirror I saw the compact truck was right behind me. OK. Some motorists stay upset for two or three blocks, some require ten blocks or more to recover their senses. Stoplight after stoplight, when I glanced into the rearview mirror I saw the man—in his early thirties, tall, white, brown hair, and dark glasses. This guy must not have a job if he has the time to follow me for miles—oh, ohhh! No beast more dangerous in the U.S.A. than an unemployed white man.

14   At this point I had to make a decision: do I forget about the trip to the pet store and head for the police station downtown, four miles away? Why should I have to let this stranger dictate my schedule for the afternoon? The man might dare to follow me to the police station, but by the time I reach the front door of the station, he'd be gone. No crime was committed; no Arizona law forbids tailgating someone for miles or for turning into a parking lot behind them. What could the police do? I had no license plate number to report because Arizona requires only one license plate, on the rear bumper of the vehicle. Anyway, I was within a block of the pet store where I knew I could get help from the pet store owners. I would feel better about this incident if it was not allowed to ruin my trip to the pet store.

15   The guy was right on my rear bumper; if I'd had to stop suddenly for any reason, there'd have been a collision. I decide I will not stop even if he does ram into the rear of my car. I study this guy's face in my rearview mirror, six feet two inches tall, 175 pounds, medium complexion, short hair, trimmed moustache. He thinks he can intimidate me because I am a woman, five feet five inches tall, 140 pounds. But I am not afraid, I am furious. I refuse to be intimidated. I won't play his game. I can tell by the face I see in the mirror this guy has done this before; he enjoys using his truck to menace lone women.

16   I keep thinking he will quit, or he will figure that he's scared me enough; but he seems to sense that I am not afraid. It's true. I am not afraid because years ago my father taught my sisters and me that we did not have to be afraid. He'll give up when I turn into the parking lot outside the pet store, I think. But I watch in my rearview mirror; he's right on my rear bumper. As his truck turns into the parking lot behind my car, I reach over and open the glove compartment. I take out the holster with my .38 special and lay it on the car seat beside me.

17   I turned my car into a parking spot so quickly that I was facing my stalker who had momentarily stopped his truck and was watching me. I slid the .38

out of its holster onto my lap. I watched the stranger's face, trying to determine whether he would jump out of his truck with a baseball bat or gun and come after me. I felt calm. No pounding heart or rapid breathing. My early experience deer hunting had prepared me well. I did not panic because I felt I could stop him if he tried to harm me. I was in no hurry. I sat in the car and waited to see what choice my stalker would make. I looked directly at him without fear because I had my .38 and I was ready to use it. The expression on my face must have been unfamiliar to him; he was used to seeing terror in the eyes of the women he followed. The expression on my face communicated a warning: if he approached the car window, I'd kill him.

18   He took a last look at me and then sped away. I stayed in the car until his truck disappeared in the traffic of Campbell Avenue.

19   I walked into the pet store shaken. I had felt able to protect myself throughout the incident, but it left me emotionally drained and exhausted. The stranger had only pursued me—how much worse to be battered or raped.

20   Years before, I was unarmed the afternoon that two drunken deer hunters threatened to shoot me off my horse with razor-edged hunting crossbows. I was riding a colt on a national park trail near my home in the Tucson Mountains. These young white men in their late twenties were complete strangers who might have shot me if the colt had not galloped away erratically bucking and leaping—a moving target too difficult for the drunken bow hunters to aim at. The colt brought me to my ranch house where I called the country sheriff's office and the park ranger. I live in a sparsely populated area where my nearest neighbor is a quarter-mile away. I was afraid the men might have followed me back to my house so I took the .44 magnum out from under my pillow and strapped it around my waist until the sheriff or park ranger arrived. Forty-five minutes later, the park ranger arrived—the deputy sheriff arrived fifteen minutes after him. The drunken bow hunters were apprehended on the national park and arrested for illegally hunting; their bows and arrows were seized as evidence for the duration of bow hunting season. In southern Arizona that is enough punishment; I didn't want to take a chance of stirring up additional animosity with these men because I lived alone then; I chose not to make a complaint about their threatening words and gestures. I did not feel that I backed away by not pressing charges; I feared that if I pressed assault charges against these men, they would feel that I was challenging them to all-out war. I did not want to have to kill either of them if they came after me, as I thought they might. With my marksmanship and my .243 caliber hunting rifle from the old days, I am confident that I could stop idiots like these. But to have to take the life of another person is a terrible experience I will always try to avoid.

21   It isn't height or weight or strength that make women easy targets; from infancy women are taught to be self-sacrificing, passive victims. I was taught differently. Women have the right to protect themselves from death or bodily harm. By becoming strong and potentially lethal individuals, women destroy the fantasy that we are sitting ducks for predatory strangers.

22   In a great many cultures, women are taught to depend upon others, not themselves, for protection from bodily harm. Women are not taught to defend themselves from strangers because fathers and husbands fear the consequences themselves. In the United States, women depend upon the courts and the police; but as many women have learned the hard way, the police cannot be outside your house twenty-four hours a day. I don't want more police. More police on the street will not protect women. A few policemen are rapists and killers of women themselves; their uniforms and squad cars give them an advantage. No, I will be responsible for my own safety, thank you.

23   Women need to decide who has the primary responsibility for the health and safety of their bodies. We don't trust the State to manage our reproductive organs, yet most of us blindly trust that the State will protect us (and our reproductive organs) from predatory strangers. One look at the rape and murder statistics for women (excluding domestic incidents) and it is clear that the government FAILS to protect women from the violence of strangers. Some may cry out for a "stronger" State, more police, mandatory sentences, and swifter executions. Over the years we have seen the U.S. prison population become the largest in the world, executions take place every week now, inner-city communities are occupied by the National Guard, and people of color are harassed by police, but guess what? A woman out alone, night or day, is confronted with more danger of random violence from strangers than ever before. As the U.S. economy continues "to downsize," and the good jobs disappear forever, our urban and rural landscapes will include more desperate, angry men with nothing to lose.

24   Only women can put a stop to the "open season" on women by strangers. Women are TAUGHT to be easy targets by their mothers, aunts, and grandmothers who themselves were taught that "a women doesn't kill" or "a woman doesn't learn how to use a weapon." Women must learn how to take aggressive action individually, apart from the police and the courts.

25   Presently twenty-one states issue permits to carry concealed weapons; most states require lengthy gun safety courses and a police security check before issuing a permit. Inexpensive but excellent gun safety and self-defense courses designed for women are also available from every quality gun dealer who hopes to sell you a handgun at the end of the course. Those who object to firearms need trained companion dogs or collectives of six or more women to escort one another day and night. We must destroy the myth that women are born to be easy targets.

■ QUESTIONS FOR ANALYSIS AND DISCUSSION

1. Why, according to Silko, do women live in a state of fear? What measures must they take to prevent personal harm? What effect does this mentality have on society as a whole?

2. How does a gun equalize the differences between men and women? Do you agree with Silko's father's comment that she and her sisters should never be

afraid because a gun "equalized all differences in size and strength" (paragraph 8)?

3. Silko points out that "more than one feminist has pointed out that rapists and serial killers help keep the patriarchy in place" (paragraph 9). How do acts of violence against women maintain the "patriarchy"? What is the patriarchy?

4. Crime experts say that most rapes are motivated by a desire for power and not really for sex. Apply this fact to the rapists Silko describes in paragraphs 11 and 12.

5. In paragraph 22 Silko comments that in many cultures, women "are not taught to defend themselves from strangers because fathers and husbands fear the consequences themselves." What does she mean? Does this statement apply to American society? Explain.

6. How does Silko's story of her trip to the pet store support her argument? Explain.

7. Throughout the essay Silko makes references to hunting. Explore the multifaceted levels of this hunting theme.

Revisionist Feminism

Susan Faludi and Karen Lehrman

The next article is the beginning a multiletter dialogue between feminist writers Susan Faludi and Karen Lehrman featured in *Slate MSN,* in which the two women discuss the meaning of "real feminism." Faludi objects to the "revisionist feminists" who seem to feel that feminism denies them their femininity. Lehrman responds by explaining that the leftist political agenda of conventional feminism has clouded the goals of the movement and has alienated both men and women.

Faludi is the author of the critically acclaimed books *Backlash: The Undeclared War Against American Women* (1991) and *Stiffed: The Betrayal of the American Man* (1998). Her articles have appeared in many journals and magazines, including *Newsweek* and *Esquire.* Karen Lehrman is the managing editor of *Consumer's Research* magazine and the author of *The Lipstick Proviso: Woman, Sex & Power in the Real World* (1997).

■ BEFORE YOU READ

Look up the word "feminism" in the dictionary. Does the definition surprise you? Does American society seem to have a different understanding of what feminism means? Explain.

■ AS YOU READ

Do Faludi and Lehrman enter this dialogue on feminism in order to reach an understanding or middle ground? What evidence is there, if any, on either side of their discussion of an attempt to reach a consensus or at least an understanding of the other's point of view?

Dear Karen,

1   I enter into this conversation with you about feminism with some misgivings. Not because I don't want to talk to you. It's just that I suspect it will be like a phone conversation where the connection's so bad neither party can hear the other through the static. I say this because in my experience, there's no getting through to the group of "feminists" (and I use that word with heavy quotation marks and highly arched brows) who are your sister travelers. I mean the group that maintains that an "orthodoxy" of "reigning feminists" (your terms) torments the American female population with its highhanded fiats, its litmus tests of "proper" feminist behavior, its regulatory whip seeking to slap the femininity out of the American girl. Christina Hoff Sommers, Katie Roiphe, Laura Ingraham, Danielle Crittenden, and the rest of the inside-the-Beltway "revisionist feminists" (as the media would have it) condemn feminism for its "excesses" over and over on the *New York Times* and *Washington Post* op-ed pages and the major TV talk shows (while complaining they are viciously "silenced" by the "reigning" feminists, who hardly ever get an airing in the aforementioned forums).

2   And you, too, Karen. Your own book-length addition to this chorus repeats the argument that feminism has turned women off by denying them the right to display and revel in their feminine beauty and sexuality. You then adorn that old can of "revisionist" contents with a fancy new label, *The Lipstick Proviso,* which you define as "women don't have to sacrifice their individuality, or even their femininity—whatever that means to each of them—in order to be equal."

3   For the longer version of my response to the "revisionists" and their charges against feminism, please see "I'm Not a Feminist But I Play One on TV." For the shorter version, to your book specifically, here 'tis:

4   Earth to Karen! Do you read me? . . . 'Cuz back on planet Earth, feminists don't "reign" and they certainly don't stop women at checkpoints to strip them of their "individuality" by impounding their lipstick (though what a pathetic "individuality" that must be if it depends on the application of Revlon to achieve it). Bulletin from the front: I wear lipstick, and I've spotted it on other feminists, too. I've watched, in fact, legions of "militant" feminists apply make-up brazenly in public ladies' rooms, and no femi-Nazi police swooped down and seized their compacts. And you know why? Because lipstick *is not what feminism is about.*

5   What's clear in your book is you feel gypped by feminism. You feel the feminists of the '60s and '70s made a promise to your generation of women that they didn't keep. Let us assume you are sincere, and I have no reason—in your case—to think otherwise. But why do you feel so betrayed? Maybe the answer lies in your definition of feminism. You write in your book that "as a young woman eager to escape the confines of a traditional household," you embraced feminism, which, you believed, "was going to turn all women into liberated women, into women who would unfailingly exhibit serene confidence, steely resolve, and steadfast courage. Unburdened by the behavioral and sartorial restrictions of traditional femininity, we would all want to trek alone through the

wilds of Indonesia, head IBM, run for president." You then go on to lament, "Yet it doesn't seem as though the first generation of women to come of age with feminism . . . has metamorphosed en masse into briefcase-toting, world-wandering Mistresses of the Universe."

6   Now here's the problem: Your definition of feminism is gleaned not from '70s feminism but from '70s advertising. In that decade, Madison Avenue and Hollywood and the fashion industry and mass media all saw a marketing opportunity in "women's lib" and they ran with it. Feminism as reinterpreted through television commercials for pantyhose and marketing manuals for Dress for Success bow ties would do just what advertising is supposed to do: Inflame your hungers and your anxieties, then offer to mollify them with a product that makes ludicrously inflated promises. So just as Hanes tried to convince shoppers that slipping on a pair of pantyhose would turn them into raving beauties with a million suitors, so the faux-feminism of Consumer America tried to convince a younger generation of women that "liberation" led to Banana Republicesque treks in the Himalayas and starring roles in the executive penthouse suite. All young women had to do to get that liberation was smoke Virginia Slims. As Christopher Lasch (that raving liberal!) wrote prophetically in 1979 in *The Culture of Narcissism*, "The advertising industry thus encourages the pseudo-emancipation of women, flattering them with its insinuating reminder, 'You've come a long way, baby,' and disguising the freedom to consume as genuine autonomy."

7   Now you are trying to reclaim that promise, proclaiming in your book that women have the "right" to liberate themselves via the marketplace. You champion women's right to express themselves through makeup, lingerie, cosmetic surgery, aerobics classes, and corsets. You even say that "entering a wet T-shirt contest" can be a "liberating" act for some women.

8   But, but, but . . . you are mad at the wrong folks. Feminists never promised you a rose garden in Lotusland, the consumer culture did. Feminism, unlike advertising, is not about gulling you into believing you could win the sweepstakes. Feminism is and always has been about women acting in the world as full-fledged citizens, as real participants in the world of ideas and policy and history. That doesn't have anything to do with wearing lipstick or not wearing lipstick or even about making obscene amounts of money. It's about insisting on the right of women to dignity, a living wage, meaningful work, and active engagement in the public arena. As for lipstick: For most women who work in the cruddy lower reaches of American employment, the problem isn't being denied the "right" to wear makeup and lingerie; it's about the right not to be *forced* to dress and act the way their male bosses demand. You may recall that flight attendants in the '60s fought one of the earliest battles of feminism's second wave so that male corporate bosses could no longer fire them over their weight, age, dress, or marital status. (Stewardesses were also, by the way, required to wear girdles—and didn't consider it liberating when their supervisors conducted company-mandated "touch checks.") Feminism, real feminism, is about freeing women to be genuine individuals—and recognizing that such individuality doesn't come in one size only or out of a bottle.

9   You propose that we cleanse feminism of political content and even "abolish" the term "women's movement." "This next wave" of feminism, you say, "needs to be primarily devoted to developing our emotional independence." Well, we certainly are in an "emotional" era. That's because we are steeped in a consumer culture where emotional manipulation is the name of the game and political analysis interferes with the Big Sell and so is discouraged. Now you are asking that feminism junk the politics and join in on the consumerizing of the American female public. Well, you can ask. You can cheerlead for that all you like, of course. And I'm sure a lot of powerful institutions will be only too glad to enable your cheerleading for their own selfish ends. But you can't call what you're asking for feminism, or progress. You can't say we've come a long way when you are still championing our "right" to stand on the stage in a wet T-shirt and be called baby.

10   . . . Am I getting through, or does this all sound like static on the line?

Sincerely,
Susan

Dear Susan,

1   Well, I think there would be much less static between us if you had read my book more carefully, did not take my words out of context, and did not lump me in with women with whom I clearly have little in common. I also think we'd have a much better connection if you'd drop the sneery, condescending tone you always seem to adopt when writing about women with whom you disagree. I respect you, I'd probably even like you if we met under slightly less fraught circumstances. Yes, I disagree with some of your philosophical and political views. But those views don't make you any less of a feminist. As long as you believe that women should have the same rights, opportunities, and responsibilities as men, you can have whatever political agenda, lifestyle, or wardrobe you wish.

2   Unfortunately, you don't seem to feel the same way about me or millions of other women. You say that "feminism, real feminism, is about freeing women to be genuine individuals—and recognizing that such individuality doesn't come in one size only or out of a bottle." But much of what you've written on the subject—in your book, magazine articles, and already in this dialogue—would indicate that you don't really mean it. And the same, I'm afraid, is true about most of the other self-appointed spokeswomen for feminism.

3   You each appear to believe that, to be allowed to use the term feminist, a woman has to adhere to a well-defined leftist political agenda, consisting of, at the very least, affirmative action, nationally subsidized day care, and "pay equity" (formerly known as comparable worth). In your *Ms.* article, you call a handful of women who happen to disagree with you politically (myself included) "pod" or "pseudo" feminists. You say that we're right-wing misogynists or pawns of right-wing misogynists. Perhaps most curiously, you imply that we're also racist. In 1992, the National Organization for Women tried to start a "women's party," offering a distinctly leftist "women's agenda." During the last election, NOW president Patricia Ireland said women should vote only for "au-

thentic" female candidates, Gloria Steinem called Texas Republican Sen. Kay Bailey Hutchinson a "female impersonator," and Naomi Wolf described the foreign-policy analysis of Jeane Kirkpatrick as being "uninflected by the experiences of the female body." The desire to enforce political conformity is even worse in academia. Many women's-studies professors regularly judge texts and opinions in terms of their agreement with the orthodox political agenda. (For an honest "insider" account, check out *Professing Feminism,* by Daphne Patai and Noretta Koertge.)

4   Fortunately, all women don't think alike, and as far as feminism is concerned they certainly don't have to. The only items on the real feminist agenda are equal rights and opportunities, a society capable of accepting the widest array of women's choices, and women strong and independent enough to make rational ones. This in no way means that feminists should "junk the politics." It means that feminism is a moral ideal; how women achieve it is a matter of political debate.

5   It's true that some of the women you mention above and in your *Ms.* article do oppose abortion rights, do deny that discrimination exists, and do believe that it is a woman's God-given duty to have children and stay home with them— all anti-feminist notions. Some have minimized the very real problems of sexual harassment and date rape, and seem far more interested in self-promotion than in the future of feminism. Yet the surveys suggest that the vast majority of women—and men—who have criticized the women's movement in recent years do believe in women's essential equality and are simply unhappy with the fact that feminism has turned into an orthodoxy, that it now means precisely the opposite of what it was intended to mean—namely, freedom.

6   Feminist theorists have gotten much better at not explicitly stating that women need to follow a certain lifestyle or dress code to be a feminist. But an implicit criticism of more traditional choices is still quite apparent. In *Backlash,* for instance, you blame the fact that women are still primarily clustered in the "pink ghetto" or low- to mid-level management positions entirely on discrimination. Some of it surely is discrimination, and some of it is due to the fact that women are still working their way up. But much of the explanation can be found in the choices of women themselves. The vast majority of women—even young women with college degrees who have grown up with nearly every option open to them—still prefer to give their families higher priority than their careers. According to the Women's Education and Research Institute (hardly a bastion of conservative thought), employed mothers are significantly more likely than fathers to want to stay at their current levels of responsibility and to trade job advancement to work part time, work at home, or have control over their work schedules. Four-fifths of mothers who work part time do so by choice.

7   The larger problem is that most feminist theorists still refuse to acknowledge that there appear to be significant biological differences between the sexes. They still seem to believe that equality with men has to mean sameness to men, that until all aspects of traditional femininity are abolished, women will not be free. Thankfully, this is far from necessary. Women, on average, may al-

ways have a stronger need than men to nurture, a need that will at times eclipse their desire for power. Restructuring the corporate world to better accommodate two-career families may certainly help women to deal with these conflicting goals, but I don't think they will ever disappear. We may not like the choices many women continue to make, but not only are they really none of our business, there's precious little we could do about them if they were.

8   Biology also still seems to be turning up in courtship (the desire of the vast majority of women to want men to pursue them), sex (the ambivalence most women have toward casual sex), and beauty (the energy most women give toward making themselves attractive). As you well know, I do not say anywhere in the book that women have to wear lipstick to be feminist or even feminine. I use lipstick as a metaphor for all of the traditionally feminine behaviors that feminist theorists have at some point condemned as being degrading and exploitative—from being a mother to staying home full time with one's children to wearing miniskirts and makeup. In *Backlash*, you implicitly argue that the desire of many women to buy feminine or sexy clothing and indulge in cosmetic products and services is wholly the result of manipulation by the beauty and fashion industries. You call women's desire for sexy lingerie "fashion regression," and argue that happy and confident women don't care about clothes. Actually, I think the desire of most women to not hide their sexuality is a sign of progress, evidence that many women now feel they no longer have to renounce a fundamental aspect of themselves in order to make a symbolic point.

9   I do not feel "gypped" by feminism. On the contrary, feminism has offered me the opportunity to live my life in a way that was considered reprehensible just 40 years ago. What I do feel is that the feminist revolution is not complete, and it's incomplete in ways that differ from the orthodox feminist line. There's still more political work to be done, to be sure, especially involving the issues of rape and domestic violence. But there's also much personal work to be done. This is a major theme of my book, yet for some reason you have chosen to purposefully misread what I wrote about it. Where do I say anything about "the consumerizing of the American female public"?

10   Of course the advertising industry exploited feminism; that's their job. But that has nothing to do with what I'm talking about. I use the term emotional independence to refer to self-development, which was a prominent part of feminist theorizing and activism in the early days of the Second Wave. Actually, it's not that surprising that you chose to ignore what I was saying and turn the focus back on how society has victimized women. Feminists have unfortunately been doing that for the past 20 years, which may partly explain why women lag so far behind in their emotional development. While enormous attention has been paid to how the "patriarchy" mistreats women, little has been written about how women mistreat themselves. Even focusing on how women should take responsibility for their problems is often dismissed as naive, sexist, or "blaming the victim."

11   (By the way, you also took my point about "entering a wet T-shirt contest" completely out of context. As you well know, I was actually saying that just because women now have the freedom to do something doesn't mean it's the

most rational thing to do. "Only each woman can decide if her actions are self-destructive and thus unfeminist," I wrote, "What is self-destructive for one woman—entering a wet T-shirt contest, for instance, or being a full-time house-wife—may be liberating for another.")

12   It's true that the orthodoxy is breaking up, and other feminist voices are finally being heard. But that's no thanks to you, Susan. I think you have focused more energy on stifling dissent than perhaps any other feminist writer. In your book, you castigate Susan Brownmiller, Betty Friedan, and Erica Jong for having the gall to suggest that the women's movement's refusal to acknowledge biological differences between the sexes is hurtful to women. You can't blame the media for the fact that two-thirds of women still don't call themselves feminists. The media may very well highlight the extremes, but it has also given Gloria Steinem, Naomi Wolf, Patricia Ireland, and yourself plenty of space and air time to alienate the majority of women through your restrictive view of feminism.

13   Feminism—real feminism—deserves to be respected and honored. Every woman today should proudly call herself a feminist. But that is not going to happen until prominent feminist writers such as yourself admit to a couple of things. One, that a Republican housewife who annually has her face lifted and daily greets her husband at the door wearing only heels can be a feminist if she knows her mind, follows her desires, and believes that every woman has the right to do the same. Two, that the notion of sisterhood is false, outdated, and sexist. Women don't "owe" each other anything: They don't have to like each other, agree with each other, vote for each other, or hire each other for feminism to succeed.

14   Three, the notion of a "women's movement" has outlived its usefulness. Men must be just as aware and involved as women—on both a personal and political level—for feminism to work. Four, women can act differently from men. Even if that means that Congress, corporate boards, and CEOs will never be 50 percent female, as long as women are making their choices freely, feminism will not be undermined. And finally, each woman is fundamentally unique. No assumptions can be made about her politics, values, goals, and beliefs.

15   Instead of fighting about whether or not feminism has turned into an orthodoxy, I think it would be far more useful if this dialogue—as well as the larger feminist debate—were focused on the complexities that women must deal with today. For instance, how does the corporate world learn to judge women strictly on their merits yet recognize the obvious differences—e.g., that women are the only ones who get pregnant? How do we help women deal with their ambivalence toward responsibility and power? How do we help women develop the strength and independence to demand boyfriends who don't abuse them, and raises that they deserve? These are tough questions, and I'd really like to know what you think about them.

Sincerely,
Karen

■ **QUESTIONS FOR DISCUSSION AND ANALYSIS**

1. Why does Faludi express "misgivings" about entering into a conversation on feminism with Lehrman? What tone does she set for the dialogue? How does Lehrman respond to this tone?

2. Summarize Faludi's argument. What is her definition of "real feminism"? Why does she object to "revisionist feminism"? Explain.

3. Summarize Lehrman's argument. What is her definition of "real feminism"? Why does she object to Faludi and other "self-appointed spokeswomen for feminism?" Explain.

4. In what ways has consumer culture clouded the goals of feminism? How has advertising exploited feminism? Explain.

5. On what points do Faludi and Lehrman agree? If you were the moderator of this dialogue, how would you use these points of agreement to help them reach a consensus?

■ **WRITING ASSIGNMENTS**

1. Write an essay exploring the effects of the perception of women as victims in the media. Some of the areas of your exploration might draw from television, film, art, advertising, newspapers, music, and other popular media. How do media representations of women enforce (or refute) the perception of women as victims and men as aggressors?

2. You have been asked to write an article about feminism at the beginning of the twenty-first century for inclusion in a time capsule to be opened at the beginning of the next century. Describe your own perception of feminism and include examples from popular culture and your experience. How do you think things will have changed in 100 years? Explain.

3. Several of the essays in this section comment that women must deal with the possibility of violence every time they leave their homes. Some feminists say that dwelling on violence against women in fact weakens them in today's society, promoting psychological and physical terrorism. Read the review of Katie Roiphe's book *The Morning After: Sex, Fear, and Feminism on Campus* by Jean Bethke Elshtain published in *First Things: A Journal of Religious and Public Life* at <www.firstthings.com/ftissues/ft9404/reviews/elshtain.html>. Do you agree with Roiphe's perspective on "co-responsibility"? Explain your viewpoint, drawing from experience and data supplied from her book, and the articles in this section.

4. Thirty years ago, men were expected to earn more than women. Do we still hold such beliefs? Poll your classmates to find out their opinions regarding income status. Do males feel that they should earn more? Would they feel less masculine if their girlfriends or wives earned more? Do females seek men with higher incomes when they consider a partner? Analyze your results and write an argument that draws conclusions from your survey and its connection to feminism in the twenty-first century.

CHAPTER 12

September 11, 2001

On the morning of September 11, 2001, the unthinkable happened. When two planes deliberately crashed into the twin towers of New York City's World Trade Center, another struck the Pentagon, and a fourth was diverted by the heroic efforts of passengers from its target into a field in Pennsylvania, American consciousness was forever changed. It was not just an attack on Americans on American soil, but an attack on the ideals that Americans hold most dear. Almost every nation lost a citizen that day. And while the world reeled from the shock, Americans overwhelmingly responded in ways that epitomized the most noble and heroic in human nature.

September 11 made us think about what it meant to be an American, and what our country stood for. It made us rethink our definitions of heroes; it stimulated unity, compassion, and patriotism. The essays and articles in this section present many perspectives on the events of September 11. Not all of them are pro-American. But they all provoke us to think about what happened that day, and how it has forever changed us.

We begin with some perspectives on how the day itself irrevocably altered our perception of safety, freedom, and security. In "This Is What a Day Means," political scientist and writer Andrew Sullivan discusses how the events of September 11 will remain forever imprinted on the nation's memory, and why we will never be the same. Jonathan Schell explores the nature of a war on terrorism, and the steps we need to take to promote the ways of peace. Nobel Peace Prize–winner Elie Wiesel reflects on how the tragic events of this day brought out the best in Americans. Instead of spreading fear and panic, explains Wiesel, the terrorists' actions as orchestrated by Osama bin Laden's Al Qaeda network generated national pride, the highest acts of heroism, and patriotism.

The next section examines this sense of patriotism as it relates to the American flag. Only days after the attacks, the flag seemed to be everywhere. Stores could not keep their shelves stocked with them. An entire industry sprang to life: Flags were pinned to lapels and stuck on bumpers and back windows. In some towns, it seemed like there was a flag flying in front of every house. Months later, Christmas lights sparkled red, white, and blue. The three essays in this section address different attitudes toward the flag and the patriotism it represents.

The final section takes a look at America's response to terrorism. Caleb Carr explains that in order to understand why America is a target for terrorists, we must first realize that our entire culture is viewed as a threat by some militant groups. Arundhati Roy details why some groups hate the United States in "The Algebra of Infinite Justice." The section closes with a roundtable discussion of six Harvard University professors who attempt to define terrorism, analyze the Bush administration's reaction to September 11, and offer some ideas on how to deal with terrorism in the future.

A DAY OF INFAMY

This Is What a Day Means

Andrew Sullivan

In the days before September 11, 2001, we took for granted our daily security. Explains Andrew Sullivan, "America was a symbol that the world need not always be the impenetrably dark place it has often been. It was a sign that someplace, somewhere, was always secure." The terrorist attacks of September 11 changed this perception. In a single day, the American concept of safety was irrevocably changed.

Sullivan is a former senior editor and current columnist for *The New Republic.* His work has appeared in many journals and magazines, including *The Wall Street Journal,* the *Washington Post,* and *Esquire.* He received his Ph.D. from Harvard University in political science and lectures in universities across the country on many different political issues. He is a contributing writer to the *New York Times Magazine,* in which this essay first appeared on September 23, 2001.

■ BEFORE YOU READ

In the next article, Andrew Sullivan examines how our concepts of safety and security have forever been changed by the events of September 11. In what ways did your personal perceptions change because of what happened that day? Explain.

■ AS YOU READ

What does America symbolize to its citizens? to other countries? Have the events of September 11 altered or reinforced this symbolism?

1   "What are days for?" the poet Philip Larkin asked. We used to know the answer to that. Days were for living, for working, for the rituals of normalcy that make up the way of life we have come to know as American. These days had their

ups and downs; they had their surprises and shocks. But they had as well a sense of reliability or modest predictability. We barely noticed these small moments of routine that, strung together, formed the ballast of a culture: the commutes to work, the family outings, the plane rides to friends, the coffee breaks and household chores. They acquired a rhythm that, although we easily forgot, took a revolution to begin, a civil war to resolve and dark and bloody wars to defend.

2   This normalcy was not the same thing as freedom; but it was quietly dependent on it. And so this security built slowly upon itself, broadening and deepening until we took it for granted, the threats to it always remote and, though involving us, not about us. We watched those threats on television, like a reality show that never fully became real. And when we saw Americans abroad in trouble or distress, we knew that there was always a hope for a homecoming, a return to safety.

3   To arrive from elsewhere onto American soil was always and everywhere a relief. It presaged the joy of security again, of family and friends and faith and work. We knew what days were for; and knew also that even when disaster struck or news shocked, the days themselves would encompass what we had to deal with. They would bracket us, shield us, support us.

4   I look at the calendar now and see the last time I felt this way. I check my voice mail and hear voices recorded before it changed. I haven't erased them. Something stops me. I want to remember their unwitting innocence—of dates fixed and dinners planned, of trips scheduled and work to be done, of assumptions of regularity that seemed banal before they ended, when they suddenly seemed more precious than the gorgeous sun that beat down on that Tuesday morning. I miss that blithe assurance that things will be what they have been—if not in degree but in kind. I miss the America that knew deeply that it was different, apart, protected, somehow open to the world and yet immune from its worst evils.

5   As any immigrant knows, this was the thrill of this country, its irresistible pull, its deepest promise. It was a symbol that the world need not always be the impenetrably dark place it has often been. It was a sign that someplace, somewhere, was always secure—as powerful an icon to those outside this continent as those within it.

6   This was the new world. It is now only the world.

7   We like to think that there are regular patterns in history, that events can be foreseen, that consequences can be predicted, that the world moves slowly from one era to another. We shrink from believing that in one instant, history can be stopped dead, or that the deepest part of a country's meaning can be altered. We do not want to contemplate the chance that history is in fact a series of unique moments, each as contingent as the last, with nothing inevitable, nothing foretold.

8   When the first tower of the World Trade Center was attacked, we thought immediately that this was an accident: because that is what the past had prepared us for. Although we had fantasized in movies or concocted in novels the scenarios in front of our eyes, we kept seeing them as if they were not actually

happening, as if by force of will we could simply negate the evidence of our senses. And even as the hours proceeded and the worst got worse, we somehow resisted that this was the case, as if we would wake the next day to find it had not really happened, that our country had not absorbed a wound deeper than even now we can fully articulate or absorb.

9   We can talk logistics and details. We can recover our dead and comfort our survivors. We can look at what shone in that day almost as brightly as the sun: the passenger heroism aboard the planes, the sacrifices of countless firefighters and policemen, the acts of dignity and courage that no one will ever truly know in the nightmare of the stricken building in the minutes before it collapsed— the last phone calls of doomed fathers and mothers and sons and daughters, taking their last moments to speak to those they loved. We know we will endure. In fact, we know that it is at moments like this one that true heroism is born and leadership forged. We can anticipate the day—not yet here—when we do not think at some point of this gaping gash in our collective soul. And we can build now a solidarity and patriotism that eclipses even that of our founders and defenders for centuries.

10   But we also know somewhere that things will never be the same, that the inviolable might of this country's promise has been assaulted by an enemy whose war has just begun.

11   Although the wound is obviously deepest here, it isn't only this country that has been altered. America is not only a place. America is an idea. The knowledge of this secure elsewhere was what kept freedom and hope alive for millions around the globe for two centuries. It was the force that broke the stalemate in the first Great War, the place from which the world dared to hope for peace after 1918. It was the beacon toward which countless immigrants traveled, in order to leave their somewhere behind. It was the rock upon which Churchill summoned the will from his people's terrified hearts to go on and win against the darkest forces that freedom had ever encountered. It was the symbol that ultimately brought down the Berlin Wall and faced terror in Tiananmen Square.

12   In this sense, what was done to America was also done to the collective consciousness of the world, to those future Americans not yet born in other parts of the globe, to those who have come to rely upon the United States as the last resort for a liberty long languishing in other somewheres. It was a place where the human past could, in dreams at least, be erased, eluded, relinquished, avenged by the sheer sight of millions of all types and creeds and races living well and freely, day in, day out. This was the dream, in the only country in which mere dreams were not derided as illusions. America's power, even when wielded across the globe, was therefore still a strangely innocent power—innocent of what true evil can bring, innocent of what real danger is. Even when we encountered it—in Flanders, in Normandy, in Auschwitz, in Moscow, in the Vietnam delta and the Iraqi desert—it was always someplace else. Never here. Not in this place. Not where freedom was reborn. This elsewhere would never just be somewhere.

13   This is what a day means. Like the day an archduke was shot in Sarajevo, when no one knew in the morning what the afternoon would have proved. Like the day of the first blitzkrieg into Poland, when denial in the dawn ceded to dread at dusk. Like the day in November 1963 when the same sense of numbness and grief swept through Americans in an instant. Like the beautiful September day, when a man heard a sound and looked up into the sky in curiosity and calm and saw the end of something we never truly appreciated until in one short day, it had already disappeared.

14   These former things have passed away. Another world began that day.

■ QUESTIONS FOR ANALYSIS AND DISCUSSION

1. According to Sullivan, how did the events of September 11 change our perspective on "what a day means"? Explain.
2. In what ways does normalcy depend on freedom? What happens when our sense of normalcy is violated?
3. Sullivan explains that America is more than just a place, it is an idea. What does he mean?
4. In paragraph 10, Sullivan states, "But we also know somewhere that things will never be the same, that the inviolable might of this country's promise has been assaulted by an enemy whose war has just begun." Respond to this statement, reflecting on America's immediate response to the terrorist attacks and its perspective now that some time has passed.

A Letter from Ground Zero

Jonathan Schell

After the attacks of September 11, 2001, a question that was foremost on everyone's mind was how to retaliate. How do we wage a war against people who have demanded no concessions and will make any sacrifice in the name of their cause? What would happen if weapons banned by most of the world—instruments of nuclear and biological warfare—fell into their hands? In the next article, Jonathan Schell discusses the delicate balance between war and annihilation, and the dangers we face in a world where weapons of mass destruction are a frightening reality.

A former writer and editor for *The New Yorker*, Schell has been nominated for a Pulitzer Prize. He is the author of many books, including *The Fate of the Earth, The Gift of Time,* and *Writing in Time.* The recipient of a Guggenheim fellowship and McArthur Foundation grant, Schell teaches literary journalism at Wesleyan University. This article first appeared in the October 29, 2001, issue of *The Nation.*

■ BEFORE YOU READ

Did September 11 make you think more about nuclear and biological warfare? What is your own opinion of these weapons? What should America's position be?

■ AS YOU READ

Schell advocates a more unified world position on the elimination of weapons of mass destruction, economic justice, and negotiated settlements of existing conflicts. Evaluate his support for these causes. Are they possible? plausible? Why or why not?

1   One month after September 11, ground zero—six blocks from where I live—remains unquiet. Inextinguishable subterranean fires belch smoke into the neighborhood, as if the ruin were an active volcano, spreading a stench whose source we do not care to think about. The global crisis set in motion by the attack has been active, too. In its fourth week, two major eruptions occurred: the beginning of the Anglo-American war on Afghanistan and the outbreak of anthrax in Florida.

2   The two events were reflected in the divided mood of the American public. On the one hand, public support for the war was strong. On the other hand, a profound, unmistakable unease was palpable in the land. Fear of weapons of mass destruction was part of it. A sheriff in the small town of Pendleton, Oregon, told a *New York Times* reporter, "What I realize now for the first time is that we can be big and bad and still be got." But fear was not the only note struck. There were expressions of worry that the Afghans would now suffer what Americans—not used to this sort of thing—had suffered. While the public found the assault in Afghanistan "inescapable and just," the *Washington Post* reported, "the jingoistic call for annihilation was heard less often than the hope that the death of innocents might be kept to a minimum." There were signs that awareness of a common peril had created a feeling of common humanity.

3   The two currents of reaction have in fact been present since the very first second of the crisis. When the attacks occurred, the thought that flashed spontaneously into millions of minds was that our world had changed forever. But what, exactly, was the change that everyone felt, and why did awareness of it come so quickly? It was, I suggest, an immediate, bone-deep recognition of the utter perishability of all human works and all human beings in the face of human destructive powers. The change was felt immediately because it was the recognition of something already known, if rarely thought about—known since 1945, when Hiroshima was destroyed by an atomic bomb. The twin towers of the World Trade Center were the most massive objects in the City of New York, perhaps in all America. If, without any warning, they could evaporate in the blink of eye, what was safe?

4   The peril of further terrorist attacks was of course uppermost in people's thoughts, but in the background were the still existing, though strangely missionless, nuclear arsenals currently in the hands of eight nations. These, too, soon obtruded onto the scene. The conceivable overthrow of the military dictatorship in Pakistan by extreme Muslim forces angry that their nation had been coerced by the United States into a supporting role in the attack on Afghanistan raised the specter that Pakistan's nuclear weapons might fall into the hands of a Taliban-like regime. Here in the United States, Billy Graham's son,

the Rev. Franklin Graham, called for their use against America's enemies. Defense Secretary Donald Rumsfeld, asked whether the United States was contemplating the use of nuclear weapons, twice declined to rule it out. On the second occasion, he even upped the ante, pointing out that during the cold war the United States had refused to rule out the "first use" of nuclear weapons. That is still US policy, notably in the event of the use of chemical or biological weapons.

5   The destruction of the twin towers, in short, was a taste of annihilation, a small piece of the end of the world. Recognition of this—let us call it the annihilation model of the shape of the crisis—educated, you might say, the viscera of the public. In the public's conscious mind, on the other hand, another model prevailed, which can be called the war model. In this model, which formed the basis for President George W. Bush's speech before the joint session of Congress, September 11 was Pearl Harbor and the starting gun for a long military conflict—"America's New War," as CNN had it. However, even the Administration soon had to recognize that the war model fit the actual situation imperfectly, at best. The death of 5,000 certainly created moral and legal justification enough for waging war. The right of self-defense is clearly recognized in international law. But not every action that is justifiable is wise. Who, in this picture, was the equivalent of Japan or Nazi Germany? Where were the targets? How were they to be hit? What could be the role of armed forces in fighting against terrorism, in which police forces have traditionally been used? (When the town of Omagh was bombed in 1998, killing twenty-nine people, Britain did not shower Northern Ireland with cruise missiles.) And in fact, in the weeks between the President's warlike speech and the launch of the attacks, the Administration back-pedaled significantly from the war model. Rumsfeld's definition of US war aims was remarkably modest and vague. It was to "create conditions for sustained antiterrorist action and humanitarian relief." Would ground troops be sent in? Would they occupy Afghanistan? Would the Taliban be overthrown? Would the Northern Alliance be installed to replace them, or perhaps the former King of Afghanistan, Mohammed Zahir Shah? If installed, would either of these seek to "root out" terrorists? Would they succeed? When it was all over, would the number of terrorists be greater or fewer than before? Even if US forces won the war in Afghanistan (no easy task) would it lose the war on terrorism? Military strategy faded into the mist of these unanswered political questions.

6   If the annihilation model had been the basis for understanding the crisis, policies of a very different character would have been adopted. The dangers of escalation—of heightened fervor in the Islamic world, of tit-for-tat strikes between Islamic forces and American troops—would have been uppermost in official minds. Military restraint then would have been the order of the day from the very beginning of the effort rather than being introduced as an afterthought. War would have been seen as a sort of self-indulgence. Political considerations—the mood and response of the world's 1 billion Muslims, for instance—would now be dominating. The fight against terrorism would take the

form of police action, conducted by the international coalition so painstakingly put together by Secretary of State Colin Powell. Military action would play a merely supporting role—in the form, perhaps, of the occasional commando raid to seize or destroy a terrorist cell when its location could be ascertained by intelligence. The model for military action, insofar as it occurred, would not be today's blitzkrieg but a siege.

7   The distinction between waging war and preventing annihilation is not a new one. The military policies of the entire cold war were based on it. Preventing annihilation was the foremost stated goal of the principal strategy of the age, the doctrine of nuclear deterrence. Policy-makers were keenly aware that actual fighting must be resisted because it could lead to oblivion for all concerned. Now the danger of annihilation has reared its head again, and once again the perils of escalation are before us. The restraint that was slowly learned in the cold war has to be relearned in this new context. This time, however, deterrence can hardly serve. Terrorists have no countries to hold hostage to retaliatory nuclear destruction. They possess only their lives, and these they throw away with their own hands.

8   New policies to address the new danger of annihilation are needed, and these originate far from the precincts of war. One is a comprehensive global effort to rid the world of weapons of mass destruction—a plan in which a readiness of the great powers to disarm would lay the foundation for unchallengeable policies of nonproliferation, which in turn would lay the basis for the tightest possible international control of these weapons' special materials and technologies. No plan can reduce the danger by 100 percent, but an 80 or 90 percent reduction of risk should be possible. Another, even vaster and more difficult undertaking is a systematic campaign to damp down and then politically resolve the world's festering local conflicts, starting with those in the Middle East. Such steps have always been desirable. Now they have become essential for survival.

9   Can such sweeping, positive ambitions have any bearing at this hour, which has turned out, for the time being, to be one of war? British Prime Minister Tony Blair, for one, thinks they can. In his speech to the recent Labour Party conference, he proposed a "politics of globalization" to complement the economics of globalization. He called for the international community to address with new resolve the conflicts in Rwanda, in Israel and Palestine, and in Ireland, among others; for action to redress the growing global gap between rich and poor; for measures to remedy global warming and other environmental ills. These were not original ideas, but to set them forth at this moment was original. Blair deserves credit merely for striking this hopeful note at a time of such foreboding. However, Blair located his vision on the far shore of victory in the war on terrorism. The danger is that if the world's response to the growing new threat of annihilation is war, the result will be new acts of annihilation. Blair has won a seat in the war councils with his backing for the United States. Perhaps at some dire turning point in the future, he will use his influence to speak up for restraint. The world is sick. It cannot be cured with America's new

war. The ways of peace—adopted not as a distant goal but as a practical necessity in the present—are the only cure.

■ QUESTIONS FOR ANALYSIS AND DISCUSSION

1. Schell comments that while support for the war effort was strong, Americans expressed hope that the death of innocent people in Afghanistan be kept to a minimum. Was this response surprising? different from that for other conflicts? What accounted for this attitude? Explain.
2. Following the attacks, many people found themselves comparing the events of September 11 to the attack on Pearl Harbor. In what ways were the attacks similar and in what ways were they different? Explain.
3. What position does Schell advocate? What is his purpose in writing this essay? Do you agree or disagree with his position? Explain.
4. What political issues does Schell connect to the events of September 11? Have these issues changed in the time that has elapsed since the attacks? Explain.

We Chose Honor

Elie Wiesel

It is the objective of terrorists to instill a sense of fear and anxiety in their victims. Experts agree that this certainly was a goal of the September 11, 2001, attacks—to send the message that no place and no one was safe. But many political and social analysts say that this plan was a colossal failure. Instead of sowing fear, the attacks resulted in widespread patriotism and self-sacrifice. The attacks unified not just the United States, but many nations, in a common cause—to stamp out terrorism.

Nobel Peace Prize recipient Elie Wiesel has written more than 40 books, including the acclaimed *Night* about his experience in a Nazi death camp. This article appeared a month after the September 11 attacks in *Parade Magazine* on October 28, 2001.

■ BEFORE YOU READ

In the next article, Wiesel writes that immediately following the attacks, he wondered, "Would this terrible act drive us apart [. . .] or draw us together as a nation?" Why could the attacks have driven us apart? Why did they draw us together? Explain.

■ AS YOU READ

The author of this essay is a recipient of the Nobel Peace Prize. Does knowing that he was bestowed this honor influence how you read his essay? Does it inform his message?

1   None of us will ever forget that sunny day in September when the United States was subjected to a manmade nightmare: a heinous terror attack unprecedented in contemporary history. It will remain shrouded in mourning in the violated memory of our country.

2   Would this terrible act drive us apart, I asked myself, or draw us together as a nation?

3   My wife and I were in a taxi in midtown Manhattan. We looked with disbelief at the gigantic clouds of smoke and ashes hanging over the lower part of the city. We listened to the radio and couldn't understand what we heard. Suddenly our hearts sank: Someone we love worked on Wall Street. Cell phones remained mute. At home, we found a message: He was all right.

4   Glued to television like so many others, we watched the first pictures. They were both surreal and biblical: the flames, the vertical collapse and disappearance of the world's two proudest towers. Many of us were stunned into silence. Rarely have I felt such failure of language.

5   I remember what I was thinking: "That's madness, madness." Two banal words, like an accursed mantra. Sheer madness. Terrorists wanted to die in order to spread death around them. They demanded neither ransom nor concessions. They proclaimed no belief and left no testament. But then what did they wish to affirm, negate or prove? Simply that life is not worth living? Some observers insisted that they were "courageous," since they wanted to die. I disagree: They wanted to kill and to do so anonymously. It would have taken more courage to live and explain why they had chosen murder.

6   More questions, many of them, came later: Faced with such immense suffering, how can one go on working, studying and simply living without sinking into despair? How is one to vanquish the fear that infiltrated our very existence? And how are we to console the families and friends of the more than 5000 victims?

7   The pictures of missing victims, the sobbing of relatives, the farewell words on cell phones, the sight of hardened journalists weeping. . . . Days and days elapsed, and the devastated site was still reminiscent of war-torn Europe in 1945.

8   I checked history books for a semblance of precedent for this terror. There may be one. In the 11th century, a certain Hasan-e Sabbah founded a secret small sect of assassins in Persia. Known as the Messengers of Death, they roamed around Islam clandestinely for years before fulfilling their mission. They killed people they did not know, for motives they themselves did not comprehend. Is Osama bin Laden a reincarnation of Hasan-e Sabbah? No. Those times and those violent "dreamers" are gone. The 21st century will not be theirs.

9   Why, then, the mass murder now? A human earthquake, it was caused by people whose faith had been perverted. There can be no justification for it. Can it be explained? Yes, by hatred. Hatred is at the root of evil everywhere. Racial hatred, ethnic hatred, political hatred, religious hatred. In its name, all seems permitted. For those who glorify hatred, as terrorists do, the end justifies

all means, including the most despicable ones. If they could, fanatics of violence would slaughter all those who do not adhere to their ideological or religious principles. But this they cannot achieve and so they resort to simply arousing fear, the goal of terrorists since they emerged in history.

10   Only this time, they failed. The American people reacted not with fear and resignation but with anger and resolve. Here and there it was misguided and misdirected: Individual Muslims were assaulted and humiliated. That was and is wrong. Collective blame is unwarranted and unjust. Islam is one of the world's great religions and most of its believers in our country are good and decent citizens. That had to be said and our leaders said it.

11   On the highest level of government, President Bush immediately charted the right path to follow by declaring war against terrorist leaders and all those who harbor and aid them. His address before the joint session of Congress made the American people experience a moment of greatness. The Senate and the House made us proud. Democrats and Republicans spoke with one voice. The White House, the State Department, the Pentagon lost no time in preparing for the battle to come. In a very short while, our entire nation and its allies were mobilized to wage a new world war whose aims are to identify, uproot, disarm and apprehend all those who were and are directly, or indirectly, linked to terrorist practitioners of mass murder.

12   One thing is clear: By their magnitude as well as by their senselessness, the terrorist atrocities constitute a watershed. Yes, life will go back to normal: it always does. But now there is a before and an after. Nothing will be the same. The political philosophy of governments, the national economy, the concern over security, the psychology of citizens, the weight of comradeship and hope: Everything has changed. One will not, as before, take a plane without considering the possibility of sabotage. Nor will one look at his or her neighbors without suspicion. We may never visit Lower Manhattan without pangs of sadness; we all know of someone who perished simply because he or she was there.

13   But the American people did not bend. Never have they been more motivated, more generous. Their behavior was praised the world over. Instead of trying to save themselves, men and women, young and old, ran to Ground Zero to offer assistance. Some stood in line for hours to donate blood. Hundreds of thousands of sandwiches, sodas and mineral waters were distributed. Those who were evacuated from their buildings were offered food and shelter by neighbors and strangers alike. Rudy Giuliani, the most admired New Yorker of the day, appealed in vain over radio and television for volunteers to stay away; they kept coming. And then, one had to see the outpouring of affection and gratitude toward policemen and firefighters to believe it.

14   And so, the terrorists achieved the opposite of what they wanted. They moved people to transcend themselves and choose that which is noble in man.

15   For in the end, it is always a matter of choice. Even when faced with the murderous madness of criminals, and in the presence of the silent agony of

their victims, it is incumbent upon us to choose between escape and solidarity, shame and honor. The terrorists have chosen shame. We choose honor.

16   I belong to a generation that thinks it knows all that is possible to know about the thousand manners of dying but not about the best way of fighting death. And I know that every death is unjust, that the death of every innocent person turns me into a question mark. Human beings are defined by their solidarity with others, especially when the others are threatened and wounded. Alone, I am on the edge of despair. But God alone is alone. Man is not and must not be alone.

17   If the terrorists believe they can isolate their living targets by condemning them to fear and sadness, they are mistaken. Americans have never been as united.

18   Nor has our hope been as profound and as irresistibly contagious.

■ QUESTIONS FOR ANALYSIS AND DISCUSSION

1. Wiesel comments that some people said that the terrorists who committed the acts of September 11 were "courageous" because they wanted to die. Why does Wiesel object to this statement? Explain.
2. How does Wiesel define evil? What does he identify as the "root" of evil? How does his definition apply to the terrorists who attacked the United States?
3. What, according to Wiesel, is the irony of the attacks of September 11? Explain.
4. How does Wiesel's choice of title reflect the American response to the attacks of September 11 that he describes in his essay? In what ways have Americans chosen honor? Do you think his viewpoint is shared by the people of other nations? Why or why not?

September 11, 2001

The cartoon on page 414 by Jeff Danziger was published by the *Los Angeles Times* immediately following the terrorist attacks in New York City and Washington, D.C. At the time of publication, the country was in a state of suspended disbelief, trying to grasp the unimaginable. The attack was meant not only to destroy the symbols of America's superpower status, but to kill as many people as possible, thereby creating widespread terror and chaos.

The "X" of his suspenders immediately draws us to the central figure of a gigantic Uncle Sam, knee-deep in building rubble and smoke and carrying the body of a woman. Since the nineteenth century, the character of Uncle Sam has served as the personification of the United States. Featured on U.S. Army recruitment posters, a strong-willed Uncle Sam pointed fingers at young men, urging them to fight for their country. But this Uncle Sam is not looking out at us: His sleeves are rolled up, and his shoulders are stooped as he surveys the destruction around him. As you examine the editorial cartoon, consider the artist's choice of character placement, shading, image, and use of symbolism.

QUESTIONS FOR ANALYSIS AND DISCUSSION

1. What is the effect of depicting Uncle Sam's sleeves rolled up? Is it a strong image of Uncle Sam? What does his clothing symbolize? How do his actions reinforce this symbolism?
2. What other icons are featured in the drawing? What is left standing in the picture, and why?
3. What is the effect of the figure in Uncle Sam's arms? Whom does she represent? Would the picture be as effective if he were carrying a man? Explain.
4. Consider Danziger's use of Uncle Sam as the central figure, rather than many editorial cartoonists' choice of Lady Liberty. Why do you think he chose this figure? What other messages are conveyed beyond what is depicted in the photo?
5. Summarize your overall feelings regarding this editorial cartoon. What message did you receive as a viewer? What does Danziger "say" through his artwork? Explain.

WRITING ASSIGNMENTS

1. The essays in this section present some intensely personal perspectives on the events of September 11, 2001, as well as wider political and social analysis. Write about your own perspective of September 11. How did you feel when you first heard about the attacks? How did you feel several months later? Did the events change you awareness of security? of patriotism? of heroism? Explain.

2. Andrew Sullivan states that on September 11, 2001, "another world began." What world does he mean? Describe the world post–September 11. How is it different? Or is it? Explain.

3. Almost every generation has experienced a moment that they later remembered exactly in terms of where they were when the disaster struck. Pearl Harbor, the assassination of John F. Kennedy, the assassination of Martin Luther King Jr., and September 11, 2001, are among such historical moments. Write an essay exploring how such events change national consciousness. Is September 11 likely to be a defining moment for your generation? Why or why not?

PATRIOTISM AND THE FLAG

The True Test of Patriotism Is Harder Than Just Waving a Flag
Eugene Kane

After September 11, 2001, flag sales soared, flags waved everywhere. For many people, this show of patriotism reflected a shared sense of unity and purpose. In the next article, *Milwaukee Journal Sentinel* staff writer Eugene Kane wonders if all the flag waving was really an expression of sincerity or a passing trend. While the current passion for Old Glory is great, says Kane, true patriotism is much more than waving a flag. This article appeared in the September 30, 2001, edition of the *Milwaukee Journal Sentinel.*

■ BEFORE YOU READ

What does the American flag symbolize to you? Did the flag take on a new or deeper meaning for you after September 11, 2001? Why or why not?

■ AS YOU READ

Why do you think people chose overwhelmingly to display flags rather than other American symbols? Was the proliferation of flag waving a demonstration of group behavior? Explain.

1   It is the easiest way to be considered a patriot these days.
2   Just wave a flag.
3   Americans have rediscovered their love affair with Old Glory. The flag has been plastered over everything—T-shirts and jackets, cars and sport utility vehicles, office buildings and shops. Some neighborhoods look as though it's Flag Day 24 hours a day.

4   It's even led to a new flag etiquette, as some organizations try to figure out if flags are appropriate in places where they weren't before. Take the news media. Several TV networks decided journalists shouldn't be wearing flag pins or putting up flags on the broadcast set.

5   The rationale: Reporters are supposed to be "objective," and wearing the flag on one's sleeve—literally or figuratively—just might lead some viewers to consider ABC or CNN a branch of official government as opposed to an independent news organization that reviews all information from the military or the CIA with appropriate cynicism.

6   In other cases, the thought was not to encourage viewers to engage in a game of "Who's more patriotic?" when one on-air personality wears the flag and the other doesn't.

7   From this corner, a general ban on flag-wearing by all journalists seems appropriate. When the Fourth Estate does its job well, we don't need to wave a flag to prove our belief in American ideals.

8   Waving a flag or wearing a flag is not only the easiest way to show patriotism these days, it's also the most superficial.

9   As recently as a few weeks ago, there were as many people wearing T-shirts that read "Jail Bait" or "Too Sexy" or the name of a popular rapper or hip fashion designer as are wearing flags today.

10   We've already proved to be a nation of consumers more than willing to turn ourselves into billboards for the next hot thing.

11   Changing the signage in times of national crisis doesn't seem that impressive.

12   Instead, the true test of patriotism appears more difficult for many to pass.

13   Flying, for example. Air travel on commercial airlines has decreased more than 50% since the terrorist attacks. At a time when it's of paramount importance to demonstrate courage and commitment that our way of life can't be eroded by an unknown danger, many Americans have wimped out big time.

14   These are the same Americans who insist it's time to bomb Afghanistan into a parking lot, who make bold statements about getting Osama bin Laden "dead or alive" and rush to declare war on somebody—anybody—with the fervor of a bunch of wanna-be John Waynes.

15   These are the same people canceling vacations and postponing airplane flights until things get a bit safer—as if things will ever again be as safe as you want them to be.

16   Another true test of patriotism is continuing to hold firm to our bedrock ideals, the tolerance of different religions and backgrounds.

17   All over the country, people of Middle Eastern backgrounds and, specifically, Muslims—or even people who just look Middle Eastern or Muslim—have been threatened and even attacked. They've been accosted by flag-waving yahoos who use the terrorism in New York and D.C. as an excuse to turn America into a place where only people "who look like us" are tolerated.

18   The rampant racial profiling of Arab and Middle Eastern "types" in the days following the hijacked planes was sad but predictable.

19   On a Northwest Airlines flight from the Twin Cities to Salt Lake City, passengers apparently refused to fly with three Middle Eastern-looking men, and they were not allowed to fly on that plane.

20   It will take time for the travel industry to find an acceptable middle ground between reasonable suspicion of foreigners from a part of the world now considered dangerous to American interests, and unfounded discrimination against innocent travelers.

21   But you need no middle ground to draw the line at the harassment of hard-working citizens with Arabic-sounding names, or Muslims practicing their religion in the peaceful and loving tradition that is followed by most of the Islamic world.

22   Being a patriot these days—more than ever before—means considering what being an American truly means.

23   It's time to understand that all dissent isn't unpatriotic.

24   We can still question our government—and President Bush—for their handling of the crisis. We can still ask questions about the apparently sorry state of most airport security, and the below-standard quality of our military intelligence that left a gaping hole for terrorist hijackers to pass through.

25   We can wonder if the much-ballyhooed **"War on Terrorism"** is going to be as ineffective as the "War on Drugs."

26   We can insist that all talk about the multibillion-dollar anti-missile defense system Bush planned to force down our throats—a system that would have been useless Sept. 11—stop right now.

27   Nothing unpatriotic about that.

28   The true test of patriotism may be how much we can put up with in a scary new world.

29   Whether it be long delays and inconveniences while traveling, increased scrutiny of our private affairs or myriad sensational rumors emerging from the Internet seemingly every day.

30   (By the way: real patriotic Americans don't manufacture a false picture of a guy posing on the World Trade Center observation deck as a plane hurtles toward it, and send the picture in an e-mail to everyone they know.)

31   The time for real patriotism is upon us; it requires more than just flag-waving.

32   Compared with the courage and strength of character that will be necessary to return to our normal way of life, waving a flag is easy.

33   In fact, if I were a terrorist still hiding from the law, there would be a giant American flag hanging outside my home right now.

34   Because if that's all you have to do—and none of the other stuff—it really doesn't mean much.

■ QUESTIONS FOR ANALYSIS AND DISCUSSION

1. Kane describes some of the many ways the American flag has been displayed and some of the new rules that accompany this display. Find out what the

official rules are for displaying the flag at <www.ushistory.org/betsy/flagetiq.htm>. Are there situations where displaying the flag is inappropriate? Do you think the rules make sense, or are they irrelevant in today's world?

2. Why does Kane fear that much of the flag displays following September 11 are "superficial"? Do you agree? Explain.

3. Who is Kane's audience? Does he keep his audience in mind as he expresses his opinion?

4. Kane comments that television journalists should not wear flag pins because such a display may send the message that they are biased. Do you agree with this point of view? Why or why not?

The Way We Live Now: 9-30-01: Recapturing the Flag

George Packer

For many American school children, the day begins with the recitation of the Pledge of Allegiance. But not everyone agrees that the flag should be saluted and revered. For some people, the flag symbolizes political values with which they don't agree. In the next article, George Packer explains why so many liberals are wary of the flag, and why the events of September 11 have made some members of the political right rethink their opinions of Old Glory.

Packer is the author of several books, including *The Village Waiting* (1988), *Central Square* (1998), and a family memoir *Blood of the Liberals* (2000). His work has appeared in *Harper's* magazine and the *New York Times*. This article first appeared in the *New York Times* in September 2001.

■ BEFORE YOU READ

In the next article, Packer explains why September 11 "made it safe for liberals to be patriots." Why do liberals shun the flag?

■ AS YOU READ

Packer states that before World War II, patriotism was part of the collective American consciousness, but the McCarthy era and Vietnam created an atmosphere where liberals and academics felt that displaying the flag was "simple bad taste." Does your view of the flag differ from your parents' and grandparents' perspective? Explain.

1   Sept. 11 made it safe for liberals to be patriots. Among the things destroyed with the twin towers was the notion, held by certain Americans ever since Vietnam, that to be stirred by national identity, carry a flag and feel grateful toward someone in uniform ought to be a source of embarrassment. The force of the blows woke us up to the fact that we are part of a national community. This heightened awareness could be the disaster's greatest legacy, one that liberals should not fear but learn to use.

2   The estrangement of liberal Americans from patriotism is a recent turn. The word "liberal" first came into political use among a group of intellectuals who supported Woodrow Wilson taking the country into World War I. In World War II, the anti-Fascist war, liberalism and patriotism were still synonymous. My late father, a law professor, quit college to enlist, served on a destroyer and was wounded in action. But by the time I was growing up, on a university campus in the 1960's, too much contrary history had intervened for patriotism to be a part of my moral education: first the McCarthy era, when patriotic slogans were used to target liberals, including my father, and then Vietnam, when American power turned so manifestly unjust.

3   We were not anti-American, but my father was too rational to trade on such ordinary virtues as courage and loyalty. This disappointed me, because as a boy I spent hours with my friends re-enacting American military glory at Guadal-canal and Omaha Beach. At the same time, I wore a peace button and had the "War Is Not Healthy for Children and Other Living Things" poster. No, war was not healthy—but it was more exciting than anything else I could think of.

4   Over time, the instinct for battlefield virtue went underground. As patrio-tism became the exclusive property of conservatives, the part of me that craved danger and commitment and sacrifice had to find an outlet in not quite satisfy-ing alternatives like the Peace Corps. But I don't want to pretend that my wari-ness of the flag was just a matter of political values. It was also a matter of culture and class. The flag was waved mainly by working-class people, for whom loyalty to the family, the tribe and the nation hadn't been eroded by the pressure of middle-class ambition and self-conscious sophistication. My family would sooner have upholstered the furniture in orange corduroy than show the colors on Memorial Day. Display wasn't just politically suspect, it was simple bad taste: sentimental, primitive, sometimes aggressive.

5   A strange thing happened after the cold war ended: patriotism all but dis-appeared from American politics. The right and the left essentially offered a choice between hedonisms: tax cuts or spending. No one asked for sacrifice; no one spoke to common purpose. Liberalism settled for irony and contempt, which mobilized no one. Not long before the attack, a friend noted that ratings for Fox News and Comedy Central were up while CNN was down. "In this coun-try we have the right wing," he said, "and we have Comedy Central."

6   Sept. 11 changed all that, instantly. That day a policeman tried to help an investment banker who had fled the twin towers and seemed to be in shock. "I'm not in shock," the banker replied. "I like this state. I've never been more cognizant in my life."

7   In the days that followed, we all witnessed an outbreak of civic-mindedness so extreme that it seemed American character had changed overnight. As flags bloomed like flowers, I found that they tapped emotion as quickly as pictures of the missing. To me, these flags didn't represent flabby complacence, but alert-ness, grief, resolve, even love. They evoked fellow feeling with Americans, for we had been attacked together.

8   Patriotism is as volatile as any emotion; once released, it can assume ugly forms. "I'm a patriot," said Frank Roque after being arrested for murdering a

Sikh in Arizona. But in the past decade, our national disorder has been narcissism, not hysteria. Anyone who wants reform should figure out how to harness the civic passion that rose from the smoking debris. Like jet fuel, it can be used for good or ill. All the calls for pacifism now issuing in e-mail petitions from the left and all the impassioned critiques of American arrogance will be irrelevant if they don't speak to Americans' patriotism.

9   Patriotism has nothing to do with blindly following leaders. But the American flag now represents a national community that came under attack, and that in turn represents, at least in the minds of the terrorists, the whole decadent civilization of the modern world. Our civilization is, of course, decadent, but it is also free enough for us to wake up to that fact. What I dread now is a return to the normality we're all supposed to seek: instead of public memorials, private consumption; instead of lines to give blood, restaurant lines.

10   My political views haven't changed since Sept. 11. Even as the sight of other people's flags stirred me, I did not go out and buy my own. Some part of me still shrinks from the display of patriotism, as if it would violate the emotion itself. I don't desire war—but I know that patriotic feeling makes individuals exceed themselves as the bland comforts of peace cannot. "The only thing needed," William James wrote in "The Moral Equivalent of War," "is to inflame the civic temper as past history has inflamed the military temper." I've lived through this state, and I like it.

■ **QUESTIONS FOR ANALYSIS AND DISCUSSION**

1. Why, according to Packer, is it "embarrassing" for liberals to be patriotic? What caused this estrangement from the flag and what it symbolizes? How did September 11 change this perspective, and is it likely to last?

2. Packer admits that his wariness of the flag was not simply a matter of political values. For him, displaying the flag was also a "matter of culture and class." What does he mean by this statement? Do you agree with the author's connections between class and displaying the flag? Why or why not?

3. How can patriotism "assume ugly forms"? What examples does the author give?

4. Who is the author's intended audience? What assumptions does he make about his readers? Cite some examples from the text to support your response.

5. How did the author's childhood and familial experiences influence his views on the flag? Have his views changed? Explain.

Rally Round the Flag

King Kaufman

In the last article, George Packer described how the patriotic feelings inspired by September 11 made it "safe" for liberals to wave flags. The next article continues this exploration from the point of view of one such liberal. King Kaufman, a senior writer at *Salon* magazine, explains, "I love Old Glory. I just wonder if I can take it back from the creeps who've waved it all my life." This article was printed in *Salon* magazine exactly one week after the attacks of September 11.

■ BEFORE YOU READ

In your opinion, was the flag-waving response following the September 11 attacks overzealous or justifiable and reasonable? Why or why not?

■ AS YOU READ

What are Kaufman's objections to the American flag? Evaluate his argument and the evidence he uses to support it.

1   Sept. 18, 2001. I'm wrestling with the American flag.

2   It's everywhere now: tiny ones riffling on car antennas, medium ones waving from porches, giant ones yawning from cranes. People are wearing them. Every Old Navy flag shirt ever bought has been pulled out of the drawer this week, and Stars and Stripes 'do rags are all the rage.

3   There's no flag flying on my porch. I don't have a flag, and they're hard to come by these days anyway—not that I've tried to get one. And if I had one, I can't figure out if I'd fly it or not.

4   See, Old Glory and I, we go way back, and we've had our problems.

5   For most of my life, the American flag has been the cultural property of people I can't stand: right-wingers, jingoists, know-nothing zealots. It's something that hypocritical politicians wrap themselves in. It's something that certain legislators would make it a crime to burn—a position that's an assault on the very freedom that the flag represents. It's something brandished at times like these by idiots who say things like, "Let's go over there and burn those rag-heads!"

6   During the Gulf War, I hated the American flag. It was everywhere then, too, on porches and car antennas and over the left breast of every uniformed athlete, all in support of a war I and many others thought to be immoral.

7   But I also love the flag. Seeing it stirs something in me, even when I'm mad at it, or disagree with those who wave it. I am, after all, an American, and despite being opposed to every single military adventure this nation has undertaken in my lifetime, I'm a patriotic one at that.

8   For me, though, patriotism is more about the freedom to criticize the government than it is about waving a piece of red, white and blue laundry around and singing "God Bless America." It's about loving our shared national personality—aggressive, impulsive and open, unimpressed with such Old World nonsense as royalty. It's about feeling at home in a country where the first question asked of new acquaintances is not "Where are you from?" but "What do you do?"; where a loutish baseball star can sit next to a president and say, "Hot as hell, ain't it Prez?" and be loved all the more for it. It's about loving this country's crazy cultural stew—that "melting pot" that we give ourselves more credit for than we should, but that really does exist.

9   For me, statements like "America right or wrong" or "America: Love it or leave it," a chestnut from my childhood, are the antithesis of what this country is all about. And those are the sentiments that the flag has come, over many years, to represent for me.

10   So you'll be surprised to hear that I have an American flag shirt, and maybe surprised to hear that I sometimes wear it—without irony!—on occasions such as the Fourth of July. First of all, it's a hell of a shirt since, after all, it's a Grand Old Flag. But I also like what it says. It says I'm an American. Not for me the pretentious Europhile weenieness that sometimes plagues my fellow middle-class American white boys. I'm a proud son of the country that's produced Bart Simpson and Ambrose Bierce, Robert Johnson and Abe Lincoln, Michael Jordan and Doc Holliday. Bruce Springsteen said something in his "Born in the U.S.A." days that stayed with me: "That's my flag too." How did the Republicans and the gun nuts and the xenophobes co-opt it?

11   There are two kinds of patriots: The "God Bless America" kind and the "This Land Is Your Land" kind. I'm the latter.

12   On the surface, the songs sound similar: simple melodies with lyrics about America's natural beauty, the mountains and deserts and "oceans white with foam" in one; the Redwood forests, Gulf Stream waters and "sparkling sands of her diamond deserts" in the other.

13   But that's only because we don't sing all the verses that Woody Guthrie wrote in his song, an answer to "God Bless America," which he hated for its sentimentality and dumb, blind devotion. Here's one of the verses school kids don't sing: "As I was walking, I saw a sign there/And that sign said 'No trespassing'/But on the other side, it didn't say nothing/Now that side was made for you and me." Another verse has "my people" at the relief office, "wondering if this land was made for you and me."

14   That song's political and social criticism, its questioning, are also part of what makes this country great. These things, as much as our culture, our national personality, our country's physical magnificence, are what the flag represents to me.

15   But when I see that flag flying from a neighbor's porch, I think, "Oh boy, right-wing nut." And I'm not hearing people singing "This Land Is Your Land" over the last week, though "God Bless America" is everywhere.

16   While I'm not quite a pacifist, I have a pretty simple, even simplistic view of war: You don't fight unless you've been attacked. So now that this country has been attacked, I agree with the vast majority that some sort of military response is warranted. This is a new feeling for me, this feeling that we're the good guys and we're fighting the bad guys. It makes sense that I'd want to fly the good guys' flag, but that flag comes wrapped around a lot of baggage.

17   There's the bell. The wrestling match continues.

■ QUESTIONS FOR ANALYSIS AND DISCUSSION

1. How would Packer respond to Kaufman's article? In what ways are their arguments similar and in what ways are they different? Whose argument seems the more compelling, and why?

2. What does the flag symbolize to Kaufman? How can he both hate the flag and love it too?

3. What connections does Kaufman make between the songs "God Bless America" and "This Land Is Your Land," and the American flag? What song does he prefer, and why? How do these songs support his argument regarding the American flag? Explain.

Box of Flags

> Just as the terrorists know that we are watching them, we know that they are watching us. When they see us in the streets, wearing the flag, they know that we are not afraid of them, and that we will defeat them.
>
> —Moses D'vila, teacher

On September 17, 2001, the *New York Times* featured the photo on page 424 to accompany the article "A Nation Binds Its Wound in Red, White and Blue." The article included quotes from many Americans explaining why they chose to display the flag. Overwhelming patriotism had made it almost impossible to purchase a full-size flag. And from sidewalk vendors in New York City, reported the *New York Times,* you could buy your patriotism "at four bucks a pop." As you study the photo, consider the context in which it was taken, the medium in which it was printed, and the article it accompanied.

■ QUESTIONS FOR ANALYSIS AND DISCUSSION

1. Did you elect to display the American flag after the September 11 terrorist attacks? Why or why not?

2. Evaluate the photo. What does it depict? What message does it convey? Is it a patriotic photo? Why or why not?

3. Would the context of this photo be different if it were featured in a newspaper in another country? What would viewers infer from the photo? What message might it convey if it were featured in a Middle Eastern newspaper?

4. Newspaper photo editors choose the photos they print very carefully. Why do you think the *New York Times* selected this photo to print? Does it tell you anything about the newspaper itself? about the photojournalist who took the picture? Explain.

■ WRITING ASSIGNMENTS

1. Currently, burning the flag is protected under the First Amendment right of freedom of expression. However, legislation has been proposed that would make this act illegal. Write an essay presenting your own viewpoint on this issue. Should burning the flag be illegal? Should it be protected under the First Amendment? Why or why not?

2. Two authors in this section explain why they object to the American flag. Write a response to one or both of these authors, in which you agree or disagree with

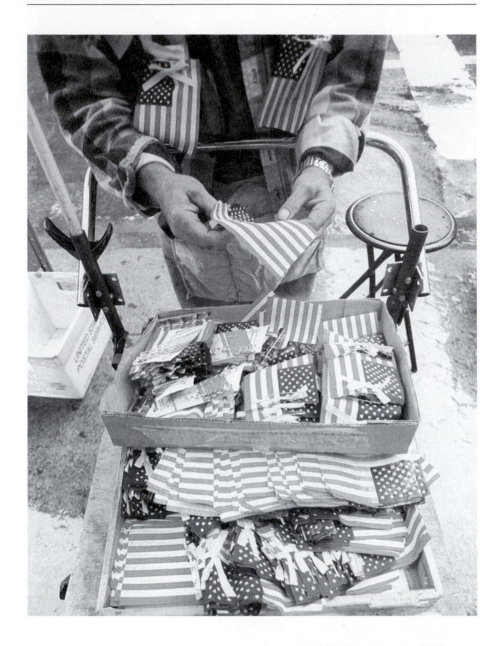

their viewpoint while presenting your own. Respond to specific points they make and provide support for your own opinion.

3. The Pledge of Allegiance, written at the end of the nineteenth century, is re-cited in many American classrooms across the country. Review the language of the pledge. Should it be recited in school? Should such recitation be manda-tory? Why or why not?

REACTING TO TERRORISM

Americans Don't Understand That Their Heritage Is Itself a Threat
Caleb Carr

Following the terrorist acts on September 11, 2001, reporters kept referring to the attack as "senseless" and "irrational." Americans asked why they were targeted by a group of people so far removed from the United States. What had we ever done to them? In the next piece, author Caleb Carr explains that the terrorist attacks on September 11 were far from irrational acts of violence. Rather, the Pentagon and the World Trade Center were carefully selected targets chosen for their symbolism. As he explains, this is a war of cultures, and America itself—and what it stands for—is the threat.

   Novelist and historian Carr is a contributing editor of *MHO: The Quarterly Journal of Military History.* He is the author of the best-selling novels *The Alienist* (1995) and *Angel of Darkness* (1998). This article appeared in a forum on terrorism in the October 14 edition of the *New York Times.*

■ BEFORE YOU READ

Consider the targets chosen by the terrorists in the September 11 attacks. What did these buildings symbolize to Americans? to the Western world? to Muslim extremists? Explain.

■ AS YOU READ

Carr is a military historian. How does he use history to support various points?

1   We have heard a great deal of talk to the effect that the world will never be the same after the attacks of Sept. 11, that we are living in a new reality, and in one sense this is true. But this is not the first great and violent historical turning point that the United States has faced. In other words, to put it as Lewis Carroll's Mad Hatter might have, we have been in this new world before.

2   America experienced just such a prolonged moment during our own Civil War, when not only armies but also civilians were slaughtered in horrifying numbers because of a long-brewing clash between a dying, slavery-based agrarian society and a vigorous, newly industrial modern state. We weathered another during the days and years following Pearl Harbor, when the majority of Americans had no idea if or where Japanese planes might strike again and were later forced (as we have lately been) to reckon with enemies who were willing to engage in suicidal attacks to achieve their purpose.

3   Yet perhaps the most immediately pertinent of such precedents is offered by a much earlier conflict. In 1814, the United States was engaged in a bitter war, on land and at sea, with the greatest power in the world, the empire from which we had originally rebelled: Great Britain.

4   Many analysts of the War of 1812 have tried to explain it as an economic or political conflict of limited importance. But it would have been hard to convince the American civilians who suffered what amounted to terrorist attacks by ruthless British raiding forces between 1812 and 1814 that the conflict was either limited or explicable. The British assaults were astoundingly savage: women and children were mutilated and murdered along with civilian men and soldiers in a deliberate attempt to break the American people's will to fight. These efforts reached their culmination in the last days of August 1814, when a squadron of British ships loaded with soldiers and sailors sailed into Chesapeake Bay and up the Patuxent River with a terrifying objective: to burn the city of Washington to the ground.

5   The British force succeeded in this goal. By the night of Aug. 24, the White House, the Capitol, the Library of Congress and many other buildings emblematic of both the newborn capital city and the infant country itself were engulfed in flames. The government had been evacuated at the last minute, its officers (including President James Madison) scattering across the countryside. British action against remaining American soldiers and civilians continued to be, in many cases, merciless.

6   The questions asked by Americans in the aftermath of this momentous event were some of the same that I have heard all over our city and country in recent days: Why here? Why this?

7   The War of 1812 had little to do with specific political grievances or economic rivalries. It was prosecuted by the British because of a deep anxiety over the spread of American democratic republicanism. Having seen the bloody anarchy that had overtaken France during its revolution and having watched the United States peacefully and dramatically multiply its territory through the Louisiana Purchase, the British Empire—a stratified society still largely controlled by its aristocracy and constitutional monarchy—had grown deeply fearful that the spread of American-style democratic rebellion would mean not only economic competition abroad but also uprisings at home. In short, the British gratuitously destroyed important structures in Washington (and killed many innocent people) because those buildings were obnoxious symbols of American values whose spread and propagation the London government feared would spell the disempowerment of their own.

8   The British were right to fear as much, for in time it was indeed the rise of the United States that set the example for populations in colonies around the world to seize their own destinies and put an end to the imperial, socially regimented system on which British power depended. True, in the 20th century the United States and Britain would become allies in order to face the the common enemies of imperial Germany and, later, Nazi and Japanese totalitarianism. Nevertheless, it was the spread of American values that put an end to the colo-

nialism and imperialism that were the practical and spiritual lifeblood of the British Empire.

9   Similarly, it is the spread of American values—individualistic, democratic, materialistic and, yes, in many ways crass and exploitative American values— that terrorist groups and the traditionalist, socially repressive societies that support them now fear. This fear has driven them to emulate the British forces of 1814 by damaging and destroying a group of structures that are among the most familiar symbols of contemporary American power.

10   Thus the why. But why here? Washington is perhaps understandable, but why New York?

11   The engine that runs the juggernaut that is expansionist American democratic capitalism (which is the force that opens the way for American cultural predominance) is housed, chiefly, in a comparatively few high-profile buildings at the southern tip of Manhattan Island. Americans look (or in the case of the World Trade Center, looked) on these buildings as some of the most distinctive symbols of all that our city and nation can achieve and have achieved.

12   Our enemies in this war, by contrast, looked at them and saw—still see— the death of their own values, their own ways of life, their effective autonomy. Such perception breeds both malice and fear. Inside those buildings, the people behind this attack believe, is where the end of the societies they come from and the values that they live by was and is being planned (whether consciously or not), and *there* is where the erosion must be stopped. The terrorist obsession with the World Trade Center was, in this light, not irrational. In fact it was, viewed in the context of a war of cultures, entirely understandable.

13   That context must now be fully realized by our side in this conflict. We must all match the sudden comprehension and bravery of the hijacked passengers aboard United Airlines Flight 93, who, realizing that their plane was going to be used as a flying weapon of mass destruction, immediately rose to challenge their captors, thus sacrificing their own lives to prevent a fourth crash that could have killed thousands more Americans.

14   The people of this country, it has often been truly said, have a very bad sense of their own heritage, and New Yorkers tend to be among the worst offenders in this area. We have been known to pull down historic structures with remarkably little concern, to crumble and pave over our past in order to make way for what we hope will be an even more profitable future. But there are moments when we must overcome this blind tendency and look to our history for both inspiration and solace. We know in our collective memory the nature of this struggle; that understanding must now move from our subconscious to the very forefront of our minds so that we can accept the full dimensions of the conflict that will very soon engulf the lives of not only New Yorkers and Washingtonians but all Americans.

15   Yes, this is war, and in all likelihood it will be a vicious and sustained one. What our enemies want is nothing short of an end to our predominance, and they will not forsake terrorism until either they attain that result or we make such behavior prohibitively, horrifyingly expensive. And this worst assault on

the United States in its history happened in New York City because it symbolizes all that those same enemies loathe and fear most: diversity, licentiousness,
avarice and freedom. Now, as we go about the process of adjusting ourselves to
this new world of terrible conflict, we can and must take heart from that one
seemingly paradoxical historical observation: both as New Yorkers and as Americans, we have been in this new world before.

▪ QUESTIONS FOR ANALYSIS AND DISCUSSION

1. According to Carr, why is the United States a target for terrorism? Is there a rationale behind such hatred? Explain.
2. Carr states that "it is the spread of American values [. . .] that terrorist groups
   [. . .] now fear" (paragraph 9). What values does he identify? Why do terrorist
   groups, and the "socially repressive" countries that support them, fear these values? Are some of these values a cause of concern to Americans as well? Explain.
3. What has history taught us about wars on values? Evaluate Carr's historical examples of when Americans have faced similar conflicts. What does history
   teach us may happen next?
4. Carr observes, "The terrorist obsession with the World Trade Center was, in
   this light, not irrational. In fact it was, viewed in the context of a war of cultures, entirely understandable." Respond to this statement. Do you agree with
   his assessment? Why or why not?

The Algebra of Infinite Justice
Arundhati Roy

In the next piece, Arundhati Roy challenges American's call for vengeance. Presenting a different viewpoint on the motivation behind the terrorist attacks, and the reaction of the United States, Roy asserts that America faces an enemy it doesn't understand, because "they don't appear much on TV."

   Roy is a political activist and the author of *The God of Small Things* (1997) and
Power Politics (2001). This article first appeared in the September 29, 2001, issue of
the British newspaper *The Guardian*.

▪ BEFORE YOU READ

What was the immediate American reaction to the September 11 attacks? Was it to
fight? to mourn? to think and debate?

▪ AS YOU READ

In the next essay, Roy poses some very strong challenges and claims against the
United States. What are her objections, and how well does she support her claims?
What evidence does she use to prove her points?

1   In the aftermath of the unconscionable September 11 suicide attacks on the Pentagon and the World Trade Center, an American newscaster said: "Good and evil rarely manifest themselves as clearly as they did last Tuesday. People who we don't know massacred people who we do. And they did so with contemptuous glee." Then he broke down and wept.

2   Here's the rub: America is at war against people it doesn't know, because they don't appear much on TV. Before it has properly identified or even begun to comprehend the nature of its enemy, the US government has, in a rush of publicity and embarrassing rhetoric, cobbled together an "international coalition against terror," mobilised its army, its air force, its navy and its media, and committed them to battle.

3   The trouble is that once America goes off to war, it can't very well return without having fought one. If it doesn't find its enemy, for the sake of the enraged folks back home, it will have to manufacture one. Once war begins, it will develop a momentum, a logic and a justification of its own, and we'll lose sight of why it's being fought in the first place.

4   What we're witnessing here is the spectacle of the world's most powerful country reaching reflexively, angrily, for an old instinct to fight a new kind of war. Suddenly, when it comes to defending itself, America's streamlined warships, cruise missiles and F-16 jets look like obsolete, lumbering things. As deterrence, its arsenal of nuclear bombs is no longer worth its weight in scrap. Box-cutters, penknives, and cold anger are the weapons with which the wars of the new century will be waged. Anger is the lock pick. It slips through customs unnoticed. Doesn't show up in baggage checks.

5   Who is America fighting? On September 20, the FBI said that it had doubts about the identities of some of the hijackers. On the same day President George Bush said, "We know exactly who these people are and which governments are supporting them." It sounds as though the president knows something that the FBI and the American public don't.

6   In his September 20 address to the US Congress, President Bush called the enemies of America "enemies of freedom". "Americans are asking, 'Why do they hate us?'" he said. "They hate our freedoms—our freedom of religion, our freedom of speech, our freedom to vote and assemble and disagree with each other." People are being asked to make two leaps of faith here. First, to assume that The Enemy is who the US government says it is, even though it has no substantial evidence to support that claim. And second, to assume that The Enemy's motives are what the US government says they are, and there's nothing to support that either.

7   For strategic, military and economic reasons, it is vital for the US government to persuade its public that their commitment to freedom and democracy and the American Way of Life is under attack. In the current atmosphere of grief, outrage and anger, it's an easy notion to peddle. However, if that were true, it's reasonable to wonder why the symbols of America's economic and military dominance—the World Trade Center and the Pentagon—were chosen as the targets of the attacks. Why not the Statue of Liberty? Could it be that the

stygian anger that led to the attacks has its taproot not in American freedom and democracy, but in the US government's record of commitment and support to exactly the opposite things—to military and economic terrorism, insurgency, military dictatorship, religious bigotry and unimaginable genocide (outside America)? It must be hard for ordinary Americans, so recently bereaved, to look up at the world with their eyes full of tears and encounter what might appear to them to be indifference. It isn't indifference. It's just augury. An absence of surprise. The tired wisdom of knowing that what goes around eventually comes around. American people ought to know that it is not them but their government's policies that are so hated. They can't possibly doubt that they themselves, their extraordinary musicians, their writers, their actors, their spectacular sportsmen and their cinema, are universally welcomed. All of us have been moved by the courage and grace shown by firefighters, rescue workers and ordinary office staff in the days since the attacks.

8   America's grief at what happened has been immense and immensely public. It would be grotesque to expect it to calibrate or modulate its anguish. However, it will be a pity if, instead of using this as an opportunity to try to understand why September 11 happened, Americans use it as an opportunity to usurp the whole world's sorrow to mourn and avenge only their own. Because then it falls to the rest of us to ask the hard questions and say the harsh things. And for our pains, for our bad timing, we will be disliked, ignored and perhaps eventually silenced.

9   The world will probably never know what motivated those particular hijackers who flew planes into those particular American buildings. They were not glory boys. They left no suicide notes, no political messages; no organisation has claimed credit for the attacks. All we know is that their belief in what they were doing outstripped the natural human instinct for survival, or any desire to be remembered. It's almost as though they could not scale down the enormity of their rage to anything smaller than their deeds. And what they did has blown a hole in the world as we knew it. In the absence of information, politicians, political commentators and writers (like myself) will invest the act with their own politics, with their own interpretations. This speculation, this analysis of the political climate in which the attacks took place, can only be a good thing.

10   But war is looming large. Whatever remains to be said must be said quickly. Before America places itself at the helm of the "international coalition against terror", before it invites (and coerces) countries to actively participate in its almost godlike mission—called Operation Infinite Justice until it was pointed out that this could be seen as an insult to Muslims, who believe that only Allah can mete out infinite justice, and was renamed Operation Enduring Freedom—it would help if some small clarifications are made. For example, Infinite Justice/Enduring Freedom for whom? Is this America's war against terror in America or against terror in general? What exactly is being avenged here? Is it the tragic loss of almost 7,000 lives, the gutting of five million square feet of office space in Manhattan, the destruction of a section of the Pentagon, the loss of several hundreds of thousands of jobs, the bankruptcy of some airline companies and the dip in the New York Stock Exchange? Or is it more than that? In

1996, Madeleine Albright, then the US secretary of state, was asked on national television what she felt about the fact that 500,000 Iraqi children had died as a result of US economic sanctions. She replied that it was "a very hard choice", but that, all things considered, "we think the price is worth it". Albright never lost her job for saying this. She continued to travel the world representing the views and aspirations of the US government. More pertinently, the sanctions against Iraq remain in place. Children continue to die.

11   Operation Enduring Freedom is ostensibly being fought to uphold the American Way of Life. It'll probably end up undermining it completely. It will spawn more anger and more terror across the world. For ordinary people in America, it will mean lives lived in a climate of sickening uncertainty: will my child be safe in school? Will there be nerve gas in the subway? A bomb in the cinema hall? Will my love come home tonight? There have been warnings about the possibility of biological warfare—smallpox, bubonic plague, an-thrax—the deadly payload of innocuous crop-duster aircraft. Being picked off a few at a time may end up being worse than being annihilated all at once by a nuclear bomb.

12   The US government, and no doubt governments all over the world, will use the climate of war as an excuse to curtail civil liberties, deny free speech, lay off workers, harass ethnic and religious minorities, cut back on public spending and divert huge amounts of money to the defence industry. To what purpose? President Bush can no more "rid the world of evil-doers" than he can stock it with saints. It's absurd for the US government to even toy with the notion that it can stamp out terrorism with more violence and oppression. Terrorism is the symptom, not the disease. Terrorism has no country. It's transnational, as global an enterprise as Coke or Pepsi or Nike. At the first sign of trouble, ter-rorists can pull up stakes and move their "factories" from country to country in search of a better deal. Just like the multi-nationals.

13   Terrorism as a phenomenon may never go away. But if it is to be contained, the first step is for America to at least acknowledge that it shares the planet with other nations, with other human beings who, even if they are not on TV, have loves and griefs and stories and songs and sorrows and, for heaven's sake, rights. Instead, when Donald Rumsfeld, the US defence secretary, was asked what he would call a victory in America's new war, he said that if he could con-vince the world that Americans must be allowed to continue with their way of life, he would consider it a victory.

14   The September 11 attacks were a monstrous calling card from a world gone horribly wrong. The message may have been written by Bin Laden (who knows?) and delivered by his couriers, but it could well have been signed by the ghosts of the victims of America's old wars. The millions killed in Korea, Viet-nam and Cambodia, the 17,500 killed when Israel—backed by the US—in-vaded Lebanon in 1982, the 200,000 Iraqis killed in Operation Desert Storm, the thousands of Palestinians who have died fighting Israel's occupation of the West Bank. And the millions who died, in Yugoslavia, Somalia, Haiti, Chile, Nicaragua, El Salvador, the Dominican Republic, Panama, at the hands of all the terrorists, dictators and genocidists whom the American government

supported, trained, bankrolled and supplied with arms. And this is far from being a comprehensive list.

15   For a country involved in so much warfare and conflict, the American people have been extremely fortunate. The strikes on September 11 were only the second on American soil in over a century. The first was Pearl Harbor. The reprisal for this took a long route, but ended with Hiroshima and Nagasaki. This time the world waits with bated breath for the horrors to come.

16   Someone recently said that if Osama bin Laden didn't exist, America would have had to invent him. But, in a way, America did invent him. He was among the jihadis who moved to Afghanistan in 1979 when the CIA commenced its operations there. Bin Laden has the distinction of being created by the CIA and wanted by the FBI. In the course of a fortnight he has been promoted from suspect to prime suspect and then, despite the lack of any real evidence, straight up the charts to being "wanted dead or alive".

17   Now Bush and Bin Laden have even begun to borrow each other's rhetoric. Each refers to the other as "the head of the snake". Both invoke God and use the loose millenarian currency of good and evil as their terms of reference. Both are engaged in unequivocal political crimes. Both are dangerously armed—one with the nuclear arsenal of the obscenely powerful, the other with the incandescent, destructive power of the utterly hopeless. The fireball and the ice pick. The bludgeon and the axe. The important thing to keep in mind is that neither is an acceptable alternative to the other.

18   President Bush's ultimatum to the people of the world—"If you're not with us, you're against us"—is a piece of presumptuous arrogance. It's not a choice that people want to, need to, or should have to make.

▪ QUESTIONS FOR ANALYSIS AND DISCUSSION

1. What is Roy's tone in this essay? Who is her audience? Does her tone detract from her message, or serve to strengthen it? Explain.
2. Roy states that if America "doesn't find its enemy [. . .] it will have to manufacture one. Once war begins, it will develop a momentum, a logic and a justification of its own, and we'll lose sight of why it's being fought in the first place." Does this statement ring true? Why or why not?
3. In paragraph 4, Roy observes, "What we're witnessing here is the spectacle of the world's most powerful country reaching reflexively, angrily, for an old instinct to fight a new kind of war." How does Roy's choice of words reveal her political stance? Explain.
4. Summarize Roy's argument in this essay. Respond to her argument, referring to her specific objections and the evidence she uses to support these objections. Does history prove her argument well founded? Why or why not?
5. What solutions does Roy offer the United States in its fight against terrorism? If she could reach the ear of the politicians she names—George W. Bush and Donald Rumsfeld—how do you think they would respond to her ideas?
6. Many Americans would take issue with the statements Roy makes about why terrorists attacked the United States and the American perspective on the world,

and her criticisms of the U.S. government. Do her criticisms surprise you? Do they represent the opinions of people outside the United States? Interview a few international students on their perception of the United States as it relates to some of the comments Roy makes in her essay.

Understanding Terrorism
A Harvard University Roundtable Discussion

Several months after the terrorist attacks of September 11, Harvard University held a roundtable discussion on the nature of terrorism and the conditions that create it. Experts on government, Islam, international law, public health, the Middle East, military strategy, civil liberties, and other fields participated in the panel discussions held at Harvard Law School. *Harvard Magazine* printed excerpts of the discussion in its December 2001 issue.

The following professors participated in the roundtable discussion: Eva Bellin, associate professor of government; Ashton B. Carter, professor of science and international affairs; Philip B. Heymann, professor of law; David Little, professor of the practice of religion, ethnicity, and international conflict; Louise M. Richardson, executive dean of the Radcliffe Institute for Advanced Study and formerly associate professor of government; and Jessica E. Stern, lecturer in public policy.

■ BEFORE YOU READ

Although most people think they know what terrorism is, they are often at a loss to define it. What is terrorism? How do we address the threat of terrorism without compromising our democratic society?

■ AS YOU READ

As an academic forum, the discussion that follows presents many different—and sometimes opposing—points of view. Evaluate how the speakers in this forum work together to address the questions presented to them. Do they reach a consensus, or are many issues left unresolved? Explain.

1   Beyond the emotional reactions necessarily provoked by the terrorist attacks of September 11 and subsequent anthrax-tainted mailings, the events demand reflective analysis and an attempt at understanding. What is the nature of this kind of terrorism, and what conditions created it? How well has the United States responded to the assault, and what measures will be most effective? Will mobilizing to reduce vulnerability to terrorism alter our democratic society? How can we detect and deter other threats—and defuse the forces that give rise to terrorist groups and acts?

2   In an effort to share some of this expertise. *Harvard Magazine* invited six faculty members to talk broadly about the causes and consequences of contem-

porary terrorism. Participants in the conversation, held November 5 at Harvard
Law School and moderated by the magazine, included:

3   **Eva Bellin** '80, associate professor of government and author of *Stalled
Democracy* (on socioeconomic obstacles to democratization in the Middle East),
who teaches courses on "The Struggle for Palestine/Israel" and "The Politics of
Islamic Resurgence";

4   **Ashton B. Carter,** Ford Foundation professor of science and international
affairs and codirector of the Preventive Defense Project at the Kennedy School
of Government, coauthor of *Preventive Defense: A New Security Strategy for America,*
and assistant secretary of defense for international security policy from 1993 to
1996;

5   **Philip B. Heymann,** J.D. '60, James Barr Ames professor of law, faculty di-
rector of the Project on Justice in Times of Transition (which has been active in
Northern Ireland and the Middle East), deputy attorney general of the United
States from 1993 to 1994, and author of *Terrorism and America: A Commonsense
Strategy for a Democratic Society;*

6   **David Little,** Th.D. '63, T.J. Dermot Dunphy professor of the practice in religion, ethnicity, and international conflict and director of initiatives in religion
and public life at the Divinity School, coauthor of *Islamic Activism and U.S. Foreign Policy,* and author of volumes on religion and nationalism in Ukraine and
Sri Lanka;

7   **Louise M. Richardson,** Ph.D. '89, executive dean of the Radcliffe Institute
for Advanced Study and formerly associate professor of government, focusing
on international relations and terrorism; and

8   **Jessica E. Stern,** Ph.D. '92, lecturer in public policy at the Kennedy School,
author of *The Ultimate Terrorists,* and, from 1994 to 1995, director for Russian,
Ukrainian, and Eurasian affairs at the National Security Council.

9   Edited excerpts of the discussion follow.

10   MODERATOR: How would you define terrorism? What's distinctive about what
Professor Carter has called the "catastrophic terrorism" visited on the United
States September 11? How does that compare to other kinds of terrorism?

11   RICHARDSON: A great deal of time has been spent trying to define terrorism.
I find it more helpful to think about several crucial characteristics of terrorism.
A terrorist act must be political, and it must be violent. It's symbolic—the victim
and the audience are not the same, so the point is to use a randomly or symbol-
ically selected target to convey a political message to another audience, usually
the government, to try to affect their behavior. Finally, and most crucially, is the
deliberate targeting of innocents. It is this tactic which sets terrorism apart
from other forms of violence, and other forms of political violence, including
guerrilla warfare.

12   So I think it makes more sense to use the *means* employed as the way of
defining terrorism, rather than the goals that are being sought, or the political
context in which the act takes place.

13   CARTER: Everything Louise said makes great sense. I think that one needs
further to distinguish the motivations that enter into mass or catastrophic terrorism from those that enter into what I'll call ordinary or traditional terrorism—the airline hijacking, the bomb in the marketplace, or hostage-taking. Not
in all cases, but at least in some important cases, the motivation for mass terror
is a vengeful or messianic one, rather than a politically purposeful one. Our attentions these days happen to be on Al Qaeda, but there are certainly groups in
the United States that have long been driven to mass terrorism by rage.

14   It's very difficult, in many of those cases, to figure out what their political
motivation is—whether there *is* a political motivation, and whether there's any
way of building a bridge to that political motivation. When the PLO began,
when the IRA began, you could at least imagine some reconciliation of the underlying situation. But when we talk about mass terrorism, we may be dealing
with truly fringe motivations that it's very difficult even to understand, let alone
to deter, or to bargain with. There will probably always be some fraction of humanity which has motivations of this kind, and which might be prone to mass
violence.

15   HEYMANN: I agree that you have to include a category of sheer destructiveness without obvious motivation, though it always carries some message. Everything carries some message. But otherwise I think Louise's description is very
good. I'd like to note that she has, in some ways, led the definition away from
any kind of moral fervor.

16   It's very important how you describe "innocents." Are police innocents?
Are manufacturers of supplies innocents? That's a very troublesome question.

17   The other troublesome question is, what if it's a nondemocratic state?
What if the French Resistance is blowing up tourists from Nazi Germany in
Paris? That might seem very justified to a lot of people. Louise says that is terrorism—it may be justified, or it may not be, but we have to call it terrorism
from the start. I think she has made a useful move there. A lot of people
would insist that terrorism be against a democratic state in some kind of fair
system.

18   RICHARDSON: Conor Cruise O'Brien made popular the argument that terrorism can only occur in a democratic state. It was designed in reaction to the
African National Congress in South Africa. Here was a group which appeared
to be committing terrorist tactics, but they were completely excluded from the
political process. So one didn't want to put them in the same category as the
IRA, who had democratic opportunities open to them, but chose not to use
them. I don't think that's very helpful, because in a sense it means that the
Basque ETA in Spain were *not* terrorists when they blew up tourists under
Franco, but *were* terrorists when they continued to blow up tourists under the
democratic regime.

19   So if one takes the means-based definition I use, you do move toward a
more normatively neutral definition of terrorism, and then you can decide
whether the terrorism of the ANC is justified or not—it's a separate question.

20   If I could come back to Ash, I would say that even most of the messianic groups in fact have political motives. Even Osama bin Laden in his speeches, while he spells out this messianic message, is also spelling out very coherent U.S. policies to which he objects, like our support of Israel and our deployment of troops in the Middle East. So I prefer to keep it staunchly in the political realm.

21   HEYMANN: What would you do with Timothy McVeigh?

22   RICHARDSON: McVeigh's goal—insofar as we knew what it was—was to limit the size of the American government.

23   LITTLE: That seems like a stretch. So, Louise, you have to have a *political* motivation somehow clearly defined in order for the group to be terrorist—what about Aum Shinrikyo [the group that released nerve gas in the Tokyo subway in 1995]?

24   RICHARDSON: Otherwise it's a criminal gang. Aum Shinrikyo had very clear political motives. They actually wanted to win political power.

25   LITTLE: I would like to mention here a definition of terrorism found in international humanitarian law. It appears in the two 1977 protocols that supplement the Geneva Conventions protecting victims of armed conflict: "The civilian population as such, as well as individual civilians, shall not be the object of attack. Acts or threats of violence, the primary purpose of which is to spread terror among the civilian population, are prohibited." Technically, this definition does not apply to the acts of September 11 since the protocols pertain to states and "organized armed groups" engaged in "sustained and concerted military operations." Still, absent a comprehensive convention on international terrorism, this is the clearest legal definition we have. So far as I know, it is the only place where the term "terror" occurs in the international humanitarian legal documents, and it is important that Al Qaeda has, it appears, deliberately committed acts prohibited by the laws of war.

26   What's interesting about this definition is the exclusive focus on the spreading of terror. There is no mention of political or other motivations, and I am inclined to think that that is the nub of the matter.

27   STERN: I think this is completely right: it doesn't matter in the least whether terrorists purport to have political motivations. What matters is the *means* they use to achieve their purported objectives. I think we should turn to the "just war" tradition, which helps us distinguish between the justness of ends and means. Every terrorist I have interviewed has told me he is certain his ends are just. But the justness of terrorists' ends is inherently subjective. If we focus on the means, we run into a lot less trouble. Terrorism as a technique—the deliberate targeting of noncombatants—is a violation of every religious tradition, as well as of international law.

28   CARTER: There are important definitional issues here, but the thing that arrests people's attention today is the prospect of catastrophic terrorism. In the broadest sense, this prospect arises from the fact that with every passing year, technology puts into the hands of smaller and smaller groups destructive power of a kind that used to be reserved to organized states. And society becomes more and

more vulnerable as it becomes more interconnected and intricate. Those two facts are going to be part of the human condition as far into the future as we can see.

29   Now it seems to me that there will always be some subset of humanity which, for whatever motives, takes that destructive power into their hands and uses it against society writ large. That, in the largest sense, is the problem. And I don't think our approach to protecting society can be based solely, or at this stage in understanding even primarily, on fathoming the motivation.

30   Louise is rightly urging us to *try* to understand the underlying motivation, even though it's complicated and various. At the end of the day, though, when it comes to mass terrorism, it's the *fact* that matters. It becomes a little bit like pornography: I know it when I see it. If a civilian airliner is going into a building, that's the kind of destructive power in a small number of hands which, for whatever motivation, we can't tolerate. It's not possible to continue to operate civil society with that danger ever present.

31   STERN: Why does it matter how many hands have access to the means of terror? It seems to me it's a moral problem, and why does the perpetrator matter? We are talking about a method of killing or warfare where states are equally as liable . . .

32   CARTER: Only because it multiplies the number of possible perpetrators. When individuals can do damage that states used to do, then you have to start worrying about every individual, and there are a whole lot more of them than there are states.

33   STERN: But what about carpet bombing specifically with the aim of terrorizing the civilian population? Does that fit into our definition? What about dropping nuclear weapons on Hiroshima and Nagasaki? I think that has to fit into our definition, because it's very clear from the documents the purpose was to terrorize the civilian population.

34   HEYMANN: The position that Louise has taken is that it may be morally identical, but whether you call it terrorism is a separate question.

35   Let me say one thing about the definition. There will be a very large number of incidents that will satisfy everyone around the table that they are terrorist. That will include the World Trade Center bombing, and the Pentagon bombing, and the Oklahoma City bombing. And there will be a number of things, such as carpet bombing a city, or nuclear attacks, or attacks on police, or attacks not in a democracy, about which there will be debate. But to a very large extent, the dilemma of the United States at the moment involves activities by Al Qaeda that we would all agree were terrorist. Then the question is whether our response is effective and morally acceptable.

36   MODERATOR: Whatever definition of terrorism you use, and however you characterize it—some of you characterize terrorism as simultaneously a crime, a war, a threat, a disaster, an emergency, a kind of politics—what do you make of the U.S. response so far to September 11, to the anthrax-laced mailings?

37   CARTER: The administration began talking about retaliation as the core of its response, but has slowly, and I think rightly, moved to a wider kind of re-

sponse in the appointment of a director of homeland security, which is really the heart of the matter.

38   One of the difficulties that the president faces is that this is a mission that doesn't really have a home in our government yet. We have a Department of Defense, whose job is war. This isn't really war. Our historical experiences of wars involve foreigners, and foreign places. Not all incidents of catastrophic terrorism will involve foreigners, and they are by definition not in foreign places. It's more than a crime, because our approach to crime is fundamentally to allow it to occur, and then arrest and prosecute the perpetrators. This is a level of destructiveness that you can't allow to take place on a routine basis, the way you allow street crime to take place. It's not a "disaster" because it's an act of man, not an act of God.

39   We have institutions that deal with war, institutions that deal with crime, and institutions that deal with disaster. This is a mixture of all three. So what you see the administration trying to do is invent a new model of government to deliver a new public service, homeland security. For 200 years, we never really needed to deliver that product on a large scale. Governor Tom Ridge [director of homeland security] is supposed to be doing that, and everybody wishes him well. But it's a tough matter, because it goes to the heart of the way we see ourselves and the way we govern ourselves. In dealing with crime we attach great protections to the citizen, and deliberately limit the reach of government, whereas war is a much more unfettered matter. We've liked that distinction throughout our history. Now we have a problem that falls between the cracks, and we don't want to start treating our own citizenry the way you treat a foreign military opponent. We have to somehow find a new way. That's the heart of what the Bush administration's trying to do.

40   So far, I don't see the administration putting together a comprehensive program that covers surveillance and detection of people and threats; preventive measures to understand motivations, and stop people from either wanting to do this, or having the means to do it; protective measures, like reinforcing air filtration systems in buildings; means to interdict, effectively, a terrorist group once you'd found it (we're obviously trying to do that in Afghanistan today); containing damage, if the worst occurs, and cleaning up after à la New York and Ground Zero; and then when it's all over, finding out who did it—typing anthrax, for example, and deciding whether to retaliate or prosecute. That entire set of activities needs to be organized and lodged somewhere in the federal government. All of those things are new. It's a deep challenge to our way of government, and it's going to require some real innovations in how we structure and conduct ourselves.

41   STERN: We need to think about this as a form of psychological warfare. When our president was talking about "crusades," he was really playing into the hands of the terrorists. I can tell you that I got a flurry of e-mails from Pakistan from the jihadis who were so excited—they had been waiting for this moment. They have been longing to fight the "Crusaders and Jews"—in other words, the West. Bin Laden himself is clearly trying to turn this into a war between Islam

and the West. In his recent communiques bin Laden has been dividing the world into two camps—the believers and the infidels—arguing that this is a religious war, not a war against terrorism.

42   The whole aim of terrorism is to get us to overreact. I think initially we appeared to be coming up with a strategy that was almost a form of psychotherapy for the American people, and a very clear overreaction.

43   What's far more important over the long term is not bombing raids, but intelligence cooperation—seeking the vulnerabilities in the terrorist network. They seek out our vulnerabilities. We need to seek out theirs. A very important one is drying up the money flows. At last, we hear today that the United Arab Emirates are cooperating with U.S. government authorities in helping to dry up the money flow. The Saudis are cooperating, perhaps not as much as they might. We need much more intelligence cooperation, covert action, diplomacy. I'll feel much better when we know *less* about what's going on in Afghanistan.

44   RICHARDSON: There are three aspects to the government's response. First is the fact that a forceful response was required. Second, this was a restrained response—more restrained than many of us would have anticipated, knowing the predilections of this administration. Third come the broader, domestic infrastructure points that Ash admirably captured.

45   It was simply imperative that we have a forceful response. I tend to look at this in international, rather than domestic terms. We have to demonstrate to the Iraqs, and the Irans, and other countries around the world that we are prepared to fight, we're prepared to assume casualties to oppose this kind of action.

46   Second, on the point that Jess just made, our reaction *has* been restrained, and it's imperative that it continue to be so. Bin Laden is acting in the way that other terrorist groups before him have acted. There is nothing he would like more than to provoke a spiral of violence. He's trying to provoke massive retaliation, which would have the effect of winning more recruits for his organization, and of supporting his interpretation of our actions to the mass Muslim publics in these regions, who at this point probably share his aspirations, but certainly don't approve of his means of achieving them.

47   I think it's an effective counterterrorism policy—this is what we've learned from the past—to drive a solid wedge between the perpetrators of the violence and the broader communities. The government has clearly been aware of the need to do that. But it's very difficult to be restrained while conducting a military operation. It requires the effort to protect civilians. It requires putting our own military at greater risk. That's a risk we have to assume in the interests of protecting civilian lives, for normative reasons, but also for pragmatic ones.

48   But I'm uncomfortable with the whole language of warfare. It's a shame that we have encountered an incident that fits our understanding of terrorism better than any we have ever encountered, and I hope will encounter, and we immediately abandon the language of terrorism and shift to the language of warfare. In doing that, we set ourselves up for failure. It's understandable why the government did it—to facilitate domestic mobilization, and to demonstrate

how seriously we take this. But warfare connotes victories, and surrender, and defeat. In this war, there appear to be three goals. One is to capture bin Laden, two is to bring down the Taliban, and three is to protect ourselves from this ever happening again. Our chances of pulling off the first two are pretty good. But our chances of protecting ourselves from ever having another terrorist attack domestically are close to nil.

49   It rather reminds me of the message the IRA once sent to Prime Minister Thatcher after they had blown up her hotel in Brighton during the Conservative Party conference and narrowly missed killing her. The next day, they sent her a message saying, "You were lucky yesterday, but we've only to be lucky once." I think we cannot cede the initiative to the terrorists, where they can demonstrate, by successfully pulling off one terrorist act in this country, that we have not, in fact, won this war.

50   HEYMANN: I also would say that we have three objectives, but the most important one we ought to have in terms of this war is to say, right off the bat, this has to be fought by law enforcement and intelligence people in the countries where the terrorists are. That's what we really need.

51   I don't think catching bin Laden is the answer, if we *could* catch him. And I don't think bringing down the Taliban is the answer, if we bring down the Taliban.

52   But I do think that a critical part of preventing this is establishing that no country will be permitted to openly tolerate sizable groups planning the destruction of American lives and buildings and property, and creating widespread fear. That fits comfortably within the UN definition of self-defense. Our objective in Afghanistan should be to make the point that there's an *immense* cost to openly supporting a terrorist group that is targeting the United States for massive terrorism.

53   LITTLE: I agree. It is interesting that the United Nations Security Council really has gone some distance toward authenticating or certifying an armed response. Whether they will continue to do that remains to be seen. But they have gone out of their way to reaffirm the need to respond against activities of the kind you describe. And there have been some other very important statements to that effect. Mary Robinson, the UN High Commissioner for Human Rights, has gone on record calling September 11 a "crime against humanity" and an assault on the rule of law, democracy, and human rights. It seems to me there is *significant* international support for some kind of armed response along these lines.

54   On the other hand, one needs to bear in mind the need for restraint and limitation if the just-war categories are to be respected. They are very relevant. Certainly, the protection against indiscriminate destruction is very important. Second, we need always to bear in mind the salience of what the just-war tradition calls "a reasonable probability of success," as we undertake this kind of action. What *are* the probabilities of doing the kind of thing Louise mentions? If, as Phil suggests, we define the mission of our military response to terrorism as primarily one of retributive punishment, that objective no doubt has a higher probability of success. At the same time, endeavoring by our efforts to restore

and advance "international peace and security," together with observance of the norms of human rights and humanitarian law, in line with explicit UN Security Council expectations, should not be lost sight of.

55   I don't think the present administration has done a very good job of authenticating its response in broader international terms. There is much work to be done to put U.S. activities within a wider international *context*.

56 MODERATOR: If we believe what has been reported about the identities of the people involved in September 11, there are lots of common ties to Saudi Arabia and Egypt. What conditions in those societies—in their politics and cultures, and in ideology or Islamic thought—are associated with this kind of international terrorism? What are the terrorists' aims?

57   BELLIN: I don't think one ought to focus exclusively on domestic conditions in Saudi Arabia or Egypt. What was really striking to me was that despite the fact that something like 14 people involved in this specific incident seemed to be of Saudi nationality, in fact the people who have been involved in these sorts of terror networks come from all over the Arab world. There are Lebanese, Egyptians, people from the UAE, from Tunisia, Algeria. Clearly, a more general phenomenon is driving these activities.

58   First, there's a general sense of hostility and anger toward the United States in the Arab world, and probably the Muslim world generally. There's a general sense of anger at the U.S.'s making expedient use of countries in the Muslim world for its short-term interests, and then discarding them when its interests shift. There's anger about the U.S. employing a double standard in its implementation of UN resolutions, and in its defense of principles of international law. There's anger at the U.S. because it seems to be the leading symbol of globalization, a force that's disrupting the lives of many. Overall, people in the region are angry over their sense of powerlessness and the humiliation they feel at the hands of what they perceive to be cavalier domination by Western forces, the U.S. in particular.

59   None of this exactly explains why you get these individual incidents of terror, because there's no correlation between this mass anger and the incidents of terror. This sort of mass anger has been building up for decades, and the instances of terror are recent and unique.

60   Rami Khoury, who is a journalist from Jordan, gave a talk a few weeks back on this topic. He presented a cogent analogy, which explains the relationship between mass anger toward the United States in the Arab and Muslim world, and distinguishes between that and the acts of the violent few. He compared this anger to the position of people in the United States who oppose abortion. Khoury pointed out that a large number of people in America, maybe even a majority, don't approve of abortion. But only a very small number of people actually commit acts of violence against abortion clinics. It's the same thing in the Arab and Muslim world: there's a vast sense of anger toward the United States, but that doesn't mean the masses of people support terrorist violence to express that anger. There is general disavowal of this kind of violence by the

masses of people in the region, even though they are quite angry at the United States.

61   I think the aims of these terrorist networks are much more expressive than programmatic. The best evidence for this is in the randomness of their targets. They go after the World Trade Center, but there was also a plan to go after a Christmas market in the French city of Strasbourg, and another to dive-bomb the Eiffel Tower. Also, the terrorists do not make specific demands, saying that if you do X, Y, or Z, we will stop hitting the World Trade Center. To the extent that any objectives are stated, they shift around. At one point it's "Let's get the U.S. out of Saudi Arabia." At another time it's "Let's give the Palestinians just treatment." Another time it's "Let's take care of children in Iraq." Just this past weekend, the situation in Kashmir was suddenly added. The demands shift because the terrorists' goal is really not to solve any one of these problems, but rather to express anger.

62   This weekend I was reading the new biography of Frantz Fanon, the premier theorist of decolonialization, who wrote *Wretched of the Earth*. I pulled out my copy again, and was struck that his arguments about violence proved so useful to me in understanding the events of September 11. Fanon talks about the cleansing value of violence. Even random violence against a perceived oppressor is seen as a redemptive act. It's a way for powerless people to feel in power, to feel that they can regain their self-respect, that they can take control of their lives. It really seems to me that these recent terrorist acts are a typical Fanonian act—just an expressive act of trying to recover a sense of power and of self-determination. That's the only way I can understand it.

63   MODERATOR: After what we have seen, are you *more* concerned about use of weapons of mass destruction, even in limited ways like anthrax in letters? Given your work on terrorism, are you concerned about the disjunction between elite thinking about the prospect of terrorism, and its recent arrival on our shores, which seemed to surprise the public despite the previous World Trade Center explosion and other plots? And what would be your most pressing piece of advice, given that there are a lot of targets in this open society, and that we may have to cope with terrorism as an enduring problem?

64   CARTER: We're being told that another shoe is likely to drop before long, well before this situation of Al Qaeda and its deeper roots is "resolved" in any way. Sadly, we might yet see truly mass destruction. One can think of two frightful possibilities. One is smallpox, and the other is a nuclear weapon, either of which would make the anthrax in the letters and the World Trade Center destruction look mild in comparison.

65   For a long time, we have had an attitude that nuclear weapons are unusable, that they are deterrents, and that nobody really is going to use them. It seems to me that we are witnessing in Al Qaeda at least one group which, were it able to obtain nuclear weapons, would use them. That's very chilling, because I remind us all that there are probably in excess of a hundred thousand nuclear weapons' worth of fissile material in the former Soviet Union. Pakistan, which we have made a front-line state in this so-called war on terrorism, is a nuclear nation and has a

few dozen nuclear weapons, and the wherewithal and expertise to make more. So I would say that the nuclear chapter here is very important.

66   The most urgent piece of advice is to look beyond Al Qaeda and Afghan-istan and Islamist extremism, and to think about catastrophic terrorism as a syndrome of the human condition that will afflict us for a very long time. I would like to see the beginnings of innovation in the way we govern ourselves that I was talking about, that program that we're all hoping for from Governor Ridge, that will allow us, over the long run, to live in a civil society of a sort that we wish to live in, and to continue to enjoy the fruits of technological progress without simultaneously living in fear that the very same technology will be used by fringes to kill a lot of people. That is the big challenge of governance in front of us, and it's never been faced on this scale in human society before.

67   HEYMANN: There were two barriers to weapons of mass destruction as ter-rorist weapons. One was the difficulty of obtaining and using them, particularly of obtaining fissile material, and of delivering biological weapons. The other was the notion that nobody really wanted to, much. We plainly have passed the second barrier with Al Qaeda. I simply can't believe that people prepared to bring down the World Trade Center would balk at a small nuclear explosion. I'm not at all sure what effect that has on others. Up until this time, we had no real effort, other than the Aum Shinrikyo, to use biological or nuclear weapons of terrorism. It may be that the barrier, once down, is down for everybody. But if we were lucky, it might survive, to some extent, for other terrorist groups. I wouldn't be optimistic, but I'm a little bit less pessimistic than Ash. We do have to go through the full range of steps that Ash described. I would be focusing an awful lot of them on the type of terrorism that Al Qaeda now represents on the theory that it amounted to a breakthrough organization—trying new things in new ways, with larger numbers of people, and larger capacities than what we've seen before.

68   The major advice I'd give would take two forms. One would be not to take the president's rhetoric too seriously. There are very difficult problems of for-eign policy. There are very difficult problems of prevention. There are very dif-ficult ethical and moral problems. I think it's very useful to have defined the is-sue as for us or against us for all terrorism, and it is, perhaps, the way to argue the PR battle. But in the long run, that's a much more moralistic form of for-eign policy than we're used to. We're going to have to be very practical about it.

69   The second thing is: don't overestimate the capabilities of our present in-stitutions. I think for the type of preparation Ash is describing, our present in-stitutions look weak in cooperation, weak in individual capacity, weak in imagi-nation. None of these things are very good.

70   STERN: I think we should divide our recommendations into those intended for the government and those intended for the American people. Advising the government, I would suggest thinking not only about the kind of catastrophic threats that Ash has very usefully defined, but also much lower-tech threats—industrial sabotage, sabotage of food-processing plants—that owners of facto-ries need to be trained to deal with, and that the government should get in-volved in. Also it is clear, unfortunately, that dissemination technologies for

biological agents are improving very rapidly, which will make the threat of cata-strophic biological terrorism far more realistic in the future. But we should also remember that technologies for countering terrorism are improving, too. The government should be providing funds to expedite research, for example, on developing DNA vaccines and improving sensors. It should also be funding im-provements in the public-health system and epidemiological surveillance. In-fectious-disease monitoring is important for distinguishing biological terrorism from a natural outbreak of disease, but also critically important for dealing with emerging, re-emerging, and antibiotic-resistant diseases, which are a very real threat today.

71   I also think it's important how we are perceived around the world. We tend to see ourselves as the white hats in the world, and that is clearly not how we're perceived. We need to think about that.

72   Finally, a few words about how the American people need to respond. We now have to deal with a higher level of risk than we're accustomed to dealing with. But we should remember that terrorism pushes all our buttons, and that we are likely, psychologically, to overreact. We should keep this risk in perspec-tive. Every time you smoke a cigarette, you reduce your lifespan by five minutes. Over a hundred Americans die every day in car accidents. We feel that we have control over these risks, and not over terrorism, but the truth is if ordinary Americans want to increase their lifespans, there are things they can do right away—stop smoking and wear seatbelts.

73   RICHARDSON: I would simply argue that doing what Ash described is not at all incompatible with trying to get inside the minds of the terrorists. We should be doing both.

74   Domestically, we can use this attack to alter people's engagement in inter-national affairs. The American population, historically, is astoundingly indiffer-ent to international affairs. One of the positive impacts of this event will be to change that. It goes without saying that we have paid way too high a price.

75   We also need to include in our debates the impact of our policies on the ground. If one had asked a hundred Americans last summer if we had troops deployed in Saudi Arabia, you'd have gotten simply random responses. The vast majority would have no idea. I think if you asked a hundred random peo-ple in the Middle East, you'd have gotten a very different outcome. Our de-ployment of troops on the ground and our support of Israel are extremely un-popular. This does *not* mean that we should abandon these policies, but it does mean that we should include in part of the debate what the impact of our poli-cies is on the ground, how they are perceived on the ground. That's the domes-tic part.

76   On the international part, again, I think we have to be focused, absolutely, on how we are perceived overseas. We have to be focused, absolutely, on waging this campaign against our enemies—and doing it in such a way that we prevent them from selling their argument, and depicting us as the evildoers here.

77   If we were to capture bin Laden, we should put him on trial. I think we should not catch and kill him. Instead, we should convene an international

court—give him an Islamic judge, Christian judges—and give him every procedural protection known to man—the point being to undermine his argument
that we are the evildoers. Here is somebody who has done us this extraordinary
evil. We have him in our hands. We could do whatever we like with him, and we
choose to hand him over, not to a national jurisdiction, but to an international
jurisdiction, again as a way of trying to undermine the argument that he and
people like him make, and to demonstrate that we mean it when we say we believe in the rule of law.

78   Finally, I would simply say that four [now five] people have died of anthrax
and we have 285 million people in this country terrified. The fact that 20,000
people will die of flu this year is having much less impact. This demonstrates
that terrorism is a very effective tactic of the weak against the strong, and shows
that it's here to stay—precisely because it is such an effective tactic in sowing
fear.

79   LITTLE: The only thing I would reemphasize is the point that I tried to
make earlier, that insofar as we are now committed to an antiterror policy,
there are important implications for the U.S. and its policies.

80   One thing that means is that we begin to clarify exactly what terrorism is.
We've made a start here, though without total consensus, and we'll need to
think more carefully and extensively about a definition. Second, this will mean
conscientiously applying a clear understanding of terrorism to our own policies
and the policies of other states and groups—even if the exercise yields some
embarrassing results. I would hate to see us focus only on protecting ourselves
from the scourge of terrorism. We have broader obligations, which require a
new commitment to international collaboration and cooperation. The strident
unilateralism of the original Bush foreign policy was deeply misguided and in
need of reform. Let us hope that out of the experience of September 11 comes
just such a new and lasting commitment on the part of the United States.

■ QUESTIONS FOR ANALYSIS AND DISCUSSION

1. What definitions of terrorism do the Harvard professors offer? What is the difference between the victim and the audience? What is the "point" of terrorism?
   Explain.
2. Why is how we describe "innocents" important? Why is this question particularly troubling? Is terrorism ever justified?
3. Stern comments that terrorism is a "moral problem." What does she mean?
   Why must we consider morality when we develop a definition of terrorism?
4. According to the panel, what difficulties does the Bush administration face in
   waging a war against terrorism? What international issues must it address?
5. What conditions in the politics and culture of the Middle East connect them
   to international terrorism? Explain.
6. What advice do the members of the Harvard panel offer Americans in coping
   with terrorism? Respond to one or more of their suggestions with your own
   viewpoint.

7. Evaluate the effectiveness of this roundtable discussion. What are its strengths and weaknesses? What did you learn and why?

■ WRITING ASSIGNMENTS

1. In the Harvard University roundtable discussion, professor Eva Bellin comments on a book by Frantz Fanon, *The Wretched of the Earth,* which discusses the "cleansing value of violence." She states, "Even random violence against a perceived oppressor is seen as a redemptive act." Explore this idea in an essay, connecting Bellin's points to the acts of September 11. If you wish, you may include an analysis of American retaliatory actions in Afghanistan.

2. Several of the writers in this section comment that the terrorist acts of September 11 were aimed at the cultural ideals and political ideology of the United States. Write an essay in which you explore these ideals. Why would the people of other countries find these ideals threatening? Do Americans force their ideology on others? If so, in what ways?

3. How has terrorism affected your life since September 11, 2001? Have you been inconvenienced at airports? Are you afraid to fly? Have you considered your vacation destination more carefully? Write an essay on the personal impact of terrorism on ordinary Americans, drawing from information provided in this chapter and your own observations and experience.

C H A P T E R   1 3

Race and Ethnicity

The United States is a union predicated on shared moral values, political and economic self-interest, and a common language. However, it is also a nation of immigrants—people of different races, ethnic identities, religions, and languages. It is a nation whose motto *e pluribus unum* ("one out of many") bespeaks a pride in its multicultural heritage. In this chapter, we explore some of the issues that arise from the diversity of our cultural and ethnic backgrounds.

By definition, stereotypes are misleading assumptions about individuals or groups based on characteristics such as race, ethnic origin, social class, religion, gender, or physical appearance. The first section in this chapter, "Stereotypes: How They Hurt," examines the complex ways in which ethnic and racial stereotypes limit our relationships with others and distort how we define ourselves. Ray Suárez begins by describing how stereotypes of Hispanics have kept this group marginalized and economically tied to the white middle-class. In "The Myth of the Latina Woman," Judith Ortiz Cofer continues this discussion on a personal level by explaining how her Puerto Rican background sometimes leads others to make assumptions about her that are negative and demeaning. Many stereotypes are perpetuated on the silver screen, a point made by Ray Hanania in "One of the Bad Guys?" Hanania explains that as an Arab American, he takes issue with the fact that in the eyes of Hollywood, he is a gun-toting terrorist. However, it is not only negative stereotypes that can harm us; even stereotypes that attribute positive qualities to certain groups, such as the assumption that Asian Americans are naturally smart, can deny individuals credit for their achievements. Ted Gup points this out in "Who Is a Whiz-Kid?"

The next section, "Assimilation," focuses on the ways our multicultural heritage can both unify and divide us. Although the United States has been a multiethnic and multiracial society since its founding, in the last few decades different groups of Americans have reasserted their ethnic and racial identities. While this attention to native roots has created greater tolerance and a celebration of differences, it has also challenged our definition of ourselves as Americans. Are we no longer the "great melting pot" that Arthur Schlesinger Jr. extols in his essay "The Return of

447

the Melting Pot"? Or, should we rethink our definitions of cultural "melting," an idea that Gregory Rodriguez advances in "Forging a New Vision of America's Melting Pot." Arturo Madrid discusses the ways diversity can both strengthen and threaten our sense of national unity. And the last essay takes a look at our desire to identify each other by ethnic group, as Jordan Lite examines in "Please Ask Me Who, Not 'What,' I Am."

The final section in this chapter addresses the issue of racial profiling, especially as it applies to African Americans. Harvard Law Professor Randall Kennedy argues that while racial profiling may seem to be based on logical premises, it is morally wrong. John Derbyshire presents another point of view in his editorial "In Defense of Racial Profiling." Bryonn Bain, a student at Harvard Law School, describes his nightmarish experience of being arrested for a crime he did not commit in "The Bill of Rights for Black Men: Walking While Black." Suspected merely because he was black, Bain explains the painful ramifications of racial profiling from a personal perspective. With "Hailing While Black," Shelby Steele completes the section, reflecting on how the simple act of hailing a cab has now become "a tableau in America's ongoing cultural war." Will a cab stop for a black man in New York City, or will Steele be yet another victim of racism?

STEREOTYPES: HOW THEY HURT

Familiar Strangers
Ray Suárez

Although Hispanics were among the very first Americans, they remain marginalized in many segments of middle-class society. In the next article, Ray Suárez observes that middle-class Hispanics are inevitably "class straddlers," economically tied to whites yet still deeply connected to their heritage. Part of the reason for this, he explains, is the influence of cultural stereotypes widely held by whites and even some Hispanics. The failure to address how these stereotypes hurt, he warns, could ultimately lead to perilous consequences for all of us.

Suárez is a Washington-based senior correspondent on the *News Hour with Jim Lehrer* and a featured speaker on the public radio program *Talk of the Nation.* A contributing editor to the national Hispanic news quarterly *Si,* he is the author of *The Old Neighborhood* (1999), from which this article was excerpted.

■ BEFORE YOU READ

In the next essay, Suárez lists many Hispanic and Latino stereotypes. Before you read his essay, try to make your own list of such stereotypes. How could these stereotypes hurt Hispanics?

■ **AS YOU READ**

In his introduction, Suárez makes the valid point that months after Christopher Columbus set foot in the Americas, the first Hispanic children were born, making them the first Americans of European decent. However, Hispanics remain marginalized by middle-class society. What reasons does Suárez give for this seemingly persistent separation?

1   We were among the first Americans. Why are we still strangers? The people you call Latinos, Hispanics, Spanish, wetbacks, and illegals drew their first breaths when an infant was yanked, wet and screaming, from his mother's womb nine months after Christopher Columbus and his hungry men alighted from their ships and walked ashore on the out-islands of the hemisphere.

2   Five hundred years later, we bus your tables, watch your kids after school, pick your strawberries, lay your sod, entertain you at Disney World, and frighten you on darkened streets. Weak of mind and strong of back, we populate your dreams of fabulous sex and immigrant invasion. We fill your jails and fight your wars. We live here for years and never learn your language, so you've got to pass "official" English and English-only laws. We veer between reckless bravado and donkeylike deference. Our men can't hold their liquor, but they can carry a tune. They beat their wives and anyone who dares insult them. Their wives turn to lard after a couple of babies, and remain sweetly compliant as they take care of yours.

3   You know us so well, it seems. Why are we still strangers? That endless wrestling match between black and white—a struggle over everything, real and symbolic—needed fresh blood. They enter from stage South. So you leave a Miami drugstore angry and resentful when a counter girl doesn't understand a perfectly simple question. Elderly home owners who can't afford to move complain about noise and cooking smells, and Catholic churches become stages for the social drama playing itself out on the streets.

4   Writers like Linda Chavez say Hispanic Americans follow the same generational trajectory as Italians, Irish, and Poles. Others, particularly in civil rights organizations like the Mexican-American Legal Defense and Educational Fund (MALDEF) and the National Council of La Raza, say something different is happening. Having the Old Country two hours away by jet, instead of across an ocean, means these new Americans don't have to slam the door on their place of origin as other immigrants have.

5   In the popular mind, the arrival of Spanish-speaking immigrants is closely associated with neighborhood decay. Reality is more subtle: Neighborhoods sag in some places, spruce up in others. Despite wildly different outcomes, a kind of reductionism is at work—a tendency to regard "arrivals" of Dominicans in Upper Manhattan, Mexicans in Chicago, Central Americans in Los Angeles as an undifferentiated metaevent.

6   They move too many people into too-small houses. Their gang's emblems will start showing up in spray paint on garages. There'll be trouble at the local

school. You won't be able to talk to your neighbors. (They may smile amiably, but they won't understand a word you say.) It's all true. It's all false.

7   A new generation of nativist critics wring their hands over millions of unassimilated residents forming a fifth column and bringing Quebec to our door. They want old-style "total immersion"—that is, throwing immigrants in at the deep end of the American pool. Their opponents, I'll call them ethnicists, want it both ways.

8   Ethnicists argue for continuing foreign-language government services, yet when Latino acquisition of English is criticized as too slow, they insist that these immigrants are learning English as quickly as other Americans did. That's *Nuestra Raza,* able to learn English quickly and not learning English, at the same time.

9   Latinos are settling in urban enclaves, yes, but it remains an open question whether they are bound to the ghetto the same way black families of similar income have been.

10   In their level of education, earnings, and consumption patterns, they resemble their gentrifying neighbors more than their Hispanic working-class *hermanos.*

11   "I'm an urbanite?" says Jerry, a 33-year-old "Mex-o-Rican" (his own term: his father is Mexican, his mother Puerto Rican) who owns a home in Chicago's Logan Square neighborhood. A high-income skilled tradesman whose wife also works outside the home, Jerry acknowledges that he had his pick of places to live. "But I feel it's important for the majority of low-income Hispanic kids in Logan Square to have someone as an example—to show that people like them can live comfortably, own a nice home. It's important for kids to see me going to work in a shirt and tie rather than heading to a construction site with a lunch bucket." Jerry is a rough Hispanic equivalent of the "race man" black intellectuals talked about in the 1950s and 1960s. He speaks Spanish at home, watches Spanish television, though not exclusively, and is learning to play the *quatro,* a small 16-string guitar as central to Puerto Rican traditional music as the banjo is to bluegrass. Yet Jerry admits that he has more in common with his white neighbors of European origin than with his Hispanic neighbors.

12   Patricia, born and raised in Ecuador, is in her 40s and until recently was executive director of a citywide agency serving Hispanics. She and her husband bought a three-flat in 1986 and used its rapid appreciation to buy other investment properties. Patricia has left Logan Square for a new home in Wilmette. "I'm representative of a group of friends who moved here as young marrieds, childless couples. At the time it seemed we would stabilize the neighborhood. But then our concerns about education and safety started to take over when we had kids, and this close-knit group of people who lived nearby is slowly eroding, and I didn't feel like I had any reason to stay around here anyway."

13   Gustavo, also in his 40s, is a senior department manager in Chicago city government. By law, he must reside in Chicago. He concludes that there is "no way" he would be living in Logan Square in five or ten years. It would be more likely, he says, to find him living in Colombia, where he grew up. "This is not a

neighborhood I consider appropriate for my daughter, Veronica." Yet Gustavo finds much to like about Logan Square. He believes the neighborhood has become a magnet for upper-income Latinos, which has contributed to his sense of comfort: "No one wants to feel isolated living in a neighborhood."

14   Middle-class Hispanics are inevitably class straddlers, especially when they are home owners. They perceive their property value to be tied to the future of "Anglo" investment in the area. They are thus economically tethered to whites, while they maintain strong emotional bonds to Hispanics. When the interests of one group conflict with those of another, must the straddlers make a choice?

15   With a strong desire to teach their children Spanish, to live in an area where Spanish is still an important language of commerce, to live near family and in the city, these Logan Square neighbors demonstrate an attitude toward assimilation far different from the one that opened the century.

16   At the other end of the social and economic continuum, yet living nearby, are Latinos—boys in particular—who are convinced that America will never provide for them.

17   The world of American Latinos, brought to you courtesy of your local late news, is populated by hard, tragic gang members who believe in little except their need to enforce their code on their block. They live among shuttered factories and empty warehouses. School becomes irrelevant before they reach their teens.

18   America is going to have to see—and reach—these young men. America's zest for "juvenile predator laws" threatens gangs like the Spanish Cobras, but new recruits seem ready to take up the spots emptied by death, imprisonment, or drift into low-wage work. These boys know their country does not know them, even if they spray their names in 10-foot letters on train stations. "We're all just niggaz out here." One nervously touches his gun for reassurance, scanning the faces in the passing car, waiting.

19   Still strangers, they are products of the lead-poisoned soil of the American city. We ignore them at our peril.

■ QUESTIONS FOR ANALYSIS AND DISCUSSION

1. Analyze Suárez's use of "we" and "you" in this essay. Who is "we"? Who is his intended audience, and how can you tell? Does his use of pronouns reinforce the separation he describes as existing between whites and Hispanics? Explain.
2. Explore the differences in assimilation between Hispanics and other groups such as Italians, Irish, and Poles. What role does location play in how Hispanics have intersected with the American middle class? Explain.
3. In paragraph 6, Suárez ends his list of Hispanic stereotypes with, "It's all true. It's all false." What does he mean? How can such stereotypes be both?
4. Who are the "ethnicists"? What do they advocate? What is Suárez's opinion of ethnicists?
5. In what ways are middle-class Hispanics "class straddlers"? How do Suárez's examples of middle-class Hispanics support his assertion that they are economically tied to whites? Explain.

The Myth of the Latina Woman

Judith Ortiz Cofer

Racial stereotypes are often based on misperceptions and a lack of understanding of another group's cultural heritage. In this essay, Judith Ortiz Cofer explores how racial stereotypes are created by cultural misunderstandings, with often insulting results. She also describes how once stereotypes are established, they can perpetuate degrading popular opinions that, in turn, may damage the self-opinion of an entire group of people.

A native of Puerto Rico, Ortiz Cofer moved to the United States when she was a young girl. Educated at both American and British universities, she is the author of several books, including the novel *The Line of the Sun* (1989), for which she was nominated for a Pulitzer Prize, and *Silent Dancing: A Partial Remembrance of a Puerto Rican Childhood* (1998). Ortiz Cofer teaches literature and writing at the University of Georgia at Athens. The following has been selected from her collection of essays *The Latin Deli* (1993).

■ **BEFORE YOU READ**

Consider the ways the media perpetuate cultural stereotypes. Think about how various media, such as television and cinema, promote cultural clichés.

■ **AS YOU READ**

Ortiz Cofer comments that certain adjectives are often used to describe individuals from her ethnic background. What is the basis for these adjectives? What other words can you cite that are used to describe the personalities of women and men from certain ethnic backgrounds?

1   On a bus trip to London from Oxford University where I was earning some graduate credits one summer, a young man, obviously fresh from a pub, spotted me and as if struck by inspiration went down on his knees in the aisle. With both hands over his heart he broke into an Irish tenor's rendition of "María" from *West Side Story*. My politely amused fellow passengers gave his lovely voice the round of gentle applause it deserved. Though I was not quite as amused, I managed my version of an English smile: no show of teeth, no extreme contortions of the facial muscles—I was at this time of my life practicing reserve and cool. Oh, that British control, how I coveted it. But María had followed me to London, reminding me of a prime fact of my life: you can leave the Island, master the English language, and travel as far as you can, but if you are a Latina, especially one like me who so obviously belongs to Rita Moreno's gene pool, the Island travels with you.

2   This is sometimes a very good thing—it may win you that extra minute of someone's attention. But with some people, the same things can make *you* an

island—not so much a tropical paradise as an Alcatraz, a place nobody wants to visit. As a Puerto Rican girl growing up in the United States and wanting like most children to "belong," I resented the stereotype that my Hispanic appearance called forth from many people I met.

3   Our family lived in a large urban center in New Jersey during the sixties, where life was designed as a microcosm of my parents' casas on the island. We spoke in Spanish, we ate Puerto Rican food bought at the bodega, and we practiced strict Catholicism complete with Saturday confession and Sunday mass at a church where our parents were accommodated into a one-hour Spanish mass slot, performed by a Chinese priest trained as a missionary for Latin America.

4   As a girl I was kept under strict surveillance, since virtue and modesty were, by cultural equation, the same as family honor. As a teenager I was instructed on how to behave as a proper señorita. But it was a conflicting message girls got, since the Puerto Rican mothers also encouraged their daughters to look and act like women and to dress in clothes our Anglo friends and their mothers found too "mature" for our age. It was, and is, cultural, yet I often felt humiliated when I appeared at an American friend's party wearing a dress more suitable to a semiformal than to a playroom birthday celebration. At Puerto Rican festivities, neither the music nor the colors we wore could be too loud. I still experience a vague sense of letdown when I'm invited to a "party" and it turns out to be a marathon conversation in hushed tones rather than a fiesta with salsa, laughter, and dancing—the kind of celebration I remember from my childhood.

5   I remember Career Day in our high school, when teachers told us to come dressed as if for a job interview. It quickly became obvious that to the barrio girls, "dressing up" sometimes meant wearing ornate jewelry and clothing that would be more appropriate (by mainstream standards) for the company Christmas party than as daily office attire. That morning I had agonized in front of my closet, trying to figure out what a "career girl" would wear because, essentially, except for Marlo Thomas on TV, I had no models on which to base my decision. I knew how to dress for school: At the Catholic school I attended we all wore uniforms; I knew how to dress for Sunday mass, and I knew what dresses to wear for parties at my relatives' homes. Though I do not recall the precise details of my Career Day outfit, it must have been a composite of the above choices. But I remember a comment my friend (an Italian-American) made in later years that coalesced my impressions of that day. She said that at the business school she was attending the Puerto Rican girls always stood out for wearing "everything at once." She meant, of course, too much jewelry, too many accessories. On that day at school, we were simply made the negative models by the nuns who were themselves not credible fashion experts to any of us. But it was painfully obvious to me that to the others, in their tailored skirts and silk blouses, we must have seemed "hopeless" and "vulgar." Though I now know that most adolescents feel out of step much of the time, I also know that for the Puerto Rican girls of my generation that sense was intensified. The way our teachers and classmates looked at us that day in school was just a taste of the cultural clash that awaited us in the real world, where prospective

employers and men on the street would often misinterpret our tight skirts and jingling bracelets as a come-on.

6   Mixed cultural signals have perpetuated certain stereotypes—for example, that of the Hispanic woman as the "Hot Tamale" or sexual firebrand. It is a one-dimensional view that the media have found easy to promote. In their special vocabulary, advertisers have designated "sizzling" and "smoldering" as the adjectives of choice for describing not only the foods but also the women of Latin America. From conversations in my house I recall hearing about the harassment that Puerto Rican women endured in factories where the "boss men" talked to them as if sexual innuendo was all they understood and, worse, often gave them the choice of submitting to advances or being fired.

7   It is custom, however, not chromosomes, that leads us to choose scarlet over pale pink. As young girls, we were influenced in our decisions about clothes and colors by the women—older sisters and mothers who had grown up on a tropical island where the natural environment was a riot of primary colors, where showing your skin was one way to keep cool as well as to look sexy. Most important of all, on the Island, women perhaps felt freer to dress and move more provocatively, since, in most cases, they were protected by the traditions, mores, and laws of a Spanish/Catholic system of morality and machismo whose main rule was: *You may look at my sister, but if you touch her I will kill you.* The extended family and church structure could provide a young woman with a circle of safety in her small pueblo on the island; if a man "wronged" a girl, everyone would close in to save her family honor.

8   This is what I have gleaned from my discussions as an adult with older Puerto Rican women. They have told me about dressing in their best party clothes on Saturday nights and going to the town's plaza to promenade with their girlfriends in front of the boys they liked. The males were thus given an opportunity to admire the women and to express their admiration in the form of *piropos:* erotically charged street poems they composed on the spot. I have been subjected to a few piropos while visiting the Island, and they can be outrageous, although custom dictates that they must never cross into obscenity. This ritual, as I understand it, also entails a show of studied indifference on the woman's part; if she is "decent," she must not acknowledge the man's impassioned words. So I do understand how things can be lost in translation. When a Puerto Rican girl dressed in her idea of what is attractive meets a man from the mainstream culture who has been trained to react to certain types of clothing as a sexual signal, a clash is likely to take place. The line I first heard based on this aspect of the myth happened when the boy who took me to my first formal dance leaned over to plant a sloppy overeager kiss painfully on my mouth, and when I didn't respond with sufficient passion said in a resentful tone: "I thought you Latin girls were supposed to mature early"—my first instance of being thought of as a fruit or vegetable—I was supposed to *ripen,* not just grow into womanhood like other girls.

9   It is surprising to some of my professional friends that some people, including those who should know better, still put others "in their place." Though rarer, these incidents are still commonplace in my life. It happened to me most

recently during a stay at a very classy metropolitan hotel favored by young professional couples for their weddings. Late one evening after the theater, as I walked toward my room with my new colleague (a woman with whom I was coordinating an arts program), a middle-aged man in a tuxedo, a young girl in satin and lace on his arm, stepped directly into our path. With his champagne glass extended toward me, he exclaimed, "Evita!"

10   Our way blocked, my companion and I listened as the man half-recited, half-bellowed "Don't Cry for Me, Argentina." When he finished, the young girl said: "How about a round of applause for my daddy?" We complied, hoping this would bring the silly spectacle to a close. I was becoming aware that our little group was attracting the attention of the other guests. "Daddy" must have perceived this too, and he once more barred the way as we tried to walk past him. He began to shout-sing a ditty to the tune of "La Bamba"—except the lyrics were about a girl named Maria whose exploits all rhymed with her name and gonorrhea. The girl kept saying "Oh, Daddy" and looking at me with pleading eyes. She wanted me to laugh along with the others. My companion and I stood silently waiting for the man to end his offensive song. When he finished, I looked not at him but at his daughter. I advised her calmly never to ask her father what he had done in the army. Then I walked between them and to my room. My friend complimented me on my cool handling of the situation. I confessed to her that I really had wanted to push the jerk into the swimming pool. I knew that this same man—probably a corporate executive, well educated, even wordly by most standards—would not have been likely to regale a white woman with a dirty song in public. He would perhaps have checked his impulse by assuming that she could be somebody's wife or mother, or at least *somebody* who might take offense. But to him, I was just an Evita or a María: merely a character in his cartoon-populated universe.

11   Because of my education and my proficiency with the English language, I have acquired many mechanisms for dealing with the anger I experience. This was not true for my parents, nor is it true for the many Latin women working at menial jobs who must put up with stereotypes about our ethnic group such as: "They make good domestics." This is another facet of the myth of the Latin woman in the United States. Its origin is simple to deduce. Work as domestics, waitressing, and factory jobs are all that's available to women with little English and few skills. The myth of the Hispanic menial has been sustained by the same media phenomenon that made "Mammy" from *Gone with the Wind* America's idea of the black woman for generations; María, the housemaid or counter girl, is now indelibly etched into the national psyche. The big and the little screens have presented us with the picture of the funny Hispanic maid, mispronouncing words and cooking up a spicy storm in a shiny California kitchen.

12   This media-engendered image of the Latina in the United States has been documented by feminist Hispanic scholars, who claim that such portrayals are partially responsible for the denial of opportunities for upward mobility among Latinas in the professions. I have a Chicana friend working on a Ph.D. in philosophy at a major university. She says her doctor still shakes his head in puzzled amazement at all the "big words" she uses. Since I do not wear my diplomas

around my neck for all to see, I too have on occasion been sent to that "kitchen," where some think I obviously belong.

13   One such incident that has stayed with me, though I recognize it as a minor offense, happened on the day of my first public poetry reading. It took place in Miami in a boat-restaurant where we were having lunch before the event. I was nervous and excited as I walked in with my notebook in my hand. An older woman motioned me to her table. Thinking (foolish me) that she wanted me to autograph a copy of my brand new slender volume of verse, I went over. She ordered a cup of coffee from me, assuming that I was the waitress. Easy enough to mistake my poems for menus, I suppose. I know that it wasn't an intentional act of cruelty, yet of all the good things that happened that day, I remember that scene most clearly, because it reminded me of what I had to overcome before anyone would take me seriously. In retrospect I understand that my anger gave my reading fire, that I have almost always taken doubts in my abilities as a challenge—and that the result is, most times, a feeling of satisfaction at having won a convert when I see the cold, appraising eyes warm to my words, the body language change, the smile that indicates that I have opened some avenue for communication. That day I read to that woman and her lowered eyes told me that she was embarrassed at her little faux pas, and when I willed her to look up at me, it was my victory, and she graciously allowed me to punish her with my full attention. We shook hands at the end of the reading, and I never saw her again. She has probably forgotten the whole thing but maybe not.

14   Yet I am one of the lucky ones. My parents made it possible for me to acquire a stronger footing in the mainstream culture by giving me the chance at an education. And books and art have saved me from the harsher forms of ethnic and racial prejudice that many of my Hispanic *compañeras* have had to endure. I travel a lot around the United States, reading from my books of poetry and my novel, and the reception I most often receive is one of positive interest by people who want to know more about my culture. There are, however, thousands of Latinas without the privilege of an education or the entrée into society that I have. For them life is a struggle against the misconceptions perpetuated by the myth of the Latina as whore, domestic or criminal. We cannot change this by legislating the way people look at us. The transformation, as I see it, has to occur at a much more individual level. My personal goal in my public life is to try to replace the old pervasive stereotypes and myths about Latinas with a much more interesting set of realities. Every time I give a reading, I hope the stories I tell, the dreams and fears I examine in my work, can achieve some universal truth which will get my audience past the particulars of my skin color, my accent, or my clothes.

15   I once wrote a poem in which I called us Latinas "God's brown daughters." This poem is really a prayer of sorts, offered upward, but also, through the human-to-human channel of art, outward. It is a prayer for communication, and for respect. In it, Latin women pray "in Spanish to an Anglo God / with a Jewish heritage," and they are "fervently hoping / that if not omnipotent, / at least He be bilingual."

■ QUESTIONS FOR ANALYSIS AND DISCUSSION

1. How did Ortiz Cofer's cultural background prevent her from "fitting in"? What differences does she describe between Puerto Rican and "white" cultures?
2. How can cultural ideology and history hinder acceptance into "mainstream" corporate and social America? Explain.
3. How have the media promoted the image of the "Latina woman"? Evaluate Ortiz Cofer's analysis of why this stereotyping occurs. Do you agree?
4. What was the "island system" of morality for Puerto Ricans? How did it both liberate and restrain them? Analyze Ortiz Cofer's connection between the island system of life and the cultural misunderstandings she encountered in urban America.
5. Explain the connection between Ortiz Cofer's poem at the end of her essay and the points she makes earlier. Is this an effective way to end the essay?
6. Why does Ortiz Cofer consider herself to be "one of the lucky ones" (paragraph 14)?

One of the Bad Guys?

Ray Hanania

Sometimes stereotypes can be more than simply insulting, they can interfere with the daily lives of the people victimized by such labels. As Ray Hanania observes in the next essay, Hollywood prefers to cast Arabs as the bad guys, terrorists who like to murder innocent people "simply because it makes [them] feel good." The perpetuation of this stereotype has caused Hanania to be the subject of FBI scrutiny and to be detained in airports, merely because of the way he looks. Life in America isn't easy, explains Hanania, when you look like "one of the bad guys."

Hanania is an Arab American and the author of *I'm Glad I Look Like a Terrorist: Growing Up Arab in America* (1996), which examines the author's perspective on how the United States treats "ethnics." His writing has appeared in many newspapers, including the *Chicago Sun Times,* the *Boston Globe,* and the *St. Louis Post Dispatch.* This article was first published in the November 2, 1998, issue of *Newsweek.*

■ BEFORE YOU READ

In the next article, Hanania comments on the negative way Hollywood depicts Arabs on film. Before you read his essay, consider the way Hollywood traditionally portrays terrorists in its movies. How can Hollywood's stereotyping of Arabs hurt people of Arab descent living in America?

■ AS YOU READ

This essay was published in 1998, almost three years before the terrorist attacks of September 11. Immediately following the attacks, many movie studios delayed the release of violent films, especially ones featuring Arabs as the bad guys. In light of the events of September 11, what new obstacles do Arab Americans face in dispelling the stereotype Hanania describes?

1   As a child in the 1960s, I thought my relatives were famous. It seemed like they were in many Hollywood movies, often playing similar roles. OK. They weren't the headliners, but they did appear alongside stars like Paul Newman ("Exodus"), Sophia Loren ("Judith") and Kirk Douglas ("Cast a Giant Shadow"). My "relatives" always played the "terrorists."

2   As I grew older, though, I realized that those actors were not my relatives, at all. They just looked like them. They have that "terrorist" look, and so do I. I can safely assure you, though, I don't have the mannerisms. I'm tired of seeing my likeness wielding an AK-47, murdering innocent women and children, getting stomped by Arnold Schwarzenegger ("True Lies"), or Harrison Ford ("Indiana Jones and the Temple of Doom"), or Kurt Russell ("Executive Decision"), and now Bruce Willis ("The Siege").

3   I'm Arab-American. And for some reason, Hollywood seems to think it's OK to portray all Arabs—and all Muslims, for that matter—as the bad guys. I don't mean just bad. I mean *really* bad. It makes me so angry I want to get in my half-track with my 50-caliber howitzer that's parked in my two-Hummer garage, drive to the center of town and start shooting! I mean, isn't that what you've come to expect Arabs to do?

4   After I was honorably discharged from the U.S. Air Force in 1975, the FBI opened a file on me. It began with the ominous suggestion that I might be involved in "suspected" terrorist organizations, but the investigation concluded two years and 23 pages later that I was concerned only about improving the condition of my community. The investigation seemed based on the assumption that because I was an Arab, I must also be a potential terrorist. Most of the juicy text was blocked out with heavy, black Magic Markered lines, so it's hard to know for sure.

5   Hollywood movies are founded on the same assumption, that the Arab is the terrorist. I once thought movies were just entertainment, but they're much more. It's at the movies that the public learns about people like me. And it's also where I compare myself to the characters on the screen and wonder if there really is something wrong with me. How did my look suddenly become something so sinister? My eyes become even darker and more deep set? My accent heavier? I begin to question myself. Why is this person who looks like me so angry he wants to murder and harm innocent people? What is it that makes him wreak havoc and wanton suffering upon an innocent world?

6   Occasionally, there is an upside to being pegged as a terrorist. Once at Miami International Airport, a gaggle of people all wearing the same light gray jackets were following me around the terminal. Finally, introducing themselves as airport security, they directed me to a room where they rifled through my bags and grilled me about my travel history. They held up the embarrassing evidence of my terrorism. Wood carved heads. Goofy-looking hats. And dirty clothes.

7   When they finally realized I was just a tourist-trap junkie, they excused themselves. Usually, it takes about 15 minutes before I am released from airport detention and I'm on my way. Meanwhile, the nonterrorist-looking commuters are left waiting in the long immigration lines, impatiently nudging luggage across the tile floor, complaining about the heat and delays. But the security officers always have a reason to stop me. At Miami, they said I looked like the suspect they were pursuing. And, they just happened to have a Polaroid picture of the "suspect." He wore a double-breasted, polyester leisure suit, with a wide-brimmed Panama hat. And he had olive skin, dark eyes and those skinny little fingers that fit neatly around the trigger of a gun, like mine do. Naturally, I was very impressed. It must be difficult to get a terrorist to stop long enough to pose for a Polaroid picture.

8   Look, I'm realistic. I don't think we can erase all of Hollywood's stereotypes. But the movies seem fixated on the exaggerated bad side of Arabs. To Hollywood, the Arab is the wife-abuser who wants to buy Steve Martin's home in "Father of the Bride II." Or the guy hanging from the missile in "True Lies" when Schwarzenegger pushes the launch button and says in his Austrian accent, "Yaw're fi-yard!" We Arabs murder innocent airline passengers in "Executive Decision" simply because it makes us feel good.

9   Even a company like Disney takes a shot at us, with these lyrics from the movie "Aladdin": "Oh I come from a land, from a faraway place, where the caravan camels roam; Where they cut off your ear if they don't like your face; It's barbaric, but hey, it's home." (Disney responded to Arab-Americans' complaints by changing the last line for the video release.)

10   Must every Arab portrayed in the movies be the villain? Why can't we be the hero just once? There are plenty of overlooked role models to choose from. The first heart-transplant surgeon is an Arab-American, Michael DeBakey. Candy Lightner, who founded Mothers Against Drunk Drivers, is Arab, too. There were at least 74 Arab passengers aboard the Titanic when it sank. Half of them drowned. Director James Cameron had a good opportunity to highlight the human side of the Arab community. Instead, he chose to highlight a make-believe Irish wedding aboard the ship, rather than include one of the three Arab weddings that actually took place.

11   Arabs are everyday people. Doctors. Teachers. Football stars and team owners. Grocery-store clerks. Engineers. Elected officials. We're the mail carriers who deliver your mail. The nurses and emergency medical technicians who hold your hand through tragedy. The clerks who help you at the bank.

12   I'm not asking Hollywood to hate someone else. That would be wrong. But, I'm asking Hollywood to be fair. Don't just show the bad. Show our good side, too. But, if that can't be done, I do have one last question: are you still mad about the Crusades?

■ QUESTIONS FOR ANALYSIS AND DISCUSSION

1. Hanania comments that the depiction of Arabs as the bad guys in movies dates back to his childhood in the 1960s. What effect did this portrayal of his

"relatives" have on Hanania? How did it shape his view of his place in American society? Explain.

2. According to Hanania, what is the "terrorist look"? How does he match this description, and how has that impacted his life?

3. Evaluate how the author presents and supports the thesis of his essay. First, identify his thesis and then analyze the supporting elements he uses to prove his point. Does the author allow for alternative points of view? Does he try to see multiple sides of the issue? Explain.

4. What concessions does Hanania request at the end of this essay? How do you think scriptwriters and casting agents would respond to his request? Explain.

Who Is a Whiz-Kid?

Ted Gup

It is easy to spot negative and damaging racial stereotypes that are often the result of intolerance, misunderstanding, and even hate. But what about so-called "good" stereotypes, in which a particular group is dubbed smart, athletic, passionate, or musical? Are stereotypes permissible if they seem positive? How can these "good" stereotypes, in fact, hurt?

Ted Gup is a former writer for the *Washington Post* and *Time* magazine. His work has also appeared in *GQ, Smithsonian, National Geographic, Mother Jones,* and *Sports Illustrated.* He is the author of *Book of Honor* (2000) about CIA operatives. The following article appeared in the April 27, 1997, issue of *Newsweek.*

■ BEFORE YOU READ

In your experience, do you think society assumes that some races are inherently superior to others? What do you think accounts for such assumptions?

■ AS YOU READ

Is perpetuating a cultural stereotype acceptable if it promotes positive images? Are all stereotypes unacceptable?

1   Shortly after joining a national magazine some years ago as a writer, I found myself watching in horror as the week's cover story was prepared. The story was about "Asian-American whiz kids," and it featured a series of six student portraits, each face radiating with an intellectual brilliance. Being new to the enterprise, I was at first tentative in my criticism, cautioning that such a story was inherently biased and fueled racial and ethnic stereotypes. My criticism was dismissed. "This is something good we are saying about them," one top editor remarked. I reduced my criticism to writing. "What," I asked, "would be the response if the cover were about 'Jewish whiz kids'? Would anyone really

dare to produce such an obviously offensive story?" My memo was ignored. Not long after, the cover appeared on the nation's newsstands, and the criticism began to fly. The editors were taken aback.

2   As a former Fulbright Scholar to China I have long taken a strong interest in the portrayal of Asian-Americans. But my interest went well beyond the academic. Even as the cover was being prepared, I was waiting to adopt my first son from Korea. His name was to be David. He was 5 months old when he arrived. That did not stop even some otherwise sophisticated friends from volunteering that he would no doubt be a good student. Probably a mathematician, they opined, with a tone that uncomfortably straddled jest and prediction. I tried to take it all with good humor, this idea that a 5-month-old who could not yet sit up, speak a word or control his bowels was already destined for academic greatness. Even his major seemed foreordained.

3   Many Asian-Americans seem to walk an uneasy line between taking pride in their remarkable achievements and needing to shake off stereotypes. The jokes abound. There is the apocryphal parent who asks "Where is the other point?" when his or her child scores a 99 on a test. Another familiar refrain has the young Asian-American student enumerating his or her hobbies: "studying, studying and more studying."

4   Several months after David arrived he and I entered a small mom-and-pop convenience store in our neighborhood. The owners were Korean. I noticed that the husband, standing behind the cash register, was eyeing my son. "Is he Korean?" he asked. "Yes," I nodded. He reached out for him and took him into his arms. "He'll be good in math," declared the man. "My God," I muttered. Not him, too!

5   It was preposterous. It was funny. And it was unnerving. Embedded in such elevated expectations were real threats to my son. Suppose, I wondered, he should turn out to be only a mediocre student, or, worse yet, not a student at all. I resented the stereotypes and saw them for what they were, the other side of the coin of racism. It is easy to delude one's self into thinking it harmless to offer racial compliments, but that is an inherent contradiction in terms. Such sweeping descriptives, be they negative or positive, deny the one thing most precious to all peoples—individuality. These stereotypes are pernicious for two reasons. First, such attributes are relative and tend to pit one race against another. Witness the seething enmity in many inner cities between Korean store owners and their African-American patrons. Stereotypes that hint at superiority in one race implicitly suggest inferiority in another. They are ultimately divisive, and in their most virulent form, even deadly. Who can forget the costs of the Aryan myth?

6   Many stereotypes also place a crushing burden on Asian-Americans. Few would deny that disproportionate numbers of Asian surnames appear each year among the winners of the Westinghouse science prizes or in the ranks of National Merit Scholars. But it might be a reflection of parental influences, personal commitment and cultural predilections, not genetic predisposition. A decade ago, as a Fulbright Lecturer in Beijing, I saw firsthand the staggering hours my Chinese students devoted to their studies. Were my students in the

United States to invest similar time in their books I would have every reason to expect similar results.

7   I have often been told that Koreans are the "Jews of Asia," a reference to both their reported skills in business and their inherent intelligence. As a Jew, I cannot help but wince at such descriptions. I remember being one of the very few of my faith in a Midwest boarding school. There were many presumptions weighing on me, most of them grounded in my religion. My own classroom performance almost singlehandedly disabused my teachers of the myth that Jews were academically gifted. I barely made it through. Whether it was a lack of intelligence or simple rebellion against expectation, I do not know. I do know that more than once the fact that I was Jewish was raised as evidence that I could and should be doing better. Expectations based on race, be they raised or lowered, are no less galling.

8   David is now in the first grade. He is already taking math with the second graders and asking me about square roots and percentiles. I think back to the Korean merchant who took him in his arms and pronounced him a math whiz. Was he right? Do Asian-Americans have it easier, endowed with some special strand of DNA? The answer is a resounding no. Especially in our house. My son David has learning disabilities to overcome and what progress he has made is individual in the purest and most heroic sense. No one can or should take that away from him, suggesting he is just another wunderkind belonging to a favored race.

9   A year after my first son arrived, we adopted his brother from Korea. His name is Matthew. Let it be known that Matthew couldn't care less about math. He's a bug man. Slugs and earthworms. I suspect he will never be featured on any cover stories about Asian-American whiz kids, but I will continue to resist anything and anyone who attempts to dictate either his interests or his abilities based on race or place of birth. Bugs are fine by me and should be more than fine by him.

■ QUESTIONS FOR ANALYSIS AND DISCUSSION

1. When Gup questioned the decision to run a cover story on "Asian-American whiz kids," his editor dismissed his concerns with the comment, "This is something good we are saying about them." What does this statement say about Gup's editor? Why do you think Gup mentions this comment?

2. What pressures do stereotypes place on children? How can stereotypes affect race relations?

3. How are stereotypes "the other side of the coin of racism"?

4. Analyze Gup's comment that stereotypes contribute to strained relationships between Koreans and blacks in inner cities. Do you agree?

5. What is the "Aryan myth"? What were its costs? Is the myth active today? If so, what is its continued impact?

6. Link some of the opinions and observations on racial stereotypes Gup makes in this article to a personal experience you had with racial stereotypes. How did stereotypes apply to the situation, and how did you handle the incident?

■ WRITING ASSIGNMENTS

1. Consider the ways in which Hollywood influences our cultural perspectives of race and ethnicity. Write an essay exploring the influence, however slight, that film and television has had on your own perceptions of race and ethnicity. If you wish, interview other students for their opinions on this issue and address some of their points in your essay.
2. Think about the ways in which the social, intellectual, topographical, and religious histories of an ethnic group can influence the creation of stereotypes. Identify some current stereotypes that are active in American culture. What are the origins of these stereotypes? Write an essay in which you dissect these stereotypes and present ways to dispel them.
3. Write an essay discussing your own family's sense of ethnic or racial identity. What are the origins of some of your family's values, practices, and customs? Have these customs met with prejudice by people who did not understand them? Explain.

ASSIMILATION

The Return of the Melting Pot

Arthur Schlesinger Jr.

What exactly is the "American melting pot"? At the turn of the century, most people felt it meant educating one's children in American schools, learning the English language, and blending into mainstream American society. But a century later, the concept of the melting pot has changed. To some groups, it symbolizes the loss of individual cultures and beliefs at the expense of a homogeneous ideal defined by the status quo. In the next piece, Arthur Schlesinger Jr. questions this new desire to challenge the ideals of *e pluribus unum*.

   Schlesinger is a well-known historian and columnist for the *New York Times*. The recipient of two Pulitzer Prizes for history, he is the author of *The Disuniting of America: Reflections on a Multicultural Society* (1992), in which he questions the rising popularity of radical multiculturalism. His most recent book is *A Life in the 20th Century: Innocent Beginnings 1917–1950* (2000). This essay was first published in *The Wall Street Journal*.

■ BEFORE YOU READ

Evaluate your feelings on multicultural education. Where do you stand on the issue?

■ AS YOU READ

How does Schlesinger use American history to support his argument? Is this an effective way to bolster his argument?

1   "What then is the American, this new man?" a French immigrant asked two centuries ago. Hector St. John de Crevecoeur gave the classic answer to his own question. "He is an American, who, leaving behind him all his ancient prejudices and manners, receives new ones from the new mode of life he has embraced, the new government he obeys, and the new rank he holds. . . . Here individuals of all nations are melted into a new race of man."

2   The conception of America as a transforming nation, banishing old identities and creating a new one, prevailed through most of American history. It was famously reformulated by Israel Zangwill, an English writer of Russian Jewish origin, when he called America "God's crucible, the great melting pot where all the faces of Europe are melting and re-forming." Most people who came to America expected to become Americans. They wanted to escape a horrid past and to embrace a hopeful future. Their goals were deliverance and assimilation.

3   Thus Crevecoeur wrote his "Letters from an American Farmer" in his acquired English, not in his native French. Thus immigrants reared in other tongues urged their children to learn English as speedily as possible. German immigrants tried for a moment to gain status for their language, but the effort got nowhere. The dominant culture was Anglo-Saxon and, with modification and enrichment, remained Anglo-Saxon.

Repudiation of the Melting Pot

4   The melting pot was one of those metaphors that turned out only to be partly true, and recent years have seen an astonishing repudiation of the whole conception. Many Americans today righteously reject the historic goal of "a new race of man." The contemporary ideal is not assimilation but ethnicity. The escape from origins has given way to the search for "roots." "Ancient prejudices and manners"—the old-time religion, the old-time diet—have made a surprising comeback.

5   These developments portend a new turn in American life. Instead of a transformative nation with a new and distinctive identity, America increasingly sees itself as preservative of old identities. We used to say e pluribus unum. Now we glorify pluribus and belittle unum. The melting pot yields to the Tower of Babel.

6   The new turn has had marked impact on the universities. Very little agitates academia more these days than the demands of passionate minorities for revision of the curriculum: in history, the denunciation of Western civilization courses as cultural imperialism; in literature, the denunciation of the "canon," the list of essential books, as an instrumentality of the existing power structure.

7   A recent report by the New York State Commissioner of Education's task force on "Minorities: Equity and Excellence" luridly describes "African Americans, Asian Americans, Puerto Ricans/Latinos and Native Americans" as "victims of an intellectual and educational oppression." The "systematic bias toward European culture and its derivatives," the report claims, has "a terribly

damaging effect on the psyche of young people of African, Asian, Latino and Native American descent"—a doubtful assertion for which no proof is vouch-safed.

8   Of course teachers of history and literature should give due recognition to women, black Americans, Indians, Hispanics and other groups who were subordinated and ignored in the high noon of male Anglo-Saxon dominance. In recent years they have begun belatedly to do so. But the *cult of ethnicity,* pressed too far, exacts costs—as, for example, the current pressure to teach history and literature not as intellectual challenges but as psychological therapy.

9   There is nothing new, of course, about the yearnings of excluded groups for affirmations of their own historical and cultural dignity. When Irish-Americans were thought beyond the pale, their spokesmen responded much as spokesmen for blacks, Hispanics and others respond today. Professor John V. Kelleher, for many years Harvard's distinguished Irish scholar, once recalled his first exposure to Irish-American history—"turgid little essays on the fact that the Continental Army was 76 percent Irish, or that many of George Washington's closest friends were nuns and priests, or that Lincoln got the major ideas for the Second Inaugural Address from the Hon. Francis P. Mageghegan of Alpaca, New York, a pioneer manufacturer of cast-iron rosary beads." John Kelleher called this "the there's-always-an-Irishman-at-the-bottom-of-it-doing-the-real-work approach to American history."

10   Fortunately most Irish-Americans disregarded their spokesmen and absorbed the American tradition. About 1930, Kelleher said, those "turgid little essays began to vanish from Irish-American papers." He added, "I wonder whose is the major component in the Continental Army these days?" The answer, one fears, is getting to be blacks, Jews and Hispanics.

11   There is often artificiality about the attempts to use history to minister to psychological needs. When I encounter black insistence on inserting Africa into mainstream curricula, I recall the 1956 presidential campaign. Adlai Stevenson, for whom I was working, had a weak record on civil rights in America but was a champion of African nationalism. I suggested to a group of sympathetic black leaders that maybe if Stevenson talked to black audiences about Africa, he could make up for his deficiencies on civil rights. My friends laughed and said that American blacks couldn't care less about Africa: That is no longer the case; but one can't escape the feeling that present emotions are more manufactured than organic.

12   Let us by all means teach women's history, black history, Hispanic history. But let us teach them as *history,* not as a means of *promoting group self-esteem.* I don't often agree with Gore Vidal, but I liked his remark the other day: "What I hate is good citizenship history. That has wrecked every history book. Now we're getting 'The Hispanics are warm and joyous and have brought such wonder into our lives,' you know, and before them the Jews, and before them the blacks. And the women. I mean, cut it out!"

13   Novelists, moralists, politicians, fabulators can go beyond the historical evidence to tell inspiring stories. But historians are custodians of professional

standards. Their objective is critical analysis, accuracy and objectivity, not making people feel better about themselves.

14   Heaven knows how dismally historians fall short of their ideals; how sadly our interpretations are dominated and distorted by unconscious preconceptions; how obsessions of race and nation blind us to our own bias. All historians may in one way or another mythologize history. But the answer to bad history is not "good citizenship history"—more bad history written from a different viewpoint. The answer to bad history is better history.

15   The ideological assault in English departments on the "canon" as an instrument of political oppression implies the existence of a monolithic body of work designed to enforce the "hegemony" of a class or race or sex. In fact, most great literature and much good history are deeply subversive in their impact on orthodoxies. Consider the American canon: Emerson, Whitman, Melville, Hawthorne, Thoreau, Mark Twain, Henry Adams, William and Henry James, Holmes, Dreiser, Faulkner. Lackeys of the ruling class? Agents of American imperialism?

16   Let us by all means learn about other continents and other cultures. But, lamentable as some may think it, we inherit an American experience, as America inherits a European experience. To deny the essentially European origins of American culture is to falsify history.

17   We should take pride in our distinctive inheritance as other nations take pride in their distinctive inheritances. Certainly there is no need for Western civilization, the source of the ideas of individual freedom and political democracy to which most of the world now aspires, to apologize to cultures based on despotism, superstition, tribalism, and fanaticism. Let us abjure what Bertrand Russell called the fallacy of "the superior virtue of the oppressed."

18   Of course we must teach the Western democratic tradition in its true proportions—not as a fixed, final and complacent orthodoxy, intolerant of deviation and dissent, but as an ever-evolving creed fulfilling its ideals through debate, self-criticism, protest, disrespect and irreverence, a tradition in which all groups have rights of heterodoxy and opportunities for self-assertion. It is a tradition that has empowered people of all nations and races. Little can have a more "terribly damaging effect on the psyche" than for educators to tell young blacks and Hispanics and Asians that it is not for them.

One Step at a Time

19   Belief in one's own culture does not mean disdain for other cultures. But one step at a time: No culture can hope to ingest other cultures all at once, certainly not before it ingests its own. After we have mastered our own culture, we can explore the world.

20   If we repudiate the quite marvelous inheritance that history has bestowed on us, we invite the fragmentation of our own culture into a quarrelsome spatter of enclaves, ghettos and tribes. The bonds of cohesion in our society are sufficiently fragile, or so it seems to me, that it makes no sense to strain them by

encouraging and exalting cultural and linguistic apartheid. The rejection of the melting pot points the republic in the direction of incoherence and chaos.

21   In the 21st century, if present trends hold, non-whites in the U.S. will begin to outnumber whites. This will bring inevitable changes in the national ethos but not, one must hope, at the expense of national cohesion. Let the new Americans foreswear the cult of ghettoization and agree with Crevecoeur, as with most immigrants in the two centuries since, that in America "individuals of all nations are melted into a new race of man."

■ QUESTIONS FOR ANALYSIS AND DISCUSSION

1. In paragraph 5, Schlesinger states that instead of working toward common goals and a common identity, we now "glorify pluribus and belittle unum." Explain what you think he means by that statement. How effective is his use of the "e pluribus unum" reference?
2. Schlesinger implies that multiculturalism isn't teaching history or literature as subjects in themselves, but as a means to promote "self-esteem." Analyze and formulate a response to this statement in which you support or refute Schlesinger's claim.
3. In paragraph 10, Schlesinger comments that it was fortunate that Irish Americans disregarded their "spokesman and absorbed the American tradition." What is the "American tradition"? Why does Schlesinger think it was important that Irish Americans assimilated into mainstream culture? Do you agree?
4. How does Schlesinger support this statement: "[W]e inherit an American experience, as America inherits a European experience" (paragraph 16). Is it true? Explain.
5. How is the subject of multiculturalism approached in your school? How is American history taught in schools today? Compare the comments Schlesinger makes to your own educational experiences with multiculturalism.

Forging a New Vision of America's Melting Pot
Gregory Rodriguez

Mexican-Americans comprise the second largest immigrant population in American history and they are poised to become America's largest minority group. Influences of Latino culture are pervading mainstream society, from style and architecture, to art and music. One Californian historian comments, "the Latinization of America is so profound that no one really sees it." In the next piece, Gregory Rodriguez explains how this group could change the way the nation views itself in the next century.

Rodriguez is a senior fellow at the New America Foundation, a nonpartisan public policy institute "dedicated to bringing exceptionally promising new voices and ideas to the fore of the nation's public discourse." He is a contributing editor to the opinion section of the *Los Angeles Times* and a political analyst for MSNBC. This article was published in the February 11, 2001, edition of the *New York Times.*

■ BEFORE YOU READ

Think about your own family's experience in the United States. Did it take them long to be accepted? Did they assimilate quickly, or did it require generations to complete? Or is the process of assimilation still a daily reality for your family? Explain.

■ AS YOU READ

How do the points made by Arthur Schlesinger Jr. in the preceding piece contrast with the issues Rodriguez addresses? Does one author seem more credible than the other? more culturally aware? Explain.

1   While visiting Ellis Island at the turn of the 20th century, Henry James wondered how the sweeping tide of immigrants would ultimately affect "the idea of" America. Comparing the incorporation of foreigners to sword- and fire-swallowing feats at a circus, James reflected on what it meant for America to share its patrimony with those "inconceivable aliens."

2   Yet throughout American history, immigrants and minority groups, seeking to make room for themselves, have broadened the definition of America. Minority experiences have acted as a powerful force in the creation of America's self-image.

3   For the first half of the 20th century, Jews were the paradigmatic American minority by which all other minority experiences were understood. In the second half, African-Americans, the descendants of a forced migration, set the standard for a racial debate that altered the nation's vision of itself. Now, with Hispanics poised to become the largest minority group, Mexican-Americans— who make up two-thirds of all Latinos in the United States—could change how the nation sees itself in the 21st century.

4   Their unique perspectives on racial and cultural synthesis may fundamentally alter the nation's attitudes, for they are the second largest immigrant group in American history—the largest when including illegal immigrants. Mexicans, themselves the product of the clash between the Old and New Worlds, could shift this country's often divisive "us versus them" racial dialogue.

5   A Census Bureau study released last month found that about 10 percent of United States residents are foreign-born, midway between the high of 15 percent at the turn of the 20th century and the low of 5 percent in 1970. And Mexicans are by far today's biggest immigrant group. As such, they are the most likely to leave a permanent imprint on the culture.

6   For instead of simply adding one more color to the multicultural rainbow, Mexican-Americans may help forge a unifying vision. With a history that reveals

an ability to accept racial and cultural ambiguity, Mexican-Americans could broaden the definition of America unlike any earlier immigrants.

7   The early 20th-century debate about the "melting pot" evolved as Jewish writers envisioned an America that might better accommodate Jews. Their historic experience as a minority prompted them to take the lead in re-imagining America for an entire wave of immigrants. The playwright Israel Zangwill, in a 1908 drama about a Jewish immigrant rejecting his faith's prohibition against intermarriage, developed the optimistic American civic faith that a fusion of ethnicities will create a stronger nation. For Zangwill, the United States was both a safe harbor and a crucible that melted Old World ethnics into a distinctly new American culture.

8   But by the 1960's, America's exclusion of African-Americans from the mainstream forged a new vision based on multiculturalism. Though it encompassed other minority groups, including women and gays, blacks gave the multicultural movement its key moral impetus. The civil rights movement had begun by advocating racial integration, but by the late 1960's its message had fused with a reemergent black separatism that fueled the nascent multicultural movement.

9   Multiculturalism—the ideology that promotes the coexistence of separate but equal cultures—essentially rejects assimilation and considers the melting-pot concept an unwelcome imposition of the dominant culture. Race became the prism through which all social issues were perceived.

10   But because their past and present is characterized by a continual synthesis, a blending of the Spanish and indigenous cultures, Mexican-Americans could project their own melting pot vision onto America, one that includes mixing race as well as ethnicity. Rather than upholding the segregated notion of a country divided by mutually exclusive groups, Mexican-Americans might use their experience to imagine an America in which racial, ethnic and cultural groups collide to create new ways of being American.

11   It was never clear where Mexican-Americans belonged on the American racial scale. In 1896, two white politicians in Texas grew worried that more Mexican immigrants would naturalize and vote. They filed suit against a Mexican-born citizenship applicant, Ricardo Rodriguez, because he was not white, and so, like Asians and American Indians, not eligible to become a citizen. Citing the Treaty of Guadalupe Hidalgo, in which citizenship was granted to Mexicans in the conquered region of the Southwest after 1848, the court rejected the suit on the grounds that Mr. Rodriguez's national origins qualified him for citizenship regardless of his racial background.

12   In the 1920 census, Mexicans were counted as whites. Ten years later, they were reassigned to a separate Mexican "racial" category, though in 1950 they were white again. Mexican-Americans and Hispanics as a whole are commonly viewed as a mutually exclusive racial, linguistic and cultural category in a country of competing minorities. But Mexican-Americans do not share the overarching ethnic narrative of Jews or the shared history of suffering that has

united African-Americans. For all the discrimination and segregation Mexican-Americans suffered in the region, the Southwest was never the Deep South. In any case, as the memoirist John Phillip Santos wrote recently, "Mexicans are to forgetting what the Jews are to remembering."

13   By the late 1990's, both the largely ethnic-Mexican Hispanic Congressional Caucus and the powerful California Latino Legislative Caucus had adopted "Latino issues are American issues" as their mantra. Mexican-Americans are using their growing political power to enter the American mainstream, not to distance themselves from it. The new chairman of the Hispanic Congressional Caucus, Representative Silvestre Reyes, Democrat of Texas, was once a high-ranking Border Patrol official and the architect of Operation Hold the Line, the labor-intensive strategy to stem illegal immigration along the West Texas border.

14   Perhaps assuming that Mexicans would (or should) follow the organizational model of Jews or African-Americans, East Coast-based foundations contributed to the founding of national ethnic-Mexican institutions. The New York-based Ford Foundation was instrumental in creating three of the most visible national Mexican-American organizations—all modeled after similar black organizations.

15   But with the exception of some scattered homegrown social service organizations and political groups, Mexican-Americans have developed little parallel ethnic infrastructure. One national survey has shown that Mexican-Americans are far more likely to join a non-ethnic civic group than a Hispanic organization. There is no private Mexican-American college similar to Yeshiva University or Morehouse College. In Los Angeles, which has the largest Mexican population in the country, there is no ethnic-Mexican hospital, cemetery or broad-based charity organization. Nor does Los Angeles have an English-language newspaper for Mexican-Americans similar to the black Amsterdam News and the Jewish Forward in New York.

16   Though the Spanish-language media is often referred to as the "Hispanic media," it generally serves first generation immigrants and not their English-dominant children and grandchildren.

17   In the late 1920's, Representative John C. Box of Texas warned his colleagues on the House Immigration and Naturalization Committee that the continued influx of Mexican immigrants could lead to the "distressing process of mongrelization" in America. He argued that because Mexicans were the products of mixing among whites, Indians and sometimes blacks, they had a casual attitude toward interracial unions and were likely to mix freely with other races in the United States.

18   His vitriol notwithstanding, Mr. Box was right about Mexicans not keeping to themselves. Apart from the cultural isolation of immigrants, subsequent generations are oriented toward the American mainstream. But because Mexican identity has always been more fluid and comfortable with hybridity, assimilation has not been an either/or proposition. For example, Mexican-Americans never had to overcome a cultural proscription against intermarriage. Just as wide-

spread Mexican-Anglo intermarriage helped meld cultures in the 19th-century Southwest, so it does today. In fact, two-thirds of intermarriages in California involve a Latino partner.

19   According to James P. Smith, an economist and immigration scholar at the RAND Corporation, by 2050 more than 40 percent of United States Hispanics will be able to claim multiple ancestries. "Through this process of blending by marriage in the U.S.," he says, "Latino identity becomes something even more nuanced."

20   The fact that people of mixed ancestry came to form a greater proportion of the population of Latin America than in Anglo America is the clearest sign of the difference between the two outlooks on race. Mexican-Americans bring the New World notion encompassed by the word mestizaje, or racial and cultural synthesis, to their American experience. In 1925, the romantic Mexican philosopher José Vasconcelos wrote that the Latin American mestizo heralds a new post-racialist era in human development. More recently, the preeminent Mexican-American essayist Richard Rodriguez stated, "The essential beauty and mystery of the color brown is that it is a mixture of different colors."

21   "Something big happens here at the border that sort of mushes everything together," says Maria Eugenia Guerra, publisher of LareDos, an alternative monthly magazine in Laredo, Texas, a city that has been a majority Latino since its founding in 1755. As political and economic power continues to shift westward, Mexican-Americans will increasingly inject this mestizo vision onto American culture. "The Latinization of America is so profound that no one really sees it," asserts Kevin Starr, the leading historian of California, who is writing a multivolume history of the state. The process of they becoming us will ultimately force us to reconsider the very definition of who we are.

■ QUESTIONS FOR ANALYSIS AND DISCUSSION

1. What is the "idea" of America? How have immigrants and minority groups broadened the "definition" of America? Does the term "melting pot" seem appropriate? Why or why not?
2. What influence does Rodriguez foresee Mexican-Americans having on national identity in the twenty-first century? Explain.
3. How do you think Ray Suárez would respond to Rodriguez's assertion that, as the second largest immigrant population, Mexican-Americans "could shift this country's often divisive 'us versus them' racial dialogue" (paragraph 4)? Refer to points from each author's essay in your response.
4. According to the author, how could Mexican-American's legacy of "mixed ancestry," in turn, influence America's melting pot?
5. In what ways are Mexican-Americans different from other immigrant populations? How could this difference ultimately provide them with more political and social power? Explain.

Diversity and Its Discontents

Arturo Madrid

In this essay, Arturo Madrid considers the ways in which people of many ethnic or racial backgrounds have been prevented from assimilating into mainstream American society. Barred from sharing in the American experience, they have been denied both voice and recognition by many of America's most powerful institutions.

Madrid is a professor at Trinity University in Texas. He holds the National Medal of the Humanities (1996) and is the founding president of the Tomas Rivers Center, a national institute for policy studies on Latino issues. The following essay is a speech he originally delivered to the American Association of Higher Education.

■ BEFORE YOU READ

What does diversity mean to you? In what ways do issues of diversity touch your daily life?

■ AS YOU READ

Evaluate the ways Madrid uses the words "exotic" and "other." What meanings do the words have in this context?

1   My name is Arturo Madrid. I am a citizen of the United States, as are my parents and as were my grandparents, and my great-grandparents. My ancestors' presence in what is now the United States antedates Plymouth Rock, even without taking into account any American Indian heritage I might have.

2   I do not, however, fit those mental sets that define America and Americans. My physical appearance, my speech patterns, my name, my profession (a professor of Spanish) create a text that confuses the reader. My normal experience is to be asked, "And where are *you* from?" My response depends on my mood. Passive-aggressive, I answer, "From here." Aggressive-passive, I ask, "Do you mean where am I originally from?" But ultimately my answer to these follow-up questions that ask about origins will be that we have always been from here.

3   Overcoming my resentment I will try to educate, knowing that nine times out of ten my words fall on inattentive ears. I have spent most of my adult life explaining who I am not. I am exotic, but—as Richard Rodriguez of *Hunger of Memory* fame so painfully found out—not exotic enough . . . not Peruvian, or Pakistani, or Persian, or whatever. I am, however, very clearly the *other*, if only your everyday, garden-variety, domestic *other*. I will share with you another phenomenon that I have been a part of, that of being a missing person, and how I came late to that awareness. But I've always known that I was the *other*, even before I knew the vocabulary or understood the significance of otherness.

4   I grew up in an isolated and historically marginal part of the United States, a small mountain village in the state of New Mexico, the eldest child of parents native to that region and whose ancestors had always lived there. In those vast and empty spaces, people who look like me, speak as I do, and have names like mine predominate. But the *americanos* lived among us: the descendants of those nineteenth-century immigrants who dispossessed us of our lands; missionaries who came to convert us and stayed to live among us; artists who became enchanted with our land and humanscape and went native; refugees from unhealthy climes, crowded spaces, unpleasant circumstances; and, of course, the inhabitants of Los Alamos, whose socio-cultural distance from us was moreover accentuated by the fact that they occupied a space removed from and proscribed to us. More importantly, however, they—*los americanos*—were omnipresent (and almost exclusively so) in newspapers, newsmagazines, books, on radio, in movies and, ultimately, on television.

5   Despite the operating myth of the day, school did not erase my otherness. It did try to deny it, and in doing so only accentuated it. To this day, schooling is more socialization than education, but when I was in elementary school— and given where I was—socialization was everything. School was where one became an American. Because there was a pervasive and systematic denial by the society that surrounded us that we were Americans. That denial was both explicit and implicit. My earliest memory of the former was that there were two kinds of churches: theirs and ours. The more usual was the implicit denial, our absence from the larger cultural, economic, political and social spaces—the one that reminded us constantly that we were *the other.* And school was where we felt it most acutely.

6   Quite beyond saluting the flag and pledging allegiance to it (a very intense and meaningful action, given that the U.S. was involved in a war and our brothers, cousins, uncles, and fathers were on the front lines) becoming American was learning English and its corollary—not speaking Spanish. Until very recently ours was a proscribed language—either *de jure* (by rule, by policy, by law) or *de facto* (by practice, implicitly if not explicitly; through social and political and economic pressure). I do not argue that learning English was appropriate. On the contrary. Like it or not, and we had no basis to make any judgments on that matter, we were Americans by virtue of having been born Americans, and English was the common language of Americans. And there was a myth, a pervasive myth, that said that if we only learned to speak English well—and particularly without an accent—we would be welcomed into the American fellowship.

7   Sam Hayakawa and the official English movement folks notwithstanding, the true text was not our speech, but rather our names and our appearance, for we would always have an accent, however perfect our pronunciation, however excellent our enunciation, however divine our diction. That accent would be heard in our pigmentation, our physiognomy, our names. We were, in short, the *other.*

8   Being the *other* involves a contradictory phenomenon. On the one hand being the *other* frequently means being invisible. Ralph Ellison wrote eloquently

about that experience in his magisterial novel *The Invisible Man.* On the other hand, being the *other* sometimes involves sticking out like a sore thumb. What is she/he doing here?

9   For some of us being the *other* is only annoying, for others it is debilitating; for still others it is damning. Many try to flee otherness by taking on protective colorations that provide invisibility, whether of dress or speech or manner or name. Only a fortunate few succeed. For the majority, otherness is permanently sealed by physical appearance. For the rest, otherness is betrayed by ways of being, speaking or of doing.

10   The first half of my life downplayed the significance and consequences of otherness. The second half has seen me wrestling to understand its complex and deeply ingrained realities; striving to fathom why otherness denies us a voice or visibility or validity in American society and its institutions; struggling to make otherness familiar, reasonable, even normal to my fellow Americans.

11   I spoke earlier of another phenomenon that I am a part of: that of being a missing person. Growing up in northern New Mexico I had only a slight sense of our being missing persons. *Hispanos,* as we called (and call) ourselves in New Mexico, were very much a part of the fabric of the society, and there were *hispano* professionals everywhere about me: doctors, lawyers, school teachers, and administrators. My people owned businesses, ran organizations and were both appointed and elected public officials.

12   My awareness of our absence from the larger institutional life of society became sharper when I went off to college, but even then it was attenuated by the circumstances of history and geography. The demography of Albuquerque still strongly reflected its historical and cultural origins, despite the influx of Midwesterners and Easterners. Moreover, many of my classmates at the University of New Mexico in Albuquerque were Hispanos, and even some of my professors were. I thought that would obtain at UCLA, where I began graduate studies in 1960. Los Angeles already had a very large Mexican population, and that population was visible even in and around Westwood and on the campus. Many of the grounds-keepers and food-service personnel at UCLA were Mexican. But Mexican-American students were few and mostly invisible, and I do not recall seeing or knowing a single Mexican-American (or, for that matter, black, Asian, or American Indian) professional on the staff or faculty of that institution during the five years I was there. Needless to say, persons like me were not present in any capacity at Dartmouth College, the site of my first teaching appointment, and, of course were not even part of the institutional or individual mindset. I knew then that we—a we that had come to encompass American Indians, Asian-Americans, black Americans, Puerto Ricans, and women—were truly missing persons in American institutional life.

13   Over the past three decades, the *de jure* and *de facto* types of segregation that have historically characterized American institutions have been under assault. As a consequence, minorities and women have become part of American institutional life, and although there are still many areas where we are not to be found, the missing persons phenomenon is not as pervasive as it once was.

However, the presence of the *other,* particularly minorities, in institutions and in institutional life, is, as we say in Spanish, a *flor de tierra:* we are spare plants whose roots do not go deep, a surface phenomenon, vulnerable to inclemencies of an economic, political, or social nature.

14   Our entrance into and our status in institutional life is not unlike a scenario set forth by my grandmother's pastor when she informed him that she and her family were leaving their mountain village to relocate in the Rio Grande Valley. When he asked her to promise that she would remain true to the faith and continue to involve herself in the life of the church, she assured him that she would and asked him why he thought she would do otherwise. "Doña Trinidad," he told her, "in the Valley there is no Spanish church. There is only an American church." "But," she protested, "I read and speak English and would be able to worship there." The pastor responded, "It is possible that they will not admit you, and even if they do, they might not accept you. And that is why I want you to promise me that you are going to go to church. Because if they don't let you in through the front door, I want you to go in through the back door. And if you can't get in through the back door, go in the side door. And if you are unable to enter through the side door I want you to go in through the window. What is important is that you enter and that you stay."

15   Some of us entered institutional life through the front door; others through the back door; and still others through side doors. Many, if not most of us, came in through windows and continue to come in through windows. Of those who entered through the front door, some never made it past the lobby; others were ushered into corners and niches. Those who entered through back and side doors inevitably have remained in back and side rooms. And those who entered through windows found enclosures built around them. For, despite the lip service given to the goal of the integration of minorities into institutional life, what has frequently occurred instead is ghettoization, marginalization, isolation.

16   Not only have the entry points been limited, but in addition, the dynamics have been singularly conflictive. Gaining entry and its corollary, gaining space, have frequently come as a consequence of demands made on institutions and institutional officers. Rather than entering institutions more or less passively, minorities have of necessity entered them actively, even aggressively. Rather than waiting to receive, they have demanded. Institutional relations have thus been adversarial, infused with specific and generalized tensions.

17   The nature of the entrance and the nature of the space occupied have greatly influenced the view and attitudes of the majority population within those institutions. All of us are put into the same box; that is, no matter what the individual reality, the assessment of the individual is inevitably conditioned by a perception that is held of the class. Whatever our history, whatever our record, whatever our validations, whatever our accomplishments, by and large we are perceived unidimensionally and dealt with accordingly. I remember an experience I had in this regard, atypical only in its explicitness. A few years ago I allowed myself to be persuaded to seek the presidency of a well-known state university. I was invited for an interview and presented myself before the

selection committee, which included members of the board of trustees. The pening question of the brief but memorable interview was directed at me by a member of that august body. "Dr. Madrid," he asked, "why does a one-dimensional person like you think he can be the president of a multidimensional institution like ours?"

18   Over the past four decades America's demography has undergone significant changes. Since 1965 the principal demographic growth we have experienced in the United States has been of peoples whose national origins are non-European. This population growth has occurred both through birth and through immigration. A few years ago discussion of the national birthrate had a scare dimension: the high—"inordinately high"—birthrate of the Hispanic population. The popular discourse was informed by words such as "breeding." Several years later, as a consequence of careful tracking by government agencies, we now know that what has happened is that the birthrate of the majority population has decreased. When viewed historically and comparatively, the minority populations (for the most part) have also had a decline in birthrate, but not one as great as that of the majority.

19   There are additional demographic changes that should give us something to think about. African-Americans are now to be found in significant numbers in every major urban center in the nation. Hispanic-Americans now number over 15 million people, and although they are a regionally concentrated (and highly urbanized) population, there is a Hispanic community in almost every major urban center of the United States. American Indians, heretofore a small and rural population, are increasingly more numerous and urban. The Asian-American population, which has historically consisted of small and concentrated communities of Chinese-, Filipino-, and Japanese-Americans, has doubled over the past decade, its complexion changed by the addition of Cambodians, Koreans, Hmongs, Vietnamese, et al.

20   Prior to the Immigration Act of 1965, 69 percent of immigration was from Europe. By far the largest number of immigrants to the United States since 1965 have been from the Americas and from Asia: 34 percent are from Asia; another 34 percent are from Central and South America; 16 percent are from Europe; 10 percent are from the Caribbean; the remaining 6 percent are from other continents and Canada. As was the case with previous immigration waves, the current one consists principally of young people: 60 percent are between the ages of 16 and 44. Thus, for the next few decades, we will continue to see a growth in the percentage of non-European-origin Americans as compared to European-Americans.

21   To sum up, we now live in one of the most demographically diverse nations in the world, and one that is increasingly more so.

22   During the same period social and economic change seems to have accelerated. Who would have imagined at mid-century that the prototypical middle-class family (working husband, wife as homemaker, two children) would for all intents and purposes disappear? Who could have anticipated the rise in teen-age pregnancies, children in poverty, drug use? Who among us understood the implications of an aging population?

23   We live in an age of continuous and intense change, a world in which what held true yesterday does not today, and certainly will not tomorrow. What change does, moreover, is bring about even more change. The only constant we have at this point in our national development is change. And change is threatening. The older we get the more likely we are to be anxious about change, and the greater our desire to maintain the status quo.

24   Evident in our public life is a fear of change, whether economic or moral. Some who fear change are responsive to the call of economic protectionism, others to the message of moral protectionism. Parenthetically, I have referred to the movement to require more of students without in turn giving them more as academic protectionism. And the pronouncements of E. D. Hirsch and Allan Bloom are, I believe, informed by intellectual protectionism. Much more serious, however, is the dark side of the populism which underlies this evergoing protectionism—the resentment of the *other.* An excellent and fascinating example of that aspect of populism is the cry for linguistic protectionism—for making English the official language of the United States. And who among us is unaware of the tensions that underlie immigration reform, of the underside of the demographic protectionism?

25   A matter of increasing concern is whether this new protectionism, and the mistrust of the *other* which accompanies it, is not making more significant inroads than we have supposed in higher education. Specifically, I wish to discuss the question of whether a goal (quality) and a reality (demographic diversity) have been erroneously placed in conflict, and, if so, what problems this perception of conflict might present.

26   As part of my scholarship I turn to dictionaries for both origins and meanings of words. Quality, according to the *Oxford English Dictionary,* has multiple meanings. One set defines quality as being an essential character, a distinctive and inherent feature. A second describes it as a degree of excellence, of conformity to standards, as superiority in kind. A third makes reference to social status, particularly to persons of high social status. A fourth talks about quality as being a special or distinguishing attribute, as being a desirable trait. Quality is highly desirable in both principle and practice. We all aspire to it in our own person, in our experiences, in our acquisitions and products, and of course we all want to be associated with people and operations of quality.

27   But let us move away from the various dictionary meanings of the word and to our own sense of what it represents and of how we feel about it. First of all we consider quality to be finite; that is, it is limited with respect to quantity; it has very few manifestations; it is not widely distributed. I have it and you have it, but they don't. We associate quality with homogeneity, with uniformity, with standardization, with order, regularity, neatness. All too often we equate it with smoothness, glibness, slickness, elegance. Certainly it is always expensive. We tend to identify it with those who lead, with the rich and famous. And, when you come right down to it, it's inherent. Either you've got it or you ain't.

28   Diversity, from the Latin *divertere,* meaning to turn aside, to go different ways, to differ, is the condition of being different or having differences, is an instance of being different. Its companion word, diverse, means differing, unlike,

distinct; having or capable of having various forms; composed of unlike or distinct elements. Diversity is lack of standardization, of regularity, of orderliness, homogeneity, conformity, uniformity. Diversity introduces complications, is difficult to organize, is troublesome to manage, is problematical. Diversity is irregular, disorderly, uneven, rough. The way we use the word diversity gives us away. Something is too diverse, is extremely diverse. We want a little diversity.

29   When we talk about diversity, we are talking about the *other*, whatever that other might be: someone of a different gender, race, class, national origin; somebody at a greater or lesser distance from the norm: someone outside the set; someone who possesses a different set of characteristics, features, or attributes; someone who does not fall within the taxonomies we use daily and with which we are comfortable; someone who does not fit into the mental configurations that give our lives order and meaning.

30   In short, diversity is desirable only in principle, not in practice. Long live diversity . . . as long as it conforms to my standards, my mind set, my view of life, my sense of order. We desire, we like, we admire diversity, not unlike the way the French (and others) appreciate women; that is, *Vive la difference!*—as long as it stays in its place.

31   What I find paradoxical about and lacking in this debate is that diversity is the natural order of things. Evolution produces diversity. Margaret Visser, writing about food in her latest book, *Much Depends on Dinner*, makes an eloquent statement in this regard:

> Machines like, demand, and produce uniformity. But nature loathes it: her strength lies in multiplicity and in differences. Sameness in biology means fewer possibilities and therefore weakness.

32   The United States, by its very nature, by its very development, is the essence of diversity. It is diverse in its geography, population, institutions, technology; its social, cultural, and intellectual modes. It is a society that at its best does not consider quality to be monolithic in form or finite in quantity, or to be inherent in class. Quality in our society proceeds in large measure out of the stimulus of diverse modes of thinking and acting; out of the creativity made possible by the different ways in which we approach things; out of diversion from paths or modes hallowed by tradition.

33   One of the principal strengths of our society is its ability to address, on a continuing and substantive basis, the real economic, political, and social problems that have faced and continue to face us. What makes the United States so attractive to immigrants is the protections and opportunities it offers; what keeps our society together is tolerance for cultural, religious social, political, and even linguistic difference; what makes us a unique, dynamic, and extraordinary nation is the power and creativity of our diversity.

34   The true history of the United States is one of struggle against intolerance, against oppression, against xenophobia, against those forces that have prohibited persons from participating in the larger life of the society on the basis of their race, their gender, their religion, their national origin, their linguistic and

cultural background. These phenomena are not consigned to the past. They remain with us and frequently take on virulent dimensions.

35   If you believe, as I do, that the well-being of a society is directly related to the degree and extent to which all of its citizens participate in its institutions, then you will have to agree that we have a challenge before us. In view of the extraordinary changes that are taking place in our society we need to take up the struggle again, irritating, grating, troublesome, unfashionable, unpleasant as it is. As educated and educator members of this society we have a special responsibility for ensuring that all American institutions, not just our elementary and secondary schools, our juvenile halls, or our jails, reflect the diversity of our society. Not to do so is to risk greater alienation on the part of a growing segment of our society; is to risk increased social tension in an already conflictive world; and, ultimately, is to risk the survival of a range of institutions that, for all their defects and deficiencies, provide us the opportunity and the freedom to improve our individual and collective lot.

36   Let me urge you to reflect on these two words—quality and diversity—and on the mental sets and behaviors that flow out of them. And let me urge you further to struggle against the notion that quality is finite in quantity, limited in its manifestations, or is restricted by considerations of class, gender, race, or national origin; or that quality manifests itself only in leaders and not in followers, in managers and not in workers, in breeders and not in drones; or that it has to be associated with verbal agility or elegance of personal style; or that it cannot be seeded, nurtured, or developed.

37   Because diversity—the *other*—is among us, will define and determine our lives in ways that we still do not fully appreciate, whether that other is women (no longer bound by tradition, house, and family); or Asians, African-Americans, Indians, and Hispanics (no longer invisible, regional, or marginal); or our newest immigrants (no longer distant, exotic, alien). Given the changing profile of America, will we come to terms with diversity in our personal and professional lives? Will we begin to recognize the diverse forms that quality can take? If so, we will thus initiate the process of making quality limitless in its manifestations, infinite in quantity, unrestricted with respect to its origins, and more importantly, virulently contagious.

38   I hope we will. And that we will further join together to expand—not to close—the circle.

■ QUESTIONS FOR ANALYSIS AND DISCUSSION

1. What does Madrid mean when he says he was not "exotic enough" (paragraph 3)? Why does he identify himself as "other"?
2. Analyze Madrid's comment in paragraph 6 that "there was a myth, a pervasive myth, that said that if we only learned to speak English well—and particularly without an accent—we would be welcomed into the American fellowship." What do you think were the origins of this myth? Who created it? Why was it just a myth after all?

3. What is "intellectual protectionism" (paragraph 24)? How, according to Madrid, does it apply to universities? What impact does it have on students of all races and backgrounds?

4. In paragraph 14, Madrid relates the tale of his grandmother as she prepared to move to an area that did not have a Spanish church. Who is the "they" mentioned in the story? Why might this story be particularly disturbing?

5. Examine Madrid's exploration of the word "quality." Do you agree with his conclusions? Explain.

6. What does "diversity" mean to Madrid? To what extent do you agree or disagree with Madrid's argument concerning diversity?

7. If Arturo Madrid and Gregory Rodriguez were to engage in a debate on the issue of assimilation, especially as it relates to the Latino population, how do you think one would respond to the other? As a first step to this exercise, summarize each writer's argument. Does one author develop a stronger case? Explain.

Please Ask Me Who, Not "What," I Am

Jordan Lite

In the next piece, Jordan Lite, a young woman who describes herself as "unclassifiable," asks why casual acquaintances seem to think it is permissible to ask about her ethnic background. As she explains, her ethnicity isn't obvious, and Lite wonders why it should matter to people she's just met. The following article appeared in the July 16, 2001, issue of *Newsweek*.

■ BEFORE YOU READ

If America truly is the great "melting pot," why are we so keen to know the details of the specific "ingredients"?

■ AS YOU READ

The author comments that the men she dates keep trying to find out "what" she is because she looks "exotic." What do you think she means? What is an "exotic" look? Against what standard is it compared?

1   I've been thinking a lot about that "Seinfeld" episode where Elaine is dating this guy and it's driving her nuts because she doesn't know "what" he is. They ultimately discover that neither is exotic enough for the other and they're so disappointed that they stop seeing each other.

2   It's the story of my life these days. Each new guy I meet, it seems, is fascinated by my ostensible failure to fall into an obvious racial category. Last year we could opt out of defining ourselves to the Census Bureau, but that option

doesn't seem to have carried over into real life. I've lost track of how many flirty men have asked me what I am.

3   The first time, I was in Iowa and snobbishly dismissed the inquiry as rural provincialism. Then it happened again while I was on a date in San Francisco, a city that prides itself on its enlightenment.

4   Isn't it rude to ask "what" someone is when you've just met? Common courtesy would suggest so. But many people seem to feel uncomfortable if they can't immediately determine a new person's racial or ethnic background.

5   Of course, I've mused over "what" a stranger might be. But it's never occurred to me that asking "What are you?" of someone I've just met would elicit anything particularly revealing about him. I ask questions, but not that one.

6   So when a potential boyfriend asks me "What are you?" I feel like he wants to instantly categorize me. If he'd only let the answer come out naturally, he'd get a much better sense of what I'm about.

7   Perhaps acknowledging explicitly that race and ethnicity play a role in determining who we are is just being honest. But I'm not sure that such directness is always well intended. After I grouchily retorted "What do you mean, 'What am I?'" to one rather bewildered date, he told me his dad was African-American and his mom Japanese, and that he ruminated all the time over how to reconcile such disparate influences. I realized then that he believed my being "different" would magically confer upon me an understanding of what it was like to be like him.

8   If you're looking for your soulmate, maybe it's only natural to want a person who has shared your experience. But for some people, "What are you?" is just a line. "You're exotic-looking," a man at a party explained when I asked him why he wanted to know. In retrospect, I think he probably meant his remark as a compliment. As a Hispanic friend pointed out, when all things Latin became the new craze, it's trendy to be exotic. But if someone wants to get to know me, I wish he would at least pretend it's not because of my looks.

9   Still, this guy's willingness to discuss my discomfort was eye-opening. He told me that he was part Korean, part white. Growing up in the Pacific Northwest, he wasn't the only biracial kid on the block. One could acknowledge race, he said, and still be casual about it.

10   Although I spent my childhood in a town lauded for its racial diversity, discussing race doesn't often feel easy to me. Maybe my Japanese classmate in the first grade could snack on seaweed without being hassled, but I can readily recall being 11 years old and watching a local TV news report about a pack of white boys who beat, then chased a terrified black teen onto a highway, where he was struck by a car and killed. The violence on TV silenced me. It seemed better not to risk asking questions that might offend.

11   Years after we graduated from our private high school, one of my good friends told me how out of place she felt as one of the few black students. Her guardedness had kept me from probing; but there's a part of me that wonders if talking with her then about her unease at school would have made me more comfortable now when people ask me about my place in the world.

12   But as it is, I resent being pressed to explain myself upfront, as if telling a prospective date my ethnicity eliminates his need to participate in a real con-

versation with me. "What are you?" I am asked, but the background check he's conducting won't show whether we share real interests that would bring us together in a genuine give-and-take.

13   In a way, I enjoy being unclassifiable. Though there are people who try to peg me to a particular ethnic stereotype, I like to think others take my ambiguous appearance as an opportunity to focus on who I am as a person. So I haven't figured out why being myself should kill any chance of a relationship. Not long ago, a man asked me about my background when we met for a drink.

14   "Just a Jewish girl from New Jersey," I said truthfully.

15   I never heard from him again.

■ QUESTIONS FOR ANALYSIS AND DISCUSSION

1. Lite notes that although the U.S. Census Bureau does not require its respondents to reveal their racial background, this latitude is often not afforded the individual in social interaction. Is it important for you to know someone's ethnic background? Is it important to your identity to share your background with others? Explain.

2. In paragraph 4, Lite asks, "Isn't it rude to ask 'what' someone is when you've just met?" Answer her question, presenting your own perspective.

3. How did the author's experiences as a child influence her "silence"? Is her reaction justifiable considering the circumstances? Is it safer to guard your ethnic background? Explain.

4. How do people react to Lite's hesitancy to answer their questions regarding her ethnicity? How does she interpret their reactions?

5. One reason why Lite resents being asked "what" she is relates to her concern that people want to "instantly categorize" her. How do we categorize people based on "what" they are? How do you think the authors of the preceding section would respond to her concerns?

Pocahontas

In 1995, Disney studios produced the animated feature *Pocahontas*. From its outset, the movie makers aimed to address rising public criticism that the studio had engaged in racial stereotyping in its two previous movies, *Aladdin* (1992) and *The Lion King* (1994). To this end, the studio carefully considered how the movie would portray Native Americans and the character of Pocahontas. This effort, according to many Native Americans, failed miserably. In fact, the Native American consultant at one time for the film, Shirley "Little Dove" Custalow McGowan, has stated that "[. . .] they said that the film would be historically accurate. I soon found out that it wasn't. [. . .] I wish Pocahontas' name wasn't on it."

It was not just Disney's loose interpretation of history that rankled many Native Americans. It was the image of Pocahontas herself, which was created from a series of paintings of Pocahontas and modeled after a number of live models including Filipino model Dyna Taylor. Primarily white male make-up artists made the final decisions on how she would ultimately appear on screen, a look *Newsweek's* Laura Shapiro described as "Native American Barbie."

Was Disney up against impossible odds? Did the studio truly try to break its history of racial stereotyping? Or did it simply provide lip service while raking in millions of dollars in sales from related toys, games, movies, and videos? Visit Disney's Web site, <http://disney.go.com/disneyvideos/disneygold/pocahontas.html> for the Pocahontas video and answer the questions that follow. You may wish to watch the movie to refresh your memory of how Pocahontas was visually portrayed.

■ QUESTIONS FOR ANALYSIS AND DISCUSSION

1. How are Native Americans traditionally portrayed in film? Try to think of as many Native American characters in film as you can. Does a stereotype exist? Did Pocahontas tap into the same Hollywood stereotypes? Explain.
2. In what ways did the Disney movie perpetuate the Hollywood stereotype of the "noble savage"? Refer to specific examples from the movie in your response.
3. Pocahontas was 11 years old when she met John Smith. How did Disney change the historical story of Pocahontas, and why?
4. The movie *Pocahontas* tells the story of an interracial love affair. Consider other films with a similar focus (such as *West Side Story, Jungle Fever*). What do different characters in each film have to say about issues of race and romance? How does Hollywood perpetuate stereotypes connected to interracial romance? Explain.
5. Analyze the video jacket for the movie. What does the image tell you about the movie? Does Pocahontas look like other Native Americans in the film? in reality? Why might Native Americans object to such a depiction of this famous woman? Explain.

■ WRITING ASSIGNMENTS

1. Several authors in this section mention the emergence of multiculturalism in the last quarter of the twentieth century. Write a paper assessing the influence of multiculturalism on your life and education. For example, how has multiculturalism changed the way we look at literature and history? Has it allowed your family a stronger sense of its own culture and history? If not, has multiculturalism influenced the way you view people of other cultures and backgrounds? Explain.
2. Access the *Salon* roundtable discussion "Hanging Separately," at <http://salon1999.com/12nov1995/feature/race.html>, regarding race relations between whites and blacks. Read the various commentaries about establishing a dialogue between the races by well-known cultural critics, including Shelby Steele and Stanley Crouch. Evaluate their responses and answer the critics directly with your own opinion. Can this discussion apply to other racial and cultural groups? Explain.
3. Many of the essays in this section refer to the concept of "mainstream" society. Write an essay in which you identify and describe mainstream society. Who is

part of it, and how do they belong in it? Who decides what is "mainstream" and what is not? Or if you wish, you may argue that such an entity does not exist in modern America.

4. Jordan Lite provides a personal perspective on the ways people identify themselves and the ways others try to identify them. Write an essay about what is important to your own sense of identity. In addition to race, you should consider other factors such as gender, age, religious background, education, etc. In your opinion, on what criteria do the people you meet judge you? How do those characteristics compare to your personal standards of identity?

RACIAL PROFILING

You Can't Judge a Crook by His Color
Randall Kennedy

Racial profiling is the practice by law enforcement of considering race as an indicator of the likelihood of criminal behavior. Based on statistical assumptions, racial profiling presumes that certain groups of people are more likely to commit—or to not commit—certain crimes. The U.S. Supreme Court officially upheld the constitutionality of this practice, as long as race was only one of several factors leading to the detainment or arrest of an individual. In the next article, law professor Randall Kennedy argues that while racial profiling may seem justifiable, it is still morally wrong.

Kennedy is a professor at Harvard Law School, where he teaches courses on the freedom of expression and regulation of race relations. Educated at Princeton, Oxford, and Yale Law School, he is a member of the bar in the District of Columbia and before the U.S. Supreme Court. He is the author of several books, including *Race, Crime, and the Law* (1998), for which he won the 1998 Robert F. Kennedy Book Award. In addition to contributing to many general and scholarly publications, he sits on the editorial boards of *The Nation, Dissent,* and *The American Prospect.* This article first appeared in *The New Republic* in 1999.

■ BEFORE YOU READ

Do you consider racial profiling justifiable? If so, under what circumstances? If not, why?

■ AS YOU READ

Evaluate Kennedy's practice of posing questions to his readers and then providing them with the answers. In what ways could this article serve as a class lecture?

1   In Kansas City, a Drug Enforcement Administration officer stops and questions a young man who has just stepped off a flight from Los Angeles. The officer has focused on this man because intelligence reports indicate that black gangs in L.A. are flooding the Kansas City area with illegal drugs. Young, toughly dressed, and appearing nervous, he paid for his ticket in cash, checked no luggage, brought two carry-on bags, and made a beeline for a taxi when he arrived. Oh, and one other thing: The young man is black. When asked why he decided to question this man, the officer declares that he considered race, along with other factors, because doing so helps him allocate limited time and resources efficiently.

2   Should we applaud the officer's conduct? Permit it? Prohibit it? This is not a hypothetical example. Encounters like this take place every day, all over the country, as police battle street crime, drug trafficking, and illegal immigration. And this particular case study happens to be the real-life scenario presented in a federal lawsuit of the early '90s, *United States* v. *Weaver,* in which the 8th U.S. Circuit Court of Appeals upheld the constitutionality of the officer's action.

3   "Large groups of our citizens," the court declared, "should not be regarded by law enforcement officers as presumptively criminal based upon their race." The court went on to say, however, that "facts are not to be ignored simply because they may be unpleasant." According to the court, the circumstances were such that the young man's race, considered in conjunction with other signals, was a legitimate factor in the decision to approach and ultimately detain him. "We wish it were otherwise," the court maintained, "but we take the facts as they are presented to us, not as we would like them to be." Other courts have agreed that the Constitution does not prohibit police from considering race, as long as they do so for bona fide purposes of law enforcement (not racial harassment) and as long as it is only one of several factors.

4   These decisions have been welcome news to the many law enforcement officials who consider what has come to be known as racial profiling an essential weapon in the war on crime. They maintain that, in areas where young African American males commit a disproportionate number of the street crimes, the cops are justified in scrutinizing that sector of the population more closely than others—just as they are generally justified in scrutinizing men more closely than they do women.

5   As Bernard Parks, chief of the Los Angeles Police Department, explained to Jeffrey Goldberg of *The New York Times Magazine:* "We have an issue of violent crime against jewelry salespeople. . . . The predominant suspects are Colombians. We don't find Mexican Americans, or blacks, or other immigrants. It's a collection of several hundred Colombians who commit this crime. If you see six in a car in front of the Jewelry Mart, and they're waiting and watching people with briefcases, should we play the percentages and follow them? It's common sense."

6   Cops like Parks say that racial profiling is a sensible, statistically based tool. Profiling lowers the cost of obtaining and processing crime information, which in turn lowers the overall cost of doing the business of policing. And the fact

that a number of cops who support racial profiling are black, including Parks, buttresses claims that the practice isn't motivated by bigotry. Indeed, these police officers note that racial profiling is race-*neutral* in that it can be applied to persons of all races, depending on the circumstances. In predominantly black neighborhoods in which white people stick out (as potential drug customers or racist hooligans, for example), whiteness can become part of a profile. In the southwestern United States, where Latinos often traffic in illegal immigrants, apparent Latin American ancestry can become part of a profile.

7   But the defenders of racial profiling are wrong. Ever since the Black and Latino Caucus of the New Jersey Legislature held a series of hearings, complete with testimony from victims of what they claimed was the New Jersey state police force's overly aggressive racial profiling, the air has been thick with public denunciations of the practice.

8   Unfortunately, though, many who condemn racial profiling do so without really thinking the issue through. One common complaint is that using race (say, blackness) as one factor in selecting surveillance targets is fundamentally racist. But selectivity of this sort can be defended on nonracist grounds. "There is nothing more painful to me at this age in my life," Jesse Jackson said in 1993, "than to walk down the street and hear footsteps and start to think about robbery and then look around and see somebody white and feel relieved." Jackson was relieved not because he dislikes black people, but because he estimated that he stood a somewhat greater risk of being robbed by a black person than by a white person. Statistics confirm that African Americans—particularly young black men—commit a dramatically disproportionate share of street crime in the United States. This is a sociological fact, not a figment of a racist media (or police) imagination. In recent years, victims report blacks as perpetrators of around 25 percent of violent crimes, although blacks constitute only about 12 percent of the nation's population.

9   So, if racial profiling isn't bigoted, and if the empirical claim upon which the practice rests is sound, why is it wrong?

10   Racial distinctions are and should be different from other lines of social stratification. That is why, since the civil rights revolution of the 1960s, courts have typically ruled—based on the 14th Amendment's equal protection clause—that mere reasonableness is an insufficient justification for officials to discriminate on racial grounds. In such cases, courts have generally insisted on applying "strict scrutiny"—the most intense level of judicial review—to government actions. Under this tough standard, the use of race in governmental decision making may be upheld only if it serves a compelling government objective and only if it is "narrowly tailored" to advance that objective.

11   A disturbing feature of this debate is that many people, including judges, are suggesting that decisions based on racial distinctions do not constitute unlawful racial discrimination—as long as race is not the only reason a person was treated objectionably. The court that upheld the DEA agent's action at the Kansas City airport, for instance, declined to describe it as racially discriminatory and thus evaded strict scrutiny.

12   But racially discriminatory decisions typically stem from mixed motives. For example, an employer who prefers white candidates to black candidates—except for those black candidates with superior experience and test scores—is engaging in racial discrimination, even though race is not the only factor he considers (since he selects black superstars). In some cases, race is a marginal factor; in others it is the only factor. The distinction may have a bearing on the moral or logical justification, but taking race into account at all means engaging in discrimination.

13   Because both law and morality discourage racial discrimination, proponents should persuade the public that racial profiling is justifiable. Instead, they frequently neglect its costs and minimize the extent to which it adds to the resentment blacks feel toward the law enforcement establishment. When O. J. Simpson was acquitted, many recognized the danger of a large sector of Americans feeling cynical and angry toward the system. Such alienation creates witnesses who fail to cooperate with police, citizens who view prosecutors as the enemy, lawyers who disdain the rules they have sworn to uphold, and jurors who yearn to get even with a system that has, in their eyes, consistently mistreated them. Racial profiling helps keep this pool of accumulated rage filled to the brim.

14   The courts have not been sufficiently mindful of this risk. In rejecting a 1976 constitutional challenge that accused U.S. Border Patrol officers in California of selecting cars for inspection partly on the basis of drivers' apparent Mexican ancestry, the Supreme Court noted in part that, of the motorists passing the checkpoint, fewer than 1 percent were stopped. It also noted that, of the 820 vehicles inspected during the period in question, roughly 20 percent contained illegal aliens.

15   Justice William J. Brennan dissented, however, saying the Court did not indicate the ancestral makeup of *all* the persons the Border Patrol stopped. It is likely that many of the innocent people who were questioned were of apparent Mexican ancestry who then had to prove their obedience to the law just because others of the same ethnic background have broken laws in the past.

16   The practice of racial profiling undercuts a good idea that needs more support from both society and the law: Individuals should be judged by public authorities on the basis of their own conduct and not on the basis of racial generalization. Race-dependent policing retards the development of bias-free thinking; indeed, it encourages the opposite.

17   What about the fact that in some communities people associated with a given racial group commit a disproportionately large number of crimes? Our commitment to a just social order should prompt us to end racial profiling even if the generalizations on which the technique is based are supported by empirical evidence. This is not as risky as it may sound. There are actually many contexts in which the law properly enjoins us to forswear playing racial odds even when doing so would advance legitimate goals.

18   For example, public opinion surveys have established that blacks distrust law enforcement more than whites. Thus, it would be rational—and not neces-

sarily racist—for a prosecutor to use ethnic origin as a factor in excluding black potential jurors. Fortunately, the Supreme Court has outlawed racial discrimination of this sort. And because demographics show that in the United States, whites tend to live longer than blacks, it would be perfectly rational for insurers to charge blacks higher life-insurance premiums. Fortunately, the law forbids that, too.

19   The point here is that racial equality, like all good things in life, costs something. Politicians suggest that all Americans need to do in order to attain racial justice is forswear bigotry. But they must also demand equal treatment before the law even when unequal treatment is defensible in the name of nonracist goals—and even when their effort will be costly.

20   Since abandoning racial profiling would make policing more expensive and perhaps less effective, those of us who oppose it must advocate a responsible alternative. Mine is simply to spend more money on other means of enforcement—and then spread the cost on some nonracial basis. One way to do that would be to hire more police officers. Another way would be to subject everyone to closer surveillance. A benefit of the second option would be to acquaint more whites with the burden of police intrusion, which might prompt more of them to insist on limiting police power. As it stands now, the burden is unfairly placed on minorities—imposing on Mexican Americans, blacks, and others a special kind of tax for the war against illegal immigration, drugs, and other crimes. The racial element of that tax should be repealed.

21   I'm not saying that police should never be able to use race as a guideline. If a young white man with blue hair robs me, the police should certainly be able to use a description of the perpetrator's race. In this situation, though, whiteness is a trait linked to a particular person with respect to a particular incident. It is not a free-floating accusation that hovers over young white men practically all the time—which is the predicament young black men currently face. Nor am I saying that race could never be legitimately relied upon as a signal of increased danger. In an extraordinary circumstance in which plausible alternatives appear to be absent, officials might need to resort to racial profiling. This is a far cry from routine profiling that is subjected to little scrutiny.

22   Now that racial profiling is a hot issue, the prospects for policy change have improved. President Clinton directed federal law enforcement agencies to determine the extent to which their officers focus on individuals on the basis of race. The Customs Service is rethinking its practice of using ethnicity or nationality as a basis for selecting subjects for investigation. The Federal Aviation Administration has been re-evaluating its recommended security procedures; it wants the airlines to combat terrorism with computer profiling, which is purportedly less race-based than random checks by airport personnel. Unfortunately, though, a minefield of complexity lies beneath these options. Unless we understand the complexities, this opportunity will be wasted.

23   To protect ourselves against race-based policing requires no real confrontation with the status quo, because hardly anyone defends police surveillance

triggered *solely* by race. Much of the talk about police "targeting" suspects on the basis of race is, in this sense, misguided and harmful. It diverts attention to a side issue. Another danger is the threat of demagoguery through oversimplification. When politicians talk about "racial profiling," we must insist that they define precisely what they mean. Evasion—putting off hard decisions under the guise of needing more information—is also a danger.

24   Even if routine racial profiling is prohibited, the practice will not cease quickly. An officer who makes a given decision partly on a racial basis is unlikely to acknowledge having done so, and supervisors and judges are loath to reject officers' statements. Nevertheless, it would be helpful for President Clinton to initiate a strict anti-discrimination directive to send a signal to conscientious, law-abiding officers that there are certain criteria they ought not use.

25   To be sure, creating a norm that can't be fully enforced isn't ideal, but it might encourage us all to work toward closing the gap between our laws and the conduct of public authorities. A new rule prohibiting racial profiling might be made to be broken, but it could set a new standard for legitimate government.

■ QUESTIONS FOR ANALYSIS AND DISCUSSION

1. Kennedy argues that racial profiling is racist. In what ways is it racist? Alternatively, how can it be defended on nonracist grounds? Is it always racist? Explain.

2. A critical reader may argue that Kennedy contradicts himself in some places, such as in paragraph 21 when he follows his argument that racial profiling is wrong with the statement that in "extraordinary circumstances" it may be permissible. Is this indeed a contradiction? Explain.

3. In paragraph 17, Kennedy presents two examples of how the law "properly enjoins us to forswear playing racial odds even when doing so would advance legitimate goals." Do these examples support his argument that all racial profiling should be illegal? Explain.

4. How plausible are the solutions Kennedy offers? For example, he proposes that that to end racial profiling, cities should hire more police officers so that the "time-saving" element of racial profiling would no longer be a factor. What issues does he not address that an opponent could use to argue against this solution? What information would you recommend he include to deflect objections? Explain.

5. Both this essay and the one that follows refer to Jesse Jackson's remark that the negative stereotyping of their own race can influence even blacks. Why do you think Kennedy includes this admission?

6. Evaluate Kennedy's observation that the practice of racial profiling keeps "this pool of accumulated [minority] rage filled to the brim." How does this reaction affect other areas of law enforcement? How can racial profiling backfire in the courtroom and in the streets? Explain.

In Defense of Racial Profiling

John Derbyshire

Racial profiling has become a hotbed of political debate. In fact, says the author of the next piece, it is all but political suicide to say anything against the dissolution of racial profiling, despite the fact that the U.S. Supreme Court has upheld the practice. In this editorial, John Derbyshire explains that racial profiling has become one of the shibboleths (or catch phrases) of our time. He argues that while we can rhetorically debate in principle why racial profiling may be morally reprehensible, it will continue to be a tool of law enforcement not because of racism, but because it is "common sense."

Political conservative Derbyshire is a contributing editor to *The National Review* and a columnist for the *National Review Online* (NRO). He is the author of *Seeing Calvin Coolidge in a Dream* (1996) and *Fire from the Sun* (2000). This essay appeared in the February 19, 2001, issue of *The National Review.*

■ BEFORE YOU READ

Derbyshire argues that much of the public outcry against racial profiling stems from its exposure as a political issue by aspiring public officials. Why is racial profiling such a popular political issue? Is there any truth to Derbyshire's assertion that "anyone who wants a public career in the United States must place himself on record as being against it"?

■ AS YOU READ

How does Derbyshire acknowledge his audience? What assumptions does he make? Does his admitted decision to "offer only those arguments likely to appeal" to his audience make his argument more, or less, effective?

1   "Racial profiling" has become one of the shibboleths of our time. Anyone who wants a public career in the United States must place himself on record as being against it. Thus, ex-senator John Ashcroft, on the eve of his confirmation hearings: "It's wrong, inappropriate, shouldn't be done." During the vice-presidential debate last October, moderator Bernard Shaw invited the candidates to imagine themselves black victims of racial profiling. Both made the required ritual protestations of outrage. Lieberman: "I have a few African-American friends who have gone through this horror, and you know, it makes me want to kind of hit the wall, because it is such an assault on their humanity and their citizenship." Cheney: "It's the sense of anger and frustration and rage that would go with knowing that the only reason you were stopped . . . was because of the color of your skin . . ." In the strange, rather depressing, pattern these things always follow nowadays, the American public has speedily swung into line behind the Pied Pipers: Gallup reports that 81 percent of the public disapproves of racial profiling.

2   All of which represents an extraordinary level of awareness of, and hostility to, and even *passion* against ("hit the wall . . .") a practice that, up to about five years ago, practically nobody had heard of. It is, in fact, instructive to begin by looking at the history of this shibboleth.

3   To people who follow politics, the term "racial profiling" probably first registered when Al Gore debated Bill Bradley at New York's Apollo Theatre in February 2000. Here is Bradley, speaking of the 1999 shooting of African immigrant Amadou Diallo by New York City police: "I . . . think it reflects . . . racial profiling that seeps into the mind of someone so that he sees a wallet in the hand of a white man as a wallet, but a wallet in the hand of a black man as a gun. And we—we have to change that. I would issue an executive order that would eliminate racial profiling at the federal level."

4   Nobody was unkind enough to ask Sen. Bradley how an executive order would change what a policeman sees in a dark lobby in a dangerous neighborhood at night. Nor was anyone so tactless as to ask him about the case of La-Tanya Haggerty, shot dead in June 1999 by a Chicago policewoman who mistook her cell phone for a handgun. The policewoman was, like Ms. Haggerty, black.

5   Al Gore, in that debate at the Apollo, did successfully, and famously, ambush Bradley by remarking that: "You know, racial profiling practically began in New Jersey, Senator Bradley." In true Clinton-Gore fashion, this is not true, but it is *sort of* true. "Racial profiling" the *thing* has been around for as long as police work, and is practiced everywhere. "Racial profiling" the *term* did indeed have its origins on the New Jersey Turnpike in the early 1990s. The reason for the prominence of this rather unappealing stretch of expressway in the history of the phenomenon is simple: The turnpike is the main conduit for the shipment of illegal drugs and other contraband to the great criminal marts of the Northeast.

6   The career of the term "racial profiling" seems to have begun in 1994, but did not really take off until April 1998, when two white New Jersey state troopers pulled over a van for speeding. As they approached the van from behind, it suddenly reversed towards them. The troopers fired eleven shots from their handguns, wounding three of the van's four occupants, who were all black or Hispanic. The troopers, James Kenna and John Hogan, subsequently became poster boys for the "racial profiling" lobbies, facing the same indignities, though so far with less serious consequences, as were endured by the Los Angeles policemen in the Rodney King case: endless investigations, double jeopardy, and so on.

7   And a shibboleth was born. News-media databases list only a scattering of instances of the term "racial profiling" from 1994 to 1998. In that latter year, the number hit double digits, and thereafter rose quickly into the hundreds and thousands. Now we all know about it, and we are, of course, all against it.

8   Well, not quite all. American courts—including (see below) the U.S. Supreme Court—are not against it. Jurisprudence on the matter is pretty clear. So long as race is only one factor in a generalized approach to the questioning

of suspects, it may be considered. And of course, *pace* Candidate Cheney; it always is only one factor. I have been unable to locate any statistics on the point, but I feel sure that elderly black women are stopped by the police much less often than are young white men.

9   Even in the political sphere, where truth-telling and independent thinking on matters of race have long been liabilities, there are those who refuse to mouth the required pieties. Alan Keyes, when asked by Larry King if he would be angry with a police officer who pulled him over for being black, replied: "I was raised that everything I did represented my family, my race, and my country. I would be angry with the people giving me a bad reputation."

Goodbye to Common Sense

10   Practically all law-enforcement professionals believe in the need for racial profiling. In an article on the topic for *The New York Times Magazine* in June 1999, Jeffrey Goldberg interviewed Bernard Parks, chief of the Los Angeles Police Department. Parks, who is black, asked rhetorically of racial profiling: "Should we play the percentages? . . . It's common sense." Note that date, though. This was pretty much the time at which it was possible for a public official to speak truthfully about racial profiling. Law-enforcement professionals were learning the importance of keeping their thoughts to themselves. Four months before the Goldberg piece saw print, New Jersey state-police superintendent Carl Williams, in an interview, said that certain crimes were associated with certain ethnic groups, and that it was naive to think that race was not an issue in policing—both statements, of course, perfectly true. Supt. Williams was fired the same day by Gov. Christie Todd Whitman.

11   Like other race issues in the U.S., racial profiling is a "tadpole," with an enormous black head and a long but comparatively inconsequential brown, yellow, and red tail. While Hispanic, "Asian-American," and other lesser groups have taken up the "racial profiling" chant with gusto, the crux of the matter is the resentment that black Americans feel toward the attentions of white policemen. By far the largest number of Americans angry about racial profiling are law-abiding black people who feel that they are stopped and questioned because the police regard *all* black people with undue suspicion. They feel that they are the victims of a negative stereotype.

12   They are. Unfortunately, a negative stereotype can be correct, and even useful. I was surprised to find, when researching this article, that within the academic field of social psychology there is a large literature on stereotypes, and that much of it—an entire school of thought—holds that stereotypes are essential life tools. On the scientific evidence, the primary function of stereotypes is what researchers call "the reality function." That is, stereotypes are useful tools for dealing with the world. Confronted with a snake or a fawn, our immediate behavior is determined by generalized beliefs—stereotypes—about snakes and fawns. Stereotypes are, in fact, merely one aspect of the mind's ability to make generalizations, without which science and mathematics, not to mention, as the snake/fawn example shows, much of everyday life, would be impossible.

13   At some level, everybody knows this stuff, even the guardians of the "racial profiling" flame. Jesse Jackson famously, in 1993, confessed that: "There is nothing more painful to me at this stage in my life than to walk down the street and hear footsteps and start thinking about robbery, then look around and see somebody white and feel relieved." Here is Sandra Seegars of the Washington, D.C., Taxicab Commission:

14   Late at night, if I saw young black men dressed in a slovenly way, I wouldn't pick them up . . . And during the day, I'd think twice about it.

15   Pressed to define "slovenly," Ms. Seegars elaborated thus: "A young black guy with his hat on backwards, shirttail hanging down longer than his coat, baggy pants down below his underwear, and unlaced tennis shoes." Now *there's* a stereotype for you! Ms. Seegars is, of course, black.

16   Law-enforcement officials are simply employing the same stereotypes as you, me, Jesse, and Sandra, but taking the opposite course of action. What we seek to avoid, they pursue. They do this for reasons of simple efficiency. A policeman who concentrates a disproportionate amount of his limited time and resources on young black men is going to uncover far more crimes—and therefore be far more successful in his career—than one who biases his attention toward, say, middle-aged Asian women. It is, as Chief Parks said, common sense.

17   Similarly with the tail of the tadpole—are racial-profiling issues that do not involve black people. China is known to have obtained a top-secret warhead design. Among those with clearance to work on that design are people from various kinds of national and racial background. Which ones should investigators concentrate on? The Swedes? The answer surely is: They should first check out anyone who has family or friends in China, who has made trips to China, or who has met with Chinese officials. This would include me, for example—my father-in-law is an official of the Chinese Communist Party. Would I then have been "racially profiled"?

18   It is not very surprising to learn that the main fruit of the "racial profiling" hysteria has been a decline in the efficiency of police work. In Philadelphia, a federal court order now requires police to fill out both sides of an $8\frac{1}{2}$-by-11 sheet on every citizen contact. Law-enforcement agencies nationwide are engaged in similar statistics-gathering exercises, under pressure from federal lawmakers like U.S. Rep. John Conyers, who has announced that he will introduce a bill to force police agencies to keep detailed information about traffic stops. ("The struggle goes on," declared Rep. Conyers. The struggle that is going on, it sometimes seems, is a struggle to prevent our police forces from accomplishing any useful work at all.)

19   The mountain of statistics that is being brought forth by all this panic does not, on the evidence so far, seem likely to shed much light on what is happening. The numbers have a way of leading off into infinite regresses of uncertainty. The city of San Jose, Calif., for example, discovered that, yes, the percentage of blacks being stopped was higher than their representation in the city's population. Ah, but patrol cars were computer-assigned to high-crime

districts, which are mainly inhabited by minorities. So that over-representation might actually be an under-representation! But then, minorities have fewer cars. . . .

The Core Arguments

20   Notwithstanding the extreme difficulty of finding out what is actually happening, we can at least seek some moral and philosophical grounds on which to take a stand either for or against racial profiling. I am going to take it as a given that most readers of this article will be of a conservative inclination, and shall offer only those arguments likely to appeal to persons so inclined. If you seek arguments of other kinds, they are not hard to find—just pick up your newspaper or turn on your TV.

21   Of arguments *against* racial profiling, probably the ones most persuasive to a conservative are the ones from libertarianism. Many of the stop-and-search cases that brought this matter into the headlines were part of the so-called war on drugs. The police procedures behind them were ratified by court decisions of the 1980s, themselves mostly responding to the rising tide of illegal narcotics. In *U.S. v. Montoya De Hernandez* (1985), for example, Chief Justice Rehnquist validated the detention of a suspected "balloon swallowing" drug courier until the material had passed through her system, by noting previous invasions upheld by the Court:

22   [F]irst class mail may be opened without a warrant on less than probable cause . . . Automotive travellers may be stopped . . . near the border without individualized suspicion *even if the stop is based largely on ethnicity.* . . .

23   (My italics.) The Chief Justice further noted that these incursions are in response to "the veritable national crisis in law enforcement caused by smuggling of illegal narcotics."

24   Many on the political Right feel that the war on drugs is at best misguided, at worst a moral and constitutional disaster. Yet it is naïve to imagine that the "racial profiling" hubbub would go away, or even much diminish, if all state and federal drug laws were repealed tomorrow. Black and Hispanic Americans would still be committing crimes at rates higher than citizens of other races. The differential criminality of various ethnic groups is not only, or even mainly, located in drug crimes. In 1997, for example, blacks, who are 13 percent of the U.S. population, comprised 35 percent of those arrested for embezzlement. (It is not generally appreciated that black Americans commit higher levels not only of "street crime," but also of white-collar crime.)

25   Even without the drug war, diligent police officers would still, therefore, be correct to regard black and Hispanic citizens—other factors duly considered—as more likely to be breaking the law. The Chinese government would still be trying to recruit spies exclusively from among Chinese-born Americans. (The Chinese Communist Party is, in this respect, the keenest "racial profiler" of all.)

The Amadou Diallo case—the police were looking for a rapist—would still have happened.

26   The best non-libertarian argument against racial profiling is the one from equality before the law. This has been most cogently presented by Prof. Randall Kennedy of Harvard. Kennedy concedes most of the points I have made. Yes, he says:

27   Statistics confirm that African Americans—particularly young black men— commit a dramatically disproportionate share of street crime in the United States. This is a sociological fact, not a figment of media (or police) imagi- nation. In recent years, victims report blacks as perpetrators of around 25 percent of violent crimes, although blacks constitute only about 12 per- cent of the nation's population.

28   And yes, says Prof. Kennedy, outlawing racial profiling will reduce the effi- ciency of police work. Nonetheless, for constitutional and moral reasons we should outlaw the practice. If this places extra burdens on law enforcement, well, "racial equality, like all good things in life, costs something." It does not come for free.

29   There are two problems with this. The first is that Kennedy has minimized the black-white difference in criminality, and therefore that "cost." I don't know where his 25 percent comes from, or what "recent years" means, but I do know that in Department of Justice figures for 1997, victims report 60 percent of robberies as having been committed by black persons. In that same year, a black American was eight times more likely than a non-black to commit homi- cide—and "non-black" here includes Hispanics, not broken out separately in these figures. A racial-profiling ban, under which police officers were required to stop and question suspects in precise proportion to their demographic rep- resentation (in what? the precinct population? the state population? the na- tional population?), would lead to *massive* inefficiencies in police work. Which is to say, massive declines in the apprehension of criminals.

30   The other problem is with the special status that Prof. Kennedy accords to race. Kennedy: "Racial distinctions are and should be different from other lines of social stratification." Thus, if it can be shown, as it surely can, that state troopers stop young people more than old people, relative to young people's numerical representation on the road being patrolled, that is of no conse- quence. If they stop black people more than white people, on the same crite- rion, that is of large consequence. This, in spite of the fact that the categories "age" and "race" are both rather fuzzy (define "young") and are both useful predictors of criminality. In spite of the fact, too, that the principle of equality before the law does not, and up to now has never been thought to, guarantee equal outcomes for any law-enforcement process, only that a citizen who has come under reasonable suspicion will be treated fairly.

31   It is on this special status accorded to race that, I believe, we have gone most seriously astray. I am willing, in fact, to say much more than this: In the

matter of race, I think the Anglo-Saxon world has taken leave of its senses. The campaign to ban racial profiling is, as I see it, a part of that large, broad-fronted assault on common sense that our over-educated, over-lawyered society has been enduring for some forty years now, and whose roots are in a fanatical egalitarianism, a grim determination not to face up to the realities of group differences, a theological attachment to the doctrine that the sole and sufficient explanation for all such differences is "racism"—which is to say, the malice and cruelty of white people—and a nursed and petted guilt towards the behavior of our ancestors.

32   At present, Americans are drifting away from the concept of belonging to a single nation. I do not think this drift will be arrested until we can shed the idea that deference to the sensitivities of racial minorities—however overwrought those sensitivities may be, however over-stimulated by unscrupulous mountebanks, however disconnected from reality—trumps every other consideration, including even the maintenance of social order. To shed that idea, we must confront our national hysteria about race, which causes large numbers of otherwise sane people to believe that the hearts of their fellow citizens are filled with malice towards them. So long as we continue to pander to that poisonous, preposterous belief, we shall only wander off deeper into a wilderness of division, mistrust, and institutionalized rancor—that wilderness, the most freshly painted signpost to which bears the legend RACIAL PROFILING.

■ QUESTIONS FOR ANALYSIS AND DISCUSSION

1. Derbyshire presents a "history" of the emergence of racial profiling to the political arena. How does this history help frame and support the rest of his discussion? Explain.

2. According to Derbyshire, what influence have politicians had on the "racial profiling" debate? How have they influenced public opinion? If Americans feel so strongly against racial profiling, why does it seem to have emerged as a political issue only as recently as ten years ago? Or does the issue, in fact, have a much longer history? Explain.

3. Both Kennedy and Derbyshire quote Los Angeles police chief Bernard Parks. Does the fact that Parks is a black law enforcement official influence your opinion of racial profiling?

4. What does Derbyshire *imply* when he says that Bernard Parks' interview with the *New York Times Magazine* was "pretty much the last time at which it was possible for a public official to speak truthfully about racial profiling"? How does he support this statement?

5. Summarize Derbyshire's argument supporting racial profiling presented in paragraphs 23 through 30. After you have summarized his points, respond to each with your own opinion.

6. According to Derbyshire, what is the "fruit" of the racial profiling hysteria? In his opinion, how does the "national hysteria about race" serve to drive Americans apart as a nation? Explain.

"Bill of Whites"

Take a look at Clay Bennett's cartoon, which originally appeared in the *Christian Science Monitor.*

"... And that's 'The Bill of Whites'..."

■ QUESTIONS FOR ANALYSIS AND DISCUSSION

1. What is happening in this cartoon? Where does the scene in the cartoon take place? Who is featured in it and what is the relationship between the characters? What is the motivation behind what the man tells the little boy?
2. What is the purpose of this cartoon? Can you tell what the author's political and social position is on this issue? Explain.
3. Evaluate the effectiveness of this editorial cartoon. In what type of publication would you expect to see it?
4. How do you think other authors in this section would respond to this cartoon? Explain.

The Bill of Rights for Black Men: Walking While Black

Bryonn Bain

On October 18, 1999, Harvard Law School student Bryonn Bain was arrested for a crime he didn't commit; for the crime, says Bain, of simply being black. Using the Bill of Rights as a backdrop, he described his experience in an essay prepared for his

Cultural Perspectives on the Law class. He later submitted this piece to the *Village Voice* who printed it as their cover story in April 2000. Over 40,000 people have responded to the article, pushing Bain to the forefront of a debate on racial profiling and justice.

A musician and poet, Bain is a graduate of Columbia University and is currently a student at Harvard Law School. He is considering legal action against the New York City Police Department. Says Bain, "I have a cause, not a complaint." He hopes that sharing his experience of being "abducted, degraded [. . .] and publicly humiliated" will lead to meaningful dialogue and public action to end racial profiling.

■ BEFORE YOU READ

Review the Bill of Rights. What rights does it defend? How much are your expectations of liberty and justice connected to this document?

■ AS YOU READ

Consider Bain's repeated use of the word "nigger" throughout his essay. How does he use this word to emphasize his point? Did anyone call him this word, or did he select it based on how his experience made him feel?

1   After hundreds of hours and thousands of pages of legal theory in law school, I have finally had my first real lesson in the Law. On Sunday, October 18, 1999, I was taken from the corner of 96th Street and Broadway by the NYPD and held overnight in a cell at the 24th Precinct in New York City. While home from school for the weekend, I was arrested for a crime I witnessed someone else commit.

2   We left the Latin Quarter nightclub that night laughing that Red, my cousin, had finally found someone shorter than his five-foot-five frame to dance with him. My younger brother, K, was fiending for a turkey sandwich, so we all walked over to the bodega around the corner, just one block west of Broadway. We had no idea that class was about to be in session. The lesson for the day was that there is a special Bill of Rights for nonwhite people in the United States—one that applies with particular severity to Black men. It has never had to be ratified by Congress because—in the hearts of those with the power to enforce it—the *Black Bill of Rights* is held to be self-evident.

3   As we left the store, armed only with sandwiches and Snapples, the three of us saw a group of young men standing around a car parked on the corner in front of the store. As music blasted by the wide-open doors of their car, the men around the car appeared to be arguing with someone in an apartment above the store. The argument escalated when one of the young men began throwing bottles at the apartment window. Several other people who had just left the club, as well as a number of random passersby, witnessed the altercation and began scattering to avoid the raining shards of glass.

Amendment I

4 **Congress can make no law altering the established fact that a black man is a nigger.**

5   My brother, cousin, and I abruptly began to walk up the street toward the subway to avoid the chaos that was unfolding. Another bottle was hurled. This time, the apartment window cracked, and more glass shattered onto the pavement. We were halfway up the block when we looked back at the guys who had been hanging outside the store. They had jumped in the car, turned off their music, and slammed the doors, and were getting away from the scene as quickly as possible. As we continued to walk toward the subway, about six or seven bouncers came running down the street to see who had caused all the noise. "Where do you BOYS think you're going?!" yelled the biggest of this muscle-bound band of bullies in black shirts. They came at my family and me with out-stretched arms to corral us back down the block. "To the 2 train," I answered. Just then I remembered that there are constitutional restrictions on physically restraining people against their will. Common sense told me that the bouncers' authority couldn't possibly extend into the middle of the street around the corner from their club. "You have absolutely no authority to put your hands on any of us!" I insisted, with a sense of newly found conviction. We kept going. This clearly pissed off the bouncers—especially the big, bald, white bouncer who seemed to be the head honcho.

Amendment II

6 **The right of any white person to apprehend a nigger will not be infringed.**

7   The fact that the bouncers' efforts at intimidation were being disregarded by three young Black men much smaller than they were only made matters worse for their egos (each of us is under five-foot-ten and no more than 180 pounds). The bouncer who appeared to be in charge warned us we would regret having ignored him. "You BOYS better stay right where you are!" barked the now seething bouncer. I told my brother and cousin to ignore him. We were not in their club. In fact, we were among the many people dispersing from the site of the disturbance, which had occurred an entire block away from their "territory." They were clearly beyond their jurisdiction (we spent weeks on the subject in Civil Procedure!). Furthermore, the bouncers had not bothered to ask anyone among the many witnesses what had happened before they attempted to apprehend us. They certainly had not asked us. A crime had been committed, and someone Black was going to be apprehended—whether the Black person was a crack addict, a corrections officer, a preacher, a professional entertainer of white people, or a student at a prestigious law school.

8   Less than 10 minutes after we had walked by the bouncers, I was staring at badge 1727. We were screamed at and shoved around by Officer Ronald Connelly and his cronies. "That's them, officer!" the head bouncer said, indicting us with a single sentence.

Amendment III

9 **No nigger shall, at any time, fail to obey any public authority figures—even when beyond the jurisdiction of their authority.**

10   "You boys out here throwin' bottles at people?!" shouted the officer. Asking any of the witnesses would have easily cleared up the issue of who had thrown the bottles. But the officer could not have cared less about that. My family and I were now being punished for the crime of thwarting the bouncers' unauthorized attempt to apprehend us. We were going to be guilty unless we could prove ourselves innocent.

Amendment IV

11 **The fact that a Black man is a nigger is sufficient probable cause for him to be searched and seized.**

12   Having failed to convince Connelly, the chubby, gray-haired officer in charge, we were up against the wall in a matter of minutes. Each of us had the legs of our dignity spread apart, was publicly frisked down from shirt to socks, and then had our pockets rummaged through. All while Officer Connelly insisted that we shut up and keep facing the wall or, as he told Red, he would treat us like we "were trying to fight back." The officers next searched through my backpack and seemed surprised to find my laptop and a casebook I had brought to the club so that I could get some studying done on the bus ride back to school.

13   We were shoved into the squad car in front of a crowd composed of friends and acquaintances who had been in the club with us and had by now learned of our situation. I tried with little success to play back the facts of the famous Miranda case in my mind. I was fairly certain these cops were in the wrong for failing to read us our rights.

Amendment V

14 **Any nigger accused of a crime is to be punished without any due process whatsoever.**

15   We were never told that we had a right to remain silent. We were never told that we had the right to an attorney. We were never informed that anything we said could and would be used against us in a court of law.

Amendment VI

16 **In all prosecutions of niggers, their accuser shall enjoy the right of a speedy apprehension. While the accused nigger shall enjoy a dehumanizing and humiliating arrest.**

17   After my mug shot was taken at the precinct, Officer Connelly chuckled to himself as he took a little blue-and-white pin out of my wallet. "This is too sharp for you to take into the cell. We can't have you slitting somebody's wrist in there!" he said facetiously. I was handed that pin the day before at the Metropolitan Museum of Art. . . . I wanted to be transported back there, where I had seen the ancient Egyptian art exhibit that afternoon. The relics of each dynastic

period pulled a proud grin across my face as I stood in awe at the magnificence of this enduring legacy of my Black African ancestors.

18   This legacy has been denied for so long that my skin now signals to many that I must be at least an accomplice to any crime that occurs somewhere within the vicinity of my person . . . this legacy has been denied so long that it was unfathomable for the cops that we were innocent bystanders in this situation . . . this legacy lay locked all night long for no good reason in a filthy cell barely bigger than the bathroom in my tiny basement apartment in Cambridge, Massachusetts . . . this legacy was forced to listen that night to some white guy who was there because he had beaten up his girlfriend the way the cops frisking my cousin had threatened to beat him down if he kept trying to explain to them what had really happened . . . this legacy is negated by the lily-white institutions where many Blacks are trained to think that they are somehow different from the type of Negro this kind of thing happens to because in their minds White Supremacy is essentially an ideology of the past.

19   Yet White Supremacy was alive and well enough to handcuff three innocent young men and bend them over the hood of a squad car with cops cackling on in front of the crowd, "These BOYS think they can come up here from Brooklyn, cause all kinds of trouble, and get away with it!"

Amendment VII

20   **Niggers must remain within the confines of their own neighborhoods. Those who do not are clearly looking for trouble.**

21   Indeed, I had come from Brooklyn with my younger brother and cousin that evening to get our dance on at the Latin Quarter. However, having gone to college in the same neighborhood, I consider it more of a second home than a place where I journey to escape the eyes of my community and unleash the kind of juvenile mischief to which the officers were alluding. At 25 years old, after leaving college five years ago and completing both a master's degree and my first year of law school, this kind of adolescent escapism is now far behind me. But that didn't matter.

22   The bouncers and the cops didn't give a damn who we were or what we were about. While doing our paperwork several hours later, another officer, who realized how absurd our ordeal was and treated us with the utmost respect, explained to us why he believed we had been arrested.

Amendment VIII

23   **Wherever niggers are causing trouble, arresting any nigger at the scene of the crime is just as good as arresting the one actually guilty of the crime in question.**

24   After repeated incidents calling for police intervention during the last few months, the 24th Precinct and the Latin Quarter have joined forces to help deal with the club's "less desirable element." To prevent the club from being shut down, they needed to set an example for potential wrongdoers. We were just unfortunate enough to be at the wrong place at the wrong time—and to fit

the description of that "element." To make matters worse from the bouncers' point of view, we had the audacity to demonstrate our understanding that for them to touch us without our consent constituted a battery.

25   As Officer Connelly joked on about how this was the kind of thing that would keep us from ever going anywhere in life, the situation grew increasingly unbelievable. "You go to Harvard Law School?" he inquired with a sarcastic smirk. "You must be on a Ball scholarship or somethin', huh?" I wanted to hit him upside his uninformed head with one of my casebooks. I wanted to water torture him with the sweat and tears that have fallen from my mother's face for the last 20 years, during which she has held down three nursing jobs to send six children to school. I wanted to tell everyone watching just how hard she has worked to give us more control over our own destinies than she had while growing up in her rural village in Trinidad. I still haven't told my mom what happened. Seeing the look on her face when I do will be the worst thing to come out of this experience. I can already hear the sound of her crying when she thinks to herself that none of her years of laboring in hospitals through sleepless nights mattered on this particular evening.

Amendment IX

26   **Niggers will never be treated like full citizens in America—no matter how hard they work to improve their circumstances.**

27   It did not matter to the officers or the bouncers that my brother is going to graduate from Brooklyn College in June after working and going to school full-time for the last six years. It did not matter that he has worked for the criminal justice system in the Department of Corrections of New Jersey for almost a year now. They didn't give a damn that I was the president of my class for each of the four years that I was at Columbia University. It did not matter that I am now in my second year at Harvard Law School. And in a fair and just society, none of that *should* matter. Our basic civil rights should have been respected irrespective of who we are or the institutions with which we are affiliated. What should have mattered was that we were innocent. Officer Connelly checked all three of our licenses and found none of us had ever been convicted of a crime.

Amendment X

28   **A nigger who has no arrest record just hasn't been caught yet.**

29   It should have mattered that we had no record. But it didn't. What mattered was that we were Black and we were there. That was enough for everyone involved to draw the conclusion that we were guilty until we could be proved innocent.

30   After our overnight crash course in the true criminal law of this country, I know now from firsthand experience that the Bill of Rights for Blacks in America completely contradicts the one that was ratified for the society at large. The afternoon before we were arrested, I overheard an elderly white woman on the

bus as she remarked to the man beside her how much safer Mayor Giuliani has made New York City feel. I remember thinking to myself then, "Not if you look like Diallo or Louima!" It's about as safe as L.A. was for Rodney King. About as safe as Texas was for James Byrd Jr. . . . and this list could go on for days. Although the Ku Klux Klan may feel safe enough to march in Manhattan, the rights of Black men are increasingly violated by the police of this and other cities around the country every day. In the context of some of these atrocities, we were rather lucky to have been only abducted, degraded, pushed around, and publicly humiliated. Nevertheless, Black people from all walks of life can have little security in a nation where police officers are free to grab Black bodies off the street at random and do with them whatever they please.

31   ADDENDUM: On Wednesday, February 23, 2000, after four court appearances over five months, the D.A.'s case against Bryonn Bain, Kristofer Bain, and Kyle Vazquez was dismissed. No affidavits or other evidence were produced to support the charges against them.

■ QUESTIONS FOR ANALYSIS AND DISCUSSION

1. How does Bain's title relate to his subject? Evaluate the effectiveness of his technique of using "articles" to demonstrate the injustice he feels and how these articles reflect his actual experience.
2. How do you feel after reading this essay? Are there particular points in the author's narrative that seem especially compelling? Do you find yourself becoming emotionally involved with his narrative? Explain.
3. Analyze Bain's use of language to convey his feelings and affect his audience. For example, consider how he repeats the word "nigger" and how, in recalling the arresting officer's comments, he puts "boys" in capital letters. How does Bain's use of language influence and sway his audience?

Hailing While Black
Shelby Steele

Many articles in this section describe how racial profiling has created a sense of social and political distrust. But has the high-profile exposure of this issue created an atmosphere where we have come to expect racism? In the next piece, Shelby Steele explains how even the simple act of hailing a cab in New York City can become fraught with social and political implications.

Steele is a research fellow at the Hoover Institution specializing in the study of race relations, affirmative action, and multiculturalism. With a Ph.D. in English and an M.A. in sociology, he is the author of *The Content of Our Character: A New Vision of Race in America* (1990), for which he was honored with the National Book Critic's Circle Award, and *A Dream Deferred: The Second Betrayal of Black Freedom in America*.

■ **BEFORE YOU READ**

Have you ever anticipated or expected that you might be mistreated due to your race, age, or gender? If so, describe the situation and its outcome.

■ **AS YOU READ**

In the next essay, Steele presents a black conservative's point of view on racial profiling and social fairness. Does the fact that Steele is black make his argument more compelling? Why or why not?

1   In Manhattan recently I attempted something that is thought to be all but impossible for a black man; I tried to hail a cab going uptown toward Harlem after dark. And I'll admit to feeling a new nervousness. This simple action—black man hailing cab—is now a tableau in America's ongoing culture war. If no cab swerves in to pick me up, America is still a racist country, and the entire superstructure of contemporary liberalism is bolstered. If I catch a ride, conservatives can breath easier. So, as I raise my hand and step from the curb, much is at stake.

2   It's all the talk these days of racial profiling that has set off my nerves in this way. Having grown up in the era of segregation, I know I can survive the racial profiling of a cabby. What makes me most nervous is the anxiety that I have wrongly estimated the degree of racism in American life. I am a conservative. But conservatism is a misunderstood identity in blacks that would be much easier to carry in a world where New York City cab drivers stopped for black fares, even after dark.

3   It is easy to believe that racial profiting is a serious problem in America. It fits the American profile, and now politicians have stepped forward to give it credence as a problem. But is it a real problem? Is dark skin a shorthand for criminality in the mind of America's law-enforcement officers? Studies show that we blacks are stopped in numbers higher than our percentage in the population but lower than our documented involvement in crime. If you're trying to measure racism, isn't it better to compare police stops to actual black involvement in crime than to the mere representation of blacks in the population? The elephant in the living room—and the tragedy in black America—is that we commit crimes vastly out of proportion to our numbers in society.

4   But I can already hear "so what?" from those who believe profiling is a serious problem. And I know that the more energetic among them will move numbers and points of reference around like shells in a shill game to show racism. In other words, racial profiling is now an "identity" issue like affirmative action, black reparations or even O. J.'s innocence. It is less a real issue than a coded argument over how much racism exists in society today. We argue these issues fiercely—make a culture war around them—because the moral authority of both the left and right political identities hangs in the balance.

5   Racial profiling is a boon to the left because this political identity justifies its demand for power by estimating racism to be high. The more racism, the

more power the left demands for social interventions that go beyond simple fairness under the law. Profiling hurts the right because it makes its fairness-under-the-law position on race seem inadequate, less than moral considering the prevalence of racism. The real debate over racial profiling is not about stops and searches on the New Jersey Turnpike. It is about the degree of racism in America and the distribution of power it justifies.

6   Even as individuals, we Americans cannot define our political and moral identities without making them accountable to an estimate of racism's potency in American life. Our liberalism or conservatism, our faith in government intervention or restraint and our concept of social responsibility on issues from diversity to school reform—all these will be, in part, a response to how bad we think racism is. The politically liberal identity I was born into began to fade as my estimate of American racism declined. I could identify with a wider range of American ideas and possibilities when I thought they were no longer painted by racism. Many whites I know today, who are trying to separate themselves from the shame of America's racist past, will overestimate racism to justify a liberal identity that they hope proves that separateness. First the estimation, then the identity.

7   Recently, after a talk on a college campus, a black girl stood up and told me that she was "frequently" stopped by police while driving in this bucolic and liberal college town. A professor on the same campus told me that blacks there faced an "unwelcome atmosphere—unwelcomeness being a newly fashionable estimation at racism's potency on college campuses today. Neither of these people offered supporting facts. But I don't think they were lying so much as "spinning" an estimation of racism that shored up their political identities.

8   We are terrible at discussing our racial problems in America today because we just end up defending our identities and the political power we hope those identities will align us with. On that day in Manhattan I caught the first cab that came along. And I should have been happy just for the convenience of good service. That I also saw this minor event as evidence of something, that I was practicing a kind of political sociology as well as catching a cab—that is the problem.

■ QUESTIONS FOR ANALYSIS AND DISCUSSION

1. Both Steele and Derbyshire label themselves as "conservatives." Do you think that Steele would agree with Derbyshire's defense of racial profiling? Why or why not?
2. What is the "elephant in the living room" to which Steele alludes in paragraph 3? How does it relate to the argument in favor of racial profiling?
3. Steele comments that racial profiling has become "an 'identity' issue like affirmative action." In what ways are these issues similar? What is the coded argument that they both veil? Explain.
4. Steele admits that the first available cab stops to pick him up, much to his relief. Do you think he would have written the same essay if the cab had passed him by instead?

■ WRITING ASSIGNMENTS

1. Look up some of the cases described by Kennedy and Derbyshire in their essays and evaluate the role racial profiling played in the corresponding legal arguments. Write an analysis of the issue based on your research. Support your analysis with additional information provided by the two authors in their essays.

2. How would Kennedy and Derbyshire debate Bain's experience? Based on the essays of the three men and drawing from their specific statements, create a fictitious debate between the three, using Bain's arrest as the subject for the debate.

3. Visit *Horizon Magazine*'s online site <www.horizonmag.com/6/racial-profiling .asp> and take the racial profiling test. Write an essay in which you discuss the test, your results, and racial profiling in America today.

4. Teenagers often complain that they are watched more closely in stores because it is believed they are more likely to be shoplifters. John Derbyshire reasons that young white males are probably more likely to be stopped by the police than elderly black females. Write an essay in which you consider the validity of other kinds of profiling, such as that based on age, income, or gender. What assumptions of criminal behavior correspond to these groups? If racial profiling is wrong, is it also wrong to profile on the basis of other criteria? Why or why not?

CHAPTER 14

What Makes a Family

The American family has always been in a state of transition, deeply influenced by the social and economic landscape. How we envision the concept of family is based largely on our personal history and the values we share. Many of our ideas regarding the "traditional family" are based on models generations old, touted by politicians and perpetuated by media archetypes. However, the role the American family plays as a social and moral barometer is undeniable. In 1996, a nation-wide poll conducted by the *Los Angeles Times* reported that 78 percent of respondents felt dissatisfied with today's moral values, with half of this group identifying divorce as a key problem.

Many sociologists tell us that our vision of family is not based on reality, but on social ideals and media images. Television programs from the 1950s and '60s rerun illusions of seemingly perfect families: polite children, neat and orderly homes, strong moral values, happy marriages, and social harmony. Such images may make us feel that our own families fall short of the ideal mark. Stepfamilies, same-sex relationships, divorce, single-parent households, and extended families force us to redefine, or at least reexamine, our traditional definitions of family. This chapter considers two aspects of family: "Rethinking the Nuclear Family" and "Gay Marriage and Partnering."

We open the chapter with an examination of how we have based our vision of the perfect family on a media-constructed ideal. In "The New Nostalgia," Rosalind Barnett and Caryl Rivers explain that this perception has serious ramifications for the current generation as they try to achieve a fabricated ideal. "What's Happening to Marriage?" an essay prepared by the National Marriage Project, presents an alternative point of view, urging young Americans to make a stronger commitment to marriage despite increasing skepticism that marriage simply doesn't last. Joel Achenbach offers a humorous yet revealing perspective on parenting in "Working Dads, Unite!" Tired of being "guilted by experts," Achenbach calls for fathers to stand up and admit that they want to spend more time at work. Stephanie Coontz describes the ways women have been scapegoated by politicians and conservatives as the source of our social problems in "Single Mothers: A Menace to Society?" We conclude the section with an essay by Dan Quayle, "Why I Think I'm Still Right," in which the former vice president contends that a two-parent traditional household is still the best environment for children.

The next section features several different viewpoints on same-sex marriage and gay partnerships. Should couples of the same gender be legally allowed to marry? What problems and benefits might result? In "Virtually Normal," Andrew Sullivan challenges the prohibition of gay marriages by asserting that such unions will only strengthen and support the institution of the family. Columnist Jeff Jacoby questions this stance in "Who Says Banning Gay Marriage Is Immoral?" Laurie Essig takes a different view as she explains why, although gay marriage is legal in her state of residence, she has no desire to marry her same-sex partner, nor can she understand why any gay couple would want to marry in the first place. And E. G. Graff walks us through the history of marriage as a cultural institution in "What's Love Got to Do With It?"

RETHINKING THE NUCLEAR FAMILY

The New Nostalgia
Rosalind Barnett and Caryl Rivers

Many Americans feel that the family is in a state of decline. Underlying this feeling is the social sense that the decay of the family is linked to the loss of "traditional family" values held in the 1950s. However, in the next article, Rosalind Barnett and Caryl Rivers tell us that we are in much better shape than we may think. Rather than apologizing for the state of our families, Barnett and Rivers say we should start appreciating our amazing adaptability. In fact, the very "problems" that critics of new family structures want us to fix may be actually creating stronger families and healthier relationships.

Barnett is a clinical psychologist and expert on dual-earner family issues, the American family, and work/family relations. She is a senior research scientist in the women's studies program at Brandeis University. Rivers is a professor of journalism at Boston University and the author of several books, including *Slick Spins and Fractured Facts* (1996). Her television drama *A Matter of Principal* won a Gabriel Award as one of the best television dramas of the year. The following article is excerpted from Barnett and Rivers's co-authored book, *He Works/She Works* (1996).

■ **BEFORE YOU READ**

Are you familiar with the television programs *Leave It to Beaver, Father Knows Best, Ozzie and Harriet,* and *The Donna Reed Show?* What kinds of families are portrayed in these programs? What was the established family structure, and how was that structure depicted in these programs? Do you think they represent family life in the 1950s?

■ AS YOU READ

Why do parents in two-earner families feel guilty? What is the source of their guilt and what social expectations perpetuate it? How founded are their fears?

1   As he drops his daughter off at a very good day-care center staffed with well-trained, caring professionals, a father worries whether he's doing the right thing. Should he or his wife stay home with their daughter, even though they can't afford to? Will day care cause some problems for his child that he can't foresee? Is he doing something dreadfully wrong because his life is so different from that of his parents back in the 1960s?

2   Guilt is the universal malady of working parents today, and one to which parents in past generations were seemingly immune. Did the woman setting out in the covered wagon for a prairie homestead worry about whether her children would be well-adjusted out there on the plains? Did the women in colonial times, whose days were filled with manufacturing the clothing and food that would keep the family alive, brood about whether she and her children were "relating" well enough? Did Victorian men worry that their children were spending too much time with nannies?

3   It's safe to say that no modern working parent has completely escaped those sudden, painful stabs of guilt. It might help to understand its roots, and we will examine them in this essay. But first, it's important to realize how this guilt feeds into the mistaken conviction that today's parents can't quite measure up to those of the past.

4   It is imperative, we believe, to understand that those of us in the two-earner lifestyle have been as good or *better* parents—not worse ones—than the Ozzie and Harriet model. The two-earner lifestyle that has emerged in the past two decades of American life has been a positive development, fitting well with current economic realities. While it has not been easy, men and women have connected to the world of work and its demands while expending considerable energies on nurturing their children. If this meant that at times they felt they had to juggle too much, that there were times they wondered if they were going to be able to do it all, they lived with that problem—and, most often, survived it in good health and good humor.

5   We are already raising a generation of children in two-earner families: if we really want them to be stressed, let's tell them that what we are doing is all wrong, that what we *should* be doing was what their grandparents did in the 1950s, and that that's the ideal they, too, should aspire to.

6   In fact, we must prepare our children for the world they will really be facing—not some rosy image of a past that never was all that wonderful, and which is not going to return. With a global economy on the horizon and with the United States continually having to compete with the Pacific Rim and Europe, we will probably continue to see a pattern of downsizing of U.S. companies as high productivity becomes the watchword of industry. Men's real wages have been declining since 1960. The median income of employed white men in

1967 was about $19,800; by 1987 it was $19,008, adjusted for changes in earning power—roughly $750 less than it had been twenty years before.[1]

7   More and more, women's wages will become essential to a family's economic survival—as they are today in so many families. The days when women worked for "extras" are long gone and are not likely to return. More and more, in such an unstable work world, men will turn to their families as a way of finding self-esteem. And women, like men, will prepare early for careers or jobs in which they will be involved for most of their lives. Economists who predict the shape of the early twenty-first century say that no longer will people remain in one job for a lifetime; the successful worker of the future will be one who is flexible, learns quickly, and can transfer skills from one work setting to another. Women may have to retool as the economy twists and turns, but few will have the chance to be full-time, lifelong homemakers.

8   Not until we accept the working woman as the norm can we adequately prepare our sons and daughters for the lives they will really be leading. Our study conclusively proves that holding up the rigid and outdated lifestyle of the 1950s as a sacred icon will only add stress to their busy and often difficult lives. Perhaps the most important finding of the study on which the book is based is the fact that for working couples, a gap in gender-role ideology is a major and consistent source of stress. It is not merely annoying when your image of the ideal family does not jibe with that of your spouse; it can be an important source of stress in your life.

9   On the whole, we do not help young women prepare for the flexible jobs that will protect their economic futures and that of their families if we plant in their heads the idea that what they really *ought* to be doing is staying home. We don't prepare young men for the deep involvement they are going to have with their families if we create in them the idea that the *real man* doesn't change a diaper or drive the kids to nursery school.

10   But the actual facts about what is good for real American couples and their families today may well be drowned out by the clamor of what we call the "new nostalgia," a combination of longing for the past and a fear of change. It not only feeds the guilt that can tie individuals in knots, but can be a major stumbling block to the creation of corporate and government policies that will help, not hinder, working families. The new nostalgia has already calcified in politics, in the media, in a spate of books that tell us we must retreat to the past to find solutions for the future. The messages of a reinvigorated right wing in politics pushes a brand of family values with which Ozzie and Harriet would have felt quite at home.

11   One steady, unblinking beacon of a message has been flashed to men and women over the past few years: Change is dangerous, change is abnormal, change is unhealthy. This message permeates our mass media, the books we read, the newscasts to which we listen, the advice from pop psychologists, the covers of news magazines. Men and women must stay in their traditional places, or there will be hell to pay.

12   The message comes in many guises. It comes from warnings that women are working themselves into sickness on the so-called second shift—the house-

work women do *after* they come home from work—doing so much that their health is in peril. It may be national magazines trumpeting the mommy track, concluding that women *must* seek achievement on a lower and slower track than men. It nests in headlines that claim women are simply unable to juggle the demands of work and home and are going to start having heart attacks just like men. It may be warnings that day care interferes with the mother-child bond—despite solid evidence to the contrary. It can be found in publications concluding that if people would just stay married or kids would stop having sex, all our social problems would disappear. It may be Robert Bly warning in *Iron John* that men have become weak, thanks to women, and they must find their warrior within.[2]

13   It is more than a backlash against the women's movement. Indeed, many of the warnings insist that men had better stay in the straitjacket of traditional masculinity. These warnings are implicit in the spate of action-adventure movies aimed at young men, in which manhood is defined as domination and mayhem, with no ongoing relationships with women or children. They are implicit also in the ease with which the word "wimp" is hurled at any political candidate who does not employ slash-and-burn macho tactics.

14   The flashing message is only intensified by widely held but outdated ideas from the behavioral sciences proclaiming that a man's emotional health is primarily based on his life at work, while a woman can only find her identity through being a wife and mother. So intense has this bias been that, until recently, social scientists rarely examined men's lives at home or women's at home.

15   The new nostalgia fuels the guilt that many working parents feel. The flames are fanned by forces that many working parents don't understand—and the media play a large role in keeping the bonfire going.

16   Never in the past were parents confronted with constant and ongoing images of how their grandparents raised children. Old folk remedies may have been passed down, mothers and grandmothers gave advice, but times changed and people changed with them. It was the natural order of things. But parents today see Ozzie and Harriet and Donna Reed and all their ilk as wonderful, ideal parents night after night on the tube. (Even the President and the First Lady, whose lives resemble most working families' more than those of the old sitcoms, admitted that one of their favorite TV shows was reruns of *The Donna Reed Show*.)

17   The power those TV parents still exercise has more to do with the durability of images than it does with today's reality. As *Newsweek* magazine points out. "The television programs of the fifties and sixties validated a family style during a period in which today's leaders—congressmen, corporate executives, university professors, magazine editors—were growing up or beginning to establish their own families. (The impact of the idealized family was magnified by the very size of the postwar generation.)"[3]

18   It can be somewhat frightening to think that the legislators who are voting on family leave plans, the aides who create policies for presidential candidates, the chairs of university departments who decide what courses should be

staffed—all have inside their heads the very same model of the way our families *ought* to be.

19   Yale historian John Demos points out that "the traditional model reaches back as far as personal memory goes for most of us who currently teach and write and philosophize."[4] And in a time when parents seem to feel a great deal of change, "that image is comfortingly solid and secure, counterpoint to what we think is threatening to the future." In other words, an unreal past seems so much more soothing than a bumpy present.

20   In the manufacture of guilt, add another potent factor: the nature of the news media. The news media don't hold a mirror up to the world, despite what news executives like to say. The media not only select which facts and images will be churned out as news, but they determine the frame in which those images will be presented. This frame is most often one of conflict, tension, and bad news. It's no wonder everyone assumes that the American family is falling apart. That's all we read or hear about.

21   Of course, what the TV news anchor *doesn't* tell you is that in the past, "family" issues were rarely part of the news. Domestic violence and child abuse were shameful secrets, rarely written about. Dramatic images of violent crime were less a part of daily life. In Washington, D.C., where Caryl Rivers grew up in the 1950s, some 90 percent of crimes by young men were committed by juveniles who were graduates of one city reform school. But you never saw their victims on the evening news—because there were no minicams to capture the mayhem on video and the kids didn't spray the streets with automatic weapons fire. Americans now consume many hours of television each day—and research shows that people who watch a lot of TV see the world as a much more frightening place than it really is.

22   One of the bad-news frames of which the media is most fond today is the decline of the family. A Nexis search of the past five years reveals 15,164 references in the press to either the breakup or the decline of the American Family, a chorus that is relentless. Do you believe that the decline of the family is absolute fact? Many Americans do. However, most media coverage of the alleged decline of the family does not answer a key question: What position of lofty perfection is the family declining *from?* There must have been a golden age of family, since the words *decline* and *breakdown* imply that very notion. But when was it? And do we really want to go back there? . . . Many Americans believe that past family life was always—and should always be—like *Leave It to Beaver, Father Knows Best,* and *Ozzie and Harriet.*

23   In fact, the 1950s *were* a golden age—economically. Never before had Americans enjoyed a period of such affluence. Women reversed a long-standing trend of moving into the workforce, and went home. One would have thought that with women in such a traditional role, social critics would have approved. Mom was by the hearth with her kiddies nestled about her. But what happened? In perhaps no decade were women savaged as thoroughly as they were in the 1950s. Sweet Mom, baking cookies and smiling, was destroying her kids—the boys, anyway. While nostalgic articles in today's media hark back to the happy 1950s, the critics of the time had no such beatific vision.

24   Social critic Philip Wylie, in his best-seller *Generation of Vipers,* coined the term "Momism." Momism, Wylie decreed, had turned modern men into flaccid and weak creatures and was destroying the moral fiber of America.[5] When American soldiers sometimes failed to resist "brainwashing" when they were captured by the Communist Chinese in Korea, it was said that their overprotective mothers had made them weak and traitorous. Children often got too much Mom and not enough Dad. The memoirs of men who grew up in the 1950s reveal that their fathers were often distant and overly involved in work.

25   It's not surprising that depression was the malady that most affected women in those years. What Betty Friedan termed "the feminine mystique" came smack up against the lengthening life span. At a time when society was telling women that home and children must be their whole lives, technology and medicine were making those lives last longer than ever before in history. Women would outlive, by many years, the childhood of their last-born, and the notion that they could spend all their time in mothering was absurd. The cultural messages and the reality of the modern world were at odds. Kept out of the world of work in the suburban cocoons, physically healthier and longer-lived than their sisters in the past, women were far more prone than men to depression, and in fact the mental health of married women had reached crisis proportions by the end of the 1960s. Statistics rolling in from all across the developed world were so grim that the noted sociologist Jessie Bernard called marriage a "health hazard" for women.[6][. . .]

26   One reason we hear so much today about how wonderful the 1950s were is that the voices of male cultural critics are those most often heard. Men and women, it seems, remember that era differently. In many ways, the 1950s were good for men. It was the first era in history in which the average middle-class man could, on his salary alone, support a lifestyle that was available only to the upper classes in the past. The mental health of men was vastly superior to that of women. The daughters of 1950s homemakers rejected en masse a lifestyle that created so much depression and anxiety, and few women today would trade their lives for that of their mothers. But many men today would gladly opt for the financial security and economic opportunities their fathers had.

27   Because the 1950s live on endlessly in rerun land, it is hard for us to accept that the decade was such an atypical time. Stephanie Coontz warns that "the first thing to understand about the Fifties family is that it was a fluke, it was a seven-year aberration in contradiction to a hundred years of other trends."[7] And Arlene Skolnick notes that "far from being the last era of family normality from which current trends are a deviation, it is the family patterns of the 1950s that are deviant."

28   Deviant? Ozzie and Harriet? Indeed they were, from the point of view of history. Theirs was an atypical era, in which trends that had been firmly established since early in the century briefly reversed themselves in the aftermath of World War II. For years, women had been moving into the workforce in increasing numbers. The high point was epitomized by Rosie the Riveter, the symbol of the women who went to work in the factories to produce the tanks and the guns and the planes needed to win the war. After the war, during the brief period of unprecedented affluence when America's economic engine was unchallenged

throughout the world, women went home, and the American birthrate suddenly jumped to approach that of India. A huge baby-boom generation grew up in middle-class affluence that no other generation had known. [. . .]

29   By the late 1970s, the 1950s were only a distant echo. The women's movement unleashed women's untapped brainpower and economic potential, and millions of women flooded into the marketplace. This movement of women into the workforce in the late twentieth century is one of the great mass migrations of history, comparable to the push westward and the move from the farms to the cities. And just as those mass movements changed not only the face of American society but the lives of individual citizens, so too did this new movement rearrange our social geography.

30   Despite the media drumbeat about the decline of the family, despite those thousands of references to its decay in the media, the American family is a thriving institution. We are both more centered on the family and more frantic about its problems than our European counterparts. Arlene Skolnick writes, "Paradoxically, Americans have a stronger sense of both familistic values and family crisis than do other advanced countries. We have higher marriage rates, a more home-centered way of life, and greater public devotion to family values."[8]

31   The notion that we can return to some mythic past for solutions to today's problems is tempting, but it is a will-o'-the-wisp that should not engage our attention. The idea that we can find in Ozzie and Harriet and their lives workable solutions for today's rapidly changing economic and social patterns is a dream. Unfortunately, when we combine the new nostalgia with the old images, it's like taking a trip with only a 1955 road map to guide us. The old landmarks are gone, little backroads have become interstates, and the rules of the road have changed beyond recognition. Absurd as this image is, it is often precisely what we do when we think about the American family. Women who hurry out to work every morning can be trapped into thinking that *this* isn't what they are supposed to be doing; men with their hands in soapsuds after dinner can remember their fathers sitting and reading the newspaper while mom did the dishes. It's easy to feel resentful.

32   But the new nostalgia is more than harmless basking in the trivia of the past—it is, in fact, a major toxin affecting the health of today's men and women.

33   The "family values" crusade of the right wing, to the degree that it succeeds in invading people's thoughts, will only add to the stress of working couples by insisting on a model from the past that is increasingly impossible to achieve in the present. One newspaper poll showed that the proportion of adults who agreed with the statement "A preschool child is likely to suffer if his or her mother works" went up between 1989 and 1991.

34   As science, that statement is nonsense. There is plenty of evidence that no child is "likely to suffer" if his or her mother goes to work. But those adults agreeing with that statement—who are likely to be working parents—will get a huge dose of unnecessary stress. The family values crusade, to the extent that it

glorifies homemakers and demonizes working mothers, will succeed only in making the lives of twenty-first-century Americans harder. The clock will not be turned back to the 1950s; that's as impossible as holding back the tide. If Americans feel guilty because they can't live up to some impossible, vanished ideal, their health will suffer.

35   The era of the two-earner couple may in fact create more closeness in families, not less. As the fast track becomes less available, men and women alike will turn to family for a strong sense of self-esteem and happiness. Divorces may decline as marriages become once again economic partnerships more like the ones they were before the industrial revolution. Today, of course, marriages will be overlaid with the demands for intimacy and closeness that have become a permanent part of modern marriage, but fewer people will be able to waltz easily out of marriage, as they might have in the days when a thriving economy made good jobs easy to come by. Middle-class couples are marrying later and many women are getting established in a career before having children. This pattern may promote more responsibility and happier marriages than those in the 1950s, when many young people felt they had to get married to have sex and discovered their emotional incompatibility only after they had children.

36   Negotiation and juggling, not the established gender roles of yesterday's marriages, are the features of modern coupledom. Who will stay home when a child is sick? Who will take over what jobs when one partner has to travel for an important meeting? Whose career will take first place? Who has to sacrifice what—and when? Such issues, ones that June and Ward and Ozzie and Harriet never had to confront, are the day-to-day problems that today's partners have to wrestle with.

37   Today's couples are facing the demands of very busy lives at home and at work. If you listen to the media tell their story, they are constantly stressed, the women are disenchanted with trying to have it all, and the men are bitter about having to do work their fathers never had to do. Some of this is true—no lifestyle offers nirvana. On the other hand, today's couples have a better chance at achieving full, rich lives than did the men and women of the sitcom generation. While it may be no picnic to juggle the demands of work and family, research shows that working women are less depressed, less anxious, and more zestful about their lives than are homemakers. Today's man may have the stress of caring for children, but his relationship with his children may be warmer and more satisfying than was his own with his father. Most men who grew up in the 1950s don't tell stories about the warm, available dads we see in the sitcoms. More often, they speak of fathers who were distant, preoccupied, and unable to communicate with their sons on more than a superficial level. Many modern fathers, in fact, set out purposely to design lives that will be the exact opposite of their distant fathers'.

38   In their lifestyle, the men and women in our study are at the opposite end of the spectrum from Ozzie and Harriet. Both are breadwinners; and if they have children, both share the nitty-gritty everyday chores of parenting. They are true partners in supporting and nurturing their children and each other.

They represent the new face of the American family, and the world they live in is not very much like the America of the 1950s.

39   Despite the ersatz glow of the new nostalgia, not much would be gained by a trip back in time—even if it were possible. How many women would want to return to the widespread depression and mental health problems of the 1950s? Catherine E. Ross, an Illinois University sociologist says, "Any plea to return to the 'traditional' family of the 1950s is a plea to return wives and mothers to a psychologically disadvantaged position, in which husbands have much better health than wives."[9] And since research shows that the emotional health of the mother has a strong impact on her children, that's one bit of time travel we don't especially want to take.

NOTES

1. Janet Riblett Wilkie, "The Decline in Men's Labor Force Participation and Income and the Changing Structure of Family Economic Support." *Journal of Marriage and the Family* 53 (February 1991).

2. Robert Bly, *Iron John* (New York: Holiday House, 1994).

3. "What Happened to the Family?" *Newsweek* Special Issue (Winter 1990/Spring 1991).

4. "What Happened to the Family?" (Winter 1990/Spring 1991).

5. Philip Wylie, *Generation of Vipers* (New York: Holt, Rinehart [AMP] Winston, 1955).

6. Jessie Bernard, *The Future of Marriage* (New York: World-Times, 1972).

7. Stephanie Coontz, *The Way We Never Were: American Families and the Nostalgia Trap* (New York: Basic Books, 1992).

8. Cited in Arlene Skolnick, *Embattled Paradise: The American Family in an Age of Uncertainty* (New York: Basic Books, 1991).

9. Quoted in Betsy A. Lehman. "Parenting Pain—But Also Joy," *Boston Globe* (February 15, 1993).

■ QUESTIONS FOR ANALYSIS AND DISCUSSION

1. What is "gender-role ideology" as described in paragraph 8? In paragraphs 8 through 14, how are traditional roles described as harmful to men?

2. What are the authors' attitudes toward changes in family roles and responsibilities? What phrases, images, and metaphors help you to identify their attitudes in paragraphs 11 through 22?

3. In paragraphs 23 through 28, the authors describe what the 1950s were really like for families. What were some of the problems these families faced? Why have we adopted this family model as the ideal?

4. What improvements do the authors see in today's families? Why do they believe that such families are becoming stronger rather than falling apart? Do you agree with their conclusions? Explain.

5. What are the author's attitudes toward the media? How important is the media's role in shaping American perceptions about the state of the family?

Families on Television

In her 1992 book, *The Way We Never Were: American Families and the Nostalgia Trap,* sociologist Stephanie Coontz addresses the influence television has on our images of ideal family life. The problem, explains Coontz, is that such visions "bear a suspicious resemblance to reruns of old television series."

> When I begin teaching a course on family history, I often ask my students to write down ideas that spring to mind when they think of the "traditional family." Their lists always include several images. One is of extended families in which grandparents [were] an integral part of family life. [. . .] In traditional families, my students write—half derisively, half wistfully—men and women [. . .] committed themselves wholly to the marital relationship, experiencing an all-encompassing intimacy that our more crowded modern life seems to preclude (8).

For over fifty years, television has broadcast into American homes idealized images of American families, families that many of us think were the norm only a few decades ago, and families against which we measure our own. Examine the two photos pictured here of the 1950s family unit of *Leave It to Beaver* and of the modern family in *Everybody Loves Raymond.* How have these programs influenced our cultural expectations of family life? How are the families featured in the programs similar, and how are they different? You may wish to watch at least one episode of each program to assist you in answering the questions that follow.

■ QUESTIONS FOR ANALYSIS AND DISCUSSION

1. What influence does television's depiction of family life have on our own personal expectations of family? When you were younger, did you ever wonder why your family wasn't like the ones shown on TV? Did you ever compare your family to the families featured on TV? Explain.
2. What is the family dynamic of *Leave It to Beaver?* What lifestyle did it promote? What expectations, if any, did it create?
3. What is the family dynamic of *Everybody Loves Raymond?* What lifestyle does it promote? Is the family structure different from *Leave It to Beaver,* or essentially the same?
4. In addition to *Everybody Loves Raymond,* how does *Leave It to Beaver* compare to other comedy shows focusing on modern family life, such as CBS's *Yes, Dear,* Fox's *Grounded for Life,* and ABC's *My Wife and Kids?*
5. In your opinion, what is the "traditional family"? How does your vision of family compare to the families featured on prime time television? Is your vision at all influenced by such programs? Explain.

What's Happening to Marriage?

The National Marriage Project

Divorce has become an American way of life. Before they reach the age of 18, nearly half of all children will see their parents' marriage terminate. What does this fact reveal about American attitudes toward marriage? In the next article, the National Marriage Project examines the current and shifting view of marriage in our society. While the authors of this article seem to accept the fact that divorced families are now an established part of the American social landscape, they disagree that we should accept this trend quietly.

The National Marriage Project at Rutgers University defines its mission as follows: "to strengthen the institution of marriage by providing research and analysis that informs public policy, educates the American public, and focuses attention on a problem of enormous scope and consequence." The project is codirected by David Popenoe, professor of social and behavioral sciences at Rutgers University, and Barbara Dafoe Whitehead, a sociologist who writes extensively on issues related to marriage and the family. Popenoe is the author of *Life Without Father* (1996) and *Disturbing the Nest* (1988). Whitehead is the author of *Divorce Culture* (1997) and *Goodbye to Girlhood* (1999).

■ BEFORE YOU READ

The next article addresses American attitudes toward marriage. What is your personal opinion of marriage and divorce? Is marriage an archaic institution, no longer practical in today's society?

■ AS YOU READ

Is marriage a life goal for you? Do you think you should be married before deciding to have a family? Do you think women's improved economic role outside the home has influenced their feelings about marriage?

1   Americans haven't given up on marriage as a cherished ideal. Indeed, most Americans continue to prize and value marriage as an important life goal, and the vast majority of us will marry at least once in a lifetime. By the mid-thirties, a majority of Americans have married at least once.

2   Most couples enter marriage with a strong desire and determination for a lifelong, loving partnership. Moreover, this desire may be increasing among the young. Since the 1980s, the percentage of young Americans who say that having a good marriage is extremely important to them as a life goal has increased slightly.

3   But when men and women marry today, they are entering a union that looks very different from the one that their parents or grandparents entered.

4   As an *institution,* marriage has lost much of its legal, religious and social meaning and authority. It has dwindled to a "couples relationship," mainly designed for the sexual and emotional gratification of each adult. Marriage is also quietly losing its place in the language. With the growing plurality of intimate relationships, people now tend to speak inclusively about "relationships" and "intimate partners," burying marriage within this general category. Moreover, some elites seem to believe that support for marriage is synonymous with far-right political or religious views, discrimination against single parents, and tolerance of domestic violence.

5   One reason Americans prize marriage so highly is that it is the source of deeply desired benefits such as sexual faithfulness, emotional support, mutual trust and lasting commitment. These benefits cannot be found in the marketplace, the workplace or on the Internet.

6   Most people aspire to a happy and long-lasting marriage. And they will enter marriage with the strong desire and determination for a lifelong and loving partnership. While they are married, most couples will also be sexually faithful to each other as long as the marriage lasts. According to the most comprehensive study of American sexual behavior, married people are nearly all alike in their sexual behavior: "once married, the vast majority have no other sexual partner, their past is essentially erased."[1]

7   However, although Americans haven't stopped seeking or valuing happy and long-lasting marriage as an important life goal, they are increasingly likely to find that this goal eludes them. Americans may marry but they have a hard time achieving successful marriages. One measure of success is the intactness of the marriage. Although the divorce rate has leveled off, it remains at historically high levels. Roughly half of all marriages are likely to end in divorce or permanent separation, according to projections based on current divorce rates. Another measure of success is reported happiness in marriage. Over the past

two decades, the percentage of people who say they are in "very happy" first marriages has declined substantially and continuously. Still another measure of success is social confidence in the likelihood of marital success. Young people, and especially young women, are growing more pessimistic about their chances for a happy and long-lasting marriage.

8   The popular culture strongly reinforces this sense of pessimism, even doom, about the chances for marital success. Divorce is an ever-present theme in the books, music and movies of the youth culture. And real life experience is hardly reassuring; today's young adults have grown up in the midst of the divorce revolution, and they've witnessed marital failure and breakdown first-hand in their own families and in the families of friends, relatives, and neighbors. For children whose parents divorced, the risk of divorce is two to three times greater than it is for children from married parent families. But the pervasive generational experience of divorce has made almost all young adults more cautious and even wary of marriage. The percent of young people who say they agree or mostly agree with the statement "one sees so few good marriages that one questions it as a way of life" increased between 1976 and 1992, while the percent of those who say it is very likely they will stay married to the same person for life decreased over the same time period for both males and females.[2]

9   Marriage is losing much of its status and authority as a social institution. According to legal scholar John Witte Jr., "the early Enlightenment ideals of marriage as a permanent contractual union designed for the sake of mutual love, procreation and protection is slowly giving way to a new reality of marriage as a 'terminal sexual contract' designed for the gratification of the individual parties."[3] Marriage has lost broad support within the community and even among some of the religious faithful. In some denominations, clergy avoid preaching and teaching about marriage for fear of offending divorced parishioners. Marriage is also discredited or neglected in the popular culture. Consequently, young adults, who desperately want to avoid marital failure, find little advice, support and guidance on marriage from the peer or popular culture or from parents, clergy or others who have traditionally guided and supported the younger generation in matters of mating and marrying.

10   This loss of broad institutional support for marriage is evident in the marital relationship itself. Not so long ago, the marital relationship consisted of three elements: an economic bond of mutual dependency; a social bond supported by the extended family and larger community; and a spiritual bond upheld by religious doctrine, observance and faith. Today many marriages have none of these elements.

11   The deinstitutionalization of marriage is one of the chief reasons why it is more fragile today. For most Americans, marriage is a "couples relationship" designed primarily to meet the sexual and emotional needs of the spouses. Increasingly, happiness in marriage is measured by each partner's sense of psychological well-being rather than the more traditional measures of getting ahead economically, boosting children up to a higher rung on the educational

ladder than the parents, or following religious teachings on marriage. People tend to be puzzled or put off by the idea that marriage has purposes or benefits that extend beyond fulfilling individual adult needs for intimacy and satisfaction. In this respect, marriage is increasingly indistinguishable from other "intimate relationships" which are also evaluated on the basis of sexual and emotional satisfaction.

12   When we look at the state of marriage today, it is useful to consider the behavior and attitudes of young women. Historically, women are the normsetters in courtship and marital relationships as well as the bearers of the cultural traditions of marriage. (To test this proposition, simply compare the amount of space devoted to marriage in women's magazines to that in men's magazines.) So women's attitudes and expectations for marriage are an important measure of overall social confidence in the institution and a weathervane of which way the marital winds are blowing.

13   What do we know about the mating and marrying behavior of young women today? For one thing, women are older when they marry. The median age of first marriage for a woman is now 25, compared to 20 in 1960. For another, women who marry today are much less likely to be virgins than women in past decades. For yet another, most young women enter marriage after having lived with a partner, though not always their marriage partner. Finally, a significant percentage of young women have children outside of marriage. Women who become single mothers are less likely to ever marry.

14   Compared to men, young women are more disenchanted with marriage. This growing pessimism is particularly pronounced among teenage girls. For high school girls who expect to marry (or who are already married), the belief that their marriage will last a lifetime has declined over the past two decades while high school boys have become slightly more optimistic. Teenage girls are increasingly tolerant of unwed childbearing. Indeed, they outpace teenage boys in their acceptance of unwed childbearing today, a notable reversal from earlier decades when teenage girls were less tolerant of nonmarital births than teenage boys.

15   Women's disenchantment should not be taken as a lack of interest in having husbands. But their growing pessimism may reflect two convergent realities. One is women's higher expectations for emotional intimacy in marriage and more exacting standards for a husband's participation in childrearing and the overall work of the household. These expectations may not be shared or met by husbands, and thus the mismatch may lead to deep disappointment and dissatisfaction. The other is women's growing economic independence. Because women are better educated and more likely to be employed outside of the home today than in the past, they are not as dependent on marriage as an economic partnership. Consequently, they are less likely to "put up" with a bad marriage out of sheer economic necessity and more likely to leave when they experience unhappiness in their marriages. Moreover, because wives are breadwinners, they expect a more equitable division of household work—not always a fifty-fifty split but fairness in the sharing of the work of the home. Thus, the

experience of working outside the home contributes simultaneously to greater economic independence and less tolerance for husbands who exempt themselves from involvement with children and the household. "I don't need a grown-up baby to take care of," is a complaint often voiced by working married mothers.

16   Not all the marriage indicators are negative. Here and there, we find modest signs of positive change in attitudes or behavior.

17   Married couples today are somewhat less likely to end up in divorce court than several years ago. After one and a half decades of sharp increase, the divorce rate has declined slightly and stabilized in recent years. Although projections based on the current rate suggest that close to half of all marriages are likely to end in divorce or permanent separation, that projection could change if the divorce rate declines in the future.

18   The rate of unwed births has declined for the third year in a row, although the ratio of unwed and marital births remains the same. Mainly as a consequence of the modest reduction in both divorce and unwed births, the percentage of children living in single parent families has remained stable in the past two years (1996–98).

19   The percentage of young Americans who say that having a good marriage is extremely important to them as a life goal has increased slightly since the 1980s.

Conclusion: Marriage Is Weakening But It Is Too Soon to Write Its Obituary . . .

20   Taken together, the marriage indicators do not argue for optimism about a quick or widespread comeback of marriage. Persistent long-term trends suggest a steady weakening of marriage as a lasting union, a major stage in the adult life course, and as the primary institution governing childbearing and parenthood. Young people's pessimism about their chances for marital success combined with their growing acceptance of unwed parenthood also do not bode well for marriage.

21   Nonetheless, there are some reasons for hope. For example, given the increased importance of marriage to teenagers, it is possible that this generation will work hard at staying happily married. The decline in the unwed birth rate is also a good sign. And there are stirrings of a larger grass-roots marriage movement. Churches in more than a hundred communities have joined together to establish a common set of premarital counseling standards and practices for engaged couples. A marriage education movement is emerging among marriage therapists, family life educators, schoolteachers and some clergy. In the states, legislators are considering or have passed bills creating incentives for engaged couples to receive premarital education. Florida now requires marriage education for high school students.

22   This is not the first time in the millennial-long history of western marriage that marriage has seemed headed for the dustbins and then recovered. Certainly it is possible that the nation is on the cusp of a turnaround in some

of the negative marital trends. Perhaps the last four decades have merely been a "great disruption," in the words of social analyst Francis Fukuyama, and Americans will respond to the weakening of marriage with renewed dedication and success in achieving the goal of a long-lasting happy marriage. The positive trends bear watching and are encouraging, but it is still too soon to tell whether they will persist or result in a comeback of this important social institution.

NOTES

1. Robert T. Michael, John H. Gagnon, Edward O. Laumann, and Gina Kolata, *Sex in America: A Definitive Survey* (Boston, MA: Little, Brown and Company, 1994), 105.
2. Norval D. Glenn, "Values, Attitudes and the State of American Marriage," *Promises to Keep: Decline and Renewal of Marriage in America,* ed. David Popenoe, Jean Bethke Elshtain, and David Blankenhorn (Lanham, MD: Rowman and Littlefield, 1996), 21.
3. John Witte, Jr., *From Sacrament to Contract: Marriage, Religion, and Law in the Western Tradition* (Louisville, KY: Westminster John Knox Press, 1997), 209.

■ QUESTIONS FOR ANALYSIS AND DISCUSSION

1. In paragraph 4, the authors state, "As an institution, marriage has lost much of its legal, religious and social meaning and authority." What do the authors mean by this assertion? Is this statement self-evident? Do you agree or disagree with them, and why?
2. Is declaring strong support for marriage discriminatory against people who are not married or who are divorced? Is such a viewpoint tolerant of domestic violence? Explain.
3. According to the authors, in what ways has popular culture reinforced a sense of "doom" regarding one's chances of having a happy marriage? Can this pessimistic attitude become a self-fulfilling prophecy? Explain.
4. Evaluate John Witte Jr.'s statement in paragraph 9 that marriage today is more of a "terminal sexual contract" between adults. Do you think this is true? Does such a pronouncement go against the evidence? Explain.
5. What reasons do the authors give for why women are less likely to want to marry or to stay married?
6. What is the long-term outlook for marriage? How does your perspective fit into the outlook the authors describe?

Working Dads, Unite!
Joel Achenbach

Although few people may admit it publicly, many parents consider work to be less demanding than family life and actually look forward to work as a needed reprieve from family demands. Parents are constantly juggling the responsibilities of work and family and dealing with social pressure to spend more time with their children. The next article takes a light look at the issue of working parents—specifically working fathers. Joel Achenbach proclaims that he would like to spend more time at work and less time with his children, and he wants more fathers to admit that they feel the same way.

Achenbach is a reporter for the *Washington Post.* He is the author of several books, including *Why Things Are and Why Things Aren't* (1996), *Captured by Aliens: The Search for Life and Truth in a Very Large Universe* (1999), and *It Looks Like a President, Only Smaller* (2001). This article first appeared in the November 1998 issue of *GQ* magazine.

■ BEFORE YOU READ

What social pressures do working parents face in today's society? Is it possible to indeed have it all—a happy family life and a successful career?

■ AS YOU READ

Would your opinion of this essay be different if a mother wrote it? Would it be as funny? truthful? Are social expectations different for working fathers than for working mothers?

1   One of my goals is to spend less time with my kids. I am sure many parents feel the same way. It's not that I don't like my kids. I enjoy their company in measured doses. A couple of my kids I like in particular and in fact there's one, the little one, the "baby," whom I find cute and adorable—maybe not as much as a year ago, when she was toddling, but still hangin' in there.

2   Just once I wish someone famous would hold a press conference on national television and say something like this: "I am making this career change with some reluctance. It has taken much soul-searching. But I have finally decided that it is time for me to spend far less time with my family. Instead I will concentrate on working, achieving and climbing the ladder of success—the way adults used to before they were guilt-tripped into staying home with these goddamned kids."

3   No one ever says anything like that.

4   Instead we live in a society that is obsessed with children—spending time with them, fostering their growth, raising them properly. Now there's no date too early to start spending time with your kids—you can begin when they're still fetuses—and no limits to the amount of caring and nurturing you should smother them with. There are books that say you should coo at your wife's belly to stimulate the little critter's brain, help him get into a decent college. When the child is born, you're expected to cancel all previously scheduled activities, notify your friends that you will not be needing their acquaintance further and devote yourself to the nurturing of a potential genius. Certainly you are not supposed to do anything as uncaring, old-fashioned and pathologically self-important as go to work.

5   If you are single and you work all the time, you feel like you are some kind of pathetic drone, and you moan to your friends, "I have no life." If you are married and you work all the time, you feel like a monster, someone who is willfully condemning his children to a life of shooting heroin.

6   What's more, men are now expected to help raise their children as though they were their own. Since the kids usually are, in fact, their own, this expectation seems to have at least some superficial basis in morality. Still, I don't think the idea has been adequately scrutinized. (Has it been reviewed by OSHA?) Let me repeat. I like spending time with my kids. (OK, I don't like playing with the dolls. The little one's dolls are all named Sally. She is apparently under the delusion that a duck can be named Sally, when the proper name for a duck is something like Frieda.) Sometimes I even read them a book or take them to the park, though during such moments I am weirdly self-aware of what I'm doing, as though a tiny voice were telling me, "You are reading to your kids!" or, "You are taking them to the park!"

7   The problem is, if you get too close to your children emotionally, you start feeling horribly guilty about going off to work, and they sense that guilt the way dogs smell fear. They become geniuses at laying on a guilt trip. They know instinctively how to adopt an expression right out of those Save the Children advertisements. Kids raised in spoiled yuppie splendor suddenly become Third World urchins with no shoes.

8   Invariably, this is successful, and instead of going to work, the guilt-stricken parent is on his knees obeying the commands of a 4-year-old who will burst into tears if he does not agree to attend her tea party. (I've labored to raise my three daughters to be as masculine as possible and have tried to show them how to hit and scream and fall off things, but every time I turn my back, they are secretly holding a tea party.)

9   The truth is, the great tension in the modern family is over who will have the privilege of getting away from the house and getting something accomplished. The best-selling book *The Time Bind,* by Arlie Hochschild, tapped into the fact that many people find the workplace calmer and more hospitable than their homes.

10   But what people seem to forget nowadays is that work is a good thing in and of itself. Work is noble! Work is as fundamental to a functioning society as child rearing. Why is it that in TV commercials these days you constantly see men in business attire cavorting with little kids, tossing them in the air, goofing off? Can't these guys get back to work? Give those kids to the nanny!

11   Of course, when I go to work, I don't actually work. Don't be absurd. "Work" is a noun that refers to a location, not to an activity. Half the people at the office are zombies from lack of sleep the night before, when their monstrous children decided to play with trucks at three in the morning. Then there's the other side of the equation: If we have to spend all our time at home raising kids, then we have to spend more time at work doing the serious goofing off that we used to do at home. Some things are not negotiable; one of them is that a man of maturity and broad interests must spend most of his time at work reading the sports section or playing solitaire on his computer or even,

if possible, sleeping. Sleeping can be tricky in a crowded office, but it can be done, especially if you master the art of sleeping with your eyes open and remember to make mumbling noises every once in a while.

12   Men in the old days really knew how to work. They would work from dawn to midnight and never see their families, and when they hit middle age they'd be awash in guilt and regret. They would hate themselves, and their children would hate them, and their wives would hate them most of all, and everyone would go into therapy. This was the American way. It was dysfunctional, to be sure, but stuff got accomplished, modern society was constructed, everyone owned a house with a big yard.

13   Now, no matter how much time we spend parenting, it is still not enough. This is the age of guilt, and if we don't feel guilty enough, some expert will come along and try to help us feel worse. The experts nag us about what we eat, what we think, how we live. A particularly ripe field is in nagging parents, who feel plenty guilty and vulnerable already. The basic message is that if we don't expose our newborns to Mozart and wave flash cards in front of their faces, they will end up like the pathetic dullards our parents were.

14   For example, recently a major metropolitan paper ran an opinion piece by some sociologist types saying that day care is harmful to the development of a child's brain. This is an extension of the long-accepted research that shows that babies deprived of maternal warmth do not develop properly. Now the researchers say that care by *anyone* other than parents—even the best, warmest, most attentive day-care providers—wreaks havoc. The child's brain does not become properly wired.

15   The researchers have offered a bold solution. They propose that both mother and father work two-thirds of a normal forty-hour workweek. They call this the four-thirds solution, because that is what you get if you add up the fractions. This is obviously meant to shame people into working fewer hours while not placing the entire guilt trip on working mothers. Because—let's be honest—as guilty as men feel these days about going off to work, most women feel worse, thanks in part to the naggers.

16   The four-thirds solution is, needless to say, still more evidence that the greatest danger to society is the advice of professional sociologists.

17   On earth, my home planet, there is something called the job market. The job market is not shaped by the good intentions of academics. My impression of the job market right now is that there is not a huge demand for two-thirds employees. The only jobs with those kind of hours pay crappy wages and provide no benefits. More to the point, a professional person does not flourish working twenty-seven hours a week, particularly when roughly fifteen of those hours must be spent, as previously noted, staring out the window and wondering what became of one's youth. My math says that leaves only twelve hours a week for actual work. The way a professional person flourishes is to work harder and better—and, yes, longer—than the person in the next cubicle.

18   It's been that simple for a few millennia now, and it's not going to change. What the sociologists don't understand (perhaps because they work in academia, where there is tenure and other such antimarket concepts) is that the

forty-hour workweek is *already* a concession to a demand for civilized balance between work and family. It's a modern luxury. Many people work longer hours, maybe fifty or sixty, not because they are workaholics but because their job requires that they kick ass. They'll work at two in the morning if that is what the task requires. They'll work in the rain. They'll work through ulcers and shingles and raging fevers. This is because if they don't, they will gradually lose the competition to the other person, who has no life whatsoever and works eighty hours a week, even through bouts of malaria.

19   Eventually, we all reach a point in life when we don't have to work quite so many hours. This point is known as one's sixties. This is when you can stop competing and start horsing around with dolls. Such a person is known as a grandparent.

20   Many of whom, I'd like to point out, are not spending nearly enough time grandparenting.

■ QUESTIONS FOR ANALYSIS AND DISCUSSION

1. What is the tone of this essay? Select a few sentences from the article and analyze them. How does Achenbach use humor to engage his audience? Explain.
2. Achenbach comments that "if you are married and you work all the time, you feel like a monster, someone who is willfully condemning his children to a life of shooting heroin" (paragraph 5). What issue is Achenbach masking with his humor? What pressures do working parents face when dealing with the conflict between work and spending more time with their children? Is this pressure more acute for fathers or mothers? Explain.
3. In paragraph 9, Achenbach notes that "the truth is, the great tension in the modern family is over who will have the privilege of getting away from the house and getting something accomplished." Although Achenbach may have made this comment in jest, it underlies an issue for many parents—the value society places on work and its connection to accomplishment. What accounts for this social value system? Why do we tend to place greater value on work done outside the home than within it? Explain.
4. What does Achenbach think of researchers' solution of having both parents work a four-thirds workweek? What does Achenbach think of researchers in general? Explain.
5. Who is Achenbach's audience? What clues reveal this audience? Do you think this essay would be as effective in magazines such as *Time, Good Housekeeping, The New Yorker,* or *Rolling Stone?* Explain.

Single Mothers: A Menace to Society?

Stephanie Coontz

Although some people may lament the loss of the perceived ideal traditional family—father, mother, and children—others have come to accept, and embrace, a variety of new family configurations, including single parenthood. In the next piece,

Stephanie Coontz objects to the stigmatization of single mothers. A single mother herself, as well as a professional family historian, Coontz points out that the castigation of single mothers provides society with someone else to blame for its problems, someone with little political and economic power to overcome such a label. She also argues that the attack on single motherhood is an attack on career mothers, divorced mothers, and women's independence itself.

Coontz is a professor of history and family studies at Evergreen State College in Olympia, Washington. She is the author of *The Way We Never Were: American Families and the Nostalgia Trap* (1992) and *The Way We Really Are* (1998). This article was first published by *Vogue* magazine.

■ BEFORE YOU READ

Does society tend to blame single mothers for its ills? Do politicians single them out as scapegoats? What is our social view of single motherhood? Is our opinion different for single fathers? If so, what accounts for this difference?

■ AS YOU READ

How does Coontz's son Kristopher contribute to her essay? Which details about Kristopher did you find the most memorable? Why do you think Coontz includes her son in her essay? Explain.

1   Every time I open the paper or turn on the news, it seems as if some politician or pundit is going on about the dire consequences of single parenthood. And it's not just conservatives who are leading the way. Today, politicians and columnists of every stripe are proudly trumpeting a new "bipartisan consensus"—single mothers are a menace, both to society and to their children. After a brief period when people stopped calling babies illegitimate simply because the father was not married to the mother, the term has come back in favor, often attached to invective so mean-spirited and cynical that it takes my breath away.

2   A *Newsweek* column called illegitimacy "the smoking gun in a sickening array of pathologies—crime, drug abuse, physical and mental illness, welfare dependency." The children of unwed mothers have been labeled a "social scourge," a "catastrophe," and a "plague." Senator Daniel Patrick Moynihan, a Democrat, believes that women who have children out of wedlock are engaging in "speciation." *Washington Post* columnist David Broder describes kids of single mothers as a whole new "breed" of human, a fearsome "species of fatherless children." Even President Clinton, himself the son of a single mother, now declares that single parenthood "is simply not right. . . . You shouldn't have a baby when you're not married. You just have to stop it."

3   Well, it's a little too late for me to just stop it. I am a never-married mother with a thirteen-year-old son. That's my boy—wrestling with all the dilemmas adolescents face in contemporary America—they're talking about: Kristopher, the social scourge. The catastrophe. The plague.

4   "You obviously didn't inherit a normal set of eardrums," I tease him, over the blare of his electric guitar, "but I don't really think you're a new species." He grins when I joke about it like this, but he reads the papers, and I can tell it hurts. Teenagers take labels very seriously. All too often they try to live up to them. Or down, as the case may be.

5   Actually, I'm luckier than most unwed mothers. Because I'm white, middle class, and an older, well-established professional, my son is sometimes afforded a sort of honorary "legitimacy." Last year, for instance, when Kris objected to a particularly cruel remark a health teacher made about single mothers, the teacher hastened to explain that she knew his mom was educated, financially secure, and clearly loving. "I'm sure your mom had good reasons for what she did."

6   In other words, I could tell Kris not to worry; he's different from those other bastards. For most of the attacks are directed at the unwed welfare mom, the teenager supposedly popping out new babies each year to get a hike of about $65 in her monthly check. These are the families that former secretary of education Bill Bennett is referring to when he proposes cutting off economic assistance to single mothers and sending their children to orphanages. That's not me and my son. If I sit back and keep my mouth shut, no one would guess that my creative, compassionate youngster is one of "those" kids. Why, then, does this rhetoric make me so angry?

7   For one thing, as a family historian I know that unwed motherhood is not the major cause of our society's problems, and eliminating one-parent families won't fix our inner cities or end the need for welfare. In fact, a recent study shows that even if we reunited every single child in America with his or her biological father, two-thirds of the children who are poor today would still be poor.

8   For another, while most of the cant about the dangers of illegitimacy is aimed at welfare mothers, I am struck by how quickly the rhetoric broadens into a more general attack on women's independence, sexual or otherwise. On television talk shows, the new family-values crusaders usually begin by castigating welfare mothers but move easily to "careerist" mothers who supposedly "rationalize material benefits in the name of children": divorced women who put "individual self-actualization" before their kids' needs; women who remarry and expose their daughters to the "severe risk" of sexual abuse by men who lack a biological "investment" in the child. One *Fortune* magazine writer even blames our social ills on modern women's rejection of "the idea that women must be 'cared for' by men." It's time, they agree, to "restigmatize" both divorced and unwed mothers.

9   Yet I know from personal experience as well as sociological research that there are hundreds of paths leading to single motherhood. Some of the stories I hear would seem irresponsible to even the most ardent proponent of women's rights; others stem from complicated accidents or miscalculations that even the most radical right-winger would probably forgive.

10   At one recent workshop that I taught on family history, I met three other never-married mothers. One was a young girl who had gotten pregnant "by accident/on purpose" in the hope that her unfaithful boyfriend would marry her.

It hadn't worked, and in the ensuing year she had sometimes left her baby unattended when she went out on dates. Jarred into self-examination after being reported for neglect, she realized that going back to school and developing job skills was a more promising way of escaping her abusive parents than chasing boys. Another, now 25, had been 15 when she became pregnant. She considered abortion, but she would have had to drive 600 miles, by herself, to the nearest provider, and she didn't even have the money for a hotel room. Both these mothers had relied on welfare assistance to get by in their early days, and one was still on food stamps as she attended school. The third was an older, well-paid professional woman who had had three wedding plans fall through. She attributed her failures with men to being caught between two value systems: She was old-fashioned enough in her romantic fantasies to be attracted to powerful, take-charge men, but modern enough in her accomplishments that such men generally found her threatening. Her last fiancé had left her pregnant at age 35. With her biological clock ticking "now or never" in her ear, she decided to have the child.

11   What government agency or morals committee should decide which of us single mothers to stigmatize and which to excuse, or which of our children should be packed off to orphanages? And what about the harmful effects of such pronouncements and penalties on the children of all single parents?

12   Most single parents don't need politicians to heap more guilt and self-doubt on our heads. We're doing that just fine on our own. Everywhere we turn we see the statistics: Children of single-parent families are more likely to drop out of school, exhibit emotional distress, get in trouble with the law, and abuse drugs or alcohol than children who grow up with two biological parents. Most single parents I talk to are consumed with guilt and fear. What they really need to hear is that single parenthood is not an inevitable sentence of doom for their children.

13   And that is just what the latest research confirms. Yes, there are disadvantages for kids of single parents, but they are often exaggerated. Most kids, from every kind of family, turn out fine, so long as their mothers are not overly stressed by poverty, ongoing conflict with the child's father, or the very stigmatization that the family-values crusaders want to magnify.

14   Of course there are significant hardships in raising a child alone, but even a "traditional" family structure does not guarantee that the two parents are responsible, involved, or stable. Every family configuration offers certain challenges and benefits. My son, for example, has always been more candid with me about what's happening at school than most of his friends from two-parent families are with their parents. But I have more trouble than those parents finding opportunities to meet with Kris's teachers or scheduling a consistent time each day to be around while he does his homework. This turns out to be a common theme for most single parents. We typically spend less time supervising our child's schoolwork or talking to teachers than do adults in two-parent families, drawbacks that may lead to lower grades for our children. But we also spend more time talking with our kids, which might explain why children from

one-parent households are often more articulate and experience themselves as more effective in the world than their two-parent peers. Single parents tend to praise good grades more than adults in two-parent families, providing an impetus for their children to do well in school. But single parents also tend to get angrier when grades fall, a reaction that may lead the child to be defiant—often lowering grades even more.

15   There are other trade-offs as well. While children of single mothers often grow up to be closer to their mothers and have more respect for working women than do kids from two-parent homes, the adolescent years can be particularly trying. When a teenager begins to demand more freedom, a single mother has no ally to take over the nay-saying when her voice gives out or to help her withstand a youth's insistence that "everybody else's parents let them. . . ." Like many single parents who have close relationships with their children, I sometimes have trouble setting firm limits, even though I've studied the problems that result when adults allow their youngsters too much say in decision-making. I worry that my son's self-confidence, and his sense that he is entitled to negotiate limits with others the way he has always negotiated them with me, might lead him to do risky things or to question authority once too often.

16   Surely it's more helpful for single parents to learn how to build on their strengths and compensate for their weaknesses than to be demonized by politicians and pundits. But taking a stand against "immoral" mothers is easier and less politically risky than tackling the problems of our inner cities or addressing middle-class concerns. Our government will spend $25 billion on Aid to Families with Dependent Children this year, compared with roughly $51 billion in direct giveaways to business and another $53 billion in corporate tax breaks. But debates over subsidies only get posed in moral terms when women's sexuality is involved. After savings-and-loan corporations failed to "just say no" to risky loans and promiscuous spending on salaries, Uncle Sam handed them $150 billion of the taxpayers' money. "Underwriting tragedy is one thing," *Washington Post* columnist Charles Krauthammer has explained. "Underwriting wantonness is quite another."

17   The new family-values crusade also appeals to those uncomfortable with the changing role of women by emphatically reestablishing men as the "heads of the household." Consult your dictionary to discover the distinction between a legitimate and an illegitimate child. According to the traditional definition, any child brought into the world without a man's name on the birth certificate is not real, not authentic, not genuine, not rightful. No matter how much love, care, and effort a woman devotes to raising her children, she can never make them legitimate. But no matter how little effort a man puts into child rearing, his name on a piece of paper makes all the difference in the world to the status of his child.

18   The ancient Greeks believed that a woman contributed nothing to the production of a child except nine months' storage. In English common law, a child born out of wedlock was a *filius nullius*—the child of no one. We haven't come very far when President Clinton remarks that unwed mothers are "raising a

whole generation of children who aren't sure they're the most important person in the world to anybody."

19   I don't want to use my personal and professional advantages to wheedle special dispensation for my son to be treated as a legitimate person. Legitimacy and respect should be the birthright of every child. Anyone needing appeal to tradition to stand up for that principle can look back more than 300 years, to the response of the Native Americans when the first family-values crusaders arrived on the shores of this continent. The Jesuit missionaries told the Montagnais-Naskapi Indians that men should take control of women's sexuality and parents should discipline their children more harshly. Otherwise, the good fathers warned, your wives and daughters may give birth to babies that do not belong to you. The Native Americans were not persuaded. "You French people love only your own children," they replied, "but we love all the children of the tribe." Wouldn't it be nice if America's politicians quit beating up on single parents and started operating from that set of family values?

■ QUESTIONS FOR ANALYSIS AND DISCUSSION

1. How does Coontz support her claim that "there are hundreds of paths leading to single motherhood" (paragraph 9)? Does Coontz persuade you of this viewpoint? Why is it an important component of her argument? Explain.

2. Coontz explains that her son is afforded a kind of legitimacy because she herself is white, educated, and middle class. How does Coontz feel about such a social reaction to her son? Explain.

3. Explain what Coontz means when she says that anti-illegitimacy rhetoric often "broadens into a more general attack on women's independence, sexual or otherwise" (paragraph 8). Does Coontz convince you of this point? Why or why not?

4. Explain how the choice of words in the author's introduction conveys Coontz's attitude to her opposition.

5. Analyze Coontz's conclusion. Why do you think she includes the anecdote about Native Americans and European Jesuits? What makes this ending particularly powerful and appropriate to Coontz's article?

Why I Think I'm Still Right

Dan Quayle

In a much-publicized speech in 1992, then Vice President Dan Quayle criticized television character Murphy Brown for having a child out of wedlock, without a father present. He condemned the character for "mocking the importance of fathers by bearing a child alone and calling it another 'lifestyle choice.'" In the next article, written for the May 28, 2001, issue of *Newsweek,* Quayle explains why almost a decade later, he still believes his position on this issue was correct.

Quayle is the author of several books, including *Worth Fighting For* (1999) and *The American Family: Discovering the Values That Make Us Strong* (1996), coauthored with psychologist Diane Medved.

■ BEFORE YOU READ

Is there something morally objectionable about a woman who decides to have a baby alone? Does it matter if the woman is financially secure and well educated? Is the decision indeed simply "another lifestyle choice"?

■ AS YOU READ

Does the fact that this article is written by a former vice president of the United States influence your opinion of his argument?

1   In 1992, I caused quite a stir by criticizing a television sitcom whose main character got pregnant by her ex-husband and then sent him packing. This was not an attack on single mothers, but a rallying cry for the role fathers should play. It just bothered me that the character didn't seem to care that there would be no father to help raise the child—fathers were presented as irrelevant. My concern has always been for the welfare of the child. Clearly, it is best to have a mother and a father, preferably in a happy monogamous relationship, actively involved in rearing and nurturing their child.

2   The recent Census numbers reflect what we already know: there is extraordinary turmoil and dysfunction in families today. What has caused this? Time pressure is one reason. With the "in touch" world we live in, the outside world intrudes on every waking hour. Time formerly spent in family activities is now spent on the computer, in front of the television, on the phone, in the car, and at the mall. We are a harried society. Economic pressure is another reason. Most of our 21st-century innovations are costly, so more parents are working. Our mobile society has caused more families to live far away from the support system of their extended families. Add to this the fact that pop culture focuses too much on tearing down institutions that give us a sense of stability and it is no wonder the traditional family structure is in decline.

3   Even so, there are encouraging signs in the Census report. The number of teenage pregnancies is in decline. Then there is the rise in the number of single dads. That is a cultural shift in which women—and the courts—are more comfortable giving custody to the parent best able to care for the child. It is heartening to see men asking to be given more care-giving responsibility for their children. Still, we should hope and pray that both parents would stay deeply and positively involved in the rearing of their children.

4   Children must have hope. Hope comes from a good education, good values, self-respect and living in a society that values every person, expects the best from each of us and does not tolerate abhorrent behavior. Faith in God fosters hope by providing a rationale for living. A two-parent household, with a mother

and a father, is still the best place to raise a child. Current reality is that many children are not being raised by two parents. Since the support system of extended families, which in the past helped to fill the void, in most cases does not exist today, we need to expand the idea of extended family to include neighbors, friends, and community. We each need to look around our community and see who needs nurturing. Is there a child who needs a grandparent figure, a father figure, a mother figure or a doting aunt or uncle? Fill that void for them.

5   The sense of belonging, of being a part of a greater whole, is what is sorely needed by so many. With the wisdom and love that is passed to others, with the hope that is engendered in a child's soul, we, as a nation, will be placed on a better path to the future.

■ QUESTIONS FOR ANALYSIS AND DISCUSSION

1. Summarize Quayle's argument. What is he advocating? How can you tell? How does he support his argument? Explain.
2. Evaluate Quayle's list of the roots of "turmoil and dysfunction in families today." How do you think the other authors in this section, such as Rosalind Barnett, Caryl Rivers, and Stephanie Coontz, would respond to this list?
3. Does Quayle contradict himself when he says that an "encouraging sign" in the census report includes the rise in the number of single dads? In light of his criticism of the television character Murphy Brown, is this assertion fair? Why or why not?

■ WRITING ASSIGNMENTS

1. What is the state of marriage in the United States today? In your own words, define what marriage is. Then address the definitions of marriage as described by the authors in this section. Write an essay evaluating the definitions of marriage offered by the authors and comparing these definitions to the American reality of marriage.
2. Select one or two of the articles in this section and write an essay in which you argue for or against its premises. As you formulate your response, pay attention to the author's personal bias, his or her tone, and how the arguments involved are supported. Address these issues in your essay.
3. Write an essay supporting or questioning Stephanie Coontz's claim that "debates over subsidies only get posed in moral terms when women's sexuality is involved" (paragraph 16). To support your position, research the congressional and public debate on social welfare programs in your state or, if you wish, across the nation.
4. What images come to mind when you hear the phrase "single father"? List as many qualities and ideas as you can. Compare your ideas concerning single mothers, as described by the authors in this section and American social ideology. How are they different? How much of that difference has to do with our cultural expectations of men's and women's roles as parents? Explain.

GAY MARRIAGE AND PARTNERING

Virtually Normal
Andrew Sullivan

Many homosexual relationships closely pattern those of more conventional hetero-sexual marriages. The partners live together, buy houses in the suburbs, raise children, and plan their retirement. These couples maintain that the natural capstone of their commitment and lifestyle should be the legalization of their relationships through marriage, which affords legal protection and social legitimacy. Opponents of same-sex marriage, including some people who are tolerant of homosexuality, say that marriage is and should remain a uniquely heterosexual institution. In his essay, Andrew Sullivan argues that marriage ought to be a legal option for gay couples desiring this kind of union.

Sullivan is a former senior editor and current columnist for *The New Republic.* His work has appeared in many journals and magazines, including *The Wall Street Journal,* the *Washington Post,* and *Esquire.* He received his Ph.D. from Harvard University in political science and lectures in universities across the country on many different political issues, including allowing gays in the military and marriage rights for homosexuals. He is the author of *Virtually Normal: An Argument About Homosexuality* (1995) from which this essay was taken.

■ BEFORE YOU READ

Do you think that gay couples should be allowed to marry? Why or why not?

■ AS YOU READ

Consider how Sullivan argues his case. What support does he use to buttress his ideas? What assumptions does Sullivan make regarding his audience and their shared set of values?

1   The most common conservative argument against same-sex marriage is that the public acceptance of homosexuality subverts the stability and self-understanding of the heterosexual family. But here the conservative position undermines itself somewhat. Since most conservatives concede the presence of a number of involuntarily homosexual persons, they must also concede that these persons are already part of "heterosexual" families. They are sons and daughters, brothers and sisters, even mothers and fathers, of heterosexuals. The distinction between "families" and "homosexuals" is, to begin with, empirically false; and the stability of existing families is closely linked to how homosexuals are treated within them. Presumably, it is against the interest of heterosexual families to force homosexuals into roles they are not equipped to play and may disastrously perform. This is not an abstract matter. It is quite common that homosexual fathers and mothers who are encouraged into heterosex-

ual marriages subsequently find the charade and dishonesty too great to bear; spouses are betrayed, children are abandoned, families are broken, and lives are ruined. It is also common that homosexual sons and daughters who are denied the love and support of their families are liable to turn against the institution of the family, to wound and destroy it, out of hurt and rejection. And that parents, inculcated in the kind of disdain of homosexuality conservatives claim is necessary to protect the family, react to the existence of gay children with unconscionable anger and pain, and actually help destroy loving families.

2   Still, conservatives may concede this and still say that it's worth it. The threat to the stability of the family posed by public disapproval of homosexuality is not as great as the threat posed by public approval. How does this argument work? Largely by saying that the lives saved by preventing wavering straights from becoming gay are more numerous than the lives saved by keeping gay people out of heterosexual relationships and allowing greater tolerance of gay members of families themselves; that the stability of the society is better served by the former than by the latter. Now, recall that conservatives are not attempting to assert absolute moral truths here. They are making an argument about social goods, in this case, social and familial stability. They are saying that a homosexual life is, on the face of it, worse than a heterosexual life, as far as society is concerned. In Harvard psychologist E. L. Pattullo's words,

> Though we acknowledge some influences—social and biological—beyond their control, we do not accept the idea that people of bad character had no choice. Further, we are concerned to maintain a social climate that will steer them in the direction of the good.

3   The issue here is bad character and the implied association of bad character with the life of homosexuals. Although many conservatives feel loath to articulate what they mean by this life, it's clear what lies behind it. So if they won't articulate it, allow me. They mean by "a homosexual life" one in which emotional commitments are fleeting, promiscuous sex is common, disease is rampant, social ostracism is common, and standards of public decency, propriety, and self-restraint are flaunted. They mean a way of life that deliberately subverts gender norms in order to unsettle the virtues that make family life possible, ridicules heterosexual life, and commits itself to an ethic of hedonism, loneliness, and deceit. They mean by all this "the other," against which any norm has to be defended and any cohesive society protected. So it is clear that whatever good might be served by preventing gay people from becoming parents or healing internal wounds within existing families, it is greatly outweighed by the dangers of unleashing this kind of ethic upon the society as a whole.

4   But the argument, of course, begs a question. Is this kind of life, according to conservatives, what a homosexual life *necessarily* is? Surely not. If homosexuality is often indeed involuntary, as conservatives believe, then homosexuals are not automatically the "other"; they are sprinkled randomly throughout society, into families that are very much like anybody else's, with characters and bodies and minds as varied as the rest of humanity. If all humans beings are, as conser-

vatives believe, subject to social inducements to lead better or worse lives, then there is nothing inevitable at all about a homosexual leading a depraved life. In some cases, he might even be a paragon of virtue. Why then is the choice of a waverer to live a homosexual rather than a heterosexual life necessarily a bad one, from the point of view of society? Why does it lead to any necessary social harm at all?

5   Of course, if you simply define "homosexual" as "depraved," you have an answer; but it's essentially a tautologous one. And if you argue that in our society at this time, homosexual lives simply *are* more depraved, you are also begging a question. There are very few social incentives of the kind conservatives like for homosexuals *not* to be depraved: there's little social or familial support, no institution to encourage fidelity or monogamy, precious little religious or moral outreach to guide homosexuals into more virtuous living. This is not to say that homosexuals are not responsible for their actions, merely that in a large part of homosexual subculture there is much a conservative would predict, when human beings are abandoned with extremely few social incentives for good or socially responsible behavior. But the proper conservative response to this is surely not to infer that this behavior is inevitable, or to use it as a reason to deter others from engaging in a responsible homosexual existence, if that is what they want; but rather to construct social institutions and guidelines to modify and change that behavior for the better. But that is what conservatives resolutely refuse to do.

6   Why? Maybe for conservatives, there is something inherent even in the most virtuous homosexual life that renders it less desirable than the virtuous heterosexual life, and therefore merits social discouragement to deter the waverers. Let's assume, from a conservative perspective, the best-case scenario for such a waverer: he can choose between a loving, stable, and responsible same-sex relationship and a loving, stable, and responsible opposite-sex relationship. Why should society preference the latter?

7   The most common response is along the lines of Hadley Arkes, the conservative commentator, who has written on this subject on occasion. It is that the heterosexual relationship is good for men not simply because it forces them to cooperate and share with other human beings on a daily basis but because it forces them into daily contact and partnership with *women:*

> It is not marriage that domesticates men; it is women. Left to themselves, these forked creatures follow a way of life that George Gilder once recounted in its precise, chilling measures: bachelors were twenty-two times more likely than married men to be committed to hospitals for mental disease (and ten times more likely to suffer chronic diseases of all kinds). Single men had nearly double the mortality rate of married men and three times the mortality rate of single women. Divorced men were three times more likely than divorced women to commit suicide or die by murder, and they were six times more likely to die of heart disease.

I will leave aside the statistical difficulties here: it's perfectly possible that many of the problems Arkes recounts were reasons why the men didn't get married, rather than consequences of their failing to do so. Let's assume, for the sake of argument, that Arkes is right: that marriage to a woman is clearly preferable to being single for an adult man; that such a man is more likely to be emotionally stable, physically healthy, psychologically in balance; and that this is good for the society as a whole. There is in this argument a belief that women are naturally more prone to be stable, nurturing, supportive of stability, fiscally prudent, and family-oriented than men, and that their connection to as many men as possible is therefore clearly a social good. Let's assume also, for the sake of argument, that Arkes is right about that too. It's obvious, according to conservatives, that society should encourage a stable opposite-sex relationship over a stable same-sex relationship.

8   But the waverer has another option: *he can remain single*. Should society actually encourage him to do this rather than involve himself in a stable, loving same-sex relationship? Surely, even conservatives who think women are essential to the successful socialization of men would not deny that the discipline of domesticity, of shared duties and lives, of the inevitable give-and-take of cohabitation and love with anyone, even of the same sex, tends to benefit men more than the option of constant, free-wheeling, etiolating bachelorhood. But this would mean creating a public moral and social climate which preferred stable gay relationships to gay or straight bachelorhood. And it would require generating a notion of homosexual responsibility that would destroy the delicately balanced conservative politics of private discretion and undiscriminating public disapproval. So conservatives are stuck again: their refusal to embrace responsible public support for virtuous homosexuals runs counter to their entire social agenda.

9   Arke's argument also leads to another (however ironic) possibility destabilizing to conservatism's delicate contemporary compromise on the homosexual question: that for a wavering woman, a lesbian relationship might actually be socially *preferable* to a heterosexual relationship. If the issue is not mere domesticity but the presence of women, why would two women not be better than one, for the sake of children's development and social stability? Since lesbianism seems to be more amenable to choice than male homosexuality in most studies and surveys, conservatism's emphasis on social encouragement of certain behaviors over others might be seen as even more relevant here. If conservatism is about the social benefits of feminizing society, there is no reason why it should not be an integral part of the movement for women to liberate themselves completely from men. Of course, I'm being facetious; conservatives would be terrified by all the single males such a society would leave rampaging around. But it's not inconceivable at all from conservative premises that, solely from the point of view of the wavering woman, the ascending priorities would be: remaining single, having a stable, loving opposite-sex relationship, and having a stable, loving same-sex relationship. And there is something deliciously ironic about the sensibility of Hadley Arkes and E. L. Pattullo finding its full fruition in a lesbian collective.

10   Still, the conservative has another option. He might argue that removing the taboo on homosexuality would unravel an entire fabric of self-understand-

ing in the society at large that could potentially destabilize the whole system of incentives for stable family relationships. He might argue that now, of all times, when families are in an unprecedented state of collapse, is not the occasion for further tinkering with this system; that the pride of heterosexual men and women is at stake; that their self-esteem and self-understanding would be undermined if society saw them as equivalent to homosexuals. In this view, the stigmatization of homosexuals is the necessary corollary to the celebration of traditional family life.

11   Does this ring true? To begin with, it's not at all clear why, if public disapproval of homosexuals is indeed necessary to keep families together, homosexuals of all people should bear the primary brunt of the task. But it's also not clear why the corollary really works to start with. Those homosexuals who have no choice at all to be homosexual, whom conservatives do not want to be in a heterosexual family in the first place, are clearly no threat to the heterosexual family. Why would accepting that such people exist, encouraging them to live virtuous lives, incorporating their difference into society as a whole, necessarily devalue the traditional family? It is not a zero-sum game. Because they have no choice but to be homosexual, they are not choosing that option over heterosexual marriage; and so they are not sending any social signals that heterosexual family life should be denigrated.

12   The more difficult case, of course, pertains to Arkes's "waverers." Would allowing them the option of a stable same-sex relationship as a preferable social option to being single really undermine the institution of the family? Is it inconceivable that a society can be subtle in its public indications of what is and what is not socially preferable? Surely, society can offer a hierarchy of choices, which, while preferencing one, does not necessarily denigrate the others, but accords them some degree of calibrated respect. It does this in many other areas. Why not in sexual arrangements?

13   You see this already in many families with homosexual members. While some parents are disappointed that their son or daughter will not marry someone of the opposite sex, provide grandchildren and sustain the family line for another generation, they still prefer to see that child find someone to love and live with and share his or her life with. That child's siblings, who may be heterosexual, need feel no disapproval attached to their own marriage by the simple fact of their sibling's difference. Why should society as a whole find it an impossible task to share in the same maturity? Even in the most homosexualized culture, conservatives would still expect over eighty percent of couples to be heterosexual: why is their self-esteem likely to be threatened by a paltry twenty percent—especially when, according to conservatives, the homosexual life is so self-evidently inferior?

14   In fact, it's perfectly possible to combine a celebration of the traditional family with the celebration of a stable homosexual relationship. The one, after all, is modeled on the other. If constructed carefully as a conservative social ideology, the notion of stable gay relationships might even serve to buttress the ethic of heterosexual marriage, by showing how even those excluded from it can wish to model themselves on its shape and structure. This very truth, of

course, is why liberationists are so hostile to the entire notion. Rather than liberating society from asphyxiating conventions it actually harnesses one minority group—homosexuals—and enlists them in the conservative structures that liberationists find so inimical. One can indeed see the liberationists' reasons for opposing such a move. But why should conservatives oppose it?

■ **QUESTIONS FOR ANALYSIS AND DISCUSSION**

1. Sullivan comments that conservatives fear homosexual marriage because it could "injure" the institution of the family. What is the basis of this concern? How does Sullivan address it? Which perspective do you support, and why?

2. Evaluate Sullivan's description of the conservative definition of sexuality in paragraph 3. Do you agree that this is a commonly held definition? How would you define "homosexual life"?

3. Sullivan expends a lot of effort addressing the views of conservatives, often referring collectively to his opposition as "they." What effect does this terminology have on the reader? Explain.

4. What is the reason, according to the author, for homosexual "depravity" (paragraphs 3 through 5)? Does his discussion of this issue strengthen or weaken the goals of his essay?

5. In paragraph 7, Sullivan introduces the arguments of conservative Hadley Arkes. How does Sullivan use Arkes's argument to support his own? Does he accurately evaluate Arkes's points? Do you agree with Sullivan's summary of Arkes's argument, that "conservatism is about the social benefits of feminizing society" (paragraph 9)? Explain.

6. What are "waverers"? What options do they have, according to Sullivan? How do these options apply to gay marriage?

7. How would different audiences receive this argument in favor of gay marriage? For example, would it be as effective in addressing a college audience as it would an older or more conservative audience? What factors could influence the successful reception of Sullivan's essay?

Who Says Banning Gay Marriage Is Immoral?

Jeff Jacoby

In the first article in this section, Andrew Sullivan argued that gay marriage should be a human right. But not everyone agrees with his point of view. Religious fundamentalists and social conservatives argue that same-sex unions are not natural or moral. Other people just do not see the need to make a conventional social institution such as marriage available to those with an unconventional lifestyle. In the next essay, Jeff Jacoby responds to the 1999 Vermont lawsuit brought by a gay couple suing for the right to marry based on the grounds that it was immoral to deny them the right to legalize their relationship. The court determined that forbidding gay marriage was an "affront to our humanity" and ruled in favor of same-sex unions. Jacoby questions their decision, wondering how morality entered the equation in the first place.

Jacoby is often called the "conservative voice" of the *Boston Globe* for which he is an editorial columnist. This article first appeared in the January 24, 2000, edition of the *Boston Globe.*

■ BEFORE YOU READ

Is marriage a moral "right," or is it a privilege granted by the state?

■ AS YOU READ

Review the discussion of logic in Part One. As you read, try to identify how Jacoby applies, or fails to apply, elements of logic in his essay. What assumptions does Jacoby make about his audience's prejudices?

1   In its long opinion in *Baker* v. *State,* the same-sex marriage case, the Vermont Supreme Court tries very hard to stay on legal ground. Writing for the majority, Chief Justice Jeffrey Amestoy begins by insisting that "the issue before the Court . . . does not turn on the religious or moral debate over intimate same-sex relationships." And for most of the next 45 pages, he confines his analysis to familiar legal territory: the rules of constitutional interpretation, the intentions of the Legislature, issues of equal protection, rights and remedies.

2   Yet by Page 44, he has arrived exactly where he said he wasn't going. The "essential aspect" of the plaintiffs' demand for a marriage license is, he writes, "fundamentally for inclusion in the family of state-sanctioned human relations." In the end, he holds that same-sex couples are entitled to the benefits and status of marriage as a matter of basic decency. Or, as a much-quoted line in the opinion puts it: Stretching the Vermont Constitution so it gives gay couples "legal protection and security for their avowed commitment to an intimate and lasting human relationship is simply, when all is said and done, a recognition of our common humanity."

3   Among those quoting that passage is *The New Republic,* which in its Jan. 10 edition vigorously endorses the opinion in Baker—with none of the court's reluctance to cast the issue in explicitly moral terms. "A ban on same-sex marriage . . . violates civil equality itself," TNR's full-page editorial asserts. It is "a moral anomaly that dehumanizes and excludes a significant portion of the human race." The "ultimate moral . . . answer" is to legalize full marriage for homosexuals, so good people must "keep marshaling the moral, religious, civic, and human reasons why it is an eminently important and noble thing to do."

4   This is the heart of the campaign for same-sex marriage—the claim that it is *immoral* not to permit men to marry men or women to marry women. Marriage statutes must be changed, the same-sex marriage advocates argue, because they are indecent, because they violate our ethical code. As slavery was

wrong—the Vermont court actually cites Dred Scott—so is it wrong to limit marriage to couples of the opposite sex.

5   Just one question: Says who?

6   If something is morally wrong, it is morally wrong always. That a society may tolerate—or embrace—an indecent practice does not make it less indecent. Chattel slavery was and is an abomination, no matter how many 19th-century Americans (or 20th-century Sudanese) thought otherwise. Suttee—the Hindu custom of cremating a deceased man together with his living widow—was evil, no matter how many Hindus believed it honorable. Apartheid was immoral, no matter how many South Africans approved of it.

7   Similarly, if barring men from marrying men is an affront to "our common humanity," as the Vermont justices write—if it is an ugly "moral anomaly," as *The New Republic* says—then it has *always* been so.

8   But where in the long record of human moral instruction do we find anyone saying such a thing?

9   All through the centuries of American slavery, there were men and women who cried out against it. There were always voices raised against suttee. Apartheid was condemned the world over.

10   And likewise every other wrongful societal practice. Europeans abused Indians in the New World? Bartolome de Las Casas, who sailed with Columbus, spent his last 50 years denouncing "the robbery, evil, and injustice" done by European colonists. Women were denied political rights? In 1777, Abigail Adams begged, "Do not put such unlimited power into the hands of husbands." From child sacrifice to anti-Semitism, from selling indulgences to selling women, there have always been moral teachers and people of conscience who refused to keep silent.

11   But where are the humanitarians and the great souls who said that limiting marriage to a man and a woman is wrong? Did Francis of Assisi plead for same-sex unions? Did the Buddha? Did Sojourner Truth? Did the Prophet Micah, who yearned for justice and kindness yearn also for male-male and female-female weddings? Did Martin Luther King, who devoted his life to "our common humanity?" Did Raoul Wallenberg, who risked all to thwart evil? Is there *anyone*—any foe of intolerance, any living saint—who decried even once the laws that kept homosexuals from marrying each other?

12   This is not an argument against same-sex marriage. (That's a different column.) It is an argument against the pretense that same-sex marriage is required as a matter of decency. There is no valid moral claim absent moral authority, and there is no moral authority for the claim that restricting marriage to opposite-sex couples is unjust.

13   It is a safe guess that no member of the Vermont Supreme Court grew up believing that the ban on same-sex marriage was a stain on society. None heard it from his pastor in church. None was taught to believe it in school. Until very recently, that idea simply did not exist.

14   By all means let us debate whether the timeless definition of marriage should be changed. But let us do so without the sham claim that *morality* clamors for a change. Our moral tradition, after all, speaks loudly and clearly about

what marriage means. And what it says—what it has always said—sounds nothing like the ruling in Vermont.

■ QUESTIONS FOR ANALYSIS AND DISCUSSION

1. Although Jacoby claims to argue only against the idea that banning gay marriage is "immoral," is his argument indeed based on a conservative perspective on morality? Why or why not? Why does defining the ban on gay marriage in this way bother Jacoby? Explain.
2. Jacoby notes that *The New Republic* quoted Vermont Supreme Court Chief Justice Amestoy's legal opinion allowing gay marriage as "a recognition of our common dignity." Why do you think he singles out this publication?
3. Discuss Jacboy's statement that "if something is morally wrong, it is morally wrong always" (paragraph 6). Do you agree with this statement? Can you prove otherwise? Explain.
4. Identify the primary points Sullivan uses to make his case in the preceding essay. How do you think Jacoby would respond to Sullivan's points in an editorial? Explain.

Family Values

Take a look at Dan Wasserman's cartoon, which originally appeared in the *Boston Globe*.

■ **QUESTIONS FOR ANALYSIS AND DISCUSSION**

1. How are the subjects in Wasserman's cartoon presented? How does Wasserman portray each character through clothing, manner, words, and typeface?
2. How do you think Andrew Sullivan and Jeff Jacoby would each respond to this cartoon? Explain.
3. What is the political stance of the cartoonist? What argument is he making in this cartoon? How compelling is his argument, and why?

Same Sex Marriage
Laurie Essig

In 1999, the state of Vermont legalized same-sex marriage. Other states are considering passing similar legislation. In the next essay, Laurie Essig explains why she isn't running off to Vermont to marry her partner Liza. Not only does she not want to marry, she can't understand why anyone would want to be bound by an institution "founded in historical, material and cultural conditions that ensured women's oppression."

Essig is a professor of sociology at Barnard College. She is the author of *Queer in Russia* (1999). This essay was published in *Salon* magazine's "Mothers Who Think" section, July 10, 2000.

■ **BEFORE YOU READ**

Why do people marry? What do they hope to gain by marriage? What does society expect from married couples as compared to unmarried couples?

■ **AS YOU READ**

Essig argues that the institution of marriage itself is far from "natural and universal." On these grounds, she objects to the institution itself. How does she defend her stance? Does she make a good point?

1   Lately straight relatives and friends have been calling to talk about Vermont and the fact that same-sex "unions" are now legal in that state. They can barely contain their excitement as they ask: "Aren't you just thrilled? You and Liza will go and get married, won't you?"

2   I hate to disappoint them. They so desperately want us to be just like they are, to aspire to nothing more nor less than legal recognition till death do us part. I couch my rejection in subjunctives: "It would be nice if we could be recognized as a family. If we were married, we would save thousands of dollars in insurance bills alone."

3   But the reality is that I don't want to marry Liza (nor she me). In fact, I'm against same-sex marriage for the same reasons I'm against *all* marriage.

4   Although we like to pretend that marriage is natural and universal, it is an institution founded in historical, material and cultural conditions that ensured women's oppression—and everyone's disappointment. Monogamous, heterosexual marriages were an invention of the Industrial Revolution's emerging middle class. The Victorians created the domestic sphere in which middle class women's labor could be confined and unpaid. At the same time, by infusing the patriarchal family with the romance of monogamy for both parties, the Victorians reduced sexual pleasure to sexual reproduction. All other forms of sex—homosexuality, masturbation, nonreproductive sex—were strictly forbidden.

5   But in the American culture of the '00s, we like to be paid for our labor and we insist on indulging in our pleasures. That's why a truly monogamous and lifelong marriage today is as rare as a Jane Austen book that hasn't been made into a movie.

6   Now don't go getting your wedding dresses in a twist. I don't care if you're married, had a huge wedding, spent $15,000 on a useless dress and let your father "give you away." I really don't care what personal perversions people partake of in their quest for pleasure.

7   What annoys me is that no one, not even queers, can imagine anything other than marriage as a model for organizing our desires. In the past, we queers have had to beg, cheat, steal and lie in order to create our families. But it's exactly this lack of state and societal recognition that gave us the freedom to organize our lives according to desire rather than convention.

8   Lesbians and gay men have created alliances and households and children together. Lesbians have bought sperm and used it to devious ends, gay men have explored sex as a public spectacle that is democratically available to all—and we have done this while forming intimate, lifelong allegiances with one another. And yes, many gays and lesbians, including me, have mimicked heterosexual marriage as best we could.

9   But why should those of us who have organized our lives in a way that looks a lot like heterosexual marriage be afforded special recognition by the government because of that? What about people who organize their lives in threes, or fours, or ones? What about my friend who is professionally promiscuous, who for ideological and psychological and sexual reasons has refused to ever be paired with anyone? What about my sister who is straight but has never in her 40-odd years seen a reason to participate in marriage? Which group will gain state recognition next? The polygamous? The lifelong celibate?

10   My point is not that we should do away with marriage but that we should do away with favoring some relationships over others with state recognition and privilege. Religions, not the state, should determine what is morally right and desirable in our personal lives. We can choose to be followers of those religions or thumb our noses at them. But the state has no place in my bedroom or family room, or in yours, either.

11   "Ah," but you say, "the state must recognize monogamous couples as more conducive to stable families and therefore better for children." Hello? Have you noticed that a huge number of marriages end in divorce? Even the suppos-

edly "happy" ones aren't necessarily cheery little islands of serenity. What were your parents like?

12   There is absolutely no evidence that monogamous, state-sanctioned couplings are more stable than other sorts of arrangements. Even if there were such evidence, couples should be recognized by the state only when they decide to become parents. Why should anyone get societal privileges, let alone gifts, when he or she marries for the fourth time at age 68 with no intention of ever becoming a parent?

13   Still, as much as I hate to admit it, I am liberal at heart. If gays and lesbians want to get married, then I don't want to stop them. I just want to lay a couple of ground rules:

14   First, do not expect me to be happy. The legalization of gay marriage does not make me feel liberated as much as it makes me feel depressed. It's sort of like getting excited about gays in the military—until I remember that I don't really care about the military as an institution.

15   Second, under absolutely no circumstances should you expect me to give you a gift for such a decision. If you're insane enough to waste money on tacky clothes and bad cake, I'm not going to underwrite your actions with a toaster oven.

■ QUESTIONS FOR ANALYSIS AND DISCUSSION

1. How does Essig field inquiries from her friends and family regarding the possibility of nuptials between herself and her partner Liza? Why doesn't she admit her feelings about marriage directly? Explain.
2. Evaluate the author's tone in this essay. Does she seek to engage or antagonize her audience? Explain.
3. Essig argues that if homosexuals are granted the legal right to marry, other alternative lifestyle groups may soon demand legal recognition as well. Does this argument seem valid? Why or why not?
4. In paragraph 10, Essig states that "religions, not the state, should determine what is morally right and desirable in our personal lives." Do you agree with her position? Why or why not?

What's Love Got to Do With It?
E. G. Graff

In the preceding article, Laurie Essig argued that the institution of marriage is steeped in historical conditions that "ensured women's oppression." As such, she cannot understand why anyone would want to embrace such an institution, legally or morally. Andrew Sullivan had previously argued that two people who wish to legally recognize their love and commitment to each other should be granted the right to marry, regardless of sexual orientation. In the next article, E. G. Graff explores the historical institution of marriage, which traditionally had very little to do with love, yet still carries sacred implications. And while the institution of marriage may have a sordid past, the author explains that her own same-sex marriage is a source of surprising joy.

Graff is a scholar at the Radcliffe Institute. She has written for the *New York Times, Ms., The Nation,* and *The Village Voice.* The following essay is an excerpt from *What Is Marriage For?: The Strange Social History of Our Most Intimate Institution* (1999).

▪ BEFORE YOU READ

In the next essay, Graff notes that when she and her partner exchanged vows, they found that "by accident we'd spilled into something sacred." What sacred meanings do we ascribe to the institution of marriage?

▪ AS YOU READ

How does Graff's outline of the history of marriage connect to her personal account of her union with her partner Madeline?

1   First comes love, then comes marriage: That grade school rhyme sums up the West's 20th-century philosophy of matrimony. But while modern folk take for granted that marriage is about love, it's really a historically peculiar—even radical—idea. In traditional marriage, people talked first about finances, trusting that once the key money matters were arranged, the couple could work out such things as companionship and sex and maybe even love. That changed with the rise of capitalism, as your family's finances were no longer decided by your wedding vows. And once you were able to make your own living, you were also able to make your own bed.

2   So who, in the history of marriage, got to say "I do"? You might smile at the question itself. But take the Romans. Their weddings included pledges exchanged by—are you sitting down?—the groom and his father-in-law. In the standard upper-class ceremony, the groom said, "Do you promise to give your daughter to me to be my wedded wife?" The bride's father answered, "The gods bring you luck! I betroth her." She said not a word. Because legal marriage was a dynastic arrangement, a way of arranging alliances and inheritances, the marriage had of course been arranged among the families—so much so that even the *son's* consent could be quite superficial.

3   According to the *Roman Digest,* "If a son marries a woman on the order of his father, that marriage is valid, although one cannot be forced to marry against one's wishes: However, it will be presumed that he chose to accept." That doesn't sound much like our active courtships, does it? But at least the groom had to open his mouth. The bride—well, "a daughter who does not openly resist her father's wishes is assumed to have consented." After all, who would have dared to stand up for her own choice, given that her family or clan was the all-powerful civil authority, the law under which she lived?

4   A thousand years after the birth of Christ, one pope insisted that the rules be changed. When one powerful noble, Jourdain, married off his daughter

against her vehement objections, the pope annulled the marriage—a shocking and urgent decision. The pope won. Within two centuries, the church had turned the standard wedding ceremony topsy-turvy. Now the girl, and not her father, had to say—out loud—"I do." He might still walk her down the aisle, but he no longer literally placed her hand in her husband's; she did that herself. As one theologian explained, "Where there is to be union of bodies there ought to be union of spirits." After reading about centuries in which men traded off their daughters' wombs like cattle—and often *for* cattle—you want to give three big cheers for the Church.

5   In practice, among the late medieval and early premodern upper classes, the children's consent was still assumed: It would have taken extraordinary willfulness for a 12-year-old girl and a 14-year-old boy to stand up against their parents (without, remember, school pals or MTV to cheer on the rebellion). One 13th-century English archbishop outlawed adolescent marriages, but since local bishops gave dispensations freely—or rather, for a reasonable price—who cared?

6   When the 16th-century Protestants sided with the parents, outlawing secret marriages and requiring parental consent, it was because they refused the idea that marriage was a private affair. Everyone's interests had to be consulted: Parents and "friends" (siblings, uncles, godparents, interested others) proposed, and marriageable adults thought seriously about the suggestions of those who cared about their welfare.

7   Oh, the Protestants did believe that, at a certain age—between, say, 22 and 25—you were old enough to marry without your parents' consent. But until then it was common sense that your parents knew better than you did, that marriage based on "such ephemeral factors as sexual attraction or romantic love was, if anything, less likely to produce lasting happiness than one arranged by more prudent and mature heads."

8   And yet, despite themselves, the Protestants started using a stealth weapon that, combined with the Catholic insistence on consent, eventually exploded into today's emphasis on marital love. The secret weapon was "holy matrimony"—that dramatic new phrase that the Protestants used endlessly in their campaign against Catholic celibacy, trotting it out in innumerable permutations, preaching it from the pulpit.

9   The startling concept of holy matrimony exploited a contradiction in Catholic theology: If consent and individual will were spiritually important, wasn't the marriage bond itself—its inner life—holy as well? Of course, some of the preaching about "holy matrimony" was done by now-married priests who had to justify to their consciences and congregations their own fall from celibacy. But things also worked the other way around: As the preacher-men married, they started to see that marriage could also be a spiritual act that pleased God.

10   Following the law of unintended consequences, the meaning of "holy matrimony" grew larger and more explosive as time went on. At first, it encompassed the idea that obedient sons and daughters, in fulfilling their duty by

marrying, were doing a holy thing. But over the centuries "holy matrimony" expanded to mean that marriage's inner life was actually more important than its forms—that the souls must meet before marriage, that the inner life must guide you to your spouse. Where once you had only veto power—your parents would nominate, and you would say yes or no—your feelings now had the power to run the entire spousal-election process.

11   Exactly when things switched from consent to choice is impossible to pinpoint, since the history of the inner life is notoriously hard to trace. But diaries, letters, and literature suggest to historians and literary scholars that an earthquake in marriage attitudes sent tremors across the 18th century. By then even the propertied classes, the ones who traditionally gave their children the least control, began to think that the children should have a say in who they married. By the late 19th century, young people began and managed their own courting, only afterwards allowing their parents a veto—a process that speeded up dramatically in the 1920s, as courtship moved from front porch to backseat.

12   In other words, for the past 400 years, young people have steadily moved out from under their parents' thumbs, until today we would be a bit shocked if adults did not select spouses for themselves. And since the middle ages, girls and women have steadily been moving forward on the question of *my body, my right to choose:* to choose to marry someone her father proposed; to choose a suitor; to choose whether or not to expose herself to pregnancy every time she had sex; to choose even whether to love a woman or a man.

13   Or to quote again that 12th-century church theologian: "Where there is to be union of bodies there ought to be union of spirits." That union of spirits, that insistence on active consent, now rules our marriage ideology—and my home life. Which brings me, finally, to offer a glimpse of my own story.

14   One day in 1991, almost against my will, I knew we were going to stand up in front of the people we love and commit ourselves to each other. Of course, it's ridiculous to say that it was against my will. I decided. Madeline, being distinctly private, wanted just to exchange rings. But an insular suburban life had strangled my childhood and my parents' marriage, and so I recoiled at the notion of privacy. Something inside me insisted on a ritual moment in full community view. It took time to write a ceremony that meant enough, but not too much. In our dearest friends' living room, we would say a few Jewish prayers, recite four favorite poems, exchange rings, speak our declarations, and, of course, kiss.

15   All of which we did, semicircles of family's and friends' eyes on us like lamps.

16   How can I describe what came next? It was nearly a delirium: By accident we'd spilled into something sacred. In that backyard in (yes) June, we kissed madly, actually forgetting we were lesbians, forgetting that the neighbors might be shocked. Madeline forgot to eat or drink. My dryly sarcastic brother cried so hard while making his toast that he could barely complete his sentences. My stepfather, who once squirmed at hearing I was queer, announced his pride in me and my friends. My mother led the blessings, cut the challah, and charmed

all my friends. To poke fun at the ceremony's earnestness, we brought out a cake topped with two brides. To our utter surprise, the ceremony brought us closer, pulling an invisible cloak around us that has warmed us during difficult times. We'd thought ourselves as committed as any couple could be: How else could we have exposed ourselves to the world's ridicule? But now even the most unnoticeable traces of doubt dissolve instantly, chased away by the memory of that day when we made our declarations so publicly, placing our love in the hands of God and everyone we knew.

17   Today, after nearly a dozen years together, each morning when I wake up and find Madeline beside me, I still feel surprised by joy. I am one of those former lit majors who has whispered the "westron wind" quatrain to my love over the phone when I'm far away. In front of that roomful of family and friends, before vowing to care for her lifelong, I spoke to her that most famous Shakespearean sonnet, that determined lifetime promise: "Let me not to the marriage of true minds / Admit impediments. Love is not love / Which alters when it alteration finds." And I've repeated it to her, alone at home, when one or another of us is disconsolate, as age slowly creeps up on us, to remind her that "Love's not Time's fool / though rosy lips and cheeks / within his bending sickle's compass come; / Love alters not with his brief hours and weeks / but bears it out even to the edge of doom."

18   Our marriage, in other words, has been bought and paid for with our society's common cultural currency: love. I adore her, I want to stand by as her perfect skin mottles and browns, as her black hair grays, as her sweet eyelids sag. I want to calm her panic when she's ill, cry in her arms when my life goes wrong, and argue over our different driving styles until we're in the grave. I cry at others' weddings because I was so happy at my own.

19   If our society believes in letting two people choose their life's partner from a sea of particular and unique individuals—if each of us is free to choose a spouse based on our own hopes for companionship, affection, friendship, and love—then how dare anyone tell me I have chosen wrong? If marriage is for, as Archbishop Cranmer wrote in 1547, "mutual society, help and comfort, that the one ought to have of the other, both in prosperity and in adversity," Madeline and I belong.

■ QUESTIONS FOR ANALYSIS AND DISCUSSION

1. How do you think Laurie Essig would respond to Graff's description of, and reasons for, her marriage to her same-sex partner? Do you think Graff's story would influence Essig's opinion of marriage? Why or why not?

2. In what ways was "holy matrimony" a "secret weapon" of Protestants? How did this weapon influence today's expectations that marriage be about love? Explain.

3. When did courtship shift from parental arrangements to young adults expressing mutual interest in each other? What role did the automobile play in revolutionizing courtship?

4. What is the historical connection between marriage and teenage rebellion? Explain.

■ WRITING ASSIGNMENTS

1. The Family Research Council openly opposes homosexuality as "unhealthy, immoral and destructive to individuals, families, and societies." Visit its Web site at <www.frc.org> and read about the Council's views on the issue of homosexual marriage. Write an essay in which you address its concerns regarding homosexual marriage's threat to the institution of the American family. Evaluate the Council's argument and present your own view for comparison and contrast.

2. Write a letter to a priest, minister, rabbi, or other religious leader. Explain why you think he or she should agree to perform a marriage ceremony celebrating the commitment of two of your best friends—a gay couple. Assume that this leader has not given much thought to the issue of gay marriage. Conversely, you may write a letter against such a marriage. You care deeply about your friends and recognize that your dissent may cause them pain, but your beliefs compel you to advise against a gay union.

3. Gay couples have been more prominent on television and other media in recent years. What images of gay life has television presented to its viewers? How do the images correspond to Andrew Sullivan's claims that gay men and women often live like heterosexual couples? Or do these images try too hard to mimic heterosexual relationships? Write an essay in which you explore the portrayal of gay relationships in the media and how this depiction may or may not influence the public on the issue of gay marriage.

4. Will legalizing gay marriage increase or decrease the problems gay men and women encounter in striving for social acceptance in America? What benefits might all gay people receive, whether or not they choose to marry? Do you think a change in the laws governing marriage will help to alter the beliefs of people who now disapprove of homosexuality? Why or why not? Explain.

CHAPTER 15

Law and Order

Violent crime is an American reality. Every evening, the nightly news reports disturbing tales of murder, rape, kidnapping, and robbery. The American crime rate surpasses that of every other country in the western world. Over 2.2 million violent crimes were reported in 2000, and the number of individuals in prison increased to 6.5 million. And while there has been a slight decrease in adult crime, juvenile crime rates have soared. In the final years of the twentieth century, over 25 percent of the people arrested for weapons offenses were males under the age of 18. And incarceration does not seem to be the answer—juvenile offenders are four times more likely to commit a violent crime again. How do we impose law and order in modern America? This chapter examines several issues connected to violent crime in America: juvenile crime, gun control, and capital punishment.

It seems as if every week the newspaper headlines report yet another violent crime committed by individuals too young to vote or to have a driver's license. The first group of readings addresses the issue of juvenile crime in America and some of the pressing and complex problems facing lawmakers, parents, and society as a whole. Why are juvenile crimes becoming more violent and deadly? Is the answer to punish juveniles as adults for committing "adult" crimes? Linda J. Collier argues that the current system is too "soft" on young offenders in "Adult Crime, Adult Time." T. Markus Funk explains why second chances are a bad idea—juveniles with criminal records are four times more likely to grow up to be adult offenders. Moreover, Funk argues that the practice of sealing juvenile criminal records endangers society, preventing law enforcement and the judicial system from making informed assessments. Margaret Talbot however, disagrees. In "The Maximum Security Adolescent," Talbot wonders what kind of society will be created when children are imprisoned with adults and we essentially condemn them to be "raised by wolves" in adult prisons with hardened criminals. And Annette Fuentes explores the new "culture of meanness" against children, in which the legal system, reacting to public pressure, is cracking down on violent kids, a system, she explains, that can only serve to make the problem worse.

Each year, there are approximately 34,000 gun-related deaths in the United States. Gunshot wounds are the single most common cause of death for women in the home, and more teenagers die from gunfire than from car accidents, making gunshot wounds the leading cause of death for teenage boys in America. However, between 2 and 3 million new and used handguns are sold each year to private citizens. The next section addresses some of the controversial issues surrounding gun control in this country. In "The Right to Bear Arms," the late Chief Justice Warren E. Burger takes a historical look at the Second Amendment and what it was designed to protect. Sallie Tisdale adopts a strong position against guns in "Zero Tolerance for Slaughter," arguing that Thomas Jefferson and Benjamin Franklin could never have imagined the violent crime rates we have today. David Kopel attacks the claims made by the antigun lobby in "An Army of Gun Lies." And criminology professor Jack Levin urges both sides in the gun debate to reach some consensus in "Gun Control Needs a Middle Ground."

In the eighteenth century B.C.E, the Babylonian king Hammurabi created a code that would serve as the foundation for law and punishment. Hammurabi's Code first records the often quoted "an eye for an eye and a tooth for a tooth" (Laws 196 & 200)—the principle of law that justifies capital punishment, which mandates the forfeiture of one's life for unjustly taking that of another. The last section of this chapter addresses the death penalty. Is it the ultimate deterrent and a fitting punishment for certain crimes? Or, does the ancient precedent for the death penalty belong in the past? Our section is framed within the context of personal perspectives on actual executions. It begins with a narrative by Steve Earle describing the final moments of a death row inmate whom he had earlier befriended. In "A Reckoning on Death Row," Jonathan Alter explains how DNA evidence has added new layers of controversy to the issue of the death penalty, a perspective with which Robert Pambianco disagrees in "Alter Falters." The section ends with a discussion on the healing the death penalty may afford families of victims. Can capital punishment grant them the closure they seek?

JUVENILE CRIME

Adult Crime, Adult Time: Outdated Juvenile Laws Thwart Justice

Linda J. Collier

With juvenile crime increasing in both frequency and severity, many states are coming down hard on juvenile offenders. Most states have amended their laws to make it easier to try violent juveniles as adults. And many states have adopted "blending sentencing" standards that allow judges to sentence juveniles to harsher punishments. However, some attorneys, such as Linda J. Collier in the next essay, contend that the new laws are still too flexible. As she explains, juveniles who commit "adult" crimes deserve adult punishment.

Collier is a lawyer who has worked in the juvenile courts. Formerly an instructor of criminal justice and political science at Cabrini College, Collier is now Dean of Public Services and Social Sciences at Delaware Community College. She is currently working on a book about juvenile justice entitled, *Where Have All the Children Gone?* (scheduled for publication in 2002). This article appeared in the April 6, 1998, edition of the *Washington Post.*

■ BEFORE YOU READ

What is an "adult" crime? How are adult crimes different from "juvenile" crimes? Can we make a distinction between them anymore?

■ AS YOU READ

Consider the types of crimes Collier cites as proof that the current juvenile justice system is outdated. Do you think these crimes are typical?

1   When prosecutor Brent Davis said he wasn't sure if he could charge 11-year-old Andrew Golden and 13-year-old Mitchell Johnson as adults after Tuesday afternoon's slaughter in Jonesboro, Ark., I cringed. But not for the reasons you might think.

2   I knew he was formulating a judgment based on laws that have not had a major overhaul for more than 100 years. I knew his hands were tied by the longstanding creed that juvenile offenders, generally defined as those under the age of 18, are to be treated rather than punished. I knew he would have to do legal cartwheels to get the case out of the juvenile system. But most of all, I cringed because today's juvenile suspects—even those who are accused of committing the most violent crimes—are still regarded by the law as children first and criminals second.

3   As astonishing as the Jonesboro events were, this is hardly the first time that children with access to guns and other weapons have brought tragedy to a school. Only weeks before the Jonesboro shootings, three girls in Paducah, Ky., were killed in their school lobby when a 14-year-old classmate allegedly opened fire on them. Authorities said he had several guns with him, and the alleged murder weapon was one of seven stolen from a neighbor's garage. And the day after the Jonesboro shootings, a 14-year-old in Daly City, Calif., was charged as a juvenile after he allegedly fired at his middle-school principal with a semiautomatic handgun.

4   It's not a new or unusual phenomenon for children to commit violent crimes at younger and younger ages, but it often takes a shocking incident to draw our attention to a trend already in progress. According to the U.S. Department of Justice, crimes committed by juveniles have increased by 60 percent since 1984. Where juvenile delinquency was once limited to truancy or

CHANGES IN THE LAW

Many state legislatures have responded to the increased incidence of violent juvenile crime by enacting tougher legislation, according to a 1996 report from the federal government's Office of Juvenile Justice and Delinquency Prevention.

- Since 1992, all but 10 states have amended their laws to make it easier to prosecute some juveniles as adults.
- Since 1992, 16 states have adopted "blended sentencing" models that allow judges to impose a combination of juvenile and adult sanctions on some young offenders.
- Legislation has given prosecutors an expanded role in determining how violent juvenile offenders should be handled.

vandalism, juveniles now are more likely to be the perpetrators of serious and deadly crimes such as arson, aggravated assault, rape and murder. And these violent offenders increasingly include those as young as the Jonesboro suspects. Since 1965, the number of 12-year-olds arrested for violent crimes has doubled and the number of 13- and 14-year-olds has tripled, according to government statistics.

5   Those statistics are a major reason why we need to revamp our antiquated juvenile justice system. Nearly every state, including Arkansas, has laws that send most youthful violent offenders to the juvenile courts, where they can only be found "delinquent" and confined in a juvenile facility (typically not past age 21). In recent years, many states have enacted changes in their juvenile crime laws, and some have lowered the age at which a juvenile can be tried as an adult for certain violent crimes. Virginia, for example, has reduced its minimum age to 14, and suspects accused of murder and aggravated malicious wounding are automatically waived to adult court. Illinois is now sending some 13-year-olds to adult court after a hearing in juvenile court. In Kansas, a 1996 law allows juveniles as young as 10 to be prosecuted as adults in some cases. These are steps in the right direction, but too many states still treat violent offenders under 16 as juveniles who belong in the juvenile system.

6   My views are not those of a frustrated prosecutor. I have represented children as a court-appointed *guardian ad litem,* or temporary guardian, in the Philadelphia juvenile justice system. Loosely defined, a guardian ad litem is responsible for looking after the best interest of a neglected or rebellious child who has come into the juvenile courts. It is often a humbling experience as I try to help children whose lives have gone awry, sometimes because of circumstances beyond their control.

7   My experience has made me believe that the system is doing a poor job at treatment as well as punishment. One of my "girls," a chronic truant, was a fos-

ter child who longed to be adopted. She often talked of how she wanted a pink room, a frilly bunk bed and sisters with whom she could share her dreams. She languished in foster care from ages 2 to 13 because her drug-ravaged mother would not relinquish her parental rights. Initially, the girl refused to tolerate the half-life that the state had maintained was in her best interest. But as it became clear that we would never convince her mother to give up her rights, the girl became a frequent runaway. Eventually she ended up pregnant, wandering from place to place and committing adult crimes to survive. No longer a child, not quite a woman, she is the kind of teenage offender for whom the juvenile system has little or nothing to offer.

8   A brief history: Proceedings in juvenile justice began in 1890 in Chicago, where the original mandate was to save wayward children and protect them from the ravages of society. The system called for children to be processed through an appendage of the family court. By design, juveniles were to be kept away from the court's criminal side, the district attorney and adult correctional institutions.

9   Typically, initial procedures are informal, non-threatening and not open to public scrutiny. A juvenile suspect is interviewed by an "intake" officer who determines the child's fate. The intake officer may issue a warning, lecture and release; he may detain the suspect; or, he may decide to file a petition, subjecting the child to juvenile "adjudication" proceedings. If the law allows, the intake officer may make a recommendation that the juvenile be transferred to adult criminal court.

10   An adjudication is similar to a hearing, rather than a trial, although the juvenile may be represented by counsel and a juvenile prosecutor will represent the interests of the community. It is important to note that throughout the proceedings, no matter which side of the fence the parties are on, the operating principle is that everyone is working in the best interests of the child. Juvenile court judges do not issue findings of guilt, but decide whether a child is delinquent. If delinquency is found, the judge must decide the child's fate. Should the child be sent back to the family—assuming there is one? Declare him or her "in need of supervision," which brings in the intense help of social services? Remove the child from the family and place him or her in foster care? Confine the child to a state institution for juvenile offenders?

11   This system was developed with truants, vandals and petty thieves in mind. But this model is not appropriate for the violent juvenile offender of today. Detaining a rapist or murderer in a juvenile facility until the age of 18 or 21 isn't even a slap on the hand. If a juvenile is accused of murdering, raping or assaulting someone with a deadly weapon, the suspect should automatically be sent to adult criminal court. What's to ponder?

12   With violent crime becoming more prevalent among the junior set, it's a mystery why there hasn't been a major overhaul of juvenile justice laws long before now. Will the Jonesboro shootings be the incident that makes us take a hard look at the current system? When it became evident that the early release of Jesse Timendequas—whose murder of 7-year-old Megan Kanka in New Jersey

sparked national outrage—had caused unwarranted tragedy, legislative action was swift. Now New Jersey has Megan's Law, which requires the advance notification of a sexual predator's release into a neighborhood. Other states have followed suit.

13   It is unequivocally clear that the same type of mandate is needed to establish a uniform minimum age for trying juveniles as adults. As it stands now, there is no consistency in state laws governing waivers to adult court. One reason for this lack of uniformity is the absence of direction from the federal government or Congress. The Bureau of Justice Statistics reports that adjacent states such as New York and Pennsylvania respond differently to 16-year-old criminals, with New York tending to treat offenders of that age as adults and Pennsylvania handling them in the juvenile justice system.

14   Federal prosecution of juveniles is not totally unheard of, but it is uncommon. The Bureau of Justice Statistics estimates that during 1994, at least 65 juveniles were referred to the attorney general for transfer to adult status. In such cases, the U.S. attorney's office must certify a substantial federal interest in the case and show that one of the following is true: The state does not have jurisdiction; the state refuses to assume jurisdiction or the state does not have adequate services for juvenile offenders; the offense is a violent felony, drug trafficking or firearm offense as defined by the U.S. Code.

15   Exacting hurdles, but not insurmountable. In the Jonesboro case, prosecutor Davis has been exploring ways to enlist the federal court's jurisdiction. Whatever happens, federal prosecutors of young offenders are clearly not the long-term answer. The states must act. So as far as I can see, the next step is clear: Children who knowingly engage in adult conduct and adult crimes should automatically be subject to adult rules and adult prison time.

■ QUESTIONS FOR ANALYSIS AND DISCUSSION

1. What is the difference between "delinquent" and "criminal"? What do the terms mean socially? What do they mean when applied to the justice system?
2. How are juveniles processed through the juvenile court system? How does the process differ from what you know of the adult system? What accounts for the differences?
3. Collier comments (paragraphs 6 and 7) that the current system of using a guardian ad litem is failing. Does she provide a solution to its shortcomings? How does Collier's experience as a guardian ad litem support her argument that juveniles who commit adult crimes must be treated as adults? Are you convinced by her example?
4. What is "Megan's Law"? Why do you think Collier cites this law in her essay? How does it contribute to her argument?
5. Collier states that her views are "not those of a frustrated prosecutor." Why does she make this distinction? If her views are not those of a prosecutor, what are they? Do you believe her statement? Explain.

Young and Arrestless: The Case Against Expunging Juvenile Arrest Records

T. Markus Funk

Many states allow or require that juvenile criminal records be expunged when a youth reaches the age of maturity (18 or 21). While expunging records was originally designed to allow juveniles who committed petty crimes a "clean slate," many states end up destroying records of violent criminal acts, including rape and murder. In so doing, says Funk, these states prevent the appropriate sentencing of young adult offenders, impede the effectiveness of law enforcement, ultimately placing everyone at risk.

Funk is a candidate for a D.Phil. in law from Oxford University, where he currently serves as a lecturer in law at Oxford's St. Catherine's College.

■ BEFORE YOU READ

Expungement is the erasure of a juvenile's criminal record when he or she reaches the age of maturity (18 in some states, 21 in others). Could expungement encourage "borderline" juveniles to commit crimes?

■ AS YOU READ

Funk points out that, according to the statistics, juvenile offenders are likely to be adult offenders as well. How is expungement connected to this issue?

1   Daniel Doe (a pseudonym) is a violent man who, like most violent men, was also a violent teen. At age 12, police arrested him for vandalizing a neighbor's house—he had destroyed the furniture, spray-painted the walls, and drowned a caged pet bird in the bathtub. Two years later, he was burglarizing an apartment when the elderly occupant returned home and confronted him. In the scuffle that ensued, the old man broke his hip. When the man died from pneumonia several days later, Daniel was charged with and convicted of involuntary manslaughter.

2   Daniel's first "adult" arrest came at age 19, when he broke into an occupied home and severely beat the 45-year-old woman who lived there. By the time he was sentenced for that attack, however, his juvenile record, pursuant to Ohio law, had been "expunged"—destroyed. For the second time, Daniel was a first-time offender. Hence, a Cleveland judge, ignorant of Daniel's violent, extensive, felonious past, sentenced him to probation. Two months later, Daniel burglarized yet another house, this time beating the 81-year-old man who lived there to death.

3   Had the judge known of Daniel's violent criminal past and his demonstrated lack of any rehabilitative potential, there's little doubt that Daniel

would have gone to the penitentiary before he had the opportunity to kill the old man.

4   But the judge didn't know because the law said that he *shouldn't* know.

5   Most states have statutory provisions that allow—or even mandate—the expungement of juvenile records once the juvenile turns a certain age. Sometimes the records are actually destroyed; sometimes they are merely "sealed." The practical effect of such legislation is to allow a minor who has committed criminal or, in the lingo of the juvenile courts, *delinquent* acts to permanently erase his or her record, usually at age 17 or 18. The stated goal of this policy is to allow the juvenile offender to enter adulthood with a proverbial clean state, thereby shielding him (or, less likely, her) from the negative effects of having a criminal record.

6   Supporters say expungement is an enlightened practice that merely forgives youthful transgressions. But expungement is actually an astonishingly counterproductive policy that benefits only young criminals. The practice prevents society from acting on the simple fact that those who have committed crimes in the past are likely to commit crimes in the future and hence should be treated differently from true first-time offenders.

7   By making it virtually impossible to collect meaningful data about juvenile delinquents, expungement also makes it difficult to evaluate crime-prevention and rehabilitation programs. Outside of the criminal justice sphere, the policy has other deleterious effects. Employers, for instance, can't know whether potential employees are prone to stealing or other criminal behaviors. Given these various costs, it's not surprising that a number of states are seriously reevaluating the sealing of juvenile records.

8   Expungement laws hearken back to a simpler past. The practice "was designed to deal with delinquents who stole hubcaps, not those who mug old ladies," notes sociologist Rita Kramer in *At a Tender Age: Violent Youth and Juvenile Justice* (1988). Gargantuan increases in violent juvenile crime underscore the point. Today's juvenile offenders are generally distinguishable from their adult criminal counterparts only by their age—an arbitrary factor indeed. Juveniles are the fastest growing segment among violent offenders. Between 1983 and 1992, according to FBI estimates, violent crime committed by juveniles increased 57 percent. Murders and non-negligent manslaughter rates jumped 128 percent, aggravated assault 95 percent, and rape 25 percent. And cohort studies discussed in Neil A. Weiner and Marvin E. Wolfgang's *Violent Crime, Violent Criminals* (1989) show that juveniles account for up to 35 percent of all male police contacts.

9   The philosophy underlying expungement legislation can be traced to what is known as the Chicago School of Criminology, which, during the 1920s and '30s, championed environmental explanations of criminality. The Chicago School (the term refers to a broad-based intellectual movement that started at the University of Chicago) rejected traditional criminological theories that focused on issues of individual morality and volition and concentrated instead on factors external to the individual. This new model viewed America as a

"criminogenic" society in which ghettos and slums taught the people who lived there how to become criminal by giving them deviant cultural values.

10   This environmental model reached its high-water mark in the early 1960s with Robert K. Merton's "Strain Theory," which posited that America's supposed obsession with ambition and economic success led to crime and deviance. Strain theory viewed delinquency as arising from the frustration felt by individuals who were unable to achieve culturally defined goals because they were denied the institutionalized means of doing so.

11   In the 1960s—the decade during which most expungement statutes currently in force were written—expungement advocates espoused what is known as the "labeling" or "social reaction" model. The labeling perspective is based on the premise that the very act of labeling those who are apprehended as "different" creates deviants who are different only because they have been "tagged" with the deviant label.

12   As criminologist Frank Tannenbaum, a prominent labeling-perspective theorist, argued in his 1983 book *Crime and the Community*, "The process of making the criminal . . . is a process of tagging, defining, identifying, segregating, describing, emphasizing, making conscious and self-conscious; it becomes a way of stimulating, suggesting, emphasizing, and evoking the very traits that are complained of." Hence, the only way to rehabilitate juvenile delinquents is to send them into adulthood with this label detached.

13   Aside from any philosophical and common-sense disagreements one may have with the labeling theorists, the major question regarding expungement is whether juvenile delinquents are "normal" kids who simply make youthful mistakes that are unlikely to be repeated in adulthood.

14   The answer is no. Delinquents are substantially different from non-delinquents. Research suggests that delinquents are more defiant, ambivalent about authority, emotionally unstable, extroverted, fearful of failure, resentful, hostile, suspicious, and defensive than non-delinquents. In their book *From Boy to Man, From Delinquency to Crime* (1987), University of Pennsylvania criminologist Marvin E. Wolfgang and his co-authors found that there is an extremely strong correlation between juvenile delinquency and adult crime, and that juvenile delinquency is the "best predictor of adult criminality." John Monahan, in his 1981 book *Predicting Violent Behavior*, has found that individuals with juvenile records are four times more likely to become adult offenders.

15   Similarly, a study tracing the criminal careers of 1,000 juvenile boys discussed in Sheldon and Eleanor Glueck's *Of Delinquency and Crime* (1974) found that 73.2 percent of those who could be located had been officially cataloged as repeat offenders within 10 years of their first appearance in juvenile court. An extensive FBI study discussed by Florida State University criminologist Gary Kleck, in *Point Blank* (1991), estimates that 74.7 percent of all murderers had arrests for violent felonies or burglaries, and murderers averaged four prior major felony arrests over a criminal career of at least six years. Those figures do not even begin to approximate the actual criminal histories of those individuals, since being arrested is itself a highly atypical consequence of violating the

law. It is also worth noting that those figures would be even higher if juvenile expungement statutes did not artificially deflate them.

16   In fact, expungement statutes also make it virtually impossible to collect the kind of data that might lead to more effective crime prevention. In a 1992 article in the *Journal of Urban and Contemporary Law,* Carlton Snow, the former dean of Willamette University College of Law, argued that expungement statutes "impinge on a democratic society's ability to inform itself about all aspects of the criminal justice system. . . . Regardless of whether juvenile records are merely 'sealed' or actually destroyed, the data becomes less available for research purpose." The result: The general public is unable to evaluate the juvenile justice system accurately, and sociologists and criminologists are left less able to study important aspects of criminal behavior.

17   And, as the case of Daniel Doe illustrates, expungement often prevents the courts from adequately assessing the danger a younger criminal poses to society.

18   The functions that judges perform at sentencing—one of which is to determine the convict's rehabilitative potential, as evidenced by his response to prior convictions—are simply too important to allow incomplete information concerning the nature and seriousness of an individual's criminal past to interfere with the proper dispensation of punishment.

19   That's one of the major points in *United States* v. *Davis,* a 1995 case involving a convicted felon's due process challenge to the United States Sentencing Guidelines' directive to consider juvenile convictions in calculating a defendant's prior criminal history. Writing for the court, Judge William J. Bauer, of the Seventh Circuit Court of Appeals powerfully stated: "[I]t is imperative that the defendant's sentence account for his criminal history from the date of birth up to and including the moment of sentencing. The consideration of the defendant's juvenile record is essential, because it is clear that the 'magic age' of eighteen, seventeen, or sixteen, whatever it may be in a specific state, cannot wipe out all previous contacts with the law. The pubescent transgressions . . . help the sentencing judge to determine whether the defendant has simply taken one wrong turn from the straight and narrow or is a criminal recidivist."

20   Expungement similarly interferes with effective law enforcement, since police officers are impeded in their efforts to identify patterns of criminal conduct. There is voluminous case law stating that arrest records serve a valuable law-enforcement purpose, that the dissemination of criminal records promotes the public welfare, and that even "unresolved" arrest records provide significant information and aid in the resolution of criminal actions. When the police are investigating criminal activity, for instance, they routinely examine the prior criminal records of potential suspects to see if there is evidence of a modus operandi. Juvenile records are routinely withheld, making the police's job that much more difficult.

21   Expungement exacts costs beyond crime and punishment. It prevents employers from making fully informed hiring decisions, such as whether applicants are likely to pilfer. Compelling employers to hire individuals without full

insight into their criminal propensities is a heavy penalty to force upon businesses. In *Privacy, Secrecy and Reputation,* Seventh Circuit Court of Appeals Judge Richard Posner says that arguments for expungement are "particularly weak in the context of employment, where competition exacts a heavy penalty from any firm that makes irrational employment decisions."

22   Perhaps more important, expungement forces employers into a very risky position from a workplace liability perspective. Under the common law, an employer has a duty to provide a safe work environment, and this duty has gradually been extended to hiring safe employees, since, in terms of legal analysis, a dangerous employee creates risks comparable to a defective machine. As Carlton Snow has pointed out, "Under the theory of vicarious liability, hiring applicants with expunged juvenile records is potentially hazardous for employers and employees alike." Since an employer can be held liable for an employee's torts while on the job, says Snow, "complete knowledge about an applicant would allow an employer to take appropriate steps to decrease any liability resulting from an employee's subsequent conduct."

23   The explosion in juvenile crime and the growing intellectual disenchantment with expungement statutes are beginning to have an effect: A number of states are rethinking the policy of sealing or destroying juvenile records. This past spring, for instance, Connecticut passed a law that allows delinquency records to be disclosed to police, school officials, social service workers, and "anyone with a legitimate interest in the information." Republican Pennsylvania Governor Tom Ridge is pushing to make "it harder to expunge juvenile records" and legislation passed last February lets judges review juvenile records before setting bail. Similar initiatives are underway in Louisiana, Texas, and Kentucky, where Democratic Governor Paul Patton has announced a plan to "lift the secrecy of juvenile court proceedings for convictions of serious felony crimes."

24   At bottom, expungement statutes are attempts to lessen the penalty that public opinion places upon former offenders. But the "stigma" of having been a juvenile delinquent should only be of concern insofar as it *incorrectly* characterizes an individual who has been able to reform his life since his brief brush with the law as a juvenile. If a former delinquent remains engaged in criminal activity, then it is clear that the juvenile justice system has failed in its goal of rehabilitation, and concern for the offender should be replaced with concern for protecting society from a predatory recidivist.

25   And even if one accepts the notion that those who have committed a juvenile indiscretion will outgrow their reckless behavior, it remains necessary to differentiate between those who in fact can be rehabilitated and those whose rehabilitative potential is negligible—i.e., career criminals.

26   But current expungement statutes rarely make such a distinction, choosing instead to delete a teenager's criminal record upon reaching majority (or sooner), regardless of whether it consists of a one-time arrest for public urination or numerous convictions for assault, burglary, or rape. While expungement may be appropriate for the one-time child offender (who presumably has been rehabilitated), it is wholly inappropriate for a young chronic criminal

who, based on numerous incidents of re-offending, shows no rehabilitative potential. As the number of offenses increases, the underlying delinquency becomes more troublesome, and it is likely that an anti-social pattern will continue throughout a criminal's adult years.

27   Given that adult criminality is often predicated upon juvenile delinquency, it follows that criminals have the most to gain, and that society has the most to lose, from any expungement scheme that allows individuals to start with a "clean slate"—or, more appropriately, a *cleaned* slate—upon reaching majority. That expungement is being challenged both intellectually and politically indicates that the costs may have finally become too much to bear.

■ QUESTIONS FOR ANALYSIS AND DISCUSSION

1. What is "recidivism"? Why do current juvenile court policies make it difficult to determine just how common recidivism is?
2. Consider the labeling theorists' point that calling a criminal a criminal encourages the label's behavior. Does this theory make sense? Explain.
3. What is "strain theory"? What connection does strain theory have to current expungement policies?
4. According to Funk, how does expungement affect the ability of a judge to sentence an offender? How does it interfere with effective law enforcement?
5. Consider the way Funk formulates this essay. How does he frame his argument? Is it logical and effective? Is his introduction an effective way of drawing in his audience? Explain.

The Maximum Security Adolescent

Margaret Talbot

Much of the media attention devoted to juvenile crime details the horror stories: angry teens shooting classmates or robbing and murdering an elderly next-door neighbor. For all the attention these crimes receive, statistics indicate that they do not represent the typical juvenile offense. In the next article, Margaret Talbot explains how these extreme cases have influenced the judicial system to cast a "wide net" when determining when to try juveniles as adults. While a majority of juveniles tried as adults are charged with violent crimes, 34 percent are prosecuted for property crimes such as burglary and petty theft, or for drugs or public nuisance offenses.

Talbot is a contributing writer for the *New York Times Magazine* and a former editor for *The New Republic* and *Lingua Franca*. She is a frequent contributor to *The New Yorker*. She is currently a senior fellow at the New American Foundation. This article was first published in the September 10, 2000, issue of the *New York Times Magazine*. The story of Jeff Stackhouse was further addressed on *60 Minutes II* in February 2001.

■ **BEFORE YOU READ**

Is punishing juveniles as adults for nonviolent crimes fair? Should the severity of the crime be considered when determining how a juvenile offender ought to be prosecuted?

■ **AS YOU READ**

Talbot points out that mentally and emotionally, most juveniles under 16 do not fully understand the consequences of their actions and lack the ability of long-term foresight necessary to make sound judgments. How does this observation apply to the cases she describes in her article? Should mental maturity be a factor when trying juvenile offenders?

1   When Jefferson Alexander Stackhouse was 3 years old, good luck entered his life for the first and maybe the last time. Abandoned as a 2-week-old infant by a schizophrenic mother, Jeff had lived by then in eight different foster homes. But in 1988, he was taken in by a woman who quickly made up her mind to love him and who adopted him two years later. The fact that Jeff came to her "with all his worldly possessions in one very small box" and called every adult female Mommy "not only broke but stole my heart," his adoptive mother, Leslie Stackhouse, says now. Leslie and her then husband, Norman, adopted two more "special needs" children, a girl named Christin and her brother, Casey, who had been taken away from abusive parents when they were toddlers. Leslie's training as a foster parent helped her to go slowly with all three, giving them time to trust her. Though Jeff was withdrawn at first, prone to banging his head against the wall and biting himself, he grew into a happy little boy with a powerful loyalty to his mother.

2   By the time he hit 14, though, Jeff was getting into the kind of scrapes that keep a mother up at night. Joe Wilson, a family friend who ran a driving school in town, thought Jeff was a good kid who was being picked on because he was small for his age. "I think he was trying to defend himself in a pretty tough neighborhood," Wilson says. Jeff and his friends in Glendale, a working-class Phoenix suburb of low-slung houses, wide boulevards and scruffy palm trees, sneaked out one hot summer evening after curfew to search for loose change in unlocked cars. Jeff was caught and went through counseling in a juvenile crime deterrence program. A couple of months later, he and another friend stole a bike, which Jeff rode to school and returned later that day.

3   Then one night, after an argument with his mom, he stalked off down the street. When Leslie caught up with him, he shoved her. His 12-year-old sister was worried enough to call the police, who arrested Jeff for assault, and Leslie figured, "O.K., maybe this isn't so bad, maybe he'll learn a lesson." What Leslie really hoped was that some official would figure out a way to get her son psychological help. Jeff was troubled, she knew—school psychologists told her he had attention-deficit disorder and depression, and though he loved to read, he

struggled in school. But Leslie, who works as a school bus driver, had never been able to afford a thorough evaluation for him.

4   By that time, Jeff was under a kind of house arrest imposed by the juvenile court—he wasn't supposed to leave home alone except to attend school. But on Feb. 23 of this year, he was arrested again. He and three other neighborhood kids his age had been "play boxing," as the police report termed it, at the school bus stop, and Jeff had given one of the boys a bloody lip. After the fight, the boy and his pals set out for Jeff's house, where they called him out on the lawn, got him in a headlock and punched him. Jeff ran into the house, found an unloaded antique shotgun that his mother kept in her closet and brought it out to wave at the other kids, shouting, "Get off my property!" The three boys headed home in a hurry. No one was hurt, and two of the three did not even want to press charges.

5   But Jeff Stackhouse's worst luck so far was to have fallen afoul of the law at this particular moment in American judicial history, a moment when the century-old notion of children and adolescents as less culpable and more amenable to rehabilitation than adults has been giving way to an altogether different view. In this new and far harsher view, child criminals are virtually indistinguishable from adult criminals: they are just as capable of forming criminal intent, just as morally responsible, just as autonomous in their actions. Since 1992, 45 states, including Arizona, have passed or amended legislation making it easier to prosecute juveniles as adults. While judges in the juvenile system have always had the authority to send particularly brutal or chronic young offenders into the adult system, state legislatures have been making it easier for less serious wrong-doers to meet the same fate. Because of changes over the last decade, 15 states now grant prosecutors the sole discretion to transfer juveniles into adult court for certain categories of offenses. Twenty-eight states have statutes that automatically remove youths charged with particular crimes—many of them violent crimes, but some property and drug offenses as well—from the jurisdiction of the juvenile system. Though many states allow only children 14 and older to be prosecuted as adults, others have set younger minimum ages—10 in Vermont and Kansas—or no lower limit at all.

6   While these reforms were often motivated by such nightmarish cases as the school massacres in Jonesboro, Ark., or Littleton, Colo., they have cast a much wider net. Though 66 percent of the juveniles prosecuted as adults in 1994 were charged with violent offenses, according to a Bureau of Justice Statistics report, the remaining 34 percent were charged with property offenses, like burglary and theft, or with drug or public nuisance offenses. As a result, the number of youths under 18 held in adult prisons, and in many cases mixed in with adult criminals, has doubled in the last 10 years or so, from 3,400 in 1985 to 7,400 in 1997. Of the juveniles incarcerated on any given day, one in 10 are in adult jails or prisons.

7   Arizona is one of the states where prosecutors can bump a juvenile case into adult court at their own discretion. It is also a state with a number of mandatory sentencing laws. Jeff Stackhouse was charged as an adult on three

separate counts of aggravated assault with a dangerous weapon. Since the boys Jeff pulled his unloaded gun on were all under 15, the prosecutor also had the option of classifying the assault as a so-called dangerous crime against children, and he did. If Jeff Stackhouse is convicted, he could be sentenced to a minimum of 30 years in prison.

8   Earlier this summer, the attorney assigned to him, a young public defender named Douglas Passon, was still hoping to get the case sent back to the juvenile court, which would most likely put Jeff in a juvenile detention facility until he is 18. That's a long shot; once a case is sent to adult court, it almost always stays there. Assuming Jeff remains in the adult system, the best-case scenario would be probation, which wouldn't get him any psychological counseling but would at least keep him out of the penitentiary. For now, the prosecutor has offered 10 years in an adult prison, which Passon thinks is no kind of deal at all. Still, he realizes "that at some point I may be asking Jeff to make up his mind about that. This is a kid who's not old enough to see an R-rated movie by himself, and we're telling him he's old enough to go to prison and get jumped in the showers. We're asking him to make decisions that will affect his entire life in ways he can't even imagine."

9   When you are 14, it's not easy to project yourself into the future with any sense of clarity; for Jeff Stackhouse, maybe that's a good thing. The present— which is to say, the Madison Street Jail in downtown Phoenix, a multistory building that resembles a particularly ugly parking garage—is overwhelming enough. I visited Jeff in jail one day in June, when it was 107 outside, but fluorescent-lighted and as weatherless as a casino inside. Jeff had been in jail since February. A jocular female guard escorted him into the room, and because I was accompanied by his lawyer, I was permitted to sit on the same side of the Plexiglas partition with him. When his mother comes, she has to sit on the other side, with the signs that say "No Kissing. No Hugging" in clear view, and as Jeff tells me, "she just cries and cries."

10   Jeff Stackhouse is short, with clear hazel eyes, a face still softened by puppy fat and no hint of a whisker. He wears a faded jail-issue jumpsuit, the old-fashioned black-and-white-striped kind, orange rubber thongs and handcuffs. He is soft-spoken and polite—sweet is the word, really. I had been wondering what somebody his age missed most in jail, and that was the first question I asked him. He said he missed his mom, his sister and his dog.

11   Jeff is housed in a unit with other juveniles, but many of them are 17 and 18, and some are gang members. There are classes for the juveniles held here, but Jeff gets nervous leaving his cell. When he does, he says, "Guys hit me in the head or take my latrine supplies, tell me they're going to beat me up. And if I hit 'em back, then I'd get in trouble and I couldn't see my mom." He has asked to be put in protective custody, but so far his request has not been granted. And even when he feels brave enough to face school, he says it's "too easy. They're doing plurals and nouns and capitalization. Third-grade work. There was a guy here—I think he was on paint chips for a while. He didn't know what the letter Y was. I kind of felt sorry for him."

12   Jeff says there is nothing he has gotten used to about being in jail, but in some small way, I see, he has already adapted. He has a tattoo now, eked out on one thin wrist with battery acid, shampoo and a staple. It says C-A-S-E-Y, which was his brother's name. When Jeff was 7, Casey, then 5, drowned in a lake near Phoenix where their dad had taken the three kids for a fishing trip on the day before Mother's Day. Jeff saw it happen. Leslie and her husband split up after that—the accident drove them apart, she says, "because I was looking for Casey in the Bible, wondering what heaven was like for him, and my husband was looking for him in the bottle"—and Jeff has hardly seen his father since. In jail, Jeff had been dreaming about Casey, and in one dream he looked down at his hand and saw his brother's name there. When he got up that morning, he told his cellmate he was ready; he wanted a tattoo. Only he is still kid enough to be embarrassed about his decision. "It was kind of dumb because my mom got real mad about it," he says glumly.

13   One hundred years ago, when progressive-era reformers first invented the idea of a separate justice system for juveniles, it was boys like Jeff they had in mind. Nearly everything about the newly created juvenile court, from its paternalistic ethos to its central tenet that juveniles were not to be confused with hardened criminals to its goal of sentencing "in the best interest of the child," represented a radical break with the past and a pledge of faith in the malleability of youth. Until then, children had been tried, sentenced, imprisoned and sometimes executed alongside adults.

14   The common-law tradition did offer some recognition that young children were different from adults. Children under 7 who committed crimes were presumed not to be responsible for them and could not be punished. But after that, the question of culpability got murkier. Those between the ages of 7 and 14 were generally thought to lack responsibility for their actions. Those between 14 and 21 were presumed capable of forming criminal intent and were therefore punishable. Yet as early as the 1820's, judges who had to sentence juveniles in criminal court worried openly about the implications of putting young people behind bars. Letting them off scot-free was neither morally nor socially acceptable, but sending them to jail or prison with adults was like consigning them, in the words of one judge, to a "nursery of vices and crimes, a college for the perfection of adepts in guilt."

15   By the turn of the century, these qualms had spread widely enough to make jury nullification a problem: jurors were acquitting young lawbreakers rather than imposing sentences that would lock them up with adults. At the same time, the emerging child-study movement and the new specialty of pediatrics helped popularize the idea that childhood was a distinct phase of life and that adolescents, in particular, moved through discrete developmental stages, which adults had a duty to try and understand. Like compulsory school-attendance laws and bans on child labor, the juvenile court was a product of this new approach to childhood. It was to be presided over by a judge in street clothes, not a black robe, seated at a desk, where he could easily put a reassuring arm around a troubled lad.

16   In 1899, Illinois established the first juvenile court; by 1925, 46 states had done the same. The idea of a justice system tailored for children sank deep roots in American culture. In fact, it was not until the late 1960's that the system came under any real questioning. Paradoxically, the assault was launched by the civil liberties left. Because the juvenile court was supposed to be helping the accused child and because it shielded his identity in a way the criminal court did not, it was liberated from the necessity for due process protections—the right to counsel, the right to confront witnesses, the privilege against self-incrimination and so forth. The trouble with this arrangement was that it offered the court nearly unlimited authority to confine youths while it devised cures for their antisocial behavior.

17   The civil liberties critique of the juvenile justice system found its most powerful expression in the Supreme Court's 1967 decision in the Gault case. On June 8, 1964, Gerald Gault, a 15-year-old boy living in Gila County, Ariz., made an obscene phone call to his neighbor, one Mrs. Cook. (He wondered, quaintly enough, if she had "big bombers.") Mrs. Cook called the sheriff, who arrested the boy; his mother came home from work and found Gerald missing, with no explanation. At two subsequent hearings, Mrs. Cook never appeared, no other witnesses were sworn and no transcript made. Yet in the end, the judge ordered Gerald committed to a juvenile facility until his 21st birthday—even though the maximum sentence for an adult who committed the same crime would have been two months in jail or a $50 fine. When the Supreme Court acted on the case, it concluded in irate language that Gerald's constitutional rights had been breached by "a kangaroo court"—and extended to juveniles all due process rights except that of a jury trial.

18   Gault was a necessary reform for a system that had become too arbitrary. But instead of leading to further constructive reforms, it led to full-scale rebellion: Gault helped open the door to the dismantling of the juvenile justice system. It galvanized a liberal movement for emancipation of minors that cast them as rights-bearing autonomous citizens, barely distinguishable from adults. It also "energized the tough-on-crime constituency," says Steven Drizin, the supervising attorney at the Children and Family Justice Center at the Northwestern University School of Law. "The juvenile court has been fighting the sound bite ever since that if you give kids adult rights, you can give them adult time, too." Of course, kids, some of them anyway, weren't helping matters. A spike in the juvenile crime rate in the early 1990's and a cluster of school shootings in the latter years of the decade all created the impression that young people were getting away with murder.

19   Even after the juvenile crime rate fell precipitously in the late 90's, this sentiment continued to gain currency, as Franklin Zimring, a criminal-law professor at the University of California at Berkeley, points out, because "a punishment gap was opening between the adult and juvenile systems. The tough-on-crime crowd had won the war in the criminal system; now they looked at the juvenile court and said, 'Hey, we've got to make it look more like the adult version.'" Increasingly, the focus was on the offense, not the offender.

20   "What I noticed," says Stephen Harper, an assistant public defender in Miami who has handled cases in which juveniles were transferred to the adult system, "is that there was much less curiosity about who a kid was, why he might have done what he did. Was there abuse in his background, neglect, a drug-addicted parent?" Indeed, as more and more states began transferring kids to adult court, it became clear that youth itself would not be considered a mitigating circumstance. There was no contemporary legal precedent for going easier on a 14-year-old than a 40-year-old in criminal court—that's what juvenile court had been for, after all. And in any case, the new mandatory sentencing laws left judges little opportunity for leniency.

21   The new attitude meant passing laws that allowed more and more kids to be sent to adult court at younger and younger ages—many of them poor, a disproportionate number of them black. It also meant breaking the old taboo against dispatching the young to adult prisons, those "nurseries of vices and crimes" that advocates of the juvenile court had long lamented.

22   The body of research on juveniles in adult prison is not especially large. [. . .] It isn't even all that easy to locate young inmates, in part because states have adopted different policies about how and where to house them. "The majority of states follow a practice of dispersing young inmates in the general prison population," says Dale Parent, a project director with the research firm Abt Associates in Cambridge, Mass., which is conducting a long-term study on juveniles in state prison systems. "They might not put a small, vulnerable adolescent in a cell with a sex offender, but other than that, they do not segregate the youth, and they have no separate programs for them. A few states have extreme segregation—physically separate housing units where youthful offenders have no contact with the adult population—or arrangements with the state juvenile facility where they spend a few years there and are transferred to prison on their 18th birthdays."

23   There are plenty of reasons to keep juvenile offenders away from the adult prison population. In general, young prisoners are more vulnerable than adults to sexual exploitation and physical brutalization. They are more likely than older inmates to commit suicide. They are more likely than young people in juvenile detention facilities to be physically assaulted and to return to a life of crime when they are set free.

24   None of this should come as any surprise. Prison populations are not only older, larger and more criminally experienced than juvenile detention populations, they are also more violent. (Nearly 50 percent of prison inmates are violent offenders, while only 20 percent of juvenile training school residents are.) Prisoners tend to be much more idle than juveniles in detention. Only one-third of state prison inmates work more than 34 hours a week, and only half take classes. In juvenile facilities, on the other hand, kids spend most of the day in school, vocational-training, group counseling, substance abuse programs and the like and are encouraged to form bonds with their counselors and teachers. When Donna Bishop, a professor of criminology at Northeastern University, interviewed minors in juvenile and adult facilities in Florida, she con-

cluded that youths in prison "spent much of their time talking to more skilled and experienced offenders who taught them new techniques of committing crime and methods of avoiding detection."

25   An earlier study that Bishop and Charles Frazier conducted in Florida points to the effects of such environments on recidivism. Thousands of young offenders are sent to criminal court in Florida each year. But because so many of those transfers come about at the discretion of prosecutors, thousands of other juveniles, charged with equally serious crimes, are not. Bishop and Frazier were thus able to match by age, race, gender, current charges and past criminal record 2,738 juveniles who had been prosecuted as adults with 2,738 who had stayed in the juvenile system. Over a period of up to two years, they found that 30 percent of the teenagers prosecuted in criminal court were rearrested; the figure for those who had gone through the juvenile system was 19 percent. Transfers also proved more likely to be arrested for more serious offenses.

26   For all these reasons, many prison and jail officials would rather they never had to deal with youthful inmates at all. "We don't want juveniles locked up with adults," says Ken Kerle, the managing editor of *American Jails* magazine, the official publication of the American Jails Association. "I don't think we're doing the country any good by going back to Square 1 and chucking the whole idea of a separate system for juveniles. You can't handle kids like you handle adults. They're mercurial; they've got a lot of emotional growing-up to do. They need education, they need exercise and they need guards who have some insight into them. Put 'em in adult facilities, and they come out worse than when they went in."

27   Last year, the American Correctional Association, the professional organization that represents prison staffs, passed a resolution in favor of limiting transfers from juvenile to criminal court as sharply as possible, holding youthful offenders only where they can be entirely separate from adults and developing new training in adolescent psychology for those prison officials who are forced to manage the very young. Corrections-industry journals, meanwhile, have been particularly blunt when it comes to laying out the practical dilemmas of treating children as adults. "If inmates under the age of 18 are housed with the general population," a writer in *Corrections Today* asked recently, "does this mean adult systems should treat them like adults in every way or does it mean that special considerations should be made to their questionable adult status? Can a youthful offender be sold tobacco products? . . . Can an incarcerated juvenile file a child-abuse complaint against prison officials?" These are far from hypothetical questions. "Unless a parent or guardian signs permission for it," says Elisa Corrado, a social worker who works with imprisoned juveniles in Miami, "they can't get a Tylenol. They're still minors, even if they're in adult prison."

28   Recent insights from neuroscience tend to support the notion that teenagers really are different from adults, and in precisely the ways anyone who has ever been a teenager might think. Researchers at the National Institutes of

Mental Health have used brain imaging, for example, to show that both the frontal lobe and the corpus callosum, the cable of nerves connecting the left and right sides of the brain, are still underdeveloped in adolescence. And they surmise that until those parts of the brain have fully matured, they can contribute to greater impulsiveness and wider and more frequent mood swings. "Teenagers," Jay Giedd of the N.I.M.H. said in a speech last year, "don't utilize inhibitory pathways as well as their parents do to moderate their impulses." (To which their parents, anyway, might say, "Duh.")

29   Still, we are unlikely to return to an era when the juvenile system held sway over all lawbreakers under 18. And besides, limbically challenged or not, a 17-year-old clearly isn't as deserving a candidate for leniency as, say, a 12-year-old. Laurence Steinberg, a Temple University psychologist who heads a research project on adolescent development and juvenile justice, would rather see the law adopt more subtle dividing lines. "Most people older than 16 are not greatly distinguishable from adults on the relevant competencies—the ability to think through future consequences, for example," he says. "On the other hand, people 13 and under really do not have these abilities. For them, adult court should not be an issue." The tricky ages, says Steinberg, are 14, 15 and sometimes 16. In that age range, some adolescents—especially those with emotional or learning difficulties, which would include many kids in the criminal justice system—are childlike in important respects, while others are quite mature.

30   There will always be some juveniles who deserve to be tried and punished in the adult system, either because their crimes are particularly coldblooded or because they have been given repeated chances to reform and repeatedly failed to do so. Even some of the staunchest advocates for juveniles concede that a few of them are irredeemably dangerous. "I'm a believer that there is true evil in the world," Darrow Soll, a former public defender and prosecutor in Phoenix told me. "I'm not so foolish as to think that every child can be saved just because of their age. But an effort has to be made. There are a few who you say no juvenile system in the world is going to be able to save. But in my experience, those are definitely the exceptions."

31   The majority of young offenders dabble in crime and grow out of the urge to do so. "Self-report studies indicate that most teenage males engage in some criminal conduct," notes Elizabeth Scott, a law professor, in a recent essay, "leading criminologists to conclude that participation in delinquency is 'a normal part of teen life.' " And think about it for a minute: did you ever do anything illegal as a teenager? (Yes, drugs and booze count.)

32   "I had juvenile referrals when I was a kid," says Soll, who is now a criminal defense attorney with a posh Phoenix firm. "And if I came into the system now, I'd probably be incarcerated. I wouldn't have gotten into the military. I wouldn't have gotten an education. I sure wouldn't have entered the bar." One of Soll's oddest moments as a public defender came when he was called upon to represent a 15-year-old boy charged in criminal court and facing a possible four-year prison sentence for stealing a golf cart and setting it on fire. "What

was weird about it was that I had done virtually the same thing when I was that age," says Soll. He is 34 and a natty dresser with a bemused, cherubic face and a roster of well-heeled clients. But he grew up working class in Glendale, Jeff Stackhouse's neighborhood.

33 "O.K., in my case, I took the golf cart and drove it into the pool at school—big prank," Soll explains. "But I went to court, and I had this Roy Bean-type judge who said, 'Son, in the old days I could have sent you into the Army, and I can't now, but that's what I'd do with you.' And I did go into the Army, and I became a paratrooper, and it was a great educational experience for me and a lot of other rough-and-tumble kids like me. A whole lot better than fending off gangs in the state pen. If I'd done that today, I'd have a felony conviction and they wouldn't even let me in the Army." He whistles under his breath. "Boy, you don't want to be the parent of a teenager these days."

34 Last month, I visited Phoenix again. Jeff was still in jail, though in protective custody at last. Not much had changed for him, though he seemed a little more comfortable and, with a sprinkling of acne on his chin, a little older. [. . .] I'm thinking that nothing good is going to come of sending Jeff to prison. Some older adolescents—16- and 17-year-olds, especially—do belong in adult court. Others in that age range would be good candidates for an innovative strategy called blended sentencing, which is now being used in 19 states. Under this practice, young offenders serve their time in juvenile facilities until they are 18 or 21, but have an additional sentence in adult prison hanging over them if officials think they still pose a danger. But any child 14 or younger—and make no mistake, it is children we are talking about—is too unformed, too vulnerable, too easily swayed, too limited in his understanding of the criminal process to be subjected to it in full force.

35 "You know," [juvenile defense lawyer Frances] Gray says, "I was a public defender in Virginia for a while, and I sometimes had to work in the juvenile court there, and I hated it—the wishy-washiness of it, the endless hearings. Now, here I am dealing with kids where they were never meant to be, in criminal court, where none of us are prepared to deal with them. And I would give my front teeth—my front teeth—to have a situation where there wasn't a final disposition, where you weren't sealing some kid's fate forever."

■ QUESTIONS FOR ANALYSIS AND DISCUSSION

1. How does Talbot's story of Jeff Stackhouse introduce and later support her argument? Is it an effective way to begin her article? Why or why not?
2. Evaluate Talbot's argument. How well does she support her points with examples and facts? Does she discuss both sides of the issue? In what ways does her argument forward the principles of consensus and dialogue?
3. Does it seem contradictory or unfair that Jeff Stackhouse was charged as an adult for a crime against children when all four boys were the same age? Why or why not?
4. Talbot notes that a nineteenth-century judge once said that sending young criminal offenders to prison with adults was like sending them to "a nursery of

vices and crimes, a college for the perfection of adepts in guilt." How does professor Donna Bishop's research a century later support the judge's observation? Explain.

5. How did the Gault case create the cracks that led to the breakdown in the juvenile court system? In what ways was the case paradoxical? Explain.

6. What risks and issues face the juvenile offender incarcerated in adult penitentiaries? In your opinion, does such a sentence impose unusually harsh penalties on the juvenile offender? Explain.

7. The American Correctional Association raises the question of just how far the system should go in treating juveniles as adults. If they have been deemed adults by the court system, do any of the rules for minors still apply? Should they be able to possess tobacco products? Choose their own medications? Present your own viewpoint on this issue, referring to information from the text to help support your position.

Crackdown on Kids
Annette Fuentes

While the headlines seem to proclaim that juvenile crime is getting worse, the author of the next article argues that it is this media attention that is shifting public opinion against the young, causing a "crackdown" on juveniles. Instead of trying to figure out how to solve the problem of juvenile crime, we would rather lock up children and forget about the underlying social issues. Such an attitude, fears Annette Fuentes, will ultimately cause far more harm than good.

Fuentes is the coauthor of *Women in the Global Factory,* written with Barbara Ehrenreich. Her articles have appeared in many publications, including *The Progressive* and the *Columbia Journalism Review.* She is currently an assistant editor of *New York Newsday.* She wrote this article for the June 15/22, 1998, issue of *The Nation,* after the shooting sprees of Kipland Kinkel, Mitchell Johnson, and Andrew Golden, but before subsequent acts of school violence at Columbine and Santana High School.

■ BEFORE YOU READ

If we prosecute juveniles as adults, should they be incarcerated *with* adults as well? Why or why not?

■ AS YOU READ

Is punishing juveniles as adults a good idea? Is it justifiable under certain circumstances, but not in others? Explain.

1   When Kipland Kinkel, Mitchell Johnson and Andrew Golden reportedly unloaded mini arsenals of guns at their classmates, they fulfilled the worst fears

about young people that now dominate the nation's adult consciousness. Kinkel, 15, of Springfield, Oregon, allegedly is responsible for the deaths of two students as a result of an incident on May 21, as well as for the deaths of his parents. Johnson, 13, and Golden, 11, were charged in connection with the March 24, 1998 deaths of four students and a teacher in Jonesboro, Arkansas. All were instantly transformed from average American boys, perhaps a bit on the wild side, into evil incarnate. Forget that Mitchell sobbed next to his mother in court, or that Drew learned to sling a shotgun from Dad and Grandpa the way many boys learn to swing a bar. "Let 'em have it" was the sentiment, with catchy phrases like "adult crime, adult time."

2   After the Arkansas incident, Attorney General Janet Reno scoured federal laws for some way to prosecute Johnson and Golden so they could be locked up till age 21 if convicted, a stiffer sentence than the state could mete out. One *Washington Post* Op-Ed called for states to adopt a national uniform minimum age for juveniles to be tried as adults for violent crimes.

3   The three boys are believed to have committed terrible deeds, no question. But twenty years ago, a Greek chorus would have been clamoring to understand why they went bad. The events themselves would have been seen as aberrations. Redemption might have been mentioned, especially since these were not career delinquents. Instead, we have proposals like the one from Texas legislator Jim Pitts, who wants his state to use the death penalty on children as young as 11. And he's got plenty of support, because this is the era of crime and punishment and accountability for all constituencies without wealth or power to shield them. And the young are such a class of people.

4   In the past two decades, our collective attitude toward children and youth has undergone a profound change that's reflected in the educational and criminal justice systems as well as in our daily discourse. "Zero tolerance" is the mantra in public schools and juvenile courts, and what it really means is that to be young is to be suspect. Latino and black youth have borne the brunt of this growing criminalization of youth. But the trend has spilled over racial and ethnic boundaries—even class boundaries, to a degree. Youth, with all its innocence and vulnerability, is losing ground in a society that exploits both.

5   In fact, youth crime has not changed as dramatically as our perceptions of it. Data from the National Center for Juvenile Justice show that between 1987 and 1996, the number of juvenile arrests increased 35 percent. Juvenile violent-crime arrests were up 60 percent, but they represent a sliver of all juvenile arrests—about 5 percent of the 1996 total of 135,100. A 1997 study by the center found that "today's violent youth commits the same number of violent acts as his/her predecessor of 15 years ago." As to whether criminals are getting younger, a 1997 report from the Justice Department answers clearly: "Today's serious and violent juvenile offenders are not significantly younger than those of 10 or 15 years ago."

6   What's more, from 1994 to 1995 there was a 3 percent decline in juvenile arrests for violent crime, and from 1995 to 1996 there was a 6 percent decline. "I have people call me up and ask. 'Why is juvenile crime down?'" says Robert Shepherd Jr., a law professor at the University of Richmond in Virginia. "I say,

'Why was it up?' It could be just one of history's cycles. Over the thirty years I've been involved in juvenile justice issues, I've seen very little change in the incidence of violent crime by kids."

7   One thing that *has* changed is the prominence of guns and their role in violence. A 1997 Justice Department report looked at homicides by youths aged 13 and 14 with and without guns. In 1980 there were 74 murders committed with guns and 68 without by that age group. In 1995 gun-related murders totaled 178; there were 67 nongun murders.

8   Exaggerated claims about juvenile crime would be a hard sell if people weren't ready to believe the worst about young people. A 1997 report from Public Agenda, a nonprofit policy group, called "Kids These Days: What Americans Really Think About the Next Generation," found that 58 percent of those surveyed think children and teens will make the world a worse place or no different when they grow up. Even kids aged 5 to 12 weren't spared, with 53 percent of respondents characterizing them in negative terms. Only 23 percent had positive things to say about children. What America really thinks about its kids, in short, is: not much.

9   The generation gap is old news, but this sour, almost hateful view of young people is different. Adults aren't merely puzzled by young people; they're terrified of them. It can't be a coincidence that the shift in adult attitudes began roughly a generation after the height of political and social movements created by young people of all colors. Policy-makers now propelling anti-youth agendas remember how effective young people can be as a force for change. Demographics and the shifting nature of U.S. families also foster the anti-youth bias. According to census statistics, the number of people under age 65 has tripled since 1900, while the population aged 65 or over has increased elevenfold. One-quarter of all households are people living alone. And children are no longer integral to family structure: In 51 percent of all families there are no children under 18 living at home. Young people are easily demonized when their worlds don't coincide with ours. The sense of collective responsibility in raising children disappears as the building blocks of community change.

10   To an older America in a postindustrial world, children have become more of a liability than an asset. Middle-class parents calculate the cost of raising kids, including an overpriced college education, as they would a home mortgage. Low-income parents are bludgeoned by policies designed to discourage having children, from welfare reform to cuts in higher-education assistance. Young people's place in the economic order is uncertain, and a threat to those elders who are scrambling for the same jobs at McDonald's or in Silicon Valley. Says Barry Feld, professor at the University of Minnesota Law School and author of *Bad Kids: Race and the Transformation of Juvenile Court,* "Parents raised kids so they could take care of them when they're old. As caring for the old has shifted to the public sector, the elderly no longer have that fiscal investment in their kids. They know Social Security will be there for them."

11   Another reason adults are willing to condemn children is that it saves them from taking responsibility when kids go wrong. Take this statistical nugget: From 1986 to 1993, roughly the same period of the youth crime "explosion,"

the number of abused and neglected children doubled to 2.8 million, according to the Justice Department. And just three years later, the total of all juvenile arrests was 2.8 million. What goes around comes around.

12   Historically, U.S. criminal law followed the definitions of adulthood and childhood laid down by William Blackstone in his *Commentaries on the Laws of England* (1765–69). Children up to 7 were considered incapable of criminal responsibility by dint of their immaturity. At 14, they could be held as responsible as adults for their crimes: the years in between were a gray area of subjective judgment on culpability. But by 1900, reformers had created a separate system of juvenile courts and reform schools based on the principles that delinquency had social causes and that youth should not be held to adult standards. Eighteen was generally held as the entryway to adulthood.

13   The current transformation in juvenile justice is no less radical than the one 100 years ago. This time, though, we are marching backward to a one-size-fits-all system for youth and adults in which punishment, not reform, is the goal. From 1992 to 1995, forty-one states passed laws making it easier to prosecute juveniles in adult criminal court, and today all fifty states have such laws. In more than half the states, children under 14 can be tried in adult court for certain crimes. In thirteen states, there is no minimum age at which a child can be tried in adult court for felonies. New York permits prosecution of a 7-year-old as an adult for certain felonies. The Hatch-Sessions bill now in the U.S. Senate continues the assault on youthful offenders. It would use block grants to encourage states to toughen further their juvenile justice procedures. One provision eliminates the longstanding mandate to separate incarcerated juveniles and adults. "You're going to see more suicides and assaults if that happens," says Robert Shepherd.

14   Violent crimes like those in Oregon and Arkansas are a rarity, but they've become the rationale for a widespread crackdown on youth at school and on the streets. If Dennis the Menace were around, he'd be shackled hand and foot, with Mr. Wilson chortling as the cops hauled his mischievous butt off to juvenile hall. In Miami recently, a 10-year-old boy was handcuffed, arrested and jailed overnight because he kicked his mother at a Pizza Hut. His mother protested the police action—it was a waitress who turned him in. The boy now faces domestic battery charges in juvenile court.

15   Last October at the Merton Intermediate School in Merton, Wisconsin, four boys aged 12 and 13 were suspended for three days and slapped with disorderly conduct citations and fines (later dropped) by the local sheriff after they yanked up another boy's underwear "wedgie style." "The boys were playing, wrestling around in the schoolyard, and there was a pile-on," says Kevin Keane, an attorney who represented one of the boys. "One kid was on the ground and the others gave him a wedgie. He wasn't hurt or upset, and they all went back to class." But the principal learned about the incident and termed it a sexual assault.

16   Anti-youth analysts prefer to think more juvenile arrests means more kids are behaving recklessly. But it's just as plausible to argue that the universe of permissible behavior has shrunk. Look at curfews, which were virtually un-

known twenty years ago. Curfews generated 185,000 youth arrests in 1996—a 113 percent increase since 1987. Disorderly conduct arrests of youth soared 93 percent between 1987 and 1996, with 215,000 arrests in 1996 alone.

17   Public schools are at ground zero in the youth crackdown. A report released in March by the National Center for Education Statistics surveyed 1,234 public schools on crime and security measures. Three-fourths have "zero tolerance" policies on drugs, alcohol and weapons, which means ironclad punishment for any transgression. Six percent of the schools surveyed use police or other law enforcement on campus at least thirty hours a week, while 19 percent of high schools have stationed cops full time.

18   Public schools are even using dogs to search for illegal drugs. The Northern California A.C.L.U. filed suit in March 1997 against the Gait, California, school district on behalf of two students and a teacher who were subjected to dog searches during a course on criminal justice. "It's a real state police-prison element introduced into the schools," says A.C.L.U. lawyer Ann Bick. "It tells kids, 'We don't trust you.' And they'll live down to those expectations."

19   If the goal is to change behavior, draconian policies aimed at young people have been a dismal failure. Half a dozen studies have shown that transferring juveniles to adult courts not only doesn't deter crime, it's more likely to spur recidivism. But if the goal of the crackdown on youth is to divert attention from the real crimes plaguing the nation—child poverty, failing educational systems, 15 million kids without health insurance—then it's a success. New York City Mayor Rudolph Giuliani uses that strategy brilliantly. In January a child was killed by a brick falling from a badly managed school construction site, and reading scores were once again abysmally low. What were Giuliani's issues? Uniforms for students and deployment of police in the schools.

20   The criminalization of young people makes no sense, of course. Kids are a national treasure and natural resource, the bearers of our collective dreams and hopes. But logic and humanity don't often determine public policies or opinion. We are sowing the seeds, the dragon's teeth, of our own comeuppance. Erasing the line between youth and adulthood without granting youths the same constitutional protections and rights of citizenship as adults sets up a powerful contradiction. And sooner or later, to paraphrase Malcolm X, the chickens will come home to roost.

■ QUESTIONS FOR ANALYSIS AND DISCUSSION

1. What is "zero tolerance?" Why is it becoming the "mantra in public schools and juvenile courts" (paragraph 4)? How does Fuentes define the term? Do you agree?
2. If juvenile crime has not, as Fuentes states, dramatically increased, why is public opinion about children and crime shifting? What reasons does she cite?
3. As examples of the "crackdown" on youth, Fuentes relates two incidents in which children seemed to be treated harshly—one in which a child was arrested for kicking his mother and another in which two boys were fined for giving another boy a "wedgie" (paragraphs 14 and 15). How do these incidents

compare with the acts committed by the children in her opening paragraphs? Does such a juxtaposition support, or undermine, her argument?

4. Evaluate Fuentes' use of statistical data and examples to support her points. Which data and examples are particularly effective? Are there any examples or facts that seem particularly ineffective? Explain.

5. Consider Fuentes' suggestion that a present day Dennis the Menace would surely be in shackles. How effective is this image? What is your reaction to it? How does it contribute to the points she is trying to make in her essay?

■ WRITING ASSIGNMENTS

1. According to Annette Fuentes, one of the reasons adults are so willing to condemn children who commit crimes is that "it saves them from taking responsibility when kids go wrong." Write an essay in which you explore the role of parental responsibility for children's behavior. Should parents be held accountable for the actions of their children? Why or why not?

2. Linda J. Collier believes that the lenient treatment of violent youth by the courts thwarts justice. Other authors in this section, such as Talbot and Fuentes, believe that incarcerating juveniles with adults *ensures* that they will be repeat offenders. Research the juvenile rehabilitation practice of your own state's judicial system. Based on youth crime and recidivism (repeat offenses), defend or challenge the current system.

3. Research some recent violent and nonviolent crimes committed by juveniles over the past year. Some good resources for statistics and information on juvenile crime are available at the National Center for Juvenile Justice Web site, <www.ncjfcj.unr.edu>. Do you think public opinion supports the changes made to the juvenile justice system? Has media exposure of violent juvenile crimes influenced public opinion? Prepare an essay in which you address the connection between media exposure of violent juvenile crime and current prosecutorial practices in the judicial system.

4. What do young offenders themselves think about juvenile crime? A survey conducted by the California Bar Association indicated that "many of the children [surveyed] saw no connection between breaking the law and consequences." Visit the "Crime Is a Choice" Web site at <www.ncpa.org/hotlines/juvcrm/tccl.htm>. Are the young offenders the predators that Collier describes, or the confused kids of Talbot's essay?

GUN CONTROL

The Right to Bear Arms
Warren E. Burger

We open the dialogue on gun control with an essay by the late Chief Justice of the U.S. Supreme Court, Warren E. Burger. Examining the historical reasons for the

Second Amendment, Burger argues that its purpose was not necessarily to guarantee individuals the right to carry weapons, but to ensure that Americans could form militias in times of military need. Despite the widely held interpretation that the Second Amendment grants us each the right to own a weapon, Burger suggests that we must more importantly consider the historical context in which it was written, and he proposes measures for reducing "mindless homicidal carnage."

Burger was appointed to the U.S. Supreme Court in 1969 and served on the bench for seventeen years. He died in 1995 at the age of 87.

■ BEFORE YOU READ

Consider the title of this essay. What does the "right to bear arms" mean to you? Why do you suppose Burger used such a title even though he advocates gun control?

■ AS YOU READ

Why does Burger focus his argument on analyzing the history of the Second Amendment? Does his strategy result in the desired persuasive effect?

1   Our metropolitan centers, and some suburban communities of America, are setting new records for homicides by handguns. Many of our large centers have up to ten times the murder rate of all of Western Europe. In 1988 there were 9,000 handgun murders in America. Last year, Washington, D.C., alone had more than 400 homicides—setting a new record for our capital.

2   The Constitution of the United States, in its Second Amendment, guarantees a "right of the people to keep and bear arms." However, the meaning of this clause cannot be understood except by looking to the purpose, the setting, and the objectives of the draftsmen. The first ten amendments—the Bill of Rights—were not drafted at Philadelphia in 1787; that document came two years later than the Constitution. Most of the states already had bills of rights, but the Constitution might not have been ratified in 1788 if the states had not had assurances that a national Bill of Rights would soon be added.

3   People of that day were apprehensive about the new "monster" national government presented to them, and this helps explain the language and purpose of the Second Amendment. A few lines after the First Amendment's guarantees—against "establishment of religion," "free exercise" of religion, free speech and free press—came a guarantee that grew out of the deep-seated fear of a "national" or "standing" army. The same First Congress that approved the right to keep and bear arms also limited the national army to 840 men; Congress in the Second Amendment then provided:

> A well regulated Militia, being necessary to the security of a free State, the right of the people to keep and bear Arms, shall not be infringed.

4   In the 1789 debate in Congress on James Madison's proposed Bill of Rights, Elbridge Gerry argued that a state militia was necessary:

. . . to prevent the establishment of a standing army, the bane of liberty . . . Whenever governments mean to invade the rights and liberties of the people, they always attempt to destroy the militia in order to raise an army upon their ruins.

5   We see that the need for a state militia was the predicate of the "right" guaranteed; in short, it was declared "necessary" in order to have a state military force to protect the security of the state. That Second Amendment clause must be read as though the word "because" was the opening word of the guarantee. Today, of course, the "state militia" serves a very different purpose. A huge national defense establishment has taken over the role of the militia of 200 years ago.

6   Some have exploited these ancient concerns, blurring sporting guns—rifles, shotguns, and even machine pistols—with all firearms, including what are now called "Saturday night specials." There is, of course, a great difference between sporting guns and handguns. Some regulation of handguns has long been accepted as imperative; laws relating to "concealed weapons" are common. That we may be "overregulated" in some areas of life has never held us back from more regulation of automobiles, airplanes, motorboats, and "concealed weapons."

7   Let's look at the history.

8   First, many of the 3.5 million people living in the thirteen original Colonies depended on wild game for food, and a good many of them required firearms for their defense from marauding Indians—and later from the French and English. Underlying all these needs was an important concept that each able-bodied man in each of the thirteen independent states had to help or defend his state.

9   The early opposition to the idea of national or standing armies was maintained under the Articles of Confederation; that confederation had no standing army and wanted none. The state militia—essentially a part-time citizen army, as in Switzerland today—was the only kind of "army" they wanted. From the time of the Declaration of Independence through the victory at Yorktown in 1781, George Washington, as the commander in chief of these volunteer-militia armies, had to depend upon the states to send those volunteers.

10   When a company of New Jersey militia volunteers reported for duty to Washington at Valley Forge, the men initially declined to take an oath to "the United States," maintaining, "Our country is New Jersey." Massachusetts Bay men, Virginians, and others felt the same way. To the American of the eighteenth century, his state was his country, and his freedom was defended by his militia.

11   The victory at Yorktown—and the ratification of the Bill of Rights a decade later—did not change people's attitudes about a national army. They had lived for years under the notion that each state would maintain its own military establishment, and the seaboard states had their own navies as well. These people, and their fathers and grandfathers before them, remembered how monarchs had used standing armies to oppress their ancestors in Europe. Americans wanted no part of this. A state militia, like a rifle and powder horn, was as

much a part of life as the automobile is today; pistols were largely for officers, aristocrats—and dueling.

12   Against this background, it was not surprising that the provision concerning firearms emerged in very simple terms with the significant predicate—basing the right on the *necessity* for a "well regulated militia," a state army.

13   In the two centuries since then—with two world wars and some lesser ones—it has become clear, sadly, that we have no choice but to maintain a standing national army while still maintaining a "militia" by way of the National Guard, which can be swiftly integrated into the national defense forces.

14   Americans also have a right to defend their homes, and we need not challenge that. Nor does anyone seriously question that the Constitution protects the right of hunters to own and keep sporting guns for hunting game any more than anyone would challenge the right to own and keep fishing rods and other equipment for fishing—or to own automobiles. To "keep and bear arms" for hunting today is essentially a recreational activity and not an imperative of survival, as it was 200 years ago; "Saturday night specials" and machine guns are not recreational weapons and surely are as much in need of regulation as motor vehicles.

15   Americans should ask themselves a few questions. The Constitution does not mention automobiles or motorboats, but the right to keep and own an automobile is beyond question; equally beyond question is the power of the state to regulate the purchase or the transfer of such a vehicle and the right to license the vehicle and the driver with reasonable standards. In some places, even a bicycle must be registered, as must some household dogs.

16   If we are to stop this mindless homicidal carnage, is it unreasonable:

1. to provide that, to acquire a firearm, an application be made reciting age, residence, employment, and any prior criminal convictions?
2. to require that this application lie on the table for ten days (absent a showing for urgent need) before the license would be issued?
3. that the transfer of a firearm be made essentially as that of a motor vehicle?
4. to have a "ballistic fingerprint" of the firearm made by the manufacturer and filed with the license record so that, if a bullet is found in a victim's body, law enforcement might be helped in finding the culprit?

17   These are the kinds of questions the American people must answer if we are to preserve the "domestic tranquility" promised in the Constitution.

■ QUESTIONS FOR ANALYSIS AND DISCUSSION

1. Given some of the more shocking instances of gun misuse reported in the news (i.e., school shootings, disgruntled employees killing coworkers), do you feel that gun laws are in need of revision? If so, what sort of changes do you feel would be effective?
2. After reading Burger's history of the Second Amendment, do you feel that the "right to bear arms" means that an individual has the right to carry a weapon, or that it applies to the right to create a state militia? Explain.

3. Burger states in paragraph 14 that "Americans also have a right to defend their homes, and we need not challenge that." How far do you think this right goes? Explain.
4. Evaluate the suggestions Burger sets forth in paragraph 16 to solve the problem of handgun homicides. Would his solutions work? Why or why not? Should there be more government regulation of handguns? Explain.
5. Do you think Burger's analogy between the registration of handguns and the registration of motor vehicles is a compelling argument?
6. Burger's argument addresses a very specific aspect of the issue of handgun control. Do you find this narrow focus advantageous or detrimental to the overall effectiveness of his argument?

Zero Tolerance for Slaughter
Sallie Tisdale

Gun control is an issue that has significantly impacted the heart of the home. Every day, says gun safety expert Gavin de Becker, about seventy-five children are injured by gunfire, with a majority of accidents occurring in the home. And adolescents are twice as likely to commit suicide if a gun is kept in the home. In the next article, Sallie Tisdale explains why she is fed up with the attitude of many legislators facing the gun lobby. Why, she asks, do we need to cater to the desires of gun enthusiasts when parents are now afraid to send their children off to school? And in a country where everything from broccoli to aspirin is regulated, why are we so lenient where weapons are concerned?

Tisdale is the author of several books, including *Stepping Westward* (1991) and *The Best Thing I Ever Tasted: The Secret of Food* (2000). Her work has been published in *Vogue,* the *New York Times, Harpers,* and *The New Republic.* She is a frequent contributor to *Salon* magazine, in which this article first appeared in May 1999.

■ **BEFORE YOU READ**

Do you feel that your personal safety is threatened by the 200 million plus firearms in circulation within our nation today? Why or why not? Do you think parents are more likely to side with Tisdale? Why or why not?

■ **AS YOU READ**

Notice Tisdale's use of language, the way she poses questions to her audience, and the words she uses to describe people who support the right to bear arms. Does her tone undercut or strengthen the force of her argument?

1   I've long been an advocate of gun control, long frustrated by the craven attitude of many legislators when faced with the gun lobby. I was glad to see,

shortly after the Littleton massacre, an editorial calling for the abolition of the Second Amendment. Donald Kaul, writing for the *Chicago Tribune*, cited Great Britain's recent ban on possession of handguns. *All* handguns. The law was passed in response to the shooting in Dunblane, Scotland, three years ago. (You remember the Dunblane shooting, numb though you may be now. A man burst into a school and killed a teacher and sixteen small children before shooting himself.) Kaul suggested that what is needed is not a vague reference to bearing arms, but an amendment to the Constitution giving Congress the authority "to regulate the sale and manufacture of firearms."

2   I was applauding Kaul all along, until he added that what's really needed is "a compromise that balanced the needs and desires of gun enthusiasts with the need of society to protect itself . . ." And there we part ways.

3   This is what I want to know: Why do we need to balance the "needs and desires of gun enthusiasts" with anything at all? It is exactly this hedged, liberal urge to satisfy everyone that has gotten us into the dreadful mess we find ourselves in today—a mess that the writers of the Constitution would have deplored. Do we really believe that Benjamin Franklin and Thomas Jefferson intended the citizens of their imagined country to be scared to send their children to school? Why must we listen to the claims of gun lovers, or make any effort at all to satisfy their irrational appetite for weapons? Why should we bow to the rage and hunger of a single-issue lobby? Why should we think *for even one more second* that freedom means the freedom to own terrifying weapons of mass destruction? The discourse on the pro-gun side of this debate becomes more and more extreme, an endgame in which each one of us—commuters, shoppers, neighbors, teachers, nurses, friends—carries a gun, concealed, ready to shoot. Is this the world we are willing to make?

4   If we don't say no, it is the world we will have.

5   I am no longer an advocate of gun control. I am an advocate of gun elimination.

6   In this strange, wonderful, unique democracy, we have freedoms no other people have enjoyed. Still, we regulate the swear words people say on the radio. We regulate toys. We regulate broccoli, aspirin and massage. We legislate which trees a homeowner can plant along their curb. We require motorcyclists to wear helmets. We insist on building permits, speed limits, and driver's licenses. We rate movies. We simply prohibit the use of marijuana. But we are afraid to say no to guns.

7   Guns are, in fact, treated in a completely different way from any other commodity, any other choice. The American government and the American public—you and me—are peculiarly passive and even hopeless in the face of the gun lobby. In just the last 10 years, 35 million *new* guns have been added to the *200 million* guns we've manufactured in this country in the 20th century. They've been added to our daily lives, to our shopping malls, neighborhoods, city parks, street corners and schools. According to the Coalition to Stop Gun Violence there is now a gun for every single adult in this country *and* for every other child. A new handgun is made in this country every 20 *seconds*. Only the

most outrageous weapons—machine guns and grenades—must be registered with the government. There are no federal safety standards for firearms. (There are clearly defined standards for stuffed animals, for Christmas tree lights and for cereal.) We allow people to buy lethal weapons at gun shows without even a swift background check. Imagine your worst nightmare, your scariest neighbor, your angriest employee or the most frightening student at your child's high school loading up on ammo this weekend at a convention center near you. It's perfectly legal. It happens all the time, and we act as though there is nothing we can do about it.

8   In fact, the United States has the weakest regulations and the highest rate of death from firearms of any industrialized country on the planet—and of many less-industrialized nations. The statistics I use come from Physicians for Social Responsibility, the Coalition to Stop Gun Violence and the Bureau of Alcohol, Tobacco and Firearms. If a pro-gun reader wants to challenge these "biased" statistics, I invite him to do so. Show me that it is not true that children in the United States are 12 times likelier to die from guns than children in other industrialized countries. Show me I'm wrong, that it isn't my daughter, my sons, your daughters and sons, your grandchildren—your hearts—who are dying. Only cars kill more of us and more of our babies. And still we stand by.

9   Why? Why do we feel a compromise of any kind is required here? Even liberals who would like to see gun control may be swayed by the fear of lost rights, of constitutional change, of interfering in private choice. Many other countries have decided that public safety comes before this particular private choice. What terrible tyrannies are these, which have banned or strictly limited the private possession of most guns? Australia. Canada. Spain. Germany. The death rate from firearms in the United States is 24 times higher than that in the United Kingdom. It is 196 times higher than that of Japan. These are not countries where the military marches in the street, enforcing curfews. These are not societies where armed criminals run amok. These are not, as the National Rifle Association likes to claim, countries on that first slippery step down the same slope the Nazis chose.

10   I am unmoved by the insistence of the gun lobby that their desire to make, sell, buy, collect and, most of all, use mutilating, lethal weapons somehow equals my need to allow them to do so. I am unmoved by claims of freedom, lifestyle or privacy in this realm. As a society, we have ignored such claims made (in remarkably similar language) by sexual predators, heroin dealers and white supremacists. Why do we think guns are different? What are we worried about, really? Perhaps we are worried that it is not a good idea to enrage people who like to wave guns about. It worries me, and it should worry you. We are a country of hundreds of millions of mostly rational people, and we are held hostage to a primitive killing urge.

11   If an American cannot be happy without collecting and shooting deadly weapons, I invite him to move to a country where he can do so. There are a number of such places—most of them class-based or religious tyrannies without many of the freedoms we enjoy here, but you can't have everything. That is the

point of a democracy, after all, one of its more subtle and vital points—you can't have everything and still be free. There are countries where you can shoot machine guns to your heart's content. Go there, if that's what you want.

12   The phrase "gun nut" is not a joke. No one needs these weapons for anything. People just want them, and they want them with such angry lust that I had to face down a little fear to write this column. I am afraid of guns; I am afraid of people who like guns, own guns for the sake of owning them and shoot them for the feeling of shooting. I am a little scared all the time. I think we all are—and should be. Is there a legislator in this country brave enough to take this on?

13   I no longer want gun control. I want an absolute ban on the manufacture, sale, possession and use of handguns and automatic weapons in this country, with long prison sentences for violations. I realize there must be exceptions. The police need guns—at least until we get rid of the hundreds of millions of guns floating around. I am not opposed to game hunting for subsistence, and I can live with hunting rifles. Single-shot rifles. It will not be an easy or swift matter to eliminate guns; 200 million weapons is a lot of metal, a lot to find. It requires money, effort, collective goals and government support. We must not feel this is a hopeless task; we must not give up or give in. It can be done. All that is really missing is our will.

■ QUESTIONS FOR ANALYSIS AND DISCUSSION

1. In her opening statements, why does Tisdale object to any compromises connected to eliminating handguns from society? On what grounds does she base her objections? Explain.

2. In paragraph 3, Tisdale states, "Do we really believe that Benjamin Franklin and Thomas Jefferson intended the citizens of their imagined country to be scared to send their children to school?" To what is she referring? How does this reference support her argument?

3. In paragraph 6, Tisdale lists several things that are regulated by the government: "We regulate the swear words people say on the radio. We regulate toys. We regulate broccoli, aspirin and massage." How does this list frame her argument against guns? Does she have a point? How might an advocate for gun rights respond to this aspect of her argument?

4. At the end of her essay, Tisdale declares, "If an American cannot be happy without collecting and shooting deadly weapons, I invite him to move to a country where he can do so" (paragraph 11). How could this argument backfire? Explain.

5. Evaluate Tisdale's methods of appealing to her audience. Does she rely on emotion? shared ideology? Does she make certain assumptions about her audience? How does she challenge her opponents? If she were one of the speakers at a gun control debate, how well do you think she would fare? Explain.

6. Do the concessions Tisdale makes in her final paragraph undermine her argument? How do these concessions compare to the statements she makes in the first three paragraphs of her essay? Explain.

An Army of Gun Lies
David Kopel

In the next piece, David Kopel challenges the arguments presented by antigun advocates as outright lies. Although "a full listing of the lies told by the antigun lobby could fill a book," says Kopel, he selects a few of the more popular ones to address in this essay. The antigun lobby, he explains, resorts to such devious measures because they cannot win their arguments otherwise.

Kopel is an adjunct professor of law at New York University School of Law and Associate Policy Analyst with the Cato Institute. He also serves as Research Director of the Independence Institute in Golden, Colorado. An attorney, Kopel is the author of several books addressing the issue of gun control, including *Guns: Who Should Have Them?* (1995) and *No More Wacos: What's Wrong with Federal Law Enforcement and How to Fix It* (1997). This article appeared in the April 17, 2000, issue of *The National Review.*

■ BEFORE YOU READ

Most writers who wish to make persuasive arguments rely on facts and statistics to back up their claims. How important are facts to forming a convincing argument? What happens when facts are skewed? How important is critical reading when determining the validity of an author's facts?

■ AS YOU READ

Consider Kopel's use of the word "factoid" when referring to statistics cited by the antigun lobby. What is the difference between a fact and a factoid? Why does he use this word, and what is its effect? Explain.

~ AttAcks people ~

1   Antigun advocates have always faced an uphill battle in this country. Americans have, to begin with, a constitutional right to gun ownership. Today, half of American households exercise this right, owning a total of about 250 million guns; and over 99 percent of those households do so in a responsible manner. To fight for major restrictions on an item that plays such a valued part in the lives of so many people looks like a nearly impossible task. So if you're really committed to the effort, and you want to win, what do you do?

2   Simple: You lie.

3   A full listing of the lies told by the antigun lobby could fill a book. A short list of the more popular ones would have to begin with the canard about the number of children killed by firearms. We are told repeatedly that 13, or 15, or

17 children every day are killed by guns. This factoid is used to conjure up pictures of dozens of little kids dying in gun accidents every week.

4   In truth, the number of fatal gun accidents is at its lowest level since 1903, when statistics started being kept. That's right: Not only is the per capita accident rate at a record low, so is the actual number of accidents—even though the number of people and the number of guns are both much larger than in 1903. The assertions about "X children per day" are based on counting older teenagers, or even people in their early twenties, as "children." The claims are true only if you count a 19-year-old drug dealer who is shot by a competitor, or an 18-year-old armed robber who is shot by a policeman, as "a child killed by a gun." As for actual children (14 years and under), the daily death rate is 2.6. For children ten and under, it's 0.4 per day—far lower than the number of children who are killed by automobiles, drowning, or many other causes.

5   If the statistic about child gun deaths is the most notorious lie, one of the most frequent has to do with gun shows. All of the antigun groups repeat, incessantly, the phrase "gun-show loophole." As a result, much of the public believes that gun shows are special zones exempt from ordinary gun laws. Handgun Control, Inc., the major antigun group, has an affiliate in Colorado that claims that the "vast majority" of guns used in crimes come from gun shows, while the Violence Policy Center calls gun shows "Tupperware parties for criminals."

6   This is all an audacious lie. First of all, the laws at gun shows are exactly the same as they are everywhere else. If a person is "engaged in the business" (as the law puts it) of selling firearms, then he must fill out a government registration form on every buyer, and get FBI permission (through the National Instant Check System) for every sale—regardless of whether the sale takes place at his gun store, at an office in his home, or at a gun show. Those who are not gun dealers by profession, but happen to be selling a gun, are not required to follow this procedure. To imply that gun dealers can go to an event called a "gun show" and thus avoid the law is absolutely false. Also false is the charge about Tupperware parties for criminals. According to a National Institute of Justice study released in December 1997, only 2 percent of guns used in crimes come from gun shows. The gun-show charge has great currency in the media, but it is not very important in itself.

7   How about the more serious charge that guns are basically dangerous to society? Public-health experts and gun-control lobbyists will tell you that most murders, including those involving guns, take place among acquaintances and are perpetrated by ordinary people; these facts supposedly indicate that ordinary people are too hot-tempered to be allowed to have guns.

8   The facts tell a different story: 75 percent of murderers have adult criminal records. As for the rest, a large number either have criminal convictions as juveniles or are still teenagers when they commit the murder; laws dealing with access to juvenile-crime records prevent full access to their rap sheets. Furthermore, the category of "acquaintance" murders is misleading. It includes drug buyers who kill a drug dealer to steal his stash, and thugs who assault each other in barroom brawls.

9   There's also a sad irony here. Domestic murders are almost always preceded by many incidents of violent abuse. If a domestic-violence victim flees the home, and her ex-husband tracks her down and tries to rape her, and she shoots him, the killing will be labeled a "tragic domestic homicide that was caused by a gun," rather than what it legally is: justifiable use of deadly force against a felon.

10   The famous factoid that a gun in the home is 43 times more likely to kill a family member than to kill a criminal is predicated on a similar misclassification. Of the 43 deaths, 37 are suicides; and while there are obviously many ways in which a person can commit suicide, only a gun allows a small woman a realistic opportunity to defend herself at a distance from a large male predator.

11   Emory University medical professor Arthur Kellermann is a one-man factory of this type of misleading data. One of his most famous studies purported to show that owning a gun is associated with a 2.7 times greater risk of being murdered. Kellermann compared murder victims in several cities with sociologically similar people a few blocks away in those cities, who had not been murdered.

12   The 2.7 factoid was trumpeted all over the country; but the study is patently illogical. First of all, Kellermann's own data show that owning a security system, or renting a home rather than owning it, are also associated with equally large increased risks of death. Yet newspapers did not start running dire stories warning people to rip out their burglar alarms or to start lobbying their condo association to dissolve. The 2.7 factoid also overlooks the obvious fact that one reason people choose to own guns, or to install burglar alarms, is that they are already at higher risk of being victimized by crime. As Yale law professor John Lott points out, Kellermann's methodology is like comparing 100 people who went to a hospital in a given year with 100 similar people who did not, finding that more of the hospital patients died, and then announcing that hospitals increase the risk of death. Kellermann's method would also prove that possession of insulin increases the risk of diabetes.

13   The media are complicit in many of these lies. Take, for example, the hysteria about so-called "assault weapons." Almost everything that gun-control advocates say about these firearms is a lie. The guns in question are not machine guns; they are simply ordinary guns with ugly cosmetics that give them a pseudo-military appearance. The guns do not fire faster than ordinary guns. The bullets they fire are not especially powerful; they are, in fact, smaller and travel at lower velocity than bullets from standard hunting rifles.

14   The media have succeeded in giving a totally different impression— through deliberate fraud. The CBS show *48 Hours* purported to show a semiautomatic rifle being converted to fully automatic—i.e., turned into a machine gun—in just nine minutes. But the gun shown at the beginning was not the same gun that was fired at the end of the demonstration. An expert from the Bureau of Alcohol, Tobacco and Firearms (BATF) later said that such a conversion was impossible. And in Denver, KMGH television filmed people firing automatic weapons and told viewers that the guns were semiautomatics.

15   The most dangerous dishonesty concerns the ultimate intentions of the antigun forces. Handgun Control claims that it merely wants to "keep guns out of

the wrong hands"; yet in 1999, it lobbied hard to preserve Washington, D.C.'s outright ban on handguns. Back in 1976, the group's then leader, Pete Shields, explained the long-term strategy to *The New Yorker:* "The first problem is to slow down the number of handguns being produced and sold in this country. The second problem is to get handguns registered. The final problem is to make possession of all handguns and all handgun ammunition—except for the military, police, licensed security guards, licensed sporting clubs, and licensed gun collectors—totally illegal."

16   Sarah Brady, the current chairwoman of Handgun Control, has said that people should not be allowed to own guns for self-defense. Yet in debates, employees of the group steadfastly deny that the organization believes in the policies articulated by its leaders. In short, they are lying about what they want to accomplish. This is understandable, to be sure; but not honorable, or right for the country.

■ QUESTIONS FOR ANALYSIS AND DISCUSSION

1. In paragraph 3, Kopel asserts that the "canard" of the antigun lobby relates to the number of children killed by guns. He argues that their claim that thirteen to seventeen children a day are killed by guns is misleading because the number includes older teenagers in its count. What examples does he give of these "older teenagers"? What limitations, if any, should be considered when contemplating this statistic?

2. A key argument made by antigun advocates is that gun shows allow guns to be sold without the same restrictions imposed when selling a gun in a store. Kopel states that gun shows are subject to the same laws as "everywhere else." Review his argument (paragraphs 5 and 6). Does he successfully debunk this "myth"? Is there anything in his argument to which opponents might object? Explain.

3. Consider the words Kopel uses to describe the claims made by the antigun lobby: "notorious lie," "audacious lie," and "dangerous dishonesty." Do these words add force to his argument? How do they serve to emphasize his feelings? Do they distract you from his argument, or compel you to consider his points?

4. What objections does Kopel have to the data produced by Emory University medical professor Arthur Kellermann? How does he support his objections to Kellerman's claims?

5. According to Kopel, what role does the media play in the dissemination of gun lies? Why would they lie?

6. How persuasive is Kopel's argument? Evaluate its strengths and weaknesses.

Antigun Protest

On September 21, 1994, demonstrators positioned over forty thousand pairs of shoes representing gunshot victims alongside the Capitol's reflecting pool in Washington, D.C. Called a "silent march," the protest was an appeal to the U.S. Congress to reduce gun violence. The shoes represented the number of Americans killed

by guns in a single year. Grouped by state, the shoes were shipped to Washington and placed around the pool by hundreds of volunteers. The ghostly and silent "protesters" served as eerie reminders to politicians and citizens alike of the extent of gun-related violence in the United States today. This photo, taken by Michelle V. Agins, originally appeared in the *New York Times*.

■ QUESTIONS FOR ANALYSIS AND DISCUSSION

1. What is the symbolism of the empty shoes? Why is this article of clothing particularly poignant? Would the effectiveness of this message have been lost if the organizers used shirts or another piece of apparel? Explain.
2. How is this photo a representation of the "public speaking out"? How did the shoes "speak out" without actually uttering a word? How can silence sometimes be more effective than speaking?
3. Describe your overall impressions of this photograph. How does it make you feel? What issues does it convey? On what levels does it operate? Explain.
4. Rereview the photograph of the shoes of gunshot victims at the Capitol building. Organizers of this "march" conveyed their message without shouting slogans or hoisting any signs. Can you think of other ways we communicate strong messages without speaking? Explain.

Gun Control Needs a Middle Ground

Jack Levin

In the next article, professor of sociology and criminology Jack Levin advocates a middle ground for gun control. He concedes that his points may "satisfy almost nobody" because the gun control debate seems to be framed in all-or-nothing terms—one is either a "gun-control zealot" or a "gun fanatic." But the facts, says Levin, speak for themselves, and if we are to ever truly address the growing problem of gun violence in this country, it is time for each side to make some compromises.

Levin is Director of the Program for the Study of Violence at Northeastern University, where he also teaches sociology and criminology. He is the author or coauthor of many books, including *Overkill: Mass Murder and Serial Killings Exposed* (1994) and *The Will to Kill: Making Sense of Senseless Murder* (2000), both cowritten with Alan Fox. He has served as an expert commentator on many television programs, including *60 Minutes, 20/20,* and *Larry King Live.* He prepared this article for the RKBA Web in August 2000.

■ BEFORE YOU READ

Levin opens his essay with a quote from Janet Reno who states that it is "common sense" to deny guns to people who should not have them. Who determines who should, and who should not, be allowed access to firearms? Is the right to bear arms in the same category as freedom of speech and religion? Can the right be taken away? If so, by whom?

■ **AS YOU READ**

Levin states that the biggest problem facing the gun control debate is the lack of flexibility on both sides of the argument. What accounts for this lack of "middle ground"? Why must the debate be "all or nothing"? Does it have to be?

1   The latest incarnation of the gun-control debate involves a new American Medical Association study that finds gun background checks do not reduce murder rates. Attorney General Janet Reno has already voiced her disagreement with the study, arguing it is "common sense" to deny guns to people who shouldn't have them.

2   The problem with the gun-control debate is that it is constantly being framed in all-or-nothing absolute terms: the NRA vs. Janet Reno or the Million Mom March, criminals vs. law-abiding citizens, or the Second Amendment vs. government repression.

3   Does gun control actually reduce violence? The truth will satisfy almost nobody because it lies in the gray area between gun-control zealots and gun fanatics. In reality, it depends on what type of control measure is being advocated and on what kind of killing is being addressed.

4   *Banning assault weapons.* Most of the large-scale massacres have been committed with semi-automatic weapons. Get rid of AK-47s and you would reduce the massive body counts. But fewer than 1 percent of all murder victims—about 200 a year—lose their lives to someone who goes on a rampage. By contrast, some 19,000 annually are killed by a single bullet in a one-on-one confrontation. Eliminating high-power semi-automatics would do almost nothing to reduce single-victim murders.

5   *Waiting periods and background checks.* Most mass killers do not mind waiting. They have typically done so for months before opening fire at a crowded shopping mall or school. A waiting period would therefore do almost nothing to reduce the possibility of a massacre. However, the Brady Law's five-day waiting requirement was effective in providing a cooling-off period for enraged lovers and friends who might spontaneously be angry enough to kill themselves or others if they had a loaded gun in their hands at the time. This effect may not always show up in overall statistics. Background checks may have an impact on the so-called secondary gun market, reducing the number of firearms sold to criminals by unlicenced dealers.

6   *Liberalizing concealed weapons laws.* If almost everybody in town is packing heat, then you'd probably be safer doing the same. Certainly, a bank robber might think twice about pulling a loaded gun if all the customers and employees have one. Remember that the next time you visit Texas, where guns are as commonplace as chicken-fried steak. But just the opposite may be true in Massachusetts, where relatively few citizens carry firearms and the real problem is not murders committed by strangers, but by friends and family members who impulsively shoot one another. A liberal concealed weapons law in the com-

monwealth might add to our murder rate by providing more of our citizens with a lethal means for resolving everyday arguments, not only at home but also in bars and on the job, not to mention the roads in and out of town during commuting hours.

7   *Gun buybacks.* The Million Mom Marchers were in favor of this measure. Gun buyback programs have some symbolic importance, but do little. People who turn in their guns can turn around and buy a more efficient model.

8   And individuals who plan to use their firearms in the near future are hardly the people who will turn them in for cash.

9   *Safety locks.* George W. Bush supports this measure. Anything that reduces the access of children to a loaded firearm might help. But it is doubtful that substantial numbers of gun owners will use gun locks, especially if they want immediate access to a weapon to defend against intruders.

10   *Education.* The National Rifle Association is really pushing this approach, yet parental and classroom instructions typically do not generalize to the playground where youngsters are more persuaded by peers. A child who is bent on revenge, belongs to a dangerous gang or deals illicit drugs might actually rely on his firearms training to instruct him in the most effective manner of killing. On the other hand, educating children about the danger of guns might reduce at least some of the accidental shootings that result in death.

11   It is often said that if we make guns difficult to obtain, then only the criminals will be able to get them. This argument makes the dubious distinction between the good guys without guns and the bad guys who use them on the good guys. Actually, most lethal injuries are inflicted not by outlaws but by people who accidentally shoot one another, leave their guns in places accessible to children or lose their cool.

12   Almost every American recognizes we need to limit the availability of firearms. But rather than continue to debate a false and divisive issue, we should now focus on determining which gun control measures are effective and which ones are a waste of our time. There is much common ground in the gun control argument, but only if we get beyond the extremists on both sides.

■ QUESTIONS FOR ANALYSIS AND DISCUSSION

1. Consider how Levin shows the pros and cons of each issue he discusses. How does this approach support the goals of his essay? How might gun control advocates such as Sallie Tisdale respond to his argument?

2. How would you characterize the tone of this essay—reasoned and objective? emotional? resigned and frustrated? Explain.

3. Levin explains why, in his opinion, banning assault weapons and imposing waiting periods won't work. How does he support these assertions? Do you agree with his logic?

4. Levin conjectures that "if almost everybody in town is packing heat, then you'd probably be safer doing the same" and observes that citizens of Texas own far

more guns than people from Massachusetts. Research gun-related crime rates in the state of Texas. How do they compare to gun-related crime rates in the Commonwealth of Massachusetts? Can you make any inferences based on your research? Explain.

5. What are the goals and intentions of the author in this article? Do you think he is more likely to take a stand for, or against, the control of firearms? Support your answer with examples from his essay.

■ WRITING ASSIGNMENTS

1. Several of the authors in this section cite frightening statistics of children using firearms to kill other children. Research this issue further, locating recent statistics on guns in schools; the number of children killed by guns; the number of children who use guns; and the number of accidental deaths caused by gunfire involving children. Your essay should either support or refute the claims made by these authors that gun ownership indeed poses a serious risk to children.

2. Write a paper in which you argue for or against gun control measures such as waiting periods, background checks, handgun bans, and so forth. As a starting point for your discussion, address one or several of the arguments you find in some of the essays in this section.

3. Do you own a gun? Would you? If you do not own a gun, can you imagine circumstances in which you might decide to buy one? If you do own a gun, do you use it for hunting, protection, or another purpose? Explain.

4. Write an essay summarizing the views of two authors in this section who present different viewpoints on gun control. Who makes the more compelling argument, and why? Remember that you can concede someone's argument without having to agree with it.

CAPITAL PUNISHMENT

A Death in Texas
Steve Earle

The debate over capital punishment is often couched in moral terms of right and wrong, or as a legal issue for politicians to debate. The next article, however, gives a personal account of one man's last days on death row. A man, says the writer, who profoundly changed over the twelve years he was incarcerated. But at the end of death row, there is only one exit.

Steve Earle is a well-known musician, with "Copperhead Road" and "The Devil's Right Hand" among his list of many country music credits. Having been in prison himself, Earle works and corresponds with many inmates. His relationship with Jonathan Nobles began when a friend asked him to write to Nobles. His personal experience as a witness to the execution of Nobles was first published in the September/October 2000 issue of *Tikkun*.

■ BEFORE YOU READ

Is punishing juveniles as adults for nonviolent crimes fair? Should the severity of the crime be considered when determining how a juvenile offender ought to be prosecuted?

■ AS YOU READ

This essay is written almost like a diary, expressing personal feelings and impressions. How does it appeal to your emotions? Does it change or influence your own viewpoint of capital punishment?

1   "Hey, man."

2   Jonathan Wayne Nobles grins at me through inch-thick wire-reinforced glass, hunching over to speak in a deep, resonant voice through the steel grate below. A feeble "What's up?" is the best I can manage. The visiting area in Ellis One Unit is crowded with other folks who have traveled, in some cases thousands of miles, to visit relatives and correspondents on Texas' Death Row. They sit at intervals in wooden chairs surrounding a cinder block and steel cage that dominates the center of the room. There are cages within the cage as well, reserved for inmates under disciplinary action and "death watch" status. Falling into the latter category, Jon must squeeze his considerable bulk into one of these phone-booth-sized enclosures.

3   It's an awkward moment for both of us. In the 10 years we have corresponded, we have never met face to face. The occasion is auspicious. Jon and I will spend eight hours a day together for the next three days and another three days next week. Then the state of Texas will transport Jon, chained hand and foot, 11 miles to the Walls unit in downtown Huntsville. There he will be pumped full of chemicals that will collapse his lungs and stop his heart forever. This is not a worst-case scenario. It is a certainty. Jonathan Nobles has precisely 10 days to live. And I, at Jon's request, will attend the execution as one of his witnesses.

4   Over the next few days a routine develops. I arrive at Ellis at 8:30 in the morning. We usually spend the first two hours talking about music, politics, religion—subjects that we have covered thoroughly enough in letters over the years to know that we have widely divergent views and tastes. We fill the long awkward silences that seem inevitable in prison visiting areas with trips to the vending machines for soft drinks, candy, and potato chips. I pass Jon's goodies to the guard on duty through a small opening in the steel mesh.

5   Inevitably, we move on to life behind bars, drugs, and recovery—topics where we share considerably more common ground. We are both recovering addicts who got clean only when we were locked up. Jon began reading about

recovery and attending 12-step meetings in prison years ago. I can remember a time, back when I was still using drugs, when the recovery-speak that filled his letters made me extremely uncomfortable. Now it is a language that we share—sort of a spiritual shorthand that cuts through the testosterone and affords us a convenient, if uncomfortable, segue to the business at hand.

6   There are arrangements to be made. If Jon's body were to go unclaimed, as is the case with half of the men executed in Texas, he would be buried in the prison cemetery on the outskirts of Huntsville. Called "Peckerwood Hill" by the locals, it is a lonely space filled with concrete crosses, adorned only with the interred inmates' prison numbers. Those executed by the state are easily identifiable by the "X" preceding their number. There are no names on the stones. Jon doesn't want to wind up there.

7   Instead, he wants to be buried in Oxford, England—a place he's never seen. One of his pen pals, a British woman named Pam Thomas, has described it to him in her letters. He likes the picture Pam paints of the springtime there, when the bluebells are in bloom. Jon says that Pam is working on permission from a landowner there. I have Plan B on the back burner. A Dominican community in Galway, Ireland, has offered Jon a final resting place. At some point in the proceedings, it dawns on me that I have spent the past hour helping a living, breathing man plan his own burial.

8   One thing Jon and I don't talk about much is the movement to abolish the death penalty. In fact, Jon is suspicious of abolitionists. We were "introduced" by a pen pal of his and an acquaintance of mine. She had heard that I sometimes corresponded with inmates and asked if she could give Jon my address. I said sure. Within a month, I received my first letter. It was a page and a half long in a beautiful flowing script. It contained a lot of the usual tough rhetoric and dark humor I had learned to expect in letters from inmates. After several readings, I realized that the jailhouse small talk was merely a medium, a vehicle for one pertinent piece of information—that Jonathan Wayne Nobles was guilty of the crimes he was charged with.

9   In 1986 Jon was convicted (almost entirely on the strength of his own confession) of stabbing Kelley Farquhar and Mitzi Johnson-Nalley to death. He also admitted stabbing Ron Ross, Nalley's boyfriend, who lost an eye in the attack. Jon never took the stand during his trial. He sat impassively as the guilty verdict was read and, according to newspaper accounts, only flinched slightly when District Judge Bob Jones sentenced him to death.

10   When Jon arrived at Ellis he quickly alienated all of the guards and most of the inmates. He once broke away from guards while returning to his cell from the exercise yard and climbed the exposed pipes and bars in the cell block, kicking down television sets suspended outside on the bottom tier. On another occasion he cut himself with a razor blade, knowing that the guards would have to open his cell to prevent him from bleeding to death. He just wanted to hit one officer before he passed out.

11   But somehow, somewhere along the line, in what is arguably the most inhumane environment in the "civilized" world, Jonathan Nobles began to change.

He became interested in Catholicism and began to attend Mass. He befriended the Catholic clergy who ministered in the prison system, including members of the Dominican Order of Preachers. He eventually became a lay member of the order and ministered to his fellow inmates, even standing as godfather at inmate Cliff Boggess' baptism. He later helped officiate at the Mass that was celebrated the night before Boggess' execution. I watched this transformation in the letters that I received.

12   The Jonathan Nobles who sits on the other side of the glass from me in September 1998 is a different man from the one the state of Texas sentenced to die almost 12 years ago. The greatest evidence of this fact is the way Jon is treated by everyone he encounters. A prison clerk, displaying genuine regret, interrupts our visit. She needs Jon to sign some papers. Jon does so and then informs me that the documents allow me to pick up his personal property and distribute it to a list of people detailed in a note the clerk will hand me on my way out. Inmate James Beathard, on his way down the line to visit with a family member, stops to talk and Jon introduces us. The guard patiently waits until the exchange is over before escorting him to his assigned cubicle. Socialization during inmate transfer is a clear violation of policy, but a lot of the rules have relaxed for Jon. He says it's like the last week of the school year. I believe it's more likely that he has earned the genuine respect of everyone here.

13   I excuse myself to go to the bathroom. The truth is, I simply need a break. On the way back I run into Father Stephen Walsh, a Franciscan friar from Boston who travels regularly to minister to the Catholic inmates at Ellis. He will serve as Jonathan's spiritual adviser, waiting with Jon in the holding cell over at the Walls until he's escorted into the death chamber itself. There, he will administer the last rites.

14   Every visit ends the same way. A guard gives us a five-minute warning, and Jon hurriedly dictates a list of "things to do" that I must commit to memory, since visitors are not allowed to bring writing instruments and paper into the unit. Then Jon presses his palm against the glass and I mirror his with mine, Jon says, "I love you. I'll see you tomorrow."

15   Over the past few days the other witnesses have arrived in Huntsville. I had dinner with Dona Hucka, Jon's aunt. She is the only blood relative to make the trip and she has driven all night to be here. Pam Thomas is in from England. Both are already on the unit when I arrive. We take turns leaning close to the glass while a prison employee takes Polaroid snapshots of each of us with Jon. The prison provides this service for the fee of eight dollars each.

16   It's 10 o'clock in the morning. There isn't much time left. At 12:30 we will be asked to leave the unit and Jon will be transported to the Walls. In the death chamber, we will be able to hear Jon over a speaker in the witness room, but this is our last opportunity to speak to him. Jon divides the remaining time between us more or less equally. I go first, Jon looks tired; the stress is showing for the first time. He leans down and motions me closer. I realize he's assessing my condition as well. "You all right, man?" I tell him that I'm okay. Jon is not convinced.

17   "I'm worried about you. You don't have to be Superman or nothin'. This is insane shit that's goin' on here today. You don't have to be strong for the women if that's what you're thinkin'. They're big girls. You need to take care of yourself."

18   "I know, Jon. I'm all right. I went to a meeting last night and my manager's here now. I've also got a couple of friends up from Houston who have done this before."

19   "Witnessed?"

20   "Yeah." That seemed to make him feel better. "Okay, but if you need to cry, it's all right. Go ahead and cry."

21   "When this is all over, I'll cry."

22   "Promise?"

23   "I promise."

24   Jon shifts gears suddenly. Back to business. He looks both ways to make sure the guard isn't watching. "Take this." With much effort he pushes a tiny slip of tightly rolled paper, the diameter of a toothpick, through the impossibly tight mesh. Somehow he pulls it off. "That's my daughter's phone number in California. My sister read it to me over the phone last night. They're going to strip search me and I can't take anything to the Walls and I'm afraid I'll forget it. Give it to Father Walsh. Then I'll have it when I make my last phone calls."

25   I poke the paper in the watch pocket of my Levi's. There are a few other requests. He wants me to call his foster mother and his sister after the execution, and send flowers to two women who worked for the prison who were kind to him over the years. I promise that I won't forget. "All right, bro. Take care of yourself and your kids. Tell Dona to come back." Hands against the glass one last time.

26   "I love you, Jonathan."

27   "I love you too, bro."

Noon

28   I head back into Huntsville. My manager, Dan Gillis, arrived last night and not a moment too soon. Suddenly, driving has become difficult. The world has taken on a kind of surrealistic patina. I need someone to drive for the rest of the day. Also waiting at the hotel are two friends from the abolition movement, Karen Sebung and Ward Larkin. Both have witnessed executions, and they have made the trip to assist in any way they can. We talk over arrangements for the transportation and cremation of Jon's body, which, as it turns out, Dan has already taken care of. I make a couple of phone calls and check my messages. Then I shower, shave, and put on a pair of black jeans, a blue short-sleeve shirt, and a black linen sport coat.

4:00

29   We leave the hotel. Dan drives us to Hospitality House, a guest residence operated by the Baptist Church for the families of inmates. Dona and Pam, as well as Pam's friend Caroline, are staying there. The two other witnesses, Bishop

Carmody of the East Texas diocese and the Reverend Richard Lopez of the Texas Department of Corrections, are already there when we arrive. We are assembled here for an orientation session to be conducted by the Reverend Jim Brazzil, the chaplain at the Walls unit. He and the warden will be the only two people inside the chamber with Jon when he dies. He goes through the execution process step-by-step so that we will know what to expect and, though it's obvious he speaks with authority, I'm not listening. I can't concentrate, so I just nod a lot. It doesn't matter. No matter how well or poorly the witnesses are prepared, they are going to kill Jon anyway.

5:05

30   Reverend Brazzil answers his cell phone. It's Father Walsh, who's over at the Walls with Jon and wants the phone number, the one that Jon passed me through the . . . oh my God. I can't find it. I was sure that I transferred the slip from my other jeans into my wallet when I changed clothes, but it's simply not there. Dan runs to the motel and checks my room, but it's hopeless. Reverend Brazzil relays the bad news to Father Walsh. I feel awful.

5:30

31   We arrive at the visitors' center across the street from the Walls unit. Karen Sebung accompanies me as far as the waiting area, where we witnesses are searched, then Dona and Pam are escorted to another room by a female officer. When they return, a large man enters the room and introduces himself as an officer of the prison's internal affairs division. If we should feel faint, he says, medical attention is available. He also warns us that anyone who in any way attempts to disrupt the "process," as he calls it, will be removed from the witness area immediately. Nothing about my body is working right. My feet and hands are cold and the side of my neck is numb.

5:55

32   The corrections officer returns. "Follow me, please." We walk across the street and through the front door of the old Gothic prison administration building. We turn left as soon as we enter and find ourselves in the waiting area of the governor's office, where we are asked to wait once again. There are two reporters there. The other three members of the press pool, along with the victims' family members, have already been escorted to the witness area, which is divided by a cinder block wall. The two sets of witnesses will never come in contact with each other.

6:00

33   We're led through a visiting area similar to the one at Ellis, then out into the bright evening sun for a moment and turn left down a short sidewalk. Another left and we enter a small brick building, built into the side of the perimeter wall. We enter the tiny room in single file. Father Walsh appears from somewhere inside the death chamber to join us. The reporters enter last, and the

door is locked behind us. I can hear the reporters scratching on their notepads with their pencils. There is only room for three of us—Dona, me, and Pam—in the front row. Dona grabs my left hand and squeezes it hard. She already has tears in her eyes.

34   Jon is strapped to a hospital gurney with heavy leather restraints across his chest, hips, thighs, ankles, and wrists. His arms are wrapped in Ace bandages and extended at his sides on boards. At either wrist, clear plastic tubes protrude from the wrappings, snaking back under the gurney and disappearing through a plastic tube set in a bright blue cinder block wall. I think I see movement behind the one-way glass mirror on the opposite wall—the executioner getting into position. Jon is smiling at us, his great neck twisted uncomfortably sideways. A microphone suspended from the ceiling hangs a few inches above his head. The speaker above our heads crackles to life and Jon speaks, craning his head around to see the victims' witnesses in the room next door.

35   "I know some of you won't believe me, but I am truly sorry for what I have done. I wish that I could undo what happened back then and bring back your loved ones, but I can't." Jon begins to sob as he addresses Mitzi Nalley's mother. "I'm sorry. I'm so sorry. I wish I could bring her back to you. And Ron . . . took so much from you. I'm sorry, I know you probably don't want my love, but you have it."

36   Turning to me, he seems to regain his composure somewhat. He even manages to smile again. "Steve, I can't believe that I had to go through all this to see you in a suit coat. Hey man, don't worry about the phone number, bro. You've done so much. I love you. Dona, thank you for being here. I know it was hard for you. I love you. Pam, thank you for coming from so far away. Thanks for all you have done. I love you. Bishop Carmody, thank you so much. Reverend Lopez and you, Father Walsh, I love you all. I have something I want to say. It comes from I Corinthians. It goes . . ." and Jon recites the lengthy piece of scripture that he agonized over for weeks, afraid he would forget when the time came. He remembers every word.

37   When he finishes reciting he takes a deep breath and says, "Father, into thy hands I commend my spirit." The warden, recognizing the prearranged signal he and Jon had agreed on, nods toward the unseen executioner and Jon begins to sing.

38   "Silent night / Holy night . . ."

39   He gets as far as "mother and child" and suddenly the air explodes from his lungs with a loud barking noise, deep and incongruous, like a child with whooping cough—"HUH!!!" His head pitches forward with such force that his heavy, prison-issue glasses fly off his face, bouncing from his chest and falling to the green tile floor below.

40   And then he doesn't move at all. I watch his eyes fix and glaze over, my heart pounding in my chest and Dona squeezing my hand. Dead men look . . . well, dead. Vacant. No longer human. But there is a protocol to be satisfied. The warden checks his watch several times during the longest five minutes of my life. When the time is up, he walks across the room and knocks on the door.

The doctor enters, his stethoscope earpieces already in place. He listens first at Jon's neck, then at his chest, then at his side. He shines a small flashlight into Jon's eyes for an instant and then, glancing up at the clock on his way out, intones, "6:18."

41   We are ushered out the same way we came, but I don't think any of us are the same people who crossed the street to the prison that day. I know I'm not. I can't help but wonder what happens to the people who work at the Walls, who see this horrific thing happen as often as four times a week. What do they see when they turn out the lights? I can't imagine.

42   I do know that Jonathan Nobles changed profoundly while he was in prison. I know that the lives of people he came in contact with changed as well, including mine. Our criminal justice system isn't known for rehabilitation. I'm not sure that, as a society, we are even interested in that concept anymore. The problem is that most people who go to prison get out one day and walk among us. Given as many people as we lock up, we better learn to rehabilitate someone. I believe Jon might have been able to teach us how. Now we'll never know.

■ QUESTIONS FOR ANALYSIS AND DISCUSSION

1. Does the fact that Jon Nobles is on "death watch status" seem strange to you? What is death watch status? Is it ironic that a man facing the last weeks of his sentence be placed on this status? Explain.
2. How do the days he spends with Jon Nobles affect Steve Earle? Does the fact that Earle himself has spent time in jail make his experience more personal?
3. Is Nobles ready to die? How does he express remorse for his crimes? Can violent criminals really change? Should concessions be made for those who do? Why or why not?
4. Review Earle's account of the final hours of Nobles's life (paragraphs 28 through 42). How does his technique build tension in the essay? Is it an effective way to impress the audience? Explain.
5. How do you think Earle feels about capital punishment? Does he come out and express his viewpoint? Does he make any personal assessments regarding Nobles's crime? Explain.

A Reckoning on Death Row
Jonathan Alter

In the next piece, Jonathan Alter, a long-time advocate for the death penalty, explains why he now feels we should proceed with caution. Only a few weeks before writing this column, Alter headed a *Newsweek* investigation on DNA testing and death row inmates. The report was troubling: In the state of Illinois alone, DNA evidence excluded thirteen people on death row for crimes they could not have committed. Alter explains that he still supports the death penalty, but only in cases where we can be absolutely certain that we are executing the right person.

Alter is a senior editor for *Newsweek* and author of its "Between the Lines" column that examines politics, media, and society at large. He is also a correspondent for NBC News. His work has appeared in many publications, including *The New Republic, Esquire,* the *New York Times,* and *Rolling Stone.* The following article appeared in the June 25, 2000, issue of *Newsweek.*

■ BEFORE YOU READ

Alter notes that at the time he wrote his column, only two states guaranteed for death row inmates the right to DNA testing. Should this be a guaranteed right for all inmates facing execution? Why or why not?

■ AS YOU READ

As you read Alter's essay, evaluate his use of evidence to support his position. Does the fact that Alter supports the death penalty overall, yet urges caution, make him a more reliable writer? Why or why not?

1   June 25—Like most people, I'm a hard-liner on crime. It makes me angry to see victims' families ignored, killers released on technicalities and "life" sentences that are more like sabbaticals. Bianca Jagger and Jesse Jackson are not going to turn me around on the death penalty.

2   But nowadays I'm a moratorium man, cast adrift on the issue along with many other Americans. First came the Illinois eye-openers, where several innocent men were released from death row. A quirk, perhaps? (Al Gore's current logic.) But it wasn't. Similar cases popped up elsewhere. Last year I interviewed a Missouri man, Roy Roberts, the night before his execution. There was no physical evidence, witnesses changed their stories and Roberts passed three lie-detector tests. I began to wonder are we really executing people without knowing for sure?

3   We are. This spring, I focused on an obscure case in Texas. The state was all set to execute Ricky McGinn, who looked very guilty but had not been given his proper DNA tests. It seemed like a no-brainer—why not find out for certain before executing him? This was the case in which [then] Gov. George W. Bush issued his first-ever reprieve. But that raised as many questions as it answered. Illinois and New York are the only states that currently allow inmates to obtain DNA testing on request, and Bush had previously turned down such testing in cases that didn't get as much publicity.

4   At least [the] presidential campaign [put] some important, if misunderstood, legal concepts back into public view. Take "reasonable doubt." It turns out that's the standard only at the original trial. After that, all the reasonable doubt in the world doesn't count without gross procedural error. And all the gross procedural error in the world doesn't count if defense attorneys don't protest early in the process. Bush insists that the system is "fair"; in fact, the system is something out of Joseph Heller or Franz Kafka.

5   Which brings us to Gary Graham, executed last week. Graham was a thug on a crime spree in 1981, and he might have killed Bobby Lambert outside a Houston supermarket. Might have. The evidence in the murder case was thin. There was no DNA, fingerprint or physical evidence. During the trial, the jury was told that Graham was arrested in possession of a 22-caliber pistol similar to the one used in the crime—but not told that the Houston police found that they were in fact different guns.

6   Of the eight witnesses who saw the killer in or near the store, seven could not identify Graham in the original police reports. He was sent to his death, contrary to the Biblical admonition, on the basis of a single eyewitness, Bernadine Skillern. Her story was convincingly told, but contradicted by two other witnesses who were never called to testify or even interviewed by the indisputably incompetent court appointed defense attorney.

7   How stacked is the deck? The higher courts, including the Supreme Court (which last week refused, 5–4, to review the case), tend to trust the original jurors—unless the original jurors have new doubts. Then their views don't matter. Three of the original jurors in the Graham case said that if they had heard all the witnesses originally, they would have voted to acquit. The higher courts were unmoved.

8   The bottom line is that the "full and fair" access to the courts that Bush brags about is now a mirage. In *Herrera* v. *Collins* (1993), the Supreme Court made it much tougher to bring a constitutional claim of innocence. And the 1996 Anti-Terrorism and Effective Death Penalty Act—pushed by the Clinton administration—sharply curtailed federal review of state cases. Despite numerous appeals, the facts of the Graham case were never formally revisited. After his 1981 trial, no court gave Graham even a short hearing on the question of his guilt or innocence.

9   That left a claim of "ineffective counsel," which is like buying a lottery ticket. The Supreme Court has only twice in two centuries granted relief on those grounds. Lower courts also routinely reject such claims, in part because they are so often the last refuge of the guilty. The courts apply what is jokingly called the "mirror test"—if it fogs up (because of the lawyer's breathing), he's "effective." The *Chicago Tribune* reported that in 43 of the 131 executions on Bush's watch—almost one third—inmates were represented by counsel publicly sanctioned for misconduct (sometimes in unrelated cases) by the state bar association.

10   The closer you look at the Texas system, the more questions it raises about Bush's leadership. One reason Texas has executed three times as many inmates as the next state (Virginia) is that Texas is one of only eight states that does not have a sentence of life in prison without parole. (Juries usually like that option.) And Texas is one of only a few states without a public-defender system. In 1995 Bush vetoed a bill that would have provided for one. He prefers a system where elected judges appoint lawyers who also often happen to be contributors to the judges' campaigns. These defense attorneys have a strong financial incentive to plead out cases and otherwise help the prosecution.

11   A new poll shows that nearly 60 percent of Texans believe the state has, at some point, executed the innocent. No matter. These voters apparently view state-sanctioned murder as a fair price to pay for maintaining the status quo. A real leader would try to take his people to a better place. Will Bush? I have reasonable doubt.

■ QUESTIONS FOR ANALYSIS AND DISCUSSION

1. Alter comments at the beginning of his editorial that "Bianca Jagger and Jesse Jackson are not going to turn me around on the death penalty." What assumptions can you make about the author based on this statement? Explain.
2. What does Alter mean when he says the current system is "something out of Joseph Heller or Franz Kafka"? How does this comment reinforce his point? What images does it create? It he taking a chance that his audience will understand who these people are?
3. What is "full and fair" access to the court system? Why, according to Alter, is it a "mirage"? What does this mean for people on death row?
4. Alter comments that one of the reasons Texas awards the death penalty so often is because jurors are not given the option recommending life in prison without parole. Should all states have this option? Explain.
5. This article was written before George W. Bush was elected president. Has the system in Texas changed at all since he left his office as governor of that state?

Alter Falters
Robert Pambianco

In the preceding article, *Newsweek* editor Jonathan Alter explains why he is changing his "hard-line" position on the death penalty—he fears that innocent people are being executed. In the next article, Robert Pambianco attacks Alter's position, arguing that innocence shouldn't even be the issue. Pambianco believes that one should assume a position based on moral convictions, not out of concern for fairness. Morality, in his opinion, is the only legitimate reason for opposing capital punishment, and anything else is just a smokescreen.

Pambianco is chief policy counsel for the Washington Legal Foundation. This article was published in the August 30, 2000, issue of *The National Review.*

■ BEFORE YOU READ

In the next piece, Pambianco states, "Morality would seem to be the only conceivable legitimate reason for opposing capital punishment." Do you agree? Is capital punishment a moral issue? Why or why not?

■ AS YOU READ

Are there benefits to the death penalty? Does it protect society? Is it an effective bargaining tool for prosecutors? Is it a deterrent? Do the benefits outweigh the risk of executing an innocent person?

1   Michael Kelly wrote not too long ago that with the exception of 13-year-old girls, there is no group more prone to group-think than the press. Confirmation of that statement can be found in the ongoing stampede of news stories about the death penalty, which stand in sharp contrast to the public's lack of concern for the issue.

2   Among the latest to join the bandwagon is Jonathan Alter, who, in last week's issue of *Newsweek,* explains his conversion to the anti-death-penalty side. Like so many of the other participants in this one-sided discussion, Alter focuses on the possibility of innocent people being executed rather than on the morality of capital punishment. Indeed, he goes to great length to underscore that he is not a criminal-coddling, bleeding-heart liberal and that his opposition is animated only by a concern for fairness. Which is a shame, because why should one be opposed to capital punishment if not out of a conviction that it is immoral? Innocence is not the issue, nor should it be.

3   For one thing, the innocence argument is just plain bogus. Innocent people are not being put to death. Can anyone guarantee that an innocent execution could never happen or that it has never happened? Of course not. But the death penalty is as close to a sure bet as you're going to get anywhere in the law. While imperfect, the system bends over backward to ensure the guilt of those executed, and people can be more certain about capital punishment than most else in life.

4   What none of the commentators who have fixated on innocence seem to grasp, is that judges love to overturn death sentences. Appeals courts make these decisions all the time not because the system is hopelessly flawed, but because the system is super cautious about executions. As it should be. All the chatter about mistakes at trials raises the obvious question: Would opponents be happier if the courts of appeals were less aggressive in their scrutiny of such cases? But enough about that, because innocence is not the issue.

5   Life is full of activities which we know with a certainty will result in people dying unintentionally—driving, flying, waging war, mountain climbing, vaccination programs, and so forth. Despite this knowledge, people and governments engage in such activities because of a determination that they are otherwise legitimate or beneficial.

6   For example, it is known that when a government sends soldiers into battle a certain number of innocent casualties will result. It is also known that there is high likelihood that a certain number of said soldiers will die as a result of friendly fire. Do such facts mean that the country should not use force to defend its interests because of that knowledge?

7   Consider another, more topical, example. Government officials know that innocent people will be killed, raped, or otherwise made the victim of a crime as a consequence of paroling prisoners. However, some jurisdictions maintain these programs because of a determination that they serve some supposedly useful purpose (a dubious proposition to be sure).

8   Of course, at a certain point such crimes would become—and in many states did become—intolerable. Certainly, in the case of capital punishment, if there was some reason to believe that innocent people were regularly being ex-

ecuted, then the innocence question would be relevant. However, nobody seriously believes that. In the overwhelming majority of capital cases, there is no credible issue of innocence, and most death-row appeals are not even based on a claim of factual innocence.

9   Boiled down, the argument about innocence is an argument for abolishing the criminal-justice system. In essence, opponents are saying that unless someone can guarantee with absolute certitude that no innocent person will ever be put to death—in other words unless the system can be shown to be infallible—it should not be allowed to operate.

10   Well, if society must be denied capital punishment because of an inability to ensure perfection in its implementation, then how can society maintain the punishment of life in prison with no possibility of parole? After all, the chances of an error in a non-capital murder case are much higher because of the safeguards and redundancies built into the capital cases. (One of the ironies about the innocence issue is that an "innocent" man—defining that term as broadly as possible—sentenced to death is much more likely to be vindicated than one sentenced to life in prison.) Applying the innocence rationale, the imperfect life sentence also should be eliminated. At a minimum, there should be a moratorium so the issue can be studied.

Placing the Risk

11   Rather than obsessing about the risk of an innocent execution, it is better to ask where risk should be placed—more accurately, on whom should it be placed.

12   It is well known that there is disagreement about the deterrent value of capital punishment, and opponents insist that deterrence cannot be proven. That is true in the sense that many different factors affect the vagaries in crime and murder rates around the country, and it is difficult to say for certain what factors are controlling. However, even if one concedes for the sake of argument that the death penalty does not have a substantial impact on the overall murder rate, common sense dictates that it deters some crimes, even if only a relative handful.

13   So, where do you want to place the risk? On the truly innocent murder victims or on the death-row prisoners who have been convicted by a jury and who will be afforded roughly eleven years of appeals in federal and state courts before the sentence is carried out—if ever?

14   Opponents of capital punishment put much faith in their assertion that nobody, especially the governor of Texas, can state with certainty that every person put to death was guilty of the crime. Very well, but how certain are they in their conviction that it's never a deterrent to murder?

15   What about the risk that opponents are wrong about deterrence? Suppose capital punishment prevents 50 murders in a year, or even ten? In terms of society's crime problems, these murders may be insignificant. Not to the 50 or the ten, however. Are opponents of capital punishment so confident in their position that capital punishment deters no crimes, that they are willing to risk those people's lives?

16   If supporters of capital punishment who believe it's a deterrent are wrong about the deterrent, the result is that people convicted of horrible brutal crimes will be executed. If opponents are wrong about deterrence and prevail in eliminating capital sentences, the result will be the murders of some number of really innocent people. That risk seems much more intolerable than the extremely remote possibility that an innocent person could be executed.

17   Make no mistake about it, deterrent or not, capital punishment saves lives. It is undisputed that murderers kill again. In states that do not have capital punishment, prosecutors are unable to use the death penalty as a negotiating chip. That is, they are unable to exchange a promise not to seek the death penalty in exchange for a guilty plea and life without parole. In those states, they almost always have to take these cases to trial and a jury. And the risk of a guilty defendant going free—free to kill again—increases accordingly.

18   Then there are the prison murders, i.e., murders of guards and other prisoners. How do you punish a murderer who is already serving consecutive multiple life sentences unless capital punishment is an option? Hint: You can't. In the absence of a possible death sentence, there is no judicial mechanism to restrain the behavior of such prisoners. They are there for life, and without capital punishment they know nothing else can ever happen to them.

19   Again, maybe this is not a large number of cases. But when talking about the death penalty, one is never talking about lots of cases. There are about 12,000 murder convictions every year, and of that number about 300 or so will be sentenced to death, and in any given year maybe 100 executions will occur. Contrary to the assertions of anti-death penalty activists, capital punishment remains reserved for a tiny group of the most cruel and violent murders, e.g., those involving multiple victims, other violent crimes, victims who are children, victims who are tortured, etc.

20   Which brings us back to the big morality issue. Alter and others emphasize that a moral objection is not the impetus for their position, this is strange. Morality would seem to be the only conceivable legitimate reason for opposing capital punishment.

21   It is, after all, a life and death issue. So how can one debate it without addressing the morality or justness of this form of punishment? And if one believes that capital punishment is just, it seems ludicrous to suggest that society should be denied this form of justice because of a theoretical possibility that in a rare case it could be misapplied.

22   Insisting that capital punishment is wrong because it is the deliberate taking of a human life is a logical, coherent position. It is not one that I share, yet I can respect those who make it. It is a view based on principles as opposed to utilitarianism.

23   The focus on innocence is a smokescreen, which trivializes and diverts attention from the real question.

24   Are there some crimes that are so heinous that it would be an injustice to impose less than the ultimate punishment? The answer is yes, but why is it that so many opponents of capital punishment want to avoid such questions?

■ QUESTIONS FOR ANALYSIS AND DISCUSSION

1. Pambianco states that Jonathan Alter is "among the latest to join the band-wagon [. . .] to the anti-death-penalty side." Based on what you read in Alter's article, is this accurate? Explain.

2. Pambianco argues that Alter chooses to focus on the possibility of innocent people being executed rather than on the morality of capital punishment. "In-nocence is not the issue; nor should it be." What does Pambianco believe should be the issue? Do you agree with this stance?

3. Evaluate Pambianco's argument in paragraphs 5 and 6 paralleling the certainty of the death penalty with other activities that we know "with a certainty will result in people dying unintentionally." Do you think the legal system would agree with his argument? Explain.

4. Pambianco states that "boiled down, the argument about innocence is an argu-ment for abolishing the criminal-justice system." What does he mean? Does he make a good point? Explain.

5. Summarize Pambianco's argument. To what does he object? How well does he support his position? How do you think Alter would respond to this piece?

"Look on the Bright Side"

Editorial cartoons, as mentioned in the chapter on visuals in Part One of this text, often deal with politically and socially charged issues. In the editorial cartoon shown on page 609, artist Drew Sheneman presents a political argument on the death penalty.

Sheneman has been the editorial cartoonist for the *Newark Star-Ledger* (a local daily newspaper in New Jersey) since 1998. Aimed at a "politically astute" audience, his work can be regularly seen in several major newspapers, including the *New York Times.* He is the recipient of several national awards for his cartoons, including the Charles Schulz Award and the John Locher award given by the Association of American Editorial Cartoonists.

■ QUESTIONS FOR ANALYSIS AND DISCUSSION

1. What argument does the cartoonist make in this drawing? How does he feel about the death penalty? What message does he hope to convey to his audi-ence?

2. What information does Sheneman's audience need to know in order to under-stand the cartoon and, thus, his point? Explain.

3. Analyze the people in the picture. What objects are they holding, and what are they doing? What are their expressions? How important are the people in this picture to the message Sheneman is trying to convey? Explain.

The Place for Vengence

Shannon Brownlee, Dan McGraw, and Jason Vest

The initial reading in this section provided a firsthand account of one man's execution. The next piece examines the issue from the perspective of victims' families. Does the death penalty give families closure? satisfaction? revenge? Should they have a voice in sentencing? The authors of the next article, prepared for the June 16, 1997, issue of *U.S. News and World Report,* explain witnessing an execution leaves many victims' families dissatisfied and still grieving for their loved ones.

■ BEFORE YOU READ

The human impulse for revenge is natural, especially in cases where a loved one is brutally murdered. If someone you loved was murdered and the killer was apprehended, would you want to see that person sentenced to the death penalty? Would you wish to witness the execution? Explain.

■ **AS YOU READ**

A central tenant of Western law is that criminals should be punished on behalf of society as a whole, and not on the part of the victim. Does this tenant surprise you? Should victims' families have the right to demand the death penalty? What if they later change their minds: Should courts listen to their opinion? Explain.

1   By the time Vicki Haack arrived at the "Death Chamber" viewing room, the man who had murdered her sister Lisa was already hooked up to the intravenous tubes. In 1986, Kenneth B. Harris, a crack cocaine addict, had entered her sister's apartment, raped and choked her, and then spent an hour drowning her in her bathtub. Now, he lay strapped to a gurney in a small, powder-blue room in the state penitentiary in Huntsville, Texas, his feet lashed together and his muscular arms extended as if on a crucifix. Haack stood against the viewing window, only 4 feet from Lisa's killer. As she watched Harris, she thought about her sister's death, and about Harris's family, who stood on the other side of a wall that divided the viewing room in half.

2   Harris showed no fear. He turned his head to the side to smile and nod at his audience. With the warden at his head and the prison chaplain at his feet, Harris apologized to both families for the pain he had caused them. Then he told the warden he was ready to die.

3   Vicki Haack wept quietly as Harris closed his eyes and expelled his last breath in two loud gasps through trembling lips. She heard Harris's sister scream on the other side of the viewing room. Six minutes later, Harris was pronounced dead.

4   After the execution, Vicki Haack said that her family had forgiven Harris. "We have no hate or bitterness in our hearts," she said. "But that doesn't mean he does not pay for his crime."

5   Go on with life. It was something the murderer himself said, though, that seemed to capture what so many family members hope to get out of an execution. Just before his death, Harris turned to Haack and said simply, "I hope you can go on with your lives and we can put an end to this."

6   Murderers are paying for their crimes with their lives in record numbers. This would seem to be what Americans want. In poll after poll, more than 70 percent say they support the death penalty, a figure that has remained consistent for at least the past decade. But while the percentages haven't changed much, the nature of the discussion has. Not long ago, it was framed in terms of practicality. Was the death penalty effective in deterring crime? Was permanently incapacitating an offender the best way to protect society? Was capital punishment fairly and evenly administered?

7   But increasingly, another argument for the death penalty is being voiced, one far more elemental. It centers not on the criminal's debt to "society" but on the right of a victim's loved ones to gain peace of mind through his death. The right, in other words, to a form of therapeutic vengeance. Death-penalty opponents have traditionally viewed this kind of personal retribution as essen-

tially barbaric. The mark of a civilized society is the ability to maintain a system of justice based on laws, not emotions—on theories of jurisprudence, not psychology. But is bringing solace to a victim really an illegitimate justification for the death penalty? And isn't providing solace a powerful form of restitution?

8   Basic emotion. The impulse for revenge is potent and natural. "When someone is executed who killed a member of your family," says Brooks Douglass, "vengeance is a part of the emotions that everyone feels." In 1979, when Douglass was 16 years old, two drifters entered the Douglass family farmhouse in Okarche, Okla, as Brooks, his parents, and his 12-year-old sister, Leslie, were sitting down to dinner. The two men, Glen Burton Ake and Steven Keith Hatch, hogtied Brooks and his parents in the living room. The family was forced to listen as the men raped Leslie in a bedroom. Then, the men sat down to eat the family's hamburger patties and mushroom gravy. Ake shot all four Douglasses in the back, before leaving with $43 in cash and the wedding rings from Brooks's parents.

9   Their parents died, but Brooks and Leslie survived to begin 18 years of anguish. Brooks testified seven times in the seven years after the attack, reliving that terrible night each time. Ake was sentenced to life in prison while Hatch got the death penalty.

10   Last August, Douglass watched Hatch's execution, an experience that evoked powerfully conflicting emotions. As Hatch died, Douglass felt as if he were watching two scenes simultaneously, his parents' deaths and that of their murderer. Before the execution, he agonized over the death penalty; afterward, he felt as if death had come too easily for Hatch.

11   The grieving process for a murder victim is somewhat like that for anyone else: disbelief, anger, grief, and then, finally for some, acceptance. But survivors of homicide victims rarely move easily through these stages. Murder often taps a well of rage that can drown out all other emotions.

12   Too easy? Richard Estell from Plano, Texas, and his wife have lived with their anger and sadness since Sept. 5, 1993, when their daughter, Ashley, 7, was abducted from a park playground as they watched their son's soccer game a few yards away. The man convicted of Ashley's rape and murder, a previously convicted sex offender, Michael Blair, delayed his execution this past spring through an appeal. When he is finally put to death, Estell plans to be there. "For me, it is partly closure and partly the focus on personal revenge," he says. "I want to see him gone." Death by lethal injection is too good for Blair, says the heartbroken father. "I can't get it out of my mind what my daughter must have felt," he says. "I'd really like to see him put in with the general prison population [where he would likely be raped himself]. That would be proper punishment."

13   Prosecutors often stoke a family's rage by telling them that only the death penalty can assuage their sorrow. "When you have lost a child, you go into a state of insanity, and you think whatever they want you to think," says Aba Gayle, 64, of Santa Rosa, Calif., whose 19-year-old daughter was murdered in 1980. "They told me, 'We are going to catch this man. We're going to convict

him, and when we have an execution, you will be healed.' The DA told me this, and the sheriff's department, also the media. And I believed them." Gayle now regrets that and is fighting to keep her daughter's killer from being executed.

14   For some survivors, the execution of a killer does quench the rage, Paula Foster's daughter, Jennifer Burns, then 21, was a bookeeper at an Arlington, Texas, nightclub when David Lee Herman shot her in the back of her head during a robbery attempt in 1989. Foster says Herman's six years on death row kept her full of hate. "When it first happened, I didn't have much anger toward him," she says. "I didn't know him. But I became more angry at him because of all the appeals. He didn't deserve to live during those six years."

15   But defeating the anger only left Foster alone with her grief. Foster says that during the trials and appeals she felt she was doing something for her daughter. Since the execution, on April 2 in Huntsville, she says, "I keep thinking, 'What can I do for Jennifer now?' The execution is another healing step. Maybe I'm finally realizing that Jennifer is really gone."

16   Grief counselors suspect that some people focus on their hatred of the killer to keep the more painful feelings of sorrow at bay. Since an appeals process can take years, survivors who nurse their rage may go more than a decade without really grieving. For some survivors, the anger is intensified by guilt. A parent fails to protect a child from a pedophile; a wife feels remorse that the last words she exchanged with her husband before his death were spoken in anger.

17   More often than not, families of murder victims do not experience the relief they expected to feel at the execution, says Lula Redmond, a Florida therapist who works with such families. "Taking a life doesn't fill that void, but it's generally not until after the execution [that the families] realize this. Not too many people will honestly [say] publicly that it didn't do much, though, because they've spent most of their lives trying to get someone to the death chamber."

18   Linda Kelley, of Houston, watched the murderer of her two children—Mark, 26, and Kara, 20—die in February 1996. "My family and I have been characterized as hatemongers for wanting to watch him," she says. "We are not hatemongers. If we were really bent on revenge, we would have gotten him ourselves at the trial. We are law-abiding citizens." She was the first survivor allowed to witness an execution under a then new Texas law. "When I was standing there watching him," she says in measured tones, "this anger came back in me. All I could think of was that he stood there and looked at my precious children and shot them in the head. I kept thinking, 'I hate you for what you did. I hate you for taking the father of my two grandbabies.'"

19   But Kelley says the execution left her unsatisfied. "You stand there and you watch a man take two gasps and it's over," she says. "I would like to have seen him humiliated a little bit. I think that he should have been brought in and strapped down in front of us. My son dies after being shot in the face and choking on his own blood. We make it too easy [on killers]."

20   Sandra Miller, 50, spent 16 years nursing her hatred of William Bonin, the "Freeway Killer" who was put to death in California in February 1996. In 1980, Miller's 15-year-old son, Rusty Rugh, a straight-A student, was abducted near

their home in Riverside, Calif., as he was about to get on a bus to go to his job after school. Rusty was beaten, raped, and murdered by Bonin. His slim body was dumped by the side of the Ortega Freeway. "The rage is unbelievable," says Miller. "I was 17 when I got pregnant with Rusty. I loved him more than life." Bonin was ultimately convicted of raping, torturing, and murdering 14 boys. On the eve of his execution, Miller wrote him a note: "I think of how I could torture you. You've brought out feelings in me I didn't know a human being could have."

21   But Bonin's death brought Miller none of the relief she had hoped for. She has spent many of the intervening years in an alcoholic haze, she says. A granddaughter born nine years ago helped patch some of her loss, but like many survivors, she couldn't move on. A measure of peace has come only since she struck up an unlikely friendship with Bonin's biographer, Alexis Skirloff. Bit by bit, Skirloff told Miller about the murderer's own brutal childhood and about what she knew of Rusty's last hours. As a result, Miller has found some compassion for Bonin, become more able to grieve for Rusty, and drawn closer to the rest of her family. "My other two kids lost their brother and then they lost their mother," she says.

22   The fury often is exacerbated by treatment of the families by the criminal justice system. Sheriff's offices inform them of the death with callous indifference to the shocking nature of the news. Family members regularly travel for hours to attend court only to discover the hearing had been postponed and they weren't notified. Andy Serpico was appalled when, after the 1979 rape and murder of his wife, Bonnie, the judge at assailant James Free's trial forced Serpico and his daughters to sit in the back row of the courtroom, while Free's weeping mother was allowed to sit next to the jury. Even more galling was when the judge forbade Serpico to tell the jury Bonnie had been a mother. "The belief was that it would be prejudicial," he says. "This is why I was very vocal through the whole process of trials and clemency hearings. Everybody would get to meet James Free, get to know James Free. I wanted people to remember that Bonnie Serpico was a real person."

23   In recent years, a victims-rights movement has tried to address this perceived imbalance. In the last decade, 15 states have followed Texas's lead in allowing victims' families to view executions. Many courts now let victims testify directly to the accused during the trial and to make statements about their pain and suffering during sentencing.

24   Of course, survivors are not the only ones seeking vengeance. Callers to a New York radio show had suggestions for punishing Susan Smith, the South Carolina mother who had drowned her two sons: "Drown her." "Cook her." "She should be fried."

25   Nor are the survivors the only ones seeking peace of mind. In a way, so is the rest of the country. While death penalty foes are quick to point out that the United States is one of the few Western countries with capital punishment, it is also true that Americans are more likely to experience violent crime than citizens of other countries.

26   Americans might not feel so vengeful if they trusted the judicial system to protect them from the worst predators. Indeed, support for the death penalty drops from 77 percent to below 50 percent when people are given a choice between the death penalty and life without parole plus restitution for victims' families. Such stiff penalties are now common. But the fear that a criminal will be prematurely released is reinforced every time someone like Charles Manson or Sirhan Sirhan, convicted under earlier laws, gets a hearing for possible parole.

27   The anxiety about violent crime, however, is out of proportion with reality. Murder victims are about as likely to be killed in cold blood by strangers as they are in the heat of an argument by a close associate. Most children are abducted or abused not by strangers but by relatives.

28   Unequal justice? Allowing fear to affect decisions about executions can lead to apparent inequities. Roughly 80 percent of those put to death in the past two decades had killed whites, though only about half of murder victims are white. This has led religious groups such as the Mennonite Central Committee to conclude that in the realm of capital punishment, "black lives are worth less than white lives." Others dispute the inequity idea, arguing that the figures don't take into account the seriousness of crimes.

29   Some theologians, like Greg Koukl of the evangelical study group Stand to Reason, discount this as a reason for abolishing the death penalty. "The answer isn't to get rid of punishment," he says, "but to make justice equal for all." As Koukl and others see it, the death penalty is warranted and religiously permissible according to passages of both the Old and New Testaments—particularly the "eye for an eye" teaching espoused in Deuteronomy. The idea of punishment "fitting" the crime is not just about vengeance, they say, but fostering a basic sense of justice.

■ QUESTIONS FOR ANALYSIS AND DISCUSSION

1. How, according to the authors, has the nature of the discussion regarding the death penalty changed? How has the focus shifted from the criminal's debt to society to the victims' families right to peace of mind? Explain. What is your own viewpoint on this shift?

2. Many of the families in this story express their feelings that the executions they witness are "too easy." What do they want instead? If their wishes were granted, do you think it would indeed give them greater satisfaction? Why or why not?

3. In what ways is the grieving process more difficult for the loved ones of murder victims? Should their grief be taken into account when passing sentence? Explain.

4. What is the connection between the American desire for vengeance and our lack of confidence in the judicial system? What do we fear?

5. If not capital punishment, what form of justice do you think victims' families would see as fit for the killers of their loved ones? What punishment(s) would you recommend? Explain.

6. Did this article change any of your own opinions regarding the death penalty? Why or why not?

■ WRITING ASSIGNMENTS

1. What are your own opinions on capital punishment? Is it a moral issue, as Pambianco asserts, or a practical one, as Alter describes? Is capital punishment permissible in some cases, or it is always wrong? Support your position with your own opinion and references to some of the key points made by authors in this section.
2. Many opponents of capital punishment argue that the government should not be in the business of taking human lives. With the advent of DNA evidence, others argue that all death row inmates be allowed the option of DNA testing. Do you think the government has the right to make judgments on life and death? If so, do you think that DNA testing should be a right for all people facing death row sentences?
3. Is capital punishment a deterrent? Research this issue. Are people less likely to kill in states with the death penalty? Report your findings using statistical data and outside resources.
4. Steve Earle ends his personal narrative with the comment, "Our criminal justice system isn't known for rehabilitation. I'm not sure that, as a society, we are even interested in that concept anymore." Write an essay in which you address Earle's comments. Interview classmates and relatives for their opinion on rehabilitation and research prison rehabilitation programs in your state. What is current public opinion regarding the rehabilitation of inmates? Has public opinion shifted over the last 20 years, and if so, why?
5. The ancient world firmly believed in the tenant "an eye for an eye and a tooth for a tooth." Research the origins of this law, including Hammurabi's Code and the biblical Book of Deuteronomy. Does the death penalty convey the spirit of these laws? Would people in the ancient world feel the American legal system is serving justice? Explain.

Ethical Issues in Medicine

Ethical and moral issues of right and wrong have challenged thinking people throughout history. Many of these issues are deeply connected to questions concerning life—when it begins, and our role in its creation and end. One cannot leaf through a newspaper or turn on the news without confronting weighty debates on issues such as stem cell research, abortion, and physician-assisted suicide. And each of these subjects has created a firestorm of moral and ethical debate. This section explores some of the various arguments associated with these very controversial subjects.

We begin with an examination of the stem cell debate, a topic that has recently received a great deal of media attention. In a society with so many cultures, religions, and social opinions, how do we decide on the important ethical issues related to stem cell research? On one side of the argument is the fact that embryonic stem cells come from human embryos, which have the potential to become human beings. Some pro-life supporters argue that ethics should compel us to not use such embryos for experimentation because of this potential. On the other hand, these stem cells may hold amazing possibilities to cure disease and save lives. Supporters of stem cell research often point out that such research *is* pro-life, because it aims to save the lives of people living with debilitating diseases.

We open the section, in James Trefil's "Brave New World," with a review of the medical technology of stem cell research, cloning, and genetic engineering, and a discussion of how the three are intertwined. Against this backdrop, we then move to examine President George W. Bush's August 2001 decision to allocate government funding to support stem cell research—but only for currently existing stem cell lines. The president explains some of the ethical issues he considered when making his decision. Kenneth L. Woodward discusses these ethical issues in greater detail, including some of the religious and commercial concerns related to stem cell research. We end the section with an essay by Michael Kinsley who states that opponents of stem cell research cannot base their argument against it on reasonable premises, because reason dictates that stem cell research makes logical sense.

Continuing our examination of life and death issues, we address the debate concerning abortion and a woman's right to choose. It is a subject about which few people are neutral and rarely reach common ground. The definition of life itself—with which scientists and lawmakers still grapple—is replete with moral, religious, political, and legal ramifications. On one side, pro-choice advocates argue that a woman has a right to choose what happens to her own body, a point made by Katha Pollitt in "Abortion in American History." On the other side, pro-life supporters take the position that abortion is murder, period, an argument made by Fred Minnick in "Abortion Is Not the Answer—Ever" and Kathleen Howley in "The Myth of the Pro-Choice Woman." But as Anna Quindlen's "Some Thoughts About Abortion" demonstrates, this subject invariably creates a conflict between heart and head, or between two moral positions.

From questions concerned with life, we move to issues associated with the end of life. The question of whether terminally ill individuals should be able to end their lives has been debated in the highest courts in this nation. Although the U.S. Supreme Court has ruled against legalizing physician-assisted suicide, some states, such as Oregon, have passed laws permitting it under special circumstances. However, these legal actions fail to reconcile the many moral and ethical concerns that continue to generate controversy about this issue. The medical profession itself is divided—conceding that while physicians have an obligation to help alleviate human suffering, exactly how far this obligation goes is a matter of debate.

The first three readings in this section feature the opinions of three physicians on this issue. Dr. Marcia Angell supports the wish of dying patients to hasten their death with medical assistance, arguing that patients have the right to "self-determination" and that physicians have the responsibility to respond with compassion to their suffering. Dr. Timothy E. Quill relates the difficult choice he made when one of his patients requested his indirect help in ending her life. Quill, an advocate for informed patient choice, challenges the laws that force doctors and their patients to pursue this option in secrecy. Dr. Herbert Hendin, a psychiatrist, disagrees, expressing strong reservations about legalizing physician-assisted suicide. It is fear of pain and the unknown, he says, that motivates the terminally ill to pursue suicide. The final article in this section gives a personal face to this ethical dilemma. Carrie Carmichael describes her own experience when a terminally ill friend asked for help in ending her life. Carmichael couldn't refuse. It is a choice that haunts her still.

STEM CELL RESEARCH

Brave New World
James Trefil

In 1932, Aldous Huxley wrote a book entitled *Brave New World* that described a utopian world state in which perfect children were created in laboratories. Today, medical technology is on the brink of amazing new breakthroughs in biological chemistry and molecular genetics. What are the moral and ethical limits of medical technology? And how do we even begin to understand the complicated science involved? In the next article, James Trefil explains the science behind stem cell, cloning, and genetic engineering research, and how these emerging biotechnologies are intertwined. As he explains, we truly have entered the "brave new world" Huxley predicted, "[but] just because we can do something [. . .] doesn't mean we should."

Trefil is a professor of physics at George Mason University. He has collaborated on many books on science and is the author of *101 Things You Didn't Know About Science and No One Else Knows Either* (1997). He is a science commentator for National Public Radio and a regular contributor to *Smithsonian Magazine,* in which this article was first published in December 2001.

■ BEFORE YOU READ

What do you know about stem cells and other emerging medical technologies such as cloning and genetic engineering? Why are these subjects so controversial? Do you have any opinion about these issues?

■ AS YOU READ

Trefil comments that the emerging medical technologies of cloning, stem cell research, and genetic engineering have raised questions not only about science and medicine, but about "the nature and value of human life." What questions does he identify in his essay, and how is science intertwined with moral and ethical issues?

1   It was not by chance that President Bush's first televised address was about stem cell research, coming as it did at the height of a summer swirling with heated debate over the issue ("one of the most profound of our time," according to the President). That and other recent debates have raised questions not only about changes in science and medicine but about such profound issues as the nature and value of human life, and whether humans have the moral right to tamper with genetic material, on the one hand, or the obligation to develop technologies that would alleviate the suffering of millions, on the other. Such questions are important, but only by understanding the science involved can we begin to address the ethical conundrums coming our way.

2   With nearly every advance in medicine, from the smallpox vaccine to organ transplants, there has been controversy over how much we should be altering nature. When Louise Brown, the world's first test-tube baby (now a healthy 23-year-old), was born in England in 1978, some people called conception outside the body immoral and tried to have the technique banned.

3   Back in the 1970s, science made advances in two areas that seemed, on the surface, unrelated—but which have veered ever closer to each other. One was a growing understanding of, and ability to manipulate, deoxyribonucleic acid (DNA), the molecule that provides our genetic code. The other involved the advent of in vitro fertilization (IVF), the technology responsible for Louise Brown and nearly a million babies since.

4   IVF is a process by which eggs are removed surgically from a woman's ovaries and fertilized with sperm in a laboratory. After undergoing a few cell divisions, several of the resulting embryos are inserted into a woman's uterus where, with luck, at least one will develop into a full-term fetus. In any one trial of IVF, as many as 10 to 20 eggs may be extracted and fertilized, and the majority of the resulting embryos are often frozen at an early stage of development, in case they will be needed for later attempts at implantation in the uterus.

5   Though IVF offered new hope to many who could not otherwise conceive, it also opened up a slew of ethical questions, beginning with the status of those embryos that remain unused in the lab. Then there is the fact that the woman who donates the egg need not be the one who carries the embryo or who raises the child. It is, in fact, possible to have as many as five adults who could claim parenthood in an IVF scenario: the sperm donor, the egg donor, the woman who carries the fetus and a couple responsible for its upbringing.

6   Still, for all the potential issues it raises, IVF was in many ways just the beginning, a relatively simple manipulation of the natural order. The closer science has gotten to deciphering our genetic makeup, the more complicated the landscape has grown.

Genes and DNA

7   By the middle of the 20th century, scientists had begun to realize that "genes"—the name given to whatever it was that passed down inherited traits—were made of DNA and that they were located on chromosomes, threadlike structures found in cell nuclei of almost all living things.

8   For molecular biologists, the second half of the 20th century was devoted to divining the structure of the DNA molecule (the double helix, discovered in 1953) and then figuring out how the molecule's fundamental components—called nucleotides—combined to form genes, how genes provided the instructions for making the molecules that allow living things to function, which genes did what, and where they were located. Just last year, scientists announced that they'd sequenced the human genome. Though they are far from figuring out what all of our genes do, they now know the order and location on our chromosomes of all of the nucleotides and have identified about half of our genes.

9   Much of the research on human DNA has focused on diseases that are prevalent in families or in certain ethnic groups—starting with such single-gene disorders as cystic fibrosis, Tay-Sachs disease and sickle-cell anemia—because medical histories of affected families were available and the fruits of such research might save, or at least improve, countless lives.

10   As our understanding of our genes has increased, so have our choices dealing with birth and conception. For several decades, couples with family histories of particular diseases have sought the advice of genetic counselors about whether to have children. With amniocentesis—a procedure in which amniotic fluid is extracted from the womb and examined—expectant mothers have long been able to determine if a developing fetus has certain chromosomal disorders. But more recent advances have brought the potential for couples to be

advised not only on the basis of family history but on the presence of genetic markers of hereditary disease in their DNA. And with IVF technology came the ability to screen embryos for chromosomal anomalies—and for specific genetic traits, including genetic diseases.

11   Along with advances in screening in recent decades, there has been a surge of research on ways to treat existing genetic disorders. That research was based largely on two great truths that had been revealed about DNA. The first is that the sole function of most genes is to give cells encoded instructions for churning out particular proteins, the building blocks of life. There are tens of thousands of different proteins in the human body—from collagen and hemoglobin to various hormones and enzymes—and each is encoded by a particular order of nucleotides in a gene. (Many diseases are caused by defective genes that don't produce their protein correctly—and treatments that introduce missing proteins have long been used for such disorders as diabetes and hemophilia.)

12   The second insight is that all living things use the same basic genetic code. Just as all the books in a great library can be written in a single language, so, too, are all living things the result of different messages "written" in the same exact DNA language—and "read" by our cells. This means that if a stretch of DNA is taken from a donor and inserted into the DNA of a host's cells, those cells will read the new message, regardless of its source.

13   Though there are endless possible applications for this phenomenon (and at least as many complicating factors), doctors found particularly promising the idea of fixing broken genes by manipulating DNA through a process known as gene therapy, a form of genetic engineering.

Gene Therapy

14   In some ways, manipulating DNA is a completely natural phenomenon. Certain kinds of viruses—including HIV and others—infect us by inserting their genetic information into our cells, which then haplessly reproduce the invading virus. In some forms of gene therapy, this kind of virus itself is engineered so that the viral gene that causes the disease and allows the virus to reproduce is removed and replaced with a healthy version of the human gene that needs "fixing." Then this therapeutic, engineered virus is sent off to do its work on the patient's cells. There are hundreds of procedures using such "viral vectors" in clinical trials today, targeting diseases that range from rheumatoid arthritis to cancer. So far there have been few, if any, real successes—and the field received a serious setback in 1999 when a patient died while undergoing gene therapy trials for liver disease.

15   But even if this form of gene therapy, or one like it, can be made to be safe and effective, it still represents a relatively short-term approach to genetic disease—compared with what is theoretically possible. After all, even if individuals can be successfully treated, their descendants would likely still inherit the gene or genes that caused their ailments. The form of gene therapy we've been discussing affects so-called somatic cells, which make up the vast majority of cells

in our body. But it is not somatic cells but germ cells—our eggs and sperm—
that pass our genes to our offspring.

Genetic Engineering

16   When talking about changing the DNA in human germ cells, scientists use the
term "germ line therapy." But in plants or animals, it's what we commonly think
of as "genetic engineering." Either way, it means altering the DNA of an organism in a way that increases the likelihood (or, in some cases, ensures) that all of
its offspring will have the same, engineered, characteristics.

17   So far, this form of genetic engineering has not been attempted on humans
(as far as we know), but it is used on nearly every other life-form—from bacteria
to plants to livestock. Virtually all insulin used to treat diabetes comes from bacteria whose DNA has been modified by the addition of the human gene for insulin, which the bacteria then produce. Plants are routinely engineered so that
they will be resistant to certain pests or diseases, withstand particular herbicides
or grow in previously unusable soils. One area of intense debate concerns the
extent to which such genetically modified organisms should be used in agriculture. In the United States, about half of the soybeans and a quarter of the corn
grown on farms have been genetically modified. While the industry and many
experts argue that products that are easier to grow or contain more nutrients
(or even produce pharmaceuticals) could help prevent worldwide hunger and
disease, critics question the possible side effects—particularly to the environment—of introducing new genes into agricultural products.

18   The truth is, there is still an inestimable amount that we don't know about
the functions of particular genes or how they work in tandem. Much of the concern about genetic engineering—in plants or in people—rests on this fact. Yet
with the promise of tomatoes that prevent cancer, salmon many times the size
of those produced in nature, even pets engineered to be nonallergenic, many
people hope that similar enhancements can be made to human genes as well.
After all, such techniques as genetic screening of embryos, gene therapy and
genetic engineering have the potential not only to prevent disease but to increase the likelihood of desired traits—from eye color to intelligence and other
attributes. (Though we're very far from custom-designing our offspring, there
are already cases of genetic screening of embryos for desired traits—including
parents seeking bone-marrow matches for older, ill children.)

Cloning

19   There are also those who see great promise in another form of custom-designed
offspring: cloning. Though most scientists oppose human cloning, three researchers caused quite a stir earlier this year when they each, independently,
announced that they were working to create human clones.

20   The modern age of cloning can be said to have begun in 1996, when Ian
Wilmut of Roslin Institute in Scotland oversaw the birth of Dolly, the first mammal known to have been produced by cloning from an adult cell. Worldwide
"Hello, Dolly" headlines announced the breakthrough, and subsequently, scientists working with goats, pigs, mice and cows followed in Wilmut's path.

21   To "create" Dolly, Wilmut and his colleagues took an unfertilized egg from a ewe and removed its chromosomal material, replacing it with a somatic cell (replete with DNA) from another ewe. In normal fertilization, when sperm and egg merge, the resulting cell—containing all the genetic information necessary—immediately starts dividing. In cloning Dolly, the somatic cell and the egg were fused with an electric current, which somehow prompted the package to act as though it were a newly fertilized egg. The resulting embryo was inserted into the uterus of a third ewe, using the techniques that had seen such success in in vitro fertilization.

22   In some respects, cloning can be likened to a construction project. The egg is like a crew of workers ready to build according to the specifications on a blueprint (DNA) once the plan is finalized and the whistle blows (fertilization). Whatever the crew sees on the blueprint, it will build. In the cloning process, scientists insert an already completed blueprint and—in the form of an electric current or some other prompt—blow the whistle.

23   But just as independent builders using the same blueprint can build slightly different structures, so cloning does not create absolute replicas. Though a newborn clone will have chromosomal DNA identical to that of the adult donor and in that way would be the adult's genetic twin, it would also be a twin developed as a fetus in a different womb, flooded with a different bath of chemicals at different points in its development, born decades later and raised in a different environment. The clone could also differ from the donor due to trace DNA in the donor's egg—in structures called mitochondria, for instance—that could affect the clone's development. (In fact, there have been recent reports of human babies who have genetic material from three adults, due to a technique that uses healthy mitochondria from a donor's egg to enhance fertility.) So, though Dolly resembled her DNA donor, other sheep that Wilmut and his colleagues have cloned vary in appearance and temperament from their DNA donors as well as from other clones developed from the same DNA.

24   It is also important to note that Dolly was born only after more than 200 other clones were spontaneously aborted or stillborn. Attempts to clone animals since have often resulted in severe birth defects—from dramatically increased birth size to enlarged organs to immune deficiencies. Going back to the blueprint analogy, Cornell professor and cloning expert Jonathan Hill adds, "It seems the cloned DNA is not only a 'used' blueprint, but one that may have certain pages stuck together, making some of the details particularly hard to read."

25   As a result of these and other factors, many scientists—and politicians—believe there should be a ban on human cloning. Others are wary that such a ban might be too restrictive, since some techniques used in cloning are also used in other promising areas of science—including applications of IVF technology and stem cell research.

Stem Cell Research

26 Cloning and stem cell research are connected in at least one important way. Every one of the trillions of cells in our bodies (including our eggs and sperm,

which have but one set instead of two) contain the same DNA. The cells in your skin, for example, contain the same gene for producing insulin as those in certain regions of your pancreas, but only the latter actually make the protein. Most of the genes in our cells are inactive, leaving only the relevant ones to do their work. Though we know little about how this occurs, we do know that there is a period early in development when the cells have yet to begin the processes of determination and differentiation into blood, muscle or any other kind of cell, and all cells can still develop into any cell in the adult. In humans, this property—called pluripotency—is lost by the end of the second week after fertilization.

27   Part of what made Wilmut's success with Dolly so extraordinary was that he seems to have been able to revert an adult sheep cell back to its pluripotent state (though with all of the unexplained complications we've already detailed). Other techniques are being pursued for isolating adult stem cells—cells that are only partially differentiated—and reverting them to a pluripotent state, or nudging them to develop in particular directions. In the meantime, there is another source of pluripotent cells: the embryo itself. Pluripotent cells from human embryos are the embryonic stem cells at the center of last summer's debate.

28   Much of that continuing debate centers on the fact that human embryonic stem cells are obtained, almost exclusively, from embryos left over from IVF. Though proponents of research on them point out that they would be destroyed anyway, many opponents believe that these embryos, though composed of just a few dozen cells, are human lives, and so should be saved.

29   The other reason that stem cells have burst into the news has to do with their exceptional promise. Scientists have learned to culture human embryonic stem cells and allow them to divide and multiply, while preventing them from switching on or off any of their genes. By exposing these stem cells to different molecular compounds, they are trying to understand how that switching process works so that they can direct this cell to become a neuron, say, or that one to become a blood cell. (These two examples, in fact, are feats at which they have already had some measure of success.)

30   Eventually, some believe, we may be able to control the development of these pluripotent cells so that we can replace tissues damaged by disease or accident. Nerve cells damaged by Parkinson's or spinal cord injury, for example, or heart tissue of cardiac patients, might ultimately be replaced by tissue grown from stem cells.

31   Some scientists see even the potential to create custom-made tissue by using stem cells that are exact matches to a particular person, thus obviating the greatest problem in transplant surgery—rejection of the implant by the host's immune system. "Therapeutic cloning," as this procedure has been called, would involve inserting a patient's own DNA into an egg and then prompting the cell and egg to fuse and start dividing, as was done in creating Dolly. Each cell in the resulting embryo, and thus its stem cells, would have exactly the same DNA as the patient, and tissues derived from these cells would match exactly the patient's own tissues.

32   Along the wide spectrum of debate, there are those for whom embryonic stem cell research is acceptable as long as embryos are used with the consent of the egg and/or sperm donors (or, in the case of therapeutic cloning, the sole DNA donor); there are those who believe it is acceptable as long as it is done with embryos that would be destroyed anyway; and there are those for whom destroying even these "extra" embryos is abhorrent, and creating embryos for research or therapy all the more so.

33   President Bush, in his August [2001] address, announced that the federal government would fund research with human embryonic stem cells but only that which uses those "lines" (cells developed from the original stem cells of a single embryo) already in existence. The scientific community has argued (and the administration has conceded) that there are fewer lines developed for research than the "more than 60" the President mentioned in his speech. Those that do exist, they say, may be inappropriate for use in human therapies, because they have been cultivated in mousecell cultures and represent a very limited gene pool. Other critics of the President's position point out that—as in many areas of research—curbing public funding does not mean that the research won't go on, just that it will go on, unregulated, under private sponsorship. Still others feel that the President was wrong to let any such research continue, let alone with public funding. Clearly, the debate isn't ending any time soon.

34   We are often reminded that just because we can do something—such as exploit the latest technology—does not mean that we should. Ian Wilmut—a vocal opponent of human cloning despite (or perhaps because of) his work with animals—offers a complementary observation: "What is 'natural,'" he points out, "is not necessarily right, and what is 'unnatural' is not necessarily wrong."

35   It is always risky navigating uncharted territory. President Bush stated it adroitly, in August, when he said: "As we go forward, I hope we will always be guided by . . . both our capabilities and our conscience."

■ QUESTIONS FOR ANALYSIS AND DISCUSSION

1. What are the "ethical conundrums" facing scientists, politicians, and the general population in regard to stem cell research, cloning, and genetic engineering? Explain.

2. How are in vitro fertilization (IVF) and stem cell research interconnected? How do they entwine with other emerging medical technologies such as cloning and genetic engineering?

3. How has medical technology influenced the way we think about reproduction?

4. Why are pluripotent cells so important? How are they different from adult stem cells? Why are they at the heart of the stem cell debate?

5. What are some of the therapeutic potentials of stem cells? Is the fact that they have "potential" but not *proven* benefit important to the debate? Do you think the stem cell debate would be different if scientists could prove that stem cells cure disease? Why or why not?

6. Trefil concludes his article with the comment that "just because we can do something [. . .] does not mean that we should." Does this statement reveal his own position on stem cell research? Based on the information he provides in this article, can you determine what his opinion is of these new medical technologies? Explain.

Remarks by the President on Stem Cell Research
George W. Bush

On August 9, 2001, President George W. Bush addressed the American public on the issue of stem cell research and, more specifically, the use of government funding to support this research. The issue had been hotly debated over the summer, with opponents stating that taxpayer dollars should not be used to support research that some people consider ethically wrong. However, supporters of government-funded stem cell research, taxpayers as well, explain that such research has the potential to save thousands, perhaps millions, of lives in the future.

For President Bush, the issue was twofold: (1) whether to fund research on existing stem cell lines and (2) what to do with embryos that could be developed into stem cell lines after being donated rather than destroyed. Should government money aid this research? What decision could he make that would acknowledge the arguments of both sides?

■ **BEFORE YOU READ**

Politicians and the public face the ethical quandary of what to do with the frozen embryos that are not implanted in a uterus. If these embryos are going to be destroyed anyway, should they not be used for a common good? Why or why not?

■ **AS YOU READ**

Bush gave this speech as both a politician and an elected president. In what ways does he attempt to please both sides of the argument? Does he allow his personal leanings to influence his judgment? Should one man have the power to decide something as important as this issue?

1   Good evening. I appreciate you giving me a few minutes of your time tonight so I can discuss with you a complex and difficult issue, an issue that is one of the most profound of our time.

2   The issue of research involving stem cells derived from human embryos is increasingly the subject of a national debate and dinner table discussions. The issue is confronted every day in laboratories as scientists ponder the ethical ramifications of their work. It is agonized over by parents and many couples as they try to have children, or to save children already born.

3   The issue is debated within the church, with people of different faiths, even many of the same faith coming to different conclusions. Many people are finding that the more they know about stem cell research, the less certain they are about the right ethical and moral conclusions.

4   My administration must decide whether to allow federal funds, your tax dollars, to be used for scientific research on stem cells derived from human embryos. A large number of these embryos already exist. They are the product of a process called in vitro fertilization, which helps so many couples conceive children. When doctors match sperm and egg to create life outside the womb, they usually produce more embryos than are planted in the mother. Once a couple successfully has children, or if they are unsuccessful, the additional embryos remain frozen in laboratories.

5   Some will not survive during long storage; others are destroyed. A number have been donated to science and used to create privately funded stem cell lines. And a few have been implanted in an adoptive mother and born, and are today healthy children.

6   Based on preliminary work that has been privately funded, scientists believe further research using stem cells offers great promise that could help improve the lives of those who suffer from many terrible diseases—from juvenile diabetes to Alzheimer's, from Parkinson's to spinal cord injuries. And while scientists admit they are not yet certain, they believe stem cells derived from embryos have unique potential.

7   You should also know that stem cells can be derived from sources other than embryos—from adult cells, from umbilical cords that are discarded after babies are born, from human placenta. And many scientists feel research on these type of stem cells is also promising. Many patients suffering from a range of diseases are already being helped with treatments developed from adult stem cells.

8   However, most scientists, at least today, believe that research on embryonic stem cells offers the most promise because these cells have the potential to develop in all of the tissues in the body.

9   Scientists further believe that rapid progress in this research will come only with federal funds. Federal dollars help attract the best and brightest scientists. They ensure new discoveries are widely shared at the largest number of research facilities and that the research is directed toward the greatest public good.

10   The United States has a long and proud record of leading the world toward advances in science and medicine that improve human life. And the United States has a long and proud record of upholding the highest standards of ethics as we expand the limits of science and knowledge. Research on embryonic stem cells raises profound ethical questions, because extracting the stem cell destroys the embryo, and thus destroys its potential for life. Like a snowflake, each of these embryos is unique, with the unique genetic potential of an individual human being.

11   As I thought through this issue, I kept returning to two fundamental questions: First, are these frozen embryos human life, and therefore, something

precious to be protected? And second, if they're going to be destroyed anyway, shouldn't they be used for a greater good, for research that has the potential to save and improve other lives?

12   I've asked those questions and others of scientists, scholars, bioethicists, religious leaders, doctors, researchers, members of Congress, my Cabinet, and my friends. I have read heartfelt letters from many Americans. I have given this issue a great deal of thought, prayer and considerable reflection. And I have found widespread disagreement.

13   On the first issue, are these embryos human life—well, one researcher told me he believes this five-day-old cluster of cells is not an embryo, not yet an individual, but a pre-embryo. He argued that it has the potential for life, but it is not a life because it cannot develop on its own.

14   An ethicist dismissed that as a callous attempt at rationalization. Make no mistake, he told me, that cluster of cells is the same way you and I, and all the rest of us, started our lives. One goes with a heavy heart if we use these, he said, because we are dealing with the seeds of the next generation.

15   And to the other crucial question, if these are going to be destroyed anyway, why not use them for good purpose—I also found different answers. Many argue these embryos are byproducts of a process that helps create life, and we should allow couples to donate them to science so they can be used for a good purpose instead of wasting their potential. Others will argue there's no such thing as excess life, and the fact that a living being is going to die does not justify experimenting on it or exploiting it as a natural resource.

16   At its core, this issue forces us to confront fundamental questions about the beginnings of life and the ends of science. It lies at a difficult moral intersection, juxtaposing the need to protect life in all its phases with the prospect of saving and improving life in all its stages.

17   As the discoveries of modern science create tremendous hope, they also lay vast ethical mine fields. As the genius of science extends the horizons of what we can do, we increasingly confront complex questions about what we should do. We have arrived at that brave new world that seemed so distant in 1932, when Aldous Huxley wrote about human beings created in test tubes in what he called a "hatchery."

18   In recent weeks, we learned that scientists have created human embryos in test tubes solely to experiment on them. This is deeply troubling, and a warning sign that should prompt all of us to think through these issues very carefully.

19   Embryonic stem cell research is at the leading edge of a series of moral hazards. The initial stem cell researcher was at first reluctant to begin his research, fearing it might be used for human cloning. Scientists have already cloned a sheep. Researchers are telling us the next step could be to clone human beings to create individual designer stem cells, essentially to grow another you, to be available in case you need another heart or lung or liver.

20   I strongly oppose human cloning, as do most Americans. We recoil at the idea of growing human beings for spare body parts, or creating life for our convenience. And while we must devote enormous energy to conquering disease, it

is equally important that we pay attention to the moral concerns raised by the new frontier of human embryo stem cell research. Even the most noble ends do not justify any means.

21   My position on these issues is shaped by deeply held beliefs. I'm a strong supporter of science and technology, and believe they have the potential for incredible good—to improve lives, to save life, to conquer disease. Research offers hope that millions of our loved ones may be cured of a disease and rid of their suffering. I have friends whose children suffer from juvenile diabetes. Nancy Reagan has written me about President Reagan's struggle with Alzheimer's. My own family has confronted the tragedy of childhood leukemia. And, like all Americans, I have great hope for cures.

22   I also believe human life is a sacred gift from our Creator. I worry about a culture that devalues life, and believe as your President I have an important obligation to foster and encourage respect for life in America and throughout the world. And while we're all hopeful about the potential of this research, no one can be certain that the science will live up to the hope it has generated.

23   Eight years ago, scientists believed fetal tissue research offered great hope for cures and treatments—yet, the progress to date has not lived up to its initial expectations. Embryonic stem cell research offers both great promise and great peril. So I have decided we must proceed with great care.

24   As a result of private research, more than 60 genetically diverse stem cell lines already exist. They were created from embryos that have already been destroyed, and they have the ability to regenerate themselves indefinitely, creating ongoing opportunities for research. I have concluded that we should allow federal funds to be used for research on these existing stem cell lines, where the life and death decision has already been made.

25   Leading scientists tell me research on these 60 lines has great promise that could lead to breakthrough therapies and cures. This allows us to explore the promise and potential of stem cell research without crossing a fundamental moral line, by providing taxpayer funding that would sanction or encourage further destruction of human embryos that have at least the potential for life.

26   I also believe that great scientific progress can be made through aggressive federal funding of research on umbilical cord placenta, adult and animal stem cells which do not involve the same moral dilemma. This year, your government will spend $250 million on this important research.

27   I will also name a President's council to monitor stem cell research, to recommend appropriate guidelines and regulations, and to consider all of the medical and ethical ramifications of biomedical innovation. This council will consist of leading scientists, doctors, ethicists, lawyers, theologians and others, and will be chaired by Dr. Leon Kass, a leading biomedical ethicist from the University of Chicago.

28   This council will keep us apprised of new developments and give our nation a forum to continue to discuss and evaluate these important issues. As we go forward, I hope we will always be guided by both intellect and heart, by both our capabilities and our conscience.

29   I have made this decision with great care, and I pray it is the right one.
30   Thank you for listening. Good night, and God bless America.

■ QUESTIONS FOR ANALYSIS AND DISCUSSION

1. Wishing to come to a solution that makes concessions to both sides of the argument, Bush decided to allow government funding to support research only on existing stem cell lines (not new ones). Evaluate this decision. Has one side "won" over another? Explain.
2. Evaluate Bush's discussion of the science involved in stem cell research. How does he consider the needs of his audience in this speech? Is understanding the science of stem cell research important to understanding his decision? Explain.
3. Bush explains that he asked himself two fundamental questions when considering what to do about stem cell research (paragraph 11). How would you personally respond to these questions? Explain.
4. In paragraphs 19 and 20, Bush explains his position regarding human cloning, especially as it pertains to growing "spare body parts." Why does he include the subject of human cloning in his speech? Is this a primary concern for opponents of stem cell research?
5. In paragraph 11, Bush explains that he wondered what to do with embryos that were "going to be destroyed anyway." Does his decision address this issue?

A Question of Life or Death

Kenneth L. Woodward

In the last piece, President Bush explained his position on stem cell research and government funding, perhaps sidestepping the ethical issue of how we should value the embryos used for stem cell research. Do we view them as human beings, or as potential cures for debilitating degenerative diseases? In the next article, Kenneth L. Woodward examines the ethical debate concerning stem cell research. Should we place more importance on cells that have the potential for human life, or people who are already alive but suffering from grave illness?

Woodward has been writing for *Newsweek's* religion section since 1964. His articles have appeared in many publications, including *Commonweal, Smithsonian,* the *New York Times,* and the *Washington Post.* He collaborated on several books and is the author of *Making Saints* (1990). This article was published in the July 9, 2001, issue of *Newsweek.*

■ BEFORE YOU READ

Should all human life be viewed as equal? Is it possible to assign different "values" to human life? Why or why not?

■ AS YOU READ

Woodward explains that in the debate over stem cell research, the first "casualty" is language itself. What does he mean by this? Evaluate Woodward's own use of language in his essay. What does his word choice tell you about his position on the issue of stem cell research?

1   In any political debate burdened by strong ethical differences, the first casualty is usually language itself. So it is with the ethical issues surrounding stem-cell research—specifically the question of whether days-old human embryos should be destroyed on the promise they offer of therapeutic answers to Parkinson's and other degenerative diseases. The words we choose to frame our arguments reveal the moral universe we inhabit. Those tiny flecks frozen in tanks of liquid nitrogen—what exactly are they? To the secular eyes of *The New York Times* editorial page, for example, they are "just clumps of microscopic cells" and thus of no intrinsic moral worth. On the other hand, what the Vatican sees is the moral equivalent of a fully developed "person" and therefore worthy of social respect and legal protection. Most everyone else sees something in between.

2   Biology and common sense alike tell us that we are dealing with human life in its earliest form. With implantation and luck (about 40 percent of embryos fail to survive naturally) each will become a genetically unique person like you and me. The ethical questions then become clear: what value should we place on human embryos, and how should their well-being be balanced with that of the millions whose acute suffering might be alleviated through stem-cell research and development? These issues are further complicated by the fact that the embryos immediately in question are all products of in vitro fertilization and most will eventually be discarded anyway.

3   Like most proponents of the "right to life," the Roman Catholic Church has at least been ethically consistent. Despite in vitro fertilization's benefits to infertile couples, the church opposes the procedure precisely because so many human embryos are automatically destined for destruction. Moreover, the church remembers how Nazi doctors experimented on Jewish prisoners who were first denied their dignity and rights as human beings and then—like the surplus human embryos—destined for fast or slow extinction. It fears the slippery slope.

4   But most Americans are more pragmatic, if not outright utilitarian. Many are inclined to believe that the good that stem-cell research promises to produce outweighs the limbolike life of unwanted human embryos now in cold storage. Sympathy naturally affects individual outlooks. A mother suffering from Alzheimer's understandably elicits more compassion than a stranger's anonymous fertilized egg.

5   When professional ethicists debate the shoulds or shouldn'ts of public policy, personal feelings carry no weight. Neither do appeals to Scriptures or other

religious authority. Even arguments of abstract moral principle, like whether noble ends ever justify ignoble means, must be tempered by considerations of concrete circumstances and probable outcomes. Thus some ethicists argue that respect for human life at least requires scientists to exhaust the therapeutic potential of adult stem cells—a procedure that no one finds objectionable—before extracting those from embryos.

6   The real danger in this debate is the almost irresistible tendency to treat human embryos as "property" ripe for commercial exploitation. After all, the interested parties are not isolated individuals arguing—as with abortion—over a private "right to choose." Nor are the beneficiaries just the sick, the aged and the prematurely infirm. Those who will benefit first are the research universities seeking funding and prestige, the pharmaceutical companies seeking new products and investors—and prominent scientists who often have financial interests in both. The federal government also has a stake: in the race to market therapies for degenerative diseases, the United States is in competition with Britain and other countries where concern about experimenting with human life is less pronounced.

7   In this wider context, the voices of religion are naturally more skeptical of promised biomedical miracles than are the scientists themselves. Mindful of human sin and the hubris of the powerful, religious ethicists are wary of any proposals that might exploit the weak to benefit. By contrast, the voices of biotechnology are Promethean, proactive and impatient with ethical restraints. Both need to exercise wisdom and prudence, always in short supply. Both stand at the edge of a new world where human beings can virtually reinvent themselves. Together with politicians and the people, they must decide what is really meant by human life and progress.

■ QUESTIONS FOR ANALYSIS AND DISCUSSION

1. How do you think Woodward would evaluate Bush's speech, specifically Bush's choice of words to explain his position? How do Bush's words reveal "the moral universe" that Woodward describes?
2. How does Woodward define the ethical argument of stem cell research? What does he say "compounds" the argument, and why?
3. Where does Woodward stand on the issue of stem cell research? Is he neutral? Does he have a religious position? an ethical one? Explain.
4. What is the Catholic Church's position on stem cell research, and why? What is a "slippery slope," and how does it relate to the church's position on stem cell research?
5. How does Woodward juxtapose the "voices of religion" with the "voices of biotechnology"? Does this juxtaposition reveal how he feels about these two groups? Explain.

Reason, Faith, and Stem Cell Research

Michael Kinsley

Can the argument against stem cell research be based on reason, or must it be based on faith-held ethics? In the next essay, Michael Kinsley argues that a logical argument cannot be put forth against stem cell research. Kinsley explains: If you chose to argue that stem cell research is unethical based on principles of faith, that's just fine with him; just don't try to tell him your argument is based on logic.

Kinsley is the editor of *Slate,* an online magazine in which this column first appeared on August 28, 2000. He is also a columnist for the *Washington Post,* a frequent contributor to *Time* magazine, and the author of several collections of essays, including *The Curse of the Giant Muffins and Other Washington Maladies* (1987) and *Big Babies: Vintage Whines* (1995). Kinsley served as editor of *The New Republic* for eight years and as co-host of CNN's *Crossfire* for six years. His work has appeared in many publications, including *Harpers, Washington Monthly, The Economist,* and *The Wall Street Journal.*

■ BEFORE YOU READ

In the next article, Michael Kinsley explores the role of reason, and the role of faith, in the stem cell debate. Can the two—reason and faith—coexist in the stem cell debate? Why or why not?

■ AS YOU READ

Kinsley refers to comments Ronald Reagan earlier made on determining when life begins. Why does he choose this particular president to quote? Is it a calculated choice, or merely incidental to his argument?

1   Opponents of the new rules for government-funded stem-cell research are right that the rules are irrational. The rules forbid government-funded researchers to extract stem cells from human embryos, but they allow those researchers—on alternate Tuesdays when the wind is from the northeast and at least three members of five different review boards have dreamed of a fish—to use stem cells extracted by others.

2   Opponents of stem-cell research believe that "a microscopic clump of cells" (the *New York Times'* description of an embryo at the stage when stem cells are removed) has the same moral claims as a fully formed human being. Proponents believe that a clump of cells has no serious moral claim compared with people who "feel want, taste grief, need friends" (Shakespeare's description of a human being). No one believes that a clump of cells is just a clump of cells in private hands but becomes a full human being in the hands of a government grantee. You don't absolve yourself of murder by hiring a hit man.

3   The answer to this objection (which the authors of the regulations cannot make) is: Of course it's not rational. It's a compromise between two logically irreconcilable positions. And it stretches democracy as far as it can be stretched in deference to the strongly held views of the losing side of an argument. It says: "You cannot have your way. You cannot impose the burden of your views on others. But at least you can know that your own tax dollars won't be spent directly on something you find immoral." This is quite a concession. It's more than opponents of wars, for example, are allowed.

4   Even the burden of this compromise is heavy on those awaiting the tremendous promise of stem-cell research. That promise has already been delayed for years by the congressional ban these new rules are designed to accommodate. The breakthroughs will be slowed by more years because of all the elaborate safeguards built in to protect those clumps of cells. Imagine being paralyzed by a spinal cord injury in your teens, watching for decades as medical treatment progresses but not quite fast enough, and knowing that it could have been faster.

5   In the endless right-to-life debate, compromise is difficult for pro-lifers because the strength of their side of the argument comes from its absolutism. (Unless it comes from faith, about which there can be no argument.) Absolutism is their logical trump card. If you don't protect every human being from the moment of conception, where do you draw the line? Anywhere you draw it is another irrational distinction, conferring humanity—and, possibly, life itself—on one organism and denying both to another that is nearly identical.

6   But absolutism is also a great weakness, because it puts you at the mercy of your own logic. Opposition to stem-cell research is the *reductio ad absurdum* of the right-to-life argument. A goldfish resembles a human being more than an embryo does. An embryo feels nothing, thinks nothing, cannot suffer, is not aware of its own existence. Embryos are destroyed routinely by the millions in the natural process of human reproduction. Yet opponents of stem-cell research would allow real people, who can suffer, to do so in service of the abstract principle that embryos are people too. If faith takes you there, fine. Reason can't.

7   Ronald Reagan used to play the logical trump card this way: If we don't know for sure when human life begins, we're like rescue workers after a mine explosion who don't know if anyone has survived. Shouldn't we assume there is life to be saved, rather than assuming there isn't?

8   The problem with this analogy is that the beginning of human life is not a factual question to which we "don't know" the answer. Biology is not going to solve this and the uncertainty is in how we choose to define it, not in some missing bit of information. Furthermore, the definition depends on why you're asking. In the context of abortion, it doesn't matter when a fetus develops hands or feet or a heartbeat. What matters is when it develops a sense of self, an ability to suffer, or—if you go that route—an immortal soul.

9   And the fact that these conditions (except for the soul) don't arrive at any clear-cut moment is not the logical argument for absolutism that pro-lifers

seem to think. We used to learn in high-school biology that "ontogeny recapitulates phylogeny": The development of each individual human being resembles the evolution of the species. Apparently, these days that is regarded as unhelpful, if not inaccurate. But even most right-to-lifers do believe in evolution and are comfortable with the idea that humanity is one end of a continuum, not a thing apart.

10   They are comfortable drawing a crisper line than nature does between humans and lesser beasts and denying human rights to animals that share many human attributes. Why is it so hard for them to accept something similar about the development of an individual human being? That we each start out as something less than human, that the transformation takes place gradually, but that it's morally acceptable to draw a line somewhere other than at the very beginning. Not just acceptable, but necessary.

11   If faith tells you otherwise, listen. But don't mistake it for the voice of reason.

■ QUESTIONS FOR ANALYSIS AND DISCUSSION

1. Evaluate Kinsley's opening paragraph. What is his tone? What does his tone tell you concerning how he feels about the rules for government-funded stem cell research? Does his opening paragraph make you want to read more of his essay? Explain.
2. What is Kinsley's opinion of the "compromise" the government made regarding stem cell research? Does he think it is fair? How does he paraphrase the president's decision (paragraph 3)? What evidence does he give that the decision is not based on "reason"?
3. What is "absolutism"? Why is it the "trump card" of pro-life supporters? Why is it also a "great weakness"? Explain.
4. Identify Kinsley's main argument. How well does he defend his position? What logical support does he provide? Is it important that Kinsley's argument be defended on logical premises? Explain.

■ WRITING ASSIGNMENTS

1. Write an essay defending or arguing against stem cell research. In your argument, address some of the issues raised by the authors in this section, as well as the position assumed by President Bush in his August 2001 speech.
2. To procure the stem cells needed to treat a genetic disease, scientists have inserted your genetic material into an empty egg cell, resulting in a fertilized embryo (like Dolly). Is the resulting embryo, which has the potential to mature into a human being, subject to the same "right-to-life" arguments made by pro-life activists? Should you have more control over the embryo because it is, essentially, a cloned "you"?
3. Several of the authors in this section raise the issue of when human life "begins" and, more specifically, when this life should hold the value and protection afforded to human beings. Why is this point so critical to the debate on

stem cell research? Write an essay in which you express your own opinion as to when life begins and connect your ideas to the issue of stem cell research.

ABORTION

Abortion in American History
Katha Pollitt

The topic of abortion is a sensitive one for many people. Few people are entirely ambivalent about this subject. For some, it is a moral and religious issue. For others, it is a social and political one. The next article reviews a book written by history professor Leslie J. Reagan, *When Abortion Was a Crime.* The book, which traces the history of abortion before the landmark U.S. Supreme Court ruling of *Roe* v. *Wade* in 1973, won a President's Book Award from the Social Science History Association. Some of the facts Reagan relates about the history of abortion in the United States may surprise you.

Katha Pollitt reviewed Reagan's book for the May 1997 issue of *The Atlantic.* Pollitt is a journalist who often writes provocative analysis on popular culture and politics. Her essays have appeared in many magazines, including *The Nation, The New Yorker, The New Republic, Mother Jones,* and *Harper's.* She has published several volumes of her essays, most recently *Subject to Debate: Sense and Dissents on Women, Politics, and Culture* (2001).

▦ BEFORE YOU READ

What do you know about the history of abortion in this country? Were abortions hard to get before *Roe* v. *Wade?* Were they available only to the wealthy? Were they dangerous? Does your sense of history of this controversial topic influence your opinion of abortion?

▦ AS YOU READ

Pollitt is reporting on a book written by another woman on abortion. Can you determine Pollitt's own position on abortion based on her review? Do you think her stance affects how she reviews the book? Explain.

1   Of all the issues roiling the ongoing culture wars, abortion is both the most intimate and the most common. Almost half of American women have terminated at least one pregnancy, and millions more Americans of both sexes have helped them, as partners, parents, healthcare workers, counselors, friends. Collectively, it would seem, Americans have quite a bit of knowledge and experience of abortion. Yet the debate over legal abortion is curiously abstract: we might be discussing brain transplants. My files are crammed with articles assess-

ing the question of when human life begins, the personhood of the fetus and its putative moral and legal status, and acceptable versus deplorable motives for terminating a pregnancy and the philosophical groundings of each one—not to mention the interests of the state, the medical profession, assorted religions, the taxpayer, the infertile, the fetal father, and even the fetal grandparent. Far-fetched analogies abound: abortion is like the Holocaust, or slavery; denial of abortion is like forcing a person to spend nine months intravenously hooked up to a medically endangered stranger who happens to be a famous violinist. It sometimes seems that the further abortion is removed from the actual lives and circumstances of real girls and women, the more interesting it becomes to talk about. The famous-violinist scenario, the invention of the philosopher Judith Jarvis Thomson, has probably inspired as much commentary as any philosophical metaphor since Plato's cave.

2   Abortion as philosophical puzzle and moral conundrum is all very well, but what about abortion as a real-life social practice? Since the abortion debate is, theoretically at least, aimed at shaping social policy, isn't it important to look at abortion empirically and historically? Opponents often argue as if the widespread use of abortion were a modern innovation, the consequence of some aspect of contemporary life of which they disapprove (feminism, promiscuity, consumerism, Godlessness, permissiveness, individualism), and as if making it illegal would make it go away. What if none of this is true? In *When Abortion Was a Crime*, Leslie J. Reagan demonstrates that abortion has been a common procedure—"part of life"—in America since the eighteenth century, both during the slightly more than half of our history as a nation when it has been legal and during the slightly less than half when it was not.

3   Until the last third of the nineteenth century, when it was criminalized state by state across the land, abortion was legal before "quickening" (approximately the fourth month of pregnancy). Colonial home medical guides gave recipes for "bringing on the menses" with herbs that could be grown in one's garden or easily found in the woods. By the mid-eighteenth century commercial preparations were so widely available that they had inspired their own euphemism ("taking the trade"). Unfortunately, these drugs were often fatal. The first statutes regulating abortion, passed in the 1820s and 1830s, were actually poison-control laws: the sale of commercial abortifacients was banned, but abortion per se was not. The laws made little difference. By the 1840s the abortion business—including the sale of illegal drugs, which were widely advertised in the popular press—was booming. The most famous practitioner, Madame Restell, openly provided abortion services for thirty-five years, with offices in New York, Boston, and Philadelphia and traveling salespeople touting her "Female Monthly Pills."

4   In one of the many curious twists that mark the history of abortion, the campaign to criminalize it was waged by the same professional group that, a century later, would play an important role in legalization: physicians. The American Medical Association's crusade against abortion was partly a professional move, to establish the supremacy of "regular" physicians over midwives

and homeopaths. More broadly, anti-abortion sentiment was connected to nativism, anti-Catholicism, and, as it is today, anti-feminism. Immigration, especially by Catholics and nonwhites, was increasing, while birth rates among white native-born Protestants were declining. (Unlike the typical abortion patient of today, that of the nineteenth century was a middle- or upper-class white married woman.) Would the West "be filled by our own children or by those of aliens?" the physician and anti-abortion leader Horatio R. Storer asked in 1868. "This is a question our women must answer; upon their loins depends the future destiny of the nation." (It should be mentioned that the nineteenth-century women's movement also opposed abortion, having pinned its hopes on "voluntary motherhood"—the right of wives to control the frequency and timing of sex with their husbands.)

5   Nonetheless, having achieved their legal goal, many doctors—including prominent members of the AMA—went right on providing abortions. Some late-nineteenth-century observers estimated that two million were performed annually (which would mean that in Victorian America the number of abortions per capita was seven or eight times as high as it is today). Reagan argues persuasively that our image of nineteenth-century medicine is too monolithically hierarchical: while medical journals inveighed against abortion (and contraception), women were often able to make doctors listen to their needs and even lower their fees. And because, in the era before the widespread use of hospitals, women chose the doctors who would attend their whole families through many lucrative illnesses, medical men had self-interest as well as compassion for a motive. Thus in an 1888 exposé undercover reporters for the *Chicago Times* obtained an abortion referral from no less a personage than the head of the Chicago Medical Society. (He claimed he was conducting his own investigation.) Unless a woman died, doctors were rarely arrested and even more rarely convicted. Even midwives—whom doctors continued to try to drive out of business by portraying them, unfairly, as dangerous abortion quacks—practiced largely unmolested.

6   What was the point, then, of making abortion a crime? Reagan argues that its main effect was to expose and humiliate women caught in raids on abortion clinics or brought to the hospital with abortion complications, and thereby send a message to all women about the possible consequences of flouting official gender norms. Publicity—the forced disclosure of sexual secrets before the authorities—was itself the punishment. Reagan's discussion of "dying declarations" makes particularly chilling reading: because the words of the dying are legally admissible in court, women on their deathbeds were informed by police or doctors of their imminent demise and harassed until they admitted to their abortions and named the people connected with them—including, if the woman was unwed, the man responsible for the pregnancy, who could be arrested and even sent to prison. In 1902 the editors of the *Journal of the American Medical Association* endorsed the by then common policy of denying a woman suffering from abortion complications medical care until she "confessed"—a practice that, Reagan shows, kept women from seeking timely treatment,

sometimes with fatal results. In the late 1920s some 15,000 women a year died from abortions.

7   This state of affairs—widespread availability punctuated by law-enforcement crackdowns, popular-press scandals, and fitful attempts at medical self-policing—persisted for decades. Unsurprisingly, the Depression, during which women stood to lose their jobs if they married or had a child, saw a big surge in the abortion rate. Reagan describes clinics complete with doctors, nurses, receptionists, and printed instructions detailing follow-up care, and "birth-control clubs," whose members would pay regularly into a collective fund and draw abortion fees from it as needed. It was only in the 1940s and 1950s that organized medicine and the law combined to force these long-standing operations out of business and to disrupt the networks of communication by which women had found their way to them. Our popular image of illegal abortion as hard to find, extremely dangerous, sordid, and expensive dates from this period, as do the notorious "abortion wards" filled with women suffering from botched operations and attempts at self-abortion (always the most dangerous method).

8   Well-connected white women with private health insurance were sometimes able to obtain "therapeutic" abortions, a never-defined category that remained legal throughout the epoch of illegal abortion. But these were rare, and almost never available to nonwhite or poor women. Even for the privileged, though, access to safe abortion narrowed throughout the fifties, as doctors, fearful of being prosecuted in a repressive political climate for interpreting "therapeutic abortion" too broadly, set up hospital committees to rule on abortion requests. Some committees were more compassionate than others: at Mount Sinai, in New York, suicide attempts were considered an appropriate indication; at other hospitals they were ignored. In one instance of particular callousness, when a teenager tried to kill herself after her request was turned down, the committee decided to hospitalize her for the rest of her pregnancy. (She eventually got her abortion, after her multiple suicide attempts proved too disruptive for the staff.)

9   The conventional wisdom today considers *Roe* v. *Wade* to be an avant-garde decision, "judicial activism" at either its enlightened best or its high-handed worst. Reagan places the decision in its historical context, showing that it was a logical response to the times. By the sixties the whole jerry-built structure of criminalization was crumbling, along with the ideology of gender and sexuality that lay behind it. Moderate reforms had already been tried; twelve states permitted abortion in instances of rape, incest, danger to physical or mental health, or fetal defect, but since most women, as always, sought abortions for economic, social, or personal reasons, illegal abortion continued to thrive (something to consider for those who advocate once again restricting legal abortion in this way). When New York State decriminalized abortion in 1970 and thousands of well-off women started traveling there to obtain safe abortions while their disadvantaged sisters continued to risk death at home, the inherent unfairness of a legal patchwork was thrown into bold relief (something to ponder for those who want to throw the issue "back to the states"). Far from foisting a radical departure on an unready nation, the Supreme Court was respond-

ing to a decade-long buildup of popular sentiment for change. The movement was spearheaded by doctors who saw firsthand the carnage created by illegal abortion (more than 5,000 deaths a year, mostly of black and Hispanic women), and whose hands were now firmly tied by the hospital committees they themselves had created. They were joined by civil-liberties lawyers, who brought to their briefs a keen understanding of criminalization's discriminatory effects; and by grassroots activists in the reborn women's movement, who by the end of the 1960s were resisting the law, forming such groups as the Society for Humane Abortion, in California, which denounced restrictions as insulting and humiliating to women, and Jane, in Chicago, which began as an abortion-referral service and ended by training its members to perform abortions themselves.

10   Legalizing abortion was a public-health triumph that for pregnant women ranked with the advent of antisepsis and antibiotics. In 1971, the year after decriminalization, the maternal-mortality rate in New York State dropped 45 percent. Today, however, the inequality of access that helped to bring illegality to an end is once again on the increase. More than 80 percent of U.S. counties have no abortion providers, and some whole states have only one or two. The Supreme Court has allowed states to erect barriers to abortion—denial of public funds for poor women's abortions, parental consent and notification requirements, mandatory delays, "counseling sessions." Anti-abortion zealots have committed arson, assault, and murder in their campaign against abortion clinics. A new generation of doctors, who have never seen a woman die from a septic abortion or been haunted by the suicide of a patient denied help, are increasingly reluctant to terminate pregnancies. Only 12 percent of medical schools teach first-trimester abortion as a routine aspect of gynecology. If Reagan is right to correlate anti-abortion activity with periods of high anxiety about feminism and radicalism generally, none of this should come as a surprise. She closes on an ominous note, sketching the possibility of a United States in which not only is abortion once again a crime but anti-abortion fanaticism brings on a Romania-style fetal-police state, complete with government-monitored pregnancies and police investigations of miscarriages.

11   One of Reagan's noteworthy findings, after all, is that the views of the American people about abortion have remained rather stable over two centuries. Attitudes toward early abortions—in the eighteenth and early nineteenth centuries those before quickening, today those in the first trimester—have always been much more permissive and matter-of-fact than attitudes toward later abortions, just as losing a pregnancy after one or two missed periods, however distressing to a woman who wants to bear a child, has always been seen as a smaller event than miscarrying at six months. Little in the American popular tradition resonates with the "pro-life" doctrine that condemns all abortions alike on the grounds that a fertilized egg is already a baby. Far from being a weird judicial concoction, as its opponents argue, *Roe* v. *Wade*'s trimester system, which gradually extends the right of states to regulate and even ban most abortions as the fetus develops, reflects this folk understanding rather well. Similarly, the general lack of enthusiasm for prosecuting those who perform abortions and the

almost total failure to prosecute and jail women for having them suggest that whatever Americans may consider abortion to be, it isn't baby killing, a crime our courts have always punished quite severely.

12   *When Abortion Was a Crime* is rich, thought-provoking, and revelatory on many levels. Perhaps its greatest achievement, though, is in a way its simplest: it puts abortion back into the context in which it actually occurs—the lives of obscure and ordinary women. If the abortion debate were really about abortion, Reagan's work would consign many of its terms to the scrap heap: it seems absurd to suggest that the overburdened mothers, desperate young girls, and precariously employed working women who populate these pages risked public humiliation, injury, and death for mere "convenience," much less out of "secular humanism" or a Lockean notion of property rights in their bodies. It's even more preposterous—not to mention insulting—to see them as standing in relation to their fetuses as a slaveowner to a slave or a Nazi to a Jew.

13   Reagan suggests that the abortion debate is really an ideological struggle over the position of women. How free should they be to have sexual experiences, in or out of marriage, without paying the price of pregnancy, childbirth, and motherhood? How much right should they have to consult their own needs, interests, and well-being with respect to childbearing or anything else? How subordinate should they be to men, how deeply embedded in the family, how firmly controlled by national or racial objectives? If she is right, and I think she is, a work of history is not going to make much of a dent in the certainties of those who would like to see abortion once again made a crime. The people who need this book the most won't read it.

▪ QUESTIONS FOR ANALYSIS AND DISCUSSION

1. Pollitt comments, "The debate over abortion is curiously abstract: we might be discussing brain transplants." Do you agree with this statement? Is the debate abstract? How do you think other authors in this section would respond to this claim? Explain.

2. What is the "famous-violinist" scenario by Judith Jarvis Thomson that Pollitt mentions in her introduction? Does this reference confuse the reader, or help clarify Pollitt's points? What assumptions does Pollitt make regarding her audience's understanding of this reference?

3. Referencing a fact from Reagan's book, Pollitt points out that abortion was seven to eight times more common in Victorian America than it is now. Does this fact surprise you? Does it influence your viewpoint on this issue? Explain.

4. Pollitt is reviewing a book in this essay, but presents many of her own opinions. How does Pollitt use the book as a backdrop for her own argument? Review the article and identify where she expresses her own opinions. Is it clear what opinions are Reagan's and which are Pollitt's? Explain.

5. In paragraph 10, Pollitt states, "legalizing abortion was a public-health triumph." On what evidence does she base this statement? Is it fact or opinion? Explain.

6. In her conclusion, Pollitt comments, "Reagan suggests that the abortion debate is really an ideological struggle over the position of women." In what ways could the abortion debate be seen in this light? Do you agree? Explain.

Abortion Is Not the Answer—Ever

Fred Minnick

In the next essay, Fred Minnick describes his parents' decision not to have an abortion when his mother was pregnant with him—a decision that was agonizing for them at the time. Despite their youth and facing an uncertain economic future, Minnick's parents left the abortion clinic and had their baby instead. Minnick's position is that abortion is always wrong. His hard-line stance, written from a very personal perspective, puts an interesting twist on the debate over abortion, the point of view of an abortion "survivor."

Minnick wrote this article when he was a freshman attending Oklahoma State University. It was first published by that school's student newspaper, *The Daily O'Collegian,* on October 18, 2000.

■ BEFORE YOU READ

In the next article, college student Fred Minnick gives a list of reasons why women have abortions—reasons with which he disagrees. If you believe abortion is wrong, is it always wrong? Is there any middle ground? If you believe it is right, is it always right? Or, are there special circumstances? Explain.

■ AS YOU READ

Identify Minnick's main argument in this essay and evaluate his supporting evidence for this argument. Is this essay likely to influence the opinions of pro-choice supporters? Why or why not?

1   In December 1977, an 18-year-old woman was faced with the choice of life or death. It began when she met a boy at a hometown IGA grocery store. He was a sacker and she was the checker. A typical small town romance and for both of them—it was love at first sight.

2   After their first month of dating they spoke of marriage and how they would spend forever with one another. Neither had much money, but they had love, which is something money cannot buy.

3   They also had a future. And, like many young people, they didn't think about the consequences of sex. All of their plans were demolished when the woman discovered she was pregnant. The boy was only 16, in high school and his only income was sacking groceries. The girl had no way of supporting a family and they both were planning to attend college.

4   Their families could not fund the baby's future, either. So the only solution was an abortion.

5   Friends of the family and co-workers raised enough money for the operation. The couple, being so young, couldn't face life with a child. They were ready to make a decision which would follow them forever.

6   To this day, she remembers the hour and a half she spent in the abortion clinic. She and her boyfriend were at the counter and the receptionist smiled as she took her money, treating her as she did all of the other teenagers. The couple waited an hour before the nurse took her to the room.

7   She says the room was cold and the clasp of the door is a sound that will forever haunt her. The boy says the moments waiting in the lobby seemed like an eternity because the clinic's policy prohibited him being with his girlfriend.

8   This was not a consultation. She was there for an abortion. No second chances.

9   This was it.

10   After each second, the two contemplated their future, individually, wondering what would happen to their relationship.

11   Fifteen minutes had passed. The doctor was running behind and he still had not visited her. After not being able to bear the time or swallow his conscience, the boyfriend broke the clinics' rules and went into his girlfriend's examination room. He clutched her hand, cried and said, "we don't have to do this. We can make it. I know we can." She bawled, hugged him and said, "thank you."

12   The doctor walked into the room moments later as the two were joined emotionally by their love and physically by their arms wrapped around one another. The couple stormed out of the clinic.

13   Eight months later, I was born.

14   Mom and dad could not tell you if they received a refund that day, but they can give you a long 20-minute story on every one of my baby pictures.

15   Mom chose my life over making things easier on her life. So no matter how prideful my Democratic views are or my liberal beliefs, I could never believe in abortion—regardless of the situation. It's a belief I have more passion for than any other, and I will never change my stance.

16   Society sugar-coats abortion, calling it pro-choice, saying it's okay to kill a child. I disagree and so should the rest of the world. Not for religious reasons, political beliefs or society's perceptions, but for humanity's sake.

17   Why not call it pro-death? Because that's what it really is. The fetus has cells, which multiply and grow, thus it's a living organism and it's a person. If life is terminated by another human, shouldn't it be murder? If a pregnant woman is slain, the killer is usually charged with two counts of murder. One count for the woman and one for the child in the womb. Are we saying it's okay to kill the baby as long as he or she is terminated by his or her mother?

18   One of four pregnant women between the ages 15–44 will have an abortion rather than have a baby. They don't think of abortion as murder. It sounds too

bad to think of it that way. Instead, they justify it by saying they don't have enough money or their future is too important.

19   Money can be earned. A future can be catered to. But an aborted baby can never be brought back to life. Sure, going through with the pregnancy would be tough, but life is too precious to give up on, no matter the costs.

20   Why give the baby up for adoption? The emotional loss is less severe and the woman can feel secure knowing she didn't give up on her baby's life. Stop and think about it. Do you really want to be responsible for his or her death?

21   Even if the woman is raped, the child should still be born. Regardless of what happened to the woman, the child still has a chance to give back to this society.

22   For the woman, the burden of rape would be heavy enough. And an abortion would only hurt her more emotionally and physically.

23   As for the men who fool around and get their girlfriends pregnant, if you're man enough to have sex, you should be man enough to support your girlfriend through a pregnancy. If not, then don't have sex. There's nothing more gutless than a guy who encourages his girlfriend to abort his child.

24   A lot of people will say, "you don't know until you're in that situation."

25   I have been. Only I was inside.

■ QUESTIONS FOR ANALYSIS AND DISCUSSION

1. How does the title of Minnick's essay relate to his subject? What is the effect of the final word following the dash in his title? How do the points in his essay support this very forceful title? Explain.
2. What is the effect of the story Minnick uses to introduce his argument? Is it particularly compelling because it is his personal story? Why or why not?
3. Minnick states that he disagrees with abortion, "Not for religious reasons, political beliefs or society's perceptions, but for humanity's sake." Why does he separate humanity from the other "reasons" in the sentence? Explain.
4. Analyze the logic behind Minnick's statement that "the fetus has cells, which multiply and grow [. . .] it's a living organism, and it's a person." How might a pro-choice person respond to his argument?
5. Minnick brings up the issue of rape in his essay—a point where some pro-life supporters diverge. He states that "even if the woman is raped, the child should still be born." Does this statement make his argument stronger, or weaker?

Advertisement—for the RU-486 Pill

"You have the freedom to choose. And now, you have another safe abortion choice," reads the full-page ad featured in a July and August 2001 advertising campaign sponsored by the National Abortion Federation (NAF) for RU-486, more commonly known as the "early option" pill. The ad ran in many national magazines, including *Self, People, Vanity Fair,* and *Glamour.* The ad created controversy from the moment of its publication. The RU-486 pill, available in clinics and from private physicians, actually costs more than a surgical abortion, but can be taken at home up to 49 days after a woman's last period. Should something like an abortion pill be advertised in magazines? Does it mean crossing a line? Or, does such an ad perform a needed public service?

You

have the freedom to choose.
And now, you have another
safe abortion choice.

The Early Option Pill has
been approved by the FDA.

It safely and effectively terminates a pregnancy, and offers yet another option for women: Mifepristone, the medical breakthrough known as RU-486 in Europe, is now available in the U.S. Taken in the first 49 days of pregnancy, the Early Option Pill works to block the effects of a hormone needed to sustain pregnancy. In U.S. clinical studies, 96% of women said they would recommend it to a friend. To find out if the option used by over half a million women in Europe is right for you—or for a referral to a quality provider—call the National Abortion Federation (NAF) hotline. At NAF, our members have provided quality care to women for over 20 years.

NATIONAL ABORTION FEDERATION

Find out if the Early Option Pill is an option for you: 1-800-772-9100 | www.earlyoptions.org

■ QUESTIONS FOR ANALYSIS AND DISCUSSION

1. If you were reading a magazine and saw this ad, would you know what it was advertising? Would you look at it?
2. Advertising for an abortion pill is by nature a difficult campaign for any advertising agency to develop. What choices did the designers make when creating this ad? Why do you think they made the choices they did? Explain.
3. Who is the audience for this advertisement? How does it appeal to its target audience?
4. Would the effect of this advertisement be different if the model were looking directly out of the photo? If a man were included in the picture? Explain.
5. What information is provided in the ad? Does the ad, in your opinion, succeed in its objective?
6. Do you think it is appropriate to advertise an abortion pill? Are your opinions influenced by your feelings about abortion, or by the ad itself? Explain.

The Myth of the Pro-Choice Woman
Kathleen Howley

In the next article, pro-life supporter Kathleen Howley explains why she objects to men who say that they feel they cannot tell a woman what to do with her body. While these men may not be pro-choice themselves, they are reluctant to intervene. Such men, says Howley, are simply quoting the party line. Others support abortion because it lets them off the hook—it gives them a way out of being responsible for their actions. Either way, says Howley, their support of abortion is misdirected and actually promotes the exploitation of women.

Howley is a syndicated columnist who often writes on issues connected to Roman Catholicism. This article was first published by the *Catholic World News* in 1996, but has been reprinted by many pro-life publications and Web sites.

■ BEFORE YOU READ

In the next article, Howley states her own position and feelings regarding abortion. What is your personal position on this issue? Do you have religious, moral, or political motivations for your position?

■ AS YOU READ

Howley relates a discussion regarding abortion she had with one man at a cocktail party. Is this a strange topic for such a party? Why do you think she mentions it was a G.O.P. party?

1   I am going to try to say this without sounding like a man-hating feminist. Here goes.

2   There are few things in life more disgusting than men who, when discussing abortion, use the phrase: "I can't tell a woman what to do with her body."

3   It's like a password. It's usually pronounced with a self-satisfied smile. They're saying, "I'm cool. I'm a supportive kinda guy. I'm sensitive to the needs of women."

4   Yea, right.

5   Sometimes, there's a slight reluctance in their voice as they recite the mantra. Those are the ones who believe that while they, personally, are opposed to abortion, they couldn't tell a woman . . . blah, blah, blah. You've heard it before, I'm sure.

6   In most cases, these guys have never, in their lives, used the words "chaste" and "dating" in the same sentence. You can bet that many of them are pretty adroit at telling a woman what to do with her body, if it happens to serve their own needs.

7   Abortion, or "choice," as it's euphemistically called, becomes a requirement, for many of them, because it has the ability to erase any unforeseen problems caused by their lack of moral discretion.

8   I was at a G.O.P. cocktail party last week, and a man used that old line on me: "I can't tell a woman what to do with her body." I gave him the logical response: "What about the body inside her womb? What if it's a male body, a little boy? Surely that can't be her body, because she can't be a man and a woman at the same time. Can you tell her, in that case?" He looked at me glumly. This was not the response he expected. He probably assumed, because I'm a young woman, that I'm pro-choice.

9   Not a wise move. Three major studies within the last four years show that women tend to be more pro-life than men.

10   Makes sense, doesn't it? We're the ones with the maternal instincts, and if we know the facts of life—meaning all the stuff you never read in the newspaper, such as what an abortion does to an unborn child—many of us come down on the side of the baby.

11   I've been around enough men to know that they occasionally daydream about great feats they would perform if, for example, they suddenly found themselves trapped, with their whole platoon, under enemy fire. It's one of the most charming qualities of men, this desire to prove themselves to be brave and fearless.

12   But, so many men fail to realize that all around them, in our modern world, are opportunities to show their valor. Every day, they are confronted with opportunities to witness to the truth—situations which, perhaps, take more courage than saving a platoon from enemy attack.

13   Once a month, I attend a rosary vigil with about 200 people in front of a local Planned Parenthood clinic. I see the women going in for abortions, some reluctantly, some being steered through the door by a man who is probably the father of the baby.

14   After about 45 minutes, some of the men come out, alone, looking relieved. They did their duty and sat in the waiting room with their significant other until it was time for the abortion, and then they get to go off—get a cup of coffee, read the paper—while she's in the recovery room.

15   What bothers me is that most of these guys are dressed as if they were on a date—as if they were on the way to the movies. Except, this date involves the destruction of their children, and the wounding of their girlfriends.

16   I'm with the early feminists when it comes to abortion. Elizabeth Cady Stanton, Susan B. Anthony, Dr. Alice Bunker Stockham, and the whole crowd of them were staunchly pro-life. They called abortion "child murder," and the "exploitation of women and children."

17   More emphatically, they pointed out that abortion primarily serves the needs of the predatory male. In a July, 1869, article in "The Revolution," the feminist newspaper edited by Elizabeth Cady Stanton and Susan B. Anthony, the latter—of current U.S. one-dollar coin fame—wrote:

18   "Guilty? Yes, no matter what the motive, love of ease, or a desire to save from suffering the unborn innocent, the woman is awfully guilty who commits the deed. It will burden her conscience in life, it will burden her soul in death; but oh! thrice guilty is he who, for selfish gratification, heedless of her prayers, indifferent to her fate, drove her to the desperation which impels her to the crime."

19   In her day, Susan B. Anthony was describing a tiny minority of men. Today, you'll run into hordes of them at just about any political cocktail party you attend.

20   But, still, there are countless other men who dare to swim against the tide—men who respect life, and respect women, at a time when neither is required by the world. Those are men who don't have to daydream about performing feats of great valor. They do it every day.

■ QUESTIONS FOR ANALYSIS AND DISCUSSION

1. Howley states that at a cocktail party, a man she was speaking to assumed that because she was a young woman, she was automatically pro-choice. Whom do we assume are pro-choice, and why?

2. What is Howley's opinion of men who state that they are pro-choice because they don't feel that they can "tell a woman what to do with her body"? What is her opinion of many men in general? Does she make the same assumptions regarding men that the man at the cocktail party made about her? Explain.

3. What is the effect of Howley's first sentence? Does it draw you into her essay? Why does she feel that her statement will make her sound like a "man-hating feminist"?

4. Evaluate Howley's title for her essay. What does it imply? How does this title relate to her essay? Explain.

5. What reasons, if any, does Howley give for her position on abortion? What reasons does she offer for why women have abortions? How would Katha Pollitt respond to the reasons she cites? Explain.

6. Why does Howley mention her monthly rosary vigil? What does she witness during this vigil? Is it important? Explain.

Some Thoughts About Abortion

Anna Quindlen

With the U.S. Supreme Court ruling on *Roe* v. *Wade* in 1973, every woman was granted the right to a legal abortion. However, the moral questions of whether or not a woman should have the choice to end a pregnancy and what considerations might justify such a termination speak to our most deeply held values and beliefs. In short, abortion may be a legal right, but is it moral to exercise this right? Like many people, Anna Quindlen grapples with these questions and finds herself in the ambivalent position of "hating the idea of abortions, [but] hating the idea of having them outlawed."

Quindlen is an award-winning columnist and novelist. The recipient of a Pulitzer Prize, Quindlen's most recent books are *Short Guide to a Happy Life* (2000) and *Black and Blue* (1998).

■ BEFORE YOU READ

Do you feel abortion should be legal? illegal? Do you feel abortion is right in some situations, wrong in others? What are your two strongest arguments in support of your position?

■ AS YOU READ

Quindlen uses personal experiences with pregnancies—her own and that of young women—to help formulate her argument. As you read, consider whether these references provide strong evidence for Quindlen's point of view or whether they are too anecdotal, too personal.

1   It was always the look on their faces that told me first. I was the freshman dormitory counselor and they were the freshmen at a women's college where everyone was smart. One of them could come into my room, a golden girl, a valedictorian, an 800 verbal score on the SAT's, and her eyes would be empty, seeing only a busted future, the devastation of her life as she knew it. She had failed biology, messed up the math; she was pregnant.

2   That was when I became pro-choice.

3   It was the look in his eyes that I will always remember, too. They were as black as the bottom of a well, and in them for a few minutes I thought I saw myself the way I had always wished to be—clear, simple, elemental, at peace. My child looked at me and I looked back at him in the delivery room, and I realized that out of a sea of infinite possibilities it had come down to this: a specific person born on the hottest day of the year, conceived on a Christmas Eve, made by his father and me miraculously from scratch.

4   Once I believed that there was a little blob of formless protoplasm in there and a gynecologist went after it with a surgical instrument, and that was that. Then I got pregnant myself—eagerly, intentionally, by the right man, at the

right time—and I began to doubt. My abdomen still flat, my stomach roiling with morning sickness, I felt not that I had protoplasm inside but instead a complete human being in miniature to whom I could talk, sing, make promises. Neither of these views was accurate; instead, I think, the reality is something in the middle. And that is where I find myself now, in the middle, hating the idea of abortions, hating the idea of having them outlawed.

5   For I know it is the right thing in some times and places. I remember sitting in a shabby clinic far uptown with one of those freshmen, only three months after the Supreme Court had made what we were doing possible, and watching with wonder as the lovely first love she had had with a nice boy unraveled over the space of an hour as they waited for her to be called, degenerated into sniping and silences. I remember a year or two later seeing them pass on campus and not even acknowledge one another because their conjoining had caused them so much pain, and I shuddered to think of them married, with a small psyche in their unready and unwilling hands.

6   I've met 14-year-olds who were pregnant and said they could not have abortions because of their religion, and I see in their eyes the shadows of 22-year-olds I've talked to who lost their kids to foster care because they hit them or used drugs or simply had no money for food and shelter. I read not long ago about a teen-ager who said she meant to have an abortion but she spent the money on clothes instead; now she has a baby who turns out to be a lot more trouble than a toy. The people who hand out those execrable little pictures of dismembered fetuses at abortion clinics seem to forget the extraordinary pain children may endure after they are born when they are unwanted, even hated or simply tolerated.

7   I believe that in a contest between the living and the almost living, the latter must, if necessary, give way to the will of the former. That is what the fetus is to me, the almost living. Yet these questions began to plague me—and, I've discovered a good many other women—after I became pregnant. But they became even more acute after I had my second child, mainly because he is so different from his brother. On two random nights 18 months apart the same two people managed to conceive, and on one occasion the tumult within turned itself into a curly-haired brunet with merry black eyes who walked and talked late and loved the whole world, and on another it became a blond with hazel Asian eyes and a pug nose who tried to conquer the world almost as soon as he entered it.

8   If we were to have an abortion next time for some reason or another, which infinite possibility becomes, not a reality, but a nullity? The girl with the blue eyes? The improbable redhead? The natural athlete? The thinker? My husband, ever at the heart of the matter, put it another way. Knowing that he is finding two children somewhat more overwhelming than he expected, I asked if he would want me to have an abortion if I accidentally became pregnant again right away. "And waste a perfectly good human being?" he said.

9   Coming to this quandary has been difficult for me. In fact, I believe the issue of abortion is difficult for all thoughtful people. I don't know anyone who has had an abortion who has not been haunted by it. If there is one thing I find

intolerable about most of the so-called right-to-lifers, it is that they try to portray abortion rights as something that feminists thought up on a slow Saturday
over a light lunch. That is nonsense, I also know that some people who support
abortion rights are most comfortable with a monolithic position because it
seems the strongest front against the smug and sometimes violent opposition.

10   But I don't feel all one way about abortion anymore, and I don't think it
serves a just cause to pretend that many of us do. For years I believed that a
woman's right to choose was absolute, but now I wonder. Do I, with a stable
home and marriage and sufficient stamina and money, have the right to choose
abortion because a pregnancy is inconvenient right now? Legally I do have that
right; legally I want always to have that right. It is the morality of exercising it
under those circumstances that makes me wonder.

11   Technology has foiled us. The second trimester has become a time of resurrection; a fetus at six months can be one woman's late abortion, another's
premature, viable child. Photographers now have film of embryos of the size of
a grape, oddly human, flexing their fingers, sucking their thumbs. Women have
amniocentesis to find out whether they are carrying a child with birth defects
that they may choose to abort. Before the procedure, they must have a sono-
gram, one of those fuzzy black-and-white photos like a love song heard through
static on the radio, which shows someone is in there.

12   I have taped on my VCR a public-television program in which somehow, in-
explicably, a film is shown of a fetus in utero scratching its face, seemingly
putting up a tiny hand to shield itself from the camera's eye. It would make a
potent weapon in the arsenal of the antiabortionists. I grow sentimental about
it as it floats in the salt water; part fish, part human being. It is almost living, but
not quite. It has almost turned my heart around, but not quite turned my head.

■ QUESTIONS FOR ANALYSIS AND DISCUSSION

1. What is Quindlen's opinion on abortion at the beginning of the essay? at the
   end of the essay? What experiences have confirmed or changed Quindlen's position?
2. Refer to paragraph 10 and discuss Quindlen's dilemma regarding the legality
   and morality of abortion.
3. What is the form of this argument? Is it mostly inductive argument or deductive argument? Support your answer with evidence from the essay.
4. Have you had any experience similar to Quindlen's regarding abortions for college students? Do you agree with Quindlen's contention in paragraph 5, "[. . .]
   I know it is the right thing in some times and places"? Why or why not?
5. Would this essay be as powerful if Quindlen had not used first-person narra-
   tion? Do you find her description of very personal situations too revealing, or
   does it help illustrate the dilemma she and other thoughtful women face?
6. Where does Quindlen state the claim of her argument? Does it adequately
   summarize the argument? Explain.
7. In paragraph 8, Quindlen describes a possible third pregnancy and the aborted
   child's characteristics. Does this undercut her argument concerning the neces-

sity of legal abortion? How do you react to her husband's comment, "And waste a perfectly good human being?"

■ WRITING ASSIGNMENTS

1. Write a letter to a friend, a college freshman, who is contemplating an abortion. Advise her by posing the questions you think she should consider when making this decision.
2. If possible, view a photograph that shows the embryo as Quindlen describes in paragraphs 11 and 12. Write an essay discussing how these images do or do not influence your own opinion of abortion. How do you think other authors in this section would respond?
3. Write an essay in which you agree or disagree with the opinions offered by one of the authors in this section. Consider the author's argument, supporting evidence, and point of view when framing your response.
4. Gather literature from groups that both support and oppose abortion. Analyze the content of the material from both sides for any logical fallacies. Write an essay describing your findings, remaining as objective as possible in your discussion.
5. Write your own review of Leslie J. Reagan's *When Abortion Was a Crime* (University of California Press, 1997). If you disagree with Katha Pollitt's review of the book, prepare your response as if for publication in *The Atlantic,* as a debate between two intellectuals.

PHYSICIAN-ASSISTED SUICIDE AND END-OF-LIFE CHOICES

The Supreme Court and Physician-Assisted Suicide— The Ultimate Right

Marcia Angell

Do terminally ill patients have the right to end their own lives? Do doctors have a moral obligation to help them? Marcia Angell writes in favor of permitting physician-assisted suicide for terminally ill patients who request it. Addressing the opposition's concerns one by one, Angell argues that respect for patient autonomy morally binds physicians to honor the requests of terminally ill patients. She explains why she hopes that eventually all states will one day allow doctors to provide the means for terminally patients to end their lives peacefully.

Formerly the executive editor of *The New England Journal of Medicine,* Angell is a senior lecturer on social medicine at Harvard Medical School. She frequently writes on ethical issues in medicine and is the author of the critically acclaimed book *Science on Trial* (1996). This essay first appeared in *The New England Journal of Medicine* in January 1997.

■ **BEFORE YOU READ**

In your opinion, what are the rights of terminally ill patients? Is there a difference between a dying patient asking to be taken off a respirator and a dying patient asking for a lethal dose of a drug?

■ **AS YOU READ**

Consider how Angell frames her argument. Does her method of addressing the opposition's views help or hinder her discussion?

1   The U.S. Supreme Court will decide later this year whether to let stand decisions by two appeals courts permitting doctors to help terminally ill patients commit suicide.[1] The Ninth and Second Circuit Courts of Appeals last spring held that state laws in Washington and New York that ban assistance in suicide were unconstitutional as applied to doctors and their dying patients.[2,3] If the Supreme Court lets the decisions stand, physicians in 12 states, which include about half the population of the United States, would be allowed to provide the means for terminally ill patients to take their own lives, and the remaining states would rapidly follow suit. Not since *Roe* v. *Wade* has a Supreme Court decision been so fateful.

2   The decision will culminate several years of intense national debate, fueled by a number of highly publicized events. Perhaps most important among them is Dr. Jack Kevorkian's defiant assistance in some 44 suicides since 1990, to the dismay of many in the medical and legal establishments, but with substantial public support, as evidenced by the fact that three juries refused to convict him even in the face of a Michigan statute enacted for that purpose. Also since 1990, voters in three states have considered ballot initiatives that would legalize some form of physician-assisted dying, and in 1994 Oregon became the first state to approve such a measure.[4] (The Oregon law was stayed pending a court challenge.) Several surveys indicate that roughly two-thirds of the American public now support physician-assisted suicide,[5,6] as do more than half the doctors in the United States,[6,7] despite the fact that influential physicians' organizations are opposed. It seems clear that many Americans are now so concerned about the possibility of a lingering, high-technology death that they are receptive to the idea of doctors' being allowed to help them die.

3   In this editorial I will explain why I believe the appeals courts were right and why I hope the Supreme Court will uphold their decisions. I am aware that this is a highly contentious issue, with good people and strong arguments on both sides. The American Medical Association (AMA) filed an amicus brief opposing the legalization of physician-assisted suicide,[8] and the Massachusetts Medical Society, which owns the *Journal,* was a signatory to it. But here I speak

for myself, not the *Journal* or the Massachusetts Medical Society. The legal aspects of the case have been well discussed elsewhere, to me most compellingly in Ronald Dworkin's essay in the *New York Review of Books*.[9] I will focus primarily on the medical and ethical aspects.

4   I begin with the generally accepted premise that one of the most important ethical principles in medicine is respect for each patient's autonomy, and that when this principle conflicts with others, it should almost always take precedence. This premise is incorporated into our laws governing medical practice and research, including the requirement of informed consent to any treatment. In medicine, patients exercise their self-determination most dramatically when they ask that life-sustaining treatment be withdrawn. Although others may sometimes consider the request ill-founded, we are bound to honor it if the patient is mentally competent—that is, if the patient can understand the nature of the decision and its consequences.

5   A second starting point is the recognition that death is not fair and is often cruel. Some people die quickly, and others die slowly but peacefully. Some find personal or religious meaning in the process, as well as an opportunity for a final reconciliation with loved ones. But others, especially those with cancer, AIDS, or progressive neurologic disorders, may die by inches and in great anguish, despite every effort of their doctors and nurses. Although nearly all pain can be relieved, some cannot, and other symptoms, such as dyspnea, nausea, and weakness, are even more difficult to control. In addition, dying sometimes holds great indignities and existential suffering. Patients who happen to require some treatment to sustain their lives, such as assisted ventilation or dialysis, can hasten death by having the life-sustaining treatment withdrawn, but those who are not receiving life-sustaining treatment may desperately need help they cannot now get.

6   If the decisions of the appeals courts are upheld, states will not be able to prohibit doctors from helping such patients to die by prescribing a lethal dose of a drug and advising them on its use for suicide. State laws barring euthanasia (the administration of a lethal drug by a doctor) and assisted suicide for patients who are not terminally ill would not be affected. Furthermore, doctors would not be required to assist in suicide; they would simply have that option. Both appeals courts based their decisions on constitutional questions. This is important, because it shifted the focus of the debate from what the majority would approve through the political process, as exemplified by the Oregon initiative, to a matter of fundamental rights, which are largely immune from the political process. Indeed, the Ninth Circuit Court drew an explicit analogy between suicide and abortion, saying that both were personal choices protected by the Constitution and that forbidding doctors to assist would in effect nullify these rights. Although states could regulate assisted suicide, as they do abortion, they would not be permitted to regulate it out of existence.

7   It is hard to quarrel with the desire of a greatly suffering, dying patient for a quicker, more humane death or to disagree that it may be merciful to help bring that about. In those circumstances, loved ones are often relieved when death finally comes, as are the attending doctors and nurses. As the Second Cir-

cuit Court said, the state has no interest in prolonging such a life. Why, then, do so many people oppose legalizing physician-assisted suicide in these cases? There are a number of arguments against it, some stronger than others, but I believe none of them can offset the overriding duties of doctors to relieve suffering and to respect their patients autonomy. Below I list several of the more important arguments against physician-assisted suicide and discuss why I believe they are in the last analysis unpersuasive.

8   *Assisted suicide is a form of killing, which is always wrong. In contrast, withdrawing life-sustaining treatment simply allows the disease to take its course.* There are three methods of hastening the death of a dying patient: withdrawing life-sustaining treatment, assisting suicide, and euthanasia. The right to stop treatment has been recognized repeatedly since the 1976 case of Karen Ann Quinlan[10] and was affirmed by the U.S. Supreme Court in the 1990 *Cruzan* decision[11] and the U.S. Congress in its 1990 Patient Self-Determination Act.[12] Although the legal underpinning is the right to be free of unwanted bodily invasion, the purpose of hastening death was explicitly acknowledged. In contrast, assisted suicide and euthanasia have not been accepted; euthanasia is illegal in all states, and assisted suicide is illegal in most of them.

9   Why the distinctions? Most would say they turn on the doctor's role: whether it is passive or active. When life-sustaining treatment is withdrawn, the doctor's role is considered passive and the cause of death is the underlying disease, despite the fact that switching off the ventilator of a patient dependent on it looks anything but passive and would be considered homicide if done without the consent of the patient or a proxy. In contrast, euthanasia by the injection of a lethal drug is active and directly causes the patient's death. Assisting suicide by supplying the necessary drugs is considered somewhere in between, more active than switching off a ventilator but less active than injecting drugs, hence morally and legally more ambiguous.

10   I believe, however, that these distinctions are too doctor-centered and not sufficiently patient-centered. We should ask ourselves not so much whether the doctor's role is passive or active but whether the *patient's* role is passive or active. From that perspective, the three methods of hastening death line up quite differently. When life-sustaining treatment is withdrawn from an incompetent patient at the request of a proxy or when euthanasia is performed, the patient may be utterly passive. Indeed, either act can be performed even if the patient is unaware of the decision. In sharp contrast, assisted suicide, by definition, cannot occur without the patient's knowledge and participation. Therefore, it must be active—that is to say, voluntary. That is a crucial distinction, because it provides an inherent safeguard against abuse that is not present with the other two methods of hastening death. If the loaded term "kill" is to be used, it is not the doctor who kills, but the patient. Primarily because euthanasia can be performed without the patient's participation, I oppose its legalization in this country.

11   *Assisted suicide is not necessary. All suffering can be relieved if care givers are sufficiently skillful and compassionate, as illustrated by the hospice movement.* I have no

doubt that if expert palliative care were available to everyone who needed it, there would be few requests for assisted suicide. Even under the best of circumstances, however, there will always be a few patients whose suffering simply cannot be adequately alleviated. And there will be some who would prefer suicide to any other measures available, including the withdrawal of life-sustaining treatment or the use of heavy sedation. Surely, every effort should be made to improve palliative care, as I argued 15 years ago,[13] but when those efforts are unavailing and suffering patients desperately long to end their lives, physician-assisted suicide should be allowed. The argument that permitting it would divert us from redoubling our commitment to comfort care asks these patients to pay the penalty for our failings. It is also illogical. Good comfort care and the availability of physician-assisted suicide are no more mutually exclusive than good cardiologic care and the availability of heart transplantation.

12   *Permitting assisted suicide would put us on a moral "slippery slope." Although in itself assisted suicide might be acceptable, it would lead inexorably to involuntary euthanasia.* It is impossible to avoid slippery slopes in medicine (or in any aspect of life). The issue is how and where to find a purchase. For example, we accept the right of proxies to terminate life-sustaining treatment, despite the obvious potential for abuse, because the reasons for doing so outweigh the risks. We hope our procedures will safeguard patients. In the case of assisted suicide, its voluntary nature is the best protection against sliding down a slippery slope, but we also need to ensure that the request is thoughtful and freely made. Although it is possible that we may someday decide to legalize voluntary euthanasia under certain circumstances or assisted suicide for patients who are not terminally ill, legalizing assisted suicide for the dying does not in itself make these other decisions inevitable. Interestingly, recent reports from the Netherlands, where both euthanasia and physician-assisted suicide are permitted, indicate that fears about a slippery slope there have not been borne out.[14,15,16]

13   *Assisted suicide would be a threat to the economically and socially vulnerable. The poor, disabled, and elderly might be coerced to request it.* Admittedly, overburdened families or cost-conscious doctors might pressure vulnerable patients to request suicide, but similar wrongdoing is at least as likely in the case of withdrawing life-sustaining treatment, since that decision can be made by proxy. Yet, there is no evidence of widespread abuse. The Ninth Circuit Court recalled that it was feared *Roe* v. *Wade* would lead to coercion of poor and uneducated women to request abortions, but that did not happen. The concern that coercion is more likely in this era of managed care, although understandable, would hold suffering patients hostage to the deficiencies of our health care system. Unfortunately, no human endeavor is immune to abuses. The question is not whether a perfect system can be devised, but whether abuses are likely to be sufficiently rare to be offset by the benefits to patients who otherwise would be condemned to face the end of their lives in protracted agony.

14   *Depressed patients would seek physician-assisted suicide rather than help for their depression. Even in the terminally ill, a request for assisted suicide might signify treatable depression, not irreversible suffering.* Patients suffering greatly at the end of life may

also be depressed, but the depression does not necessarily explain their decision to commit suicide or make it irrational. Nor is it simple to diagnose depression in terminally ill patients. Sadness is to be expected, and some of the vegetative symptoms of depression are similar to the symptoms of mental illness. The success of antidepressant treatment in these circumstances is also not ensured. Although there are anecdotes about patients who changed their minds about suicide after treatment,[17] we do not have good studies of how often that happens or the relation to antidepressant treatment. Dying patients who request assisted suicide and seem depressed should certainly be strongly encouraged to accept psychiatric treatment, but I do not believe that competent patients should be required to accept it as a condition of receiving assistance with suicide. On the other hand, doctors would not be required to comply with all requests; they would be expected to use their judgment, just as they do in so many other types of life-and-death decisions in medical practice.

15   *Doctors should never participate in taking life. If there is to be assisted suicide, doctors must not be involved.* Although most doctors favor permitting assisted suicide under certain circumstances, many who favor it believe that doctors should not provide the assistance.[6,7] To them, doctors should be unambiguously committed to life (although most doctors who hold this view would readily honor a patient's decision to have life-sustaining treatment withdrawn). The AMA, too, seems to object to physician-assisted suicide primarily because it violates the profession's mission. Like others, I find that position too abstract.[18] The highest ethical imperative of doctors should be to provide care in whatever way best serves patients' interests, in accord with each patient's wishes, not with a theoretical commitment to preserve life no matter what the cost in suffering.[19] If a patient requests help with suicide and the doctor believes the request is appropriate, requiring someone else to provide the assistance would be a form of abandonment. Doctors who are opposed in principle need not assist, but they should make their patients aware of their position early in the relationship so that a patient who chooses to select another doctor can do so. The greatest harm we can do is to consign a desperate patient to unbearable suffering—or force the patient to seek out a stranger like Dr. Kevorkian. Contrary to the frequent assertion that permitting physician-assisted suicide would lead patients to distrust their doctors, I believe distrust is more likely to arise from uncertainty about whether a doctor will honor a patient's wishes.

16   *Physician-assisted suicide may occasionally be warranted, but it should remain illegal. If doctors risk prosecution, they will think twice before assisting with suicide.* This argument wrongly shifts the focus from the patient to the doctor. Instead of reflecting the condition and wishes of patients, assisted suicide would reflect the courage and compassion of their doctors. Thus, patients with doctors like Timothy Quill, who described in a 1991 *Journal* article how he helped a patient take her life,[20] would get the help they need and want, but similar patients with less steadfast doctors would not. That makes no sense.

17   *People do not need assistance to commit suicide. With enough determination, they can do it themselves.* This is perhaps the cruelest of the arguments against physician-assisted suicide. Many patients at the end of life are, in fact, physically un-

able to commit suicide on their own. Others lack the resources to do so. It has sometimes been suggested that they can simply stop eating and drinking and kill themselves that way. Although this method has been described as peaceful under certain conditions,[21] no one should count on that. The fact is that this argument leaves most patients to their suffering. Some, usually men, manage to commit suicide using violent methods. Percy Bridgman, a Nobel laureate in physics who in 1961 shot himself rather than die of metastatic cancer, said in his suicide note, "It is not decent for Society to make a man do this to himself."[22]

18   My father, who knew nothing of Percy Bridgman, committed suicide under similar circumstances. He was 81 and had metastatic prostate cancer. The night before he was scheduled to be admitted to the hospital, he shot himself. Like Bridgman, he thought it might be his last chance. At the time, he was not in extreme pain, nor was he close to death (his life expectancy was probably longer than six months). But he was suffering nonetheless—from nausea and the side effects of antiemetic agents, weakness, incontinence, and hopelessness. Was he depressed? He would probably have freely admitted that he was, but he would have thought it beside the point. In any case, he was an intensely private man who would have refused psychiatric care. Was he overly concerned with maintaining control of the circumstances of his life and death? Many people would say so, but that was the way he was. It is the job of medicine to deal with patients as they are, not as we would like them to be.

19   I tell my father's story here because it makes an abstract issue very concrete. If physician-assisted suicide had been available, I have no doubt my father would have chosen it. He was protective of his family, and if he had felt he had the choice, he would have spared my mother the shock of finding his body. He did not tell her what he planned to do, because he knew she would stop him. I also believe my father would have waited if physician-assisted suicide had been available. If patients have access to drugs they can take when they choose, they will not feel they must commit suicide early, while they are still able to do it on their own. They would probably live longer and certainly more peacefully, and they might not even use the drugs.

20   Long before my father's death, I believed that physician-assisted suicide ought to be permissible under some circumstances, but his death strengthened my conviction that it is simply a part of good medical care—something to be done reluctantly and sadly, as a last resort, but done nonetheless. There should be safeguards to ensure that the decision is well considered and consistent, but they should not be so daunting or violative of privacy that they become obstacles instead of protections. In particular, they should be directed not toward reviewing the reasons for an autonomous decision, but only toward ensuring that the decision is indeed autonomous. If the Supreme Court upholds the decisions of the appeals courts, assisted suicide will not be forced on either patients or doctors, but it will be a choice for those patients who need it and those doctors willing to help. If, on the other hand, the Supreme Court overturns the lower courts' decisions, the issue will continue to be grappled with state by state, through the political process. But sooner or later, given the need and the

widespread public support, physician-assisted suicide will be demanded of a compassionate profession.

REFERENCES

1. Greenhouse L. High court to say if the dying have a right to suicide help. *New York Times.* October 2, 1996:A1.

2. *Compassion in Dying* v. *Washington,* 79 F.3d 790 (9th Cir. 1996).

3. *Quill* v. *Vacco,* 80 F.3d 716 (2d Cir. 1996).

4. Annas GJ. Death by prescription—the Oregon initiative. *N Engl J Med* 1994;331:1240–3.

5. Blendon RJ, Szalay US, Knox RA. Should physicians aid their patients in dying? The public perspective: *JAMA* 1992;267:2658–62.

6. Bachman JG, Alcser KH, Doukas DJ, Lichtenstein RL, Corning AD, Brody H. Anttitudes of Michigan physicians and the public toward legalizing physician-assisted suicide and voluntary euthanasia. *N Engl J Med* 1996;334:303–9.

7. Lee MA, Nelson HD, Tilden VP, Ganzini L, Schmidt TA, Tolle SW. Legalizing assisted suicide—views of physicians in Oregon. *N Engl J Med* 1996;334:310–5.

8. Gianelli DM. AMA to court: no suicide aid. *American Medical News.* November 25, 1996:1, 27, 28.

9. Dworkin R. Sex, death, and the courts. *New York Review of Books.* August 8, 1996.

10. *In re: Quinlan,* 70 N.J. 10, 355 A.2d 647 (1976).

11. *Cruzan* v. *Director, Missouri Department of Health,* 497 U.S. 261, 110 S. Ct. 2841 (1990).

12. Omnibus Budget Reconciliation Act of 1990, P.L. 101–508, sec. 4206 and 4751, 104 Stat. 1388, 1388–115, and 1388–204 (classified respectively at 42 U.S.C. 1395cc(f) (Medicare) and 1396a(w) (Medicaid) (1994).

13. Angell M. The quality of mercy. *N Engl J Med* 1982;306:98–9.

14. van der Maas PJ, van der Wal G, Haverkate I, et al. Euthanasia, physician-assisted suicide, and other medical practices involving the end of life in the Netherlands, 1990–1995. *N Engl J Med* 1996;335:1699–705.

15. van der Wal G, van der Maas PJ, Bosma JM, et al. Evaluation of the notification procedure for physician-assisted death in the Netherlands. *N Engl J Med* 1996;335:1706–11.

16. Angell M. Euthanasia in the Netherlands—good news or bad? *N Engl J Med* 1996;335:1676–8.

17. Chochinov HM, Wilson KG, Enns M, et al. Desire for death in the terminally ill. *Am J Psychiatry* 1995;152:1185–91.

18. Cassel CK, Meier DE. Morals and moralism in the debate over euthanasia and assisted suicide. *N Engl J Med* 1990;323:750–2.

19. Angell M. Doctors and assisted suicide. *Ann R Coll Physicians Surg Can* 1991;24:493–4.

20. Quill TE. Death and dignity—a case of individualized decision making. *N Engl J Med* 1991;324:691–4.

21. Lynn J, Childress JF. Must patients always be given food and water? *Hastings Cent Rep* 1983;13(5):17–21.

22. Nuland SB. *How we die.* New York: Alfred A. Knopf, 1994:152.

■ QUESTIONS FOR ANALYSIS AND DISCUSSION

1. What does Angell mean when she states that the Supreme Court's decision will be as "fateful" as *Roe* v. *Wade?* What are the similarities between abortion and

physician-assisted suicide? What are the differences? Why do you think Angell makes this connection?

2. What distinctions does Angell make in paragraphs 8 through 10 between physician-assisted suicide and euthanasia? Why does she feel that making a distinction is important? Do you agree or disagree with her distinctions?

3. In paragraph 12, Angell discusses the "slippery slope" argument held by her opponents that legalizing physician-assisted suicide will lead to its abuse. What are the abuses feared by opponents of physician-assisted suicide? Is Angell's statement that "no human endeavor is immune to abuses" (paragraph 13) a satisfactory response? Explain.

4. How does Angell's story about her own father's death influence her discussion? Is it persuasive? Does it help you understand her views?

5. Angell comments that physician-assisted suicide should be viewed from the perspective of the patient and that doctors should act "in accord with each patient's wishes." Review paragraph 15. Is decision-making power truly in the patient's hands, or is it in the doctor's? Explain.

Death and Dignity—A Case of Individualized Decision Making
Timothy E. Quill

The Hippocratic oath is a pledge dating from ancient Greece that physicians recite when graduating from medical school. In it they promise to help the sick. The oath includes phrases such as "I will not harm or injure" and "I will not give a fatal draught to anyone if I am asked." Clearly, the ethical issues surrounding physician-assisted suicide are not new ones. In the next essay, Dr. Timothy E. Quill describes the difficult decisions physicians face when dealing with terminally ill patients who wish to stop their suffering by ending their lives.

Quill is a professor of medicine and psychiatry at the University of Rochester School of Medicine and associate chief of medicine at Genesse Hospital. He is the author of several books on physician-assisted suicide and end-of-life issues, including *A Midwife Through the Dying Process: Stories of Healing and Hard Choices at the End of Life* (1996) and *Caring for Patients at the End of Life* (2001). This article was first published by *The New England Journal of Medicine*.

■ BEFORE YOU READ

What obstacles does a terminally ill patient who wishes to commit suicide face in your state? What legal issues must the patient, the patient's family, and the physician consider?

■ AS YOU READ

What does it mean to "die with dignity"? What is dignity? Why is maintaining their dignity important to so many patients?

1   Diane was feeling tired and had a rash. A common scenario, though there was something subliminally worrisome that prompted me to check her blood count. Her hematocrit was 22, and the white-cell count was 4.3 with some metamyelocytes and unusual white cells. I wanted it to be viral, trying to deny what was staring me in the face. Perhaps in a repeated count it would disappear. I called Diane and told her it might be more serious than I had initially thought—that the test needed to be repeated and that if she felt worse, we might have to move quickly. When she pressed for the possibilities, I reluctantly opened the door to leukemia. Hearing the word seemed to make it exist. "Oh, shit!" she said. "Don't tell me that." Oh, shit! I thought, I wish I didn't have to.

2   Diane was no ordinary person (although no one I have ever come to know has been really ordinary). She was raised in an alcoholic family and had felt alone for much of her life. She had vaginal cancer as a young woman. Through much of her adult life, she had struggled with depression and her own alcoholism. I had come to know, respect, and admire her over the previous eight years as she confronted these problems and gradually overcame them. She was an incredibly clear, at times brutally honest, thinker and communicator. As she took control of her life, she developed a strong sense of independence and confidence. In the previous 3 1/2 years, her hard work had paid off. She was completely abstinent from alcohol, she had established much deeper connections with her husband, college-age son, and several friends, and her business and her artistic work were blossoming. She felt she was really living fully for the first time.

3   Not surprisingly, the repeated blood count was abnormal, and detailed examination of the peripheral-blood smear showed myelocytes. I advised her to come into the hospital, explaining that we needed to do a bone marrow biopsy and make some decisions relatively rapidly. She came to the hospital knowing what we would find. She was terrified, angry, and sad. Although we knew the odds, we both clung to the thread of possibility that it might be something else.

4   The bone marrow confirmed the worst: acute myelomonocytic leukemia. In the face of this tragedy, we looked for signs of hope. This is an area of medicine in which technological intervention has been successful, with cures 25 percent of the time—long-term cures. As I probed the costs of these cures, I heard about induction chemotherapy (three weeks in the hospital, prolonged neutropenia, probable infectious complications, and hair loss; 75 percent of patients respond, 25 percent do not). For the survivors, this is followed by consolidation chemotherapy (with similar side effects; another 25 percent die, for a net survival of 50 percent). Those still alive, to have a reasonable chance of long-term survival, then need bone marrow transplantation (hospitalization for two months and whole-body irradiation, with complete killing of the bone marrow, infectious complications, and the possibility for graft-versus-host disease—with a survival of approximately 50 percent, or 25 percent of the original group). Though hematologists may argue over the exact percentages, they don't argue about the outcome of no treatment—certain death in days, weeks, or at most a few months.

5   Believing that delay was dangerous, our oncologist broke the news to Diane and began making plans to insert a Hickman catheter and begin induction chemotherapy that afternoon. When I saw her shortly thereafter, she was enraged at his presumption that she would want treatment, and devastated by the finality of the diagnosis. All she wanted to do was go home and be with her family. She had no further questions about treatment and in fact had decided that she wanted none. Together we lamented her tragedy and the unfairness of life. Before she left, I felt the need to be sure that she and her husband understood that there was some risk in delay, that the problem was not going to go away, and that we needed to keep considering the options over the next several days. We agreed to meet in two days.

6   She returned in two days with her husband and son. They had talked extensively about the problem and the options. She remained very clear about her wish not to undergo chemotherapy and to live whatever time she had left outside the hospital. As we explored her thinking further, it became clear that she was convinced she would die during the period of treatment and would suffer unspeakably in the process (from hospitalization, from lack of control over her body, from the side effects of chemotherapy, and from pain and anguish). Although I could offer support and my best effort to minimize her suffering if she chose treatment, there was no way I could say any of this would not occur. In fact, the last four patients with acute leukemia at our hospital had died very painful deaths in the hospital during various stages of treatment (a fact I did not share with her). Her family wished she would choose treatment but sadly accepted her decision. She articulated very clearly that it was she who would be experiencing all the side effects of treatment and that odds of 25 percent were not good enough for her to undergo so toxic a course of therapy, given her expectations of chemotherapy and hospitalization and the absence of a closely matched bone marrow donor. I had her repeat her understanding of the treatment, the odds, and what to expect if there were no treatment. I clarified a few misunderstandings, but she had a remarkable grasp of the options and implications.

7   I had been a longtime advocate of active, informed patient choice of treatment or nontreatment, and of a patient's right to die with as much control and dignity as possible. Yet there was something about her giving up a 25 percent chance of long-term survival in favor of almost certain death that disturbed me. I had seen Diane fight and use her considerable inner resources to overcome alcoholism and depression, and I half expected her to change her mind over the next week. Since the window of time in which effective treatment can be initiated is rather narrow, we met several times that week. We obtained a second hematology consultation and talked at length about the meaning and implications of treatment and nontreatment. She talked to a psychologist she had seen in the past. I gradually understood the decision from her perspective and became convinced that it was the right decision for her. We arranged for home hospice care (although at that time Diane felt reasonably well, was active, and looked healthy), left the door open for her to change her mind, and tried to anticipate how to keep her comfortable in the time she had left.

8   Just as I was adjusting to her decision, she opened up another area that would stretch me profoundly. It was extraordinarily important to Diane to maintain control of herself and her own dignity during the time remaining to her. When this was no longer possible, she clearly wanted to die. As a former director of a hospice program, I know how to use pain medicines to keep patients comfortable and lessen suffering. I explained the philosophy of comfort care, which I strongly believe in. Although Diane understood and appreciated this, she had known of people lingering in what was called relative comfort, and she wanted no part of it. When the time came, she wanted to take her life in the least painful way possible. Knowing of her desire for independence and her decision to stay in control, I thought this request made perfect sense. I acknowledged and explored this wish but also thought that it was out of the realm of currently accepted medical practice and that it was more than I could offer or promise. In our discussion, it became clear that preoccupation with her fear of a lingering death would interfere with Diane's getting the most out of the time she had left until she found a safe way to ensure her death. I feared the effects of a violent death on her family, the consequences of an ineffective suicide that would leave her lingering in precisely the state she dreaded so much, and the possibility that a family member would be forced to assist her, with all the legal and personal repercussions that would follow. She discussed this at length with her family. They believed that they should respect her choice. With this in mind, I told Diane that information was available from the Hemlock Society that might be helpful to her.

9   A week later she phoned me with a request for barbiturates for sleep. Since I knew that this was an essential ingredient in a Hemlock Society suicide, I asked her to come to the office to talk things over. She was more than willing to protect me by participating in a superficial conversation about her insomnia, but it was important to me to know how she planned to use the drugs and to be sure that she was not in despair or overwhelmed in a way that might color her judgment. In our discussion, it was apparent that she was having trouble sleeping, but it was also evident that the security of having enough barbiturates available to commit suicide when and if the time came would leave her secure enough to live fully and concentrate on the present. It was clear that she was not despondent and that in fact she was making deep, personal connections with her family and close friends. I made sure that she knew how to use the barbiturates for sleep, and also that she knew the amount needed to commit suicide. We agreed to meet regularly, and she promised to meet with me before taking her life, to ensure that all other avenues had been exhausted. I wrote the prescription with an uneasy feeling about the boundaries I was exploring—spiritual, legal, professional, and personal. Yet I also felt strongly that I was setting her free to get the most out of the time she had left, and to maintain dignity and control on her own terms until her death.

10   The next several months were very intense and important for Diane. Her son stayed home from college, and they were able to be with one another and say much that had not been said earlier. Her husband did his work at home so

that he and Diane could spend more time together. She spent time with her closest friends. I had her come into the hospital for a conference with our residents, at which she illustrated in a most profound and personal way the importance of informed decision making, the right to refuse treatment, and the extraordinarily personal effects of illness and interaction with the medical system. There were emotional and physical hardships as well. She had periods of intense sadness and anger. Several times she became very weak, but she received transfusions as an outpatient and responded with marked improvement of symptoms. She had two serious infections that responded surprisingly well to empirical courses of oral antibiotics. After three tumultuous months, there were two weeks of relative calm and well-being, and fantasies of a miracle began to surface.

11   Unfortunately, we had no miracle. Bone pain, weakness, fatigue, and fevers began to dominate her life. Although the hospice workers, family members, and I tried our best to minimize the suffering and promote comfort, it was clear that the end was approaching. Diane's immediate future held what she feared the most—increasing discomfort, dependence, and hard choices between pain and sedation. She called up her closest friends and asked them to come over to say goodbye, telling them that she would be leaving soon. As we had agreed, she let me know as well. When we met, it was clear that she knew what she was doing, that she was sad and frightened to be leaving, but that she would be even more terrified to stay and suffer. In our tearful goodbye, she promised a reunion in the future at her favorite spot on the edge of Lake Geneva, with dragons swimming in the sunset.

12   Two days later her husband called to say that Diane had died. She had said her final goodbyes to her husband and son that morning, and asked them to leave her alone for an hour. After an hour, which must have seemed an eternity, they found her on the couch, lying very still and covered by her favorite shawl. There was no sign of struggle. She seemed to be at peace. They called me for advice about how to proceed. When I arrived at their house, Diane indeed seemed peaceful. Her husband and son were quiet. We talked about what a remarkable person she had been. They seemed to have no doubts about the course she had chosen or about their cooperation, although the unfairness of her illness and the finality of her death were overwhelming to us all.

13   I called the medical examiner to inform him that a hospice patient had died. When asked about the cause of death, I said, "acute leukemia." He said that was fine and that we should call a funeral director. Although acute leukemia was the truth, it was not the whole story. Yet any mention of suicide would have given rise to a police investigation and probably brought the arrival of an ambulance crew for resuscitation. Diane would have become a "coroner's case," and the decision to perform an autopsy would have been made at the discretion of the medical examiner. The family or I could have been subject to criminal prosecution, and I to professional review, for our roles in support of Diane's choices. Although I truly believe that the family and I gave her the best care possible, allowing her to define her limits and directions as much as possi-

ble, I am not sure the law, society, or the medical profession would agree. So I said "acute leukemia" to protect all of us, to protect Diane from an invasion into her past and her body, and to continue to shield society from the knowledge of the degree of suffering that people often undergo in the process of dying. Suffering can be lessened to some extent, but in no way eliminated or made benign, by the careful intervention of a competent, caring physician, given current social constraints.

14   Diane taught me about the range of help I can provide if I know people well and if I allow them to say what they really want. She taught me about life, death, and honesty and about taking charge and facing tragedy squarely when it strikes. She taught me that I can take small risks for people that I really know and care about. Although I did not assist in her suicide directly, I helped indirectly to make it possible, successful, and relatively painless. Although I know we have measures to help control pain and lessen suffering, to think that people do not suffer in the process of dying is an illusion. Prolonged dying can occasionally be peaceful, but more often the role of the physician and family is limited to lessening but not eliminating severe suffering.

15   I wonder how many families and physicians secretly help patients over the edge into death in the face of such severe suffering. I wonder how many severely ill or dying patients secretly take their lives, dying alone in despair. I wonder whether the image of Diane's final aloneness will persist in the minds of her family, or if they will remember more the intense, meaningful months they had together before she died. I wonder whether Diane struggled in that last hour, and whether the Hemlock Society's way of death by suicide is the most benign. I wonder why Diane, who gave so much to so many of us, had to be alone for the last hour of her life. I wonder whether I will see Diane again, on the shore of Lake Geneva at sunset, with dragons swimming on the horizon.

■ QUESTIONS FOR ANALYSIS AND DISCUSSION

1. Imagine that you have just been diagnosed with leukemia. You must make a decision to begin or refuse treatment. If you choose treatment, you face probable hair loss, extreme nausea, weakness, exhaustion, and opportunistic infections, but you have about a 25 percent chance of survival. If you refuse, you will certainly die within the year. What choice would you make? What conditions would influence your decision? Explain.

2. In paragraph 8, Quill states that "it was extraordinarily important to Diane to maintain control of herself and her own dignity." Do you think she accomplished this objective? Was assisted suicide the only way to maintain dignity and control? Explain.

3. Quill wonders why Diane had to be alone for the last hour of her life. How would the legalization of physician-assisted suicide change a patient's final hours?

4. Why do you think Quill states in paragraph 14 that he only *indirectly* made Diane's suicide possible? How does he stand on the issue of physician-assisted suicide? How can you tell?

"Aging Hands"

This photograph taken by Nita Winter was included in an article on physician-assisted suicide featured in the Winter 2000 issue of the *Harvard Medical School Alumni Bulletin.*

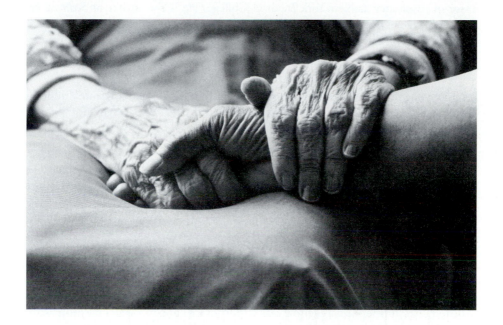

■ QUESTIONS FOR ANALYSIS AND DISCUSSION

1. Consider how the context of the photograph influences what you perceive its message to be. If this photograph were featured in a hospital ad, for example, would its "message" change?
2. What is happening in this photograph? Do you have an emotional reaction to it? Explain.
3. In what other ways could this photograph be used? Explain how you might use the photograph, its context, and the message you would try to convey.

Suicide, Assisted Suicide, and Medical Illness

Herbert Hendin

Dr. Herbert Hendin explains that all the media attention focused on the issue of physician-assisted suicide fails to address the more important issue of educating doctors to deal with the dying process as a natural part of life. He wonders if doctors sometimes elect to support euthanasia out of a desire to regain control over a situation that is essentially out of the control of medicine. He argues that patients often seek to end their lives because of fear and dread over what will happen to them as their illness progresses, rather than from actual pain and complications. He explains that the root of this fear is the loss of control, a fear many of their doctors feel as well. Euthanasia becomes the means for both patients and doctors to cope with the frustration of terminal illness rather than dealing with the illness itself.

Hendin is the executive director of the American Suicide Foundation and professor of psychiatry at New York Medical College. He is the author of *Seduced by Death: Doctors, Patients and Assisted Suicide* (1998), from which this essay is excerpted, and *The Case Against Assisted Suicide* (2002).

■ BEFORE YOU READ

Imagine your reaction if confronted with the news that you had a terminal illness. Would the option of assisted suicide be important to you? Why or why not?

■ AS YOU READ

What does Hendin say are usually patients' greatest fears regarding terminal illnesses? What drives their desire to commit suicide?

1   A few years ago, a young professional in his early thirties who had acute myelocytic leukemia was referred to me for consultation. With medical treatment, Tim was given a 25 percent chance of survival; without it, he was told, he would die in a few months. Tim, an ambitious executive whose focus on career success had led him to neglect his relationships with his wife and family, was stunned. His immediate reaction was a desperate, angry preoccupation with suicide and a request for support in carrying it out. He was worried about becoming dependent and feared both the symptoms of his disease and the side effects of treatment.

2   Tim's request speaks directly to the question at the heart of assisted suicide and euthanasia: Does our need to care for people who are terminally ill and to reduce their suffering require us to give physicians the right to end their lives?

3   Asking this question, however, helps to make us aware that neither legalizing nor forbidding euthanasia addresses the much larger problem of providing humane care for those who are terminally ill. To some degree the call for legalization is a symptom of our failure to develop a better response to the problems of dying and the fear of unbearable pain or artificial prolongation of life in intolerable circumstances.

4   People are apt to assume that seriously or terminally ill people who wish to end their lives are different from those who are otherwise suicidal. Yet the first reaction of many patients, like Tim, to the knowledge of serious illness and possible death is anxiety, depression, and a wish to die. Such patients are not significantly different from patients who react to other crises with the desire to end the crisis by ending their lives.

5   Patients rarely cite the fear of death itself as their reason for requesting assisted suicide or euthanasia, but clinicians often see such patients displace anxieties about death onto the circumstances of dying: pain, dependence, loss of

dignity, and the unpleasant side effects of medical treatments. Focusing one's fear or rage onto these palpable events distracts from the fear of death itself. Tim's anxieties about the painful circumstances that would surround his death were not irrational, but all his fears about dying amplified them.

6   Once Tim and I could talk about the possibility or likelihood of his dying— what separation from his family and the destruction of his body meant to him—his desperation subsided. He accepted medical treatment and used the remaining months of his life to become closer to his wife and parents. At first, he would not talk to his wife about his illness because of his resentment that she was going on with her life while he would likely not be going on with his. A session with the two of them cleared the air and made it possible for them to talk openly with each other. Two days before he died, Tim talked about what he would have missed without the opportunity for a loving parting.[1]

7   The last days of most patients can be given such meaning if those treating them know how to engage them. Tim's need for communication with his wife, communication that was not possible until he voiced his envy and resentment over her going on with her life while he was probably not going to be doing so, finds parallels in the lives of most dying patients.

8   In a twist on conventional wisdom, the English palliative care specialist Robert Twycross has written, "where there is hope there is life," referring not to hope of a cure, but hope of doing something that gives meaning to life as long as it lasts.[2] Virtually everyone who is dying has unfinished business, even if only the need to share their life and their death with friends, family, a doctor, or a hospice worker. Without such purpose, terminally ill patients who are not in great physical distress may be tortured by the feeling that they are only waiting to die and may want to die at once.

9   If assisted suicide were legal, Tim probably would have asked a doctor's help in taking his own life. Because he was mentally competent, he would have qualified for assisted suicide and would surely have found a doctor who would agree to his request.

10   Since the Oregon law and similar laws being considered in other states do not require an independently referred doctor for a second opinion, Tim would likely have been referred by a physician supportive of assisted suicide to a colleague who was equally supportive; the evaluation would have been pro forma. He could have been put to death in an unrecognized state of terror, unable to give himself the chance of getting well or of dying in the dignified way he did. The Oregon law is the latest example of how public frustration can lead to action that only compounds the problem; in the rush to legislate, advocates have failed to understand the problem they are claiming to solve.

11   Long before today's movement to legalize assisted suicide of patients who are seriously or terminally ill, we knew that physical illness contributes significantly to the motivation for suicide. Medical illness plays an important role in 25 percent of suicides, and this percentage rises with age: from 50 percent in suicides who are over fifty years old, to over 70 percent in suicides older than sixty.[3]

12   Most suicide attempts reflect a patient's ambivalence about dying, and those requesting assisted suicide show an equal ambivalence. The desire for death waxes

and wanes in terminally ill patients, even among those who express a persistent wish to die.[4] Some patients may voice suicidal thoughts in response to transient depression or severe pain, but these patients usually find relief with treatment of their depressive illness or pain and are grateful to be alive.[5] Strikingly, the overwhelming majority of the patients who are terminally ill fight for life until the end; only 2 to 4 percent of suicides occur in the context of terminal illness.[6]

13   Like Tim, the vast majority of those who request assisted suicide or euthanasia are motivated primarily by dread of what will happen to them rather than by current pain or suffering.[7] Similarly, in several studies, more individuals, particularly elderly individuals, killed themselves because they feared or *mistakenly* believed they had cancer than killed themselves and actually had cancer.[8] In the same way, preoccupation with suicide is greater in those awaiting the results of tests for HIV antibodies than in those who know that they are HIV positive.[9]

14   Patients do not know what to expect and cannot foresee how their conditions will unfold as they decline toward death. Facing this ignorance, they fill the vacuum with their fantasies and fears. When these fears are dealt with by a caring and knowledgeable physician, the request for death usually disappears. . . .

15   Both patients who attempt suicide and those who request assisted suicide often test the affection and care of others, confiding feelings like "I don't want to be a burden to my family" or "My family would be better off without me." Such statements are classic indicators of suicidal depression.

16   Expressions of being a burden usually reflect depressed feelings of worthlessness or guilt, and may be pleas for reassurance. Whether physically healthy or terminally ill, these patients need assurance that they are still wanted; they also need treatment for depression. If the doctor does not recognize the ambivalence, anxiety, and depression that underlie a patient's request for death, the patient becomes trapped by that request and can die in a state of unrecognized terror. . . .

17   Patients are not alone in their inability to tolerate situations they cannot control. Lewis Thomas has written insightfully about the sense of failure and helplessness that doctors may experience in the face of death;[10] such feelings may explain why doctors have such difficulty discussing terminal illness with patients. A majority of doctors avoid such discussions, while most patients would prefer frank talk.[11] These feelings might also explain both doctors' tendency to use excessive measures to maintain life and their need to make death a physician's decision. By deciding when patients die, by making death a medical decision, the physician preserves the illusion of mastery over the disease and the accompanying feelings of helplessness. The physician, not the illness, is responsible for the death. Assisting suicide and euthanasia become ways of dealing with the frustration of not being able to cure the disease.

REFERENCES

1. H. Hendin, *Suicide in America* (New York: Norton, 1995).

2. R. Twycross, "A View from the Hospice," in *Euthanasia Examined,* ed. J. Keown (Cambridge: Cambridge University Press, 1995).

3. T. B. MacKenzie and M. K. Popkin, "Medical Illness and Suicide," In *Suicide over the Life Cycle*, ed. S. J. Blumenthal and D. J. Kupfer (Washington, D.C.: American Psychiatric Press, 1990), 205–232.

4. E. J. Emanuel, D. L. Fairclough, E. R. Daniels, and B. R. Clarridge, "Euthanasia and Physician-Assisted Suicide: Attitudes and Experiences of Oncology Patients, Oncologists, and the Public," *Lancet*, 1996, 347:1,805–1,810.

5. H. Hendin and G. L. Klerman, "Physician-Assisted Suicide: The Dangers of Legalization," *American Journal of Psychiatry*, 1993, 150:143–145.

6. E. Robins, G. E. Murphy, R. H. Wilkinson Jr., S. Gassner, and J. Kayes, "Some Clinical Considerations in the Prevention of Suicide Based on a Study of 134 Successful Suicides," *American Journal of Public Health*, 1959, 49:888–889; P. Sainsbury, *Suicide in London: An Ecological Study* (New York: Basic Books, 1956); C. P. Seager and R. S. Flood, "Suicide in Bristol," *British Journal of Psychiatry*, 1955, 111:919–932.

7. H. Hendin, "Suicide and the Request for Assisted Suicide: Meaning and Motivation," *Duquesne Law Review*, 1996, 35:285–310.

8. Y. Conwell, E. D. Caine, and K. Olsen, "Suicide and Cancer in Late Life," *Hospital & Community Psychiatry*, 1990, 41:1334–1339, T. L. Dorpat, W. F. Anderson, and H. S. Ripley, "The Relationship of Physical Illness to Suicide," in *Suicidal Behaviors: Diagnosis and Management*, ed. H. L. P. Resnick (Boston: Little, Brown, 1963).

9. S. Perry, "Suicidal Ideation and HIV Testing," *JAMA*, 1990, 263:679–682.

10. L. Thomas, "Dying as Failure?" *American Journal of Political Science*, 1984, 444: 1–4.

11. D. Hendin, *Death as a Fact of Life* (New York: Norton, 1973), citing Herman Feifel, "Physicians Consider Death," unpublished manuscript presented at 1967 meeting of the American Psychological Association.

■ QUESTIONS FOR ANALYSIS AND DISCUSSION

1. Compare Tim's case to that of Timothy Quill's patient, Diane. What similarities do you see between the two patients? what differences? How soon after her diagnosis does Diane ask for "an essential ingredient in a Hemlock Society suicide"? Do you think that Hendin would feel the same about Diane's request for suicide assistance as he did about Tim's?

2. What kinds of fears and anxieties can prompt a patient to request assistance in committing suicide? How does Tim's case express Hendin's point about patient fears?

3. What does Hendin mean in paragraph 16 when he says patients' "expressions of being a burden [. . .] may be pleas for reassurance"? What are the needs for terminally ill patients besides pain control?

4. Hendin comments that some patients may seek to commit suicide because they fear the loss of control associated with terminal illness. He further comments that physicians may feel a similar frustration because they are limited in their ability to help patients. Why is the concept of control so important? What does Hendin imply is the real issue?

5. In paragraph 8, Hendin cites Robert Twycross's statement, "where there is hope there is life." How do you define "life"? Does this definition change when referring to the terminally ill? Explain.

Last Right

Carrie Carmichael

The first three essays in this section presented physicians' perspectives on physician-assisted suicide. However, many people feel that they cannot approach their physicians to discuss this possibility. For them, how they end their lives is a personal choice, made with friends and family, but still often with an edge of violence. They may shoot themselves, slice their wrists, or in the case of Carrie Carmichael's friend, jump from a building rather than face their final days in pain and helplessness. And while their suffering may end, friends and family are still left with haunting questions about what drove their loved one to make this choice.

Carmichael is a writer and performer living in New York. This essay appeared in the May 27, 2001, issue of the *New York Times Magazine*.

■ BEFORE YOU READ

In the next article, the author explains how her friend decided to commit suicide rather than face a lingering and painful death from esophageal cancer. Evaluate your own opinions of suicide. Should it be a personal choice? Or, does suicide degrade the intrinsic value of human life?

■ AS YOU READ

Carmichael presents this experience as a personal narrative. Does she present an argument? Can you determine her position on this issue? Explain.

1   Last fall, a friend asked if she could jump out my 11th-floor window. She had esophageal cancer and was planning ahead. If the chemotherapy didn't shrink her tumor, and if surgery didn't offer her continued life, she wanted something "swift and certain." Pills wouldn't be an option if she couldn't swallow anymore. She didn't have a doctor to assist her dying, so injectible morphine would be harder to get. Five years ago, she was hit by a vehicle in Mexico. "The impact didn't hurt," she told me, and she figured that hitting the ground wouldn't either.

2   We had been very close for decades and shared the major events of adult life: children's births, divorce, career crises. Nursing her husband through his protracted death from colon cancer had galvanized her. She did not want to hang on to life after the prognosis was hopeless and her pain became unrelenting. We had just sat down to a lunch I had made for us when she asked. She wanted to jump out my window because she lived in a brownstone. Her chemo-necessitated wig, picked up that morning at a shop in my neighborhood, sobered me. This was not one of our hypothetical suicide conversations—this one was real. It took my breath away, I put down my fork and said, "Let's take a look."

3   My bedrooms and living room look out on West 72nd Street. In the master bedroom, I threw up the sash. A sidewalk covering in place during some building restoration had just been removed. She was glad it was gone, she said. Nothing to break her fall. But nothing to protect pedestrians either.

4   "You couldn't be in the apartment," she ordered. "The doorman would see you leave. I would have to be here alone." She didn't want me suspected of criminal behavior.

5   "We'll see what the chemo does," I said. "And then we'll talk more." I was devastated that a woman I loved was threatened with imminent death. I wanted to be a good friend, but asking me to help her commit suicide changed everything.

6   After she left, I had second thoughts about my swift acquiescence. This was hardly a casual request. Could I sleep in my room after my friend plunged to her death from my window? Could I enter and leave passing the place where her crumpled body had lain? Which of my neighbors, which of the toddlers in strollers and kids on scooters, would see her fall?

7   On the phone a few days later, when I told her that I was waffling, she said just the offer was comforting. She felt calmer. We talked about other tall buildings with windows that open, as well as other options. Neither of us had experience with pills, injectible drugs or morphine suppositories. Nor did we know how much help she might need with any of them.

8   A few months passed and her life shrank. She moved south to live with her daughter's family. She slept much of the time, was racked with coughing and in more and more pain. My friend felt that as long as her pleasure in life was greater than her pain, she would choose to live. But she didn't want to wait until she didn't have the strength to take her own life. In February, I traveled to see her for what I knew would be the last time. "I've found a hotel with balconies," she told me during my visit. "Will you drive me there?" And I agreed. Since her family would inherit her estate, she didn't want them accused of hastening her death.

9   On the day we chose, her bag was packed and she was ready to go. As I drove onto the block, her daughter and family were saying goodbye. After they pulled away, we walked to the car. I opened the door for her. We put our seatbelts on. When we pulled up at the hotel, with the car in park, we hugged. Exchanged "I love you's." "If you change your mind, just call," I reminded her. We wept, and she waved goodbye as I turned and left. The ordinary act of dropping off a friend at a hotel was made extraordinary by her intention. I was the last person who loved her to see her alive.

10   When her friends heard how she had taken her own life, reaction was mixed. Shock at her method. Admiration of her courage. How could she do that? they asked angrily. What a legacy for her family. Thoughtless. Why didn't she cut her wrists in a warm bath? Why didn't somebody duct-tape her to her bed and find a better way? I kept quiet.

11   For my own part, I have asked myself why I did what I did. I didn't want to let her down. Although I gave her permission to take her own life, I feel guilty

that I did not find an easier way for her to die. At the same time, I'm angry that she didn't use a gentler method, one with a more peaceful end. Something easier for her. Something much easier for me.

12   So far, no punishments. No rewards. But I am haunted. I'm not at peace. Will I ever be? I know my friend is where she wanted to be, on her own terms. She had the right to take her own life, and her loved ones were right to help her, but there should have been a better way. I am left with the legacy of my friend's desperation and the prospect of my own.

■ QUESTIONS FOR ANALYSIS AND DISCUSSION

1. Having witnessed her own husband's death from colon cancer, Carmichael's friend is "galvanized" to take her own life. Does this experience make her decision to end her life seem more reasonable? Does it help the reader better understand this woman's point of view?
2. How does Carmichael react to her friend's request to jump out her 11th floor window? Why does she agree to the request? Is she motivated out of loyalty, or conviction that her friend is making a reasonable decision?
3. What concerns does Carmichael harbor considering her friend's intended use of her apartment? Why does she change her mind? Does she consider things her friend does not? Explain.
4. Could Carmichael's friend have researched her options more thoroughly? For example, in paragraph 7, Carmichael explains that her friend chooses to jump from a window because neither of them "had experience with pills, injectible drugs or morphine suppositories." Could they have researched a more "peaceful" method of death? Or, is that not the point?
5. Does Carmichael's friend have a name? What do we know about her? Why do you think details about her are so vague?
6. Analyze Carmichael's final paragraph. What troubles her the most about her friend's suicide? Explain.

■ WRITING ASSIGNMENTS

1. The patients in both Hendin's and Quill's essays were diagnosed with a form of leukemia. Imagine that a close friend has informed you that he or she has been diagnosed with this disease and is considering suicide. Write a letter in which you explain your position on suicide. Would you help this person end his or her life, as Carrie Carmichael did? Be sure to address your friend's emotions and fears about the illness and suicide, as well as your own ethical, moral, and legal concerns.
2. The Hemlock Society is a nonprofit organization representing individuals who "firmly believe control over one's death is a fundamental right, and that the option of physician aid in dying is a fundamental choice." Visit the Hemlock Society's Web site at <www.hemlock.org> and review some of its resources, including its student page. How does the Web site present the Society's views on "good death"? Depending on how you stand on the issue of physician-assisted suicide, write an essay evaluating the views expressed by the Hemlock Society.

3. Write an essay in which you describe your own position on physician-assisted suicide. Should physician-assisted suicide be legal? Would you choose this route for yourself or for a loved one? Do you think that people facing death can make informed decisions about this issue, or could they be influenced by fear and depression? Explain.

4. Does your state allow physician-assisted suicide? Research your state's position on this issue including its legal viewpoint and the official position of your state's medical board. Discuss your findings in an essay.

CHAPTER 17

Casebook: The Human Cloning Debate

When people say that they are against cloning, they usually mean human cloning in a lab. Human clones have always existed—identical twins and triplets are technically clones, each containing exact matching sets of DNA. But identical twins still start out the same way everyone else does—DNA from a sperm cell joins with DNA from an egg cell. However, in 1997, scientists at the Roslin Institute in Scotland announced that they had successfully cloned an adult sheep named Dolly. Soon after, they cloned Cedric, Cecil, Cyril, and Tuppence from cultured embryo cells—four Dorset rams that are genetically identical to one another. From that point on, everything we thought we knew about reproduction was turned upside down.

Dolly was created by a procedure known as somatic-cell nuclear transfer. Researchers took a mammary gland cell from an adult sheep and removed its nucleus, extracting the DNA. This nucleus was then inserted into an egg that had its own nucleus removed. The egg cell divided and developed into an embryo—proving that to direct embryonic development it was possible to reprogram the nuclei of adult cells, which have been differentiated to become specific cells—as a muscle cell or a blood cell. This embryo was implanted in a surrogate mother sheep, and five months later, she gave birth to a lamb. With Dolly the sperm step was skipped entirely!

After the Roslin Institute made its announcement, researchers, religious leaders, politicians, legal experts, and journalists responded to the news with strong opinions—especially as this new technology could someday relate to humans. Although the possibility of cloning does exist, the success rate for the technique that produced Dolly is extremely small—only about 0.03 percent. Moreover, most scientists are interested in human cloning as it relates to curing disease and nurturing stem cell lines. But soon after the announcement, other scientists proclaimed their intention to try and clone a human being, including the much-publicized Dr. Richard Seed—who is a physicist, not a physician. In 1997, President Bill Clinton called for the National Bioethics Advisory Commission to prepare a report on the ethical, religious, and legal issues associated with human cloning. Their recommendations were then debated by the U.S. Congress for several years.

In November 2001, while the prohibition of human cloning research was still under debate in Congress, the announcement by scientists at the Advanced Cell Technology in Massachusetts that they had achieved limited success in cloning human embryos—to be used for therapeutic and not reproductive research—caused a new uproar among politicians. In January 2002, Senator Sam Brownback (a Republican from Kansas) sought an immediate moratorium on all such research and called for renewed debate on the issue of human cloning. Brownback advocates a complete ban on all human cloning research, regardless of its intended use, a ban that would likely affect stem cell research as well.

However, not everyone is so concerned. It is unlikely that a cloned human would be a perfect replica of its DNA parent—conditions in the uterus, the health of the mother, and environmental factors can all influence fetal development. And after birth, external factors help create who we are. Supporters of human cloning research argue that scientific horror stories, such as cloning for body parts, are just that, horror stories, and will never happen in the real world. Cloning, moreover, has the potential to revolutionize medicine. Politicians such as Senator Tom Harkin (a Democrat from Iowa) are calling for legislation that would allow human cloning research for therapeutic purposes, but not for any reproductive-related activities. The articles in this section explore the multiple issues surrounding human cloning, including arguments for and against the practice. Will cloning technology reinvent how we think about human reproduction, or are we opening a "Pandora's box" full of dangers?

"Embryos-R-US"

In November 2001, Advanced Cell Technology, a privately funded research firm, announced that it had achieved some success in cloning a human embryo, with the intention of using such technology to culture stem cell lines for research purposes. Its efforts revealed how stem cell research and cloning biotechnology intersect. In the cartoon shown on page 676, Kevin Siers puts his own spin on this connection.

In 1987, while still a student at the University of Minnesota, Siers became the first recipient of the Locher Award presented by the Association of American Editorial Cartoonists. Following this award, Kevin was offered the editorial cartoonist's position on the *Charlotte Observer*'s editorial board. This cartoon was featured in the editorial pages of that newspaper.

■ QUESTIONS FOR ANALYSIS AND DISCUSSION

1. What is the cartoonist saying about the "private sector"? What does he imply motivates their research?
2. What visual clichés does the cartoon employ? How does the man's clothing and facial expression convey a character?
3. What assumptions does Siers make about his audience? Would a European reader understand the cultural conventions he uses to make his point?
4. What do we expect this man to be selling? How does Siers twist our expectations?

Baby, It's You and You and You

Nancy Gibbs

Once researchers at the Roslin Institute in Scotland announced that they had successfully cloned a sheep, they were inundated with calls from desperate parents asking if they could clone their loved ones. Says Ian Wilmut, the lead researcher who created Dolly, "I suppose this was my first sharp intimation of the effect that Dolly could have on people's lives and perceptions. Such pleas are based on a misconception: that cloning of the kind that produced Dolly confers an instant, exact replication—a virtual resurrection. This is simply not the case." Nevertheless, many people are indeed interested in human cloning—for a variety of reasons. In this article, Nancy Gibbs discusses the various reasons why people wish to pursue human cloning, and some of the arguments against it.

Gibbs is a senior editor at *Time* magazine, where she divides her time between writing major stories on national affairs and domestic policy issues for the magazine, and editing various sections of it. She has taught "Politics and the Press" at Princeton University and is a frequent guest on radio and television talk shows. This article was first published in the February 12, 2001, issue of *Time*.

■ **BEFORE YOU READ**

What do you know about human cloning? Do you think it should be banned? After reading the articles in this section, reevaluate your position. Is your answer the same? Why or why not?

■ **AS YOU READ**

Gibbs observes that many people who support human cloning seem to do so without considering the point of view of the clone. How do the examples of people who support cloning that she provides in her article support this viewpoint?

1   Before we assume that the market for human clones consists mainly of narcissists who think the world deserves more of them or neo-Nazis who dream of cloning Hitler or crackpots and mavericks and mischief makers of all kinds, it is worth taking a tour of the marketplace. We might just meet ourselves there.

2   Imagine for a moment that your daughter needs a bone-marrow transplant and no one can provide a match; that your wife's early menopause has made her infertile; or that your five-year-old has drowned in a lake and your grief has made it impossible to get your mind around the fact that he is gone forever. Would the news then really be so easy to dismiss that around the world, there are scientists in labs pressing ahead with plans to duplicate a human being, deploying the same technology that allowed Scottish scientists to clone Dolly the sheep?

3   All it took was that first headline about the astonishing ewe, and fertility experts began to hear the questions every day. Our two-year-old daughter died in a car crash; we saved a lock of her hair in a baby book. Can you clone her? Why does the law allow people more freedom to destroy fetuses than to create them? My husband had cancer and is sterile. Can you help us?

4   The inquiries are pouring in because some scientists are ever more willing to say yes, perhaps we can. Last month a well-known infertility specialist, Panayiotis Zavos of the University of Kentucky, announced that he and Italian researcher Severino Antinori, the man who helped a 62-year-old woman give birth using donor eggs, were forming a consortium to produce the first human clone. Researchers in South Korea claim they have already created a cloned human embryo, though they destroyed it rather than implanting it in a surrogate mother to develop. Recent cover stories in *Wired* and the *New York Times Magazine* tracked the efforts of the Raelians, a religious group committed to, among other things, welcoming the first extraterrestrials when they appear. They intend to clone the cells of a dead 10-month-old boy whose devastated parents hope, in effect, to bring him back to life as a newborn. The Raelians say they have the lab and the scientists, and—most important, considering the amount of trial and error involved—they say they have 50 women lined up to act as surrogates to carry a cloned baby to term.

5   Given what researchers have learned since Dolly, no one thinks the mechanics of cloning are very hard: take a donor egg, suck out the nucleus, and hence the DNA, and fuse it with, say, a skin cell from the human being copied. Then, with the help of an electrical current, the reconstituted cell should begin growing into a genetic duplicate. "It's inevitable that someone will try and someone will succeed," predicts Delores Lamb, an infertility expert at Baylor University. The consensus among biotechnology specialists is that within a few years—some scientists believe a few months—the news will break of the birth of the first human clone.

6   At that moment, at least two things will happen—one private, one public. The meaning of what it is to be human—which until now has involved, at the very least, the mysterious melding of two different people's DNA—will shift forever, along with our understanding of the relationship between parents and children, means and ends, ends and beginnings. And as a result, the conversation that has occupied scientists and ethicists for years, about how much man should mess with nature when it comes to reproduction, will drop onto every kitchen table, every pulpit, every politician's desk. Our fierce national debate over issues like abortion and euthanasia will seem tame and transparent compared with the questions that human cloning raises.

7   That has many scientists scared to death. Because even if all these headlines are hype and we are actually far away from seeing the first human clone, the very fact that at this moment, the research is proceeding underground, unaccountable, poses a real threat. The risk lies not just with potential babies born deformed, as many animal clones are; not just with desperate couples and cancer patients and other potential "clients" whose hopes may be raised and hearts broken and life savings wiped out. The immediate risk is that a backlash against renegade science might strike at responsible science as well.

8   The more scared people are of some of this research, scientists worry, the less likely they are to tolerate any of it. Yet variations on cloning technology are already used in biotechnology labs all across the country. It is these techniques that will allow, among other things, the creation of cloned herds of sheep and cows that produce medicines in their milk. Researchers also hope that one day, the ability to clone adult human cells will make it possible to "grow" new hearts and livers and nerve cells.

9   But some of the same techniques could also be used to grow a baby. Trying to block one line of research could impede another and so reduce the chances of finding cures for ailments such as Alzheimer's and Parkinson's, cancer and heart disease. Were some shocking breakthrough in human cloning to cause "an overcompensatory response by legislators," says Rockefeller University cloning expert Tony Perry, "that could be disastrous. At some point, it will potentially cost lives." So we are left with choices and trade-offs and a need to think through whether it is this technology that alarms us or just certain ways of using it.

10   By day, Randolfe Wicker, 63, runs a lighting shop in New York City. But in his spare time, as spokesman for the Human Cloning Foundation, he is the

face of cloning fervor in the U.S. "I took one step in this adventure, and it took over me like quicksand," says Wicker. He is planning to have some of his skin cells stored for future cloning. "If I'm not cloned before I die, my estate will be set up so that I can be cloned after," he says, admitting, however, that he hasn't found a lawyer willing to help. "It's hard to write a will with all these uncertainties," he concedes. "A lot of lawyers will look at me crazy."

11   As a gay man, Wicker has long been frustrated that he cannot readily have children of his own; as he gets older, his desire to reproduce grows stronger. He knows that a clone would not be a photocopy of him but talks about the traits the boy might possess: "He will like the color blue, Middle Eastern food and romantic Spanish music that's out of fashion." And then he hints at the heart of his motive. "I can thumb my nose at Mr. Death and say, 'You might get me, but you're not going to get all of me,' " he says. "The special formula that is me will live on into another lifetime. It's a partial triumph over death. I would leave my imprint not in sand but in cement."

12   This kind of talk makes ethicists conclude that even people who think they know about cloning—let alone the rest of us—don't fully understand its implications. Cloning, notes ethicist Arthur Caplan of the University of Pennsylvania, "can't make you immortal because clearly the clone is a different person. If I take twins and shoot one of them, it will be faint consolation to the dead one that the other one is still running around, even though they are genetically identical. So the road to immortality is not through cloning."

13   Still, cloning is the kind of issue so confounding that you envy the purists at either end of the argument. For the Roman Catholic Church, the entire question is one of world view: whether life is a gift of love or just one more industrial product, a little more valuable than most. Those who believe that the soul enters the body at the moment of conception think it is fine for God to make clones; he does it about 4,000 times a day, when a fertilized egg splits into identical twins. But when it comes to massaging a human life, for the scientist to do mechanically what God does naturally is to interfere with his work, and no possible benefit can justify that presumption.

14   On the other end of the argument are the libertarians who don't like politicians or clerics or ethics boards interfering with what they believe should be purely individual decisions. Reproduction is a most fateful lottery; in their view, cloning allows you to hedge your bet. While grieving parents may be confused about the technology—cloning, even if it works, is not resurrection—their motives are their own business. As for infertile couples, "we are interested in giving people the gift of life," Zavos, the aspiring cloner, told *TIME* this week. "Ethics is a wonderful word, but we need to look beyond the ethical issues here. It's not an ethical issue. It's a medical issue. We have a duty here. Some people need this to complete the life cycle, to reproduce."

15   In the messy middle are the vast majority of people who view the prospect with a vague alarm, an uneasy sense that science is dragging us into dark woods with no paths and no easy way to turn back. Ian Wilmut, the scientist who cloned Dolly but has come out publicly against human cloning, was not trying

to help sheep have genetically related children. "He was trying to help farmers produce genetically improved sheep," notes Hastings Center ethicist Erik Parens. "And surely that's how the technology will go with us too." Cloning, Parens says, "is not simply this isolated technique out there that a few deluded folks are going to avail themselves of, whether they think it is a key to immortality or a way to bring someone back from the dead. It's part of a much bigger project. Essentially the big-picture question is, To what extent do we want to go down the path of using reproductive technologies to genetically shape our children?"

16   At the moment, the American public is plainly not ready to move quickly on cloning. In a TIME/CNN poll last week, 90% of respondents thought it was a bad idea to clone human beings. "Cloning right now looks like it's coming to us on a magic carpet, piloted by a cult leader, sold to whoever can afford it," says ethicist Caplan. "That makes people nervous."

17   And it helps explain why so much of the research is being done secretly. We may learn of the first human clone only months, even years, after he or she is born—if the event hasn't happened already, as some scientists speculate. The team that cloned Dolly waited until she was seven months old to announce her existence. Creating her took 277 tries, and right up until her birth, scientists around the world were saying that cloning a mammal from an adult cell was impossible. "There's a significant gap between what scientists are willing to talk about in public and their private aspirations," says British futurist Patrick Dixon. "The law of genetics is that the work is always significantly further ahead than the news. In the digital world, everything is hyped because there are no moral issues—there is just media excitement. Gene technology creates so many ethical issues that scientists are scared stiff of a public reaction if the end results of their research are known."

18   Of course, attitudes often change over time. In-vitro fertilization was effectively illegal in many states 20 years ago, and the idea of transplanting a heart was once considered horrifying. Public opinion on cloning will evolve just as it did on these issues, advocates predict. But in the meantime, the crusaders are mostly driven underground. Princeton biologist Lee Silver says fertility specialists have told him that they have no problem with cloning and would be happy to provide it as a service to their clients who could afford it. But these same specialists would never tell inquiring reporters that, Silver says—it's too hot a topic right now. "I think what's happened is that all the mainstream doctors have taken a hands-off approach because of this huge public outcry. But I think what they are hoping is that some fringe group will pioneer it and that it will slowly come into the mainstream and then they will be able to provide it to their patients."

19   All it will take, some predict, is that first snapshot. "Once you have a picture of a normal baby with 10 fingers and 10 toes, that changes everything," says San Mateo, Calif., attorney and cloning advocate Mark Eibert, who gets inquiries from infertile couples every day. "Once they put a child in front of the cameras, they've won." On the other hand, notes Gregory Pence, a professor of philosophy at the University of Alabama at Birmingham and author of *Who's Afraid of*

Human Cloning?, "if the first baby is defective, cloning will be banned for the next 100 years."

20   "I wouldn't mind being the first person cloned if it were free. I don't mind being a guinea pig," says Doug Dorner, 35. He and his wife Nancy both work in health care. "We're not afraid of technology," he says. Dorner has known since he was 16 that he would never be able to have children the old-fashioned way. A battle with lymphoma left him sterile, so when he and Nancy started thinking of having children, he began following the scientific developments in cloning more closely. The more he read, the more excited he got. "Technology saved my life when I was 16," he says, but at the cost of his fertility. "I think technology should help me have a kid. That's a fair trade."

21   Talk to the Dorners, and you get a glimpse of choices that most parents can scarcely imagine having to make. Which parent, for instance, would they want to clone? Nancy feels she would be bonded to the child just from carrying him, so why not let the child have Doug's genetic material? Does it bother her to know she would, in effect, be raising her husband as a little boy? "It wouldn't be that different. He already acts like a five-year-old sometimes," she says with a laugh.

22   How do they imagine raising a cloned child, given the knowledge they would have going in? "I'd know exactly what his basic drives were," says Doug. The boy's dreams and aspirations, however, would be his own, Doug insists. "I used to dream of being a fighter pilot," he recalls, a dream lost when he got cancer. While they are at it, why not clone Doug twice? "Hmm. Two of the same kid," Doug ponders. "We'll cross that bridge when we come to it. But I know we'd never clone our clone to have a second child. Once you start copying something, who knows what the next copies will be like?"

23   In fact the risks involved with cloning mammals are so great that Wilmut, the premier cloner, calls it "criminally irresponsible" for scientists to be experimenting on humans today. Even after four years of practice with animal cloning, the failure rate is still overwhelming: 98% of embryos never implant or die off during gestation or soon after birth. Animals that survive can be nearly twice as big at birth as is normal, or have extra-large organs or heart trouble or poor immune systems. Dolly's "mother" was six years old when she was cloned. That may explain why Dolly's cells show signs of being older than they actually are—scientists joked that she was really a sheep in lamb's clothing. This deviation raises the possibility that beings created by cloning adults will age abnormally fast.

24   "We had a cloned sheep born just before Christmas that was clearly not normal," says Wilmut. "We hoped for a few days it would improve and then, out of kindness, we euthanized it, because it obviously would never be healthy." Wilmut believes "it is almost a certainty" that cloned human children would be born with similar maladies. Of course, we don't euthanize babies. But these kids would probably die very prematurely anyway. Wilmut pauses to consider the genie he has released with Dolly and the hopes he has raised. "It seems such a profound irony," he says, "that in trying to make a copy of a child who has died tragically, one of the most likely outcomes is another dead child."

25   That does not seem to deter the scientists who work on the Clonaid project run by the Raelian sect. They say they are willing to try to clone a dead child. Though their outfit is easy to mock, they may be even further along than the competition, in part because they have an advantage over other teams. A formidable obstacle to human cloning is that donor eggs are a rare commodity, as are potential surrogate mothers, and the Raelians claim to have a supply of both.

26   Earlier this month, according to Brigitte Boisselier, Clonaid's scientific director, somewhere in North America, a young woman walked into a Clonaid laboratory whose location is kept secret. Then, in a procedure that has been done thousands of times, a doctor inserted a probe, removed 15 eggs from the woman's ovaries and placed them in a chemical soup. Last week two other Clonaid scientists, according to the group, practiced the delicate art of removing the genetic material from each of the woman's eggs. Within the next few weeks, the Raelian scientific team plans to place another cell next to the enucleated egg.

27   This second cell, they say, comes from a 10-month-old boy who died during surgery. The two cells will be hit with an electrical charge, according to the scenario, and will fuse, forming a new hybrid cell that no longer has the genes of the young woman but now has the genes of the dead child. Once the single cell has developed into six to eight cells, the next step is to follow the existing, standard technology of assisted reproduction: gingerly insert the embryo into a woman's womb and hope it implants. Clonaid scientists expect to have implanted the first cloned human embryo in a surrogate mother by next month.

28   Even if the technology is basic, and even if it appeals to some infertile couples, should grieving parents really be pursuing this route? "It's a sign of our growing despotism over the next generation," argues University of Chicago bioethicist Leon Kass. Cloning introduces the possibility of parents' making choices for their children far more fundamental than whether to give them piano lessons or straighten their teeth. "It's not just that parents will have particular hopes for these children," says Kass. "They will have expectations based on a life that has already been lived. What a thing to do—to carry on the life of a person who has died."

29   The libertarians are ready with their answers. "I think we're hypercritical about people's reasons for having children," says Pence. "If they want to re-create their dead children, so what?" People have always had self-serving reasons for having children, he argues, whether to ensure there's someone to care for them in their old age or to relive their youth vicariously. Cloning is just another reproductive tool; the fact that it is not a perfect tool, in Pence's view, should not mean it should be outlawed altogether. "We know there are millions of girls who smoke and drink during pregnancy, and we know what the risks to the fetus are, but we don't do anything about it," he notes. "If we're going to regulate cloning, maybe we should regulate that too."

30   Olga Tomusyak was two weeks shy of her seventh birthday when she fell out of the window of her family's apartment. Her parents could barely speak for a week after she died. "Life is empty without her," says her mother Tanya, a com-

puter programmer in Sydney, Australia. "Other parents we have talked to who have lost children say it will never go away." Olga's parents cremated the child before thinking of the cloning option. All that remains are their memories, some strands of hair and three baby teeth, so they have begun investigating whether the teeth could yield the nuclei to clone her one day. While it is theoretically possible to extract DNA from the teeth, scientists say it is extremely unlikely.

31   "You can't expect the new baby will be exactly like her. We know that is not possible," says Tanya. "We think of the clone as her twin or at least a baby who will look like her." The parents would consider the new little girl as much Olga's baby as their own. "Anything that grows from her will remind us of her," says Tanya. Though she and her husband are young enough to have other children, for now, this is the child they want.

32   Once parents begin to entertain the option of holding on to some part of a child, why would the reverse not be true? "Bill" is a guidance counselor in Southern California, a fortysomething expectant father who has been learning everything he can about the process of cloning. But it is not a lost child he is looking to replicate. He is interested in cloning his mother, who is dying of pancreatic cancer. He has talked to her husband, his siblings, everyone except her doctor—and her, for fear that it will make her think they have given up hope on her. He confides, "We might end up making a decision without telling her."

33   His goal is to extract a tissue specimen from his mother while it's still possible and store it, to await the day when—if—cloning becomes technically safe and socially acceptable. Late last week, as his mother's health weakened, the family began considering bringing up the subject with her because they need her cooperation to take the sample. Meanwhile, Bill has already contacted two labs about tissue storage, one as a backup. "I'm in touch with a couple of different people who might be doing that," he says, adding that both are in the U.S. "It seems like a little bit of an underground movement, you know—people are a little reluctant that if they announce it, they might be targeted, like the abortion clinics."

34   If Bill's hopes were to materialize and the clone were born, who would that person be? "It wouldn't be my mother but a person who would be very similar to my mother, with certain traits. She has a lot of great traits: compassion and intelligence and looks," he says. And yet, perhaps inevitably, he talks as though this is a way to rewind and replay the life of someone he loves. "She really didn't have the opportunities we had in the baby-boom generation, because her parents experienced the Depression and the war," he says. "So the feeling is that maybe we could give her some opportunities that she didn't have. It would be sort of like we're taking care of her now. You know how when your parents age and everything shifts, you start taking care of them? Well, this would be an extension of that."

35   A world in which cloning is commonplace confounds every human relationship, often in ways most potential clients haven't considered. For instance, if a woman gives birth to her own clone, is the child her daughter or her sister?

Or, says bioethicist Kass, "let's say the child grows up to be the spitting image of its mother. What impact will that have on the relationship between the father and his child if that child looks exactly like the woman he fell in love with?" Or, he continues, "let's say the parents have a cloned son and then get divorced. How will the mother feel about seeing a copy of the person she hates most in the world every day? Everyone thinks about cloning from the point of view of the parents. No one looks at it from the point of view of the clone."

36   If infertile couples avoid the complications of choosing which of them to clone and instead look elsewhere for their DNA, what sorts of values govern that choice? Do they pick an uncle because he's musical, a willing neighbor because she's brilliant? Through that door lies the whole unsettling debate about designer babies, fueled already by the commercial sperm banks that promise genius DNA to prospective parents. Sperm banks give you a shot at passing along certain traits; cloning all but assures it.

37   Whatever the moral quandaries, the one-stop-shopping aspect of cloning is a plus to many gay couples. Lesbians would have the chance to give birth with no male involved at all; one woman could contribute the ovum, the other the DNA. Christine DeShazo and her partner Michele Thomas of Miramar, Fla., have been in touch with Zavos about producing a baby this way. Because they have already been ostracized as homosexuals, they aren't worried about the added social sting that would come with cloning. "Now [people] would say, 'Not only are you a lesbian, you are a cloning lesbian,'" says Thomas. As for potential health problems, "I would love our baby if its hand was attached to its head," she says. DeShazo adds, "If it came out green, I would love it. Our little alien . . ."

38   Just as women have long been able to have children without a male sexual partner, through artificial insemination, men could potentially become dads alone: replace the DNA from a donor egg with one's own and then recruit a surrogate mother to carry the child. Some gay-rights advocates even argue that should sexual preference prove to have a biological basis and should genetic screening lead to terminations of gay embryos, homosexuals would have an obligation to produce gay children through cloning.

39   All sorts of people might be attracted to the idea of the ultimate experiment in single parenthood. Jack Barker, a marketing specialist for a corporate-relocation company in Minneapolis, is 36 and happily unmarried. "I've come to the conclusion that I don't need a partner but can still have a child," he says. "And a clone would be the perfect child to have because I know exactly what I'm getting." He understands that the child would not be a copy of him. "We'd be genetically identical," says Barker. "But he wouldn't be raised by my parents—he'd be raised by me." Cloning, he hopes, might even let him improve on the original: "I have bad allergies and asthma. It would be nice to have a kid like you but with those improvements."

40   Cloning advocates view the possibilities as a kind of liberation from travails assumed to be part of life: the danger that your baby will be born with a disease that will kill him or her, the risk that you may one day need a replacement organ and die waiting for it, the helplessness you feel when confronted with un-

bearable loss. The challenge facing cloning pioneers is to make the case convincingly that the technology itself is not immoral, however immorally it could be used.

41   One obvious way is to point to the broader benefits. Thus cloning proponents like to attach themselves to the whole arena of stem-cell research, the brave new world of inquiry into how the wonderfully pliable cells of seven-day-old embryos behave. Embryonic stem cells eventually turn into every kind of tissue, including brain, muscle, nerve and blood. If scientists could harness their powers, these cells could serve as the body's self-repair kit, providing cures for Parkinson's, diabetes, Alzheimer's and paralysis. Actors Christopher Reeve, paralyzed by a fall from a horse, and Michael J. Fox, who suffers from Parkinson's, are among those who have pushed Congress to overturn the government's restrictions on federal funding of embryonic-stem-cell research.

42   But if the cloners want to climb on this train in hopes of riding it to a public relations victory, the mainstream scientists want to push them off. Because researchers see the potential benefits of understanding embryonic stem cells as immense, they are intent on avoiding controversy over their use. Being linked with the human-cloning activists is their nightmare. Says Michael West, president of Massachusetts-based Advanced Cell Technology, a biotech company that uses cloning technology to develop human medicines: "We're really concerned that if someone goes off and clones a Raelian, there could be an overreaction to this craziness—especially by regulators and Congress. We're desperately concerned—and it's a bad metaphor—about throwing the baby out with the bath water."

43   Scientists at ACT are leery of revealing too much about their animal-cloning research, much less their work on human embryos. "What we're doing is the first step toward cloning a human being, but we're not cloning a human being," says West. "The miracle of cloning isn't what people think it is. Cloning allows you to make a genetically identical copy of an animal, yes, but in the eyes of a biologist, the real miracle is seeing a skin cell being put back into the egg cell, taking it back in time to when it was an undifferentiated cell, which then can turn into any cell in the body." Which means that new, pristine tissue could be grown in labs to replace damaged or diseased parts of the body. And since these replacement parts would be produced using skin or other cells from the suffering patient, there would be no risk of rejection. "That means you've solved the age-old problem of transplantation," says West. "It's huge."

44   So far, the main source of embryonic stem cells is "leftover" embryos from IVF clinics; cloning embryos could provide an almost unlimited source. Progress could come even faster if Congress were to lift the restrictions on federal funding—which might have the added safety benefit of the federal oversight that comes with federal dollars. "We're concerned about George W.'s position and whether he'll let existing guidelines stay in place," says West. "People are begging to work on those cells."

45   That impulse is enough to put the Roman Catholic Church in full revolt; the Vatican has long condemned any research that involves creating and experimenting with human embryos, the vast majority of which inevitably perish.

The church believes that the soul is created at the moment of conception, and that the embryo is worthy of protection. It reportedly took 104 attempts before the first IVF baby, Louise Brown, was born; cloning Dolly took more than twice that. Imagine, say opponents, how many embryos would be lost in the effort to clone a human. This loss is mass murder, says David Byers, director of the National Conference of Catholic Bishops' commission on science and human values. "Each of the embryos is a human being simply by dint of its genetic makeup."

46   Last week 160 bishops and five Cardinals met for three days behind closed doors in Irving, Texas, to wrestle with the issues biotechnology presents. But the cloning debate does not break cleanly even along religious lines. "Rebecca," a thirtysomething San Francisco Bay Area resident, spent seven years trying to conceive a child with her husband. Having "been to hell and back" with IVF treatment, Rebecca is now as thoroughly committed to cloning as she is to Christianity. "It's in the Bible—be fruitful and multiply," she says. "People say, 'You're playing God.' But we're not. We're using the raw materials the good Lord gave us. What does the doctor do when the heart has stopped? They have to do direct massage of the heart. You could say the doctor is playing God. But we save a life. With human cloning, we're not so much saving a life as creating a new being by manipulation of the raw materials, DNA, the blueprint for life. You're simply using it in a more creative manner."

47   A field where emotions run so strong and hope runs so deep is fertile ground for profiteers and charlatans. In her effort to clone her daughter Olga, Tanya Tomusyak contacted an Australian firm, Southern Cross Genetics, which was founded three years ago by entrepreneur Graeme Sloan to preserve DNA for future cloning. In an e-mail, Sloan told the parents that Olga's teeth would provide more than enough DNA—even though that possibility is remote. "All DNA samples are placed into computer-controlled liquid-nitrogen tanks for long-term storage," he wrote. "The cost of doing a DNA fingerprint and genetic profile and placing the sample into storage would be $2,500. Please note that all of our fees are in U.S. dollars."

48   When contacted by *TIME,* Sloan admitted, "I don't have a scientific background. I'm pure business. I'd be lying if I said I wasn't here to make a dollar out of it. But I would like to see organ cloning become a reality." He was inspired to launch the business, he says, after a young cousin died of leukemia. "There's megadollars involved, and everyone is racing to be the first," he says. As for his own slice of the pie, Sloan says he just sold his firm to a French company, which he refuses to name, and he was heading for Hawaii last week. The Southern Cross factory address turns out to be his mother's house, and his "office" phone is answered by a man claiming to be his brother David—although his mother says she has no son by that name.

49   The more such peddlers proliferate, the more politicians will be tempted to invoke prohibitions. Four states—California, Louisiana, Michigan and Rhode Island—have already banned human cloning, and this spring Texas may become the fifth. Republican state senator Jane Nelson has introduced a

bill in Austin that would impose a fine of as much as $1 million for researchers who use cloning technology to initiate pregnancy in humans. The proposed Texas law would permit embryonic-stem-cell research, but bills proposed in other states were so broadly written that they could have stopped those activi-
50   ties too.

"The short answer to the cloning question," says ethicist Caplan, "is that anybody who clones somebody today should be arrested. It would be barbaric human experimentation. It would be killing fetuses and embryos for no purpose, none, except for curiosity. But if you can't agree that that's wrong to do, and if the media can't agree to condemn rather than gawk, that's a condemnation of us all."

■ QUESTIONS FOR ANALYSIS AND DISCUSSION

1. What reasons does Gibbs list for why people are interested in human cloning? Are these the same reasons cited by researchers? How are the expectations of the general population different from those of the scientific world?
2. What "backlash" do "responsible" scientists fear will occur as a result of human cloning research? Are their fears well founded? Explain.
3. What are some of the misconceptions people seem to have about cloning themselves? Explain.
4. Gibbs notes that the issue of human cloning is "so confounding that you envy the purists at either end of the argument." What are the opinions of the "purists"? Do you find one side of the argument more compelling than another? Explain.
5. Ian Wilmut observes that there is a tragic twist to parents' desire to clone their dead children—the success rate is so miniscule that they are more likely to end up with another dead child. Should parents be able to pursue this option? Is any chance—no matter how remote—worthy of the risk? Why or why not?
6. In paragraph 20, Doug Dorner states that he "wouldn't mind being a guinea pig." Would the donor of the cells used to create a human clone be the guinea pig? Or, is the clone the real guinea pig?
7. In paragraph 29, Gregory Pence comments that cloning is "just another reproductive tool" now available to us. Respond to his statement expressing your own viewpoint.

Cloning and the Human Self
Chet Raymo

When Ian Wilmut's team of researchers created Dolly, several scientists, including Severino Antinori and Panayiotis Zavos, announced that they would immediately try to apply this technology to create a human being. Wilmut responded publicly, indicating that cloning for human reproduction would be "criminally irresponsible." But few scientists doubt that someone will actually succeed in this pursuit, although we may never know how many failures will occur before the "success story" is announced. In the next piece, Chet Raymo explains how he underestimated "cloning fever" and the questions it raises about what it means to be human in this age of biotechnology.

Raymo teaches physics at Stonehill College in North Easton, Massachusetts. He is the author of several books on science, including *Skeptics and Believers: The Exhilarating Connection Between Science and Religion* (1998). This article appeared in the March 20, 2001, edition of the *Boston Globe*.

■ BEFORE YOU READ

Is biotechnology eroding our definition of what it means to be human? Could the way we view ourselves, and our sense of identity, change because of this new technology? Why or why not?

■ AS YOU READ

How does Raymo "define" the human self? Do you agree with his line of thinking?

1   I started writing this column on cloning six months ago, then put it aside.

2   At that time I said, "Cloning by nuclear transfer is not easy. Dolly [the Scottish sheep] was the sole success out of 277 attempts. The success rate for all cloning experiments is only a few percent. Most clones die in the womb or at birth, many with abnormalities. Given these difficulties, the cloning of humans would not seem to be an immediate prospect."

3   No one, it seemed to me then, would try cloning a human when the odds against success were so long. The birth of a deformed child or the wreckage of so many embryos had the potential to bring the house down on the heads of the cloning researchers. Cloning is controversial in the best of circumstances; failure would be a public relations (and moral) catastrophe.

4   I underestimated how quickly cloning fever would advance. Today, the media are full of reports of imminent human clones. Perhaps the most serious venture is that proposed by reproductive physiologist Panos Zavos of the University of Kentucky and Italian fertility doctor Severino Antinori. They intend to try cloning a human baby sometime within the next few years. For all we know, someone else may already have tried.

5   The brave new world of human cloning is presumably upon us.

6   The ethical, philosophical and theological debates will now begin in earnest.

7   At the heart of the debates is a question that has been around since the dawn of time: What is the human self?

8   This much is certain: The human self is not a "thing," like a chair or a motorcycle. Every cell in a human body is replaced every year or two; some organs are renewed on a weekly or monthly basis. Old cells make new ones, then expire. The material stuff of the human self blows in and out of the body like an unceasing wind.

9   What lets a self endure is not atoms but information.

10   Every cell in a human body contains an arm's length of DNA that, in principle, contains the biochemical blueprint for building a replica of the body. In fact, day by day, hour by hour, cell by cell, a living creature clones itself. For example, the cells in the irises of a person's eyes come and go; that's atoms. But the genes determine that the eyes stay brown or blue or green; that's information.

11   A person's genetic code could be transcribed into an electronic data bank (or carved on stone tablets if you had enough stone) and used a hundred or a thousand years from now to create a physical replica of the person. In principle, creating a future clone would not require the preservation of actual DNA, only the information contained therein. Information is potentially immortal.

12   Of course, no human clone will be a perfect replica of the original person, even if the genetic information is exactly preserved. The expression of genes is dependent upon the chemical environment in which they are expressed. A clone might be subtly different at birth from the DNA donor, as an identical twin can be subtly different from his or her sibling.

13   But, even if physical replication were exact, the clone would certainly not replicate a human self. After all, identical twins are physical clones, and no one doubts that they qualify as separate and unique human selves. A human self is more than a genome.

14   A self is also a rich store of conscious and unconscious memories, an always growing ensemble of experiences somehow stored as webs of neurons in the brain. In principle, this is information, too. A wiring diagram showing the connections and potentiation of every one of the myriad neurons in the brain might also be stored in a computer or carved in stone and used a thousand years from now to reproduce even the adult mental states of a future clone, although how this might be done is not even remotely imaginable.

15   The essence of the self then is information—information embodied in that flux of flowing matter called life, partly inborn, partly acquired through experience. As the ancients guessed, the soul is immaterial and potentially immortal, but they were apparently wrong about the ability of that immaterial thing to express itself in the absence of matter. Information must be stored in a physical medium if it is to endure.

16   Dolly was news. The first human clone will be a sensation, and will focus a sharp fierce light on the nature of the human self. No one likes to think about these things. We prefer to think of the human soul as a sort of dreamy, ethereal thing that visits the world of matter briefly and then goes off to sit on a cloud and play a harp. The gritty biotechnical future promises something rather different.

■ QUESTIONS FOR ANALYSIS AND DISCUSSION

1. Why did Raymo think that no one would ever attempt to clone a human being? What made him change his mind?
2. What kind of argument does Raymo make in this essay? Is it logical? theoretical? How does the way he frame his argument lead to his conclusion?

3. What, in Raymo's opinion, "lets the self endure"? Do you agree? Explain.
4. Raymo teaches physics at a college in Massachusetts. How does his essay reflect his profession and the way he approaches his interpretation of what it means to be human? Explain.

Human Cloning: Don't Just Say No
Ruth Macklin

While many ethicists have expressed concern that human cloning is rife with moral and medical pitfalls, not everyone is so concerned. Supporters of human cloning argue that we should be able to use new technology as we see fit, as a matter of personal choice. In the next article, Ruth Macklin wonders why Americans are so eager to ban human cloning. Even if it offers no direct benefit to humanity, why ban it?

Macklin is a professor of bioethics at the Albert Einstein College of Medicine at Yeshiva University. This article was published in March 1997 in *U.S. News and World Report,* soon after the announcement of Dolly's birth was made by researchers at the Roslin Institute.

■ BEFORE YOU READ

Would you opt to clone a loved one if you knew that it could be successfully done? If so, who would you clone? If not, why?

■ AS YOU READ

Are so many people opposed to human cloning because it poses legitimate risks, or because it is intellectually upsetting? What is at the root of their objections? Explain.

1   [The] news that scientists had cloned a sheep sent academics and the public into a panic at the prospect that humans might be next. That's an understandable reaction. Cloning is a radical challenge to the most fundamental laws of biology, so it's not unreasonable to be concerned that it might threaten human society and dignity. Yet much of the ethical opposition seems also to grow out of an unthinking disgust—a sort of "yuk factor." And that makes it hard for even trained scientists and ethicists to see the matter clearly. While human cloning might not offer great benefits to humanity, no one has yet made a persuasive case that it would do any real harm, either.

2   Theologians contend that to clone a human would violate human dignity. That would surely be true if a cloned individual were treated as a lesser being, with fewer rights or lower stature. But why suppose that cloned persons wouldn't share the same rights and dignity as the rest of us? A leading lawyer-ethicist has suggested that cloning would violate the "right to genetic identity." Where did he come up with such a right? It makes perfect sense to say that

adult persons have a right not to be cloned without their voluntary, informed consent. But if such consent is given, whose "right" to genetic identity would be violated?

3   Many of the science-fiction scenarios prompted by the prospect of human cloning turn out, upon reflection, to be absurdly improbable. There's the fear, for instance, that parents might clone a child to have "spare parts" in case the original child needs an organ transplant. But parents of identical twins don't view one child as an organ farm for the other. Why should cloned children's parents be any different?

Vast Difference

4   Another disturbing thought is that cloning will lead to efforts to breed individuals with genetic qualities perceived as exceptional (math geniuses, basketball players). Such ideas are repulsive, not only because of the "yuk factor" but also because of the horrors perpetrated by the Nazis in the name of eugenics. But there's a vast difference between "selective breeding" as practiced by totalitarian regimes (where the urge to propagate certain types of people leads to efforts to eradicate other types) and the immeasurably more benign forms already practiced in democratic societies (where, say, lawyers freely choose to marry other lawyers). Banks stocked with the frozen sperm of geniuses already exist. They haven't created a master race because only a tiny number of women have wanted to impregnate themselves this way. Why think it will be different if human cloning becomes available?

5   So who will likely take advantage of cloning? Perhaps a grieving couple whose child is dying. This might seem psychologically twisted. But a cloned child born to such dubious parents stands no greater or lesser chance of being loved, or rejected, or warped than a child normally conceived. Infertile couples are also likely to seek out cloning. That such couples have other options (in vitro fertilization or adoption) is not an argument for denying them the right to clone. Or consider an example raised by Judge Richard Posner: a couple in which the husband has some tragic genetic defect. Currently, if this couple wants a genetically related child, they have four not altogether pleasant options. They can reproduce naturally and risk passing on the disease to the child. They can go to a sperm bank and take a chance on unknown genes. They can try in vitro fertilization and dispose of any afflicted embryo—though that might be objectionable, too. Or they can get a male relative of the father to donate sperm, if such a relative exists. This is one case where even people unnerved by cloning might see it as not the worst option.

6   Even if human cloning offers no obvious benefits to humanity, why ban it? In a democratic society we don't usually pass laws outlawing something before there is actual or probable evidence of harm. A moratorium on further research into human cloning might make sense, in order to consider calmly the grave questions it raises. If the moratorium is then lifted, human cloning should remain a research activity for an extended period. And if it is ever attempted, it should—and no doubt will—take place only with careful scrutiny

and layers of legal oversight. Most important, human cloning should be governed by the same laws that now protect human rights. A world not safe for cloned humans would be a world not safe for the rest of us.

■ QUESTIONS FOR ANALYSIS AND DISCUSSION

1. Macklin comments that most of the negative ethical concerns stemming from the announcement that scientists had cloned a sheep emanated from the "yuk factor," the idea that this technology could be used on humans. What does she mean? Based on what you have read in this section thus far, do you agree with her?

2. Macklin presents a scenario in which a couple with a dying child may opt to clone that child. She argues that a child with such parents would not be any less loved or worse off than a child normally conceived. Discuss this idea. What problems, if any, does it present? Is it ethical?

3. What arguments can be made for, and against, Macklin's scenario of cloning a dearly loved dead child? Consider this question as if you were the parent of such a child.

4. In her closing paragraph, Macklin comments that "in a democratic society, we don't usually pass laws outlawing something before there is actual or probable evidence of harm." Is this argument logical when applied to human life? How would you respond to this statement?

Creepy and Inevitable: Cloning Us

Adam Pertman

In 1979, the first test-tube baby was conceived in a lab by in vitro fertilization (IVF). At the time, medical ethicists and the general population responded with grave concerns over the new technology. Were we tampering with nature? Were we playing God? Could this technology someday backfire in ways we might not expect? Questions that, explains the author of the next essay, seem to be echos of questions we are now asking about human cloning. Adam Pertman discusses how the scientific community is grappling with the ethical dilemmas created by this new technology. Twenty years after the birth of the first test-tube baby, we seem comfortable with the idea of IVF. Might we feel the same way about human cloning in another twenty years?

Pertman is a writer for the Focus section of the *Boston Globe,* in which this article first appeared on March 18, 2001.

■ BEFORE YOU READ

In the next piece, Pertman asks how cloning research can ever be banned. What one country may forbid, another may allow. Or, renegade scientists may continue to pursue such research on their own. Can cloning technology truly be banned, or is it inevitable?

■ AS YOU READ

Pertman notes that 20 years ago, we asked the same questions about test-tube babies and IVF that we are now posing about human cloning. Will human cloning follow the same path as IVF? Will it become more acceptable as time passes? Why or why not?

1   Today's explosively worded arguments over human cloning sound eerily like echoes suspended in time for a quarter-century.

2   When the world got word in 1981 that the first test-tube baby had been "created" in Britain, everyone from medical ethicists to infertility authorities to ordinary citizens wondered aloud—and loudly—whether we were entering dangerous moral and scientific territory.

3   "What sort of children will we produce if we tamper with nature?" they asked. "Will this technology simply allow the most affluent among us to reproduce their egos?" And, of course: "Are we trying to play God?"

4   That debate reverberated through the international research community in the 1980s, when a top French biologist, Jacques Testard, abandoned his career after devising a process for freezing embryos.

5   "Let's stop pretending that research is neutral and that only its applications can be called good or bad," Testard warned in a farewell statement. "I will go no further and will attempt no breakthroughs."

6   Other scientists have not followed his lead.

7   Six years ago, for example, a controversial infertility doctor helped a 62-year-old woman in Italy become the oldest woman ever to become pregnant; her son had died at the age of 17, and she believed another child would ease her pain. A debate raged over the ethics and morals of that procedure, too.

8   Now that same Italian doctor, Severino Antinori, has lit another bonfire by announcing that he and an American colleague, Panayiotis Zavos, are conducting research that will yield a human clone within two years.

9   Since hearing that news a couple of weeks ago, during a fertility conference in Rome, scientists have derided the two men as modern-day Frankensteins. Ethicists have condemned them as corrupt. The Vatican has described their experiments as "grotesque." All the critics have suggested a singular response: a worldwide ban (which some governments already have instituted) to prevent human cloning from ever happening.

10   Yet, just as in-vitro fertilization has long since become routine, and frozen embryo transfers are slowly starting to take place, human cloning also is going to happen. Right or wrong, openly or clandestinely, sooner or later, technologies that are devised invariably are used. And when the technology in question promises to satisfy a primal urge—becoming a parent—while offering the pros-

pect of big payoffs—people reportedly have offered to pay huge sums to become guinea pigs—then its advent becomes inevitable.

11   "No question about it," says Robert Lanza, vice president for medical and scientific development at Advanced Cell Technologies Inc. in Worcester.

12   Lanza, whose company is at the cutting edge of cloning techniques, cringes at the idea of using them to make genetic duplicates of human beings. He also worries that the disclosure of even one failed human effort will cause a public backlash against all forms of the procedure.

13   "It's outrageous and unethical. The people who want to do this, to say the very, very least, are irresponsible. They should lose their medical license," says Rudolph Jaenisch, a pioneer in cloning at the Whitehead Institute for Biomedical Research in Cambridge. Asked if he believes the experimenters will do what they promise, Jaenisch sighs his reply: "Absolutely they will."

14   So, if the mainstream nightmare vision is going to materialize, in two years or in 20, why aren't scientists, religious leaders, and politicians trying to establish monitoring mechanisms to guard against abuses? Why aren't they writing regulations to promote good practices, or drafting laws to punish wrongdoers and keep honest people honest, rather than focusing their efforts solely on preventing the inevitable?

15   The biggest reason appears to be that most critics find the very notion of human cloning so heinous, and the potential consequences so catastrophic, that they oppose its use under any circumstances. Many say they fear that advocating anything other than an outright ban would effectively legitimize the research, thereby inducing current researchers to accelerate their efforts and, worse, luring more of them into this brave new world.

16   The detractors' concerns, by any measure, are sobering.

17   Some are moral and religious, including profound questions about creating life without the participation of male and female components—a line no previous high-tech infertility treatment has ever approached. Others range from the visceral (finding it creepy to think of growing a human being out of a skin cell) to the intellectual (should egomaniacs be allowed to replicate themselves, or should depressed parents be permitted to replace a deceased child with a new, identical "twin"?)

18   Then there are the ethical and practical objections.

19   Experiments, by their very nature, often fail. Thousands of animals died before and after birth, emerged deformed, developed physical and neurological abnormalities, and exhibited all sorts of other small and large problems before Dolly the cloned sheep arrived in 1997. And animals are still dying, or experiencing dire difficulties, as cloning research continues.

20   "Are we going to allow human beings to go through these sorts of horrors?" says Jaenisch. He adds that the early development of cloned cells is so different from that of normally produced embryos that the resulting animal invariably is born with or later develops some defect.

21   Jaenisch says the process of producing human clones will probably be even easier than doing so with other mammals because of medicine's long experi-

ence nurturing fetuses created with in-vitro techniques. But he cautions that while "the efficiency may be higher, the underlying biological problem is not solved by being more efficient."

22   The defenders of human cloning reject all these objections. They insist their critics are unfairly trying to impose their conservative social and religious views, and antiquated ones at that, onto scientists whose only sin is utilizing the most modern methods available to try to counteract infertility.

23   If the critics' anxiety is about possible abuse, some cloning advocates suggest imposing standards and passing laws to punish offenders. Moreover, they maintain the benefits of human cloning will be so important that they are worth the risks involved in the research required to make it a reality.

24   "We should be trying to get the world prepared to receive this technology, not just arguing about whether it's right or wrong," says Zavos, who runs a successful fertility business in Kentucky and says more than 600 couples have signed up for his team's human-cloning project. "The genie is out of the bottle. So let's develop criteria with which we can deal with this issue. That's what I'm challenging the world to do."

25   Nearly everyone interviewed on this subject agrees that, for several reasons, the first person to successfully produce a cloned baby will probably do so surreptitiously. "It's naive to think there aren't people out there who already haven't done it, or at least are attempting to," says Michael Bishop, president of Wisconsin-based Infigen, Inc., one of the nation's foremost developers of advanced cloning technologies for animals.

26   Secrecy seems probable partly because the researcher would know that any disclosure about such work could shut it down, and probably stigmatize everyone involved—from the scientist to the parent to the child.

27   At least as important, closed doors hide mistakes; that is, if one or more flawed beings were created (or died) through cloning, no one would have to know. In this scenario, an announcement would only be made once a seemingly healthy person was produced, or perhaps even after he or she was several years old to ensure that no problems had arisen.

28   "In fact, I think when we find out about successful cloning, it will be for more than one to show that it's not some kind of a fluke," says Randolfe H. Wicker, chief executive officer of the Human Cloning Foundation, an organization that advocates the procedure. Wicker is a onetime gay-rights activist who sees this new technology as the ultimate fertility tool for everyone—but especially for men, because they can't impregnate themselves, as women can, with other people's eggs or sperm.

29   Wicker is also a libertarian who believes only the scientists affected should work out the ethical and procedural guidelines for cloning. "Government messes up everything it touches; it should keep its hands off the rights of people who want to reproduce in this fashion," he says.

30   William Hoffman, the communications director for the Institute of Medical Biotechnology, has tracked this raging debate about cloning for years. While he believes that everyone involved means what they say, he also suspects

there is an underlying reason for many opponents' views: an instinctive fear of the unknown.

31   Essentially, while he harbors reservations about the motives of some researchers ("Are they in it for the money?") and has concerns about some consequences ("Will we stigmatize the cloned children the way we used to do with adoptees?") Hoffman thinks society will work through the issues as the process becomes real and, therefore, demystified.

32   Even some opponents of human cloning agree with the notion.

33   Bishop, for instance, says monitoring and regulation probably will replace the calls for bans once human clones become reality. And he takes issue with critics like Jaenisch, asserting that many cloned animals are born without defects—indicating the same is possible for humans.

34   The questions surrounding human cloning go on and on; they are as weighty as they are extensive. Should it be permitted on a more limited basis, for example, to produce vital organs that can keep people alive? If—or when—a whole person is duplicated, how will that alter our most fundamental understandings of what constitutes life, family, and self?

35   It is largely because we, as individuals and a society, haven't even begun to grapple with such issues that many ethicists argue human cloning shouldn't be permitted to take place. At least not yet.

36   "It's irresponsible and it's unethical in the practice of medicine," says George Annas, chairman of the Health Law Department at Boston University's School of Public Health. Annas suggests the licenses of doctors who engage in the practice should be revoked, their papers should not be published, and laws should be passed imposing heavy penalties on them.

37   But Annas, who believes some "renegades" will clone humans anyway, also leaves the ethical judgment door ever-so-slightly ajar. Asked if he thought a ban should last forever, he replied, "Well, at least for right now."

■ QUESTIONS FOR ANALYSIS AND DISCUSSION

1. Several of the authors in this section comment that objections to human cloning include the criticism that we are "playing God." Address this issue. Are scientists playing God? Explain.

2. In what ways does human cloning compare to in vitro fertilization? Are the two similar, or completely different, issues?

3. Why are Drs. Severino Antinori and Panayiotis Zavos considered "corrupt" by many ethicists? If they succeed in cloning a healthy human child, do you think public opinion would change? Why or why not?

4. Dr. Zavos states that "we should be trying to get the world prepared to receive this technology, not just arguing about whether it's right or wrong." Respond to this statement. Does he have a point, or is he trying to circumvent the issues? Explain.

5. Does Pertman express a personal opinion on human cloning in this article? Can you tell where he stands on the issue? What clues does he give that reveal his point of view?

Should Human Cloning Be Permitted?

Patricia A. Baird

Many of the authors in this section focus on how human cloning can benefit, or harm, individuals. In the next piece, Dr. Patricia A. Baird explains why such a perspective is "dangerously" incomplete. The ramifications of human cloning must be viewed in their entire *social* context. How will human cloning affect our society, not just in the present, but generations down the line? How would a cloned child be viewed by society, and how might he or she feel about being a clone? If we pursue human cloning, will future generations look back on our actions as reckless and irresponsible? And why endanger the future if there is no true need to create human clones in the first place?

Baird is a geneticist and head of the Department of Medical Genetics at the University of British Columbia. She frequently writes on the social, ethical, and health consequences connected to human reproductive biology and genetics, and the resulting implications for public policy. Baird presented this paper to an ethics committee created by the California state legislature to address the issue of human cloning. The committee invited individuals to present their recommendations on human cloning and the reasons for their positions. This abridged version of Baird's presentation was published in the June 2000 issue of the *Annals of the RCPSC* (the Royal College of Physicians and Surgeons of Canada).

■ BEFORE YOU READ

Baird raises some important questions about the well-being of a cloned person: that individual's self-identity and how he or she would fit into a society where most people were not cloned. She also wonders how society would treat cloned people. How well do you think a cloned person would assimilate into our society today? Would he or she become the object of curiosity? a celebrity? a freak? Would he or she ever be able to lead a normal life? Explain.

■ AS YOU READ

How is Baird's argument different from others in this section? What issues does she address that the other writers do not?

A Qualitatively Different Type of Reproduction

1   Producing humans by somatic-cell nuclear-transfer cloning differs from sexual reproduction—it separates reproduction from recombination. Normally, in an outbred species such as humans, we cannot predict what the overall characteristics of an embryo will be. In sexual reproduction, it is unpredictable which combination of the parents' thousands of genes will occur. To date, in creating the next generation, we have had to give ourselves over to chance. But if nuclear transfer is used, the nucleus can be taken from an adult whose characteristics are known—and the process reproduces the biology of the former individual. It becomes possible to select by known characteristics which humans

will be copied. The new technology allows the asexual replication of a human being, the ability to predetermine the full complement of a child's nuclear genes, and the easier alteration of the genes of prospective individuals. Cloning is a change in the integrity of our species, and we must think about the long-term consequences.

Public Reaction to Human Cloning

2   Cloning used to produce a human is rejected by the overwhelming majority of people. Polls on new scientific developments have limitations, but the Economist reported that over 90 percent of Americans were opposed to human cloning.[1] Other polls have shown similar results.[2,3] Polls, however, are affected by how the questions are asked, so an in-depth approach is needed. Many experts believe that lay people cannot understand complicated scientific topics, but there are data showing that they can assimilate and make judgments about complex issues. The Wellcome Trust did a qualitative focus-group study, and reported that opposition to human cloning was "nearly universal" among participants.[4] Most were against the idea of using cloning for reproductive purposes, stemming from concerns for the children and society, as much as from fears about interfering with nature. When over 90 percent of citizens in a democracy oppose human cloning, it is difficult for a government to justify a policy that permits it. There are a few people, however, who would pursue cloning because they see potential advantages for themselves.

Foreseeable Requests for Cloning

3   There are foreseeable situations where individuals may want to pursue cloning, for example, for couples where both are infertile and have neither eggs nor sperm, or where the male produces no sperm. Given that there are new treatment techniques using cells from testicular biopsy, such problems are rare. A second example is where a lesbian couple might wish to use one partner's body cell and the enucleated egg of the other to produce a child together. In these scenarios, there are other options available to form a family—such as sperm donation, egg and embryo donation, or adoption. Other situations where cloning may be pursued is when a couple's child is dying or is killed, and they want to replace him or her by using one of his or her cells in nuclear-transfer cloning; or when a clone could provide a genetically compatible organ for transplantation. There will be instances where people wish to pursue cloning for particular reasons.[5–7]

4   The arguments about physical and psychological harm to clones have also been well delineated.[8,9] For example, with regard to possible physical harms, congenital malformations, handicap, early death, increased risk of cancer, premature aging, and death have all been raised. Possible psychological harms to cloned individuals (replicands) have also been outlined, including diminished individuality, a sense of foreclosed future, or a disturbed sense of identity. An important part of human identity is the sense of arising from a maternal and a paternal line while at the same time being a unique individual. Many children

who are adopted, or conceived from donor insemination, show a deep need to learn about their biological origins. Making children by cloning means that they do not have this dual genetic origin, they are not connected to others in the same biological way as the rest of humanity. The first person born this way would have to cope with being the first not to come from the union of egg and sperm. Social, family, and kinship relationships that support human flourishing have evolved over millennia—but there is no way to place replicands. Is the DNA source the twin? The mother? The father?

Widening the Frame

5   Most debate on human cloning focuses on a weighing of harms and benefits to individuals. This is a dangerously incomplete framing. Looking at the issue as a matter of reproductive technology choice, although it focuses on individual autonomy, reproductive freedom, and protection of children, means that other issues are omitted.[10] We need to shift from the framing as individual choice, to a framing that reveals how permitting cloning affects future generations and society. I am reminded of one of the consultations of the Royal Commission on New Reproductive Technologies with an aboriginal group in Canada. They told the commission about their seventh-generation rule. They said that when they had to make a big decision in their community, they always considered what the consequences were likely to be in the seventh generation. This is a useful perspective to have, because viewing cloning as a personal matter inappropriately minimizes potentially serious social consequences. Individual choices in reproduction are not isolated acts—they affect the child, other people, and future generations. The wider consequences must be considered because we all have a stake in the type of community that we live in. We do not want it to be one where the use of cloning commodifies children, commercializes family formation, or increases social injustice. Cloning raises issues about the future of our species. We have not yet found the wisdom to deal with hunger, poverty, and environmental degradation—we are unlikely to have the wisdom to direct our own evolution.

6   Nuclear-transfer cloning allows third parties to choose the genotypes of people who will be cloned. Before, when two people mated, no one could control which genes the child received out of a myriad of possibilities. This lottery of reproduction has been a protection against people being predetermined, chosen, or designed by others—including parents.

7   Cloning directs the production of human beings in an unprecedented way. When a child of a particular genetic constitution is "made," it is easier to look on him or her as a product, rather than a gift of providence. If we can, and some people do, make children "to order," it is likely to change the way we view children.

8   An impetus to developing nuclear-transfer cloning for producing animals has been that it could then be combined with genetic enhancement—genes could be added to give the animals desired traits. Genes are inserted into cells in culture, then the cells screened to pick the ones that have incorporated the

desired genes. These altered cells are used as the donors of nuclei for cloned animals. It is then possible to create transgenic cloned animals with commercially desirable genetic traits (for example, heavier meat yield or production of insulin in the milk).[11]

9   Reproduction by nuclear-transfer cloning makes it possible to think about genetically enhancing humans. A person's cells could be cultured, genes inserted, and those cells taking up the desired genes used to produce a cloned "improved" individual. We could insert genes for viral-disease resistance, or to protect against baldness or degenerative diseases, or insert genes related to height or intelligence. If nuclear-transfer cloning is permitted, what will stop genetic enhancement being used eventually? There would be strong individual motivation to have a taller or disease resistant child. We would then be taking human evolution into our own hands. Are we wise enough to manage it or the social consequences? Most people will want their child to be brighter, taller, disease-resistant—so this technology could make people more standard, based on individual choices and market forces. If it works, it is likely to become used more often than just occasionally.

10   Who would have access to cloning or genetic improvements? Everyone? It is likely that those with financial resources would have access, but not other people, because cloning or enhancement would have to be provided as a socially underwritten "good" if it were to be available to everyone. And it is unlikely that most countries would provide publicly supported cloning, given that there are few social benefits and many potential harms.

11   If cloning or enhancement technology were provided as a public good to ensure equality of access, the government would have to decide in what circumstances people may clone themselves, and what traits were desirable. Docility? Height? Ability to provide a tissue transplant? Unless the market is to decide, criteria as to who may clone themselves, and a regulatory body will be needed.

12   If cloning is used, will we undermine the unconditional parental acceptance of offspring that is central to nurturing human beings? Parental acceptance is likely to become conditional when we are able to program for certain characteristics. If cloning technology or genetic enhancement is permitted, people with disabilities, or members of racial or ethnic minorities, will be affected differently, and in a way unlikely to lead to greater equality and respect.

13   There are forces favouring the use of cloning—particular individuals will pursue it, and it will benefit financially those who provide it, so it is likely to be marketed to the public.

14   All members of the public have a stake in whether cloning is permitted, because if cloned people exist, the changes affect everyone. Even though a majority do not want to allow it, if it is permitted, we would all live in a world where people are cloned. Even though initially, individuals on whom cloning technology had a direct impact would be a minority, their collective experiences would influence social values. In public policy-making, it is inappropriate to subordinate every consideration to the question of whether it helps a couple to have a

family. Society has a legitimate role in deciding whether cloning will be used. The far-reaching nature of this choice means more voices must be involved in making decisions. The decisions should not be taken preemptively by a clinical facility or a group of scientists who ignore the wishes of the rest of the community. We need the perspectives not just of those who are knowledgeable in biology or science; we also need the perspectives of sociologists, humanists, and citizens from a variety of life experiences. On something that affects our species' future, it would be valuable to have the perspectives of people from many countries.

Conclusions Regarding Policy

15   There is no compelling case to make people by asexual means; human reproductive cloning is without potential benefits to almost all citizens, and other options are available in most situations. Many institutions have come to this conclusion; the prospects of making human beings by cloning have elicited concern in many countries, and there have been calls for a worldwide ban on cloning used to produce humans by many political and religious leaders, and by organizations such as the World Health Organization, the World Medical Organization, the American Medical Association, and UNESCO. Nineteen countries in the Council of Europe have signed an agreement that bans human cloning. Medicine, science, and technology are worldwide endeavours, so this is an issue facing humans as a species. For this reason, WHO is making an international effort to co-operate on guidelines for cloning in humans.

16   History shows that where there is a demand for a new service and the ability of a few to pay for it, unless there is legislation, there will be professionals willing to provide it. There is licensing of fertility clinics in several European countries, but in some other countries, reproductive technologies are highly commercialized and little regulated. If human cloning were permitted in the United States, it would likely proceed in the billion-dollar private reproductive-medicine sector. In this market-driven context, its use is unlikely to be controlled. It is now possible to peruse catalogues if you wish to buy eggs or surrogate pregnancies, so it seems likely that if human cloning is permitted in the United States, it is only a matter of time before pressure from individuals with specific interests would open up the field. Legislation is needed to ban the implantation into a woman of an egg cell that has had its nucleus transferred from a body cell. When such legislation is written, its wording should not inadvertently ban non-reproductive cloning research, or animal cloning research that may be of benefit, and that many people see as acceptable.

17   How we use cloning is not an individual or medical matter. It is a matter of social policy that cannot be viewed in a narrow framework of reproductive technology and individual choice. How we choose to use this technological capacity will shape society for our children, their children, and after. How it is used is likely to entrench existing inequalities, and create new ones.

18   In conclusion, using nuclear-transfer cloning to allow people to have a child introduces a different way of reproduction for our species. Once we breach this

barrier, it leaves us with no place to stop. Given all the problems outlined, the reasons for permitting cloning to produce a person are insufficiently compelling. Even in the few circumstances where the case for human cloning seems justified, there are alternative solutions. We are at an appropriate stopping place on a slippery slope. Not all reasons why a person might wish to copy his or her cells are unethical, but given there are other options open to people wishing to form a family, concerns about individual and social harms from cloning are strong enough that it is not justified to permit it. These issues affecting the creation of the next generation are important for the future of our species; we must deal with them wisely. I hope we can.

REFERENCES

1. Whatever next? *The Economist* 1997 March 1;79–81.

2. Time/CNN poll. 1997 March.

3. International Food Information Council. *Wirthlin group quorum survey,* 1997 March 21–24.

4. *Public perspectives on human cloning, medicine in society program.* The Wellcome Trust, 1999 June (http://www.wellcome.ac.uk/en/1/awtpubrepcln.html).

5. McGee G. *The human cloning debate.* Berkeley: Berkeley Hills Books, 1998.

6. Hummer J, Almeder R. *Human cloning. Biomedical Ethics Reviews.* Totowa: 1998.

7. Andrews L. *The clone age: 20 years at the forefront of reproductive technology.* New York: Henry Holt, 1999.

8. Wilson JQ, Kass L. *The ethics of human cloning.* Washington: American Enterprise Press, 1999:10(2).

9. Cloning human beings. Report of the national bioethics advisory commission. *Hastings Centre Report* 1997:27(5).

10. Baylis F. Human cloning: three mistakes and a solution. Unpublished manuscript.

11. Pennis E. After Dolly, a pharming frenzy. *Science* 1998:279;646–8.

■ QUESTIONS FOR ANALYSIS AND DISCUSSION

1. What does Baird mean when she says that human cloning will create a change in the "integrity" of reproduction? What does this word mean? What does it imply when used this way? Explain.

2. In general, do you find Baird's argument to be effective? Why or why not? What strategies does she use in arguing her point?

3. What is the "seventh-generation rule"? How does Baird apply it to the issue of human cloning? Do you think her use of this rule is an effective way to support her argument? Explain.

4. Baird comments that "we have not yet found the wisdom to deal with hunger, poverty, and environmental degradation—we are unlikely to have the wisdom to direct our own evolution." Are these examples parallel? Why or why not? Does she make a good point? Explain.

5. Is human cloning likely to "change the way we view children"? Why or why not? Frame your answer in terms of how society may view cloned children.

6. In paragraphs 9 through 11, Baird raises questions about creating "improved" babies who possess the genetic traits we prefer, that is, creating children who

are taller, brighter, or more disease-resistant. Why does she feel such an application of this nuclear-transfer cloning would be harmful? Explain.

7. Baird raises the question: If there is no real need to clone a human, why do it at all? Respond to her statement by expressing your own opinion on this aspect of the cloning debate.

8. Analyze Baird's conclusion. How does she end her argument? What ideas and points does she leave with her audience?

Yes, Human Cloning Should Be Permitted
Chris MacDonald

In the previous article, Dr. Patricia Baird, a geneticist at the University of British Columbia, explains why the case for human cloning is "insufficiently compelling" and suggests that it could even endanger the fabric of society. In the next piece, ethicist Chris MacDonald explains why he disagrees with Baird's argument. He feels that Baird is too severe in her condemnation of human cloning and fails to provide sufficient evidence that human cloning should be banned. Moreover, he disagrees with her point that if the majority of society wishes to ban something, we should heed their voice. In principle, he explains, a majority shouldn't impose its viewpoint on a minority, and this applies to human cloning as well.

MacDonald teaches ethics, philosophy, and moral theory at Dalhousie University in Halifax, Nova Scotia. His research spans health-care ethics, professional ethics, business ethics, and moral theory. This response to Patricia Baird's paper was published in the October 2000 issue of the *Annals of the RCPSC* (the Royal College of Physicians and Surgeons of Canada).

■ BEFORE YOU READ

MacDonald argues that just because most people (90 percent) want to ban human cloning, we should not bend to majority rule because such concessions can be dangerous. Do you agree? Why or why not?

■ AS YOU READ

Because no one has actually cloned a human being, much of the debate on this issue is theoretical. Are hypothetical arguments sufficient grounds to create laws against something like human cloning? Why or why not?

1   Patricia Baird's discussion of human cloning (*Annals RCPSC, June 2000*) challenges the prospect of nuclear-transfer cloning for the purposes of human reproduction. Baird reviews a long list of familiar worries about human cloning, but the most striking feature of her discussion is its frankness in placing the onus of justification on the shoulders of those who would permit human cloning. The reasons for permitting cloning, she argues, are "insufficiently compelling," so cloning should be prohibited. The implication is that any new

technology should be forbidden unless and until enough justification can be found for allowing its use.

2   Baird is to be commended for her frankness. But the onus is misplaced, or at least too severe. One need not be a single-minded defender of liberty to think that, contrary to Baird's implication, we need good reasons to limit the actions of others, particularly when those actions do no clear and specific harm. The fact that a portion of society—even a majority—finds an activity distasteful is insufficient grounds for passing a law forbidding it. For example, it is presumably true that at one point, roughly 90 percent of the public (the same proportion that Baird says is against human cloning) was opposed to homosexuality. Does (or did) this justify action on the part of government to ban homosexual lifestyles? Surely not.

3   There may be a flaw in my analogy. Human cloning, according to critics, has harmful effects (or at least risks). Indeed, Baird suggests that the arguments regarding potential physical and psychological harm to clones have been "well delineated." In fact, a convincing case has yet to be made for the claim that the physical and psychological risks to clones are more severe than, or different in kind from, those faced by children produced in more traditional ways. Identical twins live with the psychological "burden" of not being genetically unique. Children born to women over 35 are at an increased risk of genetic illness. Children resulting from in-vitro fertilization or other reproductive technologies live with the knowledge that their origins were unusual. They may even live with the knowledge that their genetic profile has been manipulated (for example, through pre-implantation selection of embryos). Human cloning for reproductive purposes is another novel—and as yet untested—medical technology. As such, it should be approached with caution. Thorough animal trials should be completed before attempts on humans are contemplated. But this is true of any new medical technology.

4   Baird worries about the shift that human cloning might provoke in the way that we view children. This in turn would change the type of community that we are. The central worry is that human cloning "commodifies" children (i.e., that cloning may make us think of children as a commodity or product to be bought and sold). Why would cloning have this effect? Is it simply because it is likely to be expensive, so that it costs money to have children? Surely this is insufficient to worry us. Raising children already costs money—the statistics show us how many hundreds of thousands of dollars it costs to raise a child through to adulthood. Yet no one has suggested that we see our children as products, or love them any less. (In the mid 1940s—before publicly funded health care—my grandparents sold their car to pay the hospital bill related to my father's birth, so "purchasing" the birth of a child is nothing new!)

5   Baird argues that an "important part of human identity is the sense of arising from a maternal and a paternal line while at the same time being a unique individual." Yet without supporting evidence, this sounds like pop psychology. And we can reply in kind: most people I know do not identify with both their maternal and paternal lineages. One of my friends, who was raised by a single

mother, identifies with her maternal eastern European heritage, and not with the French paternal heritage implied by her surname. Another friend identifies with his father's black heritage, rather than with his maternal Chinese lineage, despite his Asian physical features. Such patterns are not unusual. Dual heritage may be normal, but it hardly seems central to our conception of ourselves as humans. And identical twins seem none the worse for the knowledge that they are not genetically unique individuals. Claims about challenges to what makes us "human" may be powerful rhetorical devices, but they must be substantiated if they are to be convincing.

6   Baird is correct to exhort us to look beyond harms to identifiable individuals, to the social implications that human cloning might have. As a comparison, think of fetal sex selection. Most of us think that sex selection is a bad thing—not because of any purported harm to the child, but because we worry about the social implications of valuing children of one sex over those of another. So Baird rightly reminds us that focusing on potential harms to individuals constitutes a "dangerously incomplete framing" of the problem. Furthermore, cloning (and genetic technology in general) is sufficiently new—and its implications sufficiently poorly understood—to warrant a healthy respect, and even the allowance of a margin of safety. But this does not suggest the need for the ban that Baird (with others) proposes. What these worries suggest is a need for caution, for discussion, and for regulation. For instance, laws limiting the number of clones that might be created from one individual, restricting the combination of cloning with genetic modification, and defining lines of parental obligation, would alleviate many of the concerns associated with human cloning. (Françoise Baylis argues that cloning is so likely to be used in combination with gene transfer that we should think of cloning as an enhancement technology rather than as a reproductive technology, in her article "Human cloning: three mistakes and a solution," which has been accepted for publication in the *Journal of Medicine and Philosophy.*)

7   What I have said here should not be taken as an absolute defence of human cloning in all circumstances. (Indeed, there may be only a few circumstances in which cloning is appropriate.) Nor have I suggested that public monies should be spent on cloning research. All I have suggested is that a ban on research leading toward human cloning is unwarranted by the arguments raised thus far. Caution and discretion are warranted; a ban is not.

8   Finally, I worry that Baird's point of view exemplifies the way in which human reproductive cloning is being singled out, among cloning-related techniques, as a bogeyman. Almost in chorus, scientists are pleading with regulators not to place restrictions on cloning experimentation per se. At the same time, most scientists seem to be more than willing to swear off reproductive cloning, and indeed to wring their hands over the moral implications of its use. Yet this has the air of a too-hasty concession. The scientific community seems to be too willing to condemn one unpopular application of cloning technology, on the basis of too little convincing argumentation, to appease those who oppose cloning technology in general. But human cloning for reproductive purposes

has legitimate, morally acceptable applications—for example, for infertile couples, and for gay couples. And none of the criticisms have been convincingly made. We should not let reproductive human cloning be abandoned as the moral sacrificial lamb of the cloning debate.

■ QUESTIONS FOR ANALYSIS AND DISCUSSION

1. MacDonald presents an analogy between the acceptance, or nonacceptance, of homosexuality and the controversy over human cloning. Are these two subjects similar? Does this support his point? Why or why not?
2. In paragraph 3, MacDonald argues that no convincing case has been made that human clones would suffer more physical and psychological risks than children "produced in more traditional ways." How do you think Patricia Baird would respond to this claim? other authors in this section? Explain.
3. How does MacDonald argue against Baird's essay? Identify the points he selects to argue against and how he addresses these points. Does he address all the points in Baird's piece? Explain.
4. What is MacDonald's thesis? What does he advocate?
5. Consider the perspective from which McDonald writes. Baird is a medical professional, MacDonald an ethicist. Does he convince his audience that he has the credentials to debate this issue? Is it important to Baird's argument that she is a geneticist? Does the fact that MacDonald is not a physician himself undercut his argument? Why or why not?

■ WRITING ASSIGNMENTS

1. Many politicians are calling for a ban on human cloning. Research the issue online at Web sites such as <http://bioethics.gov>, <www.ornl.gov> and <www.nsplus.com/nsplus/insight/clone/clone.html> and other sites you locate through common search engines (using for instance, "human cloning," "ethics," and "cloning debate" as your key words). How has the cloning debate changed since the announcement of Dolly's creation? Is a moratorium on human cloning likely to be implemented within the next few years? Explain.
2. In 1997, the National Bioethics Advisory Board recommended against research in human cloning because of the dangers it would pose for a child born as a result of such reproductive technology. In 2000, researchers reported that Dolly's cells appear to be aging slightly faster than expected, perhaps because she was cloned from a six-year-old adult sheep. Through online and library research, track Dolly's development. If Dolly were human, what biological and social problems might she face? Based on your research, can you make a recommendation for or against human cloning?
3. Ruth Macklin argues, "While human cloning might not offer great benefits to humanity, no one has yet made a persuasive case that it would do any real harm, either." Based on the information you have learned in this chapter and online research, write an essay in which you address Macklin's statement.
4. One of the arguments against human cloning is that the technology could be abused to create clones of exceptional people, such as athletes, geniuses, and su-

permodels. Write an essay in which you discuss the likelihood of such an application of cloning technology. Who are possible candidates for cloning, and
why?

5. Is there such a thing as "genetic identity"? Should we have such a right? How
   might our genetic identity be violated? Could we someday arrive at a point
   where "identity theft" is more than a case of stolen credit cards? Write an essay
   exploring the concept of genetic identity and what it might mean for the future.

6. Dr. Patricia Baird suggests that human cloning technology might lead to the
   creation of "genetically enhanced" humans—a possibility to which she objects.
   However, if such technology was successfully applied, could it be considered
   parental irresponsibility *not* to genetically alter offspring? For example, if a
   woman has the gene for breast cancer and bears children without genetic engineering to prevent the transmission or activation of this gene, could she potentially face a charge of manslaughter if her daughter develops the disease?

CREDITS

Photo Credits

Page 177: Museo del Prado, Madrid. Copyright © 1998 Estate of Pablo Picasso/Artists Rights Society (ARS), New York.

Page 180: Printed by permission of the Norman Rockwell Family Agency. Copyright © 1943 the Norman Rockwell Family Agency.

Page 184: Courtesy Callard & Bowser-Suchard Inc.

Page 186: Courtesy Shreve, Crump & Low.

Page 187: Reproduced with the permission of The Timberland Company for educational purposes only. Timberland and (the tree logo) are trademarks or registered trademarks of the Timberland Company. Copyright © 2001 The Timberland Company. All Rights Reserved.

Page 189: Copyright © Tribune Media Services, Inc. All Rights Reserved. Reprinted with permission.

Page 191: Photo appears courtesy of Brooklyn Paper Publications, Inc.

Page 192: Reprinted with permission.

Page 193: AP/WIDE WORLD PHOTOS.

Page 195: Republished with permission of Globe Newspaper Company, Inc., from the January 11, 2002 edition of *The Boston Globe*.

Page 336: Photo appears courtesy of Saturn Corporation.

Page 338: Photo appears courtesy of *Upside* Magazine.

Page 340: Photo appears courtesy of Brian Hurley. Writer: Bryant Johnson; Art Director: Will Roth.

Page 381: Copyright © 2002 The New Yorker Collection from cartoonbank.com. All Rights Reserved.

Page 414: Photo reprinted with permission.

Page 423: Justin Lane/NYT Pictures.

Page 497: Clay Bennett. Copyright © 1999 The Christian Science Monitor.

Page 517 (left): Copyright © 2000 Universal Studios.

Page 517 (right): Copyright © 2002 CBS Worldwide Inc. All Right Reserved.

Page 543: Dan Wasserman. Copyright © Tribune Media Services, Inc. All Rights Reserved. Reprinted with permission.

Page 590: Michelle V. Agins/NYT Pictures.

Page 609: Drew Sheneman of the Newark Star-Ledger.

Page 644: Photo appears courtesy of the National Abortion Federation.

Page 665: Copyright © Nita Winter (415) 339-1310.

Page 676: Reprinted with special permission of North American Syndicate.

Text Credits

Joel Achenbach. "Working Dads, Unite!" *GQ,* November, 1998. Copyright © 1998 by Joel Achenbach. Reprinted by permission of Don Congdon Associates, Inc.

Jonathan Alter. "A Reckoning on Death Row." *Newsweek*, June 25, 2000. Copyright © 2000 Newsweek, Inc. All rights reserved. Reprinted by permission.

Marcia Angell. "The Supreme Court and Physician-Assisted Suicide—The Ultimate Right." *New England Journal of Medicine,* January 2, 1997. Copyright © 1997 Massachusetts Medical Society. All rights reserved.

Bryonn Bain. "The Bill of Rights for Black Men: Walking While Black." *The Village Voice*, April 4, 2000.

Patricia A. Baird. "Should Human Cloning Be Permitted?" *Journal of The Royal College of Physicians and Surgeons of Canada,* June 2000. Reprinted by permission.

Martha Balash. "Schools Can Help to Prevent Teen Pregnancy." Reprinted by permission of the author.

Rosalind Barnet and **Caryl Rivers.** "The New Nostalgia," from *He Works/She Works.* Copyright © 1996 by Rosalind Barnet and Caryl Rivers. Reprinted by permission of the authors.

Darren Beals. "Violent Culture: The Media, the Internet, and Placing the Blame." Reprinted by permission of the author.

Shannon Brownlee. "The Place for Vengeance." *U.S. World and News Report,* June 16, 1997. Copyright © 1997 U.S. News and World Report, L.P. Reprinted with permission.

Warren E. Burger. "The Right to Bear Arms." *Parade,* 1990. Reprinted by permission of author.

Carrie Carmichael. "Last Right." The *New York Times,* May 20, 2001. Reprinted by permission of the author.

Caleb Carr. "Americans Don't Understand That Their Heritage Is Itself a Threat." The *New York Times,* October 14, 2001. Copyright © Caleb Carr. Reprinted by permission of William Morris Agency, Inc. on behalf of the author.

James C. Carter. Letter to the Editor. *Times-Picayune,* October 24, 1997. By permission of the author.

Judith Ortiz Cofer. "The Myth of the Latina Woman: I Just Met a Girl Named María." *The Latin Deli: Prose and Poetry.* Copyright © 1993 by Judith Ortiz Cofer. Reprinted with the permission of The University of Chicago Press.

Linda J. Collier. "Adult Crime, Adult Time: Outdated Juvenile Laws Thwart Justice." The *Washington Post,* April 6, 1990. Reprinted by permission of the author.

Stephanie Coontz. "A Menace to Society?" *Vogue,* December, 1994. Reprinted by permission.

John Derbyshire. "In Defense of Racial Profiling." *National Review Magazine,* February 9, 2001. Copyright © 2001 by National Review, Inc., 215 Lexington Avenue, New York, NY 10016. Reprinted by permission.

John Ellis. "The Consequences of 'Carnage as Entertainment.'" Appeared in *The Boston Globe,* May 23, 1998. Reprinted by permission of the author.

Steve Erle. "Death in Texas." *Tikkun,* September/October 2000. With permission from Tikkun.

Laurie Essig. "Same-Sex Marriage: I Don't Care If It Is Legal, I Still Think It's Wrong—and I'm a Lesbian." *Salon.com,* July 10, 2000. Reprinted with permission.

Susan Faludi and **Karen Lehrman.** "Revisionist Feminism." Copyright © *Slate.* Distributed by United Feature Syndicate, Inc.

Kathryn Steward and **Corina Sole.** Letter to the Editor. The *Washington Post,* October 5, 1996. Reprinted by permission of the authors.

Ray Suarez. "Familiar Strangers." From *The Old Neighborhood.* The Free Press, 1999. Reprinted by permission.

Andrew Sullivan. "This Is What a Day Means." The *New York Times Sunday Magazine,* November 23, 2001, © Andrew Sullivan, reprinted with the permission of The Wylie Agency.

Andrew Sullivan. "Virtually Normal." From *Virtually Normal, Same Sex Marriage,* by Andrew Sullivan Vintage Books, 1997. Used by permission of Alfred A. Knopf, a division of Random House, Inc.

Margaret Talbot. "The Maximum Security Adolescent." The *New York Times Sunday Magazine,* September 1, 2000. Copyright © 2000 Margaret Talbot, reprinted with the permission of The Wylie Agency, Inc.

Deborah Tannen. "I'm Sorry, I Won't Apologize." The *New York Times Sunday Magazine,* July 21, 1996. Copyright © Deborah Tannen. Reprinted by permission.

Deborah Tannen. "A War of Words." The *Washington Post,* Weekly Edition, March 23, 1998. Reprinted by permission of author.

Sallie Tisdale. "Zero Tolerance for Slaughter." *Salon,* May 6, 1999. Reprinted by permission.

James Trefil. "Brave New World." *Smithsonian,* December 2001. Reprinted by permission of the author.

Joseph Turow. "Targeting a New World." Chapter I, from *Breaking Up America.* The University of Chicago Press, 1997. Reprinted by permission.

James Twitchell. "Two Cheers for Consumerism." From *Lead Us into Temptation: The Triumph of American Materialism.* Columbia University Press, 2000. Reprinted by permission.

"Understanding Terrorism: A Harvard Roundtable Discussion." *Harvard Magazine,* February 2002. Reprinted by permission.

Robert Wachbroit. "Human Cloning Isn't as Scary as It Sounds." Copyright © 1997 The Washington Post Company, Inc. Reprinted by permission.

Henry Wechsler. "Binge Drinking Must Be Stopped." Appeared in *The Boston Globe,* October 2, 1997. Reprinted by permission of Henry Wechsler, Ph.D., Principal Investigator, Harvard School of Public Health, Director of College Alcohol Studies.

Elie Wiesel. "We Chose Honor." *Parade,* October 28, 2001. Reprinted with permission of the author.

Kenneth Woodward. "A Question of Life." *Newsweek,* July 9, 2000. Copyright © 2000 Newsweek, Inc. All rights reserved. Reprinted by permission.

INDEX

Page numbers followed by an *f* refer to figures.

"A Question of Life or Death" (Woodward), 629–631
Questions
  anticipating, in argument essay, 109
  asking before writing, 69–70
  interview, preparing, 205
Quill, Timothy E., 659
  "Death and Dignity—A Case of Individualized Decision Making," 659–664
Quindlen, Anna, 376, 648
  "The Comfort of Friends," 376–380
  "Some Thoughts About Abortion," 648–650
Quotation, in research notes, 222–223

Radio programs, citing, 240
"Rally Round the Flag" (Kaufman), 420–422
Raymo, Chet, 687–688
  "Cloning and the Human Self," 687–689
Reading(s)
  analyzing, 39–41
  annotating, 35, 36f–37f
  arguing with, 41–42
  critical, 28–29
  deliberation about, 48–49
  personal experience and, 34–35
  previewing, 29–31
  skimming, 31–34
  summarizing, 35, 37–39
  two or more, creating dialogue between, 42–48
Reason, appeal to, 122
"Reason, Faith, and Stem Cells" (Kinsley), 632–634
Reasons
  creating, 9–11
  definition of, 16
  presenting in argument essay, 108
  examples of, 112, 116
Rebuttals, in Toulmin model, 155–156
"A Reckoning on Death Row" (Alter), 601–604
Red herring, 58, 146
Reference works, documentation of, 234–235
References, 230

Reilly, Don, 380
  "Stopping for Directions" (cartoon), 380–381
"Remarks by the President on Stem Cell Research" (Bush), 625–629
Research
  evaluating sources, 214–221
  incorporating, 224–226
  locating sources, 209–214
  note taking during, 221–223
  search strategy, 206–209
Research paper(s),
  characteristics of, 203
  drafting, 223–226
  presentation of, 226–227
  revising, 226
  sample, 240–259
Respect for audience, showing, 82
Restroom symbols, 365
"The Return of the Melting Pot" (Schlesinger, Jr.), 463–467
Reviews, 212
  documentation of, 237
Revising, research paper, 226
"Revisionist Feminism" (Faludi and Lehrman), 394–400
Rewriting, 62
"The Right to Bear Arms" (Burger), 578–581
Rivers, Caryl, 508
  "The New Nostalgia," 508–516
Rockwell, Norman, 179
  "Freedom of Speech" (painting), 179–182
Rodell, Susanna, 355–356
  "Bump and Grind: Little Girls Strut Their Stuff," 355–358
Rodriguez, Gregory, 467–468
  "Forging a New Vision of America's Melting Pot," 467–471
Roiphe, Katie, 382
  "The Independent Woman and Other Lies," 382–387
Roy, Arundhati, 428
  "The Algebra of Infinite Justice," 428–432

"Same Sex Marriage" (Essig), 544–546
Samuelson, Robert J., 90
  "Media Have Fallen for Misguided Anti-smoking Campaign," 90–92